THE BOUNDARYLESS CAREER

THE BOUNDARYLESS CAREER
A New Employment Principle
for a New Organizational Era

Edited by

Michael B. Arthur

Denise M. Rousseau

New York   Oxford
OXFORD UNIVERSITY PRESS
1996

Oxford University Press

Oxford   New York
Athens   Auckland   Bangkok   Bogota   Bombay
Buenos Aires   Calcutta   Cape Town   Dar es Salaam
Delhi   Florence   Hong Kong   Istanbul   Karachi
Kuala Lumpur   Madras   Madrid   Melbourne
Mexico City   Nairobi   Paris   Singapore
Taipei   Tokyo   Toronto

and associated companies in
Berlin   Ibadan

Library of Congress Cataloging-in-Publication Data
Arthur, Michael B. (Michael Bernard), 1945–
The boundaryless career : a new employment principle for a new
organizational era / by Michael B. Arthur and Denise M. Rousseau.
p.   cm.
Includes bibliographical references and index.
ISBN 0-19-510014-X
1. Career development.   2. Organizational change.   I. Rousseau,
Denise M.   II. Title.
HF5381.A8314   1996
650.1—dc20   96-25423

1 3 5 7 9 8 6 4 2

Printed in the United States of America
on acid-free paper

Preface

In 1995, IBM's hostile bid of $3.5 billion for Lotus was accepted. The major prize was the collaborative software package "Notes," as well as a stronger competitive position against market leader Microsoft. A battle among "core firms" looms, in an industry recently considered a haven for entrepreneurial start-ups. Has the software industry shifted so quickly from small-firm opportunism to large-firm domination? If so, does it signal a similar trend for other industries? And does it signal a demise for careers—boundaryless careers—fashioned on alternative assumptions?

On all three questions we say *no . . .* or, at least, *not yet!* The Lotus story contrasts with broader patterns of disaggregation in the computer industry. The success of Lotus's Notes is predicated on a strategy to collaborate with outside specialist firms—and, thereby, four times as many people as Lotus provides—in installing the product. We find the story of the fourfold increase in non-Lotus employees, and the influence of people over Lotus strategy, the more interesting and unexplored phenomenon.

Other industries continue to thrive on the kind of decentralized arrangements, and employment mobility within them, that are chronicled, for example, in Michael Porter's (1990) *The Competitive Advantage of Nations.* Governments continue to seek industrial development or regeneration through regional networks of small-firm specialists. This despite the centrality of large hierarchical firms—and, through them, a presumed "industrial state"—in so much twentieth-century political and economic thought.

But reversion to assumptions of large-firm dominance would be premature for another reason: Large hierarchical firms continue to bias the way we think about employment over time—that is, about careers. How can we appreciate the potential of alternative forms of employment if we haven't given those forms adequate attention? And how can we reasonably evaluate what have traditionally been called "organizational careers," in the absence of competing ideas? This book, therefore, offers a compendium of such ideas, designed to bring alternative career forms—what we call *boundaryless careers*—into clearer focus.

This compendium originates from, and is principally authored by, contributors from the United States. However, we in no way wish to convey the idea that boundaryless careers are in any way peculiar to the United States, or that we should look principally to the United States for new ideas. On the contrary, we hope, through the publication of this book, to promote debates about boundaryless careers in the international arena.

With the above having been said, our first acknowledgment goes to the contributing authors who have joined us in this venture. It was their enthusiasm that drove this project forward. It was their openness to new ideas, from their own disciplines and beyond, that gave this book its emergent character. Not least, it was their collective willingness to revisit old assumptions, and to suffer the editors' prompting along the way, that led to this book's publication.

Herb Addison of Oxford University Press has been a particular source of support; so, too, has Cary Cooper, who commissioned a preceding special issue of the *Journal of Organizational Behavior*. Several of this book's authors also gave feedback on our ideas, or on earlier drafts of other people's chapters. Special thanks go to Robert DeFillippi, who was in at the start of our deliberations and is still a trusted adviser at the end. Further thanks go to Colleen Jones, Daniel Baranowski, Andrea Larson, Barbara Lawrence, Toni King, David Tuerck, and John Van Maanen, all of whom helped with either the development of ideas or direct review activity. Herbert Simon and John Van Maanen have been interested and gracious enough to author some brief comments for prospective readers.

We are particularly indebted to John Wiley and Sons, for giving us their gracious permission to draw freely from the July 1994 special issue of the *Journal of Organizational Behavior*. Four chapters and parts of chapter 1 are based on that material, although all that work has been revised and updated for this book. We are also indebted to the Academy of Management for sponsoring a symposium—at its 1993 annual meeting—that first gave life to the notion of boundaryless careers. Both Priscilla Rosati, at Suffolk University, and Carole McCoy, at Carnegie Mellon University, gave extraordinary help in bringing this book to press.

Despite all the help received, responsibility for the book's editing is our own. Also, both editors contributed equally to this work in the fullest sense: Neither of us could have done anything *near* half of the work alone!

August 1995
Boston, Massachusetts   M.B.A.
Pittsburgh, Pennsylvania   D.M.R.

Contents

Contributors

Howard E. Aldrich
  Department of Sociology
  University of North Carolina at
    Chapel Hill

Michael B. Arthur
  School of Management
  Suffolk University
  Boston

Lotte Bailyn
  Sloan School of Management
  Massachusetts Institute of Technology
  Cambridge

Ted Baker
  Department of Sociology
  University of North Carolina at
    Chapel Hill

Michael H. Best
  Center for Industrial Competitiveness
  University of Massachusetts at Lowell

Allan Bird
  College of Business
  California Polytechnic State University
  San Luis Obispo

Ronald S. Burt
  Graduate School of Business
  University of Chicago

Bee Leng Chua
  Department of General Business
    Management
  The Chinese University of Hong Kong

Robert J. DeFillippi
  School of Management
  Suffolk University
  Boston

Jerome R. Ellig
  Program on Social and Organizational
    Learning
  George Mason University
  Fairfax, Virginia

Joyce K. Fletcher
  Department of Cooperative Education
  Northeastern University
  Boston

Nanette Fondas
  Fuqua School of Business
  Duke University
  Durham, North Carolina

Robert Forrant
  Center for Industrial Competitiveness
  University of Massachusetts at Lowell

Cherlyn Skromme Granrose
  Center for Organizational and
    Behavioral Sciences
  Claremont Graduate School
  Claremont, California

Douglas T. Hall
  School of Management
  Boston University

Monica S. C. Higgins
  Harvard Business School
  Boston

Paul M. Hirsch
  J. L. Kellogg Graduate School of
    Management
  Northwestern University
  Evanston, Illinois

Candace Jones
  Organization Studies Department
  Carroll School of Management
  Boston College
  Chestnut Hill, Massachusetts

Raymond E. Miles
  Haas School of Business
  University of California at Berkeley

Shazia Rafiullah Miller
  Center for Urban Affairs and Policy
    Research
  Northwestern University
  Evanston, Illinois

Anne S. Miner
  School of Business
  University of Wisconsin–Madison

Philip H. Mirvis
  Sandy Spring, Maryland

Charles Perrow
  Sociology Department
  Yale University
  New Haven, Connecticut

Holly Raider
  Naugatuk, Connecticut

David F. Robinson
  Department of Management and
    International Business
  University of Wisconsin–Madison

James E. Rosenbaum
  Center for Urban Affairs and Policy
    Research
  Northwestern University
  Evanston, Illinois

Denise M. Rousseau
  H. John Heinz III School of Public
    Policy and Management
  Graduate School of Industrial
    Administration
  Carnegie Mellon University
  Pittsburgh

AnnaLee Saxenian
  Department of City and Regional
    Planning
  University of California at Berkeley

Mark Shanley
  Management and Strategy Department
  Kellogg Graduate School of
    Management
  Northwestern University
  Evanston, Illinois

Charles C. Snow
  Department of Management and
    Organization
  The Pennsylvania State University
  University Park

Tojo Joseph Thatchenkery
  Program on Social and Organizational
    Learning
  George Mason University
  Fairfax, Virginia

David Thomas
  Graduate School of Business
    Administration
  Harvard University
  Boston

Pamela S. Tolbert
  School of Industrial and Labor Relations
  Cornell University
  Ithaca, New York

Karl E. Weick
  School of Business Administration
  University of Michigan
  Ann Arbor

THE BOUNDARYLESS CAREER

1

Introduction: The Boundaryless Career as a New Employment Principle

MICHAEL B. ARTHUR AND DENISE M. ROUSSEAU

Work gets done. Time passes. Careers—sequences of work experiences over time—unfold. A career depicts the person, the elementary unit in work arrangements. Careers invoke relationships within and among firms. Careers spell economic and social outcomes. Put simply, everyone who works has a career. And everyone's life outside work is connected to the career. As lives are lived, a focus on careers, rather than on jobs, insists that we account for time and its implications. Careers matter!

They matter more because of the new economy, which is characterized by interdependent work activities in both the national and global arenas. It is an economy influenced by changing technology and more dynamic than most people have previously seen. It is an economy in which opportunity, insecurity, flexibility, and uncertainty coexist, thereby confusing workers and policymakers alike. A better understanding of work and time, and so of careers, is a critical need. But traditional concepts about work and time—such as job security—suggest little more than disorder, or even chaos, in the new economic era. New concepts, and new models of success in life and work, are urgently needed to help us interpret what's going on.

The *boundaryless* career is one such new concept, and the principal one that this book promotes. The boundaryless career does not characterize any single career form, but, rather, a range of possible forms that defies traditional employment assumptions. Accordingly, the term *boundaryless* distinguishes our concept from the previous one—the "bounded," or organizational, career.[1] That view saw people in orderly employment arrangements achieved through vertical coordination in mainly large, stable firms. The meaning of careers, and their

3

influence on the economy, was subordinated to those firms: Getting along meant doing what the firm wanted; getting ahead meant being grateful for opportunities the firm brought your way. The organizational career appeared to be the dominant employment form through the mid-1980s. It isn't dominant any more.

Firms today cannot promise a lifelong career, or anything close to it; people can no longer expect such a prospect. But one good thing about the organizational career model was that most people understood it. The logic of vertical coordination—and of job grades, promotions, demotions, plateauing, and fast-tracking, to service that logic—was found everywhere. So, too, was a logic of orderly levels, of people only mattering within the structure of firms; "peripheral" firms only mattering because of "core" firms; both kinds of firms only mattering in industry sectors; and sectors only mattering in nation-states. For better or worse, the emergent logic of what Galbraith (1971) labeled the "industrial state" contributed to a shared understanding—among people and the firms that employed them; and among the vast array of social commentators who cared, one way or another, about career effects. No such logic exists today.

It is easy, and emotionally satisfying, to reject a logic that no longer holds true. Doing so provides a *tabula rasa* of fresh opportunity. It is far harder to replace that logic with something more helpful in the new organizational era. What should employers and employees, politicians and voters, ambassadors and host nations, and the largely separate branches of academic inquiry make of each other if the old assumptions don't apply? What should we try to salvage from the old assumptions? What should we do about the familiar ways of thinking that developed around those assumptions? What can we know about the future, and about technologies, world events, and innovations that have not yet arrived? How can we help to make careers more useful, more effective, more livable, in the new era?

We do not offer stock answers in this volume. What we do offer is a community of scholars brought together from a variety of disciplines and by a shared interest in the questions posed. The common focus is on the boundaryless career; the common agenda is to better comprehend its properties and possibilities in the years ahead. The broader purpose is to develop more useful employment models for the "new organizational era" to which our title refers.

This introduction explores the broad significance of boundaryless careers. These careers are contrasted with traditional organizational career assumptions still prevalent in current research. We propose the boundaryless career as a vehicle for exploring a principal, yet neglected, meaning of organization, concerned with the organizing *process*. We argue that the case for a boundaryless-careers agenda is further supported by the prognoses of change to a postindustrial model of employment. We briefly introduce the themes of networking, learning, and enterprise as illustrative boundaryless-career phenomena. Finally, we discuss the organization of this book and its contributing authors.

The Significance of Boundaryless Careers

The term *career* means the unfolding sequence of a person's work experiences over time (Arthur, Hall, and Lawrence, 1989).[2] This meaning draws on a long tradition of inquiry, but usage of the term can be confusing. What we mean is that the principal difference between *careers* and *jobs* is not—as some would have it—that work breaks down neatly into higher- and lower-status categories, so that, for example, lawyers and managers have careers but secretaries and factory workers do not.[3] Rather, the principal difference is that the career concept insists that we note the significance of *time* for all who participate in work arrangements. Time affects, for example, employment stability, skills and experience gained, relationships nurtured, and opportunities encountered. In contrast, the concept of the job—as well as its derivatives such as job satisfaction, job analysis, and job design—makes no such insistence. The more dynamic the economy, the more relevant is this difference, and, we contend, the more valuable is a career perspective.

Put simply, *boundaryless* careers, are the opposite of "organizational careers"—careers conceived to unfold in a single employment setting. Direct evidence of the significance of boundaryless careers stems from several sources. For example, the median employment tenure for all U.S. workers is just four-and-a-half years, and, for managers and professionals, just six years (Maguire, 1993). In Japan, the supposed bastion of lifetime employment, the median for male workers is only eight years (Cheng, 1991). Firms with under 500 employees—the antithesis of large firms, in which organizational careers are most viable—account for 56% of U.S. private-sector employment (Small Business Administration, 1992), predicted to rise to 70% by the year 2000 (U.S. Department of Labor, 1992). Patterns of new-job creation indicate that small firms are adding to, and large firms subtracting from, the pool of career opportunities (Birch, Haggerty, and Parsons, 1993).[4] New-job creation has in turn been estimated to represent only one tenth of overall career moves into new employment (Bureau of Labor Statistics, 1989). Large firms of over 500 employees account for only 30% of employment in the United Kingdom and other European countries (Storey, 1994), only 15% of employment in Japan, and proportionally even less in Hong Kong, Taiwan, and Singapore (Cestells, 1992).[5] Further boundaryless-career effects stem from large-firm decentralization into autonomous employment groups, and from internal service departments that are being pushed to compete with outside suppliers (Bridges, 1994).

Beginning in about 1984, various reports began to corroborate the demise of the industrial state—and so of organizational careers—that the employment statistics suggest. Communities of small European firms were competing with large firms through interfirm networks and flexible specialization (Piore and Sabel, 1984). Silicon Valley, in California, was nurturing regional success based on employee mobility and new-firm formation rather than on large-firm expansion (Rogers and Larsen, 1984). Economists took on America's "bigness complex," and, in particular, the relative inability of large firms to deliver innovations (Brock and Evans, 1986). One of the authors of *In Search of Excellence* chimed in to declare that "the era of sustainable excellence" was now over (Peters, 1987). Conventional wisdom about Japanese success was challenged by reports that so-called peripheral firms, and careers initiated within them, were the seedbed of that country's innovations (Friedman, 1988). If "giant" firms were to "learn to dance," it would be through careers that functioned without the employment security of the past (Kanter, 1989). The "competitive advantage of nations" was seen to stem from industry clusters of firms, and from employment mobility within clusters, rather than from solo firms (Porter, 1990). "Intelligent enterprise" was described as involving wholesale disaggregation of established firms and the "voluntary" association of capable people "who don't *have* to work for a particular company" (Quinn, 1992). Perhaps the most influential management commentator since World War II reversed his 50-year-old position that firms should take responsibility for their employees' social welfare (Drucker, 1994).

In sum, the old picture of stable employment, and organizational careers associated with it, has faded, and a new picture of dynamic employment and boundaryless careers calls for our attention. This does not deny the organizational career as a legitimate base of inquiry; but it does suggest an alternative point of departure, and one which acknowledges the unpredictable, market-sensitive world in which so many careers now unfold. However, much of the foundational work previously applied to organizational careers can still be used to inform the boundaryless-career perspective. The same may be said, as this book will make clear, about a range of other standpoints with indirect, yet powerful, messages about how careers are viewed.

The Specifics of Boundaryless Careers

Within the general meaning of boundaryless careers—as being the opposite of organizational careers—lie several specific meanings, or emphases. The most prominent of these is a case where a career, like the stereotypical Silicon Valley career, moves across the boundaries of separate employers. A second meaning occurs when a career, like that of an academic or a carpenter, draws validation—and marketability—from outside the present employer. A third meaning is involved when a career, like that of a real-estate agent, is sustained by external networks or information. A fourth meaning occurs when traditional organizational career boundaries, notably those involving hierarchical reporting and advancement principles, are broken. A fifth meaning occurs when a person rejects existing career opportunities for personal or family reasons. A sixth meaning depends on the interpretation of the career actor, who may perceive a boundaryless future regardless of structural constraints. A common factor in the occurrence of all these meanings is one of independence from, rather than dependence on, traditional organizational career arrangements.

The variety of meanings behind the boundaryless career is consistent with earlier research on careers, and, in particular, work initiated at Massachusetts Institute of Technology (MIT) in the mid-1970s (Hall, 1976; Schein, 1978; Van Maanen, 1977a).[6] This work emphasized four themes equally applicable to both organizational- and boundaryless-career concepts. Two of these themes have already been introduced: The first affirms a definition of "career" that applies to *all workers,* and all sequences of work roles; the second asserts that the *time* dimension be recognized as a key mediator of employment relationships. The third theme emphasizes the career as a focus for interdisciplinary study; economics, management and organization studies, political science, psychology, and sociology should all contribute to our understanding of how careers unfold. The fourth theme involves seeing the career from both *subjective* and *objective* perspectives. The subjective view refers generally to the individual's own interpretation of his or her career situation; the objective refers to institutional—firm or societal—interpretations of the same career situation.[7] Taken together, the four themes define a unique place for career studies in the economics and organizational studies arenas, and serve the study of all careers, including boundaryless careers, equally well.

An Organizational Careers Legacy

However, there is a greater legacy suggested in the MIT work that does not concur with the boundaryless career perspective. A key element in this legacy is reflected in the terms used in the titles of the foundational texts: *Careers in Organizations* (Hall, 1976): *Organizational Careers* (Van Maanen, 1977a); and *Matching Individual and Organizational Needs* (Schein, 1978). The titles reflect what Van Maanen (1977b: 4) described as being "for the most part [a] complementary" match between career studies' interest in unfolding individual identity and "the nature and workings of complex organizations."[8] Two further elements are suggested less by the MIT initiative than by concurrent assumptions about the organizations referenced. One widespread assumption was that these organizations and their environments were relatively stable. Another assumption was that organizational structures were inherently hierarchical. In affirmation, Kanter's *Men and Women of the Corporation* (1977) focused on careers in an established, supposedly representative, corporate hierarchy.

In a preceding journal article (Arthur, 1994), we argued that popular studies from the early 1980s—notably Peters and Waterman's (1982) *In Search of Excellence* and companion works reporting Japanese success—emphasized organizational, rather than boundaryless, career assumptions.[9] But those popular reports were symptomatic of a broader problem found in surrounding economic and organizational assumptions. Prominent frames of reference—for example, in economics, on transaction costs (Williamson, 1975); in organization theory, on resource dependency (Pfeffer and Salancik, 1978); and in strategic management, on industry structure (Porter, 1980)—offered mutually reinforcing arguments. The arguments suggested, or were taken to suggest, why firms should make, not buy; expand, not contract; absorb, not spin off; control, not coexist; and in general, leverage hierarchical rather than market-centered principles. Such theories discounted the role of the person—as an industry or occupation participant, as a contributor to strategy, or as a trusted agent. Companion studies that spanned internal labor markets, employee commitment, organization culture, and leadership reinforced a presumption of employee dependence on the employer firm. The ideas from these works were progressively converted into research agendas and employment practices. They constitute—if we may coin the term—an *Orwellian* legacy of interdependent ideas about the dominance of large, bureaucratic forms of organization that prevailed largely unchallenged until the symbolic passing of "1984," referring to George Orwell's book with its extreme depiction of the top-down bureaucratic form.

The Research Response

What, though, is the extent of this legacy today? We sampled five interdisciplinary journals to examine, first, all empirical research on careers (that is, on how work unfolds over time) for the periods 1980–1989 and 1990–1994; and, second, a subsample, taken from the same journals, of all research on work and employment, but where the time dimension was not a central concern.[10] Our sampling, summarized in Table 1.1, reveals that more than 80% of articles on careers, and almost 75% of articles from 1990, presume environmental stability;[11] that more than 75% of articles on careers presume an intrafirm focus with this focus in turn subordinating the subjective perspective on careers to the objective perspective;[12] that around 75% of articles are also restricted to managerial-, professional-, or hierarchical-career issues; and that larger firms with over 500 employees command far more attention then their smaller counterparts, even though on aggregate the latter employ more people. One difference in the more recent 1990s sample is that studies of occupational subjects have increased, somewhat moderating the large-firm bias of earlier research. However, the emphasis over both periods, and, most remarkably, the second

Table 1.1 Studies of Careers, Work, and Employment in Five Interdisciplinary Journals

Theme	Research on Careers				Research on Work and Employment[1]	
	1980–1989		1990–1994		1990–1994	
	Number	%	Number	%	Number	%
Environmental stability[2]	43	93	43	74	71	67
Intrafirm focus	36	78	44	76	97	91[3]
Hierarchical assumptions[4]	35	76	47	81	70	66[5]
Size						
Large firms (> 500 employees)	21	46	21	36	42	40
Smaller firms (< 500 employees)	7	17	5	9	13	12
Mixed-size firms[6]	2	4	9	16	26	25
Occupational or industry sample	14	30	23	40	22	21
Experimental research	—	—	—	—	7	7
Total number of articles	46	100	58	100	106	100

[1] Subsample of a sample of 150 articles—30 per year from each journal.
[2] Presumed wherever environmental change was not signaled in the article.
[3] Five additional articles could not be reasonably classified.
[4] Includes career studies restricted to managerial and professional employees.
[5] Twenty-six additional articles could not be reasonably classified.
[6] Includes occasional best estimates from the data provided.
SOURCES: Empirical research from the *Academy of Management Journal, Administrative Science Quarterly, Journal of Management, Journal of Management Studies,* and *Journal of Organizational* (formerly *Occupational*) *Behavior.*

period, is clearly on organizational- rather than boundaryless-career assumptions.

The evidence from studies on work and employment—that is, on the systems and practices through which careers unfold—is even more graphic. A sample of over 100 such studies still presumes environmental stability occurring more often than change, and emphasizes large firms over small- and medium-size firms. A body of work on topics such as job redesign, employee empowerment, and internal change does challenge traditional hierarchical assumptions, but only in less than half the number of studies that reaffirm those assumptions. Most striking of all is the nearly complete absence of studies on work and employment that look beyond the boundaries of the single firm.[13] When people's mobility is acknowledged, it is viewed as an internal problem for the firm—that is, as "turnover," "propensity to leave," or "willingness to relocate." Recruitment of new talent is similarly neglected except for entry-level employees or for CEOs. In its studies of employment, the field of organizational studies remains constrained inside the "black box" of the single firm, just as economics appears constrained outside that box.

Limitations of organizational studies research are being more broadly acknowledged. Journal gatekeepers lament the lack of research response to "cataclysmic changes" in industry arrangements (Daft and Lewin, 1993), and question "whether past theories and research apply to new organizational forms and realities" (Smith, Carroll, and Ashford, 1995). The "radical industry transformation" of recent years is described as escaping the attention of managers and academics alike (Prahalad and Hamel, 1994). The prognoses for new research emphasize the significance of more adaptive and interdependent arrangements among firms, and of shifting work arrangements. Yet these prognoses continue to treat employment as an issue that is internal to the single firm. They therefore continue to neglect the boundaryless career phenomenon.

The Meaning of *Organization*

There are two principal definitions of the term *organization* in modern dictionaries. The longest established definition refers to "the act or process of organizing." The second definition refers to "a group of people that has a more or less constant membership."[14] As Drucker (1993) has pointed out, the second definition—referring to "the" organization as an entity—has been in use only since the 1950s, and this usage correlates closely with the era of the industrial state. However, it is this second definition that has dominated, and indeed been a presumption, in organizational research.

The notion of the boundaryless career invites a reconnection with the more traditional meaning of organization as *process*. Instead of the largely static view of the single firm, we are invited to think of *organization* in a more dynamic sense. *Organization* in this sense is seen as stemming from, rather than constraining, the behavior of people and firms. Although this sense has been explored before (e.g., by Weick, 1979; Miles and Snow, 1986; Reddy and Rao, 1990), it has not made its way into the mainstream of scholarly ideas, nor into the flow of employment research those ideas inspire. Yet it is a sense that returns the meaning of organization to the action verb from which it stems, accommodating shifting interfirm relations, and more adaptive forms of employment in support of those relations. It is the sense in which the title of this book heralds a "new organizational era."

The meaning of *organization* has been similarly constrained by economic thought. The orthodox economics emphasis on equilibrium among firms has reinforced assumptions of stable, constant membership groups. So-called evolutionary economics employs the same linguistically recent meaning that sees the organization as synonymous with the firm (see, e.g., Nelson and Winter, 1982). Work on labor markets has bifurcated into "external" and "internal" labor market views that reinforce the same meaning. The economic principles behind "competitive strategy" were predicated on the few, seemingly intransigent, firms that held market power, rather the many firms that did not (Williamson, 1991). Popular "game theory" approaches frequently define "players" as firms rather than as the individuals on which the theory depends (e.g., Samuelson and Nordhaus, 1992). When it blurs or loses the distinction between people and firms, economics also loses touch with how people and firms can contribute to one another—that is, with how the *process* of organization can unfold.

We submit that both economics and organization studies can collaborate on the meaning of *organization* that they have largely forgotten. And we submit the study of boundaryless careers as a catalyst for such collaboration to occur.[15]

Pendulum or Paradigm Shift?

There are some who say that what we have experienced is a temporary phenomenon. They argue that the data, for example, on the collapse of large firms, and the growth in the number of small firms, have been exaggerated. Economies need a healthy base of "core" firms, and of traditional employment systems within those firms (as argued, for example, by Harrison, 1994). A related argument sees a bifurcation in learning and income opportunities between privileged and underprivileged workers, and a social obligation to support the latter group (Reich, 1991, Freeman, 1993). Both arguments can suggest a renewed focus on employment security and, in turn, on firms as custodians of workers' careers.

In contrast, a community of futurists sees technological and global forces continuing to dismantle corporate or government "empires" (Toffler, 1990) and the careers they once hosted. The futurists (e.g., Drucker, 1993) suggest a paradigm shift from an "industrial society" to a "knowledge society," where accrual of skills and knowledge shifts power to the person rather than to a hierarchical position. A related theme is one of paradox, whereby people will have greater freedom to act on their own, but fewer external rules to act by (Handy, 1994; Naisbett, 1994). Multiple "new crafts" are reported to be already responding to the new employment realities (Barley, 1992), as are emerging forms of employment contracting (Rousseau, 1995). Of course, the image of the knowledge society suggests a crucial task for the boundaryless-careers agenda—namely, to confront job and career situations that inhibit knowledge accumulation.

The debate about the scope and scale of future career changes is unlikely to end soon. However, the debate has been hampered on both sides by the widespread assumption of a linear cause-effect relationship—namely, that changes manifested in firms create career effects.[16] In contrast, the study of boundaryless careers can transcend problematic cause-effect assumptions, and in turn highlight interdependencies between the person and the firm. For instance, such interdependencies are strongly suggested in recent writings on networking, learning, and enterprise. These topics are briefly introduced below, both to suggest prominent possibilities for the future study of boundaryless careers, and to anticipate recurrent themes throughout this volume.

Networks and Learning

The boundaryless career perspective suggests that people take responsibility for their own career futures. If they are to do so, "cultivating networks" and gaining access to other people's knowledge and resources are fundamental steps (Hirsch, 1987). Meanwhile, individual networks develop into social networks at the level of the firm, and define interfirm dependencies and exchange relationships (Burt, 1992; Granovetter, 1985). As a result, network relations simultaneously serve the career interests of individual actors and the strategic interests of firms. Both sets of interests are affected by the flow of information and influence, as well as by direct career movements, to new employer situations (Nohria, 1992).

Networks also serve as learning systems (Powell and Brantley, 1992), again with consequences for both individuals and firms. Learning over the course of a career prospectively adds to a person's employment value, or human capital (Becker, 1964). Meanwhile, learning through "communities-of-practice" (Brown and Duguid, 1991) can have a two-way effect, as people draw learning from, and infuse learning into, the work groups they join. Also, learning becomes embedded in a firm's "routines" (Nelson and Winter, 1982) which—like a Broadway play—can still be performed after an individual actor moves on (and takes the benefit of his or her experience to another setting).

A broader influence of learning occurs at the level of the industry region—first, in promoting "a pool of skilled and specially trained personnel" through whom new business can be formed; and second, in creating regional advantages as "the stock of knowledge and skill . . . accumulates as firms imitate each other and personnel move among firms" (Porter, 1990). The associated career mobility can be prompted by both individuals and firms—by individuals, in that the more they learn, the more employable they are likely to be elsewhere (Drucker, 1992); and by firms, in that "great jobs"—with high levels of learning—are, by their nature, not guaranteed jobs (Kanter, 1991).

Bringing in Enterprise

The theme of individual enterprise has drawn limited attention in the wake of the MIT initiative, and lacks a prominent place in the careers research reported in Table 1.1. Both Schein's (1978) "creativity" career anchor and Derr's (1986) "getting high" career-success map accommodate enterprise, which is also one of six basic career interests identified by Holland (1985). However, the common suggestion is that enterprise is one of several options, rather than a necessary element, in people's career behavior.[17]

A stronger case for enterprise—in the broad sense of pursuing distinctive, personally relevant opportunities—can be built from other views. One view draws on persistent ideas about human potential, or uniqueness, and the associated discomfort with externally defined goals (Shepard, 1984). A supporting view stems from Axelrod's (1984) influential demonstration of the alignment between enlightened self-interest and communal interest.[18] A third view concerns the relevance of individual discovery (Kirzner 1992), which, by its nature, cannot be anticipated in present job arrangements. A fourth view sees personal enterprise as the path to the expression of deeply held identities and values (Freeman and Gilbert, 1988). All these views point to enterprise as more of an integral, rather than an optional, component of people's career behavior.

A related view of enterprise stems from studies of the sister concept of entrepreneurship. This work has usually focused on the founding of new firms, and has attributed the founding to a single party, or entrepreneur (e.g., Smith and Miner, 1983).[19] However, recent interpretations are broader. They go beyond the archetype of the lone entrepreneur in their views of new-firm formation. They see entrepreneurship as a property of the firm as a whole, and as an enduring, rather than a preliminary, concern in a firm's existence (Best, 1990). They also see entrepreneurship as a concern of teams (Stewart, 1989), or as a process involving interdependent efforts among firms (Starr and Macmillan, 1990). Further, they see entrepreneurship as a principal concern of people pursuing modern-day, network-sensitive careers (Kanter, 1989).

The Boundaryless Career: An Interfirm Concept

We are suggesting that the dropping of organizational career assumptions, the separate but simultaneous treatment of the person and the firm as units of analysis, and the greater appreciation of person-firm interdependencies can inform a new careers agenda. It is an agenda that views firms as being changed by, as well as bringing change upon, people's careers. And it is an agenda that sees activities such as individual networking, learning, and enterprise as interwoven with the activities of firms. Common to all these opportunities is the suggestion that careers—and, prominently, boundaryless careers—constitute the threads that bind people and firms, and, in turn, broader industrial and economic activities.

Envisioning the boundaryless career as a thread helps us introduce its multiple properties. First, the thread accumulates the individual properties of texture, color, and strength that reflect the person's cumulative aptitudes, experience, and reputation in a developing career. Second, threads develop further properties of size, pattern, and resilience when woven into the shifting fabric of the firm. In these terms, and with the added observation that new threads join the fabric and old threads leave, the boundaryless career and the organizational career are similar concepts. However, the distinctiveness of the boundaryless career appears when we extend this metaphor to interfirm activities. We are encouraged to see how threads enter and leave the fabric of the firm, and how further cooperation (binding) and competition (tension) among firms are stitched together through people's career behavior. Taking an even broader view, we are encouraged to see how shifting patterns in interfirm relations contribute to the changing tapestry of industry regions, sectors, and, ultimately, national and international economies. To better understand this tapestry, there is a need to better understand the properties of the essential threads—boundaryless careers—from which it is woven. Each of the chapters in this book makes a distinct attempt to do so.

Organization of the Book

This book is organized into five parts. We will briefly introduce the contributing authors to highlight the relevant and distinctive expertise they bring to the boundaryless careers arena.

Part I offers contrasting explorations of the boundaryless career phenomenon. AnnaLee Saxenian has uncovered differences behind the relative success of the Silicon Valley, California, high-technology district, versus its counterpart in the Route 128 area of Massachusetts, including differences in the career signals each district transmits (Saxenian, 1994). Karl Weick has been a persevering advocate of a relatively unstructured view of organizing and of associated "self-designing" firms; he has also directly addressed the implications for career behavior in such firms (Weick, 1979; Weick and Berlinger, 1989). Candace Jones has made a special study of independent filmmaking, and of the network ties behind successive project contracts (Jones, 1993). Anne Miner has persistently explored—most recently, with her coauthor, David Robinson—how career behavior through "idiosyncratic jobs" contributes to broader innovation processes (see Miner, 1990).

Part II emphasizes the new organizational forms associated with boundaryless careers. Raymond Miles and Charles Snow coauthored a groundbreaking article, in 1986, explaining popular reports of the "horizontal" or "virtual" organization, and have subsequently explored what might be labeled horizontal, rather than vertical, employment arrangements (see Miles, 1989). Robert DeFillippi is broadly cited for his contribution to the competency-based view of the firm, and has subsequently considered related career competencies with coauthor Michael Arthur (Reed and DeFillippi, 1990; Arthur, Claman, and DeFillippi, 1995). Howard Aldrich draws on his past writing on the "population ecology" of firms, and on issues of small-firm entrepreneurship (Aldrich, 1979; Aldrich and Fiol, 1994), to explore contingency worker issues with coauthor Ted Baker. Allan Bird brings together two streams of interest concerned with Japanese views of "the learning organization" and with Western views of career behavior (see Beechler and Bird, 1993).

In part III the focus shifts to the contexts and processes behind boundary-less careers. Jerry Ellig is a specialist in market-based economics (see Gable and Ellig, 1994), with growing interest—most recently, with coauthor Tojo That-chenkery—in commensurate market-based employment. Holly Raider is engaged in the study of interfirm research-and-development activity, while Ronald Burt has developed a distinctive "structural holes" view of network relations (Burt 1992). Cherlyn Granrose has, for some years, focused on Asian career systems (see Granrose, 1995), and shares a particular interest, with coauthor Bee Leng Chua, in the career systems of the expatriate Chinese. Paul Hirsch (1987) joined here by Mark Shanley was one of the first to chronicle the trau-matic career effects of large-firm restructuring, and the psychological as well as physical dislocations for those involved.

Part IV introduces some concepts in human development. Philip Mirvis has chronicled the disruptions stemming from large-firm merger activities (Mirvis and Marks, 1992), and coauthor Douglas (Tim) Hall remains a continuing ad-vocate of "protean" career behavior (Hall, 1976, 1993). Lotte Bailyn—joined here by coauthor and current research collaborator Joyce Fletcher—has been persistently concerned with how employment arrangements can accommodate and benefit from shifting work and family priorities (Bailyn, 1993). David Thomas has, for some years, chronicled minority career experiences and their underlying relationships (see Thomas and Alderfer, 1989), while Monica Hig-gins developed an early specialization in how timing affects helping relation-ships. Nanette Fondas's writing links the study of managerial-career behavior and the emerging feminization of managerial work (Fondas, 1993; Fondas and Stewart, 1994).

Part V considers the re-engineering of institutions that lend meaning to ca-reer behavior. Charles Perrow is a seasoned observer of the organizational soci-ety, as well as a relatively recent advocate of small-firm networks (Perrow, 1991; 1992). Economist Michael Best focused on regional communities of firms in his *The New Competition* (1990), while Robert Forrant was spending ten years on the shop floor observing blue-collar career experiences. Pamela Tolbert has studied the interplay of occupational and organizational structures in work arrangements (Tolbert and Stern, 1991). James Rosenbaum, an authority on how company career "tournaments" create successive groups of winners and losers, has since examined preparatory career influences in education and ap-prenticeship systems (Rosenbaum, 1984, 1992).

It is fashionable, in current American political circles, to claim a distinction between "reactionaries" and "revolutionaries." The distinction, whatever its merits, places those wishing to promote constructive debate in the horns of a dilemma. One horn has us sticking with ideas from the past, while the other horn has us rejecting ideas from the past, in preparing for the future. We submit that neither horn does much good without reference to the other. The threads of our own ideas, like the threads of the careers we study, need to link the past to the future, to bring the best from one arena to avail the other. That is the spirit in which this book and its contributors' chapters are offered.

Our contributors have taken the concept of the boundaryless career and applied their particular expertise to it. They have done so largely without regard for established academic reputations—including their own—and in a spirit of openness to the years ahead.

Notes

1. Our definition is separate from, but historically connected to, General Electric Chairman and CEO Jack Welch's musings about "the boundaryless organization," reported, for example, by Tichy and Sherman (1993). Our term was picked up as the theme for the 1993 Academy of Management meeting in Atlanta, where the notion of the boundaryless career was first explored (Arthur, 1994).

2. This definition is drawn in turn from earlier work at Massachusetts Institute of Technology in organization studies (Van Maanen, 1977a), at the University of Chicago in sociology (Hughes, 1958), and at Columbia University in educational psychology (Super, 1957). However, we have changed the qualifier from "evolving" (Arthur, Hall, and Lawrence, 1989) to "unfolding" to suggest less orderly or less predictable career progression.

3. Some would still draw a distinction between *careers* and *jobs* (e.g., Yogev and Brett, 1985); however, such a distinction is inconsistent with the definition of *career* adopted here and in the preceding work cited in note 2.

4. Birch et al. (1993) claim U.S. firms with under 500 employees created 5.9 million net new jobs, and larger firms lost 2.4 million net jobs, over the 1987–1991 period.

5. The more usual statistic seen for Japan is 81–82% employed in firms with under 300; 85% at a cutoff size of 500 employees is an estimate.

6. The core group included Bailyn, whose own book from that era appeared somewhat later (Bailyn, 1980).

7. This duality of perspectives distinguishes career studies from related social science perspectives, where subjective and objective views are often represented as opposite ends of the same continuum (e.g., Burrell and Morgan, 1979).

8. As noted later in this chapter, Hall concludes with the idea of the "protean career," which is managed by the career actor across multiple settings and is explicitly "*not* what happens to the person in any one organization" (Hall, 1976: 201, emphasis in original).

9. *In Search of Excellence* expressed its "major concern" as being "with how big companies stay alive, well, and innovative" (Peters and Waterman, 1982: 22). *The Art of Japanese Management* saw the large corporation "as a dominant organization in society" (Pascale and Athos, 1981: 24) and adopted "giant" Matsushita Electric Company as its principal exemplar. *Theory Z* emphasized vertically integrated "zaibatsu" arrangements whereby smaller "satellite" firms existed "largely at the pleasure and the mercy of the major firms" and with "little hope of ever growing into major competitors" (Ouchi, 1981: 21).

10. The five journals we studied all cover the range of years sampled. The selection of interdisciplinary journals probably means that psychological studies of careers are underrepresented. The final list of selected articles and their subjects is available from the authors.

11. Studies of race, gender, and work-family issues were difficult to classify since the question arises about whether the choice of subject itself implied social change. It was decided to classify these articles as implying stability, unless social change was otherwise emphasized. However, even if these articles were taken as evidence of social instability, they often presumed organizational stability in their recommendations.

12. A typical example would be when subjective variables (for example, personal

career aspiration) are compared to objective variables (for example, hierarchical job level), out of concern about existing organizational arrangements.

13. The original sample included 150 articles, as noted in Table 1.1. The remaining 43 articles did include subsets on populations of firms and strategic alliances that had a multifirm flavor, but did not explore related work and employment implications.

14. The definitions quoted are from Webster's Third New International Dictionary (1985), Springfield, Mass.

15. This having been said, as the editors we were uncomfortable to impose a single meaning of *organization* on authors who are accustomed to using the term in their own way. However, all authors contribute one way or another to our understanding of the *process* of organization, and all are clear in their own use of the term.

16. An interesting exception is the debate involving Gilder's (1989) "breakthrough" thesis—that new firms prosper from career moves—and Florida and Kenney's (1990) "follow-through" thesis—that established firms suffer. Both hypotheses concur that boundaryless careers influence firms.

17. Some would argue that autonomy, and, therefore, a broader literature (e.g., Deci and Ryan, 1985) fit in here. However, we see a distinction between being left alone and seeking opportunity when left alone!

18. In a computer simulation of unfolding relationships (Axelrod, 1984), "tit for tat"—trust 'em once, and if they trust you back, trust 'em again—beat all other approaches. Axelrod's research was at the level of the person, and applies directly to career behavior. However, like much work in economics, it has been adopted at the level of the firm (Morgan, 1986) and even the nation-state (Kahn and Zald, 1990).

19. This is despite the insistence of early economists (e.g., Mises, 1949 and even Schumpeter 1951) that entrepreneurship referred to a business function, not an individual actor.

References

Aldrich, H. E. 1979. *Organizations and Environments*. Englewood Cliffs, N.J.: Prentice Hall.

Aldrich, H. E., and Fiol, M. C. 1994. Fools rush in? The institutional context of industry creation. *Academy of Management Review*, 19: 645–670.

Arthur, M. B., ed. 1994. *The Boundaryless Career*. Special Issue, *Journal of Organizational Behavior*, 15, 4.

Arthur, M. B.; Claman, P. H.; and DeFillippi, R. J. 1995. Intelligent enterprise, intelligent careers. *Academy of Management Executive*, 9, 4: 7–22.

Arthur, M. B.; Hall, D. T.; and Lawrence, B. S. 1989. *Handbook of Career Theory*. New York: Cambridge University Press.

Axelrod, R. 1984. *The Evolution of Cooperation*. New York: Basic Books.

Bailyn, L. (with E. H. Schein). 1980. *Living with Technology: Issues at Mid-Career*. Cambridge, Mass.: MIT Press.

Bailyn, L. 1993. *Breaking the Mold*. New York: Free Press.

Barley, S. R. 1992. "The new crafts: The rise of the technical labor force and its implications for the organization of work." Working Paper WP05. National Center on the Educational Quality of the Workforce, University of Pennsylvania.

Becker, G. 1964. *Human Capital*. New York: Columbia University Press.

Beechler, S., and Bird, A. 1993. The best of both worlds? An exploratory study of human resource management practices in U.S.-based Japanese affiliates. In N. Campbell, ed., *The Global Kaisha*. Oxford, Eng.: Blackwell.

Best, M. H. 1990. *The New Competition*. Cambridge, Mass.: Harvard University Press.

Birch, D.; Haggerty, A.; and Parsons, W. 1993. *Who's Creating Jobs?* Cambridge, Mass.: Cognetics, Inc.

Bridges, W. *JobShift*. Reading, Mass.: Addison-Wesley, 1994.

Brock, W. A., and Evans, D. S. 1986. *The Economics of Small Business*. New York: Holmes and Meier.

Brown, J. S., and Duguid, P. 1991. Organizational learning and communities-of-practice: Toward a unified view of working, learning, and innovation. *Organization Science*, 2: 40–56.

Bureau of Labor Statistics. 1989. *Occupational Outlook Quarterly*, Summer.

Burrell, G., and Morgan, G. 1979. *Sociological Paradigms and Organizational Analysis*. London, Heinemann.

Burt, R. S. 1992. *Structural Holes*. Cambridge, Mass.: Harvard University Press.

Cestells, M. 1992. Four Asian tigers with a dragon head: A comparative analysis of the state, economy and society in the Asian Pacific Rim. In R. P. Applebaum and J. Henderson (eds.), *States and Development in the Asian Pacific Rim*. Newbury Park, Calif.: Sage, pp. 33–70.

Cheng, M. T. 1991. The Japanese permanent employment system. *Work and Occupations*, 18, 2: 148–171.

Daft, R., and Lewin A. 1993. Where are the theories for the new organizational forms? An editorial essay. *Organization Science*, 4, 1: i—vi.

Deci, E. L., and Ryan, R. M. 1985. *Intrinsic Motivation and Self-Determination in Human Behavior*. New York, Plenum.

Derr, C. B. 1986. *Managing the New Careerists*. San Francisco, Jossey-Bass.

Drucker, P. F. 1994. The age of social transformation. *Atlantic Monthly*, November, 53–80.

Drucker, P. F. 1993. *Postcapitalist Society*. New York: HarperCollins.

Drucker, P. F. 1992. The new society of organizations. *Harvard Business Review*, September-October, 95–104.

Florida, R., and Kenney, M. 1990. *The Breakthrough Illusion: Corporate America's Failure to Move from Innovation to Mass Production*. New York: Basic Books.

Fondas, N. 1993. The feminization of American management. In Dorothy Moore, ed. *Academy of Management Best Paper Proceedings*, pp. 358–362.

Fondas, N., and Stewart, R. 1994. Understanding differences in general management jobs. *Journal of General Management*, 17, 4: 1–12.

Freeman, R. B., ed. 1993. *Working Under Different Rules*. New York: Russell Sage Foundation.

Freeman, R. E., and Gilbert, D. R. 1988. *Corporate Strategy and the Search for Ethics*. Englewood Cliffs, N.J.: Prentice Hall.

Friedman, D. 1988. *The Misunderstood Miracle: Industrial Development and Political Change in Japan*. Ithaca, N.Y.: Cornell University Press.

Gable, W., and Ellig, J. 1994. *Introduction to Market-Based Management*. Fairfax, Va.: Center for Market Processes, George Mason University.

Galbraith, J. K. 1971. *The New Industrial State*, 2d ed. New York: Houghton Mifflin.

Gilder, G. *Microcosm*. 1989. New York: Simon and Schuster.

Granovetter, M. 1985. Economic action and social structure: The problem of embeddedness. *American Journal of Sociology*, 91: 481–510.

Granrose, C. S. 1995. Careers of Japanese and expatriate Chinese managers in U.S. multinational firms. *Journal of Asian Business*, 10, 4: 1–21.

Hall, D. T. 1976. *Careers in Organizations*. Santa Monica, Calif.: Goodyear.

Hall, D. T. 1993. The "new career contract": alternative career paths. Paper read at Fourth German Business Congress on Human Resources, Cologne.

Handy, C. 1994. *The Age of Paradox*. Boston, Harvard Business School Press.

Harrison, B. 1994. *Lean and Mean: The Changing Landscape of Corporate Power in the Age of Flexibility*. New York: Basic Books.

Hirsch, P. 1987. *Pack Your Own Parachute*. Reading, Mass.: Addison-Wesley.

Holland, J. L. 1985. *Making Vocational Choices,* 2d ed. Englewood Cliffs, N.J.: Prentice Hall.

Hughes, E. C. 1958. *Men and Their Work*. Glencoe, Il.: Free Press.

Jones, C. 1993. Toward an understanding and theory of network organizations. Ph.D. diss., University of Utah, Salt Lake City.

Kahn, R. L., and Zald, M. N., eds. 1990. *Organizations and Nation States*. San Francisco: Jossey-Bass.

Kanter, R. M. 1977. *Men and Women of the Corporation*. New York: Basic Books.

Kanter, R. M. 1989. *When Giants Learn to Dance: Mastering the Challenges of Strategy, Management and Careers in the 1990s*. New York: Basic Books.

Kanter, R. M. 1991. Globalism/localism: A new human resources agenda. *Harvard Business Review,* March-April, 9–10.

Kirzner, I. 1992. *The Meaning of Market Process*. New York: Routledge.

Maguire, S. R. 1993. Employer and occupational tenure: An update. *Monthly Labor Review,* June, 45–56.

Miles, R. E. 1989. Adapting to technology and competition: A new industrial relations system for the 21st century. *California Management Review,* Winter.

Miles, R. E., and Snow, C. C. 1986. Organizations: New concepts for new forms. *California Management Review,* 28, 3: 62–72.

Miner, A. S. 1990. Structural evolution through idiosyncratic jobs: The potential for unplanned learning. *Organization Science,* 1: 195–210.

Mirvis, P. H., and Marks, M. L. 1992. *Managing the Merger*. Englewood Cliffs, N.J.: Prentice Hall.

Mises, L. von. 1949. *Human Action,* 3d ed. New Haven, Conn.: Yale University Press.

Morgan, G. 1986. *Images of Organization*. Newbury Park, Calif.: Sage.

Naisbett, J. 1994. *Global Paradox*. New York: Morrow.

Nelson, R. R., and Winter, S. G. 1982. *An Evolutionary Theory of Economic Change*. Cambridge, Mass.: Belknap/Harvard University Press.

Nohria, N. 1992. Is a network perspective a useful way of studying organizations? In N. Nohria and R. G. Eccles, eds., *Networks and Organizations*. Boston: Harvard Business School Press, pp. 1–22.

Ouchi, W. G. 1981. *Theory Z*. Reading, Mass.: Addison-Wesley.

Pascale, R. T., and Athos, A. G. 1981. *The Art of Japanese Management*. New York: Simon & Schuster.

Perrow, C. 1991. A society of organizations. *Theory and Society,* 20: 725–762.

Perrow, C. 1992. Small firm networks. In N. Nohria and R. G. Eccles, eds., *Networks and Organizations*. Boston: Harvard Business School Press, pp. 445–470.

Peters, T. J. 1987. *Thriving on Chaos*. New York: Knopf.

Peters, T. J., and Waterman, R. H. 1982. *In Search of Excellence: Lessons from America's Best-Run Companies*. New York: Harper and Row.

Pfeffer, J., and Salancik, G. R. 1978. *The External Control of Organizations*. New York: Harper and Row.

Piore, M. J., and Sabel, C. F. 1984. *The Second Industrial Divide: Possibilities for Prosperity*. New York: Basic Books.

Porter, M. E. 1980. *Competitive Strategy*. New York: Free Press.

Porter, M. E. 1990. *The Competitive Advantage of Nations*. New York: Free Press.

Powell, W. W., and Brantley, P. 1992. Competitive cooperation in biotechnology: Learning through networks? In N. Nohria and R. G. Eccles, eds., *Networks and Organizations*. Boston: Harvard Business School Press, pp. 366–394.

Prahalad, C. K., and Hamel G. 1994. Strategy as a field of study: Why search for a new paradigm? *Strategic Management Journal*, 15(S), Summer, 5–16.

Quinn, J. B. 1992. *Intelligent Enterprise*. New York: Free Press.

Reddy, N. M., and Rao, M. V. H. 1990. The industrial market as an interfirm organization. *Journal of Management Studies*, 27: 43–59.

Reed, R., and DeFillippi, R. J. 1990. Causal ambiguity: Barriers to imitation and sustainable competitive advantage. *Academy of Management Review*, 15: 88–102.

Reich, R. B. 1991. *The Work of Nations*. New York: Knopf.

Rogers, E. M., and Larsen, J. K. 1984. *Silicon Valley Fever: Growth of High-Technology Culture*. New York: Basic Books.

Rosenbaum, J. E., 1984. *Career Mobility in a Corporate Hierarchy*. New York: Academic Press.

Rosenbaum, J. E., et al. 1992. *Apprenticeship in America: Guidelines for Building an Effective System*. William T. Grant Foundation, Commission on Youth and America's Future, Washington, D.C.

Rousseau, D. M. 1995. *Psychological Contracts in Organizations*. Newbury Park, Calif.: Sage.

Samuelson, P. A., and Nordhaus, W. D. 1992. *Economics*, 14th ed. New York: Mc-Graw-Hill.

Saxenian, A. 1994. *Regional Advantage: Culture and Competition in Silicon Valley and Route 128*. Cambridge, Mass.: Harvard University Press.

Schein, E. H. 1978. *Career Dynamics: Matching Individual and Organizational Needs*. Reading, Mass.: Addison-Wesley.

Schumpeter, J. A. 1951. Economic theory and entrepreneurial history. In R. V. Clemence, ed., *Essays of J. A. Schumpeter*. Port Washington, N.Y.: Kennikat Press.

Shepard, H. A. 1984. On the realization of human potential: A path with a heart. In M. B. Arthur; L. Bailyn; D. J. Levinson; and H. A. Shepard, *Working With Careers*. New York: Graduate School of Business, Columbia University, pp. 25–46.

Small Business Administration 1992. *The State of Small Business*. Washington, D.C., Government Printing Office.

Smith, K. G.; Carroll, S. J.; and Ashford, S. J. 1995. Intra- and interorganizational cooperation: Toward a research agenda. *Academy of Management Journal*, 38, 7–23.

Smith, N. R., and Miner, J. B. 1983. Type of entrepreneur, type of firm, and managerial motivation: Implications for organizational life cycle theory. *Strategic Management Journal*, 4: 325–340.

Starr, J. A., and Macmillan, I. C. 1990. Resource cooptation via social contracting: Resource acquisition strategies for new ventures. *Strategic Management Journal*, 11(S): 79–92.

Stewart, A. 1989. *Team Entrepreneurship*. Newbury Park, Calif.: Sage.

Storey, D. J. 1994. *Understanding the Small Business Sector*. London: Routledge.

Super, D. E. 1957. *The Psychology of Careers*. New York: Harper & Row.

Thomas, D. A., and Alderfer, C. P. 1989. The influence of race on career dynamics: Theory and research on minority career experiences. In M. B. Arthur; D. T. Hall; and B. S. Lawrence, eds., *Handbook of Career Theory*. New York: Cambridge University Press, pp. 133–158.

Tichy, N. M., and Sherman, S. 1993. *Control Your Destiny or Someone Else Will*. New York: Doubleday.

Toffler, A. 1990. *Powershift*. New York: Bantam.

Tolbert, P. S., and Stern, R. 1991. Organizations of professionals: Governance structures in large law firms. In P. S. Tolbert; S. R. Barley; and S. B. Bacharach, eds., *Organizations and Professions*. Greenwich, Conn.: JAI Press, pp. 97–117.

U.S. Department of Labor. 1992. Quoted in T. Pouschine and M. Kripalani. I got tired of forcing myself to the office. *Forbes,* 149, 11: 104–114.

Van Maanen, J., ed. 1977a. *Organizational Careers: Some New Perspectives*. New York: Wiley.

Van Maanen, J. 1977b. Introduction: The promise of career studies. In J. Van Maanen, ed. *Organizational Careers: Some New Perspectives*. New York: Wiley, pp. 1–12.

Weick, K. E. 1979. *The Social Psychology of Organizing*, 2d ed. Reading, Mass.: Addison-Wesley.

Weick, K. E., and Berlinger, L. R. 1989. Career improvisation in self-designing organizations. In M. B. Arthur; D. T. Hall; and B. S. Lawrence, eds., *Handbook of Career Theory*. New York: Cambridge University Press, pp. 313–328.

Williamson, O. E. 1975. *Markets and Hierarchies: Analysis and Antitrust Implications*. New York: Free Press.

Williamson, O. E. 1991. Strategizing, economizing and economic organization, *Strategic Management Journal*, 12(S): 75–94.

Yogev, S., and Brett, J. 1985. Patterns of work and family involvement among single- and dual-earner couples. *Journal of Applied Psychology*, 70: 754–768.

I

EXPLORING THE NATURE OF BOUNDARYLESS CAREERS

Boundaryless careers by definition take many forms. The first part of this book is intended to highlight some of the essential elements boundaryless careers share. Two of its chapters provide strong industry-specific illustrations, while the remaining two chapters offer what may be viewed as complementary, and more generalizable, ideas. Taken together, the four chapters explain how skilled observation of boundaryless career practices can stimulate new, more enlightened, theory and career development opportunities.

We begin with AnnaLee Saxenian's "Beyond Boundaries: Open Labor Markets and Learning in the Silicon Valley." As the title suggests, Saxenian covers what may be the most frequently cited of all examples of regional economic success. But what distinguishes her description is its explicit claim to learning advantages that emanate from boundaryless-career behavior. This behavior, and the career motivation behind it, depend centrally on participation in social networks. These networks not only transcend company and industry lines but also blur the boundaries between the economy and community life. The region and its relationships—rather than the individual firm—thus define opportunities for individual and collective advantage. Saxenian suggests that such open labor markets provide an important competitive advantage over traditional internal labor markets because they generate multiple opportunities for experimentation and collective learning.

Karl Weick's "Enactment and the Boundaryless Career: Organizing as We Work" is, in a sense, a social-psychological response to Saxenian. With the Silicon Valley as a prime example, we are drawn toward the process of enactment as a central explanation for how boundaryless careers create new relationships and ways to work. Weick's essential theme is that boundaryless careers shape firms at least as much as boundaryless firms shape careers. As firms become less bounded, people must wrestle with uncertainty and incomplete information. The result is that people fill in the blanks, being helped along the way by the forces of individual personality and interpersonal relationships. People making sense of uncertainty enact a structure in which to work. Microlevel processes shape macrolevel organizing. Weick describes how people organize while they work, through processes of enactment and learning, individually and collectively, creating career scripts and institutions that ultimately can act to constrain them. Cycles of enactment are endemic as people respond to organizational and life transitions.

Candace Jones's "Careers in Project Networks: The Case of the Film Industry" provides a second illustration of the nature of boundaryless careers. Her particular focus is on independent filmmaking, which has persistently outstripped the major studios in both innovation and production success. Drawing on in-depth interviews and archival data from the independent film industry, Jones offers insights into how boundaryless careers are experienced and organized into a project network. Subcontractors and their selection, training, and socialization provide the infrastructure that builds and maintains project networks. Projects are essential building blocks in boundaryless careers, and from these we derive two important career patterns—those of the free agent and the team member.

David Robinson and Anne Miner conclude this first part with an approach that might be applied to the collective learning that independent filmmakers have achieved. Their chapter, "The Evolution of Careers as Organizations Learn," reverses the usual perspective, and focuses on how organizational and population-level learning affect individual job changes and careers. Collective learning increasingly drives individual careers. Ongoing organizational learning requires variation (for discovery and change), selection (making choices among new routines), and retention (memory). Although some observers predict boundaryless careers will arise primarily from independent agents negotiating short-term contracts, Robinson and Miner disagree. They maintain that collective learning processes involve unexpected links between social networks and careers. The result is a set of complex, diverse patterns of employment, including both highly fluid and relatively stable jobs.

2

Beyond Boundaries: Open Labor Markets and Learning in Silicon Valley

ANNALEE SAXENIAN

According to local mythology, William Hewlett, cofounder of the Hewlett-Packard Company, routinely offered the following advice to newcomers to Silicon Valley: "If you want to succeed here you need to be willing to do three things: change jobs often, talk to your competitors, and take risks—even if it means failing." Speaking with the authority of one of the region's oldest and most respected entrepreneurs, Hewlett was able to highlight the distinctive features of the labor markets in this northern California region: the pervasiveness of interfirm mobility; the importance of the informal social networks that transcend firm boundaries, and the high rates of firm formation (and failure). Hewlett recognized that successful careers in Silicon Valley are rarely built within the boundaries of a single firm; rather, they are defined by the ability of an individual or a team to define new markets, technologies, products, and applications. As one local semiconductor executive reportedly noted: "Many of us wake up in the morning thinking that we work for Silicon Valley, Inc."

This chapter argues that the region and its relationships, rather than the firm, define opportunities for individual and collective advances in Silicon Valley. It suggests that open labor markets—and the corresponding career paths—offer important competitive advantages over traditional corporate job ladders in a volatile economic environment. The essential advantage of regional, rather than firm-based, labor markets lies in the multiple opportunities they provide for learning.

Learning occurs in Silicon Valley as individuals move between firms and industries, acquiring new skills, experiences, and know-how. It occurs as they exchange technical and market information in both formal and informal forums, and as shifting teams of entrepreneurs regroup to experiment with new technologies and applications. Learning occurs as firms of different sizes and specializations jointly solve shared problems. Above all, learning occurs through failure, which is as common as success. In short, learning in Silicon Valley is a collective process that is rarely confined within the boundaries of individual firms and ultimately draws from the resources of the region as a whole.

The case of Silicon Valley offers important lessons for students of work organization. The region provides a clear example of boundaryless careers in action. And while much of the scholarly research on work and employment concerns the often wrenching transition from traditional organizational job ladders to less-bounded labor markets, this transition has been avoided in Silicon Valley. Indeed, from the earliest days, careers in Silicon Valley had few boundaries. As a result, the Silicon Valley experience provides important insights into both the social and institutional prerequisites and the learning advantages of boundaryless careers.

In contrast with standard economic models of labor-market behavior that rely on atomistic assumptions concerning individual job searches and human capital, this essay emphasizes the social embeddedness of labor markets (Granovetter, 1988, 1995). It demonstrates the extent to which career mobility in Silicon Valley depends centrally on participation in local networks of social relations. These networks not only transcend company and industry lines, but also blur the boundaries between the economy and local social life. In the words of one theorist of open labor markets:

> Individuals secure their long-term employability through participation in neighborhood groups, hobby clubs, or other professional and social networks outside the firm. Only those who participate in such multiple, loosely connected networks are likely to know when their current jobs are in danger, where new opportunities lie, and what skills are required to seize them. The more open corporate labor markets become, the greater the economic compulsion to participate in the social activities they organize. (Sabel, 1991)

Although these words were not written to describe Silicon Valley, they certainly could have been.

In the following section, I describe the origins of the technical community in Silicon Valley—one that supports open labor markets. Subsequent sections demonstrate how the region's social and professional networks support high rates of job mobility and contribute to ongoing experimentation, entrepreneurship, and collective learning at the regional level. In the final section, I contrast Silicon Valley's labor markets with those of the region's leading technology competitor, Boston's Route 128, where firms have, until recently, maintained more traditional organizational boundaries and career paths. While the comparison cannot be fully developed here, research suggests that these differences help account for the divergent fortunes of these two regional economies (Saxenian, 1994).

The Origins of a Technical Community in Silicon Valley

Silicon Valley's early engineers and scientists saw themselves as the pioneers of a new industry in a new region. They were at once forging a new settlement in the West, and advancing the development of a revolutionary technology—semiconductor electronics. As newcomers to a region that lacked prior industrial traditions, Silicon Valley's pioneers had the freedom to experiment with institutions and organizational forms, as well as technologies. These young engineers, having left behind families, friends, and established communities, were unusually open to risk-taking and experimentation.[1]

The shared experience of working at the Fairchild Semiconductor Corporation also served as a powerful bond for many of the region's early semiconductor engineers. During the 1960s, it seemed as if every engineer in Silicon Valley had worked there.[2] Even today, many of the region's entrepreneurs and managers still speak of Fairchild as an important managerial training ground and applaud the education they got at "Fairchild University." Similar, shared professional experiences continued to reinforce the sense of community in the region even after individuals had moved on to different, often competing, firms.

A poster of the Fairchild family tree, which traces the genealogy of the scores of Fairchild spin-offs, hangs on the walls of many Silicon Valley firms. This family tree symbolizes the complex mix of social solidarity and individualistic competition that characterizes Silicon Valley. The tree graphically illustrates the common ancestry of the region's semiconductor companies and reminds engineers of the personal ties that enabled people, technology, and money to frequently recombine into new ventures. The importance of these overlapping, quasi-familial ties is reflected in continuing references, more than three decades later, to the "fathers" (or "grandfathers") of Silicon Valley and their offspring, the "Fairchildren."[3]

At the same time, the family tree glorifies the risk-taking and competitive individualism that distinguish the region's business culture. Silicon Valley's heroes are the successful entrepreneurs who have taken aggressive professional and technical risks—the garage tinkerers who created successful companies. These entrepreneurial heroes are celebrated for their technical achievements and for the often considerable wealth that success has brought them.

The informal cooperation among Silicon Valley engineers predates the semiconductor industry. Stanford Dean of Engineering Frederick Terman actively pursued a vision of building a "community of technical scholars" around Stanford during the 1940s and 1950s in order to enhance the region's industrial base. He promoted collaboration between the university and local technology firms, in a variety of ways: providing start-ups with financial support and low-rent space in the newly created Stanford Industrial Park; offering continuing technical education for employees of local companies; and encouraging ongoing interaction between businesses and university faculty and students. His support of engineering students such as William Hewlett, David Packard, and the Varian brothers exceeded traditional professorial encouragement of promising graduate students.

These students in turn extended this tradition of assistance in their relations with other firms in the region, providing encouragement, advice, computer time, space, and even financing to new entrepreneurs. A San Jose journalist noted later:

> As their company grew, both Hewlett and Packard became very involved in the formation and growth of other companies. They encouraged entrepreneurs, went out of their way to share what they learned, and were instrumental in getting electronics companies to work together on common problems . . . Largely because of them, there's an unusual spirit of cooperation in the local electronics industry.[4]

The shared identities that grow out of these social and professional networks underlie the common practices of information exchange among the region's producers. The Wagon Wheel bar in Sunnyvale, a popular watering hole where engineers met during the 1960s and 1970s to exchange ideas and gossip, has been termed "the fountainhead of the semiconductor industry." As Tom Wolfe described it:

> Every year there was some place, the Wagon Wheel, Chez Yvonne, Rickey's, the Roundhouse, where members of this esoteric fraternity, the young men and women of the semiconductor industry, would head after work to have a drink and gossip and brag and trade war stories about phase jitters, phantom circuits, bubble memories, pulse trains, bounceless contacts, burst modes, leapfrog tests, p-n junctions, sleeping sickness modes, slow-death episodes, RAMs, NAKs, MOSes, PCMs, PROMs, PROM blowers, PROM blasters, and teramagnitudes, meaning multiples of a million millions. (1983: 362)

By all accounts, these informal conversations were pervasive, and served as an important source of up-to-date information about competitors, customers, and changes in markets and technologies. Local entrepreneurs came to see social relationships and even gossip as crucial aspects of their businesses. In an industry characterized by vigorous technological change and intense competition, informal communication was often more valuable than formal, but less timely, forums, such as industry journals.

Informal information exchange was not limited to after-hours discussions, but continued on the job. Competitors consulted each other on technical matters with a frequency unheard of in other areas of the country. According to one executive: "I have people call me quite frequently and say, 'Hey, did you ever run into this one?' and you say, 'Yeh, seven or eight years ago. Why don't you try this, that or the other thing?' We all get calls like that" (Braun and Macdonald, 1978: 130).

Information exchanges also occurred at frequent gatherings organized by the Western Electronics Manufacturers Association (WEMA) and at other industry conferences and trade shows. According to the president of WEMA: "Easterners tell me that people there don't talk to their competitors. Here they will not only sit down with you, but they will share the problems and experiences they have had" (Bylinsky, 1976).

A variety of more- and less-formal gatherings of specialists also served as forums for exchange. The Homebrew Computer Club, for example, was founded in 1975 by a group of local microcomputer enthusiasts who had been influenced by the counterculture ethic of the 1960s. They placed a notice on bulletin boards inviting those interested in computers to "come to a gathering of people with like-minded interests. Exchange information, swap ideas, help work on a project, whatever . . . " (Levy, 1984: 194). Within months, the club's regular membership had reached about 500, mostly young "hackers," who came to meetings to trade, to sell or give away computer hardware and software, and to get advice. The club became the center of an informal network of microcomputer experts in the region that survived even after the group itself folded. Eventually, more than 20 computer companies, including Apple Computer, were started by Homebrew members.

While Homebrew is a particularly well-known example, it was not exceptional—such groups continue to be pervasive in Silicon Valley. The CEO of a semiconductor-materials firm noted: "There are people gathered together once a month or once every two months to discuss every area of common scientific interest in the Valley. Around every technological subject, or every engineering concern, you have meeting groups that tend to foster new ideas and innovate. People rub shoulders and share ideas" (Delbecq and Weiss, 1988).

Social Networks and Open Labor Markets

The region's dense social and professional networks are not simply conduits for the dissemination of technical and market information. They also function as highly efficient job-search networks, contributing to the unusually high rates of interfirm mobility in the region. Gathering places like the Wagon Wheel served as informal recruiting centers and as listening posts; job information flowed freely along with shoptalk. As one engineer reported: "In this business there's really a network. You just don't hire people out of the blue. In general, it's people you know, or you know someone who knows them" (Gregory, 1984: 445).

Engineers in Silicon Valley shifted so frequently between firms that mobility not only became socially acceptable; it became the norm. The preferred career option in Silicon Valley was to join a small company or a start-up company, rather than an established firm with a good reputation. In fact, the superiority of innovative, small firms over large corporations became an article of faith among the region's engineers.

By the 1970s, Silicon Valley was distinguished by the highest levels of job-hopping in the nation. Average annual employee turnover in local electronics firms exceeded 35% and was as high as 59% in the region's small firms (American Electronics Association 1981). It was almost unheard of for a technical professional in Silicon Valley to have a career in a single company. An anthropologist studying the career paths of the region's computer professionals concluded that job tenures in Silicon Valley averaged two years. One engineer there explained:

> Two or three years is about max [at a job] for the Valley because there's always
> something more interesting across the street. You don't see someone staying twenty
> years at a job here. If they've been in a small company with 200 to 300 people for
> 10 or 11 years, you tend to wonder about them. We see those types coming in
> from the East Coast. (Gregory, 1984: 216)

The region's engineers developed loyalties to each other and to advancing
technology, rather than to individual firms or even industries. In the words of
the cofounder of LSI Logic: "Here in Silicon Valley there's far greater loyalty to
one's craft than to one's company. A company is just a vehicle which allows
you to work. If you're a circuit designer it's most important for you to do
excellent work. If you can't in one firm, you'll move on to another one." [5]

When John Sculley, who was recruited from the East Coast in 1985, became the CEO of Apple Computer, he was amazed by the extent to which
mobility had become a norm in Silicon Valley:

> The mobility among people strikes me as radically different than the world I came
> from out East. There is far more mobility and there is far less real risk in people's
> careers. When someone is fired or leaves on the East Coast, it's a real trauma in
> their lives. If they are fired or leave here it doesn't mean very much. They just go
> off and do something else . . . (Delbecq and Weiss, 1988: 37)

The geographic proximity of firms in Silicon Valley facilitated these high
levels of mobility. Moving from job to job in Silicon Valley did not disrupt
personal, social, or professional ties as much as it could elsewhere in the country. According to one engineer:

> If you left Texas Instruments for another job, it was a major psychological move,
> all the way to one coast or the other, or at least as far as Phoenix. Out here, it
> wasn't that big a catastrophe to quit your job on Friday and have another job on
> Monday. This was just as true for company executives. You didn't necessarily have
> to tell your wife. You just drove off in another direction on Monday morning.
> You didn't have to sell your house, and your kids didn't have to change schools.
> (Hanson, 1982)

As another Silicon Valley executive put it, "People change jobs out here without
changing car pools." Ironically, many of these Silicon Valley job-hoppers may
well have led more stable lives than the upwardly mobile "organization men"
of the 1950s who were transferred from place to place by the same employer.

Local technology companies in turn competed intensely for experienced engineering talent. They offered bonuses, stock options, high salaries, pleasant
work conditions, interesting projects, and other incentives to attract good people from their competitors. Early efforts to take legal action against employees
who left firms to join new companies proved inconclusive or protracted, and
most firms came to accept high turnover as a cost of business in the region.
In fact, employees often left for new opportunities with the blessings of top
management, and with the understanding that if the change didn't work out,
they could return. Such understandings created an important safety net for local engineers.

As individuals move from firm to firm in Silicon Valley, their paths overlap repeatedly: A colleague might become a customer or a competitor; today's boss could be tomorrow's subordinate. Individuals move both within and between industry sectors—from semiconductors to personal computers, or from semiconductor equipment to software. They move from established firms to start-ups, and vice versa. And they move from electronics producers to service providers, such as venture-capital or consulting firms—and back again.

Professional loyalties and friendships generally survive this turmoil. Few presume that the long-term relationships needed for professional success will be found within the four walls of any particular company. Many rely on trade shows, technical conferences, and informal social gatherings to maintain and extend their social and professional networks. In the words of the CEO of a local semiconductor firm:

> The network in Silicon Valley transcends company loyalties. We treat people fairly and they are loyal to us, but there is an even higher level of loyalty—to their network. I have senior engineers who are constantly on the phone and sharing information with our competitors. I know what my competitors say in their speeches and they know what I say in private conversations.[6]

Informal exchange and collaboration thus coexist with fierce interfirm competition in Silicon Valley to support careers that are rarely confined to individual companies.

In the words of anthropologist Kathleen Gregory:

> Negotiating a career in Silicon Valley is best viewed as an intricate free-form dance between employees and employers that rewards continuous monitoring, but cannot be fully choreographed. Careers in computing do not take place by design, but are emergent and negotiated between ever changing individuals and employers. (1984: 205)

Learning through Experimentation (and Failure)

Starting a new firm became increasingly legitimate in Silicon Valley with the emergence of successive generations of successful role models. The generations of entrepreneurial start-ups depicted by the Fairchild family tree were replicated during the 1960s, 1970s, and 1980s in one sector after another—from computers and disk drives to networking, software, and multimedia.[7] This proliferation of successful new ventures depends upon and, in turn, reproduces a regional culture of risk-taking and open exchange.

The culture of Silicon Valley accords the highest status to those who start firms. Not only is risk-taking glorified in the region, but failure is socially acceptable. And the successes of generation after generation of start-ups reinforce the belief that anyone can be a successful entrepreneur; there are no boundaries of age, economic status, or social status that preclude the possibility of a new beginning. Unlike elsewhere, there is little embarrassment or shame associated with business failure. In fact, the list of individuals who have failed, even repeatedly, only to succeed later, is well known in the region. As Apple CEO John Sculley put it: "In Silicon Valley, if someone fails, we know they're in all likelihood going to reappear in some other company in a matter of months" (Mc-Kenna, 1989: 85). New ventures in Silicon Valley are typically started by engineers who have acquired operating experience and technical skills while working in other firms in the region. The archetypal Silicon Valley start-up is formed by a group of friends and/or former colleagues with an idea for a new product or application. Some are frustrated by the difficulties of pursuing their ideas within an established firm; others simply seek new challenges. They seek funding and advice from local venture capitalists—often former entrepreneurs and engineers themselves—and rely on an ever-expanding circle of specialized suppliers, consultants, university researchers, and market researchers for additional assistance in starting the new enterprise. As they grow, they often recruit employees from their networks of professional friends and acquaintances.

In short, the region's social and technical networks operate as a kind of superorganization, through which individuals, in shifting combinations, organize a decentralized process of experimentation and entrepreneurship. Individuals move between firms and projects without the alienation that might be expected from such a high degree of mobility, because their social and professional relationships remain intact (Gregory, 1984). In Silicon Valley, the region and its networks, rather than individual firms, are the engines of technological advance.

Widespread job mobility and open information exchange accelerate the diffusion of technological capabilities and understandings in the region. Departing employees are typically required to sign nondisclosure statements that prevent them from revealing company secrets. However, much of the useful knowledge in the industry grows out of the experience of developing technology. When engineers change companies, they take with them the know-how and skills acquired at their previous jobs. What distinguishes Silicon Valley is the extent to which the region's networks ensure the rapid spread of knowledge and skill within a localized industrial community.[8]

Experimentation—and even failure—are recognized in Silicon Valley as critical opportunities for learning. One executive recruiter notes: "Everybody knows that some of the best presidents in the valley are people that have stumbled."[9] In the words of another commentator:

> The value of failure is its role in the learning process; unless failure is possible, no learning is possible . . . ; in the realm of ideas, unless falsification is possible, learning isn't possible. As a matter of fact, in information theory, no information is transmitted unless negation is possible, and so the tolerance of failure is absolutely critical to the success of Silicon Valley. If you don't tolerate failure, you can't permit success. The successful people have a lot more failures than the failures do.[10]

Larry Jordan, vice president of marketing at semiconductor-producer Integrated Devices Technology, describes how the learning that occurs through the area's continuing recombinations strengthens the region's industrial fabric:

> There is a unique atmosphere here that continually revitalizes itself by virtue of the fact that today's collective understandings are informed by yesterday's frustrations and modified by tomorrow's recombinations. . . . Learning occurs through

these recombinations. No other geographic area creates recombinations so effectively with so little disruption. The entire industrial fabric is strengthened by this process.[11]

This localized process of recombination encourages both technological and organizational innovations. Many more technical paths are pursued in Silicon Valley than would occur either in the traditional large firm or in a region with less fluid social and industrial structures, because of the relative ease of new-firm formation. Within most large firms (or stable regions), a single technical option is selected and pursued—typically leaving many viable alternatives untapped. Over time, the organization becomes increasingly committed, or locked in, to a particular trajectory. On the other hand, a more flexible regional economy continues to generate and pursue technological alternatives.

While it could no longer be said, by the 1980s and 1990s, that "everyone knows everyone" in Silicon Valley, local executives still regard the density and openness of the region's social and professional networks, and the corresponding frequency of informal exchanges, as a crucial advantage. According to one local manager:

> Over a lunch conversation or a beer, you'll learn that company A or company B has a technology that you want, and you'll find out about it. If it fits your needs, you'll build it into your next product. Even if you don't, you get a lot of pointers from networking: you learn about the latest start-ups and you learn about people, about who's good and who's not. You also learn about technology. You learn about things that are possible. You sometimes learn that what you thought wasn't possible can in fact be done. So you just call the people up and learn more. You might not call your competitor directly, but you can call people in the supply base, and they'll share anything.[12]

Technical information thus continues to be diffused rapidly in the region, along with the tacit technological capabilities and understandings that move as engineers move, paving the way for new opportunities and enterprises.

This environment of open communication also facilitates collaboration with customers. An executive at a semiconductor firm claims that a sophisticated local customer base is absolutely critical to his firm:

> When we come out with the specs for a new product, we take them to a series of companies that we have relations with and that have good technical horsepower, and they'll give us feedback on the features they like and don't like. It's an iterative process: we define a product, we get feedback and improve it, we refine it and develop associated products. The process feeds on itself. And the fact that these customers are nearby means that the iterations are faster; rapid communication is absolutely critical to insuring fast time-to-market.[13]

Another executive comments similarly on the importance of sophisticated customers being in close proximity for a process of mutual learning and adaptation:

> It's not necessary that our customers are geographically close, but the fact that the valley has some of the leaders in systems and computers is a vital part of the cross-pollination process. We use others' existence to create our own existence: our form is vitally affected by their presence. We change and so do they.[14]

These interactive relationships between customers and vendors foster cross-fertilization, learning, and innovation along the entire production chain in Silicon Valley, from semiconductors to disk drives and software, and to final systems.

This is not to suggest that conflicts are absent in Silicon Valley. The very intensity of competition among local producers is a continuing spur to imitation and technological innovation. Competitive rivalries are often highly personalized, as status is defined as much by technical excellence as by market share. And by the 1980s, lawsuits and conflicts over intellectual property were commonplace in the region.[15]

Yet even as competitive pressures intensify, an underlying loyalty and a shared commitment to technological excellence unify the members of this industrial community. Local firms compete intensely for market share and technical leadership, while simultaneously relying on the collaborative practices that distinguish the region. The paradox of Silicon Valley is that competition demands continuous innovation, but innovation requires interfirm cooperation. Nothing is prized more than individual initiative and technological advances, which are impossible without access to the information, ideas, and experience that reside in the valley's dense social and professional networks.

Thus, while Silicon Valley's high rates of job mobility and new-firm formation may lead to losses for individual firms, they also foster a dynamic process of industrial adaptation in the region. Knowledge of the latest techniques in design, production, and marketing is diffused rapidly throughout the area. And the ease of recombining new ideas with existing skill and know-how ensures that firms in the region will pursue a multiplicity of technological opportunities, many of which would have been bypassed under a more stable industrial regime.

A Passing Phase?

Observers often conclude that Silicon Valley's open labor markets and collaborative practices are appropriate only to the early stages of an industry life cycle, when firms are small and technologies fluid. Once the industry matures, the argument goes, and companies gain in scale and self-sufficiency, they will abandon local relationships (Harrison, 1994; Markusen, 1985). The obvious implication is that over time, Silicon Valley's largest firms will establish internal labor markets and more traditional organizational boundaries.

A comparison with the Route 128 region in Massachusetts—where firms compete in the same technology sectors as Silicon Valley and yet have failed to adapt successfully to changing markets—suggests that open labor markets are not simply a passing phase. Rather, they are a component of a flexible and enduring alternative to the traditional organizational model, one that, under conditions of market and technological volatility such as those of the present, offers important competitive advantages.[16]

As late as the 1980s, the most desirable career path on Route 128 was to move up the corporate ladder of a large company with a good reputation. Whereas interfirm mobility was by then a way of life in Silicon Valley, Route

128 executives were more likely to consider job-hopping unacceptable and to express a preference for professionals who were "in it for the long term." The employees of the region's technology firms were, in turn, very loyal, generally expecting to stay with a company for the long term. What little mobility occurred in the region tended to be between established, relatively safe, companies.

This difference in career patterns was reflected in the regional compensation practices. In Silicon Valley, the early firms like Hewlett-Packard (H-P) and Intel offered their employees profit-sharing plans and generous stock options in order to attract and motivate talented individuals. Today, while there is little interest in retirement plans because company tenures are so short, stock options are typically available to all employees—from the rank and file to top managers. One venture capitalist described stock as "the mothers' milk of Silicon Valley" and suggested that local firms would lose their competitive edge if people didn't have equity ownership in their firms.[17] In the Route 128 area, by contrast, even recent graduates worry primarily about gaining a comfortable pension, and it is rare for firms to offer stock options to employees, except perhaps to top executives.

The practice of leaving a large company to join a small firm or a promising start-up, so common in Silicon Valley, was virtually unheard of on Route 128. As one veteran employee of Honeywell put it:

> There is tremendous loyalty to the company and tremendous will to make things succeed within the company [on Route 128]. There were pockets of brilliance at Honeywell, but these individuals never took the leap to go off on their own or join another company. I stayed at Honeywell for more than twenty years. I had lots of opportunities to leave, but I never took them seriously because I had too many personal commitments and business ties. When I finally left, it was like an 8.5 on the Richter scale. Everyone was shocked, they just couldn't believe it![18]

Indeed, while there were a handful of high-profile entrepreneurs in the region, starting a company on Route 128 was still regarded as extremely risky. A former Digital Equipment Corporation (DEC) executive who is now based in Silicon Valley reports similarly: "We never talked about start-ups back East. Out here we're always talking about who's doing what, what's succeeded. As a result, everyone in Silicon Valley is motivated to do start-ups, while on the East Coast nobody is."[19] Not surprisingly, local engineers have a hard time identifying gathering spots or opportunities on Route 128 for socializing or informal information exchanges. Indeed, most report that work and social life remain largely separate in the region.

The comparison of the leading computer firms in the two regions—Silicon Valley's H-P and Route 128's DEC—demonstrates the competitive advantages of open labor markets. DEC, which relies almost exclusively on internal labor markets and long-term employment, has failed to keep pace with its California counterpart, which features open boundaries and integration into regional networks. Both DEC and H-P were comparably sized companies in 1990 and the largest and oldest private-sector employers in their respective regions. Yet by 1995, H-P had decisively surpassed DEC technologically and had established itself as the second largest computer company in the nation, after IBM.

Corporate performance has multiple causes, to be sure, but the differences in the firms' organization—and, in particular, the openness of their boundaries—help explain these differences in performance. While H-P actively participates in local labor markets and the social life of the region, and, in so doing, helps to reproduce the open labor markets of Silicon Valley, DEC has historically maintained clear boundaries between itself and the regional economy. This comparison suggests the limits of bounded organizations in the current environment.

For close to 50 years, Hewlett and Packard actively encouraged their employees to involve themselves in the region and its rich professional and social networks. Following the model of H-P's founders, successive generations of H-P executives have maintained congenial relations with individuals who leave the firm (and, at times, even assisting them with start-ups); they have rewarded the creation of outside relationships; and they remain active participants in local civic and political affairs.

DEC, by contrast, detached itself almost completely from the region. By the late 1960s, DEC was the largest employer in the town of Maynard, yet none of the firm's senior management belonged to the local chamber of commerce, and CEO Ken Olsen discouraged his managers from participating in community affairs. One observer has described DEC as "a sociological unit, a world unto itself" (Rifkin and Harrar, 1990: 106). Indeed, executives at the company are quick to point out that DEC does not see itself as part of the Route 128 region or even New England but, rather, as part of the national and global economies.

Not surprisingly, this insularity is reflected in labor markets and career paths. Promotions at DEC have historically come almost exclusively from building strong internal relations, not from success in dealing with the external world. According to one long-time employee: "Getting hired into DEC . . . is like getting married: you meet your wife's mother and father and her aunts, uncles and cousins. It is a bonding process to an extended group of peers, as well as executives higher up and workers lower down" (Rifkin and Harrar, 1990: 119). Strong bonds of mutual support developed between DEC employees, creating intense loyalty and dedication to the organization. As a result, the rate of employee turnover at DEC was among the lowest in the computer industry.

While engineers who left H-P—or most other Silicon Valley firms—typically stayed in touch with former colleagues for the rest of their careers, those who left DEC were ostracized and cut off from the DEC community. They were often labeled failures, rather than being seen as potential resources. And once having left, they had no option of returning. According to one executive who did leave: "If you're stupid enough to cut yourself off from the mother church, Digital's attitude is, 'Don't bother to come back.' " (Rifkin and Harrar, 1990: 121). The closed nature of the DEC corporate culture thus ensured that all of the social and professional relationships that mattered were inside the firm.[20]

The blurring of organizational boundaries does not simply benefit individual firms, but also contributes directly to the health of the regional economy. While Hewlett-Packard served as a prolific training ground for Silicon Valley entrepreneurs, DEC's inward-looking organization was less conducive to developing entrepreneurial skill. H-P's decentralized and quasi-autonomous divisions provided the autonomy and general management responsibilities that are essential for a start-up. As a result, former H-P executives were responsible for starting more than 18 firms in Silicon Valley between 1974 and 1984, including such notable successes as Rolm, Tandem, and Pyramid Technology.

In contrast, DEC's matrix organization—which represented only a partial break from traditional functional corporate hierarchies—stifled the development of managerial skill and initiative in the Route 128 region. The matrix demanded continuous negotiations to reach a consensus, and despite the addition of cross-functional relations among product groups, final authority remained highly centralized in the firm (Schein, 1985). With the exception of its acrimonious split with Data General, it is difficult to identify successful spin-offs from DEC. As one local venture capitalist noted:

> It's well known among the venture capital community here that it is a significant disadvantage to hire anyone from DEC onto a startup management team. The matrix management and decision by consensus means that a manager who's been at DEC for a long time is going to be indecisive.[21]

H-P and DEC are not exceptions in their regions, rather, they reflect widespread differences in corporate organization between Silicon Valley and Route 128. Management scholars Delbecq and Weiss (1988) conclude that Silicon Valley firms tend to be organized as highly decentralized confederations of autonomous work teams, linked by intense informal communications. They argue that the critical unit in the region is not the firm, but the "loosely coupled engineering team," which they define as a "set of individuals with a strong sense of entrepreneurship, joined around a project mission associated with technology-driven change, who remain in contact frequently and informally with multiple levels and functions within the company through intense informal communications." This characterization—loosely linked engineering teams embedded in dense informal networks—applies to life outside as well as inside Silicon Valley companies; indeed, it is an apt characterization of the organization of the regional economy.

Route 128's technology firms, by contrast, are more stable, formal, and orderly organizations. While a handful of firms, including DEC, consciously experimented with decentralized forms of organization, Weiss and Delbecq (1987) conclude that most Route 128 firms rely on a "formal, vertical structure," and that their management styles are "conservative and top-down oriented," as compared to their Silicon Valley counterparts.

The experience of a DEC research lab in Palo Alto during the mid-1980s illustrates some of these differences. DEC employees who had previously worked on the East Coast were amazed as they began to participate in Silicon Valley's social and technical networks. One engineer concluded:

> DEC definitely relates differently to the regional economy in Silicon Valley than in Route 128. DEC is the largest employer in Route 128 and you come to think that the center of the universe is North of the Mass Pike and East of Route 128. The thinking is totally DEC-centric: all the adversaries are within the company. Even

the non-DEC guys compete only with DEC. DEC Palo Alto is a completely different world. DEC is just another face in the crowd in Silicon Valley.[22]

He described his years with the DEC group in Palo Alto:

> We had an immense amount of autonomy, and we cherished the distance from
> home base . . . and all the endless meetings. It was an idyllic situation, a group
> of exceptionally talented people who were well connected to Stanford and to the
> Silicon Valley networks. People would come out from Maynard and say [that]
> "this feels like a different company." The longer they stayed, the more astounded
> they were.[23]

DEC was ultimately unable to assimilate the lessons of its geographically distant
Palo Alto research group, in spite of the group's technical advances, and, in
1992, DEC transferred it back to its Maynard headquarters. Not surprisingly,
many of the key employees of the lab left DEC to work for Silicon Valley companies.

In short, Route 128 firms like DEC strictly defended their corporate boundaries at a time when job mobility and open information sharing were widely
accepted practices in Silicon Valley. Networking and informal exchanges on
Route 128 occurred almost exclusively within the large firms, not between them.
As a result, information about labor and product markets remained trapped
within the boundaries of individual firms, rather than being diffused rapidly
through local social and professional networks, as in Silicon Valley. This insularity deprived the Route 128 region of many of the opportunities for collective
learning that distinguish Silicon Valley.

The ultimate irony is that when the Route 128 economy faltered in the late
1980s and engineers began to leave DEC and the region's other large firms
(often involuntarily), many chose to go to Silicon Valley, rather than staying in
the region. As one local venture capitalist noted: "We always worked on the
theory that there were good people in the old traditional companies and that
they were ready to come out, if we had the money. Now we wake up to find
that half of them moved to California to start their companies."[24]

Conclusions

The blurring of the boundaries between firms provides a regional advantage for
Silicon Valley. Open labor markets allow individuals and firms to experiment
and to learn by continually recombining local knowledge, skills, and technology.
And the resilience of the regional economy suggests that the learning advantages
of open labor markets—when embedded in a rich fabric of social relationships—
outweigh their costs. Silicon Valley's professional networks minimize the search
and switching costs incurred by high rates of interfirm mobility. In other words,
they provide both the social capital (see chapter 11) and the informational signals (see chapter 21) needed to ensure career success outside internal labor
markets.

As individuals change project teams and companies in an open labor market like Silicon Valley, they also blur the boundaries between firms and the

institutions of the surrounding community, thereby undermining the distinction between work and social life and between the economy and civil society. For career success, individuals in Silicon Valley rely on bars, health clubs, hobbyists' clubs, technical and professional associations, training programs, community colleges, universities, and a variety of other networks that cross company lines and reach from the economy into social and even family life. As a result, the success of local firms is linked to the reinvigoration of the local community. The nature of the relationship is nicely captured by Best and Forrant's term *community-based career* (see chapter 19).

Silicon Valley firms continue to outperform competitors with traditional corporate boundaries that are located in the Route 128 area and elsewhere. The question remains, however, about the extent to which this model of open labor markets embedded in social networks will be diffused. Will the more traditional bounded organization continue to dominate and absorb civil society (see chapter 18), or will the boundaries between firms and between the economy and society become increasingly blurred with the dismantling of internal labor markets? While the Silicon Valley model is still far from widespread, businesses and policymakers in regions from Washington to Texas are attempting to foster the relationships that distinguish Silicon Valley. They may well have more success than older industrial regions that have deeply entrenched organizational boundaries to overcome. The regions that succeed will be those that create the social and institutional fabrics that can support both companies and careers that know no boundaries.

Notes

1. This interpretation of Silicon Valley's origins is not a substitute for more systematic historical accounts. See, for example, Saxenian, 1994; Malone, 1985; Freiberger and Swaine, 1984; Rogers and Larsen, 1984; Hanson, 1982.

2. Fewer than two dozen of the 400 men that attended a 1969 semiconductor-industry conference, held in Sunnyvale, had never worked for Fairchild. "Silicon Summit," *Electronic News*, September 26, 1969, p. 1.

3. See Andrew Pollack, "Fathers of Silicon Valley Reunited," *New York Times*, April 15, 1988, which describes the gathering in Palo Alto to mark the sale of Fairchild Semiconductor. Three decades after its founding, the company's founders were honored by more than 1,000 "Fairchildren"—all former Fairchild employees.

4. James J. Mitchell, "H-P Sets the Tone for Business in the Valley," *San Jose Mercury News*, January 9, 1989, pp. 1D-2D

5. Interview with Robert Walker, vice president and chief engineering officer, LSI Logic Corporation, May 2, 1988.

6. Interview with Robert Swanson, CEO, Linear Technology Corporation, June 24, 1991.

7. William Hewlett and David Packard were the original garage-entrepreneur heroes of Silicon Valley, but each technological generation produces new heroes—Intel's Robert Noyce, Apple's Stephen Jobs, and Silicon Graphics' Edward McCracken are among the best known, but there are scores more.

8. The ongoing diffusion of experience and know-how ultimately enhances the viability of the region's new ventures. A 20-year study of 400 firms, conducted between 1967 and 1987 by Albert Bruno at the University of Santa Clara's School of Business,

found that while only 75% of American manufacturing firms survive their first two years of business, 95% of the technology firms formed in Silicon Valley during the 1970s and 1980s survived their first six years of business; cited in *New York Times,* March 7, 1988.

9. Jack Yelverton, cited in Cheryll Aimee Barron "Silicon Valley Pheonixes," *Fortune,* November 23, 1987, pp. 130–134.

10. Cited in Richard Karlgaard, "George Gilder Interview," *Upside,* October 1990, p. 52.

11. Interview with Larry Jordan, vice president, marketing, Integrated Devices Technology, August 7, 1990.

12. Interview with Tom Furlong, RISC workstation manager, Digital Equipment Corp., Palo Alto, February 11, 1991.

13. Interview with marketing manager, Chips & Technologies, July 25, 1990.

14. Interview with Larry Jordan, vice president of marketing, Integrated Devices Technology, September 5, 1990.

15. Moreover, the pressure to be the first to market with new products and technologies underlies an unusually hard-driving work ethic in the region. The intense peer pressure among individuals in an ambitious and talented professional community drives many Silicon Valley engineers to work unusually long hours; this is evident in high rates of divorce and burnout.

16. This is my argument in a 1994 book. For more evidence on the competitive advantages of flexible network systems, see Best (1993) and Sabel (1989).

17. William Unger, of the Mayfield Fund, quoted in Ron Wolf, "Valley Execs Take Stock—and Moderate Salaries" *San Jose Mercury News,* June 28, 1992, p. 2D.

18. Interview with Paul DeLacey, vice president, operations, Boston Technology, February 4, 1991.

19. Interview with Jeffrey Kalb, CEO, MasPar Corp., January 10, 1991.

20. This was, in part, a result of vertical integration: The firm designed and manufactured internally virtually all of the software and hardware components for its computers. Faced with intense competitive pressures in the 1990s, DEC has been forced to become less self-reliant and build more external alliances.

21. Interview with Ted Dintersmith, general partner, Aegis Fund, December 11, 1990.

22. Interview with Joe DeNucci, vice president, Entry Systems Group, MIPS Computer Systems, March 25, 1992.

23. Interview with DeNucci.

24. Howard Anderson, president, Yankee Group, and general partner, Battery Ventures, cited in "Stalwart Venture Capitalists Keep Eyes on Future," *Mass High Tech.* March 11, 1991, p. 3.

References

American Electronics Association. 1981. "Statement of Pat Hill Hubbard." In *Technical Employment Projections.* Palo Alto, Calif.: American Electronics Association

Angel, D. 1989. "The Labor Market for Engineers in the U.S. Semiconductor Industry." *Economic Geography* 65, 2 (April): 99–112

Best, M. 1990. *The New Competition: Institutions of Industrial Restructuring.* Cambridge: Harvard University Press.

Braun, E., and S. Macdonald. 1978. *Revolution in Miniature: The History and Impact of Semiconductor Electronics.* Cambridge, Eng.: Cambridge University Press.

Bylinsky, G. 1976. *The Innovation Millionaires: How They Succeed.* New York: Scribner.

Delbecq, A., and J. Weiss. 1988. "The Business Culture of Silicon Valley: Is It a Model for the Future?" In J. Weiss, ed., *Regional Cultures, Managerial Behavior and Entrepreneurship*. New York: Quorum Books.

Freiberger, P., and M. Swaine. 1984. *Fire in the Valley: The Origins of the Personal Computer*. Berkeley: Osborne-McGraw Hill.

Granovetter, M. 1988. "The Sociological and Economic Approaches to Labor Market Analysis." In G. Farkas and P. England, eds., *Industries, Firms, and Jobs*. New York: Plenum Press.

Granovetter, M. 1995. *Getting a Job: A Study of Contacts and Career,* 2d ed. Chicago: University of Chicago Press.

Gregory, K. 1984. "Signing Up: The Culture and Careers of Silicon Valley Computer People." Ph.D. diss., Northwestern University.

Hanson, D. 1982. *The New Alchemists: Silicon Valley and the Microelectronics Revolution*. Boston: Little Brown.

Harrison, B. 1994. *Lean and Mean: The Changing Landscape of Corporate Power in an Age of Flexibility*. New York: Basic Books.

Levy, S. 1984. *Hackers: Heroes of the Computer Revolution*. Garden City, N.Y.: Anchor Press/Doubleday.

Malone, M. 1985. *The Big Score: The Billion-Dollar Story of Silicon Valley*. New York: Doubleday.

Markusen, A. 1985. *Profit Cycles, Oligopoly, and Regional Development*. Cambridge: MIT Press

McKenna, R. 1989. *Who's Afraid of Big Blue?* Reading, Mass.: Addison-Wesley.

Rifkin, G., and G. Harrar. 1990. *The Ultimate Entrepreneur: The Story of Ken Olsen and Digital Equipment Corporation*. Rocklin, Calif.: Prima Publishing.

Rogers, E., and J. Larsen, 1984. *Silicon Valley Fever: Growth of High Technology Culture*. New York: Basic Books.

Sabel, C. 1989. "Flexible Specialization and the Reemergence of Regional Economies." In P. Hirst and J. Zeitlin, eds., *Reversing Industrial Decline? Industrial Structure and Policy in Britain and Her Competitors*. Oxford, Eng.: Berg.

Sabel, C. 1991. "Moebius-Strip Organizations and Open Labor Markets: Some Consequences of the Reintegration of Conception and Execution in a Volatile Economy." In P. Bourdieu and J. Coleman, eds., *Social Theory for a Changing Society*. Boulder, Colo.: Westview Press.

Saxenian, A. 1994. *Regional Advantage: Culture and Competition in Silicon Valley and Route 128*. Cambridge, Mass.: Harvard University Press.

Schein, E. 1985. *Organizational Culture and Leadership*. San Francisco: Jossey-Bass.

Weiss, J., and A. Delbecq. 1987. "High Technology Cultures and Management: Silicon Valley and Route 128." *Group and Organization Studies* 12, 1: 39–54.

Wolfe, T. 1983. "The Tinkerings of Robert Noyce: How the Sun Rose on Silicon Valley" *Esquire*, December, 346–374.

3

Enactment and the Boundaryless Career: Organizing as We Work

KARL E. WEICK

Mary Catherine Bateson captures the theme of this chapter in her comments about deviant resumes:

> "Resumes full of change show resiliency and creativity, the strength to welcome new learning; yet personnel directors often discriminate against anyone whose resume does not show a clear progression. Quite a common question in job interviews is, 'What do you want to be doing in five years?' 'Something I cannot now imagine' is not yet a winning answer. Accepting that logic, young people worry about getting 'on track,' yet their years of experimentation and short-term jobs are becoming longer. If only to offer an alternative, we need to tell other stories, the stories of shifting identities and interrupted paths, and to celebrate the triumphs of adaptation." (1994: 83).

This chapter is a story of shifting identities. Its message is that interrupted career paths can be opportunities. When people make sense of these interruptions and use them as occasions for improvisation and learning, "triumphs of adaptation" occur. The vehicle for converting shifts and interruptions into adaptations is the boundaryless career, which I view as improvised work experiences that rise prospectively into fragments and fall retrospectively into patterns—a mixture of continuity and discontinuity.

A crucial shift in traditional careers is the disappearance of external guides for sequences of work experience, such as advancement in a hierarchy. In their place, we find more reliance on internal, self-generated guides, such as growth, learning, and integration. As a result of this shift, more of the influence over organizing devolves to the level of interaction and small groups, since the boundaries of organizations have become more permeable, more fluid, more dynamic, and less distinct. Nowadays, an organization is known by its organizing, just as the organizing effort is known by the interactions that comprise it.

This emerging pattern of continuing collective experiments, short-term jobs, and retrospective acts of improvisation (Gioia, 1988) constitutes one meaning of the term *self-designing systems*. The continuous updating inherent in such systems is a significant source of the adaptation that Bateson wants to celebrate.

The patterns that comprise the boundaryless career are seen to start on a smaller scale, and are more local, more tentative, and more subtle, than are the patterns associated with traditional, externally defined careers. But the fact that these newer patterns start small does not mean that they are trivial. On the contrary, precisely because they are patterns in a world of fragments, they can influence the expectations that distal stakeholders use when they define what constitutes work. A career system begins to form when stakeholders take the logic that was handed to them by the people who first enacted it, and redirect it to the enactors in the form of expectations, requests, meanings, and images that define what their enactment meant. As these relations between enactors and stakeholders continue to unfold and recycle, they generate histories, movements from novices to experts, older and newer participants, increasing explication of tacit understandings, more integration, and more internalization, all of which are changes that mimic a career system. What is different now is that work experience is more decoupled from specific organizations, more proactive and enactive, more indistinguishable from organizing, more portable, more discontinuous, less predictable, and more reliant on improvisation.

This map of boundaryless careers in boundaryless organizations is an extension of the map that Lisa Berlinger and I first drew in 1989 when we suggested that the growing importance of self-designing systems, such as entrepreneurial start-ups in Silicon Valley (Delbecq and Weiss, 1988), was likely to reshape the meaning of career systems and career development. We argued that images of career planning and advancement would be replaced by images of improvisation and learning. We argued further that as hierarchies became less available to mark progress in objective careers, this void would be filled by greater reliance on milestones in subjective careers, such as an increase in competence. These subjective milestones would serve as proxies for advancement, development, and upward movement. Thus, a change in competence would substitute for a change in job title. More significant, this shift from a position-based career system to a system based more on skill, competence, and experience should place more control over the design of the organization in the hands of the people who are building subjective careers. Organizations that incorporate this experience in an ongoing redesign program should themselves have more adaptability than those that ignore it. In a quiet, subtle inversion, the boundaryless career enacts the boundaryless organization.

The suggestion that career development can have a significant effect on the structure and processes of organization is relatively rare in career literature. For example, Nystrom and MacArthur (1989) categorized the 155 propositions they culled from the *Handbook of Career Theory* (Arthur, Hall, and Lawrence, 1989), and found that 135 of them treated the organization as the independent variable and careers as the dependent variable. Of the remaining 20 propositions suggesting that causation ran in the other direction, 25% of them appeared in the chapter on self-designing systems that Berlinger and I wrote in the *Hand-*

book of Career Theory. As Nystrom and MacArthur noted, the organizational properties that are highlighted when causation flows from careers to organizations differ from those highlighted when causation flows the other way. In our chapter, for example, the independent variable of careers had an effect on the organizational variables of self-design, adaptability, innovation, rigidity, and change, whereas organizations had an effect on careers through the independent variables of self-design, incompleteness of design, idea overload, and professionalization.

I conclude four things from this discussion. First, the literature on careers is relatively silent about the ways in which career development affects the form and functioning of organizations. Second, boundaryless careers in boundaryless organizations shape one another. Third, to capture how career development shapes organizational form requires that one pay attention to organizational properties that are often invisible when people examine organizations as independent variables. And fourth, the very fact that boundaries are in flux means that whatever structuring does come to define career systems may originate in unexpected places and have unexpected effects.

The rest of this chapter is organized in the following way: After a brief look at examples of boundaryless careers and organizations, I suggest, following Bell and Staw (1989), that as organizations become less bounded, they function more like weak situations. One result is that micro-level phenomena such as personality dispositions, tightly coupled interpersonal routines, and cohesive alliances have greater effects on outcomes and structure. To describe more systematically the way in which these effects are achieved, I then introduce the concept of enactment and show how it can give form to weak situations. A crucial point in my discussion builds on Barley's (1989) suggestion that career scripts mediate this structuring. Having suggested that boundaryless careers can be understood as moments of enactment that leave defining traces in social systems, I then suggest several ways to refine this basic theme.

Images of Boundaryless Life

Recent descriptions of boundaryless organizations and careers have taken a variety of forms: They are described as an increased outsourcing of activities and as distributed boundary spanning (DeFillippi and Arthur, 1994); as having greater reliance on just-in-time employees (Barner, 1994); as stemming from the growing influence of informal divisions of labor, information networks, adhocracies, flat structures, structural chaos, strong cultures, professional autonomy, self-regulation, decentralization, and trust (Thompson, 1993); as a movement to career systems that resemble those associated with baseball teams (Sonnenfeld, 1989); and as the creation of such diverse forms as the community, the federation, the octopus, the mobile, the tangled web, and the skyscraper (Power, 1988: 72). Behind most of these depictions is the assumption that organizations will increasingly need to leverage diverse knowledge resources, and that to do so, they will need to lose some of their bureaucratic form and discipline.

The weakening of boundaries in careers has also been described with evocative images. Bateson (1994: 82) describes the growing number of people who live with multiple discontinuities and make multiple fresh starts as the "zigzag people." Among such people, she numbers immigrants, refugees, displaced housewives, foreclosed farmers, bankrupt entrepreneurs, and people with obsolete skills. To think of oneself as a perennial consultant (Peters, 1992: 218), or as a business of one, or as a person "who has learned to acquire additional specialties rapidly in order to move from one kind of job to another" (Drucker, 1994: 68), is to edge toward a mindset appropriate for boundaryless careers. Mirvis and Hall (1994: 377), quoting the indelicate imagery of people who are more attached to their work than to organizations, suggest that the boundaryless career is "just sex, not marriage." Nicholson and West (1989: 190) make the important empirical point that even though boundaryless careers seem novel, in fact, conventional career moves have been rare for a long time (for example, data from the 1970s and 1980s suggest that 10% of moves were lateral or simple promotions; 50% involved a change in status and function; and 50% occurred between organizations). In the context of these examples, it seems reasonable to define boundaryless careers as "sequences of job opportunities that go beyond the boundaries of single employment settings" (Defillippi and Arthur, 1994).

Boundaryless Organizations as Weak Situations

One way to understand the growing influence of career development on organizational form is to argue that the loosening of organizational boundaries has transformed strong situations, which used to be well defined by structured, salient cues, into weaker situations that are now ambiguous, with fewer salient guides for action. When situations weaken, behavior tends to be guided by more tightly coupled structures, such as enduring personality dispositions (Bell and Staw, 1989; see Carson, 1989; 228–229, for a contrasting perspective). I suggest that the set of structuring mechanisms includes more than individual dispositions. It is this larger set of possibilities that includes mechanisms by which career development shapes social systems.

The distinction between strong and weak situations was proposed by Mischel (1968) and is generally understood in terms of the following elaboration:

> Psychological 'situations' (stimuli, treatment) are powerful to the degree that they lead everyone to construe the particular events in the same way, induce *uniform* expectancies regarding the most appropriate response pattern and require skills that everyone has to the same extent . . . .Conversely, situations are weak to the degree that they are not uniformly encoded, do not generate uniform expectancies concerning the desired behavior, do not offer sufficient incentives for its performance, or fail to provide the learning conditions required for successful genesis of behavior. (Mischel, 1977: 347)

Some commentators, such as Thompson (1993) and Perrow (1993), argue that organizations have always generated strong situations and continue to do so. They note that, whereas centralized organizations once exerted top-down

control, local and lower management increasingly exercise operational autonomy, but still within a more tightly controlled framework. Observers who see
organizations as generating weaker situations refer to other trends. Knowledge
creation as a newer route to adaptability (e.g., this volume; Bird, Nonaka and
Takeuchi 1995) is neither well understood nor consistently implemented. Thus,
organizations moving toward this goal should be less well structured. Efforts to
downsize have removed knowledgeable people, which has resulted in "an erosion of company knowledge stores over time" (Bird, this volume). With less
knowledge, but more demand for knowledge creation, organizations moving
toward this goal should indeed be less well structured. With greater demand for
updating of knowledge, organizations now need knowledge workers more than
knowledge workers need them (Drucker, 1994: 71). This reversal of dependency, if recognized, should heighten uncertainty.

While organizations may seem to create strong situations, especially in the
face of control over job security and centralized information processing, they
also create more conflicting practices (e.g., airline cost-cutting threatens safety);
these encourage a greater variety of interpretations, diverse expectations, contra-
dictory incentives, and shifting definitions of competencies that are needed. Organizational situations may not be weak, but they are weakening. And guides
for action may lie elsewhere.

Guides for action may in fact lie in personality disposition and in collective
improvision. People make sense of uncertainty on a small scale by a stable process of collective trial and error that resembles an evolutionary system (Weick,
1979). And it is this small and tight learning process that imposes structure on
larger and looser situations. Both stable personality dispositions and the stable
collective improvisation of local evolution are sources of structure when situations weaken and work experience comes in fragments. The restructuring originates from the bottom up. Starting with more intense assertion of personality
and collective improvisation, the restructuring first strengthens situations and
then redraws organizational boundaries. As people work, they organize within
weak situations. As they organize, they organize the weak situations into
stronger ones. And stronger situations lay down traces of larger organizations.
These traces are formed out of work and organizing and reflect both influences.
Local coping and local scripting of that coping into careers constrain and define
coping and scripting on a larger scale. People enact the stronger situation, which
then constrains them.

Whether the shaping is driven by individual or collective action is less crucial than the fact that microstrength shapes macroweakness. Such reversals of
causation should not be read as triumphs of the individual spirit in a crass
capitalistic world of coercive organizations. Nor should they be read as human-
istic wishful thinking. They should be read instead as straightforward extrapola-
tions of responses to uncertainty that locate an important source of organizational design in the attempts of interdependent actors to make sense of recurring
work transitions.

Collective enactment can create enduring changes in social systems, including broad-scale institutions. As I have noted, people enact and sustain images of

a wider reality that justify what they are doing collectively (Weick, 1993: 16). When boundaries begin to dissolve, traditions become less prescriptive and institutions become less structured. Traditional career scripts (e.g., internal labor markets) become less suitable as guides for action and interaction. Nonetheless, interactions become *more* patterned as people collectively pursue learning in order to cope with ambiguity (e.g., by forming local alliances and obtaining work using regional networks). These patterns come to exert more influence over career scripts and institutions. That is the theoretical significance of a shift from bounded to boundaryless careers. Significant structuring originates in more micro levels and modifies more macro levels.

Institutions imply that there is some sort of logic to the boundaryless organization. What is significant is that this is not a logic that awaits discovery, even though it often seems that way. Instead, it is a logic waiting to be constructed retrospectively out of the organizational traces laid down during action and interaction. Selective retention of adaptive enactments (Weick, 1979) provides the pattern that enacts a career script that in turn becomes institutionalized as a boundaryless career. Thus, a boundaryless career comes to mean organizing rather than organization; small projects rather than large divisions; enaction rather than reaction; transience rather than permanence; self-design rather than bureaucratic control; and struggles for continuity rather than struggles for discontinuity. I do not mean to imply that organizations and institutions are simply passive containers in these developments. I do mean that they are not as monolithic as others contend and that enactment shapes both career scripts and institutions.

Refinements of Enactment

To think more clearly about boundaryless careers by using the themes of enactment and organizing, one must be alert to subtleties in what is already a moderately complex set of ideas. For example, the concept of enactment suggests that individuals are agents of their own development, but not simply because they are active, controlling, and independent. People also organize cooperatively in order to learn. This continual mixing of agency and communion (Bakan, 1966; Marshall, 1989) manifests itself in the reciprocity between individual and organizational needs (Arthur & Kram, 1989); between personal change and role development (Nicholson and West, 1989: 188); between strategic choices and market cues (Porac, Thomas, and Baden-Fuller, 1989: 399); and between imposed and evolved jobs (Miner, 1987).

While the relations are reciprocal in the sense of codetermination, this codetermination is also asymmetrical. The basic asymmetry is one in which microdynamics shapes macrostructures. As the situations they confront weaken, people increasingly enact their social constraints, including career systems. What I have added to Bell and Staw's (1989) argument is a larger set of processes that potentially is capable of structuring the void left by weakness. I have also added the more important possibility that these newly influential processes come to dominate and define the weak situations, thereby strengthening them. Once strengthened, these situations now create conformity as well as deviation, which means that people live careers partly in response to their own constructions.

Implicit in the story of boundaryless careers are subtleties of acceptance, organizing, and identity, which I now want to introduce. These refinements suggest some of the conditions under which the story I propose is more or less likely to unfold. These refinements provide leads for research. But they also illustrate ways of talking that can be used by people trying to make sense of the boundaryless careers they are living.

Enactment and Communion

Although I described enactment as a mixture of agentlike control and communionlike, cooperative learning, the idea of enactment tends to evoke images of unmitigated agency. Such images include having expectations of self-assertion, wanting to be judged by concrete achievement, changing the environment to match preconceived images, showing independence, doing, having feelings of outer rather than inner development and of separation rather than affiliation.

To develop a richer sense of enactment, organizing, and boundaryless careers, I need to pursue an intriguing footnote in Bailyn's (1989) attempt to summarize major themes in the *Handbook of Career Theory*. Her note 10 reads:

> There are a number of interesting commonalities between certain of the chapters in this handbook. One of the more intriguing is that between the Weick and Berlinger chapter on the self-designing career and the ones by Gallos and Marshall on women. Is an organization based on principles of communion—of "being" and "caring"—a self-designing organization? Is it possible that people whose dominant mode is communion will fit more easily into such organizations than do those whose behavior is guided more by agency? (p. 487)

Communion is about tolerance, trust, being oriented to the present, and noncontractual cooperation. What is striking is the way in which career plans influenced by communion differ from the future-oriented and goal-dominated plans of an agent perspective. In the following description of communion, notice the extent to which it is synonymous with organizing to learn:

> [The keynotes of communion are] flexibility, openness to opportunities and right timing as the person and appropriate environment meet. This process is not usually change seeking but change accepting. Individuals must be prepared for transformation, to lose and gain definitions of self. . . .Communion is essentially present oriented, concerned with the next appropriate step when choices are made rather than looking beyond. People may have "dreams" but hold them lightly, using them as visions of possibility rather than as aspirations that have to be realized. (Marshall 1989: 287–288)

Communion is about readiness and adaptability just as agency is about initiative and adaptation. Both are invaluable to a boundaryless career and, in tandem, complement each other. Marshall suggests that a powerful means to integrate both sets of values is to practice "communion enhanced by agency." By this, Marshall means that "communion can draw on agency to supplement, protect, support, aid, focus, and arm it" (p. 280). Essentially, one says, "I choose to go with the flow." The agency of choosing is integrated with the communion of accepting "flows." As the act of organizing controls and enacts changes into scripts, situations, organizations, and institutions, agency dominates and is mitigated by communion. But, when these enacted changes then shape the meaning of growth, learning, and development, communion once more dominates and is enhanced by agency. Thus, an unfolding boundaryless career combines the communion of organized learning, the agency of environmental control, the communal acceptance of the environments and scripts thus created, and the agency of further structuring of initiatives driven by new recognition of what remains to be known and done.

There are several implications of using the concept of communion to enrich our understanding of careers and enactment. First, if weak situations evoke overlearned dispositions, and if overlearned dispositions tend to be pure rather than mixed, then career systems built to cope with boundaryless careers should be stronger on agency than on communion if they are enacted by men rather than women. Changes in the demographics of projects organized around learning should change the nature of the career system. Second, individual experiences organized around learning may themselves vary in the ratio of agency to communion. As the ratio of communion to agency increases, so, too, should the incidence of learning. What remains unclear is the extent to which that learning will then diffuse and become structured into scripts, situations, and institutions. Third, the recurrent suggestion that "people skills" are an asset in boundaryless careers reflects a reality in which the communion that enables organizing, learning, and trust also supplies the continuities that span the discontinuities created by shifting boundaries. The problem here is that, even though these skills play a major role in knowledge creation, they tend to be overlooked. Marshall puts it this way:

> Communion sees itself, including its actions, as part of a wider context of interacting influences. It tends not to assume personal accomplishment when events turn out favorably and is certainly less likely to be able to identify its contribution. This may be significant but largely invisible and difficult to disentangle because work has been largely pursued through influence, by shaping environments for others or in mutually empowering relationships. Action based in communion may therefore go unrewarded by formal organizational systems. (1989: 285)

A fourth implication of an enriched view of enactment is that one's capability for learning is dependent on the adequacy with which one can alternate between and integrate assertion and acceptance. To notice what has changed is to be attentive and accepting; to change what is noticed is to be focused and assertive; and to notice what has been changed by one's actions is to return to attentive acceptance. If continuous learning is the hallmark of a boundaryless career, then those who can integrate communion and agency should develop faster than those who can't. They develop faster because they learn more.

Fifth, people who face the loss of boundaries and value communion would not necessarily create new structure immediately to reverse these losses. What they might do instead is come to terms with uncertainty and recast it as a realm of possibilities. In fact, action might unfold with a minimum of conceptual pre-meditation, in the interest of heightened sensitivity to whatever the loss of boundaries might hold. People might be less likely to reconstruct hierarchies and more likely to construct heterarchies. "A heterarchy has no one person or princi-ple in command. Rather, temporary pyramids of authority form as and when appropriate in a system of mutual constraints and influences. The childhood game of paper, stone and scissors provides a simple illustration: paper wraps stone, stone blunts scissors, scissors cut paper. There is no fixed hierarchy, but each is effective, and recognized, in its own realm. In this way different values can take primacy in an individual's career pattern at different stages" (Marshall, 1989: 289). Organizing for learning that is structured heterarchically should legitimate a greater variety of perspectives, should blend agency with commu-nion, and should mean more rapid adaptation.

A sixth implication is that people with strong dispositions, favoring agency, control, and predictability, should be bothered sooner by the loss of boundaries and situational structure than would people disposed toward communion. Those with an agency mind-set should persist longer in treating boundaryless organizations as if they still had traditional boundaries, and boundaryless ca-reers as if they still were about hierarchical advancement. The admonition to get closer to the customer should be especially galling to people with an agency mind-set, who are more inclined to enact customers who want whatever the enactor has to offer.

Finally—and with a touch of irony—organizations and careers with fewer boundaries should favor either agency or communion. Either value, when pur-sued intensely, creates new boundaries, either those of the entrepreneur or those of the community. Framed in this way, efforts to cope with boundaryless careers could create even more intense conflicts over themes of independence versus the community, since either one can restore some of the structure that was lost. Integration may become more difficult and seem less necessary unless continu-ous learning becomes a dominant value. Continuous learning requires both agency and communion. To learn is to accept in order to change; to enact in order to be guided; to say in order to see; to organize in order to differentiate. To define boundaryless careers as a chance to fuse agency and communion is to turn a threat and a male response of control into an opportunity and a female response of integration.

Enactment and Organizing

I have repeatedly described the process of organizing (to learn) as a stable, bounded process in a boundaryless world. Organizing consists of self-designing cycles of enactment-selection-retention, in which retained outcomes partially shape subsequent action. Interaction is the feedstock for organizing, and learn-ing is often the outcome. When situations weaken, people revert to the relative stabilities of organizing. This means that in a boundaryless world, organizing should be more common, more influential, and more visibly embodied in both career systems and organizations. The purpose of this section is to refine the understanding of organizing in ways that tie it more closely to careers. Specifically, I will briefly explore three ideas: expectation enactment, the institutionalization of projects, and reciprocity during development.

Expectation Enactment

The idea of role occurs repeatedly in the careers literature and was central in Barley's discussion of career scripts. Barley (1989: 50) distinguishes between role and identity, defining the former as the interaction structure of a setting, and the latter as stable definitions of self that enable people to enact roles. Fondas and Stewart (1994) have elaborated the idea of roles by citing the concept of expectation enactment, suggesting that under certain conditions, people teach others how to interact with them. A manager enacts expectations by defining criteria for successful job performance or by shaping the expectations others hold about acceptable behavior or career prospects.

Expectation enactment is central to organizing and boundaryless careers, for at least two reasons. First, the process of teaching-learning that is involved in expectation enactment seems to follow roughly the sequence of enactment-selection-retention that is associated with organizing. Thus, when people organize to learn, they may organize to enact expectations and learn from feedback. Expectation enactment done locally on a small scale may be the template for related processes on a larger scale. Second, the variables assumed by Fondas and Stewart (1994: 92, figure 2) to influence expectation enactment share an interesting property: Virtually all of them strengthen as boundaries weaken, which should mean that as organizations become less bounded, there is more expectation enactment. For example, with fewer boundaries and weaker boundaries, distances between people, in terms of authority, decrease: role-set diversity increases; focal managers take more risks and, of necessity, adopt a more internal locus of control; focal managers and people in the role-set interact more and are more interdependent; and the organization itself displays more change in size, more mission ambiguity, and more variability in job definitions. All of these influences move in the direction of producing greater expectation enactment.

Projects

Organizing lies behind expectation enactment and gives it shape, just as it may also give shape to projects. Projects are relatively pure occasions of organizing. And one way to view boundaryless careers is as a "project-based game as in a checkerboard" (Peters, 1992: 220). Boundaryless careers consist of the repeated reaccomplishment of organizing in order to learn. And the reaccomplishment takes the form of a series of projects. People gain experience from both the content of what they do and the way they organize to do it. These experiences enlarge the repository of ideas that Alan Bird describes, and the knowledge of why, how, and whom, as described by Arthur and DeFillippi. Boundaryless careers become defined in terms of movements among projects and within projects.

While projects may be a dominant organizational form and may best be understood by closer attention to organizing than to organization, it remains possible to stratify projects and the assignments within them. I mention this because it is easy to confuse a loss of boundaries with a loss of differential authority and to forget that small differences in influence can amplify. The principle of hierarchy dies slowly—if ever—which means that organizing to learn may retain vestiges of advancement, upward movement, and tournaments. The hierarchies being "ascended" in a boundaryless career, however, become project based rather than organization based. Even successful replacement of hierarchies by heterarchies does not preclude informal ranking of required expertise and differential influence over the process.

The point is that in boundaryless organizations, the meaning of a boundaryless career shifts from advancement to learning and knowledge acquisition—but not entirely. Substitutes for hierarchical advancement can still be discerned. If a boundaryless career is a checkerboard career, there are stronger and weaker pieces, positions, and configurations, and there are moves that gain power and moves that lose it. To remove boundaries is to mobilize more primitive, more overlearned sources of structure, including personality and basic forms of organizing. Implicit in organizing is differentiation (Sherif and Sherif, 1964: chap. 7); and implicit in differentiation is the potential for advancement, plateauing, and descent.

Reciprocity during Development

If projects are an important medium through which organizing is expressed, if projects take a more conspicuous social form in boundaryless careers, and if life in projects comes to define career scripts, then we may understand boundaryless careers better if we translate organization-level formulations into project-level formulations. Arthur and Kram's (1989) discussion of individual-organizational reciprocity provides an example of how to do this.

Arthur and Kram (1989) argue that as adults develop, their dominant needs change from needs to explore to needs to advance, ending with needs to protect. If each of these needs are met when they are salient, the person will offer the organization exuberance, directedness, and stewardship, respectively. These offerings, when aggregated, enable the organization to adapt, achieve objectives, and maintain the internal structure (pp. 294–296). Tensions arise when individual needs are ahead or behind of organizational stages. For example, the individual has progressed to the advancement need, but the organization needs adaptation, and so the poor fit is expressed by the individual as boredom at the prospect of movement to an earlier stage, and by the organization as worry and a paralyzing thought that it will be drawn to a more advanced stage for which it is ill-prepared.

I suggest that in a boundaryless world, Arthur and Kram's development sequence continues to unfold, but it does so more quickly, with more intensity, in smaller gatherings. A lifetime of development is compressed into the lifetime of a project, just as the "seasons" of an organization become compressed into the seasons of a project.

One implication is that life in a boundaryless career is likely to be volatile. The volatility arises because timing now assumes more importance. Short projects pass through stages rapidly, and the chances that project stages will match individual stages are lower because the length of time during which a match can occur is shorter. With shorter intervals for a reciprocal fit to occur, more of the time may be filled with the mismatches and the attendant anxiety produced by boredom and worry. Whether individual development leads or is behind the development of projects will be influenced by a host of factors, the discussion of which is beyond the scope of the point I want to make: My point here is that projects are the medium through which organizing is expressed.

As a boundaryless career unfolds and experience accumulates, individuals may steadily outdistance the start-up needs of new projects for adaptation, unless these new projects are so novel that individuals have no choice except to explore. It is also possible, however, that when people shuffle in and out of a project, but the project itself continues, then advanced project needs for achievement and maintenance may be thwarted by newcomers who explore rather than implement, and who offer diffuse exuberance in a setting that needs focused attention. In either case, mismatches persist and produce strong feelings and weak learning.

If we play by the rules sketched by Arthur and Kram, the "remedy" would seem to be greater discontinuity from project to project. With greater discontinuities, it is more likely that individual and collective needs will coincide (that is, exploration, advancement, and adaptation line up); that reciprocity will be established, and that learning will occur.

Enactment and Continuity

Two descriptions frame the issue discussed in this final section, on refinements:

> The transfer of learning relies on some recognizable element of continuity—a woman describing her patchwork of careers for me recently remarked wryly on a continuity between work as a kindergarten teacher, a teacher of the deaf, and dean for "Greek life" (fraternities) on a university campus! (Bateson, 1994: 86).

> "Salman Rushdie, in discussing that quest [for coherence in self], describes personal meaning as a "shaky edifice we build out of scraps, dogmas, childhood injuries, newspaper articles, chance remarks, old films, small victories, people hated, people loved"; and then adds that "perhaps it is because our sense [of that meaning] is constructed from such inadequate materials that we defend it so fiercely, even to the death." (Lifton, 1993: 88)

The concept of a career has at least two sides to it, a personal side and a public side (Barley, 1989: 46). The personal (internal) side is characterized by a felt identity or an image of self, whereas the public (external) side is characterized more by official position, the institutional complex, and styles of life. The issue addressed in this section is: What happens to the personal side when the public side consists of fragments (Mirvis and Hall, 1994: 369), and when a person is tempted to say, "I'm not quite anything" (Lifton, 1993: 52)? Boundaryless careers generate fragments in search of continuity.

The importance of continuity in boundaryless careers arises for several reasons. First, people without any sense of continuity whatsoever should experience substantial ongoing states of arousal that interfere with learning. The same should hold true for organizations whose identity is up for grabs (e.g., see Dutton and Dukerich, 1991).

Themes of continuity are also crucial because learning itself is a process that builds on similarities and differences between the present and the past (e.g., stimulus generalization). With no continuity, there is no learning. Instead, in the interest of economy, there is simply reaction without either cumulation or repetition.

A third reason that we need to think carefully about continuity is that if organizing is enacted into enduring career scripts and institutions, then these newer career systems create novel continuities with which people have little familiarity. When people enact new continuities, the necessity to learn increases, rather than decreasing. If people enact a self-designing system, they are able to spot a "recognizable element of continuity" only with the passage of time and action.

If the construction of continuity is crucial for a boundaryless career, how do people accomplish it? There are several possibilities, some of which I will discuss briefly. To begin with, no single experience provides a pure case of continuity or discontinuity. As Michael puts it, "There are many pasts" (1985: 95). Bateson (1994) has capitalized on the fact that continuity lies partly in the eyes of the beholder, by having people interpret their own life history twice, focusing first on continuity ("Everything I have ever done has been heading me for where I am today"), and then on discontinuity ("It is only after many surprises and choices, interruptions and disappointments, that I have arrived somewhere I could never have anticipated"). She finds that tales of continuity and discontinuity can be constructed from the same facts (e.g., "Sure, I've had the same job for thirty years, but meanwhile consider the turnover in my body's cells"); that the tales are not mutually exclusive (e.g., "I have always enjoyed tackling the unknown"); and that some tales focus on different aspects of the person's life (e.g., the person keeps the same spouse but has different jobs), while some show a preference for continuity but recognize discontinuity (e.g., "I have always been a writer, but I shifted from being a poet to being a journalist"). Thus, one way to deal with the apparent fragments of a boundaryless career is to look more closely for sources of continuity.

Continuities also can be highlighted if one recasts the nature of a boundaryless career itself. Consider Defillippi and Arthur's description:

> The ideal-typical boundaryless career is characterized by a career identity that is employer-independent (e.g., "I am a software engineer"), the accumulation of employment-flexible know-how (e.g., how to do work in an innovative, efficient, and/or quality enhancing way), and the development of networks that are inter-organizational (e.g., occupational or industry-based), non-hierarchic (e.g., communities of practice) and worker enacted. (1994: 320)

Adoption of this mind-set should enable people to span specific settings and to derive continuity from self-descriptions that are more like those of professionals with their core beliefs, values, and skills that are not organization-specific. Those who view their boundaryless life in ways that simulate the work of a professional see themselves as people who "have technical skills transferable across organizations, recognized apart from hierarchical status, and with opportunity decoupled from promotion within a single organization" (Kanter, 1989: 510).

As I noted earlier, boundaryless careers may have their own unique continuities. Probably the most obvious new continuity is learning: "Learning is the new continuity for individuals, innovation the new continuity for business" (Bateson, 1994: 83). There is a hitch in this seemingly seamless picture of learning as the new continuity. The problem is that organizations are often poor places to learn.

Norms of compassion encourage the vulnerability that is a precondition for learning; yet, organizations are often unsafe and devoid of compassion. Organizations violate these norms in order to be lean and mean, but thereby increasing the odds of their becoming dumb and dated. Michael (1985: 101) makes this very clear when he talks about a challenge that has been repeatedly ignored by those (e.g., Huber, 1991) who attempt to specify the nature of organizational learning—namely, the role of compassion in learning. Michael suggests that acknowledging and experiencing the personal and organizational life of the learner depend on being open to unfamiliar ideas and experiences and on being increasingly interdependent. Both requirements demand exceptional degrees of vulnerability. But being vulnerable can lead to a humane world only if the norms of compassion are observed. Otherwise, those willing to risk a learning stance will be destroyed by the power-hungry and hostile people. He suggests that everyone needs all the clarity they can muster, regarding their ignorance and finiteness, and all the support they can obtain in order to face the upsetting implications of what their clarity reveals to them. "A compassionate person is one who, by virtue of accepting this situation, can provide others as well as self with such support. Learning how to establish such norms will be as difficult as it is unavoidable" (Michael, 1985: 101).

Just as communion is crucial to collective learning, as I have noted here, pure agency isn't sufficient for boundaryless organizations. Pure agency tends to encourage raw assertions of power as well as an unwillingness to become vulnerable in order to learn (remember, Karl Deutsch defined power as "the ability not to have to learn"). Both tendencies reduce the knowledge creation that Drucker feels will become commonplace. Drucker is wrong in this prediction, unless much more fundamental changes occur than simply those associated with the rational recognition that knowledge and learning are sources of competitive advantage. Organizational and career advantage, in the face of fewer boundaries, is more likely to favor those who shift to a more complicated sense of themselves and their capabilities, including their capability for compassion.

As a final source of continuity, I want to reiterate that continuity may lie in higher-order, more-abstract capabilities such as mutability itself (e.g., see Zurcher, 1977), adaptability, improvisation, or being a generalist. What endures across varying experiences is a constancy of being a quick study, of fitting in, of making do in ways that add value. The constancy is continuous swift adaptation made possible by ongoing enhancements of adaptability. These enhancements of adaptability occur as people articulate and make explicit their tacit knowledge, and transform explicit knowledge into tacit knowledge that enlarges their understanding (Bird, this volume). The tension here, again, involves trade-offs. To be an adaptable generalist may be to sacrifice an in-depth specialty and a higher degree of temporary adaptation. In some industries, it may be possible to specialize in being a generalist, especially if problems routinely are nonroutine (e.g., see Pacanowsky, 1995). What seems to be true of boundaryless careers is that either orientation seems to be adaptive: There seem to be opportunities for the adaptability of the generalist and for the adaptation by the specialist. Where the opportunities seem to disappear is for people who blend the two orientations, rather than alternating between purer expressions of the two. As is often the case in complex environments, evolution favors treating ambivalence as the optimal compromise (Campbell, 1965: 304–306).

Conclusion

Boundaryless organizations seem more and more to generate discontinuous episodes of growth, during which people organize to learn. This macrochange is reflected in career scripts that increasingly focus on organizing, learning, enactment, projects, self-design, tools for continuity, cycles, knowledge acquisition, networks, reputations, self-management, benchmarking of skills, and self-reliance. Careers still mean journeys, but the destinations are no longer fixed levels in a hierarchy, but fluid positions of expertise in a heterarchy organized around collective learning. While all of this sounds minimally structured, what I have tried to show is that the structure of boundaryless careers comes from moments during which people organize in order to learn. When people do this, they enact both the learning process, and its outcomes, into the scripts, organizations, and institutions that subsequently constrain them. Macrocareer systems come to resemble microorganizing.

Career success comes to be defined in terms of things like amount of learning accumulated; meaningfulness of continuities constructed; ability to create and manage organizing; comfort in returning to the novice role over and over; ability to explicate what had previously been known only tacitly; tolerance for fragmentary experience; skill in making sense of fragments retrospectively in ways that help others make sense of their fragments; willingness to improvise, and skill at doing so; persistence; compassion for others struggling with the uncertainties of a boundaryless life; and durable faith that actions will have made sense, even though that sense is currently not evident. People skilled in these ways are likely to find a series of challenging projects that, when strung together, simulate traditional advancement. The difference is that the transitions from project to project are more dramatic and more discontinuous.

There is basically no substitute for trial and error in dealing with surprise.

When large organizations are surprised, smaller groups organize for improvisation and experimentation, to deal with the surprise. In doing so, these smaller groups essentially replace organization with organizing. This change provides the infrastructure that shapes boundaryless organizations so that they look and function more like the self-designing systems that dealt with the surprise in the first place. This shift to self-design becomes embodied in scripts and institutions that become the hallmark of life in the boundaryless organization. Thus, coming full circle people adapt to the life of continuous learning that they implanted in the first place to cope with the loss of boundaries.

References

Arthur, M. B.; Hall, D. T.; and Lawrence, B. S. (eds.). (1989). *Handbook of Career Theory*. New York: Cambridge University Press.

Arthur, M. B., and Kram, K. E. (1989). Reciprocity at work: The separate yet inseparable possibilities for individual and organizational development. In M. B. Arthur; D. T. Hall; and B. S. Lawrence (eds.), *Handbook of Career Theory* (pp. 292–312). New York: Cambridge University Press.

Bailyn, L. (1989). Understanding individual experience at work: Comments on the theory and practice of careers. In M. B. Arthur; D. T. Hall; and B. S. Lawrence (eds.), *Handbook of Career Theory* (pp. 477–489). New York: Cambridge University Press.

Bakan, D. (1966). *The Duality of Human Existence*. Boston: Beacon.

Barley, S. R. (1989). Careers, identities, and institutions: The legacy of the Chicago School of Sociology. In M. B. Arthur; D. T. Hall; & B. S. Lawrence (eds.), *Handbook of Career Theory* (pp. 41–65). New York: Cambridge University Press.

Barner, R. (1994). The new career strategist: Career management for the year 2000 and beyond. *The Futurist, 28* (5), 8–14.

Barr, P. S., Stimpert, J. L.; and Huff, A. S. (1992). Cognitive change, strategic action, and organizational renewal. *Strategic Management Journal, 13,* 15–36.

Bateson, M. C. (1994). *Peripheral Visions: Learning along the Way*. New York: HarperCollins.

Bell, N. E., and Staw, B. M. (1989). People as sculptors versus sculpture: The roles of personality and personal control in organizations. In M. B. Arthur; D. T. Hall; and B. S. Lawrence (eds.), *Handbook of Career Theory* (pp. 232–251). New York: Cambridge University Press.

Browning, L. D., Beyer, J. M., and Shetler, J. C. (1995). Building cooperation in a competitive industry: SEMATECH and the semiconductor industry. *Academy of Management Journal, 38,* 113–151.

Campbell, D. T. (1965). Ethnocentric and other altruistic motives. In D. Levine (ed.), *Nebraska Symposium on Motivation* (pp. 283–311). Lincoln: University of Nebraska Press.

Carson, R. C. (1989). Personality. *Annual Review of Psychology, 40,* 227–248.

Delbecq, A. L., and Weiss, J. (1988). The business culture of Silicon Valley: Is it a model for the future? In J. Hage (ed.), *Futures of Organizations* (pp. 123–141). Lexington, Mass.: Lexington Books.

Dreyfuss, H. L., and Dreyfuss, S. E. (1986). *Mind over Machine*. New York: Free Press.

Drucker, P. F. (1994). The age of social transformation. *Atlantic Monthly*, November, pp. 53–80.

Dutton, J. E., and Dukerich, J. M. (1991). Keeping an eye on the mirror: Image and identity in organizational adaptation. *Academy of Management Journal, 34,* 517–554.

Fondas, N., and Stewart, T. (1994). Enactment in managerial jobs: A role analysis. *Journal of Management Studies, 31* (1), 83–103.

Gioia, T. (1988). *The Imperfect Art.* New York: Oxford University Press.

Gowler, D., and Legge, K. (1989). Rhetoric in bureaucratic careers: Managing the meaning of management success. In M. B. Arthur; D. T. Hall, and B.S. Lawrence (eds.), *Handbook of Career Theory* (pp. 437–453). New York: Cambridge University Press.

Huber, G. P. (1991). Organizational learning: The contributing processes and the literature. *Organization Science, 2* (1), 88–115.

Kanter, R. M. (1989). Careers and the wealth of nations: A macro-perspective on the structure and implications of career forms. In M. B. Arthur; D. T. Hall; and B. S. Lawrence (eds.), *Handbook of Career Theory* (pp. 506–522). New York: Cambridge University Press.

Kress, G., and Hodge, R. (1979). *Language as Ideology.* London: Routledge and Kegan Paul.

Lifton, R.J. (1993). *The Protean Self.* New York: Basic Books.

Marshall, J. (1989). Re-visioning career concepts: A feminist invitation. In M. B. Arthur; D. T. Hall; and B. S. Lawrence (eds.), *Handbook of Career Theory* (pp. 275–291). New York: Cambridge University Press.

Michael, D. N. (1985). With both feet planted firmly in mid-air: Reflections on thinking about the future. *Futures,* April, pp. 94–103.

Miner, A. S. (1987). Idiosyncratic jobs in formalized organizations. *Administrative Science Quarterly, 32,* 327–351.

Miner, A. S. (1990). Structural evolution through idiosyncratic jobs: The potential for unplanned learning. *Organization Science, 1* (2), 195–210.

Mirvis, P. H., and Hall, D. T. (1994). Psychological success and the boundaryless career. *Journal of Organizational Behavior, 15,* 365–380.

Mischel, W. (1968). *Personality and Assessment.* New York: Wiley.

Mischel, W. (1977). The interaction of person and situation. In D. Magnuson and N.S. Endler (eds.), *Personality at the Crossroads.* Hillsdale, N.J.: Erlbaum.

Nicholson, N. (1984). A theory of work role transitions. *Administrative Science Quarterly, 29,* 172–191.

Nicholson, N. (1987). The transition cycle: A conceptual framework for the analysis of change and human resources management. In K. M. Rowland and G. R. Ferris (eds.), *Research in Personal and Human Resources Management,* vol. 5, Greenwich, Conn.: JAI.

Nicholson, N., and West, M. (1989). Transitions, work histories, and careers. In M. B. Arthur; D. T. Hall; and B. S. Lawrence (eds.), *Handbook of Career Theory* (pp. 181–201). New York: Cambridge University Press.

Nonaka, I., and Takeuchi, H. (1995). *The Knowledge-creating Company.* New York: Oxford University Press.

Nystrom, P. C., and MacArthur, A. W. (1989). Propositions linking organizations and careers. In M. B. Arthur; D. T. Hall; and B. S. Lawrence (eds.), *Handbook of Career Theory* (pp. 490–505). New York: Cambridge University Press.

Pacanowsky, M. (1995). Team tools for wicked problems. *Organizational Dynamics, 23* (3), 36–51.

Perrow, C. (1993). *"Dartmouth Speech."* Mimeographed. Yale University, Department of Sociology.

Peters, T. (1992). *Liberation Management.* New York: Knopf.

Porac, J. F. Thomas, H., and Baden-Fuller, C. (1989). Competitive groups as cognitive communities: The case of Scottish knitwear manufacturers. *Journal of Management Studies, 26,* 397–416.

Power, D. J. (1988). Anticipating organization structures. In J. Hage (ed.), *Futures of Organizations* (pp. 67–79). Lexington, Mass.: Lexington Books.

Quinn, J. B. (1992). *Intelligent Enterprise.* New York: Free Press.

Sherif, M., and Sherif, C. W. (1964). *Reference Groups: Exploration into Conformity and Deviation of Adolescents.* New York: Harper and Row.

Smircich, L., and Stubbart, C. (1985). Strategic management in an enacted world. *Academy of Management Review, 10* (4), 724–736.

Sonnenfeld, J. A. (1989). Career system profiles and strategic staffing. In M. B. Arthur; D. T. Hall; and B. S. Lawrence (eds.), *Handbook of Career Theory* (pp. 202–226). New York: Cambridge University Press.

Thompson, P. (1993). Postmodernism: Fatal distraction. In J. Hassard and M. Parker (eds.), *Postmodernism and Organizations* (pp. 183–203). Newbury Park, Calif.: Sage.

Wallas, G. (1926). *The Art of Thought.* New York: Harcourt Brace.

Weick, K. E. (1969). *The Social Psychology of Organizing.* Reading, Mass.: Addison-Wesley.

Weick, K. E. (1979). *The Social Psychology of Organizing,* 2d ed. Reading, Mass.: Addison-Wesley.

Weick, K. E. (1983). Managerial thought in the context of action. In S. Srivastava (ed.), *The Executive Mind.* (pp. 221–242). San Francisco: Jossey-Bass.

Weick, K.E. (1987). Substitutes for corporate strategy. In D. J. Teece (ed.), *The Competitive Challenge* (pp. 221–233). Cambridge, Mass.: Ballinger.

Weick, K. E. (1993). Sensemaking in organizations: Small structures with large consequences. In J. K. Murnighan (ed.), *Social Psychology in Organizations: Advances in Theory and Research* (pp. 10–37). Englewood Cliffs, N.J.: Prentice Hall.

Weick, K. E., and Berlinger, L. (1989). Career improvisation in self-designing organizations. In M. B. Arthur; D. Hall; and B. S. Lawrence (eds.), *Handbook of Career Theory* (pp. 313–328). New York: Cambridge University Press.

Weick, K. E., and Bougon, M. G. (1986). Organizations as cause maps. In H. P. Sims, Jr., and D. A. Gioia (eds.), *Social Cognition in Organizations* (pp. 102–135). San Francisco: Jossey-Bass.

Zemke, R. (1994). The new middle manager: Learning to cover the bases. *Training,* August, pp. 42–45.

Zurcher, L. A., Jr. (1977). *The Mutable Self.* Beverly Hills: Sage.

4

Careers in Project Networks:
The Case of the Film Industry

CANDACE JONES

Faced with the demise of traditional careers, individuals are increasingly en-gaged in jobs comprised of short-term projects, rather than in permanent em-ployment arrangements (Bridges, 1994; Huey, 1994; O'Reilly, 1994; Richman, 1994a, 1994b). This radical shift in responsibility and action in worklife is transforming our notion of careers and work organization. Understanding what these changes mean and how they are being played out is a critical issue for practitioners and organizational scholars.

A good source for examining transformed careers and work organization is the U.S. film industry. Since the late 1950s, it has experienced many of the changes contemporary firms are facing, such as the downsizing of the work force, the subcontracting of work, and the need to operate in increasingly uncer-tain and competitive environments (Balio, 1985). For over two decades, work in the film industry has been organized around projects and informal personal networks, rather than around traditional hierarchies and in-house human re-source departments. Thus, the industry is being referred to as a network organi-zation (Hirsch, 1972; Miles and Snow, 1986; Powell, 1990; Reich, 1991).

The film industry's network organization is constantly being created and re-created. Firms and subcontractors combine for a specific project, disband when the project is finished, and then combine for new projects—often with differing participants. Self-employed subcontractors move from project to proj-ect, while the role of the company is to finance and distribute the finished prod-uct (the film). Thus, careers move across firms, rather than within a firm. The film industry provides an empirical base and model for understanding how changes in employment affect careers and interfirm organization.

Since we have little understanding of these new interfirm careers, key ques-tions remain unanswered. For example, how are careers and work organized within this fluid and decentralized industry? What skills and knowledge are needed for career success in an organizational system in which the right to participate is renegotiated with each new project? How do projects and careers interact to maintain a network organization? Are boundaryless careers in project networks characterized by marketlike relations—a series of one-night stands—among subcontractors and firms, or by repeated interactions, among subcontractors and firms, that enhance learning and innovation? Is the industry open, with competition defining success, or closed, with key players defining and promoting a chosen few?

This chapter attempts to answer these questions and provide some insight into the processes and structures of interfirm careers and organization. Using a variety of data, I examine two aspects of careers in project networks. The first aspect concerns how individuals are trained and socialized for boundaryless careers. The data suggest that the boundaryless career provides the foundation on which project networks are organized and maintained. New recruits chosen have the interpersonal skills needed for project-based organizing, as well as the technical skills needed for the craft. They are then socialized into the industry culture.

The second aspect of careers involves identifying what career patterns are successful in a project network. A career pattern results from relations among subcontractors and within traditional firms. The individual free agent who works among many different subcontractors and across a variety of firms typifies the most common career pattern in the film industry. However, much elite, high-status work involves being a member of a production team. Overall, careers within the industry are highly competitive, with many participants entering to compete, but with few succeeding and remaining in the industry's elite inner core. The industry is stratified by subcontractors who work among elite firms and those who do not.

This chapter seeks to extend revisionary ideas about careers, organizations, and networks. The emphasis is on the boundaryless career—defined by movement across the boundaries of separate firms, validation from the market rather than the employer, and cross-organizational networks of information (Arthur, 1994: 296)—rather than on the traditional hierarchical career. Also, the lesson taken from industries such as film (Faulkner, 1987), construction (Eccles, 1981), and semiconductors (Saxenian, 1990) is that conceptualizing the firm as the organization is outmoded. Rather, work is organized around the project rather than the firm; the "employees" are subcontractors who move from project to project or across firms, over time (Faulkner, 1987; Eccles, 1981; Peterson and Berger, 1971). Thus, the new network forms of organization are an interfirm phenomenon.

This chapter also emphasizes a particular network type—the project network—used extensively in the film, music, and construction industries. The project is the organizing mechanism, and teams are comprised of diversely skilled members who work for a limited period to create custom and complex products or services (this is adapted from Faulkner and Anderson, 1987: 880, and Goodman and Goodman 1976: 494). The "organization" producing the product—the film—typically involves multiple firms and subcontractors and is neither formally nor legally defined. Further, the organization is a temporary one and constructed around the desired product or service, usually involving complex and pioneering endeavors (Faulkner and Anderson, 1987; Powell, 1990; Ring and Van de Ven, 1992).

Project networks have two main characteristics that relate to the task and to the environment. First, the task is complex and nonroutine, which requires many individuals to join in creating the product or service; this high level of mutual responsibility is called team interdependence. For example, making a film requires coordinating the efforts and talents of hundreds of subcontractors from a variety of backgrounds (e.g., actors, lighting crew, storyboard artists, set designers, musicians, and accountants). Emphasis on horizontal information flows facilitates the speed and sharing of information among parties and cuts down on the time required to do complex tasks (Clark and Fujimoto, 1989; Imai, Nonaka, and Takeuchi, 1985).

Second, the project network usually operates in an uncertain and dynamic environment, primarily due to unpredictable and rapidly shifting consumer demands. The film industry uses independent producers, and networks to facilitate product innovation and adaptation (Robins, 1993), as is the case in the music industry (Peterson and Berger, 1971), and the Italian fashion industry (Piore and Sable, 1984: 215). In essence, project networks permit resources to be reallocated with ease among members within the network. Thus, they are adaptive to changing environmental demands.

For the individual entrepreneur (or subcontractor), project networks provide more varied work, opportunity, and development potential than do traditional firm careers. Not only do the interpersonal networks allow skilled entrepreneurs access to exciting projects among myriad firms, but the boundaryless quality of the new career enhances both skill and reputation, due to increased experience in different work settings and exposure to a variety of tasks and people. However, these boundaryless careers often make significant demands on time, energy, and lifestyle.

The approach here integrates two distinct perspectives—the experiences of subcontractors and archival industry data—to answer questions about how careers and organization interact in the film industry. Empirical data for my discussion derive from three sources. First, I conducted two-to-three-hour, in-depth interviews with five individuals who have been in the film industry since the late 1970s: a casting coordinator—Cate; a cinematographer—Bruce; a grip/electrician—Bryan; a producer—Tim; and Leigh, a film commissioner for the state of Utah, and treasurer of the Association of Film Commissioners International (Jones, 1988).[1] The interviews took a long time to gather, for two reasons. First, since work is project based, many of the participants were involved in differing projects both in and outside Utah at the time. Thus, interviews had to be arranged according to their timetables. Second, to get an interview, even using the film commissioner (who knew these people as the entry person), often took 20–30 phone calls to the same person. The reasons for this became clear once they granted the interviews: They give access to the industry according to a person's persistence and motivation. I had to prove that I was both persistent and motivated to do the interviews, before some of them would grant me the time. However, once they granted me the time, they were incredibly generous and gave me several hours and follow-up questions and responses.[2] My second source is extensive historical data in the form of interviews and ethnographic research on the film industry. For example, research on studio musicians' careers is a key source (Faulkner, 1985, 1987). Third, I compiled a data base of 2,744 subcontractors, and their film credits for the 606 feature films that were released and distributed in the United States from 1977 to 1979[3]—a time when, film historians suggest, the industry network structure was already established (Ellis, 1990: 437–439). Film credits indicate the experience and status of film subcontractors. They are akin to publication credits in academia.

Boundaryless Careers in Project Networks

In this section I explore case studies and prior literature, to derive a model identifying four career stages; and I explain how the skills and competencies needed at each stage maintain the project network. In essence, the career is a conduit for organizing work, in which each stage of the career provides the foundation for the informal organization of a project network. By identifying how individuals are socialized into careers, we can understand the structures and processes of organizations.

Beginning the Career: Getting Access through Interpersonal Skills and Perseverance

A career in the film industry is a difficult process, due to a lack of the traditional recruiting and selection practices that initiate most careers. Yet, the film industry's exposure to potential recruits is pervasive: Tabloid tales are splashed across checkout counters; television dramas are filled with beautiful people who have glamorous lives; and stars are paraded across theater screens throughout the world. This media coverage draws individuals to the film industry and toward glamour, hope, and dreams of success. Translating these dreams into reality requires hard work and an ability to get your foot in the door. The "mechanics of the process are straightforward. Small armies of investors, artists and technicians qualify themselves and compete for projects" (Faulkner and Anderson, 1987: 883). However, how one qualifies oneself to get access and experience is less clear.

Gaining entry and experience (credits) is difficult for two reasons: It is intensely competitive, and no clear-cut steps or entry routes exist for newcomers. Getting credits is indeed an intensely competitive process. According to Dezso Magyar, director of the AFI's (American Film Institute's) Center for Advanced Film and Television Studies, only 5% to 10% of the 26,000 film-school graduates who obtain degrees each year actually gain employment in the film industry (Hubbell, 1991). Since no clear-cut steps or entry routes exist, varied backgrounds, including Broadway theater, network television, music videos, and film schools, are used to launch careers and gain entrance into the film industry. The burden on newcomers is to seek out successful subcontractors who will help place them in their first project. Bryan, the grip/electrician explains: "There's no tried and true way to get started. You have to go find people you like who make movies. . . . It's getting the first job that is the hardest."

Those who get their foot in the door are sorted out by two attributes: good interpersonal skills and being highly motivated. Good interpersonal and communication skills are critical for career success in the film industry because of the highly interdependent and ambiguous nature of the work. Tim, the producer, expresses this well: "If I like them, that's 90% of it. When you work that many hours, under that much stress, and you get some jerk, he makes life miserable. You want someone with whom you click and can communicate." Further, tasks are ambiguous because they are rough ideas, on paper, that have to be translated into tangible products. Cinematographer Bruce explains that it is "very subjective. People's styles and tastes differ tremendously. And if you can get that translation from paper to physical, tangible product, then you're successful. However, a lot of things can go wrong in between." This emphasis on interpersonal skills is also important in scoring film music (Faulkner 1987: 13) and in theater (Goodman and Goodman, 1972).

Newcomers are also screened by their motivation and persistence. Commitment and passion are indeed necessary to carry one through the industry's long hours, low pay, constant travel, and other lifestyle compromises. Leigh, the film commissioner, describes how "you can tell, after their [the newcomers'] first production, if they are going to make it, if they have the passion for it to carry them through the 18-hour days. I knew I did because I felt energized and excited by it." Bruce, the cinematographer, warns new recruits that "if money is the reason you work hard, don't get into this business. You can make a hell of a lot more money by being a stockbroker." The grip/electrician, Bryan, emphasizes this issue: "It's not an 8-to-5 thing. I rarely work a month that I don't work a lot of nights. Sometimes I work both days and nights in the same week. You may go from [filming] church devotional to a heavy-metal music video in one week. You get unusual circumstances. People who are challenged by and able to handle those kinds of demands make good people. That's why you have to seek it for yourself."

Film is a demanding career. Since each new job must be negotiated, one must have a high performance level on the job. As Bruce, the cinematographer says, "You need very competent players to perform. If someone is draggin' their ass, then you need to replace them with someone who can do it. You hire them once and if they don't do a spectacular job, you hire someone else next time." Bryan warns recruits, "In the grip electric area [where crews set up and run the lighting for films], people get a little bit of experience at the bottom [entry level]. Eighty percent never make it and 20% finally get to a place where they can start making some money." Bryan's perception is confirmed by the archival data I used: Fully 69% of subcontractors who worked on the 606 films, during the 1977–1979 period, made only one feature film. This low rate of success in consistently finding projects is not simply an artifact of a three-year period. Faulkner and Anderson (1987: 894), in a study of producers and directors over 15 years, found that 64% of producers and 50% of directors had only a single credit. Clearly, individuals must constantly compete and prove themselves for opportunities. In the film industry, insiders give opportunities to newcomers who have the skills and motivation needed for project-based organizing. Excellent interpersonal and communication skills are critical because work is coordinated in production meetings, the tasks are ambiguous and highly interdependent, and freelance work requires informal communication networks for identifying future work. Persistence and high levels of motivation and commitment are critical due to the intense competition for opportunities; and due to lifestyle demands, such as constant travel and unusual work schedules and the incessant search for new projects.

Crafting the Career: Learning Technical Skills and Being Socialized into the Industry Culture

Landing a first job is only the beginning of one's work in a project network. Crafting a career requires that one learn not only the skills and roles, to perform tasks successfully in the industry, but also the industry culture, since these values, norms, and ground rules replace the bureaucratic control of a corporate hierarchy. From an individual's perspective, learning the craft and learning the industry culture occur simultaneously because the culture identifies how one's career is to evolve: through on-the-job experience, where one starts with low-level, menial tasks, and works one's way up to more prestigious, challenging, and interesting tasks based on past performance.

In the film industry, new recruits start at the bottom of the totem pole and slowly work their way up through extensive on-site training. They do menial tasks and work long hours for minimal pay, to learn the skills and roles of the medium. The film commissioner recalls "90-hour weeks for $2.00 an hour" at Sunn Classic. Tim, the producer, also worked at Sunn Classic and recounts his experience as an apprentice film editor: "It was like bootcamp. . . . I never had any time off for two years." He started in film editing, went into sound editing, then went into syncing dailies (matching the sound and picture). He moved into public television, then acting, prosthetic work [make-up], and, finally, into production. This learning process took between five and seven years. Similarly, Bruce's first job was cleaning and rolling 100-foot electrical cords; his second, loading film and maintaining equipment. Neither of these was related to the creative process, but they taught him how to handle the equipment. His third job was editing. Finally he got some "seat time"—to shoot film—which is what he wanted to do all along. He talks about "the hard learning years with marginal pay and long hours. You just can't put a price on it, because of the experiences you're exposed to." These experiences mirror Faulkner's (1987: 54) interviews with film composers. Most spent years in paying their dues—helping colleagues; doing a few episodes on TV, a TV series, a TV pilot, and finally a feature film. He found that "newcomers are matched to routinized and low-risk work." The benefit of such intensive on-the-job training is that individuals are exposed to the many roles and tasks needed to complete the project—which, in turn, enhances coordination. In sum, the film industry values on-the-job training in a variety of technical tasks and organizational roles that enhance coordination of diverse functions; it requires long hours to internalize the industry culture; and people move to more challenging projects based on prior performance.

This process involving intensive hours invokes the questioning of old values, breaks down resistance to new values, and is common in the socialization of professionals (Light, 1979) and managers (Pascale, 1985). Since the film industry places newcomers in the position of seeking out and choosing their own socialization agents, it provides a powerful socialization strategy for teaching newcomers the industry culture—what work is done, how its done, and how members are to act while doing it. Working with knowledgeable insiders is typical of systems that require passage through inclusionary boundaries (Van Maanen and Schein, 1979: 234). This intense socialization creates common understandings, values, and goals that guide behavior, rather than written rules or regulations (Ouchi, 1979; Tompkins and Cheney, 1985). Because the film industry is loosely structured, geographically dispersed, and occupationally varied (including actors, costume designers, musicians, and electricians), the coordination among these varied and diverse members depends upon a set of shared values. The industry culture establishes common understandings, routines, and conventions (Becker, 1982) among differing parties, so that rules for working together do not have to be re-created for each film (Faulkner, 1987: 92–93). This allows previously unacquainted individuals to work together in temporary organizations (Becker, 1982; Goodman and Goodman, 1972, 1976).

In essence, the industry culture establishes not only the parameters for how careers and work are experienced, but also the foundation for coordinating and organizing work. It also allows for extensive movement of participants among firms and other subcontractors, since values, norms, and organizational roles are shared.

Navigating the Career: Building Reputations and Creating Contacts

Three challenges confront the freelance professional during this stage: establishing one's reputation by consistently producing quality work; expanding one's skill base by getting more challenging projects; and developing a network of personal contacts by initiating and maintaining relationships. Building a reputation and developing a network evolve simultaneously—a reputation is established by performing quality work involving a variety of circumstances and people.

Each job requires a participant to secure another invitation to do a movie; thus, building and maintaining a reputation are critical steps. Bruce explains that he trains his production assistants to understand the importance of quality and hard work:

> Technically there are things that are bad, and pretty soon, if they show up too often, you're not going to get work anymore. That's not just from me but from the whole industry. If somebody develops bad habits—is lazy or indifferent— we'll say, "Gee, that guy doesn't bring much to the party does he? Let's not invite him next time."

Tim, the commercial producer, says, "You can't afford to do schlocky productions. Your profile is critical." Bryan, the grip/electrician, says, "You build your reputation every day. You're only as good as your last job. If your last job was good, people remember you and you get good recommendations." In the film industry, those "with successful performances and track records move ahead in their careers, those with moderate reputations do not, those with poor reputations experience employment difficulties" (Faulkner and Anderson, 1987: 881). A critical lesson is that if one does not produce quality work, one will be replaced and lose future opportunities to work in the industry.

Along with performing quality work, one must seek out projects that challenge and expand one's skills. In project networks, the individual, not the boss or organization, is responsible for developing and enhancing skills. "You have to continually work to get better," says Bruce, the cinematographer "Otherwise, you'll get passed up by everybody else. You have to keep up with technology and have a contemporary visual sense. It's like fashion; it keeps changing all the time—styles of lighting design and composition." Challenging work that expands skills provokes a tension: Work must challenge, but not exceed, the capacity to perform it effectively. Poor performance hurts one's reputation, which has been so painstakingly built.

The key to getting more projects is building and maintaining a network with people who make movies. Opportunities and recommendations for jobs come through informal communication channels. Often these chains of communication and recommendations involve two or three people. For example, Cate, the casting person, got her job as assistant to the extras coordinator on John Huston's movie *Wise Blood* by learning that a friend's friend was working on the movie. The friend called her friend, who recommended that Cate get the job. This reliance on informal networks for sources of information is also critical to other industries with project-based organizational systems, such as music (Becker, 1982: 87) or construction (Bresnen et al., 1985: 113–114). The importance of informal contacts and information flows mirrors Weick's (1979: 97–98) view that the essence of organizing is interpersonal communication, because it creates structures and affects what gets done.

In project networks, subcontractors must constantly seek new projects. The 1977–1979 archival data show that the film industry is characterized by people who move extensively among firms for work; only 19% of participants who made two or more films worked exclusively for one firm. Thus, 81% of subcontractors who repeatedly have work move among firms and fellow subcontractors. This movement creates the conditions for effective information flow across the industry, because people know one another, may interact repeatedly, and talk about these interactions (Granovetter, 1985: 490). Thus, project networks are structurally suited to dispersing information widely and quickly—information about reputations and jobs. Leigh, the film commissioner, implies this when she says, "We're a big industry but a small industry, because we talk to one another."

Being associated with commercially successful films defines one's status and role relationships within the industry. Cate describes the "ticket" to her success as creating a "genuine look for the director" in her casting of extras for *Footloose*. The commercial success of this film opened up opportunities for her. If your movies don't perform well, your status and relationships within the industry change dramatically. Ned Tanen, chief of Universal and then Paramount, explains that as a studio chief, "You only need two or three expensive movies that don't do well within a given year, and your legitimacy is very suspect" (quoted in Kent, 1991: 52). The industry aphorism is: "You're only as good as your last credit." Given the unpredictability of what makes a movie successful and the difficulty in consistently working on hits, roles and status among industry participants are redefined as careers fluctuate with the movie's market success.

Maintaining the Career: Extending the Profession and Balancing It with Personal Needs

Once they are established in careers, project-network participants face two key challenges: to act in ways that maintain and extend the network organization, and to balance professional demands with personal needs. The first challenge of maintaining the project network's viability as an organizational form is comprised of three tasks: identifying and training new members; establishing workshops that develop talent in the field; and coordinating events such as film festivals, which integrate the industry by exposing diverse participants to one another, and which establish standards within the industry by identifying exemplars of excellent work and role models. These organizational demands change the roles, skills, and focus the more senior members.

Identifying and training new members shift one's role and focus from developing oneself to developing others. The protégée thus becomes the mentor. Often this is achieved by setting up informal seminars and training programs for newcomers. "I am currently extending myself a little by giving informal seminars to the up-and-coming people in the business," says Bruce. He asks potential entrants who seek him out, "Why do you want to be involved in film production? What does it do for you?" Tim explains his training process and criteria: "I tell those who want to get experience to write me a letter explaining what they want out of this industry, what their goals are, what they want to do; and then, if I like what they say, I'll interview them." Clearly, the socializing agent chooses recruits who have similar values and goals. This allows for "concertive control" where explicit written rules and regulations are replaced by a common understanding of values, objectives, and tasks, and a "deep appreciation of the organization's mission" (Tompkins and Cheney, 1985: 184). Because insiders select and train newcomers with similar goals and values, the project network is replicated and maintained. Indeed, the project network has been used for decades in film, construction, and theater.

Senior members of project networks extend the industry by establishing workshops or coordinating film festivals. These events integrate industry members, showcase current work, and provide role models. Robert Redford, who established June Lab, was cited as a role model by my interviewees. June Lab is a script-development workshop at Sundance, where beginning screenwriters are invited to develop their scripts, with help from established screenwriters and critics. In addition, Redford's involvement with the United States Film Festival in Park City, Utah, was a critical factor in establishing it as a premier event for showcasing independent productions. It also serves as a mechanism for matching creative filmmakers with the distribution channels of film studios.

The second challenge at this stage of one's career is to maintain some sense of balance between personal and professional life. The constant demands of performing quality work, seeking new projects, and maintaining a personal network of relations can consume the energies and lives of project-network participants. It is not uncommon for people involved with film projects to work 12-to-18-hour days. Ed Limato, the agent for Mel Gibson, Richard Gere, and Michelle Pfeiffer, explains that "you really have to eat it, breathe it, every waking moment of the day. . . . It's an eighteen-hour job" (quoted in Kent, 1991: 22). For those who wish to be an elite member in their industry, the profession becomes their life. For others, balancing professional demands with a personal life is critical. Their personal life acts as both a retreat from, and a source of, renewal for the incessant professional demands.

My interviewees had all chosen to balance professional and personal lives. Bruce describes how "you reach a point where you are creatively drained." He deals with this by separating work and home life. "When I go home and the day is over, it's time to rest and leave the job behind," says Bruce. Tim describes the consequences of not balancing the professional and the personal: "People get so enthralled with working in the business that they can't be rational about when to stop. You can't do drugs to keep going; eventually, you'll go crazy. There are so many alcoholics and drug addicts who were not that way when they started in the business, but they end up that way because they work constantly. They have no personal lives. They travel. They're gypsies. They don't have any foothold in their lives. What they call home is an apartment somewhere. They don't have any meaningful relationships. It's a tough, tough road to hoe." Boundaryless careers in project networks typically place high demands on participants in two ways: first, the tasks require enormous creative energy; and second, getting consistent work in projects requires time, travel, and maintaining numerous contacts. These demand high levels of energy and commitment, which may create problems of balancing personal needs with professional demands.

Career Stages and Project Networks: Careers as Conduits for Organizing

The stages and training within the career both produce and reproduce the informal organizing needed to coordinate work in project networks. Table 4.1 shows how the career stages, the skills and competencies needed at each stage, and the requirements of project networks interact to maintain the informal organization. Although this table is derived primarily from film-industry data, it identifies career stages, skills and competencies, and organizational requirements applicable to other industries, such as high technology, fashion, consulting, music, and construction, as well as professions such as medicine, academics, and law.

At the beginning of the career, as I have noted, individuals are sorted by interpersonal and communication skills since work is coordinated through production meetings and mutual adjustment among project members. Motivation and perseverance are essential since individuals must compete for projects, and

Table 4.1 Interaction of Boundaryless Careers and Project Networks

Career Stage and Primary Issues	Skills and Competencies	Organizational Requirements
BEGINNING: Getting access to the industry or profession	· Identifying gatekeepers to gain entrance · Demonstrating interpersonal skills · Showing motivation and persistence	· Attracting new entrants to regenerate organization · Sorting potential entrants by their interpersonal skills and motivation
CRAFTING: Learning required skills and industry culture	· Learning technical skills and roles · Assimilating industry culture—norms and values · Demonstrating reliability and commitment	· Training in a range of technical skills and roles facilitates coordination of complex projects. · Inculcating industry culture allows interfirm movement and enhances coordination among multiple participants.
NAVIGATING: Building reputation and personal networks	· Establishing reputation through quality work · Expanding one's skills and competencies · Developing and maintaining personal contacts	· Defining status order as new members enter and older members shift positions · Negotiating membership relations among participants
MAINTAINING: Extending the profession and balancing the personal	· Mentoring and sponsoring others · Balancing personal needs and professional demands	· Providing forums to develop members' skills · Coordinating industry events to expose and integrate members · Setting standards for skills and competencies in the industry

since each new job is negotiated. Thus, a career in project networks is a series of competitions and negotiations for work. In stage two—crafting the career—paying dues, through menial work and long hours, teaches the new recruits the requirements of the medium. The long hours in the socialization process are critical for breaking down old values and facilitating the adoption of the industry culture. Intense socialization into the industry culture allows individuals with diverse backgrounds and functions to coordinate their activities.

The third stage—navigating the career—establishes the reputation and contacts required for continued work in the industry. The need to renegotiate for each job creates movement of subcontractors among firms and one another. This movement makes informal communication channels effective in dispersing information about reputations throughout the industry. Data on reputations, interpersonal communication, and movement from project to project interact to sustain a system in which the work organization is constantly created and re-created with each new project.

The fourth stage—maintaining the career—demands that the focus shift from developing oneself to developing others and to maintaining the industry. Senior members must now mentor and sponsor newcomers, provide workshops to develop junior members, and coordinate events to establish standards, showcase talent, and provide role models. The challenge for the individual is to balance one's personal needs with one's professional demands. In summary, stages of the boundaryless career in project networks sort, train, and socialize individuals on key skills essential for maintaining an interfirm organization.

Career Patterns in a Project Network Industry

Few formal boundaries exist in industries characterized by project networks, such as films, construction, and music. However, there are definite social structures—repeated patterns of interaction—within the film industry that separate powerful individuals and firms from the majority of subcontractors and firms, who remain on the periphery of the industry (Faulkner, 1987; Jones, 1993). Since the industry's structure is defined by the patterns of recurrent and nonrecurrent interactions, a clear understanding of the development of boundaryless careers depends on increasing our knowledge of what career patterns prevail, and of the industry social structure within which these careers arise.

Career Patterns of Subcontractors: Competitive Entrepreneur or Creative Team Member?

An unanswered question is whether boundaryless careers in project networks are characterized by marketlike relations—involving a series of one-night stands—among subcontractors and firms (Kanter, 1989) or by teams with repeated interactions that enhance learning and innovation (Miner and Robinson, 1994). Clique analysis is a good way to see whether there are strong and intimate interactions, or short-term and limited ones, and whether members have common purposes and goals (Burt, 1980: 97). A clique analysis of the subcontractors for 1977–1979 shows that only 14% (373 out of 2,744) work repeatedly with other subcontractors in teams. This suggests that marketlike relations—free agency—may dominate the film industry.

However, examination of interaction among subcontractors identified two kinds of relations: free agents and team members. Of the 282 successful subcontractors—defined as those who made three or more films in three years—36% engaged in free-agent careers, whereas 64% participated as members of teams (see Table 4.2). Although only 14% of all film subcontractors engaged in repeated interactions, 64% of successful subcontractors use repeated interactions in teams as the basis for their career. This suggests that free-agent relations dominate and tend to be used by many who are less successful (work less often than once a year), and that more successful subcontractors tend to be team members.

Further analysis suggests that employment relations are even more complex. Four different types of firm-subcontractor employment relationships can be identified: market, hybrid, dominant, and exclusive. Market relationships (36% of the total) involve those subcontractors who work only once for a firm. Hybrid relationships (27%) involve working repeatedly for one or more firms, but for no one primary firm. Dominant relationships (26%) involve dependence on a primary firm for two-thirds or more of the subcontractor's work. Lastly, the traditional exclusive employment relationship is relatively rare—only 11% of all subcontractor-firm relationships. These two subcontractor orientations and four types of employment relationships interact to create eight different career patterns within the film industry (frequencies are shown in the cells of Table 4.2). The most common career patterns involve hybrid teams, which work repeatedly, but not exclusively, for firms; market teams, which move across firms; and individuals who act as free agents.

There is a further suggestion: that certain career patterns are more viable for some skills and competencies than others. Table 4.2 also breaks the subcontractor roles into three primary organizational roles—managerial, technical, and support. Managerial skills are performed in the producer and director roles; they organize, control, and direct the resources for the film project. Technical skills are performed by the cinematographer, the editor, and the production designer, who are responsible for the technical aspects of filmmaking (lighting, set construction, camera work). Support is provided primarily by the assistant director, who administers and does whatever tasks are needed by the director. Managerial skills and competencies occurred most often with team career patterns (the average occurrence was 38%, across cells 5 through 8) and occurred significantly less so with free-agent career patterns (the average was 24%, across cells 1 through 4). Technical skills and competencies were most likely with hybrid relationships and with either free-agent or team orientations (cells 2 and 6, 65% and 61%), and were least likely with exclusive relationships (cells 4 and

Table 4.2 Career Orientations, Employment Relations, and Organizational Competencies

Subcontractor Relations	Employment Relation (Subcontractor-Firm)			
	Market: Subcontractor works once with each firm	Hybrid: has repeated work with one or more firms	Dominant: does two-thirds of work with one firm, but works with other firms	Exclusive: works with one firm only
Free Agent	Cell 1 18%	Cell 2 6%	Cell 3 11%	Cell 4 1% 36%
	Technical 58%	Technical 65%	Technical 39%	Technical 0%
	Managerial 18%	Managerial 11%	Managerial 32%	Managerial 33%
	Support 24%	Support 24%	Support 29%	Support 67%
Team	Cell 5 18%	Cell 6 21%	Cell 7 15%	Cell 8 10% 64%
	Technical 51%	Technical 61%	Technical 51%	Technical 39%
	Managerial 35%	Managerial 25%	Managerial 40%	Managerial 50%
	Support 14%	Support 14%	Support 9%	Support 11%
	36%	27%	26%	11% N-282

9, 0% and 39%). The support role was a likley career path for free agents with exclusive employment relations (67%). Interestingly, support is less likely as a career strategy for subcontractors with team career orientations (average: 12% across cells 5 through 8).

These career patterns suggest a variety of strategies that subcontractors may use in project networks. The key insight is that career patterns appear to result from a matching of employment relations, subcontractor orientations, and organizational roles. For example, technical skills and competencies are well suited for hybrid relations, because these provide both continuity and exposure for new people and work challenges that extend and enhance technical skills. In contrast, managerial skill and competencies facilitate work of developing teams that are needed to make an elite product (e.g., films by Woody Allen or Robert Altman), or are needed to establish efficient routines for several low-budget films (e.g., by Sunn, New World, or Walt Disney). Support skills, and the coordination they provide, may be more important when free agents dominate production arrangements.

Cores and Peripheries: Developing Long-Term Access to Projects

It is untrue that project networks have no structures at all. In industries with extensive subcontracting and permeable firm boundaries, tightly knit relations exist in the inner cores, which are connected to loosely woven interactions on the peripheries. The peripheries of the industry's social structure are open; those individuals with the necessary skills and desire, and those firms with the necessary capital, may enter. In contrast, the industry's inner cores, where the high-status, high-paying work occurs, are restricted. Only a small percentage of people both enter and remain within the industry's inner core for most of their careers. For example, in the film industry, from 1965 to 1980, only 7% of the film producers made 40% of the films, while 64% made only one film (Faulkner and Anderson, 1987: 894).

One way to identify the varying cores and peripheries within the industry social structure is through a k-core analysis (Scott, 1991: 112; Seidman, 1983) among industry participants. K-core analysis allows us to assess varying degrees of interconnectedness by locating areas of tightly and loosely woven interactions—as one moves to the inner cores, there is an increase in contact among subcontractors and firms. Thus, those within the inner cores have rich informal communication networks concerning jobs and opportunities. In contrast, those on the periphery interact with the least frequency and have poor informal communication networks concerning jobs and opportunities. As Faulkner explains, "working on the periphery is an odd mixture of nearness and remoteness; . . . the newcomer is near in that he has contact with many members of his occupation, but remote in that such contact is occasional, incidental, rather than a result of solid ties" (1987: 120).

A k-core analysis of the film industry in the 1977–1979 period reveals distinct areas—an inner core, a semi-periphery, and a periphery—that are defined by subcontractors who work for the major studios, the minor studios, and fly-by-night firms. In the inner cores, 80% or more of the subcontractors work exclusively for the seven major studios. Thus, these relationships are more densely connected, and subcontractors, on average, made three films in the three-year period. These inner cores are inhabited by the elite, who have greater compensation, skill, experience, stability of employment, and access to resources (Balio, 1985; Faulkner, 1987). In contrast, around 50% of subcontractors on the periphery work for the fly-by-nights and the minor studios. And working for the 32 minor studios and the 142 fly-by-nights makes the interactions less cohesive and less likely to provide good information on subcontractors' skills and reputations. On average, the fly-by-nights make only 1.19 films; they are indeed transitory firms and cannot be counted on to build a career. The periphery is comprised of lower-paid jobs, less skill, and experience, and have unstable and tenuous employment (Balio, 1985; Faulkner, 1987). Further, around 50% in the semiperipheral area work for the minor firms, 25% for the major studios, and 25% for the fly-by-nights. Clearly, the semiperiphery links the cores and the periphery through direct and indirect relations.

In summary, the social structure of the film industry reveals a small set of firms—the seven major studios—who share a relatively large elite group of subcontractors. For subcontractors, inclusion in this elite inner core provides more challenging work, prestige, better pay, and access to resources within the industry. As Raider and Burt point out in chapter 11, movement among firms and other elite subcontractors provides greater social capital for these subcontractors, who have better access to information and to job opportunities at the elite firms. However, prior success does not guarantee a place in the inner core. One's position in the inner core must be reaffirmed with a successful performance on each new project. What these data do point out is that few consistently perform and excel at the high levels required to remain within the inner core for their entire careers.

Conclusion

Boundaryless careers and project networks are interfirm phenomena that force us to reframe our understanding of both careers and organization. This movement across firms requires individuals to develop skills such as interpersonal communication and knowledge of the industry culture, which facilitate the informal coordination of work. Since individuals must constantly compete for projects, one's reputation and informal networks of contacts are critical for continued employment. Thus, individuals have a much greater responsibility for seeking experiences that maintain and extend their skills. Although a variety of career strategies are available in project networks, two strategies appear most successful: developing key technical skills for which others will want you, or becoming a valued member of one or more production teams. In short, these new careers and organizations provide more challenge and variety in one's work, but also more responsibility and a proactive pursuit of success in one's career.

ACKNOWLEDGMENTS: I would like to thank Michael Arthur and Benyamin Lichtenstein for comments on earlier drafts.

Notes

1. Leigh, the film commissioner, identified the four other subcontractors who were to be interviewed, on the basis of their quality credits and consistent work. The film commissioner seeks to increase film production in the state, and his office also organizes the U.S. Film Festival in Park City, Utah. The interviews were done during a five-month period in 1988 and were semistructured; the questions were: (1) Tell me about what you do in the film industry. (2) How did you get started? (3) What makes a career successful in the film industry? (4) Do you help newcomers get started? What about them makes you decide to help them? (5) What advice do you give these newcomers? The data were content analyzed, included in a report, and fed back to the informants, who then assessed the data for accuracy and understanding of the film industry. This acts as a validity check on the data and interpretations.

2. See Jones (1993) for more information about data collection and methods of analysis.

3. Film credits are recorded in the film-industry periodical *Willis' Screen World.* Since a three-year period for examining career patterns may be perceived as too short a time span to obtain valid results, I examined whether this short period skewed the data for the 2,074 subcontractors with only one film credit. The career histories of the 2,074 subcontractors were checked against Katz's *Film Encyclopedia.* Further, since production in film projects typically lasts from six to twelve weeks, and only directors are guaranteed a salary for a minimum of ten weeks, subcontractors who work less than once a year, on average, will have a hard time making a living. Indeed, the most productive subcontractors made between 12 and 13 films in the three-year period.

References

Arthur, M. B. 1994. "The boundaryless career: A new perspective for organizational inquiry." *Journal of Organizational Behavior*, 15: 295–306.

Balio, T. 1985. *The American Film Industry*, 2d ed. Madison: University of Wisconsin Press.

Becker, H. S. 1982. *Art Worlds*. Berkeley: University of California Press.

Bresnen, M., A. Wray, A. Bryman, A. D. Beardsworth, J. Ford, and E. T. Keil, 1985. "The flexibility of recruitment in the construction industry: Formalisation or re-casualisation?" *Sociology*, 19 (1): 108–124.

Bridges, W. 1994. "The end of the job." *Fortune*, September, 19: 62–72.

Burt, R. 1980. "Models of network structure." *Annual Review of Sociology*, 6: 79–141.

Clark, K. B., and T. Fujimoto. 1989. "Lead time in automobile product development: Explaining the Japanese advantage." *Journal of Engineering and Technology Management*, 6: 53.

Eccles, R. G. 1981. "The quasifirm in the construction industry." *Journal of Economic Behavior and Organization*, 2: 335–357.

Ellis, J. C. 1990. *A History of Film*, 3d ed. Englewood Cliffs, N.J.: Prentice-Hall.

Faulkner, R. R. 1987. *Careers on Demand: Composers and Careers in the Hollywood Film Industry*. New Brunswick: Transaction Books.

Faulkner, R. R., and A. B. Anderson. 1987. "Short-term projects and emergent careers: Evidence from Hollywood." *American Journal of Sociology*, 92: 879–909.

Faulkner, R. R. 1985. *Hollywood Studio Musicians: Their Work and Careers in the Recording Industry*, 2d ed. Lanham, Md: University Press of America.

Goodman, P. L., and R. A. Goodman. 1972. "Theater as a temporary system." *California Management Review*, 15 (2), 103–108.

Goodman, R. A., and P. L Goodman. 1976. "Some management issues in temporary systems: A study of the professional development and manpower—the theater case." *Administrative Science Quarterly*, 21 (3), 494–500.

Granovetter, M. 1985. "Economic action and social structure: The problem of embeddedness." *American Journal of Sociology*, 91: 481–510.

Hirsch, P. M. 1972. "Processing fads and fashions: An organization-set analysis of cultural industry systems." *American Journal of Sociology*, 77: 639–659.

Hubbell, J. 1991 "Celluloid sheepskins." *American Film*, April: 11.

Huey, J. 1994. "Waking up to the new economy." *Fortune*, June, 27: 36–48.

Imai, K.; I. Nonaka; and H. Takeuchi. 1985. "Managing the new product development process: How Japanese companies learn and unlearn." In K. B. Clark et al. (eds.), *The Uneasy Alliance*, pp. 337–375. Cambridge, Mass.: Harvard Business School Press.

Jones, C. 1988. *"Selection and socialization of film professionals."* Mimeographed. University of Utah, Salt Lake City.

Jones, C. 1993. *"Toward an understanding and theory of network organizations."* Ph.D. diss. University of Utah.

Kadushin, C. 1976. "Networks and circles in the production of culture." *American Behavioral Scientist*, 19: 769–784.

Kanter, R. M. 1989. *When Giants Learn to Dance: Mastering the Challenges of Strategy, Management and Careers in the 1990s*. New York: Basic Books.

Kent, N. 1991. *Naked Hollywood*. New York: St. Martin's.

Light, D., Jr. 1979. "Surface data and deep structure: Observing the organization of professional training." *Administrative Science Quarterly*, 24: 551–558.

Miles, R. E., and C. C. Snow. 1986. "Organizations: New concepts for new forms." *California Management Review*, 28 (3): 62–73.

Miner, A., and D. F. Robinson. 1994. "Organizational and population level learning as engines for career transitions." *Journal of Organizational Behavior*, 15: 295–306.

O'Reilly, B. 1994. "What companies and employees owe one another." *Fortune*, June 13: 44–57.

Ouchi, W. G. 1979. "A conceptual framework for the design of organizational control mechanisms." *Management Science*, 25 (9): 833–848.

Pascale, R. 1985. "The paradox of 'corporate culture': Reconciling ourselves to socialization." *California Management Review*, 27: 26–41.

Peterson, R. A., and D. G. Berger. 1971. "Entrepreneurship in organizations: Evidence from the popular music industry." *Administrative Science Quarterly*, 10 (1): 97–106.

Piore, M. J., and C. F. Sabel. 1984. *The Second Industrial Divide*. New York: Basic Books.

Powell, W. W. 1990. "Neither market nor hierarchy: Network forms of organizing." In B. Staw and L. L. Cummings (eds.), *Research in Organizational Behavior*, pp. 295–336. Greenwich, Conn.: JAI.

Reich, R. R. 1991. *The Work of Nations*. New York: Alfred Knopf.

Richman, L. R. 1994a."How to get ahead in America." *Fortune*, May: 46–58.

Richman, L. R. 1994b. "The new work force builds itself." *Fortune*, June: 68–79.

Ring, P. S., and A. H. Van de Ven. 1992. "Structuring cooperative relationships between organizations." *Strategic Management Journal*, 13: 483–498.

Robins, J. A. 1993. "Organization as strategy: Restructuring production in the film industry." *Strategic Management Journal*, 14: 103–118.

Saxenian, A. 1990. "Regional networks and the resurgence of Silicon Valley." *California Management Review*, 33 (1): 89–112.

Scott, J. 1991. *Social Network Analysis: A Handbook*. Newbury Park, Calif.: Sage.

Seidman, S. B. 1983. "Network structure and minimum degree." *Social Networks, 5*: 269–287.

Tompkins, P. K., and G. Cheney. 1985. "Communication and unobtrusive control in contemporary organizations." In R. McPhee and P. K. Tompkins (eds.), *Organizational Communication: Traditional Themes and New Directions*. Beverly Hills: Sage.

Van Maanen, J. 1979. "People processing: Strategies for organizational socialization." *Organizational Dynamics*, 7: 19–36.

Van Maanen, J., and E. H. Schein. 1979. "Toward a theory of organizational socialization." In B. Staw (ed.), *Research in Organizational Behavior*, pp. 287–365. Greenwich, Conn.: JAI.

Weick, K. 1979. *The Social Psychology of Organizing*, 2d ed. New York: Random House.

5

Careers Change as Organizations Learn

DAVID F. ROBINSON AND ANNE S. MINER

Many formalized organizations have moved toward more fluid departmental boundaries and individual jobs (Weick and Berlinger, 1989; Nonaka, 1990). Scholars have drawn attention to the recent increase in joint ventures, outsourcing, research consortia, and other complex organizational forms in the United States (Contractor and Lorange, 1988; Aldrich and Sasaki, 1994), and to the extended presence of contingent workers (Pfeffer and Baron, 1988; Barnett and Miner, 1992). Taken together, these trends imply a blurring of the traditional boundaries, both within and among organizations—taken for granted in much of the prior career research.

Some have argued that this shift to boundaryless organizations—defined here as organizations whose membership, departmental identity, and job responsibilities are ambiguous—will produce a pattern of unstructured careers (e.g., see Kanter, 1989). They propose that careers will primarily follow a pattern of independent agents involved in short-term contracts, and accompanied by unfettered flows of information within and among organizations. Individuals will move rapidly between roles and develop little organizational attachment.

In this chapter, we develop a different prediction. We argue that boundaryless organizations will not produce atomistic careers similar to those of independent agents. Instead, we suggest that boundaryless organizations will increase the number of job transitions created by organizations seeking to discover new knowledge. However, other job transitions will occur because firms seek to "harvest" their current knowledge and to retain proven routines. These job transitions will remain structured in many cases.

Our chapter turns around the traditional focus on how learning by individuals may impact organizational change. We argue that organizations should be seen as learning entities. We describe three key processes underlying simple trial-and-error learning by organizations: the variation, selection, and retention of organizational routines, or of repeated patterns of activities. To survive and prosper in the current era, firms will need to engage routinely in all three processes throughout the organization. We then consider how learning processes will affect individual job changes within individual organizations and populations of organizations. Finally, we consider how these processes will change the way that social interaction and information use interweave with job mobility.

To illustrate two of the key learning processes, consider the following explanations and examples: *Variation,* or discovery of new knowledge through experimentation with different actions, allows a firm to learn what it needs to do to survive and prosper. Firms can deliberately act to increase the amount of variation in their current activities, which can, in turn, directly affect individual careers. In product development, for example, firms will sometimes create separate development teams, all charged with solving the same problem (Quinn, 1986). Having several teams working independently generates more potential new-product and new-process routines than having a single team. Imagine, for example, that a firm creates three such teams to design a new pocket-sized portable telephone. If fifteen employees were promoted to the positions making up those teams, rather than the five required for one team, then ten of these promotions are the direct result of the firm's extra effort to generate variation, or knowledge discovery.

A related example helps explain how careers may also be affected by *retention* processes, or the firm's efforts to harvest prior learning. Take the portable phone designed in the above example, but assume now that the firm discovered a more efficient general manufacturing method during production, and sought to use this method with its other products as a "best" practice. Jobs created to spread this best practice would focus primarily on ensuring that the new production methods were consistent across settings and employees (avoiding variation). In this example, the organization seeks to exploit consistently what it has learned (as expressed in the new manufacturing routine), and career changes will occur in support of that imperative. Specifically, the promotions will go to candidates who most closely match the predefined skill sets of these new jobs.

We propose that while a great deal of traditional career theory has focused on mobility patterns driven by retention processes (emphasizing specialization and job consistency), organizations have actually routinely sustained variation processes as well. However, organizations have often segregated these processes into separate research-and-development or creative-job groups. Increased movement toward boundaryless organizations will lead to greater emphasis on variation-related mobility throughout organizations and create novel types of career transitions.

The shift to boundaryless organizations will also affect the role of social interaction and information in mobility processes. For example, accidental social contact between scientists may lead to knowledge creation, which in turn will change their careers. Employees who embody key parts of organizational memory will play more critical roles in the knowledge-based organization, yet may be more deeply linked to external networks of information than in traditional competitive settings. Paradoxically, this may create a small core of jobs that are more stable and protected than others (Barnett and Miner, 1992).

To explore these claims, we briefly review the traditional logic of career-mobility processes, define boundaryless careers, and introduce organizational and population-level learning. We then develop our arguments using illustrative material from an exploratory study of career transitions in several knowledge-intensive organizations. We conclude by describing how the learning perspective provides a vital platform for research on boundaryless careers, and by outlining key managerial dilemmas faced by firms that depend on learning for their survival and prosperity.

Theoretical Framework

In this chapter, we define a career as the "evolving sequence of a person's work experiences over time" (Arthur, Hall, and Lawrence, 1989: 8). Much theorizing about careers has envisioned (or tacitly assumed) fixed lattices of positions with clear and stable boundaries and purposes (Weber, [1922] 1968; Baron, 1984; Arthur, Hall, and Lawrence, 1989).

In contrast to these assumptions, considerable field observation reveals that many jobs never had such stable lattices for progression (Osterman, 1984; Miner, 1987). In addition, organizations in the industrialized world have recently become more fluid. Joint ventures, research consortia, outsourcing of activities, and contingent employment arrangements have proliferated, blurring external organizational boundaries (Aldrich and Sasaki, 1994; Osterman, 1984; Belous, 1989). Within firms in the United States, decentralization and increasing emphasis on cross-functional coordination and teams have blurred previously rigid departmental boundaries (Imai, Nonaka, and Takeuchi, 1985; Maidique and Zirger, 1988). Finally, many American employers have moved to more general job descriptions, emphasizing key work values, rather than precise, predetermined duties (Souder, 1987).

The Boundaryless Organization

In this chapter, we use the term *boundaryless organization* to refer to organizations whose membership rules, departmental identity rules, and job-responsibility rules are ambiguous. Other guides for action, such as shared values, however, may be strong ones. We define a boundaryless career as a career that unfolds unconstrained by clear boundaries around job activities, by fixed sequences of such activities, or by attachment to one organization. One might imagine that job transitions within boundaryless careers would be limited only by dynamic interactions between economic free agents (Spence, 1974; Schelling, 1978). However, we propose that organizational factors will still drive individual career transitions, but the underlying logic will be that of organizational and population-level learning.

Organizational and Population-Level Learning

Over 30 years ago, Cyert and March ([1963] 1992) first proposed that organizations are learning systems, in which actions with apparently useful results become incorporated into standard operating procedures. There is now a widespread consensus that we can observe several levels of learning. Individuals within organizations learn new skills and values. Groups can learn norms and practices, even, in some cases, without the conscious awareness of the individual participants (Hutchins 1991). Whole organizations can learn and sustain new routines and values, even though the individuals within them come and go (Levitt and March, 1988). Here, organizational memory consists of the behavioral routines, scripts, standard operating procedures, and even the physical plant of the organization (Walsh and Ungson, 1991). Finally, populations, or collections of organizations, can learn, as when firms in an industry widely adopt a new technology (Miner and Haunschild, 1995).

Theorists have proposed many definitions of organizational learning. Here, we define learning as the patterned transformation of a system, arising from the acquisition or retention of knowledge. Knowledge is either behavioral or informational. The process of experimenting with, and then adopting, flexible time rules for employees is an example of *behavioral* learning. In contrast, *informational* learning occurs when a research department simply becomes aware of a new chemical formula. Learning does not necessarily lead to adaptation. Nor is learning always helpful; it can be dangerous, especially if causality is attributed to events that are only accidentally related. This is superstitious learning (Levitt and March, 1988).

Our discussion of learning's effects on transitions follows that of Miner (1990), in that we conceptualize learning as an evolutionary process (Nelson and Winter 1982). Change (learning) unfolds through the recycling of variation, selection, and retention processes (Campbell, 1969; Weick, 1979; Aldrich, 1979). In our earlier example of three competing new-product-development teams, the separate team efforts would constitute a variation step. A "shoot-out" in which the teams presented their plans, and the firm selected only one for production, would represent a selection phase. Finally, emphasis on consistency in the production of the new design would constitute retention.

Impact of Learning Processes on Career Transitions

Instead of beginning with individual learning and looking at its aggregate impact, we turn the question around. We ask, "If organizations must sustain collective learning to survive and prosper, how will this affect the kinds of transitions individuals make between jobs over time?" We want to consider systematically how organizational learning can produce individual career transitions.

Transitions are defined as significant changes in employees' formal jobs, such as the creation of new positions, moves to different jobs, or moves to different organizations. Formal transitions have been the major focus of most empirical research on careers in the sociology, economics, and management literatures (Spillerman, 1977; Barney and Lawrence, 1989; Rosenbaum, 1989; Stewman and Konda, 1983). Below, we examine the impact of organizational and population-level learning on career transitions.

Research Strategy

To explore the potential impact of organizational learning on boundaryless careers, we followed an inductive agenda. We conducted 24 semistructured interviews of business and university-based professionals at a small spin-off technology firm, a medium-sized scientific-equipment manufacturer, and two universities. We targeted knowledge-intensive organizations, and selected subjects on the basis of their known or anticipated involvement in technological or organizational change. In two institutions, people other than the authors selected the subjects, at our request. During the selection process, we had no prior information on subjects' career transitions. Subjects were asked to describe their work experiences, in a set of open-ended questions. In analyzing their responses, we focused on career transitions between and within organizations.

Impact of Organizational Level Learning Processes on Career Transitions

Variation

For learning to occur, organizations need sources of varied routines, to provide a pool of innovative ideas from which new routines can be selected (March, 1991). Traditionally, organizations institutionalize the search for variation in research laboratories and development departments. Typically, job duties in such systems are ambiguous in the sense that clearly defined sets of activities cannot be specified in advance. Instead, broad levels of responsibility or independence are specified.

In the boundaryless organization, the descriptions of what is to be done are ambiguous throughout the organization, not just in a few specific departments. The organization may not know in advance what needs to be done, but needs to generate variation to permit trial-and-error learning and the discovery of new information. Discovery processes can produce internal career transitions for individuals throughout the organization. Consider the following career shift described to us by Terry Jenner, an engineer who was originally trained in high-energy physics:

Jenner gained a reputation for creating innovative and effective solutions after he successfully completed three projects outside his area of expertise. Jenner made a job transition when he was subsequently promoted to a new position, where he was asked to come up with new uses for surplus equipment and for factories that would soon be idled by new, more productive machinery.

Jenner's transition is an example of variation generated within the firm in order to solve a serious and ill-defined problem of underutilized equipment. The organization did not know how to utilize the idled machines, but it was aware of Jenner's ability to innovate, from his track record.

Job transitions arising from organizational discovery also occur in administrative areas and can involve creating new tactics and goals for the organization. One employee, for example, convinced a school of engineering to adopt new hiring and skills-development goals for nonacademic employees, which also resulted in a new, formal position and several promotions for her. Miner (1987) found that even a bureaucratized university created 7–12% of new nonfaculty, nonresearch jobs around individual skills and interests. These were new positions, not predefined by the administration, which shows a nontrivial impact for merely one of many potential mechanisms for variation.

The career moves of participants in our study suggest that organizational discovery drives interorganizational career transitions as well. For example:

Barry Fitzer, a chemist, gained experience in a consumer-products company, working with absorbent materials at a time when the materials were just being developed. That experience was valued by Standard Chemicals, a supplier of bulk industrial materials that wanted to start manufacturing consumer-products but was unfamiliar with the materials' properties. Fitzer experienced a career transition when Standard Chemicals hired him away from the consumer-products company to gain experience with the new materials.

It is important to note that the organization, in recruiting Fitzer, was not hiring him to implement an already well-focused set of actions. Instead, the firm sought to gain a general competence, by using his transition as a way to discover unknown potential in a particular material. Fitzer's transition can be seen as one step in his firm's search for variation through importing external competencies, or "grafting"—in contrast to internal trial-and-error learning (Huber, 1991). The discovery of new goals may also occur through interorganizational transitions. Search committees for senior positions sometimes use extremely broad position definitions, looking to the candidates themselves to propose a vision of the new organizational goals.

Finally, we suggest that the discovery process can generate transitions producing new, hybrid types of jobs and roles. Consider, for example, the following developments in the career paths of two individuals:

William Garrett, a researcher working in a medical facility, developed insight into how a mosquito-borne disease might affect a person infected with the disease. Garrett's insight eventually provided a new understanding of the disease and led to an improved diagnostic test, replacing flawed tests currently generating $70 million in sales for other firms.

Garrett established a relationship with a university faculty member, who became Garrett's adviser in his pursuit of a doctoral degree. The faculty adviser, Sharon Dalton, was interviewed by the management of the medical facility and required to sign a royalty agreement, before Garrett was allowed to collaborate with her as his doctoral adviser. Dalton experienced a career transition as she became a consultant in designing the test. As a consultant, she received grants to perform some of the needed animal testing in her university laboratory. Dalton also shares in the royalties now being earned by the disease test.

Upon completing his Ph.D., Garrett was promoted to the post of director of research for the medical facility. The promotion, in part, recognized his professional accomplishments (numerous publications; appointment to the editorial board of a science journal) and gave him sufficient status to promote further research by the organization.

In this case, two people began with distinct roles within distinct organizations: One was an employee of a medical facility and one a university professor. Because of the medical facility's interest in discovering products with important potential, the professor shifted to a hybrid situation combining her ongoing attachment to the firm with traditional faculty duties. The researcher/student indeed became a director of research and was appointed to an editorial board by his peers. These career transitions were not the product of preexisting routines: The faculty member did not have the situation of a consulting firm seeking such relationships, nor did the student anticipate a promotion to the directorship.

Selection

Organizational learning requires not only variation, but also selection. Some routines and information are retained, while others are not. In the previous section, we noted that employees may make transitions to parallel research teams as the organization seeks variation. Imagine that after a year, the firm conducted a "shoot-out" to determine what product design it would use. Employees on the successful design team were promoted to new positions for its further development, while members of the unsuccessful teams moved elsewhere in the firm (Quinn, 1986). The organizational selection process for choosing product designs, in turn, produced these job transitions.

Over time, some jobs are selected for survival and others are eliminated (Miner, 1990, 1991). This process produces transitions for individuals. Whole groups of jobs are sometimes retained or destroyed through broader processes of reorganization, zero-base budgeting exercises, or cutbacks.

In a boundaryless organization, some jobs represent experiments that the organization can later review and discard or strengthen. Recall Terry Jenner from a previous example of variation:

Jenner's employer decided to experiment with encouraging the creativity and innovativeness that Jenner had shown in completing several challenging projects. The firm had Jenner teach departments how to improve creative-idea generation and problem solving. After two years, most of the departments had been trained and the innovation-training function was disbanded. Jenner was then promoted to yet another new project.

In this case, in the variation phase, the firm established a new innovation department. In the selection phase, the firm determined that the department was no longer necessary and disbanded the training department.

Retention

Nearly all learning theorists have noted the trade-offs between generating enough variation to permit further learning, and maintaining retention (or consistency) mechanisms to capture the value of prior experiments (March 1991). Organizational variation and selection processes without retention (memory) cannot produce learning, because the organization cannot harvest the value of its prior experimentation.

Recall the example of competitive new-product-development teams and the "shoot-out" for selection of a specific product design. After prototype development and test production runs, imagine that the organization moves into a manufacturing mode. On the production floor, the organization will seek consistency in the behavior of people and machines.

Traditional career research has not been wrong, but has simply mistaken one aspect of organizational learning—use of effective retention mechanisms—as the only motivator of career patterns. For example, detailed job descriptions, formalized selection systems, elaborate compensation systems, and career ladders formed a retention system firms used to replicate useful activities. Lifetime employment practices also encourage consistency and are alternatives to formalized job descriptions (Miner, 1990). Socialization of employees can produce consistency without formal mechanisms or incentives (Barley, 1986).

Our interviews suggest that the relative importance of retention mechanisms versus variation mechanisms may decline. As firms decentralize and stress entrepreneurship, proportionally more employees can expect promotions or reassignments as the organization pursues variation. However, even in fast-moving companies, some employees will be promoted, in part because of the continuity they provide.

Transitions from firms emphasizing retention mechanisms may arise because employees find the mechanisms unacceptable. For example:

Bill Stevens, operations manager at Maxcon, a growing biotechnology firm, left the company and started a new, much smaller firm, Biotechnics. Maxcon's bureaucracy had grown complex; he was limited in his job duties; and the internal approval process for new products became frustrating to him. He complained that he no longer had the freedom to address multiple issues, and that he no longer personally knew the people with whom he worked. His solution was to launch a new company with several other former Maxcon employees. At Biotechnics, Stevens, as the operations manager, is in touch with the whole development process.

In this case, an employee made a transition to a new, smaller organization, in part because his job activities became routinized, and the institutionalization of approval processes and other activities created a personally unacceptable work environment.

Impact of Population-Level Learning on Transitions

We have considered how organizational learning processes can affect individual career transitions in the boundaryless organization. Observational and interview data point to an often overlooked additional stimulus for individual career transitions: population-level learning. A "population" can be thought of as a group of organizations, such as those firms in a particular industry, small biotechnology firms, large multinational corporations or school districts in metropolitan areas. Generally, the firms in a population share a common feature or interest, although this is not required.

Population-level learning is defined as the systematic change in the nature and mix of routines in a population of organizations (Miner and Haunschild, 1995). To make the idea of population-level learning concrete, we can consider a hypothetical population of child-care centers over a 20-year period. At first, the newly established centers all require that parents become significantly involved in operating a cooperative center. Ten years later, commercial day-care centers appear, which do not require parental involvement, and use marketing practices. After ten more years, nearly all centers use marketing practices and few require parental involvement. The nature and mix of routines enacted in the population of centers have changed systematically.

If the population-level shift occurred because the cooperative centers failed, but the commercial ones survived, this would be considered population-level learning through selection of whole organizations. Alternatively, if the cooperative centers copied the commercial centers, then population-level learning through interaction, or shared experience, occurred.

Variation

At the population level, variation occurs through the creation of new organizations, or the introduction of new sets of routines into the population at large (Lant and Mezias, 1990). These events can produce career transitions for individuals. For example, Haveman and Cohen (1994) reported significant employee movement into and out of the California savings and loan industry as firms were born, or died. The technological change that occurs as industries adopt new technology, such as computer-aided design (CAD), or adopt practices such as total quality management, also leads to career transitions, as firms abolish old skills and adopt new skills.

In technology-driven industries, small firms often provide the population with variations in product and manufacturing routines. Large firms wait until the early trial-and-error learning has been carried out by the small firms, and then adopt their practices or acquire the small firms. This variation process produces career transitions for some individuals. For example:

Sarah Bright was one of the original founders of a rapidly growing biotechnology firm called Maxcon. Bright left Maxcon to join Crystal, Inc., a massive pharmaceutical firm that sought her broad competencies in biotechnology manufacturing methods. The pharmaceutical firm had stayed out of these product areas until it concluded there was enough experience to invest major capital in developing products.

Bright's transition, while part of the discovery process for Crystal, is also part of the population-learning process, as larger firms capture new processes by hiring people like Sarah Bright.

In some cases, populations of organizations explicitly pursue a process of collective variation by forming *research consortia* (Aldrich and Sasaki, 1994). Organizational boundaries blur when scientists work at a consortium for several years. As a result, transitions sometimes occur when participants move to other firms through contacts made at the consortium, even though strong norms may exist to discourage such transitions. Interorganizational transitions may also occur through employee involvement in firms' experiments with joint ventures, outsourcing, and contract research (Contractor and Lorange, 1988).

Selection

In population-level learning, market, government, or even accidental forces, such as war, may lead to the demise of entire organizations over time. Careers of founding entrepreneurs and their employees are directly affected when firms fail. Haveman and Cohen (1994) have shown that nearly one half of all transitions that managers made among California savings-and-loan firms, over a 20-year period, were due to failing firms.

Learning also occurs through the *selection of new routines* by the population of organizations. Selection of practices can result from the efficiency or superiority of a particular method (for example, adoption of mass production by the auto industry). Individual organizations may develop these routines through experience; however, the selection of a particular routine by a population is often influenced by other organizations and institutions. Certain practices may be required by governmental regulations. Some practices are voluntarily adopted to make organizations seem more legitimate to stakeholders, such as banks, customers, and/or regulators (DiMaggio and Powell, 1983).

Firms do not consider every routine for possible adoption. For example, government agencies, consultants, and trade associations (Aldrich and Sasaki, 1993) act as selection "filters" by choosing certain practices to spread among their client firms. Business schools, through their curriculum decision-making process, select certain routines—total quality management (TQM), for example—to disseminate among their population of students, who are in turn hired by firms. Selection of new routines leads to career transitions, such as those experienced by individuals who obtained new positions established by firms to comply with government affirmative-action policies (Edelman, 1992).

Retention

As boundaryless organizations proliferate, we expect individuals to be used increasingly to transfer new practices to firms. Retention of these practices will generate career transitions. The following example shows how government regulation leads firms to internalize and retain the routines of their regulators:

Tony Jacobs worked for two Florida-based public utilities, in the area of rate regulation. He later spent ten years on the Indiana public-service commission, regulating similar utilities. Then, tired of the utilities business, Jacobs became a commercial pig farmer.

After a few years of losing money and hating the smell of pigs, Jacobs returned to the utility business. This time, he went to work for Merman Consumer Products, a manufacturing company that used a great deal of energy in making its products. Merman valued Jacobs's regulatory expertise and used it to limit the utilities' attempts to increase Merman's utility rates.

Jacobs, in this instance, represents a "carrier" of certain values and procedures. His role was to teach his new organization the routines of the regulatory body, even as he helped the organization resist regulation.

The retention process may lead to substantial numbers of job transitions in areas where there is rapid and strong diffusion throughout the population. In the present era, trainers who offer TQM skills may find multiple openings as organizations seek, retain, and harvest value from these competencies. Trainers who teach with traditional management-planning tools may find transitions difficult.

Learning as a Moderator of Other Factors in Career Transitions

The general idea that social interaction will affect career transitions has a long intellectual history. Weber ([1922] 1968) contrasted "offices" for which candidates were selected on the basis of merit, with cases in which personal and family connections determined both governmental and commercial positions. Granovetter (1986) suggested that "weak" ties (casual social connections) can convey the existence of potential openings, and the subtle features of both candidates and organizations that facilitate matches.

Organizational Learning and Social Interaction

As organizational boundaries become more diffuse, learning processes may influence the ways in which social interaction affects careers. For example, one scientist reported that, in developing a new product, he seeks informal relationships with vendors to learn about the latest technical developments in a field. Small technology-based firms sometimes cultivate the personal linkages of their scientists to university scientists, to keep a pipeline to technological frontiers. In both cases, social interaction permits the employee to use very current information that can lead to high performance levels and related career transitions.

In addition to the direct effects of social interaction, chance social events can intertwine with organizational learning to affect career transitions in more subtle ways. For example:

John Durst, a theoretical chemist, had a chance conversation with a colleague (an experimental chemist). Both scientists were surprised to find that the National Bureau of Standards published statistics, on the magnesium dioxide molecule, that did not agree with their understanding of the molecule. Using his knowledge of theory, Dr. Durst was able to compute what he thought the numerical measure of this particular property of magnesium dioxide should be. His colleague then designed an experiment that confirmed Durst's theoretical estimate.

A radio astronomer heard about the results (relevant to his work on star formation), and the three scientists began a triangular collaboration. The resulting work formed a key basis for Durst's career promotions, as well as for the careers of the others. Their collaboration also helped develop an atmosphere of intradepartmental cross-fertilization at the university and elsewhere as their careers unfolded.

In this case, a social interaction occurred accidentally and was not a form of deliberate intelligence gathering. Yet it shaped the direction of the science work done by three people over a period of decades, including the career transitions they made across and within universities. It appears likely that the interaction of chance social contacts, knowledge discovery, and career paths will become increasingly important under boundaryless conditions.

Population-Level Learning and Social Interaction

We anticipate that population-level learning will also affect the role of social interaction in careers. Where organizational boundaries and membership status are fluid, retention processes are harder to maintain. If a firm, for example, subcontracts a substantial amount of work and depends heavily on temporary employees, it becomes more difficult to institutionalize effective routines. In these situations, recruiting from social networks may be used to actually replace some aspects of stable jobs in organizations and serve as a retention mechanism for prior learning.

Consider, for example, political organizations that are assembled to work only for a specific period and completely disappear at the end of a campaign. If all the competencies and routines needed to run the campaign had to be devised anew each time, such organizations would not be effective. However, these organizations typically call on people and routines from other campaigns, often recruiting from informal social networks. The population-level memory, then, lies in the social network, rather than within bounded organizations.

Common interests provide a basis for the formation of informal networks that can play surprisingly strong roles in determining career outcomes. For example, recent descriptions of the formation of the "digerati"— professionals interested in digitalization—tend to support the role of social networks as a collective retention vehicle, and lead to the creation of homogeneous groups (Keegan, 1995). Increased homogeneity of backgrounds and interests of key players in organizations may be an unintended outcome of the use of networks as retention vehicles.

The Risks of Social Interaction

An important corollary of our framework is that learning processes will not lead to completely unfettered communication between organizations. For example, firms may cooperate in research consortia designed to develop precompetitive technologies, but they then fiercely compete in the marketplace with products from that technology (Contractor and Lorange 1988). Indeed, boundaryless organizations still exist in competitive environments, and communication will still be limited by the desire to control access to secrets that maintain competitive advantage.

Informal social interaction, as a source of crucial information, represents both an opportunity and a danger for the firm and its intellectual property. Subjects in our interviews had developed sophisticated approaches to managing their social information exchanges. One scientist carefully estimated how much information he could reveal on current projects; this allowed him to communicate with colleagues at conferences, without providing competitors with enough knowledge to surpass his work. Several subjects informally exchanged information only with trusted colleagues who would protect their organizational and personal interests.

Implications for Careers

The shift toward boundaryless organizations will not produce a cataclysmic shift from lockstep, ordered careers to random patterns of career transitions inside and between organizations. Our arguments above portray a world in which careers continue to be driven in part by organizational and population-level learning. Discovery or knowledge creation (variation processes), previously salient chiefly to the careers of research scientists, will drive aspects of many more careers. However, many careers will continue to unfold through transitions between structured jobs and roles. Below, we consider the implications of our learning framework for theoreticians and managers.

Impact on Career Theory

We believe that the focus on boundedness in prior career theory derived in part from the boundaries we set on our own theorizing and data collection. Career theories have frequently focused on ordered careers within large American organizations. Their industrial relations practices assumed a taken-for-granted status in many organizational theories. Also, modeling sequential movement in structured career systems is less complex than the dynamic modeling called for by learning theory and a mobile workforce.

From the learning perspective, old theories focusing on bureaucratic careers (Osterman, 1984) are not wrong, but, instead, are seen as research on systems designed to retain organizational practices (memory). In contrast, studies of scientific and entrepreneurial careers are considered research on systems that generate and capture variation (Shenhav, 1991).

We suggest that viewing boundaryless organizations and careers from a learning perspective raises four especially important issues: the interaction of careers with organizations and with each other; unintended learning outcomes; the role of timing; and the impact of learning-related variables on careers.

Interaction with Organizations

Career theorists have long noted that organizations that socialized employees into fixed systems overlooked the degree to which employees modified these systems (Van Maanen and Schein, 1979). Recent models specifically link career transition and organizational adaptation. The models suggest that a "modest level of turnover" increases exploration (variation) and can improve collective knowledge through diversity introduced by new players (March, 1991: 79). As we have explored in this article, these organizational learning processes may produce career transitions. At the same time, individuals may be learning as well. The interaction of individual and organizational learning processes offers an important frontier for further exploration.

Networks and Unintended Outcomes

There are also important potential unintended outcomes of organizational learning processes if networks of individuals become the repository of much collective learning. Will this jeopardize the survival of organizations or cause increased use of informal networks of influence, such as family or social networks? Will the nature of social networks enhance homogeneity, by race and sex, in workplace settings, in contrast to current ideologies favoring diversity? Research will be needed to address these issues.

Timing

As populations of organizations learn, there is an implied window of opportunity in which a new practice may be adopted. This is a familiar feature of evolutionary and learning processes (Levitt and March, 1988). Systematic adoption of new processes, and accidents of timing in which technologies combine in unforeseen ways, will both affect the careers of individuals. Technological evolution provides a natural starting place for formulating more precise learning and career propositions, while tackling difficult modeling problems raised in studying careers as dynamic processes.

New Variables

Finally, the learning framework also points to new sets of variables worthy of study. For example, the nature and duration of membership in particular teams (Shenhav, 1991), and the type of "project champion" role involved, if any (Day, 1994), will potentially affect career transitions. Involvement with emerging technologies may make individuals highly valued by other firms, while employees involved in failed or unneeded projects may lose their positions.

Implications for Managers and Individual Employees

We have focused on the effects of organizational learning on specific types of job transitions made by individuals. What are the implications of our approach for sequences of such events—for the long-term careers of individuals?

Boundaryless organizations will have more flexible work arrangements than traditional employers have. However, employees who leave the workforce may risk having their skills become obsolete, which could limit their future opportunities. Increased opportunities for employees to make career transitions will lead to interesting careers, but employees will need to learn to use social networks and political skills to find the best employment opportunities (Salancik and Pfeffer, 1977). For employees with highly valued skills, compensation may increasingly be set by a bidding process involving organizations, rather than by a single firm's salary hierarchy. This may lead to some highly paid positions and to equity concerns among lower-paid employees. Employees will need to be able to negotiate for compensation, as well as for favored assignments that will build their skills portfolio. It will be increasingly important for employees to recognize projects with future value, and to be able to leave projects that look unpromising for the employees' future development.

The learning framework directs managers to focus primarily on two issues: how to enhance variation processes without losing the value of consistency and how to deal with the expanded number of other entities that serve as the organizational retainers of routines and information. Firms may become more nimble, in being able to hire highly talented individuals from other organizations in their network, thereby avoiding the lengthy process of developing talented employees in-house. However, those same firms risk losing highly skilled employees to transitions originating through that very same network. Indeed, personnel may become increasingly important as retainers of organizational routines, yet the risk of losing key employees to other firms will increase.

Managers will be challenged to minimize the disruptions that employee transitions cause among established work teams; this will make socialization of employees increasingly important as a means of smoothing transitions, retaining key employees, and instilling guiding organizational values into personnel (Roberts and Fusfeld, 1981). Socialization here is not the cynical cooptation of employees, but an effort to enhance employee understanding of the dynamics of organizational survival and prosperity. Observers of firms that rely on organizational learning for competitive advantage emphasize that rigid roles must be replaced by guiding values (Imai, Nonaka, and Takeuchi, 1985). Management has a unique role in creating and sustaining such values; yet it cannot necessarily count on long-term employee affiliation as their source.

At the same time, employees may not be so inclined to act in their employers' best interest, as they were in more stable career situations. Employees will be less accountable for the long-term implications of their decisions as they make more frequent transitions to new positions or employers. Employees may move on to new positions before the results of their actions are fully realized. Some employees will see their futures as being more dependent on their knowledge and skills, and will allocate resources to acquire these competencies (now making them more valued by other organizations and more available for transitions). This may be especially true if the employer has mixed success in meeting employee development needs or has trouble honoring past commitments to employees.

If employees change employers more often, it would not be surprising to see a decline in loyalty to the firm, combined with uncertainty over what needs to be done as job boundaries and duties are blurred (Lawless and Price, 1992). Firms will face an increased risk of loss as employees choose to act in their own best short-term interest (this is often described as "agency" problems); the firm will thus be exposed to the risks of liability in cases of negligence or thefts of trade secrets by exiting employees. Indeed, longstanding norms about who should harvest the value of intellectual property may need to be renegotiated in a world in which information is increasingly important but organizational affiliations are increasingly fluid or unclear. For example, some firms have created novel compensation incentives in which employees receive equity interests in new products, or share in licensing income from inventions. These formal incentives can have unintended outcomes if they lower the morale of other employees, however. Managers of firms that use learning as a key competitive advantage, then, will face tough but intriguing dilemmas requiring innovative solutions.

Conclusion

In this chapter, we have offered a view of organizations, as learning systems within populations of organizations, which themselves are learning systems. We have argued that both organizations and populations of organizations learn through the selection and retention of new subunits and routines.

We have proposed that a logic of learning underlies career patterns, both as a cause of individual job transitions, and as a moderator of the ways that social interaction affects careers. We suspect that even in large, bureaucratized organizations, careers have been driven by the logic of organizational learning more than has previously been emphasized (Miner, 1991). We believe variation and trial-and-error learning processes are often masked by retroactive accounts of stable and purposeful behavior. For example, strategy theorists initially applauded Honda's introduction of minibikes in the United States as a product of good planning, but they later discovered it occurred primarily through improvisation (Pascale, 1984). Nonetheless, we have proposed that the logic of learning will increasingly drive career dynamics as organizations move away from sharp and stable boundaries for membership, internal structure, and roles.

The learning framework provides an important platform for research on boundaryless careers, by providing a way in which to look at whole career systems over time and across nations; by suggesting precise and nonobvious implications of learning processes; and by highlighting important questions about social interaction, information use, and careers. This perspective directs managers to two key issues for the current era: how to generate variation without losing key elements for the retention of what is learned; and how to enhance firm survival and prosperity in the face of the proliferation of other repositories for learning and information. The learning framework does not undermine the centrality of interaction and personal meaning in careers. Instead, it highlights the fact that these issues are played out in a dynamic context in which both organizational boundaries and goals unfold over time. This vision implies that managers must function as the facilitators of such learning systems, rather than as mere agents of control (Miner, 1994), and it offers theorists a powerful lens for the study of careers in the current era.

ACKNOWLEDGMENTS: The authors thank Michael Arthur, Denise Rousseau, and Mary Zellmer for their helpful contributions to this chapter; and John Wiley & Sons for permission to use our article from the *Journal of Organizational Behavior's* special issue on boundaryless careers, from which this chapter is adapted.

References

Aldrich, H. E. (1979), *Organizations and Environments.* Englewood Cliffs, N.J.: Prentice-Hall.

Aldrich, H. E. and Sasaki, T. (1995), R&D consortia in the United States and Japan. *Research Policy*, 24, 2: 301–316.

Aldrich, H. E. and Sasaki, T. (1993). Governance structure and technology transfer management in R&D consortia in the United States and Japan. Paper read at Japan Technology Management Conference, Ann Arbor, Mich.

Arthur, M. B.; Hall D. T.; and Lawrence, B. S., eds. (1989). *Handbook of Career Theory.* New York: Cambridge University Press.

Barley, S. K. (1986). Technology as an occasion for structuring: Evidence from observations of CT scanners and the social order of radiology departments. *Administrative Science Quarterly*, 31: 78–108.

Barnett, W., and Miner, A. S. (1992). Standing on the shoulders of others: Career interdependence in job mobility. *Administrative Science Quarterly*, 37: 262–281.

Barney, J. B., and Lawrence, B. S. (1991). Pin stripes, power ties and personal relationships: The economics of career strategy. In M. B. Arthur; D. T. Hall; and B. S. Lawrence, eds., *Handbook of Career Theory*. New York: Cambridge University Press, pp. 417–436.

Baron, J. N. (1984). Organizational perspectives on stratification. *Annual Review of Sociology*, 10: 37–69.

Belous, R. (1989). *The Contingent Economy: The Growth of the Temporary, Part-Time and Subcontracted Workforce*. Washington, D.C.: National Planning Association.

Campbell, D. (1969). Variation and selective retention in sociocultural evolution. *General Systems*, 16: 69–85.

Contractor, F. J., and Lorange, P. (1988). Why should firms cooperate? The strategy and economics basis for cooperative ventures. In F. J. Contractor and P. Lorange, eds., *Cooperative Strategies in International Business*. Lexington, Mass.: Lexington Books, pp. 3–28.

Cyert, R. M., and March, J. G. ([1963] 1992). *A Behavioral Theory of the Firm*, 2d ed. Oxford, Eng.: Blackwell.

Day, D. L. (1994). Raising radicals: Different processes for championing innovative corporate ventures, *Organization Science*, 5, 2.

DiMaggio, P. J., and Powell, W. W. (1983). The iron cage revisited: Institutional isomorphism and collective rationality in organizational fields, *American Sociological Review*, 48: 147–160.

Edelman, L. (1992). Legal ambiguity and symbolic structures: Organizational mediation of civil rights law. *American Journal of Sociology*, 97, 7: 1531–1576.

Granovetter, M. (1986). Labor mobility, internal markets, and job matching: A comparison of the sociological and economic approaches. In R. V. Robinson, ed., *Research in Social Stratification and Mobility*. Greenwich, Conn.: JAI Press, vol. 5, pp. 3–39.

Haveman, H. A. and Cohen, L. E. (1994), The ecological dynamics of careers: The impact of industry dynamics and industry demography on career mobility in the California savings and loan industry. *American Journal of Sociology*, 100.

Huber, G. P. (1991). "Organizational learning: The contributing processes and the literatures." *Organization Science*, 2, 1 (February): 88–114.

Hutchins, E. (1991). Organizing work by adaptation. *Organization Science*, 2, 1 (February).

Imai, K.; Nonaka, I.; and Takeuchi, H. (1985). Managing the new product development process: How Japanese companies learn and unlearn. In K. B. Clark et al., eds., *The Uneasy Alliance*. Cambridge, Mass.: Harvard Business School Press.

Kanter, R. M. (1989). Careers and the wealth of nations: A macro-perspective on the structure and implications of career forms." In M. B. Arthur; D. T. Hall; and B. S. Lawrence, eds., (1989), *Handbook of Career Theory*. New York: Cambridge University Press, pp. 506–522.

Keegan, P. (1995). The Digerati. *New York Times Magazine*, May 21: 38–88.

Lant, T. K., and Mezias, S. J. (1990). Managing discontinuous change: A simulation study of organizational learning and entrepreneurship. *Strategic Management Journal*, 11, 147–179.

Lawless, M. W., and Price, L. (1992). An agency perspective on new technology champions. *Organization Science*, 3, 3 (August).

Levitt, B. S., and March, J. G. (1988). Organizational learning. *Annual Review of Sociology*, 14, 319–340.

Maidique, M. A., and Zirger, B. J. (1988). The New Product Learning Cycle. In K. Gronhaugh and G. Kaufmann, eds., *Innovation: A Cross-Disciplinary Perspective.* Oslo: Norwegian University Press.

March, J. G. (1991). Exploration and exploitation in organizational learning. *Organization Science,* 2, 1 (February).

Miner, A. S. (1994), Seeking adaptive advantage: Evolutionary theory and managerial action. In J. V. Singh and Joel A. Baum, eds., *Evolutionary Dynamics of Organizations.* Oxford University Press, 76–89.

Miner, A. S. (1991). Organizational evolution and the social ecology of jobs. *American Sociological Review,* 56, 772–785.

Miner, A. S. (1990). Structural evolution through idiosyncratic jobs: The potential for unplanned learning, *Organization Science,* 1, 2: 195–210.

Miner, A. S. (1987). Idiosyncratic jobs in formalized organizations, *Administrative Science Quarterly,* 32 (September): 327–351.

Miner, A. S., and Haunschild, P. (1995). Population level learning. In B. M. Staw and L. L. Cummings, eds., *Research in Organizational Behavior.* Greenwich, Conn.: JAI Press.

Miner, A. S., and Robinson, D. F. (1994). Organizational and population level learning as engines for career transitions. *Journal of Organizational Behavior,* 15: 345–365.

Moorman, C., and Miner, A. S. (1995). The impact of organizational memory on new product performance and creativity. Paper read at, Wharton Conference on Innovation in New Product Development, May, at Univeristy of Pennsylvania.

Nelson, R. R., and Winter, S. G. (1982). *An Evolutionary Theory of Economic Change.* Cambridge, Mass.: Harvard University Press.

Nonaka, I. (1990). Redundant, overlapping organization: A Japanese approach to managing an innovation process. *California Management Review,* 32 (spring): 27–38.

Osterman, P. (1984). White-collar internal labor markets. In P. Osterman (ed.), *Internal Labor Markets:* Cambridge, Mass.: MIT Press, 163–189.

Pascale, R. T. (1984). The Honda Effect excerpted from *Perspectives on Strategy:* The real story behind Honda's success. *California Management Review,* 26 (spring): 47–72.

Pfeffer, J., and Baron, J. N. (1988). Taking the workers back out: Recent trends in the structuring of employment. In B. M. Staw and L. L. Cummings, eds., *Research in Organizational Behavior.* Greenwich, Conn.: JAI Press, pp. 257–303.

Quinn, J. B. (1986). Innovation and corporate strategy: Managed chaos. In M. Horwich, ed., *Technology in the Modern Corporation: A Strategic Perspective.* New York: Pergamon Press, pp. 167–183.

Roberts, E. B., and Fusfeld, A. (1981). Staffing the innovative technology based organization. *Sloan Management Review,* 22, 3: 19–34.

Rosenbaum, J. E. (1979). Tournament mobility: career patterns in a corporation. *Administrative Science Quarterly,* 24: 220–241.

Salancik, G. R., and Pfeffer, J. (1977). Who gets power and how they hold on to it. In M. L. Tushman, and W. L. Moore, eds., *Readings in the Management of Innovation.* Cambridge, Mass.: Ballinger.

Schelling, T. (1978). *Micromotives and Macrobehavior.* New York: Norton.

Shenhav, Y. (1991). Expected managerial careers within growing and declining R&D establishments. *Work and Occupations,* 18, 1 (February): 46–71.

Souder, W. E. (1987). *Managing New Product Innovations.* Lexington, Mass.: D. C. Heath.

Spence, A. M. (1974). *Market Signaling: Informational Transfer in Hiring and Related Screening Processes*. Cambridge, Mass.: Harvard University Press.

Spillerman, S. (1977). Careers, labor market structure and socioeconomic achievement. *American Journal of Sociology*, 83: 551–593.

Stewman, S., and Konda, S. L. (1983). Careers and organizational labor markets: demographic models of organizational behavior. *American Journal of Sociology*, 88: 637–685.

Van Maanen, J., and Schein, E. H. (1979). Toward a theory of organizational socialization. In B. M. Staw, ed., *Research in Organizational Behavior*. Greenwich, Conn.: JAI Press, 1: 209–264.

Walsh, J. P., and Ungson, G. R. (1991). Organizational memory. *Academy of Management Review*, 16: 57–91.

Weber, M. ([1922] 1968), *Economy and Society—An Outline of Interpretive Sociology*, edited by G. Roth, and C. Wittich. New York: Bedminster Press.

Weick, K. E. (1979). *The Social Psychology of Organizing*. Reading, Mass.: Addison-Wesley.

Weick, K. E. and Berlinger, L. R. (1989). Career improvisation in self-designing organizations, in M. B. Arthur; D. T. Hall; and B. S. Lawrence, eds., *Handbook of Career Theory*. New York: Cambridge University Press.

II

THE COMPETITIVE ADVANTAGES OF KNOWLEDGE BASED IN BOUNDARYLESS CAREERS

Global competitiveness and changing technology drive changes in work and workers. A key force in shaping the experiences boundaryless workers acquire over a lifetime is the competitive pressure that puts a premium on distinctive competencies of both firms and workers. Each of the chapters in part II addresses the link between these two levels of analysis, as well as the implications of the knowledge-based or competency-driven view. A particularly important implication is the transition from bounded to boundaryless career arrangements.

Raymond Miles and Charles Snow's "Twenty-first Century Careers" points out that organizational form dictates the source of required competencies. The authors detail the "waves" of organizational forms that have altered the competency sources and their accessment. In the earliest forms, competencies resided in specialized members (e.g., crafts and skilled trades). Moving to second-, third-, and fourth-wave forms of organization, Miles and Snow describe the shift of competencies to organizational procedures and rules, and then to the captured competencies of internal labor markets. They forecast what we already see signs of: fourth-wave forms of organization, termed "cellular," for the strength of their components and the flexibility and power of their networks, providing umbrellas for deeply skilled occupational groups allied with others of distinctly different capabilities.

Robert DeFillippi and Michael Arthur extend our exploration of the competency theme in "Boundaryless Contexts and Careers: A Competency-Based Perspective." Beginning with a competency-based view of the modern firm, they differentiate among three forms of knowing—knowing *why,* knowing *how,* and knowing *whom*—which constitute people's developing career competencies. The implications for boundaryless careers are explored by references to changing firm, occupational, and industry community contexts, all of which can be seen to promote boundaryless career behavior. The authors close with a comparison of bounded-versus-boundaryless career profiles, and a proposed list of shared values underlying boundaryless-career employment contracting.

Ted Baker and Howard Aldrich offer a more cautionary perspective in "Prometheus Stretches: Building Identity and Cumulative Knowledge in Multiemployer Careers." Taking a life-course perspective, Baker and Aldrich explain how fundamental changes must occur in people's sense of self, and in their relations with family, peers, and colleagues, as they choose and are forced into work settings with new and often unfamiliar demands. Developing the concept of "career heterogeneity," these authors describe how the number of employers, the extent of knowledge cumulation, and the role of personal identity specify outcomes of career processes occurring over the course of people's lives. Based on these dimensions, a model of career patterns is presented that explicates the forms careers take, and the broader institutional forces that affect the quality of people's lives.

Allan Bird's "Careers as Repositories of Knowledge: Considerations for Boundaryless Careers" argues for a reconceptualization of the meaning of careers. He envisions careers as accumulations of information and knowledge, rather than as simple progressions of work experiences. Drawing on theories characterizing firms as knowledge creators, Bird links the knowledge individuals acquire in multiemployer career moves to the value-creating activities of firms. Boundaryless careers require that individuals take more responsibility in managing their work experiences and the knowledge-creating activities that derive from them. A down side is also noted by Bird: As knowledge resides in people, turnover can impair the firm's knowledge base. Career management thus again becomes a concern of both individuals and firms.

Organizational learning has been widely held to give firms a distinctive, nonreplicable competitive advantage. Our authors suggest that a firm's ability to gain this advantage is inherently tied to accessing people, and to offering experiences appropriate for their ability to access future career-building experiences. Traditional ways of categorizing competencies—skills, years of experience, patents held, and procedures in place—fall short of capturing the meaning of career-based competencies. In the new organizational era, our authors argue there will be new ways of gaining knowledge and new knowledges, previously neither considered nor counted.

6

Twenty-First-Century Careers

RAYMOND E. MILES AND CHARLES C. SNOW

A career is described as the evolving sequence of a person's work experiences over time (Arthur, Hall, and Lawrence 1989). Effective careers benefit individuals, organizations, and society. From the individual's perspective, an effective career is one that allows the full development and utilization of potential. Effective careers in organizations are achieved when individual competencies and organizational needs are consistently matched. From society's perspective, effective careers not only enhance individual and organizational achievement, but they also integrate individuals into their communities and help them become better citizens (Wilensky, 1961).

Over the course of American business history, major shifts have occurred in career patterns and expectations, and even more changes are on the horizon. The shape of both past and future careers, we believe, can be largely explained by the continuing evolution of organizational form. An organization's form—its configuration of strategy, structure, and management processes—determines the mix of career competencies appropriate for a particular era and locates responsibility for their development and application. More specifically, our argument rests on three key ideas.

1. *Organizational form dictates core managerial competencies.* The earliest professional careers were built on two core competencies: a body of commonly understood technical knowledge, generated and controlled by members of the profession; and a set of norms that provided the basis for self-governance. Organizational careers, by contrast, shifted the control of technical- and governance-competency development from the individual to the organization. In business organizations, a third competency, commercial knowledge and skills, became essential to career success.

2. *Each organizational form requires its own mix of managerial competencies.* As organizational forms increased in complexity, the required

mix of technical, commercial, and governance competencies changed. In general, each new organizational form required an increasing proportion of organization members to acquire and apply commercial and self-governance competencies, in addition to their technical skills. Newer organizational forms, such as the network, have required their members to use collaborative skills. In organizations of the future, we will see a reversal of the trend toward complexity as more individuals will work as independent professionals in settings characterized by self-management.

3. *Organizational form dictates how careers are managed.* The locus of responsibility for managing an individual's career has shifted over time. Early companies assumed broad responsibility for planning and directing all programs of competency acquisition and application. In today's companies, this responsibility is being increasingly shared by the firm's managers and its employees. In tomorrow's organizations, many of which will be multifirm ones, most individuals will assume responsibility for their own competency and career development.

In the following sections, we will explore the simultaneous evolution of careers and organizational forms, dividing the long history of organizations into time periods that Toffler (1981, 1990) has called "waves." Second-wave careers, for example, are those found in the traditional, hierarchically organized companies that dominated the U.S. economy from the time of the Industrial Revolution (around 1860) to the 1970s. Third-wave organizational forms are those that emerged from the dramatic transformations of the 1970s and 1980s, and are typically referred to as network organizations. Many networks consist of multifirm groups in which career movement proceeds horizontally, rather than vertically. Fourth-wave careers will take place in organizations of the future. Although the profile of a fourth-wave career is not fully apparent at this time, the experiences of today's pioneering individuals and organizations suggest that future careers may recapture many of the original characteristics of the classic professions. In the final section, we will explore the changes that third- and fourth-wave organizations imply for companies, labor institutions, and for those individuals who wish to pursue careers involving the newest organizational forms.

Careers in Second-Wave Organizations

Toffler's (1981) second wave encompasses the economic and sociocultural transformations that flowed across the American economy from the Industrial Revolution until well into the second half of the twentieth century. During this period, the small, owner-managed business firm gave way to the large, multilevel corporations that took the United States into, and ultimately to the forefront of, world manufacturing and distribution. Eventually, these corporate giants developed a widespread and particular way of doing business. (See Table 6.1.)

Foremost in the second-wave business prescription was a "do-it-yourself"

Table 6.1 Business Prescriptions

Second Wave (1860–1970)	Third Wave (1975–1995)	Fourth Wave (2000–)
Do everything yourself.	Do only what you do best, and outsource noncore operations to specialist firms.	Be able to do anything, anytime, anywhere.
Get better by getting bigger.	Get better by increasing mutually beneficial relationships among suppliers, customers, and partners.	Get better by competing and collaborating simultaneously.
Manage by using administrative mechanisms such as policies, rules, and procedures.	Manage by using market mechanisms such as profit centers and competitively determined prices.	Self-manage by means of continuous knowledge creation and empowerment.

mentality—firms sought to gain full control over all business ventures, pushing many to engage in extensive vertical integration. Also, as these companies grew, they added more and more levels of management hierarchy in order to keep operations under control. The metaphor usually used characterized second-wave firms as a tall, steep organizational pyramid. And, lastly, in the name of efficiency, managers were expected to make decisions and to allocate resources by following predetermined policies, rules, and procedures.

The big second-wave companies changed not only the way business was conducted, but the way people spent their working lives. For managers and employees alike, careers were defined in company-specific terms, and involved a lifetime of movement up the corporate pyramid, as individuals developed and exercised the skills required for personal and corporate success.

Prior to the emergence of corporate careers, the traditional concept of a career could be traced to the classic, or "free," professions, and to military and government service. Careers in the free professions, such as medicine, law, teaching, and the clergy, were built on systematic knowledge acquired through a long period of education and apprenticeship training; and on a "service ideal" in which a client's interests take precedence over personal or commercial profit (Wilensky, 1964). The free professions, which date back to the late Middle Ages in Europe, are found today throughout the world. Individuals in these classic professions have had substantial education and training; have pursued a limited number of well-specified jobs over their lifetime; and have adhered to an explicit code of ethics. For much of their history, the free professions existed apart from bureaucratic organizations and managerial oversight.

The military, during the Renaissance and afterward, provided professional careers for a dispossessed European aristocracy (Wilensky, 1964). Similar to the free professions, the military offered its officers a lifetime career. However, unlike the free professions, soldiers pursued their careers within organizations. Later, civil-service organizations arose in which individuals could pursue a lifetime career in government. Both military and civil-service careers were characterized by clearly defined jobs and ranks, as well as by prescribed criteria for promotion.

Careers in Functionally Organized Firms

In America, the classic professions, and, to some extent, military and government careers, followed many of the traditions of their European predecessors. The corporate career came into prominence at the turn of the century as large, single-business firms were created in response to the emergence of nationwide markets, which had been made possible by the establishment of transcontinental railroads and communications systems.

Railroad firms pioneered the earliest corporate careers and the second-wave organizational invention called the functional structure (Chandler, 1965). The key to success for the railroad, steel, and other large firms of the early 1900s was the harnessing of the technical competence and capital equipment that achieved efficient mass production of standard goods and services. The functional form of organization grouped people together in departments representing a particular technical specialty. In functional firms, most organization members accumulated a set of technical skills, closely linked to specific company processes, as they moved from junior to senior status within their respective departments. For most managers and employees of functionally organized companies, the opportunity to develop and apply governance and commercial skills was extremely limited.

At any given time, only a handful of individuals in the functional firm were called upon to practice governance skills—the ability to exercise responsible self-direction and self-control in the pursuit of organizational goals. These were the managers in charge of each of the major functions. Indeed, in recognition of both the limited number of highly rewarding managerial positions in functional firms, and the lack of interest or ability of some individuals to move into management, some firms created dual career ladders so that technical specialists could obtain higher pay and status without moving from their specialty to a managerial position.

Similarly, only top managers were expected to acquire and use broad commercial skills—those involving the setting of product and marketing strategies; the responses to new technological capabilities; and the making of important investment decisions. While many people in a functional firm may be employed in designing and producing a product or service, as well as in making and accounting for sales, the typical position deals with only a specialized fragment of an efficient, routinized process.

Corporate Careers in the Divisional Organization

The divisional form of organization was developed from the period after World War I through the 1950s (Chandler, 1962). This period was defined by growing consumer sophistication and the emergence of the United States as the dominant industrial power after World War II. The key to company success in this period was the assemblage of expanding marketing and managerial competence into increasingly sophisticated organizational packages.

The divisional form of organization was created to pursue diversification—to use accumulated company know-how to take the firm into new product and new market areas, where it could add value. The divisional form, invented at General Motors in the 1920s and used early on in mass retailing by Sears, Roebuck, offered new career opportunities for many organization members as the form spread to other firms and industries. In the divisional form, instead of a single unified structure organized by function, the firm was divided into largely self-contained units (divisions) that could operate independently. Each division focused on a given market and operated with considerable autonomy as it pursued goals approved by corporate management. With each division responsible for much of its own market strategy and resource allocation, the new form substantially increased opportunities for careers leading to "general management" positions—that is, those at the top of divisions requiring technical, governance, and commercial competencies. The "top management" experience obtained by many managers in the divisional organization provided the firm with a resource for further investment—a reservoir of high-quality managers with commercial and governance competencies that could be used to create new divisions targeted at new markets. Careers in divisionalized firms were enhanced by moving managers from smaller to larger divisions and by using experienced managers to create new divisions.

In most divisionalized firms, management maintains overall responsibility for career development. Because of the sporadic creation and acquisition of new divisions in this type of organization, careers may progress less predictably than those in a stable functional hierarchy. However, the sheer number of general-management jobs that needed to be filled on a regular basis in the 1950s allowed certain divisionalized firms to become highly regarded for their management-development philosophies and programs. So-called academy companies, such as General Electric, Procter and Gamble, and Sears, Roebuck, were known for producing high-caliber managers who possessed a complete repertoire of technical, commercial, and governance skills. Perhaps more than any other company in the 1960s and 1970s, Hewlett-Packard (H-P) fostered the widespread accumulation of general-management skills by encouraging engineers and other technical specialists to pursue their ideas all the way to commercialization. Successful "intrapreneurs" at H-P ended up running the divisions they had created (Packard, 1995).

Corporate Careers in the Matrix Organization

Following the rapid growth of the U.S. economy after World War II, many firms focused on harvesting their gains and learning how to respond to a more complex, changeable domestic and global marketplace. The divisional form had allowed firms to pursue market opportunities quickly and effectively, but at the cost of redundancy and other inefficiencies. Increasingly, firms felt the need to be both efficient and responsive in the deployment of a common set of resources—to seek scale economies in stable areas of operation, and to pursue innovations in new or changing areas. What emerged from their efforts was a new, "mixed" organizational form, the matrix.

The matrix form of organization, which was developed primarily in the aerospace industry in the late 1950s and early 1960s (Mee, 1964), incorporated key elements of both the functional and divisional structures. In a matrix organization, project (program or brand) managers used resources from functional departments to perform services for a particular customer or set of clients. In the matrix form, individuals developed and upgraded their technical competencies in their "home" functional department. In addition, they were exposed to commercial and governance matters when they were temporarily assigned to project or program groups.

In attempting to keep customers satisfied by effectively managing multifunctional resources and meeting budgets, project managers in matrix organizations developed and utilized many of the same general-management skills used by divisional managers in a diversified firm. In later, global matrix systems, country managers played the project-management role in their interactions with global functional and product divisions, responding to local needs by drawing on the resources of companywide units. Country managers, too, thus developed a complete complement of technical, commercial, and governance competencies.

Because they were often operating in remote locations or on specialized projects or products, the careers of many matrix-organization members involved shared responsibility. While the renewal of technical skills was presumably the responsibility of functional-department managers, both project managers and functional-unit heads participated in performance evaluation and other career-related decisions for matrix members. Moreover, some members of matrix organizations felt the need to play a more proactive role in their career development, and they lobbied for assignments to specific projects that fit their particular competencies and career objectives. In fact, some more advanced matrix firms, such as TRW, offered members opportunities to "manage" their own careers by encouraging contact between project leaders and matrix members.

In sum, as second wave organizational forms evolved from functional to divisional and matrix units, each new form required a somewhat broadened array of commercial and governance competencies in order to operate with maximum effectiveness. Nevertheless, the typical career profile remained essentially the same throughout this period, with its defining characteristic being movement up a pyramidical hierarchy, usually within the same company, or, at most, a few companies (see Table 6.2). In the most progressive second-wave firms, some members began to reacquire the breadth of competence exercised by owner-managers and professionals, while still enjoying the security of a large firm. Soon, however, as the third wave began to sweep across these older organizational forms, companies began to trade guaranteed security for vastly greater opportunities to develop and apply a broader range of career competencies.

Careers in Third-Wave Organizations

The 1970s marked the beginning of the end of the one-company lifetime career that had begun over a century earlier. In virtually every industry, the forces of globalization and rapid technological change required older companies to rethink their existing organizational structures and supporting human-resource

Table 6.2 Career Profiles

Second Wave	Third Wave	Fourth Wave
Stay with a single employer.	Work for multiple employers while practicing your technical specialty.	Work as a self-employed professional.
Move up the corporate hierarchy.	Move across projects to obtain experience.	Expand professional expertise.
Rely on company-specific technical competence.	Rely on commercial, governance, and collaborative skills as well as technical skills.	Rely on technical, commercial, collaborative, and governance skills.
Let employer define career progress.	Define career progress with employer.	Define one's own career progress.

management systems (Miles and Snow, 1984a, 1984b). Competitors were cutting costs, improving quality, and speeding up deliveries. New products were hitting the market at a faster rate than the typical firm could imagine, much less match. Second-wave companies that had succeeded by the careful planning and coordination of vast arrays of internal resources were discovering that the synergies their systems were designed to produce were costing more to achieve than they were worth in the marketplace.

With incredible swiftness, a new competitive prescription firmly established itself. Unlike the second-wave belief that a firm should do everything itself, the third-wave approach was to "do only what you do best" and then outsource noncore operations to other specialist firms (see Table 6.1). Unlike older firms that had grown by adding layers of management hierarchy, third-wave firms grew by increasing the number of beneficial relationships among their suppliers, customers, and partners. And, finally, instead of managing according to policies and rules, third-wave companies created organizational arrangements that relied heavily on market forces to make decisions and allocate resources.

By the middle of the 1980s, two related trends were clearly visible. First, mature second-wave firms were downsizing and delayering at a pace never before seen, trying to achieve the flexibility and speed of their more nimble competitors. Second, managers in a variety of industries were honing the design of a new organizational form called the network (Miles and Snow, 1986; Thorelli, 1986). Network structures emerged to allow the small firms in newer industries to act big and the older firms in hypercompetitive industries to act small. Small firms in industries such as computers and biotechnology kept a tight focus on their core competencies, and then found upstream (e.g., suppliers) and downstream (e.g., retailers) partners to join them, as needed, to produce completed goods and services quickly and with cost effectiveness. Older firms in industries such as automobiles and home appliances moved toward network arrangements as they began outsourcing to just-in-time suppliers who could produce parts, components, and services in a better and cheaper fashion than these mature firms could accomplish in-house (Case, 1990).

A complete network "organization" is composed of three main elements, each of which adds immediate or potential value to a business (Miles and Snow, 1994). These elements are: (1) the individual network firm, which occupies one or more points along the industry value chain; (2) the set of individual firms activated for the delivery of a particular product, service, or business; and (3) the broader set of firms arrayed along the value chain and available as partners for future products or services. (See Figure 6.1.) Thus, the total "value-added capability" (Miles, Snow, and Miles, 1995) of a network organization is the sum of an individual firm's competencies, the joint or synergistic abilities of the firm and its currently connected partners, and the availability of resources in potential partners across the entire network (which serve all firms as latent assets held at low shared cost).

A network organization, however, is only as strong as its weakest link. If some firms within the network have less knowledge about available resources than others have, the others must carry excess resources to meet their own current and future needs. If some firms have poor connecting skills, thus raising the transaction costs for current and future partners, the resources of these firms lower the total network's value. And if the internal resources of a given network firm cannot be freely and easily deployed, its resources cannot be fully utilized by either its current or potential partners. When these various intra- and interfirm competencies are fully developed, a different metaphor than the traditional pyramid can be invoked to portray a network firm and its operating processes.

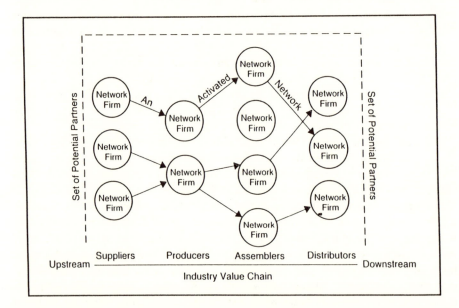

Figure 6.1   A complete network organization. Reprinted by permission from Raymond E. Miles and Charles C. Snow, *Fit, Failure, and the Hall of Fame: How Companies Succeed or Fail* (New York: Free Press, 1994).

The Spherical Structure
In the most advanced networks, firms are learning to share technical and market information freely, thus assuring the availability of resources across the network and widespread knowledge of that availability. In addition, advanced-network firms are constantly honing their ability to connect with specialist firms along the industry value chain quickly and at the lowest possible cost. These firms have come to realize the value of substituting various forms of trust for more expensive forms of control (Handy, 1995; Miles and Creed, 1995). In some advanced-network firms, continuous investment in training and education is allowing a "spherical" structure to replace the traditional organizational pyramid (Miles and Snow, 1995).

The spherically structured network firm has the capacity to connect quickly and efficiently with multiple partners along the industry value chain, thus assuring the fullest utilization of its own internal resources and the most agile response to the network as a whole. We use the metaphor of a fully rotatable sphere because it illustrates a firm's ability to rapidly send the resources required for any connection to the exact point where they are needed. At the most rudimentary level, the ability of a Nordstrom's salesperson to escort a customer to another department, and, if necessary, to begin the selling process by introducing the customer to another salesperson, fulfills the spherical metaphor. Similarly, faced with the need to explain the development of a major new product to a group of investment analysts, one company sent an R&D team—rather than a management group—to make the presentation. Individuals and teams in a spherical firm are indeed broadly trained and empowered to diagnose situations and to deploy their own resources as well as those of the entire firm.

A spherical firm's teams, all of which possess technical, commercial, and self-governance competencies, can enrich an entire activated network. Nike, for example, makes a variety of investments all along its particular network. It invests in its upstream partners by sending its own technicians to work in manufacturing plants, to bring them up to Nike's performance standards. Also, together with some of its more developed manufacturing partners, Nike coparticipates in the design of new athletic footwear. At the downstream end, Nike permits some of its most valued retailers to place orders directly with its manufacturing partners. Nike's trust in both its manufacturing and retailing partners thus increases the flexibility and speed of adaptation across the entire network.

A Third-Wave Career Profile
As both new and old firms began to adopt network structures and practices, human resource utilization and career expectations changed to fit the new organizational form. For entrepreneurs, and for some young engineers and scientists, the network form of organization provided a quick route to positions of importance and impact. Many of these technical specialists formed their own small firms and then linked themselves, more or less permanently, to other firms along the industry value chain. In larger firms, the use of flexible network structures

brought more people, proportionally, into decision-making roles; and the ability to quickly assemble substantial resources from several linked firms allowed network organizations to compete favorably with more established companies. Although career paths were less obvious, and therefore riskier, than in second-wave organizations, the payoffs in both dollars and feelings of achievement were attractive to many people.

In the downsized and delayered second-wave firms attempting to achieve networklike flexibility and efficiency, careers, in the short run at least, were often frustrating and painful. The presumably secure jobs of several million middle managers were swept away as firms cut back to their core businesses by eliminating both staff and operating departments. Managerial and staff specialists, well endowed with company-specific technical knowledge but not equipped with commercial and governance skills, were at least temporarily unemployable. Similarly, semiskilled personnel in plants and offices saw their operations either transferred to "contingent" workforces of part-time and temporary employees or outsourced entirely.

By the beginning of the 1990s, it was clear that the third-wave revolution had driven many careers out of the middle of large pyramidical hierarchies and had replaced them with new careers in which people worked across the boundaries of smaller networked companies. Third-wave careers were likely to involve short-term participation in multifirm projects (Jones, 1995); validation of performance by the market, rather than by company superiors (Arthur, 1994); and heavy use of personal and professional networks (Saxenian, 1990, 1994). Moreover, across-the-network careers tended to flourish in those settings where the regional or industry infrastructure provided both interfirm job information and mechanisms to minimize the frictional costs of personnel movement—for example, the regional technology clusters of Silicon Valley, in northern California; New Jersey's "Princeton Corridor"; and Utah's "Software Valley" (Bahrami and Evans, 1995). Within these regions, job information is widely available, and personnel movements are quick and frequent.

Emergence of a New Competency Set

Along with a general shift from intraorganizational to interorganizational careers, the third wave (network) organization demanded a new set of competencies considered crucial to the operation of the network firm itself and to the development and maintenance of its relationships with upstream and downstream partners. This new competency set consists of collaborative knowledge and skills.

Competence in collaboration essentially involves three main factors. The first factor includes *referral* skills, which must be used both within the network firm and across its partners (and, in some instances, even its competitors). Just as a medical doctor is professionally obligated to refer a patient to the proper specialist, or just as a consultant steers an inquiring company toward another consulting firm with the needed expertise, individuals and teams in network companies must be able to diagnose situations and act as a broker between clients and resources. Such a referral process, of course, relies heavily on continuously upgraded knowledge and information.

Another set of collaborative skills involves competence in *partnering*—the ability to create networks, negotiate contractual arrangements, produce mutually beneficial outcomes, and so on. For a number of years, General Electric has taught partnering skills as part of its highly renowned Work-Out Program.

The final set of collaborative skills is known as *relationship management*. In broad terms, this refers to giving high priority to the needs and preferences of key customers and partners. For example, PepsiCo assigns to top executives the responsibility for maintaining contact with certain customers, or Boeing involves key customers in the new aircraft design process, or Novell financially assists a supplier by buying its inventory in advance—all of these actions represent attempts to maintain valued relationships. In multifirm network organizations, relationship management is clearly an important part of managing the activated network. However, the underlying philosophy of relationship management can be easily extended to include potential partners among the broader array of specialist firms within the industry.

In essence, in the Third Wave, or network, firm, the smaller permanent workforce (relative to a second-wave company) has a highly visible, but limited, set of internal career opportunities. To the extent that the firm is spherically structured, organization members acquire governance skills and commercial knowledge, along with their technical competencies. Due to widely practiced individual and team self-governance, there are fewer traditional managerial positions, and a network firm's members must consider outside advancement opportunities as well as internal career moves. The network firm focuses on providing members with a full set of skills, knowledge, and experience so that their employability is enhanced, both within and outside the firm. Education and training beyond current needs are provided to guarantee network firm adaptability and to enhance member employability. Members are expected to participate in the design of their own career paths and to make personal investments that accompany those made by their current network employer.

Because much of the work in network firms occurs in association with value-chain partners, effective organization members will also possess strong collaborative skills. Moreover, members of multifirm networks are constantly in contact with external learning opportunities that not only broaden their commercial skills, but also provide information about job availability throughout the activated network and outside it. Increasingly, job information will be deliberately and actively shared by firms in a network organization to promote a rich and varied "internal" labor market. Indeed, one could easily imagine the spread of network-related professional credentialing processes to facilitate member mobility across firms, as is already the case in the film and television industries (Jones, 1995).

Careers in Fourth-Wave Organizations

If second-wave organizations built and utilized management hierarchies, and third-wave organizations flattened and disaggregated them, fourth-wave firms will seek to eliminate hierarchies altogether. Today, in a few pioneering settings—particularly those of professional services—minimalist organizations are being created that merely house and facilitate the activities of entrepreneurial professionals. One of the most interesting organizations in this regard is Technical and Computer Graphics (TCG), located in Sydney, Australia (Mathews, 1992, 1993). It clearly has many spherical features, but it is also one of the best available examples of what may turn out to be a fourth wave of organizational evolution.

TCG: A Fourth-Wave Organization?

TCG is a multifirm network that, by practicing sophisticated entrepreneurship, project leadership, and self-governance, has become the largest privately owned computer service business in Australia. It is a highly interactive group of 13 small companies with combined annual revenues of approximately $50 million and a staff of 200. TCG is a world-class innovator in portable data terminals, computer graphics, bar-coding systems, electronic data interchange, and other applications of information and communications technology.

Within TCG, new-product development is called "triangulation," meaning that it involves a three-cornered partnership among a TCG firm, a similar technology-based firm outside TCG, and a major customer (see Figure 6.2). New product development can begin anywhere within the network, because each of the 200 technical specialists in the 13 member companies is expected to search constantly for new product or new service opportunities. When an

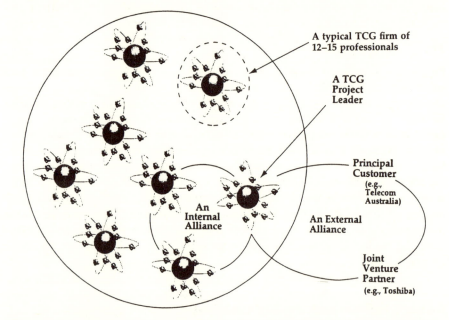

Figure 6.2 Technical and Computer Graphics' network organization. Reprinted by permission of Raymond E. Miles and Charles C. Snow, "The New Network Firm: A Spherical Structure Based on a Human Investment Philosophy," *Organizational Dynamics*, spring 1995, p. 8.

opportunity appears to have concrete potential, the initiating TCG firm becomes the project's leader.

The project's leader first locates two main types of external partners: a joint-venture partner who provides equity capital in exchange for a share of the product's future success; and a principal customer whose large advance order wins it contractual rights and provides additional cash needed to pursue the product's development. Next, the project leader seeks the participation of other appropriate TCG firms in the product development process. A TCG firm is free to join or not join the venture, depending on its level of interest and production capacity. After these external and internal alliances have been formed, the project-leader firm serves as the gateway through which information and resources flow for the remainder of the venture. At any given time, many triangulation processes such as this are under way at TCG.

In the multifirm TCG network organization, every individual is expected to be an entrepreneur and a sometime project leader who is able to apply technical, commercial, and leadership skills. Also, every individual in the various TCG firms works closely, as part of a self-managed team, with other professionals in the network. Consequently, strong collaborative and self-governance skills exist throughout the organization. Although the total network staff of 200 individuals is small, by most company comparisons, TCG nevertheless has a global reach. And, perhaps most important from a career perspective, TCG has very few operating rules and no pyramidical management hierarchy. In short, TCG is an organization in which everyone is a technical professional and businessperson —and in charge of his or her own career.

The Cellular Organization

Fourth-wave organizations, we believe, are only beginning to be recognized as such, and an understanding of them requires a new metaphor that captures their distinctive characteristics and competencies. An appropriate metaphor to describe an organization like TCG must go beyond the somewhat mechanistic notion of the fully rotatable sphere and become truly organic. Therefore, we offer the metaphor of the "cellular" organization. A cell in any living organism, because it possesses all the fundamental functions of life, can act alone. However, by acting in concert with other cells, it is capable of performing more complex functions. Similarly, a cellular organization is made up of cells (self-managing teams, autonomous business units, etc.) that could exist on their own, but by interacting with other cells, can produce a more potent and competent organism. Common knowledge and information are shared by all the cells in a manner, akin to human DNA, that reflects heredity and guides development.

The cellular metaphor has a number of qualities that relate to our discussion of an organization such as TCG, whose "cells" are the small firms of professionals who are able to act effectively both within and outside the organization. TCG firms are held together not by a command structure, but by a common understanding—a written "constitution" that describes rights and responsibilities and provides guiding principles for most internal and external interactions. (See Table 6.3.) New entrants in the network are guided by this

Table 6.3 TCG's Governance Principles

1. Mutual Independence
   The TCG network consists of independent firms whose relations are governed by bilateral commercial contracts. It is open to new entrants who are prepared to abide by the rules. There is no internal hierarchy.

2. Mutual Preference
   Member firms give preference to each other in the letting of contracts. Contracts may be made outside the group, against a competitive bid from a member firm, when circumstances warrant (e.g., work overload or a signal to the member firm that it has to lift its game).

3. Mutual Noncompetition
   Member firms do not compete head-to-head with each other. Such self-denial helps to establish trust among member firms.

4. Mutual Nonexploitation
   Member firms do not seek to make profits from transactions among themselves.

5. Flexibility and Business Autonomy
   The flexibility of the network as a whole derives from the capacity of member firms to respond to opportunities as they see fit. They do not need to ask for group approval to enter into any transaction or new line of business, provided the proposed innovation does not breach any rules.

6. Network Democracy
   There is no overall corporate owner. Nor is there any central committee or other formal governance structure. However, member firms can hold equity in each other as well as in third-party joint venturers.

7. Expulsion
   A firm may be expelled from the network if it willfully disobeys the rules. Expulsion can be effected simply by severing all commercial ties with the miscreant member.

8. Subcontracting
   There are no "subcontractor-only" firms within the TCG group. Each member firm has access to the open market, and indeed is expected to bring in work from outside the network.

9. Entry
   New members are welcome to join the network but are not to draw financial resources from the group. New members must obtain capital from banks rather than through equity from other member firms. It is membership in the network that serves as collateral for the bank loan.

10. Exit
    The network places no impediments in the way of a departing firm. However, there is no market for shares held in TCG member firms. Hence, departure arrangements have to be negotiated on a case-by-case basis.

SOURCE: Reprinted by permission of Raymond E. Miles and Charles C. Snow, "The New Network Firm: A Spherical Structure Based on a Human Investment Philosophy," *Organizational Dynamics,* spring 1995, p. 9.

common heritage. Indeed, they were selected largely because their cell structure was similar to that of the established TCG firms.

The common heritage of cells is the knowledge base that gives the larger organism many shared response capabilities. For the cellular metaphor to be truly apt, the lengthy process of evolution must be compressed so that knowledge stored within and across cells can be quickly expanded and applied. For example, as a given TCG firm works with an external customer and a venture partner, it might well have all of the resources it needs within itself. However, by accepted protocol, it recruits internal partner firms (cells) to both augment and support its skills, and also to share the knowledge gained by the application of TCG skills. Within each firm, members rotate roles, with each member expected to take entrepreneurial initiatives and provide support to other firms' members.

To complete the cellular metaphor, the organization is designed to facilitate continuous growth and renewal. A cellular organization is an appropriate form in those settings where creative and entrepreneurial activities are valued, and where the resources needed to implement these activities are available through the sharing of knowledge, skills, and learning opportunities within a set of complementary teams or firms. Thus, the cellular organization does not "use" its members. Instead, it is used by them to facilitate their own business initiatives.

A Fourth-Wave Career Profile

In the cellular firm, the organization functions not as an employer, but as a facilitating mechanism to promote the application and enhancement of the professional skills of its membership. It has some of the key properties of the classic guilds and professional associations, such as the sharing of knowledge and the accepting of responsibility for members' competency and performance. Within the cellular organization, members take full charge of their own career, enjoying the learning opportunities provided by their own initiatives and those of their fellow members. A common bond promotes full self-governance as well as a sense of service and professional allegiance.

Most cellular organizations will be small and will emerge in knowledge-intensive services. Therefore, extensive education will be a prerequisite for both initial and continued membership. Cellular organizations will offer their members seminars featuring both internal and external experts and covering the latest theoretical and applied developments. They also will encourage sabbaticals to upgrade member competency, and will create joint funds to finance such leaves. As always, what emerges is up to the members, as they draft the constitution by which they agree to abide.

Tomorrow's Industrial Relations System

Although organizational forms have always shaped careers, both firms and their members are part of a larger, evolving industrial relations system—the broad set of mechanisms and institutions a society uses to create, develop, and maintain an effective workforce. In the United States, we use a mix of public and private mechanisms to attract and allocate workers, managers, and professionals for our myriad firms and agencies. In order to fully understand what careers will be like in the twenty-first century, one must examine them as they interact with the three key groups in the industrial relations system: individuals, companies, and institutions (Miles, 1989).

Much of our current industrial relations system emerged during the heyday of second-wave organizations. Hiring and training practices, as well as pay and benefits programs, were created to build and maintain stable workforces for the early producers of goods and services. From the 1920s through the period following World War II, company pension plans and vacation and health-care programs tied employees to a particular firm and limited their mobility. Most government pension and health-care programs lagged behind developments in the more progressive firms, and although they were designed to be portable, government programs have never been viewed as substitutes for company efforts.

As the principal providers of employee work skills, most second-wave firms focused their training programs on company-specific knowledge and routines. Only where apprenticeship programs were available for established trades did training exceed company requirements. Thus, not only did rewards and benefits limit mobility, but work experience and training made employees valuable primarily to their own companies.

For lower-level employees, government policy expected career actions to be regulated, at least in part, through collective bargaining between unions and management. Union processes also became company and/or industry oriented as large firms began to dominate mature industries. Those firms became favorable targets for organizing efforts, and when several were organized, other companies in the industry tended to follow suit. Common wage rates reduced competitive pressures, and big union locals focused on assuring members' job rights and privileges as they moved up internal career ladders.

However, during the third-wave transformations of the 1980s, large companies no longer served as the primary creators of new jobs and, instead, were rapidly downsizing and refocusing. Competitive pressures squeezed salaries and benefits and toughened companies' collective bargaining stances as well as their efforts to resist employee unionization. Smaller firms, increasingly becoming the providers of new jobs, were more difficult to organize, and employers in many newer industries were often able to prevent unionization. Further, smaller firms, wherever possible, sought to hire already-trained personnel in order to avoid the heavy costs of internal training staff, and many argued that they could not match the reward and benefits packages of large companies.

Thus, a second-wave industrial relations system, aimed primarily at providing secure jobs for loyal employees, was no longer aligned with a third-wave workplace that demanded flexible skills and portable reward and benefits packages. As conditions heralding a fourth-wave industrial environment continue to unfold, our present industrial relations system will move further and further out of touch.

Some companies are, as we have noted, beginning to realize that heavy investments in human assets are crucial to their long-term success, but human capital is probably still being depleted more rapidly than it is being replaced in most firms. Moreover, most unionized employees cannot expect short-run help from their own associations. Unions are gradually revamping their structures and services to stem the tide of lost memberships and to organize and serve new industries; but union redesign efforts are proving to be every bit as difficult as those being conducted by major firms. At a time when union skill certification and interfirm job-mobility information services could make an important contribution, unions are struggling simply to survive.

Clearly, an industrial relations system that fits the needs of companies and their members in the twenty-first century demands new roles for each of its major players. In our view, major changes need to be made at all system levels. First, recruitment, work orientation, and the achievement of basic knowledge and skill levels will become a tripartite responsibility of companies, government agencies, and employees and their union organizations. Regional skill centers supported by area companies of all sizes, as well as most unions, will recruit members and provide a wide range of training, with the help of subsidies and assistance from local, state, and federal agencies. These centers will serve as orientation and selection mechanisms for new workforce members and as re-training and placement arenas for experienced employees. Further, these centers will define new skill sets and their certification processes. Some of these pro-cesses will be industry specific, but others will have broad applicability. For example, some providers of temporary office personnel are beginning to offer new skill classifications, and companies and unions will likely see the value of assisting in the creation of certifiable skill categories that promote mobility and raise overall job performance.

Second, communications mechanisms will be created at the regional, indus-try, and, ultimately, national levels, to match people to jobs. Informal personal and professional networks that serve regional industry groups are already at work (e.g., in Silicon Valley). So, too, are electronic networks that carry business information to companies, such as the CommerceNet in Silicon Valley (*Business Week,* 1994). These networks could easily be used to exchange regional job information and individual resumes. If regional mechanisms are in place, the electronic hardware is already available to provide on-line national data inter-change.

Finally, along with the company and institutional changes needed to im-prove interfirm career mobility, individuals also must change. Increasingly, indi-viduals will have to assume responsibility for their own career planning and development, by working proactively with employers to design a sequence of experiences that offers ever-more challenging learning opportunities. This means that individuals will have to be aware of the learning resources available to them and of how to access those resources. Computer and networking skills will be essential for personal success. In addition, individuals who wish to have effec-tive fourth-wave careers must be committed to acquiring the full range of com-petencies discussed above—technical, commercial, governance, and collabora-tive skills.

Conclusion

We have argued that major shifts in career patterns have been shaped by the evolution of organizational forms, which in turn interact with broad institu-tional forces. A lengthy period of aggregation, in which companies incorporated and systematized individual skills and behaviors, has been followed by a period of rapid and significant disaggregation, in which teams and individuals in smaller, more flexible organizations are being reempowered to exercise techni-cal, commercial, collaborative, and self-governance skills.

The earliest second-wave organizations succeeded by shaping human competencies to meet capital-equipment needs and to adjust to narrowly focused organization structures. These organizations added value by incorporating technical, governance, and commercial skills in routines and procedures that could be quickly learned and passed along to new members. Organization members were among the "tools" assembled by second-wave firms to carry out their operating routines.

Third-wave organizations shifted the focus from the achievement of scale economies (based on repeatable routines) to the achievement of scope economies (based on flexible routines). The network organization could succeed only to the extent that its members could rotate human and capital resources to meet the various demands of its partners along the industry value chain. Organization members were still "tools," but they were increasingly self-directing tools possessing much of the knowledge that was essential to their own utilization. In the network form, the organization and its members have moved toward a more balanced interdependence.

In fourth-wave organizations, individual and organizational roles will be reversed—the organization will become a tool of its members. Created voluntarily and governed by its own code of conduct, the organization will facilitate the generation and retention of knowledge and skills retrievable by any and all of its "owners." Its members will be very much like the self-directing professionals of the preorganizational period. However, instead of acting as free-standing professionals, they will magnify their own competencies and resources by linking them to others of a similar mind and talent. No one will need to leave these organizations in order to advance their careers, exercise self-direction, or pursue creative new applications of his or her skills.

The most futuristic organizational arrangement, the cellular form, has the potential to be a constantly renewing system in which all learning is shared, and in which all members can entrepreneurially assemble resources and invest them in new ventures. In a fully developed cellular form, one can imagine members' careers and organizational processes becoming essentially indistinguishable.

References

Arthur, Michael A. 1994. "The Boundaryless Career: A New Perspective for Organizational Inquiry." *Journal of Organizational Behavior,* 15: 295–306.
Arthur, Michael A., Douglas T. Hall, and Barbara S. Lawrence. 1989. *Handbook of Career Theory.* Cambridge, England: Cambridge University Press.
Bahrami, Homa, and Stuart Evans. 1995. "Flexible Re-Cycling and High-Technology Entrepreneurship." *California Management Review,* 37 (spring): 62–89.
Business Week. 1994. "Truck Lanes for the Info Highway," April 18: 112–114.
Case, John. 1990. "Intimate Relations." *INC.,* August: 64–72.
Chandler, Alfred D., Jr. 1962. *Strategy and Structure: Chapters in the History of the American Industrial Enterprise.* New York: Doubleday.
———. *The Railroads: The Nation's First Big Business.* New York: Harcourt, Brace, and World.
Handy, Charles. 1995. "Trust and the Virtual Organization." *Harvard Business Review,* May–June: 40–50.

Jones, Candace. 1995. "Careers in Network Organizations: The Case of the Film Industry." Working paper, Boston College.

Mathews, John. 1992. *TCG: Sustaining Economic Organisation Through Networking.* New South Wales, Australia: Industrial Relations Research Centre, University of New South Wales.

———. 1993. "TCG R&D Networks: The Triangulation Strategy." *Journal of Industry Studies,* 1: 65–74.

Mee, John F. 1964. "Ideational Items: Matrix Organization." *Business Horizons,* 7: 70–72.

Miles, Raymond E. 1989. "Adapting to Technology and Competition: A New Industrial Relations System for the 21st Century," *California Management Review,* 31 (winter): 9–28.

Miles, Raymond E., and W. E. Douglas Creed. 1995. "Organizational Forms and Managerial Philosophies: A Descriptive and Analytical Review." In L. L. Cummings and Barry M. Staw, eds., *Research in Organizational Behavior,* vol. 17. Greenwich, Conn.: JAI Press, pp. 333–372.

Miles, Raymond E., and Charles C. Snow. 1984. "Fit, Failure, and the Hall of Fame." *California Management Review,* 26 (spring): 10–28.

———. 1984. "Designing Strategic Human Resources Systems." *Organizational Dynamics,* summer: 36–52.

———. 1986. "Network Organizations: New Concepts for New Forms." *California Management Review,* 28 (spring): 62–73.

———. 1994. *Fit, Failure, and the Hall of Fame: How Companies Succeed or Fail.* New York: Free Press.

———. 1995. "The New Network Firm: A Spherical Structure Based on a Human Investment Philosophy." *Organizational Dynamics,* spring: 5–18.

Miles, Raymond E., Charles C. Snow, and Grant Miles. 1995. "How Do Organizations Add Value?" Working paper, University of California, Berkeley.

Packard, Dave. 1995. *The HP Way: How Bill Hewlett and I Built Our Company.* New York: HarperCollins.

Saxenian, AnnaLee. 1990. "Regional Networks and the Resurgence of Silicon Valley." *California Management Review,* 33 (fall): 89–112.

———. 1995. *Regional Advantage.* Cambridge, Mass.: Harvard University Press.

Thorelli, Hans B. 1986. "Networks: Between Markets and Hierarchies." *Strategic Management Journal,* 7: 37–52.

Toffler, Alvin. 1981. *The Third Wave.* New York: Bantam Books.

———. 1990. *Powershift.* New York: Bantam Books.

Wilensky, Harold L. 1961. "Orderly Careers and Social Participation: The Impact of Work History on Social Integration in the Middle Mass." *American Sociological Review,* 26: 521–39.

———. 1964. "The Professionalization of Everyone?" *American Journal of Sociology,* 70: 137–158.

7

Boundaryless Contexts and Careers: A Competency-Based Perspective

ROBERT J. DEFILLIPPI AND MICHAEL B. ARTHUR

Some observers have noted how careers are increasingly characterized by interfirm mobility (MaGuire, 1993; Pfeffer and Baron, 1988; Kanter, 1989a, 1989b). U.S. workers typically experience ten employers over their adult lives (Topel and Ward, 1992). Japanese male workers—despite their country's reputation for lifetime employment—typically experience six employers (Cheng, 1991). Yet recent reviews of career research report a preponderance of studies focused on single employment settings (Feldman, 1989; Ornstein and Isabella, 1993); even occupational career perspectives, on general managers, for example (McCall, Lombardo, and Morrison, 1988), or on scientists and engineers (Raelin, 1991), have been premised on the unfolding of careers in a single firm.

Part of the explanation for the continued preponderance of intrafirm studies may lie in the relative speed with which the fixed lattices of job positions and stable career paths have been eliminated (Bridges, 1994; Dalton, 1989). However, the elimination of intrafirm career paths may not imply an absence of job opportunities for affected workers. Instead, career paths may involve sequences of job opportunities that go beyond the boundaries of single employment settings. Such careers paths are defined here as boundaryless careers.[1]

Traditional ideas on employment emphasize stability, hierarchy, and clearly defined job positions for career progression. However, these ideas respond to a model of organization that has come under increasing scrutiny (see chapter 1; and Williamson, 1991). Alternative ideas emphasize continuous adaptation of firms—and so of careers—to a hypercompetitive, rapidly changing environment (D'Aveni, 1994; Nohria and Berkeley, 1994). Prominent among alternative ideas is a focus on the cultivation of human-resource-based competencies. This competency-based view of the firm emphasizes that collective employee competencies link a firm's past and present activities, and, in turn, extend to future strategic possibilities (Hamel and Heene, 1994; McGrath, MacMillan, and Venkataraman, 1995; Reed and DeFillippi, 1990).

An emerging theme behind the competency-based view of the firm is a retreat from old ideas about vertical coordination. That is, instead of relying on centralized or corporate decisionmaking, firms, or business units, are seen to benefit from voluntaristic, market-based interaction with partners, suppliers, and customers.[2] This horizontal model of "intelligent," market-based coordination is seen as a better way of accommodating each firm's unique and shifting interests (Halal, 1994; Pinchot and Pinchot, 1993; Quinn, 1992). However, current writings on career and human resource management—including those on "strategic human resource management" (e.g., Schuler, 1992)—persist in emphasizing a vertically coordinated, hierarchic approach. In this chapter, we challenge the apparent inconsistency between the firm-centered and person-centered levels of analysis. We do so by arguing that competency accumulation at the level of the person is better served by boundaryless career principles. In turn, we argue that competency accumulation through boundaryless careers can make a critical contribution to the unfolding competencies of firms and their host industries. New employment principles, and new underlying values, will be needed if this critical contribution is to be achieved.[3]

First, we present a view of career competencies that is inspired by the competency-based view of the firm. Next, we explore employment, occupational, and industry-community contexts to suggest how career competencies unfold, and with what boundaryless career implications. We subsequently examine profiles of bounded versus boundaryless careers, and the interdependence we find among the competency dimensions. Finally, we propose a set of five values on which new employer-employee relations can be built, and from which mutual benefits from boundaryless careers can accrue.

Career Competencies

Our thinking on career competencies is drawn from the recent stream of work about firm competencies, and their strategic and competitive implications. This work cites overlapping arenas of competency that are broadly related to a firm's culture, know-how, and networks (Hall, 1992). Each arena of firm competency suggests a matching arena of career competency, which we introduce below as *knowing-why, knowing-how,* and *knowing-whom* competencies, respectively.

Knowing-why competencies, like Derr's (1986) career success maps, answer the question "Why?" as it relates to career motivation, personal meaning, and identification.[4] Accordingly, people's beliefs, values, and identities are the targets for the persistent, frequently tacit, messages to employees that stem from a firm's culture (Barney, 1986; Fiol, 1991). The recognition that corporate cultures influence knowing-why competencies has led to renewed interest in culture change (Kilmann, Saxton, and Sherpa, 1985; Schein, 1992). A common proposal involves eliciting greater employee identification with the firm, as in

Senge's (1991) argument to incorporate employees' "personal visions" into a "shared vision" of the firm as a whole.

However, the conception of boundaryless careers invites different possibilities. Weick and Berlinger (1989) encourage employees of modern-day adaptive firms to decouple their identities from their jobs and work settings. Bridges (1994) counsels workers to develop an identity that provides a sense of psychological integration into a work world of continuing change and fragmentation. Mirvis and Hall (in chapter 14 of this book) equate "psychological success" with people's abilities "to make sense of their constantly changing work agenda and to integrate their work experiences into a coherent self-picture." This sense-making ability—shaped by knowing-why career competencies—may involve occupational or nonwork identification or achievements. Or it may involve personal interests, such as balancing work and family demands, or getting free from hierarchical authority over the nature and content (or hours) of one's work (Bailyn, 1993).

Knowing-how competencies reflect career-relevant skills and job-related knowledge, and explain how people contribute to a firm's repertoire of overall capabilities (Nelson and Winter, 1982). A further insight from the firm-based competency literature indicates how people's knowing-how competencies are embedded in and reinforced by a firm's know-how or "routines" (Nelson and Winter, 1982; Pentland and Rueter, 1994). These established ways of converting collective know-how into product or service outputs have a two-way effect for the individual employee. Knowing-how competencies that do not get reinforced will fade in the organization's "memory," and thus lose value for both the firm and the employee (Miner and Robinson, 1994). Conversely, the accumulation of new competencies will be influenced by the collective learning efforts of the firm (Cohen and Levinthal, 1990).

Knowing-whom competencies reflect the growth of career-relevant networks, and refer to how people contribute to interfirm communication (Nohria, 1992). The competency-based view of the firm highlights three major benefits of network activity. The first involves the network as a resource used to draw on the separate expertise of other firms (Perrow, 1992). The second is that the network is a repository for attained reputations, which can increase the flow of new business (Lado, Boyd, and Wright, 1992). The third is that the network is a source of new learning, and, consequently, improved competitive advantage (Powell, 1990). For each and all of these benefits, the firm is dependent on the networking efforts of its members.

However, firm-centered views largely overlook the distinct benefits of network activities for the individual career. A person may capitalize on the supplier and customer networks of the firm to gain access to new contacts, or pursue new job opportunities (Rousseau and Wade-Benzoni, 1994). A person may strengthen his or her own position in a current or rival firm through unique relationships forged with key customers or suppliers (Von Hippel, 1988). A person may use network access to gather career-relevant information. In these instances, a firm's network serves as a distinct resource for the employee's career (Pfeffer, 1989).

The firm-based competencies perspective acknowledges that individual competencies lie behind the competencies of the firm. It also acknowledges that firms can add competencies through recruitment (Simon, 1991), or lose competencies through unwanted resignations (Hall, 1992). However, we emphasize here a broader dependence of firm competencies on individual career behavior. Knowing-why, knowing-how and knowing-whom competencies are forms of knowledge assets (Winter, 1987) that share a common characteristic: Their value is not intrinsic, but is dependent on their being employed in settings that recognize their potential contribution and provide corresponding opportunities. From a career standpoint, the interest of the person is in finding such employment settings, whether within or outside one's present firm. The possibilities for doing so, as we will discuss below, extend across the employment, occupational, and industry-community contexts in which boundaryless careers unfold.

Employment Contexts for Boundaryless Careers

Multiple changes in employment contexts reflect a new era of interfirm competition in both the national and global markets. The changes reflect not only corporate restructuring and downsizing, but also a range of new organizing principles developed in response to the new era. These principles imply distinct changes in the kinds of career competencies that will be encouraged.

Layoffs from corporate downsizing and restructuring directly challenge the career competencies of affected workers. These workers are explicitly told that their investments in knowledge and skills (knowing how) and in intrafirm relationships (knowing whom) are no longer valued. The common struggle to reduce identification with the old employer (knowing why) also translates into a distrust of prospective new employers. Moreover, this loss of identification often applies to people whose jobs have been spared, but who relate to the plight of former colleagues. These people also frequently perceive lowered future job security for themselves (Heckscher, 1995; Hirsch, 1987).

However, Quinn (1992) asserts that the primary task of modern service and technology firms is to optimally cultivate and leverage the firm's knowledge-based core competencies, which largely reside in the intelligence (knowing how), motivation (knowing why), and information networks (knowing whom) of the firm's workers.[5] Such knowledge-based firms invite new patterns of organization to attract, keep, and leverage key people as knowledge resources (Sveiby and Lloyd, 1987). Several recent proposals for organizing so-called knowledge workers follow.

Hedlund (1994) prescribes an N-form (network-form) corporate structure, in which knowledge workers are assigned to, and rotated among, diverse projects in temporary constellations or project teams comprising multifunctional, multidivisional and multinational sources of expertise. Proponents of internal, market-based organization insist that all line and staff units and their workers should be held strictly accountable for market-based performance, while being given the autonomy to form voluntary entrepreneurial teams, and collaborative networks or confederations of internal entrepreneurs (Pinchot and Pinchot, 1993; Halal, 1994).

The starburst form of organization results when a company constantly splits off units that represent newly created competencies (Quinn, 1992). Within such starburst firms, workers with valued knowing-how abilities are encouraged to seek career opportunities in split-off or sold-off units that can better utilize and reward their specialized skills than the parent firm can. Affected workers are also encouraged to identify with the higher level of risk-taking that the star-burst form of employment implies.

A pattern in emerging new industries—an example is optical electronics—involves the formation of firms that require the integration, or "fusion," of for-merly separate technologies and competencies (Kodama, 1992). Fusion firms demand that their workforce at all levels (from senior managers to front-line workers) be actively involved in searching for new technological knowledge both inside and outside the host industry. Those workers who can integrate their own competencies with other people's and can develop networks spanning both employment and technological boundaries, are most likely to gain career recognition and rewards in fusion-oriented employment contexts.

Handy (1990) sees outsourcing as part of a broader trend in which pre-viously large firms are shifting to having a core group of permanent employees. Activities outside the firm's "core competence" will be contracted to outside specialists, temporary employees, or contingent workers. This suggests that there will be more opportunities for people to develop entrepreneurial compe-tencies formerly prohibited within more vertically integrated settings.

Consistent with the above trends, Kanter (1989a) predicts a decline in pure-type bureaucratic careers and a growth in professional and entrepreneurial ca-reers. Heckscher (1995) found that those middle managers who reported a pro-fessional career orientation were most successful in coping with a decline in job security and further career opportunities. Kanter (1989b) also acknowledges that careers may involve sequential or concurrent combinations of bureaucratic, professional, and entrepreneurial competencies developed in response to em-ployment circumstances.

Common to the above trends is a distinct view of entrepreneurship, which looks beyond the founders or leaders of firms. This view sees entrepreneurship as a process involving multiple actors whose competencies contribute to the collective entrepreneurial success of the firm (Best, 1990; Reich, 1987).

Indeed, these changes in employment contexts encourage the emergence of new career competencies. From a *knowing-why* standpoint, employment con-texts are disconfirming traditional beliefs about the stability of jobs and employ-ment. They are also inviting people to identify with new arrangements, such as joint ventures or spin-off activities, and to adopt a more entrepreneurial ap-proach in their work behavior. Regarding *knowing-how*, emerging employment contexts are demanding continuous changes in people's skills and knowledge, including the pursuit of new knowledge through supplier, customer, or other interfirm arrangements. Regarding *knowing-whom*, revised expectations about information gathering and exchange relations are exposing people to new career possibilities in both their overall competency accumulation and their choice of employment setting.

Occupational Contexts for Boundaryless Careers

The study of occupational careers (Slocum, 1966) foundered in the 1970s and 1980s, as most attention became refocused on organizatonal careers. However, as we have already noted, occupational (or professional) career investments can provide an attractive alternative to dependency on employers. Also, there is growing evidence that occupations serve as platforms for new learning, and, in turn, for continuing boundaryless-career activities.

Occupations have served as a traditional basis for the attainment of credentials, and of subsequent career mobility. Crafts people with certified skills are likely to enjoy greater interfirm career opportunities than are uncertified semi-skilled or unskilled blue-collar workers (Thomas, 1989). Kanter (1989a) has recently observed a broad trend of occupational-skill standardization and credentialing facilitating boundaryless careers for a variety of nonelite occupational groups, such as nurses' aides.

Current trends involving the demise of job security, the pace of technological change, and the career actor's interest in employability are converging to promote the continuous pursuit of new knowing-how competencies. Such "extended occupational learning" (Hendry, Arthur, and Jones, 1995) lies beyond the pursuit of formal credentials. It occurs in what Van Maanen and Barley (1984) describe as occupational communities—that is, groups of people brought together through shared work experiences. Occupations form natural "communities of practice," through which shared learning occurs, often regardless of formal organizational position (Brown and Duguid, 1991; Orr, 1990). Occupations thus provide a context for tacit (knowing-how) learning to emerge, and for experienced workers to mentor younger charges. Also, occupational networks and formal membership groups sustain complementary (knowing-whom) activities, through which further identification (knowing-why) and learning (knowing-how) take place.

The accounting profession has evolved explicit interfirm career paths for its new recruits, who frequently start in one of the Big Six public-accounting firms. Young accountants typically gain experience (knowing-how) while gaining exposure to a range of clients (knowing-whom), who are also prospective employers. These arrangements benefit all parties. Young accountants can leverage their Big Six work experience for entry into a client firm. The Big Six firm retains the goodwill of its clients, and an invisible network of former employees who are strategically positioned within the firm's client base (Rousseau and Wade-Benzoni, 1994).

A second example of interfirm occupational career paths stems from Starbuck's (1992) characterization of "knowledge-intensive" firms. Such firms' competencies are embodied in their members' skills, which invariably become visible to clients through work performance. As a result, management consulting, software writing, investment banking, and law practices are among the kinds of firms vulnerable to a loss of competencies to customers and/or competitors (Eccles and Crane, 1988; Stinchcombe and Heimer, 1988).

These observations illustrate the importance of occupations to our career-competencies view. Regarding knowing-why competencies, people's traditional identification with their occupation can be reinforced by shared experiences in technological change, and by participation in learning communities focused on distinct occupational problems. The importance of knowing-how competencies is reinforced by expanded credentialing activity; by evidence of high occupational commitment; and by evidence that occupational skills are transferable to industry competitors or former clients. Further, occupational communities foster significant knowing-whom competencies that provide a reference group for shared problem solving, and a continuing support group for people making interfirm career moves.

Industry Communities and Boundaryless Careers

The preceding discussion of employment and occupational trends does not imply that boundaryless careers evolve without constraints. One of the most significant constraints is the availability of alternative employment opportunities. Thus, various accounts of industry communities—defined here as geographic concentrations of interdependent firms and occupations—invite particular attention for the career possibilities they create.[6]

The geographic concentration of an industry provides for regional accumulation of specialized skills that may not be widely available elsewhere. Teece (1980) has argued that skill advantages accrue for large multiproduct firms, because workforce competencies can be better matched to the greater variety of tasks that are performed. However, Goldstein and Gronberg (1984) claim similar interfirm advantages accrue through the skill concentration of related firms located within the same geographic region. A local workforce may accumulate competencies that are specialized for the industry, yet generalized to the needs of multiple firms within the region (Piore and Sabel 1984). A person with experience in one firm may be presocialized and pretrained to perform similar tasks in another firm (Spender, 1989). Firms within the region may thus economize on the costs of retraining, and may share the benefits of industry experience accumulated by the regional workforce.

Porter (1990) extends this point to build an argument for new-firm formation. Drawing on a comparative study of industry regions within nations, he argues that the geographic concentration of rivals stimulates the development of skilled human resources. In turn, this facilitates new-firm formation by providing an abundant supply of skilled and experienced labor. A geographic concentration of domestic rivals also triggers special programs in local schools, universities, technical institutes and training centers. These promote an educational philosophy and infrastructure that further support the skill needs of the industry. Moreover, Porter (1990) argues that geographically concentrated firms are more likely to enjoy rich information flows among their workforces, translating knowing-whom competencies into greater diffusion of industry-specific know-how and innovation.

Peters (1992) suggests that most of tomorrow's work may be done by multifirm project teams. Project teams are similar to communities of practice, in that they provide a reference point for interpersonal communication (knowing-whom) and new learning (knowing-how). However, interfirm project teams bring together representatives from different specializations and from different organizations. Also, projects and the multifirm networks that support them are impermanent. The project-based view gives rise to a vision of a "checkerboard career" (Peters, 1992: 220), in which a person moves freely between employers as new projects occur. This checkerboard vision (knowing-why) of the boundaryless career may be reinforced by thoughtful employers, preferring to "have energized individuals . . . for two or three exciting years . . . rather than 25 dull years" (Peters, 1992: 220). Jones (in chapter 4 of this volume) provides empirical evidence of project-based boundaryless career processes and outcomes in her study of filmmaking projects.

We should note that industry communities can differ in their career competencies. In particular, Saxenian (1989, 1994) has illustrated divergent career patterns stemming from the Cambridge (England) and Silicon Valley, (California) high-technology regions. Cambridge, fueled by traditional government contracting policies and large-firm domination, has encouraged workers' identification, information exchange, and interaction to be constrained inside employer firms. Silicon Valley, steeped in the high-tech, entrepreneurial culture of California, has evolved institutional practices (i.e., use of hands-on venture capitalists, network-intensive social forums, and extensive interfirm cooperation and spin-off formation) that attract and reward workers who accumulate industry-specific, rather than employer-specific, career competencies.

Our observations suggest that people seeking to maximize career opportunities outside their present employment setting are likely to discover a greater density of opportunities in industry communities. Moreover, because these communities tend to share industry-specific values and beliefs, the corresponding knowing-why competencies of industry participants will make transferability between employers less costly. A similar point applies to transferable knowing-how competencies, which include both direct job knowledge and broadly shared industry recipes (Spender 1989). Extensive interfirm communication and interpersonal networks, facilitated by the density of firms, nurture knowing-whom competencies relevant to prospective future employment settings. Also, the interconnectedness of the social networks of the industry region increases the likelihood that indirect ties (e.g., friends of friends) will supply needed information on career opportunities. However, industry community traditions may still discourage boundaryless career behavior, and promote alternative competencies emphasizing intrafirm depth, rather than interfirm breadth, of career activities.

Bounded-versus-Boundaryless Competency Profiles

Our knowing-why, knowing-how, and knowing-whom career-competency perspective draws on previously separate streams of research on career-relevant values, skills, and social networks. Each form of career competency can contribute to the propensity of an individual to pursue a career in which subjectively defined career success is associated with intentional or voluntary changes of employment settings. Accordingly, Table 7.1 suggests two contrasting competency profiles for bounded versus boundaryless careers. The ideal typical bounded career is characterized by an employment context–based career identity (e.g., "I am an IBM engineer"); the accumulation of employment-specialized knowing-how skills (e.g., how to work "the IBM way"); and the development of networks that are intraorganizational (e.g., the IBM family), hierarchic (e.g., the IBM chain of command), and employer prescribed.

By contrast, the ideal typical boundaryless career is characterized by a ca-

Table 7.1   Competency Profiles of Boundaryless versus Bounded Careers

	Career Profile	
Competency	Bounded	Boundaryless
Knowing-why		
Identity	Employer-dependent	Employer-independent
Knowing-how		
Employment context	Specialized	Flexible
Knowing-whom		
Locus	Intrafirm	Interfirm
Structure	Hierarchic	Nonhierarchic
Process	Prescribed	Emergent

reer identity that is independent of the employer (e.g., "I am a software engineer"); the accumulation of employment-flexible know-how (e.g., how to do work in an innovative, efficient, and/or quality-enhancing way); and the development of networks that are independent of the firm (e.g., occupation or industry based), nonhierarchic (e.g., communities of practice), and worker enacted.

Our perspective suggests that asymmetries in the development of boundaryless-career competencies may constrain the realization of a boundaryless career. For example, deficiencies in social networks (knowing-whom) may preclude boundaryless-career mobility by preventing people outside one's current employment setting from recognizing or advocating the value of one's expertise (knowing-how) to prospective employers. Similarly, a person whose career identity (knowing-why) is highly bound to a current employer may underutilize his or her work activities and social networks in efforts to identify and exploit career opportunities outside the current employment context. Finally, a person whose employment skills are too narrowly customized to the requirements of his or her current employer may have difficulty identifying with, or exploring, interfirm opportunities.

Future careers research will be able to elaborate on the bounded versus boundaryless career-competency profiles outlined in Table 7.1, and will generate a richer compendium of competency-based career profiles. These will extend our understanding of the interplay between boundaryless career competencies and the changing organizational, occupational, and industry-community contexts in which careers are evolving.

Shared Values in Competency-Based Boundaryless Careers

The preceding discussion suggests several underlying values for harmonizing the design of competency-based firms and boundaryless careers. These values most directly affect firms' culture and workers' knowing-why competencies, respectively. However, they are values that also interact with broader competency-accumulation efforts by both people and firms. These values complement what we have elsewhere called "new career paradigm" employment principles (Arthur, Claman, and DeFillippi, 1995). They offer a basis for shared understanding in modern, frequently tacit, employment contract arrangements.

First, *voluntarism* is an important underlying value for both competency-driven firms and boundaryless careers. Voluntarism asserts that the most effective choices are those freely made without bureaucratic or hierarchic constraints. Thus, firms and their workers will most effectively develop and utilize their competencies when they are free to make self-interested, informed choices. Voluntarism places a greater burden on both a firm's culture and the responding employee (knowing-why) competencies. Firms should establish clear missions and articulate visions that inspire and guide the development of projects and other work initiatives. Similarly, boundaryless workers should choose to commit to employment contexts and projects that are consistent with, and supportive of, their personal identity and aspirations. Such commitments are durable only when both the employer and employee perceive a mutual interest in a continued association, and where either party remains free to terminate the employment contract when mutual interests no longer prevail.

The exercise of freedom also implies greater responsibility for the consequences of free choices, so that freedom from bureaucratic constraint must be balanced by a commitment to *market discipline:* This value asserts that work performance should be assessed in terms of its market-based outcomes, and places a greater burden on workers' knowing-how competencies and their aggregation in firms. Firms need to focus on the accumulation and leveraging of those core competencies with which they can maintain a competitive advantage. Activities in which the firm is relatively incompetent must be either upgraded or eliminated. Similarly, workers must cultivate skills that are valued by the marketplace, and for which the worker is competitively competent. Bridges (1994) advises workers to view their current employment situation as a market consisting of both the internal market of their current employer and the external market served by their current employer. According to Bridges, both markets must be satisfied for the worker's developing competencies to retain their worth.

A third value behind the competency-based perspective is one of *leverage*. Competency-based theories of the firm suggest that competencies should be leveraged through their application to new market opportunities that lie beyond those in which the competencies were originally applied. Exercising leverage should therefore be a persistent theme in a firm's relations with both current and prospective trading partners. Similarly, a competency-based career perspective recommends that workers leverage competencies toward obtaining new employment opportunities. Such opportunities may exist among suppliers, customers, and competitors of one's present firm, as well as in alternative industry contexts that value the skills being accumulated. To fully realize leveraging opportunities, both firms and their workers need to cultivate extensive multiindustry networks of contacts and information sources. Hence, valuing leverage requires that both firms and people invest in knowing-whom competencies.

Competency-based theory also suggests *collaboration* as a value for both firms and employee careers. The value of collaboration brings increased demands upon firms' network, and people's knowing-whom, competencies. Competency-based firms should utilize outsourcing, collaborative alliances, and partnership relations to achieve what vertically integrated hierarchic organizations achieved through internal competency development. Similarly, competency-specialized workers should benefit from collaborative partnerships in performing tasks that are beyond workers' current expertise. Also, firms and workers should be able to participate productively as members of multifunctional and, increasingly, multifirm project teams. Such collaborative projects require that firms and their workers possess knowing-whom competencies in order to identify and select appropriate collaborative or outsourcing partners. Collaboration also requires that a firm and its participating workers develop knowing-how competencies related to collaborative project participation.

A further value associated with the competency-based view is *resiliency*. Bridges (1994) defines resilience in terms of the ability to quickly let go of the outdated, learn the new, and bounce back from disappointment. Because markets for both firm- and worker-embodied competencies are increasingly uncertain and rapidly changing, the productive lives of many competencies are rapidly declining. As a result, firms and their workers are required to increasingly invest in upgrading their skills in order to be competitively viable. More worrisome is the increasing likelihood that competencies that were acquired in the past may be rendered obsolete by unanticipated technological and market discontinuities. Under these circumstances, both firms and workers must indeed reengineer and reinvent their competencies more fundamentally, or face market rejection.[7]

Some observers call on firms to provide the infrastructural support needed to foster a career-resilient workforce (Waterman, Waterman, and Collard, 1994). Other observers recommend that government play a proactive role in assuring workers access to reskilling opportunities (Bridges, 1994). Yet other observers place their trust in the development of voluntary associations that will supply reskilling and competency-enhancing opportunities (Heckscher, 1995). The competency-based career perspective suggests that workers themselves assume primary responsibility for evaluating the market potential of their current competencies, and that they proactively invest in new competencies that are more in tune with prevailing technological and market trends. Such resilience thus becomes part of the set of overall career competencies of the boundaryless-career worker, and draws on the traditional American cultural virtue of self-reliance.

However, it should be noted that in societies that place greater emphasis on collective identity and collective achievement, prescriptions for boundaryless careers may similarly emphasize collective, rather than individual, enterprise. For example, Granrose and Chua (in chapter 12 of this book) suggest that family members of ethnic Chinese businesses define boundaryless career and learning opportunities in terms of what is good for the family as a whole.

Conclusion

This chapter has argued that recent competency-based views of the firm can be usefully harnessed for the study of boundaryless careers. We have proposed that cumulative career competencies are embodied in people's beliefs and identities (knowing-why), skills and knowledge (knowing-how) and networks of relationships and contacts (knowing-whom). Our explorations have covered boundaryless career implications of current employment, occupational and industry community contexts. We have compared boundaryless versus bounded career competency profiles and identified the interdependencies between competency dimensions. Finally, we have identified competency-based values compatible with the design of both modern-day firms and boundaryless careers.

In closing, we offer this career competency perspective as a basis for new dialogue and experimentation. And in the spirit of this chapter, we particularly welcome responses from readers reaching beyond their own—or their discipline's—traditional boundaries. Elaboration of the ideas we propose may be best achieved by collaborative, even if temporary, efforts. Such efforts would surely be consistent with the kinds of careers we seek to promote.

Notes

1. An employment setting, as viewed in this chapter, is any setting with independent authority to enact employment contracts. This can mean either an independent firm or a business unit of a larger firm, in which employment responsibility is decentralized. The latter meaning can be linked to General Electric President Jack Welch's vision of the "boundaryless organization," that is, of multiple, high-autonomy employment settings (Hirschhorn and Gilmore, 1992). Moves both within and outside these settings would represent boundaryless career behavior.

2. In this chapter the term *firm* is applied to both legally independent and largely autonomous business units.

3. Readers can refer to a previous version of this chapter (DeFillippi and Arthur, 1994) for research implications, and to a related article (Arthur, Claman, and DeFillippi, 1995) for a more contractual perspective on the employment relationship.

4. We prefer the term *knowing why* to the term *know why* (used in the previous version), to better signal the dynamic economy in which boundaryless careers unfold.

5. A related article (Arthur, Claman, and DeFillippi, 1995) applied the concept of intelligence more broadly to all three competency areas.

6. We use the term *industry,* rather than *industrial,* to signal our interest in communities defined by a shared, rather than multiple, industry affiliations.

7. Unlike firms, whose passing may be viewed as evidence of market efficiency, the obsolescence of the competencies of a significant proportion of a population's workforce is a catastrophe, and a long-term threat to economic, political, and social stability.

References

Arthur, M. B. 1992. "Career theory in a dynamic context." In D. H. Montross and C. J. Shinkman (eds.), *Career Development in the 1990s: Theory and Practice.* Springfield, Ill.: Charles C. Thomas, pp. 65–84.

Arthur, M. B.; P. H. Claman; and R. J. DeFillippi. 1995. "Intelligent enterprise, intelligent careers." *Academy of Management Executive* 9 (4): 7–20.

Bailyn, L. 1993. *Breaking the Mold.* New York: Free Press.

Barley, S. R. 1992. "The new crafts: The rise of the technical labor force and its implication for the organization of work." Working paper (WP05), University of Pennsylvania, National Center on the Educational Quality of the Workforce.

Barney, J. 1986. "Organizational culture: Can it be a source of sustained competitive advantage?" *Academy of Management Review* 11: 656–665.

Bennett, A. 1990. *The Death of the Organization Man.* New York: Morrow.

Best, M. H. 1990. *The New Competition: Institutions of Industrial Restructuring.* Cambridge, Mass.: Harvard University Press.

Bolles, R. N. 1993. *What Color Is Your Parachute?* Berkeley, Calif.: Ten Speed Press.

Bridges, W. 1994. *JobShift.* Reading, Mass.: Addison-Wesley.

Brown, J. S., and P. Duguid. 1991. "Organizational learning and communities of practice: Toward a unified view of working, learning, and innovation." *Organization Science* 2 (1): 40–56.

Cheng, M. T. 1991. "The Japanese permanent employment system." *Work and Occupations* 18 (2): 148–171.

Cohen, W. M., and D. A. Levinthal. 1990. "Absorptive capacity: A new perspective on learning and innovation." *Administrative Science Quarterly* 35: 128–152.

Dalton, G. W. 1989. "Developmental views of careers in organizations." In M. B. Arthur; D. T. Hall; and B.S. Lawrence (eds.), *Handbook of Career Theory.* New York: Cambridge University Press, pp 89–109.

D'Aveni, R. 1994. *Hypercompetition.* New York: Free Press.

Derr, C. B. 1986. *Managing the New Careerists.* San Francisco: Jossey-Bass.

Drucker, P.F. 1994. "The age of social transformation." *Atlantic Monthly,* November: 53–80.

Eccles, R., and D. Crane. 1988. *Doing Deals: Investment Banks at Work.* Boston: Harvard Business School Press.

Feldman, D. C. 1989. "Careers in organizations: Recent trends and future directions." *Journal of Management* 15 (2): 135–156.

Fiol, C. M. 1991. "Managing culture as a competitive resource: An identity-based view of sustainable competitive advantage." *Journal of Management* 17: 191–211.

Goldstein, G. S., and T. J. Gronberg. 1984. "Economies of scale and economies of agglomeration." *Journal of Urban Economics* 16: 91–104.

Hall, D. T. 1984. "Human resource management and organizational effectiveness." In C. J. Fombrun; N. M. Tichy; and M. A DeVanna (eds.), *Strategic Human Resource Management.* New York: Wiley.

Hall, R. 1992. "The strategic analysis of intangible resources." *Strategic Management Journal* 13: 135–144.

Halal, W. E. 1994. "From hierarchy to enterprise: Internal markets are the new foundation of management." *Academy of Management Executive* 8 (4): 69–83.

Hamel, G., and A. Heene. 1994. *Competence-Based Competition.* Chichester, Eng.: John Wiley.

Handy, C. 1990. *The Age of Unreason.* Boston: Harvard Business School Press.

Harrison, B. 1994. *Lean and Mean.* New York: Basic Books.

Heckscher, C. 1995. *White Collar Blues: Management Loyalties in an Age of Corporate Restructuring.* New York: Basic Books.

Hedlund, G. 1994. "A model of knowledge management and the N-form corporation." *Strategic Management Journal* 15, Special Issue: 73–90.

Hendry, C.; M. B. Arthur; and A. M. Jones. 1995. *Strategy through People: Adaptation and Learning in the Small-Medium Enterprise.* New York: Routledge.

Hirsch, P. 1987. *Pack Your Own Parachute.* Reading, Mass.: Addison-Wesley.

Hirschhorn, L., and T. Gilmore. 1992. "The new boundaries of the 'boundaryless' company." *Harvard Business Review* May-June: 104–115.

Kanter, R. M. 1989a. *When Giants Learn to Dance.* New York: Simon and Schuster.

Kanter, R. M. 1989b. "Careers and the wealth of nations: A macro perspective on the structure and implications of career forms." In M. B. Arthur; D. T. Hall; and

B. S. Lawrence (eds.), *Handbook of Career Theory*. New York: Cambridge University Press, pp. 506–522.

Katzenbach, J. R., and D. K. Smith. 1993. *The Wisdom of Teams*. New York: Harper Business.

Kilmann, R. H.; M. J. Saxton; and R. Serpa (eds.). 1985. *Gaining Control of Corporate Cultures*. San Francisco: Jossey-Bass.

Kodama, F. 1992. "Technology and the new R&D." *Harvard Business Review* July-August: 70–78.

Kram, K. E. 1985. *Mentoring at Work*. Glenview, Ill.: Scott, Foresman.

Lado, A. A.; N. G. Boyd; and P. Wright. 1992. "A competency-based model of sustainable competitive advantage: Toward a conceptual integration." *Journal of Management* 18 (1): 77–91.

Lewis, J. 1990. *Partnerships for Profit: Structuring and Managing Strategic Alliances*. New York: Free Press.

Maguire, S. R. 1993. "Employer and occupational tenure: An update." *Monthly Labor Review* June: 45–56.

McCall, M.; M. Lombardo; and A. Morrison. 1988. *The Lessons of Experience: How Successful Executives Develop on the Job*. Lexington, Mass.: Lexington Books.

McGrath, R.G.; I. C. MacMillan; and S. Venkataraman. 1995. "Defining and developing competence: A strategic process paradigm." *Strategic Management Journal* 16 (4): 251–276.

Miles, R. E., and C. C. Snow. 1986. "Network organizations: New concepts for new forms." *California Management Review* 28: 62–73.

Miner, A. S. 1990. "Structural evolution through idiosyncratic jobs: The potential for unplanned learning." *Organization Science* 1: 195–210.

Miner, A. S., and D. F. Robinson. 1994. "Organizational and population level learning as engines for career transitions." *Journal of Organizational Behavior* 15: 345–364.

Mirvis, P. H., and D. T. Hall. 1994. "Psychological success and the boundaryless career." *Journal of Organizational Behavior* 15: 365–380.

Nelson, R. R., and S. G. Winter. 1982. *An Evolutionary Theory of Economic Change*. Cambridge, Mass.: Belknap/Harvard University Press.

Nohria, N. 1992. "Is a network perspective a useful way of studying organizations?" In N. Nohria and R. G. Eccles (eds.), *Networks and Organizations*. Boston: Harvard Business School Press, pp. 1–22.

Nohria, N., and J. Berkeley. 1994. "An action perspective: The crux of the new management." *California Management Review* 36: 70–92.

Ornstein, S., and L. Isabella. 1993. "Making sense of careers: A review (1989–1992)." *Journal of Management* 19: 243–267.

Orr, J. 1990. "Sharing knowledge, celebrating identity: War stories and community memory in a service culture." In D. S. Middleton and D. Edwards (eds.), *Collective Remembering: Memory in Society*. Beverly Hills: Sage, pp.169–189.

Perrow, C. 1992. "Small Firm Networks." In N. Nohria and R. G. Eccles. *Networks and Organizations*. Boston: Harvard Business School Press, pp. 445–470.

Peters, T. 1992. *Liberation Management*. New York: Knopf.

Pentland, B. T., and H. H. Rueter. 1994. "Organizational routines as grammars of action." *Administrative Science Quarterly* 39: 484–510.

Pfeffer, J. 1989. "A political perspective on careers: Interests, networks, and environments." In M. B. Arthur; D. T. Hall; and B. S. Lawrence (eds.), *Handbook of Career Theory*. New York: Cambridge University Press, pp. 380–396.

Pfeffer, J. 1994. *Competitive Advantage through People*. Boston: Harvard Business School Press.

Pfeffer, J., and J. N. Baron. 1988. "Taking the workers back out: Recent trends in the structuring of employment." In B. M. Staw (ed.), *Research in Organizational Behavior*. Greenwich, Conn.: JAI Press, 10: 257–303.

Pinchot, E., and G. Pinchot. 1993. *The End of Bureaucracy and the Rise of the Intelligent Organization*. San Francisco: Berrett-Koehler.

Piore, M. J., and C. F. Sabel. 1984. *The Second Industrial Divide*. New York: Basic Books.

Porter, M. E. 1990. *The Competitive Advantage of Nations*. New York: Free Press.

Powell, W. W. 1990. "Neither market nor hierarchy: Network forms of organization." In B. Staw (ed.), *Research in Organizational Behavior*. Greenwich, Conn.: JAI Press, 12: 295–336.

Prahalad, C. K., and G. Hamel. 1994. *Competing for the Future*. Cambridge, Mass.: Harvard University Press.

Quinn, J. B. 1992. *Intelligent Enterprise*. New York: Free Press.

Raelin, J. 1991. *Clash of Cultures*. Boston: Harvard Business School Press.

Reed, R., and R. J. DeFillippi. 1990. "Causal ambiguity: Barriers to imitation and sustainable competitive advantage." *Academy of Management Review* 15 (1): 88–102.

Reich, R. B. 1987. "Entrepreneurship reconsidered: The team as hero. *Harvard Business Review* May-June: 77–83.

Reich, R. B. 1991. *The Work of Nations*. New York: Knopf.

Rousseau, D. 1995. *Psychological Contracts in Organizations*. Newbury Park, Calif.: Sage.

Rousseau, D., and K. A. Wade-Benzoni. 1994. "Linking strategy and human resource practices." *Human Resource Management* 33 (3): 463–489.

Saxenian, A. 1989. :The cheshire cat's grin: Innovation, regional development and the Cambridge case." *Economy and Society* 18: 448–477.

Saxenian, A. 1994. *Regional Advantage: Culture and Competition in Silicon Valley and Route 128*. Boston: Harvard University Press.

Schein, E. H. 1992. *Organizational Culture and Leadership*. San Francisco: Jossey-Bass.

Schneider, B., and A. M. Konz. 1989. "Strategic job analysis." *Human Resource Management* 28 (1): 52–63.

Schuler, R. S. 1992. "Strategic human resource management: Linking the people with the strategic needs of the business." *Organizational Dynamics* summer: 18–31.

Senge, P. M. 1990. *The Fifth Discipline*. New York: Doubleday.

Simon, H. A. 1991. "Bounded rationality and organizational learning."*Organizational Science* 2: 125–134.

Slocum, W. L. 1966. *Occupational Careers*. Chicago: Aldine.

Spender, J. C. 1989. *Industry Recipes*. Oxford, Eng.: Blackwell.

Starbuck, W. H. 1992. "Learning by knowledge-intensive firms." *Journal of Management Studies* 29 (6): 713–740.

Stinchcombe, A., and C. A. Heimer. 1988. "Interorganizational relations and careers in computer software firms." In I. H. Simpson and R. L. Simpson (eds.), *Research in the Sociology of Work*, vol. 4: *High-Tech Work*. Greenwich, Conn.: JAI Press, pp. 179–204.

Sveiby, K. E., and T. Lloyd. 1987. *Managing Know-How*. London: Bloomsbury Publishing.

Teece, D. J. 1980. "Economies of scope and the scope of the enterprise." *Journal of Economic Behavior and Organization* 1: 223–247.

Thomas, R. J. 1989. "Blue collar careers: Meaning and choice in a world of constraints." In M. B. Arthur; B. S. Lawrence; and D. T. Hall (eds.), *Handbook of Career Theory*. New York: Cambridge University Press, pp. 354–379.

Topel, R. H., and M. P. Ward. 1992. "Job mobility and the careers of young men." *Quarterly Journal of Economics* 107: 439–479.

Van Maanen, J., and S. R. Barley. 1984. "Occupational communities: Culture and control in organizations." In B. M. Staw (ed.), *Research in Organizational Behavior*, vol. 6. Greenwich, Conn.: JAI Press.

Von Hippel, E. H. 1988. *The Sources of Innovation*. New York: Oxford University Press.

Waterman, R. H.; J. A. Waterman; and B. A. Collard. 1994. "Toward a career-resilient workforce." *Harvard Business Review* July-August: 87–95.

Weick, K. E., and L. R. Berlinger. 1989. "Career improvisation in self-designing organizations." In M. B. Arthur; D. T. Hall; and B. S. Lawrence (eds.), *Handbook of Career Theory*. New York: Cambridge University Press, pp. 313–328.

Williamson, O. E. 1991. "Strategy, economizing, and economic organization." *Strategic Management Journal* 12 (S): 75–94.

Winter, S. 1987. "Knowledge and competence as strategic assets." In D. J. Teece (ed.), *The Competitive Challenge*. Cambridge, Mass.: Ballinger, pp. 159–184.

8

Prometheus Stretches: Building Identity and Cumulative Knowledge in Multiemployer Careers

TED BAKER AND HOWARD E. ALDRICH

In American society, work is an important context for the expression and further development of both identity and knowledge. The temporal organization is embedded in peoples' work histories, which are generically labeled "careers" (Arthur, 1994: 297), and in this chapter, we use concepts from the life-course perspective to examine recent historical changes in career patterns. The life-course perspective has developed among a variety of social and behavioral sciences during the 1980s and 1990s, and "refers to the social patterning of events and roles over the life-span, a process ever subject to the interaction of individual behavior with a changing society" (Elder and Caspi, 1990). This perspective directs our attention to historical influences that affect processes of identity formation and expression within careers, and to how knowledge is accumulated and put to use.

Career Heterogeneity

Most Americans build their careers as employees, working as members of organizations. Since the late 1970s, organizational policies in the United States and elsewhere have increasingly emphasized "employment flexibility" (Brodsky, 1994; Harrison, 1994). Until the early 1990s (Lawlor, 1994), contingent and temporary employment grew very rapidly (Belous, 1989). Further, a recent study of job stability in the United States (Swinnerton and Wial, 1995) found that job stability for the period of 1987–1991, decreased—modestly, but statistically significantly—from the years 1979–1983. We interpret this evidence as suggesting—with some ambiguity—that the lifetime number of employers for which the average American worker will work is probably increasing. What are the consequences of this change for workers and their careers?

The career histories of Americans manifest a great deal of heterogeneity across three dimensions: numbers of employers, extent of knowledge cumulation, and the role of personal identity. We have derived these three dimensions from our reading of the July 1994 special issue of the *Journal of Organizational Behavior*, through the lens of the life-course perspective. The first dimension is simply the number of employers (including spells of self-employment) included in a person's work history. The second dimension is the extent to which the knowledge and competencies that employees gain is cumulative over the course of their careers. At one extreme, little that is learned in one period of employees' work histories is pertinent to their activities in a later period of their careers. Toward the other extreme, each job builds, in fundamental ways, on what workers have learned in previous jobs.[1]

The third career dimension is the extent to which employees themselves play an instrumental role in structuring their work histories through their personal identities, and the extent to which work histories structure personal identities. Our use of the identity concept draws on social-psychological notions of authenticity and self-efficacy.[2] Authenticity denotes the belief that people have some sense of a "core or essential self," to which they are motivated to remain true (Gecas and Burke, 1995: 57; Gecas, 1986: 141; Gergen, 1991). This idea also resonates with Hall's (1971, 1986) notion of a "core" identity that represents the common component among multiple and easily changeable subidentities. Self-efficacy "refers to the perception or experience of oneself as a causal agent in one's environment" (Gecas and Burke, 1995: 47). Self-efficacy has been tied to a wide variety of outcomes by social psychologists (Gecas and Seff, 1989; Mortimer and Lorence, 1979; Bandura, 1977).[3]

Concepts of the self that are very similar to our notion of identity have frequently been criticized by postmodernist thinkers: "Postmodern society . . . is viewed as inimical to the maintenance of the bounded, private, centered self striving for agency and authenticity" (Gecas and Burke, 1995: 57; see also Gergen, 1991). Instead, some analysts "assume that the social form and historical content of the self are derived sociohistorical productions" (Weigert, 1988: 263). The structural changes that we evaluate as threats to identity would be seen by postmodernists as simply elements of the transition toward postmodernity. Thus, some readers might view our concept of identity as historically contingent, dated, and no longer applicable. In contrast, our point of view is that identity, as we have described it, captures elements of the modern self that are of continuing—and perhaps even greater—importance as people try to build meaningful careers.

The three career dimensions—identity, knowledge cumulation, and multiple employers—specify outcomes of career processes that take place over the course of peoples' lives. The dimensions should be thought of as continuous variables describing a three-dimensional space within which very few points (representing individual career patterns) are impossible to reach, but in which job clusters tend to occur. Guided by the life-course perspective (Elder and O'Rand, 1995: 454–455), we view career processes as interactions of people's agency—which refers to their abilities to make choices and influence their own lives—with changing structures of constraints and opportunities. Increasing job instability should push the clustering of careers outward along the multi-employer dimension.

Table 8.1 shows the career dimensions. First, it represents careers built around one or a few employers; and, second, it represents multiemployer careers. The cells of this table are not filled with job lists, but, rather, with illustrative work-history sequences. Emerging career patterns may reflect some underlying propensity for boundarylessness, but, prior to the end of a work history for any individual, it is not possible to firmly identify a career as boundaryless. Someone could work for IBM for 30 years, retire, and then build a boundaryless career. This is ever more true in the face of increasing variance in what retirement means in the United States (Henretta, 1992; O'Rand and Henretta, 1982). Because Table 8.1 is filled with examples of work histories from our research, and represents individuals who are still working, these are actually only career segments, not completed careers. In the context of modern careers, the meaning of any single job is ambiguous in the extreme.

Table 8.1   Career Dimensions and Work-History Sequences

Role of Personal Identity	Cumulation of Knowledge	
	Low	High
	Single or Few Employers	
Low	Cell 1 4 years in army, then 35 years as school janitor	Cell 2 33 years in Government Systems Division at IBM ("organization man," identity submerged in organization identity)
High	Cell 3 Production manager in large paper-goods company; describes his way of doing job as highly idiosyncratic, but stable over a number of years	Cell 4 Corporate attorney in rapidly growing organization, plans to remain after 12 years (professionals embedded in organizations)
	Multiple Employers	
Low	Cell 5 Data-entry clerk, to supervisor, to telemarketer, to data-entry clerk, across 3 employers	Cell 6 Public accounting, to CPA, to corporate controller, while wanting to be an operating manager (people who do what they are good at, just because they are good at it)
High	Cell 7 Union electrician, moving from a project for one electrical contractor, to another project for another contractor, year after year	Cell 8 Highly skilled software engineer moving from one assignment to another as an independent contractor

The top portion of the table describes careers characterized by employment stability. For example, cell 1, representing low identity and low cumulation of knowledge, lists a man who has spent most of his work life as a janitor. He describes his own work history not as a career, but as a very stable and secure job. Cell 2, representing low identity and high knowledge cumulation, describes what used to be called the "organization man," a person whose identity has been submerged in the identity of the firm. Cell 3, indicating high identity and low cumulation, is represented by a man who has spent a number of years managing a department in a large firm; he has not learned a great deal from month to month, but feels that he brings something to it that "the other production managers here don't have." Cell 4, representing high identity and high cumulation—which (perhaps along with cell 2), we think, are traditional career goals of many Americans—shows the example of a corporate attorney who has spent 12 years in a rapidly growing company and plans to remain with this firm. His professional career is thus embedded in a corporation.

The table's bottom portion describes career possibilities that will become more common because of employment flexibility. Cell 5, representing low identity and low cumulation, describes a woman who has moved from job to job, and across employers, with little sense of a connection between jobs or to her sense of identity. Cell 6, representing low identity and high cumulation, shows a man who trained to be an accountant, and who has developed a lucrative financial-management career, while wanting to be an operating manager. This cell represents people who move across employers, repeatedly ending up doing what they are good at, regardless of whether it's what they want to do. Cell 7, representing high identity and low cumulation, describes a union electrician who takes pride in his craft, but who performs very similar tasks, year after year, across a wide variety of projects and electrical contractors.

The boundaryless career offers an enticing vision of individual initiative, relative independence from a hierarchy, and the building of a sense of community through voluntary association and networks. Employees who are able to build work lives characterized by high interemployer mobility, high cumulation of competencies, and high identity fall into cell 8. We label this single category that of the "boundaryless career." In contrast to several of the authors cited above, we are concerned with what we see as the challenges facing people who try to build boundaryless careers.

In the early 1960s, sociologist Harold Wilensky (1961: 523) defined a career as "a succession of related jobs, arranged in a hierarchy of prestige, through which persons move in an ordered (more or less predictable) sequence." Wilensky found a great deal of what he termed "disorderliness" in a study of the careers of middle- and working-class white men in the Detroit area. He also found that disorderly careers predicted reduced integration between individuals and the broader communities in which they lived. The concept of the boundaryless career and the analysis of its consequences closely parallel Wilensky's work. The main difference between our concept and Wilensky's is that clearly structured organizational career paths have been eroded over the decades since Wilensky's study, reflecting important changes that have taken place in the structure of employment since Wilensky's analysis. The challenges resulting from these changes are the main independent variables in this chapter. For those people who manage to create order—identity and knowledge cumulation—across their work histories, a boundaryless career is the reward. Those who are unable to construct this order for themselves end up with something less, as reflected in cells 5–7 of Table 8.1.

The Emergence of Boundarylessness

Boundaryless career patterns reflect the results of people's attempts to come to terms with changes in the opportunity structures they face. Despite the attractive philosophical case that can be made for the freedoms of a boundaryless career, there is little evidence that Americans have made a sudden ideological and cultural shift to placing a higher value on moving from job to job and from employer to employer. In their analysis of changes in job stability during the 1980s, Swinnerton and Wial (1995: 302) found that changes in job-retention patterns of low-seniority workers from 1979 to 1991 were "more readily interpretable as a result of changes in employers' layoff behavior than as a consequence of changes in workers' propensities to quit."

Individuals have not become less stable as employees; instead, employment has become more flexible. A range of reasons has been offered to explain increases in employment flexibility over the last 30 years (Brodsky, 1994: 53). These include the continuing globalization of product and labor markets; changes in the economic policies of governments concerned with domestic growth; and the increased variability of consumer demand and market segmentation—all of these have combined with more sophisticated use of information technology. *Flexibility* has been used to describe a wide variety of observed employment patterns. Underlying employment flexibility are the practices that slow the growth of jobs offering long-term employment and the possibility of a career with a single employer. Such practices increase the growth of jobs that may not last very long or offer employees much in the way of a clear next step.

Much of the growth of flexible-employment patterns is relatively recent, and the apparent increase in boundaryless career patterns is even newer. For example, Mirvis and Hall (1994: 368) found only slight suggestions of a movement toward boundaryless careers during the period from the 1960s through the 1980s. The emergence of employment flexibility has preceded the emergence of boundaryless careers, although the length of the lead time can be disputed. Until this point, the direction of causality has been one-sided: Changes in social structure, in the form of flexible patterns of employment, have created a challenge for people who are trying to build what they view as successful lives and work histories. We will argue here that the the challenge facing individual workers may be great.

Research Methods

We wanted to learn about how people deal with building careers across multiple employers; thus, we chose to conduct open-ended, semistructured interviews with people in circumstances in which we expected multiple-employer careers to be the modal condition. The length of our interviews ranged from 20 minutes to more than five hours, and averaged about 90 minutes. In all, we spoke with 82 people. We interviewed 32 local entrepreneurs in two industries: computer training and environmental consulting. The interviewees included 21 employees of the entrepreneurs' firms; eight hiring managers in large firms (over 20,000 employees); five software engineers who were then working as independent contractors; plus 16 people who had lost their jobs (in large firms involved in information-technology services and commercial banking) and had recently begun the process of looking for new work. We would expect to see more experience with boundaryless-career activities in this sample than in a similar-size, randomly selected group, but we believe that the people we interviewed represent a reasonably diverse group, in terms of age, ethnicity, gender, and organizational roles. The sample is not educationally heterogeneous, as virtually everyone with whom we spoke has at least a four-year college degree. All interviews took place between October 1993 and February 1995.

An Individual's Structural and Historical Position

We have borrowed a number of concepts from life-course theorists to orient our discussion in a way that emphasizes the historical and temporal ordering of the events and problems we attempt to analyze. Historical influences may be classified into three types of effects: cohort, period, and maturation. A cohort effect describes the differential impact of a historical event or change on younger people as compared to older people. A period effect occurs when social change has similar effects on different age cohorts. Maturation effects describe the impact of the secular process of aging. The next two sections of this chapter describe cohort and period effects. Because we spoke with very few people who were over 55, we do not have a separate section on maturation effects. [4]

Cohort Effects

People in different age cohorts, and in different marital and parental circumstances, may be differentially affected by the emergence of circumstances requiring the construction of boundaryless careers. What differences should we expect to see between people who have been employed for a number of years and those who are closer to the beginning of their careers?

Changes in patterns of employment have stronger effects on people who are in their mid- or late-career years. If we think of the process of building a lifelong work history as being influenced by rules, in the form of institutional regulations and behavioral norms, then we can conceptualize the emergence of flexible-employment practices as a *change in the rules*. It's one thing for the rules to change at the beginning of a career, but it's quite another for them to change after people have followed the same unchanging rules for 20 years.

Several institutionalized links between people's work lives and their lives as a whole are affected by the extent to which employment relations are stable.

These include a variety of seniority benefits, pension portability, benefit vesting periods, health-insurance portability and preexisting health-condition problems, and retirement-planning expectations.

To the extent that benefits accrue on the basis of seniority, a boundaryless career pattern reduces the availability of such benefits to an individual. Mundane examples include waiting periods before being able to apply internally for jobs, and gradual accrual of sick-pay and vacation benefits. Another common example occurs when employers include employment tenure in decisions about what workers get to keep their jobs in cases of involuntary layoffs.

Pension portability exists if an employee, when moving to another employer, is able to maintain "credit" for years of work with a previous employer. In defined-contribution plans, portability may be less of a problem, because specific funds may be available, in an account established by one employer, to roll over into another employer's plan or into an IRA. In defined-benefit plans, retirement benefits are often a function of years of employment (with a single employer), multiplied by the highest salary earned. A 1991 government study found that only about 13% of people covered under defined-benefit pension plans had any form of interemployer pension portability (Foster, 1994). A person with an identical work and salary history, but who worked, for example, for two employers for a period of 15 years each rather than for one employer for 30 years, would, even if the two employers had identical-defined benefit pension plans, likely end up with much smaller total pension benefits.

Vesting refers to the process by which employees gain equity in the pension plans offered by their employers. Under the Employee Retirement Income Security Act of 1974, private, single-employer retirement plans may vest participants 100% after five years, or 20% after three years, with an additional 20% vesting being provided each year until full vesting at seven years. Umbrella plans that are coordinated across multiple employers (for example, in some unionized industries) are allowed to provide no vesting for the first nine years of participation, with 100% after ten years (Foster, 1994). Obviously, if people end up working for a larger number of employers, while pension systems remain unchanged, they are at an increased risk of getting reduced benefits under defined-benefit plans, and of completely losing a portion of benefits each time they leave an employer prior to vesting. To the extent that people who are late in their careers allow their expectations about income from defined-benefit plans to condition their personal-savings behavior, any unexpected change in employers prior to expected retirement may be a substantial problem. Unexpected changes in patterns of lifelong accumulation of retirement benefits violate the expectations and outcomes of even those who plan quite deliberately for retirement.

Health insurance figures in the career plans of many workers, as our interviews made clear. One very successful senior employee of an entrepreneurial firm surprised us by explaining that he wanted to change jobs, and had another opportunity, but that a moderately serious, preexisting medical condition made moving from one employer-sponsored medical plan to another a problem. The preexisting condition also kept him from jumping to full-time involvement with a business he was operating on the side.

In addition to whether they are early or late in their careers, other basic social aspects of peoples' lives influence whether they will be able to build a boundaryless career. We consider these characteristics as part of the cohort effects, because they are influenced by age-graded norms—for example, the culturally appropriate age at the time of a first marriage—that vary between birth cohorts.

Marriage and the presence of children may have a substantial impact on how a person is affected by the results of employment flexibility. We have already discussed the importance of pension and medical-insurance benefits and how these are intertwined with employment stability. Employees commonly include their spouse under their employer's medical plan, generally at a group rate. Thus, a married person whose spouse works at a good job may be well positioned to avoid some potential medical-insurance pitfalls accompanying more frequent changes of employers. Further, if one spouse can support the family financially, at least temporarily, the other spouse can take career risks that might otherwise seem foolish. By contrast, a spouse tied to a local job may severely limit a couple's geographic mobility if they are in search of new opportunities.

Similar circumstances surround the presence of children. Having two working spouses makes getting adequate insurance coverage for the kids more likely. However, people with children enrolled in school usually try to avoid moving them around frequently, causing another drag on geographic mobility and thus reducing parents' abilities to exploit boundaryless career opportunities in another locale. A more profound set of problems arises in cases where both parents have unrewarding jobs, or where only one parent is employed, or in single-parent households.

Period Effects

Three sets of period effects are of interest: changing norms regarding multiemployer careers, threats to the cumulation of knowledge across job sequences, and threats to the maintenance of a stable identity in careers.

Changing Norms

Structural changes in employment patterns, particularly increases in flexibility, occurred *prior* to the emergence of boundaryless careers. Norms have emerged more quickly for employer, than for employee, behavior, in the sense that employers accept the termination of unwanted employees as a routine management practice, but are still uncertain about how to interpret multiple job changes by employees. The terms "layoffs," "downsizing," "reengineering," and "flexibility" have become commonplace in the 1990s as firms have reduced their workforces during times of economic recession and times of recovery. As Mirvis and Hall noted, "At this point, . . . movement toward the boundaryless organization is well ahead of acceptance of the boundaryless career" (1994: 377).

With a single exception, none of the employers we interviewed expressed any sense of an obligation to provide continued employment for people they hire. Employers did not deny that they would feel personally uncomfortable with eliminating people's jobs for economic reasons, but nonetheless, each felt that downsizing is a legitimate business response to changing circumstances. The one entrepreneur who believed himself obligated to provide employment security has been unable to bring himself to hire any permanent employees, and instead, relies on subcontractors. Our tentative conclusion is that the planned elimination of jobs is currently seen as nonstigmatizing and legitimate among employers.

By contrast, terminated employees have not been as fortunate. Across the board, employers we interviewed described those who have lost their jobs as carrying a stigma. One large-company middle manager described it to us in the following terms:

> Everybody knows that when you have a layoff, you use it as a chance to get rid of the people you wanted to get rid of anyway, but couldn't document or hadn't bothered documenting as bad employees [which is done to meet company standards for terminating employees]. If you don't have much dead wood, you hope they make you use a seniority list, because then you can say it's out of your control. But these days, it's typically not done by seniority, and you can pretty much get rid of everyone you want to get rid of, along with some people you'd like to keep, because normally, you have to go deeper than just the dead wood.

Over time, the stigma attached to involuntary job losses may change. Elimination of jobs through restructuring was legitimated very quickly, as it meshed with the "employment-at-will" doctrine underlying labor law in the United States. If the routine and legitimated elimination of jobs continues, we would expect increased acceptance of the status of "involuntary job loser" as increasing numbers of people fall into this category. The process has probably already begun.

Cumulation of Knowledge

Knowledge cumulation may be analyzed along three dimensions: knowledge quantity, the efficiency of its acquisition, and its transferability. First, although it is never simple to measure the quantity of what someone has learned, some jobs do provide more learning opportunities than others. Second, the efficiency of the cumulation process can be assessed by measuring what proportion of the knowledge gained on a job is firm specific. Efficiency of cross-employer cumulation is then calculated by dividing the amount of non-firm-specific knowledge gained on a job by the total knowledge gained. In a multiple-employer career framework, firm-specific knowledge is at risk of becoming wasted knowledge. Third, transferability refers to the proportion of non-firm-specific knowledge that is applicable to future work in other organizations.

Quantity and transferability are contingent not only on a specific job and employment setting, but also on an individual job holder's characteristics, including work and education history. For example, in our interviews with employees of a computer-training company, most of the employees who were at their first or second jobs after college spoke at length about how much they found themselves learning. One of these, Marlene, had previously worked for several other training companies, and now had exactly the same formal job as much younger employees had. She talked mainly about how effectively she was able to apply previously acquired technical training skills to her current job. Accordingly, she was learning very little, and spoke of the beginnings of boredom with her work.

Movement between jobs with very high knowledge transferability may result in a very low cumulation of additional knowledge. Efficiency is less contingent on personal history, and is more directly a feature of job and industry settings: Some jobs are tied, in unique ways, to particular companies, whereas others have very similar knowledge requirements from firm to firm.

Threats to Cumulation

Career cumulation of knowledge is probably enhanced to the extent that reductions in average levels of job tenure mean that workers are more likely to stay only a short time at a job where nothing is learned. However, multiple employer patterns may create conditions promoting two forms of waste: inefficient knowledge acquisition and ineffective transferability.

Inefficiency results when employees repeatedly invest in learning only firm-specific knowledge. Being fully competent at a job often requires an understanding of the larger context in which it is embedded. Some new firm-specific learning may be required for each new position in the same firm, but it is unlikely to approach that which is required for a new job with a new employer.

Ineffective transferability occurs when very little of the knowledge gained in prior positions is applicable to a future position. Lack of transferability may occur by chance when employees deliberately take on new types of jobs because they desire to "do something different"; and many employees we interviewed, particularly those at relatively low job levels, have taken this approach to changing jobs. Because they have jobs that can be learned in a relatively short time, and that quickly bore them, they decide to move on to other jobs that they can learn quickly. However, people trying to build careers across several employers must balance the potential stagnation and boredom of high transferability against the threat of losing all previously acquired competence, if they move to a position for which prior work has been poor preparation.

Career paths within single organizations tend to have two qualities that may be lacking in multi-employer career paths. First, the degree of transferability of competence between jobs is generally high, because managers take this into account in setting up and adjusting internal labor markets and career paths. Second, the human resource management literature emphasizes not only the difficulties employers face in selecting from among job candidates, but also the difficulties recruits face in obtaining useful information about a job before they accept it and work at it for a while (Taylor and Giannantonio, 1993). Employees within a firm learn about a new job with the same employer much more easily than about jobs in different organizations. Compared to internal moves, then, interorganizational job changes are less likely to match expectations and more likely to offer unanticipated challenges to one's knowledge and identity.

Career ladders within firms allow both employees and employers to exploit investments in firm-specific knowledge over time (Althauser and Kalleberg, 1981). Firms tend to invest more in training employees whom they anticipate will be around for a long time than in training employees who are likely to leave in the near future (DeFillippi and Arthur, 1994: 316). Likewise, if they expect to build a career with the same employer, it makes little sense for employees to worry about whether the knowledge they gain is firm specific. In the age of the boundaryless career, both of these assumptions are violated: Employers need to worry more about gaining returns on investments in employee development, and employees need to worry more about the efficiency of their knowledge cumulation. Everything else being equal, we would expect a reduction in employer-sponsored investment in training, and an increase in employee concern about cumulation.

Workers whose skills are based on a rapidly changing state of the art, and who are not learning new skills quickly enough at work, might find themselves pursuing additional education throughout their lifetime. Indeed, continuing vocational education might become a seemingly permanent component of employees' personal lives. Many of the software engineers we interviewed continue to take night classes, year after year, to maintain the currency of their skills (Miles and Snow, 1995). Several of the computer-training firms we studied provide training for employees wishing to learn new skills, but only on the employees' own time, not on company time. Recent studies have suggested that employed Americans are dedicating an increasing number of hours to their work (Schor, 1991). If people use their own time to develop and maintain vocational knowledge, the increased-time burden represents a further encroachment of work into formerly personal time. Alternatively, to the extent that what it means to be competent changes over time, those who have been repeatedly exploiting old skills will end up effectively losing ground to others who have been learning new skills.

Identity and Threats to Identity

Our concept of identity combines the notions of authenticity and self-efficacy. Similar to Hall (1971: 65–66; 1986), who built on earlier work by Kurt Lewin (1936), we believe that the development of an identity-enhancing career is facilitated by circumstances that allow people to set and work toward challenging, but attainable, goals that fit in with their sense of who they are. Such achievements provide personal evidence that their unfolding careers are coherent reflections of how they understand themselves. In a single employer setting, the ability to set and achieve such goals will be heavily influenced by the nature of job tasks and the degree of autonomy. People whose job tasks fit in with their sense of core identity, and who are able to take a lead role in setting and accomplishing challenging goals, will develop careers that are high on the identity scale. We also agree with Hall (1971: 66), who noted that this "choice-initiated cycle of career development" may be "self reinforcing and continuing." In other words, success in setting and achieving personally meaningful goals will support further attempts to express identity through work activities. Over time, identity is both a determinant and an outcome of work careers as they are experienced by employees.

For people to construct boundaryless careers, they must express and build their identity across a series of employers. They must achieve a sense of authenticity and self-efficacy through the structuring and evolution of the path from one employer to another over time, as well as through the individual jobs that make up work histories. We see three main categories of threats involving identity in multiple-employer contexts: inability to get a good job, inability to escape a good job, and inability to escape aspects of an identity that has worked well in the past.

The first threat is simply the inability to get or keep a job that will allow people to develop skills compatible with their identity. Among people with multiple-employer careers, this is by far the most significant source of their failure to construct a successful boundaryless career. Several of the women we interviewed appear to have fallen into this situation, as a result of frequently derailing their careers in order to follow their husbands. For some people, such behavior might be the expression of their identity, but the women we studied did not understand it this way.

Workers' modal responses to questions about how they make sense of their careers fall somewhere between the feeling that "I've never really put it all together before, like I just did for you," and, "It doesn't really make any sense, does it?" Even people who believe they can detect an individual, personally sensible pattern in their work histories generally told us that they don't feel they very strongly influenced the path their career has taken. This is a failure of self-efficacy. Only one person with more than seven years of work experience told us that her work history has been faithful to her vision of how she wanted to build her career.

The second threat to identity is almost exactly the opposite of the first—an inability to escape from a self-chosen rut.[5] We spoke several times with Curt (a person with multiple employers, high cumulation, low identity), who studied accounting in college, went into public accounting, became a CPA, and then a corporate controller. Fairly early in this process, Curt decided he would really like to be an operating manager, and made several attempts to move in that direction. However, he kept getting promoted into better and more lucrative financial jobs. He finally took a step down with his employer to get an operating-management job.

The third threat involved the interaction of identity and the emergence of a boundaryless career—escaping an old identity—can be understood by using the life-course concepts of control cycles, situational imperatives, and accentuation (Elder and O'Rand, 1995). Life-course theorists have suggested: "When social change creates a disparity between claims and resources, goals and accomplishments, the corresponding loss of control prompts efforts to regain control. The entire process resembles a control cycle—losing control is followed by efforts to restore control over life outcomes, a process featuring reactant behavior" (Elder and O'Rand, 1995: 468). Recall that our concept of identity is derived from the social psychological notion of self-efficacy. The idea of "losing control" can be directly interpreted, therefore, as an interruption, or breaching, of identity in one's career.

Situational imperatives are changes in circumstances that result in a substantial reduction in an individual's personal control (Elder and O'Rand, 1995: 468). Researchers have found that during times of transition, particularly during stressful periods, prominent individual characteristics tend to become even more pronounced. Elder and Caspi (1990) labeled this the "accentuation principle." When long-established identities are threatened, people tend to rely more heavily on what has worked in the past, rather than changing their sense of self, or searching productively for new ways of coping.

Many midcareer members in our sample may be characterized as people who are "still imbued with expectations of upward mobility and look . . . forward to mastering a job and then savoring the intrinsic and material satisfactions of seniority" (Mirvis and Hall, 1994: 386). These people believe that if they work hard and do a good job, then they will be able to build a career with a single employer, or a very limited number of employers. Maintaining a stable employment pattern is an important component of their identities, and they have some sense of control over their future.

Members of this group are often faced with a situational imperative, as changing patterns of employment may require that they try to continue building their careers across multiple employers, in the face of increased uncertainty about what constitutes competence. Violation of their sense of control over their careers and their future results in attempts to regain control. Major elements of what they believe to be their competencies include hard work, loyalty, and flexibility toward their employers. Over time and with previous employers, these competencies have been encouraged and rewarded. As the rules change, attempts to regain control may take place through a redoubling of hard work and loyalty, accentuating the traits that formerly improved their chances of success—just as these traits have lost their efficacy. Their identity is thus challenged, and they attempt to restore it by doing what used to work. We then have the sad specter of employees who are emphasizing loyalty at the very time their employers are devaluing it.

Who Wins on the Boundaryless Frontier?

We have focused on obstacles to the building of boundaryless careers. We may also ask: "Who is likely to succeed in turning the emergence of the boundaryless career into an opportunity?" In this section, we try to suggest some aspects of structural positioning that may contribute to the building of careers that include multiple employers, knowledge cumulation, and expressions of identity.

First, we would expect people who are beginning—or in the early stages of—their careers to have an advantage over people who are already established in organizationally bounded careers. One reason for this advantage is that people who have spent large amounts of time in bounded careers are unlikely to have developed the "meta-skills" (Hall, 1986; Mirvis and Hall, 1994) that are useful in learning from the experience of moving from employer to employer. These include the psychological skills stressed by Hall, as well as skills such as an ability to learn new roles quickly, and to operate effectively in the midst of the ambiguity that is common at the start of a new job.

People who self-consciously and reflexively build boundaryless careers from the beginning are more likely to avoid inappropriate attitudes and orientations than others. Such people will be less likely to develop some of the characteristics associated with successful bounded careers, such as unconditional loyalty, personal identification with an employer, and the potentially ill-considered belief that an employer will provide adequate skill development and acceptable career paths. The absence of these learned characteristics will make people less likely to accentuate personal characteristics at a time when they are most dysfunctional, such as when they are faced with changing situational imperatives.

Second, people who have started more recently—or will start in the future—to build boundaryless careers will probably fare better than those who started in an earlier era. To the extent that some of the institutional barriers to boundaryless careers, such as the lack of portability of pensions and health insurance, are reduced over time, people who are building boundaryless careers today have an advantage over those whose early careers were built under the old institutional order.

Third, the dynamics of household formation and dissolution play a role in making boundaryless careers more or less likely for men and women. Members of families consisting of two spouses with good jobs, each able to cover the other's insurance needs and pay the bills during spells of unemployment or reeducation, should be well positioned to attempt to build a boundaryless career. Such households, however, today constitute a minority of all American family units. About 55% of all households in the United States consist of a married couple (Ahlburg and De Vita, 1992). In 1940, almost 70% of families were traditional, "husband-employed, wife-homemaker" families, but by 1990, that figure had dropped to only 20% (Ahlburg and De Vita, 1992: 25).

The presence of school-age children may reduce a worker's willingness to move. The presence of both children and a nonworking spouse may reduce someone's willingness to make voluntary changes that appear to involve taking on the increased risk of spells of unemployment. The less each spouse is tied to the current geographic location, the more the other is able to take advantage of opportunities in other places. Sarah, one of our interviewees, followed her husband's career to several new locations, and was then promised that they would stay put for a few years, for her to develop her career. When her husband then accepted another transfer, Sarah remained behind and ended the marriage. Single parents with bad jobs are, of course, ill-positioned to construct boundaryless careers.

Fourth, people who have early careers in organizations that do not hold out the promise, or provide the internal structures, to support organizationally based careers may be more likely to learn quickly that there are rewards associated with changing jobs across employers. People who plan for, and make, changes voluntarily and opportunistically may thereby be less likely to end up losing work involuntarily, thus avoiding the associated stigma. Again, people who involuntarily lose work several years from now may find that it is has become less of a problem.

Fifth, because maintaining and building skills in a boundaryless career can be a continuous and time-consuming investment, we expect that people whose sense of identity is not involved in a variety of other time-consuming activities, such as parenting, hobbies, or community work, will be better positioned to take advantage of boundaryless-career opportunities. These people will be better able to give undiluted priority to their work lives.

Conclusions

A boundaryless career, in our view, is a work history that is high on all three career dimensions: identity, cumulation of knowledge, and multiple employers. We have argued that a potential long-term increase in boundaryless career behavior is being driven by people's responses to recent increases in flexible labor practices among employers, and that building a multiemployer career requires overcoming challenges to personal identity and cumulation of knowledge over time.

In her review of recent work on job mobility and career processes, Rosenfeld (1992: 53–54) called for greater incorporation of life-course concepts into this literature. In this chapter, we have borrowed from life-course theory to help us understand the emergence of changes in employer behavior, which were followed by changes in the behavior of those attempting to build careers.

We find that flexible employment practices are broadly seen as fully legitimate, and that boundaryless careers are probably becoming more accepted. Institutional and political inertia in such areas as pensions and insurance continue to be a problem, particularly for members of older cohorts.

We have speculated about what types of personal and social resources might position some people to take good advantage of current changes in patterns of employment and careers. People in younger cohorts should be able to take advantage of institutional changes, and we predict such changes will move in the direction of providing better support for multiple-employer careers. Younger workers will also be learning their career-management skills and metaskills during a time when a boundaryless career is less anomalous than it was during the early careers of people in older cohorts. Because of the increased career-long personal investment required for success on the boundaryless frontier, people with a single-minded focus and an identity built mainly around their work should be well positioned for successful boundaryless careers.

Changes in people's career values and behavior reflect alterations in the human resource environments in which organizations operate. Over time, some organizations will become better at attracting and utilizing boundaryless-career builders, and some organizations will become worse. This may lead to the emergence of differences in organizational forms. We speculate that organizations that make effective use of interorganizationally mobile workers may be characterized by intensive use of temporary project teams and recruitment of employees through social networks.

The challenge of building a boundaryless career may lessen significantly during the next decade or two. Over long periods of time, we expect that structural changes in employment patterns will both influence and be influenced by changes in cultural and institutional conditions. Thus, for example, any history of changes in women's patterns of labor-force participation over the last century would have to take into account the interaction of changes in opportunities, achievement, ideology, regulatory frameworks, and the ways young women are brought up and educated, with all of these occurring in varying contexts of resistance and inertia. If flexible-employment practices continue to develop, we expect to see reciprocal influences between the institutions that develop around boundaryless careers, the expectations and values that employees bring to their jobs, and employment patterns within and among organizations.

Notes

1. This dimension is very similar to DeFillippi and Arthur's (1994: 309) notion of "know-how," and is nearly identical to Bird's (1994: 309) concept of careers as repositories of knowledge.

2. These two aspects of identity are reflected in Hall's concept of "psychological success," which "refers to the experience of achieving goals that are personally meaningful to the individual, rather than those set by parents, peers, an organization, or society" (Mirvis and Hall, 1994: 366).

3. We believe that this concept is similar to Arthur's (1994: 302) concept of "enterprise," to DeFillippi and Arthur's (1994) notion of "knowing why," and to Bird's (1994) discussion of the blurring of work and private lives among entrepreneurs.

4. In general, though, we think age is an important variable. Recent research has documented the increasing variability and ambiguity of retirement processes (Henretta, 1992; O'Rand and Henretta, 1982), and we consider this to be part of the overall emergence of careers as boundaryless. We would also expect age itself to influence career activities through its impact on health, vitality, and changing priorities. In our discussion, age should not be confused with career stage; although there is obvious overlap, the two variables have independent effects.

5. We suspect that failure to construct a successful boundaryless career, due to this type of identity failure, is harder to detect than other failures, especially in personal interviews. We will refrain from discussing the thorny issues involved in trying to decide under what conditions people might be confused about whether they have achieved a sense of identity in their careers. For our exploratory research, we have taken them at their word.

References

Ahlburg, Dennis A., and Carol J. De Vita. 1992. "New realities of the American family." *Population Bulletin* 47 (2). Washington, D.C.: Population Reference Bureau.

Althauser, Robert P., and Arne L. Kalleberg. 1981. "Firms, occupations, and the structure of labor markets: A conceptual analysis." Pp. 119–149 in Ivar Berg (ed.), *Sociological Perspectives on Labor Markets.* New York: Academic Press.

Arthur, Michael B. 1994. "The boundaryless career: A new perspective for organizational inquiry." *Journal of Organizational Behavior* 15: 295–605.

Bandura, Albert. 1977. "Self-efficacy: Toward a unifying theory of behavioral change." *Psychological Review* 84 (2): 191–215.

Belous, Richard S. 1989. "How human resource systems adjust to the shift toward contingent workers." *Monthly Labor Review* (March): 7–12.

Bird, Allan. 1994. "Careers as repositories of knowledge: A new perspective on boundaryless careers." *Journal of Organizational Behavior* 15: 325–344.

Brodsky, Melvin M. 1994. "Labor market flexibility: A changing international perspective." *Monthly Labor Review* (November): 53–60.

DeFillippi, Robert J., and Michael B. Arthur. 1994. "The boundaryless career: A competency-based perspective." *Journal of Organizational Behavior* 15: 307–324.

Elder, Glen H., Jr., and A. Caspi. 1990. "Studying lives in a changing society: Sociological and personological explorations." Pp. 201–247 in A. I. Rabin; R. S. Zucker; R. A. Emmons; and S. Frank (eds.), *Studying Persons and Lives*. New York: Springer.

Elder, Glen H., Jr., and Angela M. O'Rand. 1995. "Adult lives in a changing society." Pp. 452–475 in Karen S. Cook; Gary Alan Fine; and James S. House (eds.), *Sociological Perspectives on Social Psychology*. Boston: Allyn and Bacon.

Foster, Ann C. 1994. "Portability of pension benefits among jobs." *Monthly Labor Review* (July): 45–50.

Gecas, Viktor. 1986. "The motivational significance of self-concept for socialization theory." *Advances in Group Processes* 3: 131–156.

Gecas, Viktor, and Peter J. Burke. 1995. "Self and identity." Pp. 4–67 in Karen S. Cook; Gary Alan Fine; and James S. House (eds.), *Sociological Perspectives on Social Psychology*. Boston: Allyn and Bacon.

Gecas, Viktor, and Monica A. Seff. 1989. "Social class, occupational conditions and self-esteem." *Sociological Perspectives* 32: 353–364.

Gergen, Kenneth J. 1991. *The Saturated Self: Dilemmas of Identity in Contemporary Life*. Basic Books.

Hall, Douglas T. 1971. "A theoretical model of career subidentity development in organizational settings." *Organizational Behavior and Human Performance* 6: 50–71.

Hall, Douglas T. 1986. "Breaking career routines: Midcareer choice and identity development." Pp. 120–159 in Douglas T. Hall et al. (eds.), *Career Development in Organizations*. San Francisco: Jossey-Bass.

Harrison, Bennett. 1994. *Lean and Mean: The Changing Landscape of Corporate Power in the Age of Flexibility*. New York: Basic Books.

Henretta, J. C. 1992. "Uniformity and diversity: Life course institutionalization and late-life exit." *Sociological Quarterly* 33: 265–279.

Lawlor, Julia. 1994. "Boom in temp-worker hiring eases." *USA Today* (February 28): 4B.

Lewin, Kurt. 1936. "The psychology of success and failure." *Occupations* 14: 926–930.

Miles, Raymond E., and Charles C. Snow. 1995. "The new network firm: A spherical structure built on a human investment philosophy." *Organizational Dynamics* (spring): 5–18.

Mirvis, Philip H. and Douglas T. Hall. 1994. "Psychological success and the boundaryless career." *Journal of Organizational Behavior* 15: 365–380.

Mortimer, Jeylon T., and Jon Lorence. 1979. "Occupational experience and the self-concept: A longitudinal study." *Social Psychology Quarterly* 42: 307–323.

O'Rand, Angela M., and J. C. Henretta. 1982. "Delayed career entry, industrial pension structure, and retirement in a cohort of unmarried women." *American Sociological Review* 47: 365–373.

Rosenfeld, Rachel A. 1992. "Job mobility and career processes." *Annual Review of Sociology* 18: 39–61.

Schor, Juliet B. 1991. *The Overworked American: The Unexpected Decline of Leisure*. New York: Basic Books.

Swinnerton, Kenneth A., and Howard Wial. 1995. "Is job stability declining in the U.S. economy?" *Industrial and Labor Relations Review* 48, 2: 293–304.

Taylor, M. Susan, and Cristina A. Giannantonio. 1993. "Forming, adapting and terminating the employment relationship: A review of the literature from individual, organizational and interactionist perspectives." *Journal of Management* 19, 2: 461–515.

Weigert, Andrew J. 1988. "To be or not: Self and authenticity, identity and ambivalence." Pp. 263–281 in Daniel T. Hall et al. (eds.), *Self, Ego and Identity: Integrative Approaches*. New York: Springer-Verlag.

Wilensky, Harold L. 1961. "Orderly careers and social participation: The impact of work history on social integration in the middle mass." *American Sociological Review* 30: 521–539.

9

Careers as Repositories of Knowledge: Considerations for Boundaryless Careers

ALLAN BIRD

The traditional notion of a career as something that occurs within a single firm, or that consists of an obvious sequence of positions, no longer holds. In fact, one response to the appearance of boundaryless firms is the increasing growth in what has come to be known as boundaryless careers. To fully understand the implications of these emerging trends, a new perspective is required.

This chapter argues for a reconceptualization of careers that would consider them repositories of knowledge (Arthur, 1992), shifting emphasis away from work experience per se and to the information and knowledge that is created therefrom.

Defining *career* is not easy. Within the disciplines of psychology, sociology, political science, economics, history and geography, Arthur, Hall, and Lawrence (1989) identify 11 separate descriptions of what constitutes a career. Common to all of these definitions is the notion that a career is "the evolving sequence of a person's work experiences over time" (Arthur et al., 1989: 8).

However, work experiences do not a career make. In its deeper meaning, *career* conveys more than a chronology of positions held. The element missing in traditional definitions of careers can be found in the information and knowledge acquired as a result of an evolving sequence of work experiences.

I define careers as accumulations of information and knowledge embodied in skills, expertise, and relationship networks that are acquired through an evolving sequence of work experiences over time. Although work experiences constitute the primary mechanism through which careers occur, they do not in themselves represent career. The nature or quality of a career is indeed defined by the information and knowledge that is accumulated.

Syntactic and Semantic Aspects of Careers

One way of understanding the relationship between knowledge and work experiences, within the context of careers, is to borrow two word concepts: syntax and semantics. *Syntax* refers to "the way in which words are put together to form phrases, clauses, or sentences" (*Merriam Webster's Collegiate Dictionary*, 1977: 1183), whereas semantics has to do with meaning or content. The syntactic aspect of a career is its structure, which is exhibited in the career's sequence of work experiences. Most of the research on careers addresses syntactic aspects. For example, Rosenbaum's (1984) study of careers among a cohort of nearly 4,000 workers in a single large firm analyzes them in terms of such things as the number of hierarchical levels involved in advances and the length of stay at each level. These dimensions represent structural aspects of an individual career.

A syntactic view of careers assumes universality and reduces contextual dependency. All careers possess properties such as the length of time in a given position, and this can be interpreted without necessarily referring to situational factors, such as the nature of the position, or where it is located within the firm. Even when situational factors are included, these are still often syntactic qualities because they delineate the structure of a career.

In contrast, the semantic aspect of careers addresses their content: It is concerned with the content and meaning of work experiences. Semantic aspects of careers are not easily universalized—they are inextricably embedded in context. The content of a career is located in what is learned from experiences—in the information, knowledge, and perspectives that are acquired or changed over time, as a result of the experiences. For example, two employees might both work for three years as tellers in the same bank. The syntactic aspects of their careers are similar—the same position, the same bank, the same length of time. In semantic terms, however, there may be substantial differences as a result of the specific relationship networks developed, skills acquired, and expertise accumulated.

It is important to point out that the syntax-semantics contrast is not the same as the subjective-objective-view distinction suggested by Hughes (1937). *Syntax* in this case denotes the form or structure of the career, which may be similar to Hughes's objective view of a career. However, semantics is not concerned with the *meaning* of a career in the subjective sense of an interpretation of work experiences, but with the content of a career.

Nor is the conceptualization of careers as repositories of knowledge a simple reaffirmation of the importance of personal career development or of the potential that work experiences provide for self-realization (Shepard, 1984). It focuses on individual and organizational learning, particularly the cumulation of individual knowledge through work experiences. Moreover, it directs attention away from factors that have traditionally been of interest to careers researchers, and to hitherto unaddressed factors such as how one's knowledge relates to the firm; how work experiences are integrated and synthesized; or how the knowledge accumulated can be applied in new ways.

Careers and Firms as Knowledge Creators

The notion of careers as repositories of knowledge is consistent with recent theoretical developments coming from Japan (Itami, 1988; Kagono, Nonaka, Sakakibara, and Okumura, 1985; Nonaka and Takeuchi, 1995). Two streams of work are particularly relevant to our consideration of the career concept.

Itami (1988) analyzes the strategic ramifications of information, concluding that competition is based on differentiation between firms. Regardless of whether firms compete on the basis of cost, quality, or product differentiation, a firm's chosen strategy is essentially aimed at making its products or services different from those of its competitors. The ability to differentiate is embodied in a firm's information. Ultimately, all advantages are informational—in the form of a routine or process; in the form of an organizing structure; or in the form of a product or service.

One implication of this perspective for career theory is that to remain competitive and ensure the ability to differentiate, firms must develop their employees in ways that enhance the supply of information and knowledge within the firm. Employees add value by creating information through their work experiences. Firms accomplish this by structuring work experiences: Job rotation, on-the-job training, and the development of relationship networks within and outside the firm comprise ways in which knowledge embedded in individual careers can be shaped to serve a firm's information needs.

A second line of research (Nonaka and Takeuchi, 1995) challenges the fundamental assumptions underlying U.S.-based organization theory, which is predicated on a belief that firms are processors of information. The key activity of managers is the use of information in making decisions that direct firm activities. The concern noted is with how managers use information in the light of bounded rationality (March and Simon, 1956), localized alternative-information searching, and sequential attention to multiple firm objectives (Cyert and March, 1963).

In contrast, Nonaka and Takeuchi (1995) view the primary function of a firm as knowledge creation. Firms create knowledge by shaping employees' first-hand work experiences and then drawing out this experiential learning in ways that allow it to be shared throughout the firm. The key activity of managers is to give direction to the knowledge-creating activities of employees. As with Itami (1989), the implication is that firms remain competitive by creating knowledge, and that employee experiences are critical to that process.

Explicit Knowledge and Tacit Knowledge

Discussion of careers as repositories of knowledge requires a consideration of how knowledge is created, and the way in which the knowledge creation process within firms relates to individual careers. We will begin by first comparing two types of knowledge.

Explicit knowledge can be transmitted to others through formal, systematic language (Polanyi, 1966). It is impersonal and independent of context. A mathematical equation is explicit knowledge because it conveys knowledge by means of a language that is impersonal (it is not rooted in any person or situation), formal (there are rules governing the structure of equations), and systematic (mathematical symbols are used).

In contrast, tacit knowledge refers to the understanding embedded in people's experiences, which is difficult to communicate to others. It is necessarily personal because it is attained through firsthand experiences and is deeply rooted in action and commitment (Nonaka, 1991a). It is accessible to its possessor primarily in the form of intuition, speculation, and feeling. Tacit knowledge is the sum of an individual's understanding, as described by Polanyi when he states, "We know more than we can tell" (1966: 4).

Two aspects of tacit knowledge are relevant to its application to careers. First, tacit knowledge has a cognitive dimension that is reflected in traditional beliefs, paradigms, schemata, or mental models (Nonaka 1990). This cognitive dimension helps us make sense of the world around us, influencing how we perceive and define the world. The second is a technical dimension that consists of skills, crafts, and know-how that are situation-specific. Most tacit knowledge, particularly the cognitive dimension, remains beyond our ability to make it explicit (Winogard and Flores, 1986).

Types of Knowledge Creation

There is a difference between information and knowledge. Information may be thought of as an acquired asset ("flow") and knowledge as a base ("stock"). For example, someone may explain to me the proper way to write an essay. As I receive the explanation, I am acquiring information, but the information imparted to me comprises only a portion of the knowledge I have. Another portion comes from me. In the process of receiving, categorizing, and interpreting the information provided, it is personalized—that is, it is transformed into something different and new, as a result of being joined together with what I already know, and of being colored by the specific context in which I receive it. In other words, when I hear someone's explanation, new information is acquired and knowledge is created.

Nonaka (1991a) argues that the interplay between tacit and explicit knowledge gives rise to the creation of new knowledge. He identifies four types of knowledge creation (see Figure 9.1).

1. Tacit to Tacit. One form of knowledge creation involves the transmittal of tacit knowledge between individuals. When an apprentice, for example, studies under a master craftsman, learning occurs not only through spoken words or instructions, but through observation and imitation as well. Socialization of the apprentice leads to knowledge creation through the expansion of the knowledge base to someone new, who modifies what is learned with their own understanding. Because it remains as something "more than can be told," however, socialization leads to little actual new knowledge being created. Moreover, the transmittal itself is time consuming and not easily delivered to many people.

2. Explicit to Explicit. Explicit knowledge can be easily transmitted—its explicitness makes it easy to combine with other knowledge. Bringing items of

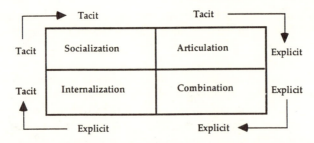

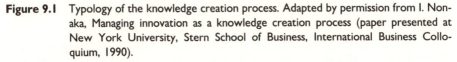

Figure 9.1 Typology of the knowledge creation process. Adapted by permission from I. Nonaka, Managing innovation as a knowledge creation process (paper presented at New York University, Stern School of Business, International Business Colloquium, 1990).

explicit knowledge together is indeed referred to as "combination." For example, collecting information about the financial performance of various business units brings about the creation of new knowledge: how the firm as a whole is performing. Although combination creates new knowledge through synthesis, as in tacit-to-tacit knowledge transmittals, the volume of new knowledge created tends to be small.

The most profound knowledge creation occurs when knowledge changes from tacit to explicit or from explicit to tacit. It is at this nexus that individual careers, as reflected in work experiences, have the potential to make significant contributions to firms.

3. Tacit to Explicit. The conversion of tacit knowledge to explicit knowledge—"articulation"—is significant because it makes possible the sharing of knowledge that was previously inaccessible. In a furniture company, when a master cabinetmaker is able to articulate the thinking and techniques behind a particular style of woodworking, that information can be widely disseminated within the firm. Designers can incorporate this newly created knowledge into future products, or other cabinetmakers can produce pieces of comparable workmanship.

4. Explicit to Tacit. When employees acquire explicit knowledge and then apply it to their own unique situations, the result is an expansion of their tacit-knowledge base. This "internalization" leads to a reframing of knowledge that constitutes knowledge creation in its own right. Moreover, the transference from explicit to tacit leads to self-renewal and deepens commitment. A total self-renewal of the individual employees constitutes a self-renewal of the firm itself. The tacit-to-tacit and explicit-to-tacit knowledge creation types may appear similar in some ways. The difference between socialization and internalization lies in the primary informational source contributing to knowledge creation. In the tacit-to-tacit quadrant (socialization), the primary information source contributing to new knowledge creation is the master. New knowledge is being created through replication, with the receiver's knowledge base contributing little. In the explicit-to-tacit quadrant, it is the receiver's knowledge base that contributes the bulk of the information, while the explicit serves as a leavening agent, obliging the receiver to see things in a different light or think in a different way.

Nonaka (1991b) outlines how each type of knowledge creation plays itself out, in his description of how a product-development team at the Matsushita Electric Company created a new bread-making machine for the home. Though a prototype had been developed, the bread it produced was considered unacceptable, with a hard crust and a doughy inside. One team member, Ikuko Tanaka, suggested that the company study the technique of the Osaka International Hotel's baker, who had a reputation for making excellent bread. As an apprentice with the baker, Tanaka noticed that he used a distinctive technique of stretching the dough when kneading it. Returning to the product-development team, Tanaka shared her insights. After several modifications in the design, Matsushita developed the "twist dough" method. The new machine set a sales record for kitchen appliances. Nonaka continues:

1. First, [Ikuko Tanaka] learns the tacit secrets of the Osaka International Hotel baker [socialization].
2. Next, she translates these secrets into explicit knowledge that she can communicate to her team members and others at Matsushita [articulation].
3. The team then standardizes this knowledge, putting it together into a manual or workbook and embodying it in a product [combination].
4. Finally, through the experience of creating a new product, Tanaka and her team members enrich their own tacit knowledge base [internalization]. In particular, they come to understand in an extremely intuitive way that products like home bread-making machines can provide genuine quality. That is, the machine must make bread that is as good as that of a professional baker. (1991b: 99)

Although all four types of knowledge creation are useful and contribute to firms, articulation and internalization are the most critical types because they provide greater benefit over time. Both are also the most critical for individuals because the self must be actively involved: first, in articulating one's understanding of things; and second, in internalizing what is learned, thereby changing one's own knowledge.

The Knowledge-Creation Process

The last piece of the puzzle involves the process by which knowledge creation is activated. Nonaka (1991a) suggests that the process occurs across three organizational levels, with each exhibiting critical properties that contribute to the overall process. These are presented in Table 9.1.

1. **The Individual Level.** The individual level is characterized by action and reflection, with the critical property being autonomy. Individuals need freedom to combine action and thought in using their own discretion. Autonomy allows for experimentation—trial and error—in both action and thought. Actions can clarify thoughts, and thoughts can make sense of actions (Weick 1979). The product of interplay between thought and action is the extension of an individual's tacit-knowledge base and is reflected in intuitive approaches to problem solving.

Table 9.1   Levels of Organizational Knowledge Creation

Level	Critical Property	Factors Related to Knowledge Creation
Firm	Structure	Competitive resource allocation
Group	Interaction	Direct dialogue
Individual	Autonomy	Action and deliberation

SOURCE: Adapted, by permission, from I. Nonaka, Managing the firm as an information creation process. In *Advances in Information Processing in Organizations*, Vol. 4 (Greenwich, Conn.: JAI Press, 1991), pp. 239–275.

2. The Group Level. Discussion encourages the drawing out of tacit knowledge. The critical property at this level is interaction. In a dialogue, ideas must be made concrete. It is a dynamic process in which members try out various interpretations and meanings (Nonaka 1991a). Through discussion, unity and coherence in meaning and understanding converge in an explicit form, which, by extension, others can understand and assimilate.

3. The Firm Level. At the firm level, the critical property is structure. Structure moderates the extent and nature of relationships between groups, as well as the degree of autonomy available to individuals. Structure also serves as a regulating mechanism in resource allocation. A particular group's access to money, materials, or people gives direction to the nature of interaction in the knowledge-creation process. Competition for resources acts as a stimulus for knowledge creation that benefits the firm and promotes greater access to resources.

The knowledge-creation process requires the critical properties of all three levels, if it is to be effective. A situation of individual autonomy without interaction leads to an inability to articulate tacit knowledge. In the absence of structure and the influence of resource allocation, individual autonomy and group interaction lead to knowledge creation that may have little value for the firm.

Careers and Knowledge Creation

If we envision careers as accumulations of knowledge embodied in the skills, expertise, and relationship networks that are acquired through an evolving sequence of work experiences over time, the view of firms as knowledge creators suggests several implications. First, it emphasizes the semantic aspects of a career: what changes have occurred in the four knowledge-creation types—that is, what new knowledge was created.

The juxtaposition of a new conception of careers with a notion of firms as knowledge creators leads to a greater emphasis on the experiential dimension of careers. A career is no longer a sequence of positions; rather, it must be thought of in terms of work experiences themselves, which are not coextensive with given positions. In Nonaka's (1991b) example of the bread-maker development team, Tanaka experienced all four knowledge creation types, in the process greatly expanding her knowledge, skills, expertise, and relationship network.

Under the traditional definition, Tanaka's membership in the development team constituted one position in a sequence of work experiences. Such a characterization devalues the significance of the variety of experiences she had, along with the impact they are likely to have on subsequent work experiences.

Viewing careers as knowledge repositories requires a change in approach in studying the syntactic aspect of careers. Rather than focusing on positions or jobs, the structure of careers should be studied in terms of events that affect an individual's store of knowledge. The four knowledge creation types provides one taxonomy for classifying work experiences. Indeed, Tanaka's experiences with the development team provide an example of how the taxonomy can be applied. Her experiences further suggest that there may be cycles or patterns of work experiences that are relevant to the evolution of a career.

A further implication of this approach is that it provides an integrated view of careers. Historically, theories of career have adopted one of two models (Rosenbaum, 1989): An individualistic model argues that individuals are the motive actors determining career direction; in contrast, the structural model contends that careers are an aspect of the structure of a firm and are determined by firm policies and internal labor markets (Slocum, 1974). These two models become integrated, and the relationship between the two is made transparent, when firms are viewed as knowledge creators. Individuals are the main agents of change, because it is their action and thought that give rise to newly created knowledge. Simultaneously, experiences are context-specific, and it is firms that provide the structure within which experiences occur. The individual and the firm are inextricably linked.

Thinking about careers as repositories of knowledge is not without its challenges. Several issues remain that, though beyond the scope of this chapter, warrant discussion here. First, we need to address the relationship between knowledge creation and traditional career outcomes—that is, promotions, plateaus, and salaries. It is reasonable to conclude that there is some relationship between knowledge creation and enhancing one's status, as well as improving chances for promotion. Given current downsizing trends, the demand for increased individual contributions to a firm's value-added activities has the effect of tightening the connection between individual knowledge creation and career outcomes.

Boundaryless Careers

The notion of boundaryless careers emerges in response to the common view of careers as being bounded: in firms; and in well-defined roles, positions, or jobs. Recent developments in information and telecommunications technology, organizational forms, labor markets, and changing personal values confirm that a view of careers as taking place solely within firms is no longer sufficient to encompass the increasing range of work experiences that people currently encounter (Keichel, 1995).

This section discusses the implications of boundaryless careers for a knowledge-oriented view of careers and firms, and vice versa. Attention is given to how such careers may affect knowledge acquisition by the individual and firm. Three lines of inquiry are pursued. The first asks, "What are the implications of boundaryless careers for different types of knowledge creation?" The second pursues the question of how boundaryless careers may affect the process of knowledge creation—specifically, how such careers may influence autonomy at the individual level, interaction at the group level, and structure and values at the firm level. The third reverses the question and asks, "What are the implications of a knowledge perspective for boundaryless careers?"

The Effect of Boundaryless Careers on Types of Knowledge Creation

Socialization (Tacit to Tacit)

Tacit-to-tacit knowledge transmittal is characterized by observation, imitation, and practice. Socialization creates new knowledge through the transmittal of skills and expertise, as well as values and ways of understanding. This activity is frequently carried out within firms, particularly with regard to new members. New employees, formally and informally, learn the ropes and acquire a sense of how things work. Specialized skills and knowledge may be passed on through apprenticeships and informal on-the-job training. Problems with the transference of tacit knowledge arise when employees shorten their stay. Older, knowledgeable employees may leave, taking their tacit knowledge with them, before passing it on to those who follow. Newer employees may stay for a shorter period, discouraging older employees from investing time in passing on knowledge. The result may be an erosion of company knowledge stores over time.

The research on newcomers (Louis, 1980) suggests another potential difficulty: Newcomer experiences consist primarily of tacit-to-tacit knowledge transmittal. Individuals who find themselves entering new firms frequently may develop rich stores of tacit knowledge, as a result of experiencing a variety of socialization events. However, transitions are stressful and as they accumulate, people are inclined to resist learning new ways (Storti, 1989). Knowledge creation through socialization interactions may thus diminish as the number of job changes rises. The marginal increase in one's knowledge may approach zero.

The most critical forms of knowledge imparted through socialization are traditional beliefs, paradigms, or mental models. These are embedded in organizational cultures and are evident in phrases such as "the IBM way of doing things." These sense-making structures give direction to knowledge creation activities.

In the case of boundaryless careers, the source of work experiences leading to an inculcation of traditional beliefs and paradigms becomes uncertain. Will an individual be with a firm long enough to acquire such learning, or will substitutes arise from somewhere else? Evidence from Silicon Valley, where interfirm mobility has historically been quite high, suggests that professional values and beliefs may substitute for organizational ones. Miner and Robinson (1994) suggest a related development, noting that some corporations serve as breeding grounds for managers in a given industry: Procter and Gamble and GE have performed this function in the past in their respective industries; GE and Proctor and Gamble managers were recruited by other firms, and then exerted strong

influence within the companies they entered. As boundaryless careers proliferate, it is unclear whether such companies can continue to serve as primary purveyors of tacit-to-tacit knowledge transfer.

The tacit-to-tacit knowledge transfer may also take place in reverse, with
new employees socializing current ones. Don Baylor's stint with the Boston Red
Sox is one unintended example of how this works (Arthur, 1994: 1):

> In 1986 the Boston Red Sox recruited an aging slugger named Don Baylor. It was
> clearly a short-term arrangement; the club wanted an experienced right-handed
> hitter, in return for which Baylor was offered a one-year contract and expected to
> be a relatively minor contributor to the team. Baylor, however, did more than
> expected. Claiming respect from both senior and junior players, he *quickly im-*
> *pressed his experience and personality upon the team.* It was Baylor who initiated
> a "kangaroo court" whereby players sat in judgment of their teammates' errors in
> the field, and imposed escalating fines for repeat offenders. Players took their self-
> discipline seriously, but inevitably in good spirit . . . . With Baylor as informal
> leader, the Boston Red Sox made it to the World Series. (Emphasis added)

Baylor passed on his tacit knowledge of how to play baseball, educating his
teammates and reframing their knowledge. Perhaps because of the emergence of
free agency and the specialized nature of skill development in professional
sports, similar cases of *intended* socialization are many. More recently, the NBA
Philadelphia 76ers acquired a 20–year-veteran center, Moses Malone, to develop their rookie franchise player, Shawn Bradley—Malone's job is to tutor
Bradley in the NBA style of play.

Combination (Explicit to Explicit)

In an era of boundaryless careers, work experiences of the explicit-to-explicit
knowledge transfer type are likely to diminish greatly. To a large extent, knowledge creation through the combining of information that has already been made
explicit is an analytical exercise that can be carried out through the use of computers and expert systems. In fact, turning more of this type of activity over to
computers, automated systems, and expert systems frees people to concentrate
on the more dynamic tacit-to-explicit and explicit-to-tacit knowledge creation
undertakings (Nonaka, 1991a).

Articulation (Tacit to Explicit)

It is highly probable that the most critical form of knowledge creation that
individuals with boundaryless careers may undertake is that of articulation—
making explicit the tacit knowledge they bring to the different firms they work
in. Firms gain a competitive advantage through their ability to set themselves
apart from their competitors (Itami, 1988). As employees develop diverse bases
of tacit knowledge, they are able to help a company differentiate through the
articulation of that knowledge. Whether through downsizing or the adoption of
new organizational forms, the smaller size of firms heightens the importance of
any individual to a firm's differentiating activities.

One potential difficulty with frequent interfirm mobility is that tacit knowledge may not be fully or even adequately articulated before an individual moves

on. As Hedberg notes, "Complex, fast-moving industrial societies appear to afford bad conditions for learning" (1981: 13). Yet these are the conditions under which complete articulation of tacit knowledge is essential, because it is this knowledge that a firm requires.

Failure to fully articulate tacit knowledge may also lead to difficulties in dispersing that information throughout the company. GM experienced this problem when it tried to disseminate the knowledge acquired by GM managers who were seconded to NUMMI, the Toyota-GM joint venture (Keller, 1989). Due to a failure to make explicit what the managers knew about cooperative-management techniques, the lessons of NUMMI were misrepresented to, and misunderstood by, the rest of the company.

Internalization (Explicit to Tacit)

The increased interfirm mobility associated with the boundaryless career may also exert significant influence on how explicit knowledge is internalized. With frequent movement within or between firms, internalization of new knowledge may become divorced from the development of a commitment to a firm. The self-renewal that is derived from expanding one's tacit knowledge base may be seriously diminished.

Keller (1989) found an example of this: When it became apparent that the NUMMI plant was successful because of the cooperative-management techniques Toyota had introduced, GM managers and shop foremen from the Van Nuys plant were sent to learn the techniques; although Fremont GM managers were ready and able to teach the new techniques, Van Nuys employees could only stay for two weeks. This was an insufficient amount of time for them to absorb and internalize what they were learning. Upon their return to the Van Nuys plant, few managers were able to apply what they had learned; nor were their ways of understanding management-labor relations altered.

This example emphasizes the potential difficulty that boundaryless careers present for both firms and individuals. For the firm, employees may be less committed, and the application of new knowledge poorly implemented. For the employee, the result may be superficial mimicry, rather than internalization, with an accompanying loss of opportunity for self-renewal.

The Effect of Boundaryless Careers on the Knowledge-Creation Process

The impact of the boundaryless career may be even more dramatic when it comes to the process of knowledge creation, and the critical properties involved in that process. Influence is most obvious at the intersection of individual autonomy, group interaction, and firm structure and values.

The Individual Level

The boundaryless career brings about greater autonomy for the individual, granting wider discretion in both thought and action. Individuals become the main agents in career direction and progression. In turn, the responsibility to develop tacit knowledge falls squarely on the individual.

While increased freedom in work experiences offers a great opportunity, it also brings on great risks (Kanter, 1989). Autonomy in thought and action is necessary, however, since individuals may have difficulty in determining what work experiences will lead to *relevant* tacit knowledge. A critical aspect of the knowledge-creation perspective is that new knowledge should be of value in helping the firm to differentiate itself (Itami, 1988). The critical question is, "What sorts of tacit knowledge do firms need?" Heightened interfirm mobility will afford a greater opportunity for a fit between an individual's tacit knowledge and a variety of the firm's needs. Simultaneously, there is less clarity as to what types of knowledge fits individuals should pursue.

Another concern is the tendency individuals have for avoiding learning under complex or turbulent conditions (Hedberg, 1981). The uncertainty associated with greater freedom is likely to result in greater individual stress, leading, in turn, to a falling back on overlearned and first-learned behaviors. Rather than knowledge creation, individuals may end up locked into repetitive, dysfunctional behaviors.

The Group Level

Greater autonomy may lead to people's development of broader tacit-knowledge bases. But tacit knowledge is valuable only if it can be made explicit. This requires interaction with others. In the boundaryless career, interaction is more loosely structured, and is less likely to be situated within the firm. Instead, it occurs within a person's own network of acquaintances, across companies, or through professional gatherings and conferences, which have always been a venue for discussion. Lynn, Piehler, and Kieler (1993), for example, note that Japanese engineers have extensive interfirm networks that are an important conduit for the exchange of ideas and information. Japanese engineers are active in attending professional conferences, and these also serve as venues for dialogue and exchange. Similarly, Larsen (1993) found that many women entrepreneurs possessed extensive personal networks, which they used prolifically for information exchange and discussion.

The Firm Level

Boundaryless careers are also characterized by less structure (Kanter, 1989) and by fewer, weaker firm-based values. Although the influence of individual firms may wane, this does not mean that collective organizational influence will become insignificant. The presence of network organizations and complex webs of strategic alliances may impose a structure of its own. The analogy of bone and cartilage captures the difference between structure imposed by an individual firm, and that provided by a group of loosely connected firms: Single-firm structures tend to be rigid, while collective structures allow more flexibility. Rose and Ito (1993) describe such a situation in Japanese industrial groupings, when they note that webs of parent-subsidiary relationship create a family of firms that—because they all bear the "genetic imprint" of the original parent firm—

bear a strong resemblance to one another in underlying values and organizing principles. Careers within the family of firms may be boundaryless in that there is fluid movement between member companies. Nevertheless, the structure that shapes the knowledge-creating activities of individual careers is a weak one.

Firms may also exert influence over the values that give meaning to independent knowledge-creating actions by developing soft cultures. Kreiner and Schultz (1993) describe how EUREKA, a pan-European program established by 19 countries and the European Community in 1985, used symbols to infuse its members, who were separated by geography, nationality, and culture, with a common set of values and understandings. They describe symbols as functioning in three ways to bring people together and give them a sense of commonality and direction. Symbols served as categorizing devices, reorienting people's consciousness to what actions meant. The symbols also served as a magnetizing device, drawing people in with the opportunity for collaboration. In this sense, symbols serve as a signaling mechanism, bringing people to the firm through self-selection. Finally, symbols act as a licensing device allowing highly autonomous actors to proceed along disparate trajectories that appear to fragment the company. Symbols license such behaviors because they imply that the final objective is the same, and that eventually such trajectories will arc back and converge.

Kreiner and Schultz's (1993) work raises interesting questions about how boundaryless careers may be affected by soft cultures. Their findings also suggest that there may be substitutes for structure. These may exist in the form of collective organizational networks, as seen in Japan, or may grow out of professional or industry values and standards. DeFillippi and Arthur (in chapter 7 of this book) pick up on the latter possibility, by proposing a set of values that competency-based firms and boundaryless careers may share. These include preferences for voluntarism, market discipline, leverage, and collaboration. Educational training may also provide the underlying foundation for shaping knowledge creation in individual careers.

Using a Knowledge Perspective to Think about Boundaryless Careers

A knowledge creation perspective enlightens and enlarges our understanding of boundaryless careers, and the ways in which they may affect firms and the people who work in them. First, it provides a logic that integrates the phenomena of careers with the larger organizational context within which they take place. Second, it focuses attention on the semantic, or content, aspect of such careers, compelling both individuals and firms to address distinctions between careers in terms of what is learned.

The Knowledge Creation Logic of Boundaryless Careers

The complementary notions of competitive advantage being predicated on information, and of firms maintaining viability through knowledge creation, provide a framework for understanding boundaryless careers and their relationship to firms. Nonaka (1991) describes the organizational knowledge creation process in terms of three levels. With boundaryless careers, the levels may be blurred or may disappear, but the properties remain critical.

Structure

With the boundaryless career, structure is not imposed by any one firm, but by a group of firms. Boundaryless careers are marked by greater latitude as to where individuals can participate in knowledge-creating activities. Individuals define the structure within which they pursue their careers, doing so through the strategic choices they make about their career domain. Careers can be limited to a company, or to an industry, or not at all. The essential criteria for domain choice are driven by personal assessments about the fit between skills, expertise, and network- and knowledge creation opportunities.

Career-domain decisions are not made in a vacuum. The structure of a given industry or market affects the availablity of resources and their allocation, influencing, in turn, the knowledge creation activity possiblilities within an industry or market. Consequently, initial decisions about domain constrain future possibilities. In boundaryless careers, paths and trajectories are shaped not by fixed lattices within firms, but by available venues for knowledge creation, given the current state of one's knowledge base.

Interaction

For the boundaryless career, interaction occurs not just within the confines of firm-imposed groups, but also within one's professional and social networks, whose boundaries are not coterminous with those of any firm. Networks provide an opportunity for discourse, and a forum in which information can be gathered and disseminated. Although these activities are possible within the context of a traditional career within a single firm, with a boundaryless career, the choice of networks resides with the individual. There may be constraints on network choices, but greater latitude is likely.

Autonomy

More than anything else, boundaryless careers are characterized by autonomy. As a result, they have the potential to generate large quantities of tacit knowledge. While this may enlarge an individual's overall knowledge base, sorting out what knowledge is appropriate for a particular firm or job comprises a critical activity in the boundaryless career.

The Semantics of Boundaryless Careers

Thinking about boundaryless careers as knowledge repositories compels us to focus on firm and job changes in terms of the effect those changes have on an individual's opportunity to create or use knowledge. The motivation behind career moves may not be the need for more money or higher status. It may be an opportunity to learn new things, or to use what someone already knows but cannot apply in a current position. Individuals who voluntarily pursue such careers may be driven by a stronger desire to learn and experiment than those who do not.

A related consideration is how boundaryless careers may develop either within or between firms. Firms that impose rigid structural constraints on their knowledge-creating activities may inadvertently encourage people to cross over into other firms. Even at the height of their success, automotive firms in Detroit experienced higher rates of turnover than other manufacturing firms. The rigid structure of assembly-line work discouraged active mental involvement in the job (Cole, 1979), suggesting little opportunity for knowledge creation or use. Lower levels of turnover and higher levels of job involvement in Japanese automotive firms may be consequences of allowing for greater flexibility in knowledge creation activities. Quality-control circles and self-managed work groups afford workers greater autonomy and provide a location for interaction, both critical components in articulating tacit knowledge. Japanese companies may provide a venue for boundaryless careers within a single firm (Koike, 1994). In this case, the boundaryless aspect of the career is that the employee conceptualizes "a boundaryless future regardless of the structural constraints" (Arthur, 1994).

A knowledge perspective encourages us to confront the nature of work experiences, and what people and firms learn from them. Certain boundaryless careers may be associated more with specific types of knowledge creation. For example, boundaryless careers in Silicon Valley are probably driven by firms and individuals focused on articulation—the concern is with the tacit knowledge that an individual brings to the job, and how it can be made explicit with regard to a firm's special needs. By contrast, clerical temps, and firms that hire them, seem focused on combination—linking explicit knowledge. The temp brings in skills and expertise that are impersonal and independent of context, combining them with tasks that are standardized.

Not all boundaryless careers are voluntary choices (Fierman, 1994). Many people are forced into such careers due to downsizing and restructuring. Adjustment to boundarylessness, and the satisfaction one feels with a new career type, may stem from the type of knowledge creation one participates in. Internalization and articulation may be less stressful and may require less adjustment, because they entail highly personal experiences associated with development and growth. By contrast, socialization and combination may be more stressful and may require a greater adjustment.

If knowledge creation types are associated with certain types of boundaryless careers, then significant career events may occur during a transition from one knowledge creation type to another. Career plateaus may occur not when persons are locked in jobs, but when their knowledge creation activities rarely change.

Nonaka and Takeuchi (1995) suggest that the knowledge creation process occurs in a spiral fashion, cycling through each quadrant. The boundaryless career may play out this spiraling cycle across numerous firms. Perceptive individuals may find they are able to leverage the move from one firm to the next by identifying what type of knowledge creation they will be engaged in, thereby determining their contribution to the firm.

Boundaryless careers may also encourage people to adopt a more holistic way of thinking about their work. Dyer (1993) notes that entrepreneurial behavior often leads to a blurring of work and private lives. Individuals in boundaryless careers are more likely to see connections between work and nonwork activities, because repeated transitions break down the mental mind-sets that people establish when they are locked into structures and routines. Information gleaned from vocational and avocational experiences commingle more easily. An example of this is found in the experience of Tess in the movie *Working Girl*. She sees connections that others miss because she makes no distinction between work and nonwork. She develops an idea for a merger as a result of pooling information from work with that acquired through her hobby. She creates new knowledge by combining information about the needs of a client with those of a radio station—the knowledge that there is a fit between the two—leading to a mutually beneficial relationship.

Conclusion

The intersection of boundaryless careers and firms as knowledge creators brings us back to the notion of careers as repositories of knowledge, suggesting an additional permutation: boundaryless careers themselves as knowledge creators. This possibility raises several significant implications.

Knowledge creation within firms is predicated on autonomy, interaction, and structure, with each function being carried out at a different level. The role of managers is to coordinate knowledge-creation activities across levels (Nonaka and Takeuchi 1995). However, in boundaryless careers, individuals take over much of the "managerial" responsibility for creating knowledge—it is the individual who assumes responsibility for exploiting autonomy, generating interaction, and imposing structure.

This raises questions about the future function of firms and the managers within them. Keichel (1995) notes that in emerging network organizations, individuals self-organize and manage, remaining part of a project or a team only as long as they add value. As with everyone else, managers are viable only to the extent that they, too, contribute something unique. This is not to suggest that they are superfluous. Firms can contribute the structure and venue for knowledge creation. Managers can add value by proposing a vision that induces creativity; by delineating broadly defined organizational values; and by allocating resources. They can also provide arenas for a competition of ideas, advance new ideas themselves, and synthesize the real and the ideal. Nevertheless, it would appear that boundaryless careers greatly reduce the scope of a manager's duties, while simultaneously increasing the significance of that portion which remains.

In a related vein, boundaryless careers create tension in the juxtaposition of individuals' interests with those of the firm, when it comes to the coordination of knowledge-creating factors. Indeed, on whose behalf is the knowledge creation process being managed—firms or individuals? The answer would seem to be that tension is resolved naturally through a market discipline (see chapter 7 in this book) in which individual and firm are aligned through mutual self-interest, a sort of knowledge-creating "invisible hand." Particular careers and firms remain connected only insofar as they move in the same direction. The real gains and losses in knowledge may only become apparent at the community level.

Finally, the concept of firms as knowledge creators originated in Japan, where lifetime employment, job rotation, on-the-job training, intercompany secondment, intensive socialization, and an emphasis on employee development are all commonplace. Although Nonaka and Takeuchi (1995) argue that a knowledge creation approach is universal, and cite evidence from U.S. companies such as 3M and GE to support their cause, how well it applies is subject to debate. Their detailed analysis of Tanaka's experience and the subsequent multiplier effects for Matsushita are predicated on the basis of what might best be described as "quasi-boundaryless careers within a single firm." Whether the same effects yield for careers that cross firm boundaries remains to be seen. Bird and Beechler's analysis (1995) of managerial practices among Japanese subsidiaries in the United States indicates that many adopt a modified version of their Japanese approach, because of an inability to cope with the independent, self-reliant behavior of U.S. employees. Knowledge creation may take on a different dynamic when workers are highly individualistic and assume substantial responsibility for their careers.

The developments pushing more individuals into boundaryless careers may be greater than many are able to handle (Fierman, 1994). It is possible that only the more entrepreneurial ones will thrive; others will struggle to get by. In light of America's move toward an information society (Drucker, 1993), acquiring a deeper understanding of boundaryless careers, and how they relate to knowledge creation, should be among those items high on the lists of organizational scholars and practitioners alike.

References

Arthur, M. B. 1994. The boundaryless career: A new perspective for organizational inquiry. *Journal of Organizational Behavior*, 15: 295–306.

Arthur, M. B. 1992. East meets west again: Some thoughts about careers, cultures and competitiveness. Address delivered to the Academy of Management Meeting, Careers Division, Las Vegas, Nev.

Arthur, M. B.; Hall, D. T.; and Lawrence, B. S. 1989. *Handbook of Career Theory*. New York: Cambridge University Press.

Bird, A. and Beechler, S. 1995. Links between business strategy and human resource management strategy in U.S.-based Japanese subsidiaries: An empirical investigation. *Journal of International Business Studies*, 26: 23–46.

Cole, R. 1979. *Work, Mobility and Participation*. Berkeley: University of California Press.

Cyert, R., and March, J. 1963. *A Behavioral Theory of the Firm*. New York: McGraw-Hill.

Drucker, P. 1993. *Post-Capitalist Society*. Oxford, Eng.: Butterworth-Heineman.

Dyer, W. G., Jr. 1993. Toward a theory of entrepreneurial careers. Brigham Young University Working paper.

Fierman, J. 1994. The contingency work force. *Fortune,* January 24: 30–36.

Hedberg, B. 1981. How organizations learn and unlearn. In P. C. Nystrom and W. H. Starbuck (eds.), *Handbook of Organizational Design,* vol. 1: *Adapting Organizations to Their Environments,* pp. 3–27. New York: Oxford University Press.

Hughes, E.C. 1937. Institutional office and the person. *American Journal of Sociology,* 43: 404–413.

Itami, H. 1988. *Invisible Assets.* Tokyo: Toyo Keizai.

Kagono, T.; Nonaka, I.; Sakakibara, H.; and Okumura, A. 1985. *Strategic versus Evolutionary Management.* Amsterdam: Holland-Elsevier.

Kanter, R. M. 1989. Careers and the wealth of nations: A macro-perspective on the structure and implications of career forms. In M. B. Arthur; D. T. Hall; and B. S. Lawrence (eds.), *Handbook of Career Theory,* pp. 506–521. New York: Cambridge University Press.

Keichel, W. 1995. A manager's career in the new economy. *Fortune, April 4:* 68–72.

Keller, M. *Rude Awakening: The Rise, Fall, and Struggle for Survival of General Motors.* 1989. New York: HarperCollins.

Koike, K. Learning and incentive systems in Japanese industry. 1994. In M. Aoki, and R. Dore (eds.), *The Japanese Firm: Source of Competitive Strength,* pp. 41–65. New York: Oxford University Press.

Kreiner, K., and Schultz, M. 1993. Soft cultures: The symbolism of cross-border organizing. Paper presented at the Academy of Management Meeting, Managerial and Organizational Cognition Interest, Atlanta.

Larsen, A. 1993. The challenges of control, purpose, and definition of the entrepreneurial firm using a network approach. Paper presented at the Academy of Management Meeting, Careers Division, Atlanta.

Louis, M. R. 1980. Surprise and sense making: What newcomers experience in unfamiliar organizational settings. *Administrative Science Quarterly,* 25: 226–251.

Lynn, L. H.; Piehler, H. R.; and Kieler, M. 1993. Engineering careers, job rotation, and gatekeepers in Japan and the United States. *Journal of Engineering and Technology Management,* 10: 53–72.

March, J., and Simon, H. 1956. *Organizations.* New York: McGraw-Hill.

Merriam Webster's Collegiate Dictionary. 1977. Springfield, Mass.: Merriam-Webster.

Miner, A. S., and Robinson, D. F. 1994. Organizational and population level learning as engines for career transitions. *Journal of Organizational Behavior,* 15: 345–364.

Nonaka, I. 1991a. Managing the firm as an information creation process. *Advances in Information Processing in Organizations,* 4: 239–275. Greenwich, Conn.: JAI Press.

Nonaka, I. 1991b. The knowledge-creating company. *Harvard Business Review,* 69, 6: 96–104.

Nonaka, I. 1990. Managing innovation as a knowledge-creation process: A new model for a knowledge-creating organization. Paper presented at International Business Colloquium, New York University, Stern School of Business.

Nonaka, I., and Takeuchi, H. 1995. *The Knowledge-Creating Company.* New York: Oxford University Press.

Polanyi, M. 1966. *The Tacit Dimension.* London: Routledge and Kegan Paul.

Rose, E. L., and Ito, K. 1993. The genealogical structure of Japanese firms: Parent-subsidiary relationships. NYU Working Paper Series, Mgmt-93–94. New York University, Stern School of Business.

Rosenbaum, J. E. 1989. Organization career systems and employee misperceptions. In

M. B. Arthur; D. T. Hall; and B. S. Lawrence (eds.), *Handbook of Career Theory*, pp. 329–353. New York: Cambridge University Press.

Rosenbaum, J. E. 1984. *Career Mobility in a Corporate Hierarchy*. New York: Academic Press.

Shepard, H. A. 1984. On the realization of human potential: A path with a heart. In M. B. Arthur; L. Bailyn; D. J. Levinson; and H. A. Shepard, *Working with Careers*. New York: Graduate School of Business, Columbia University, pp. 25–46.

Slocum, W. 1974. *Occupational Careers*. Chicago: Aldine.

Stevenson, H. H., and Jarillo, C. 1990. A paradigm of entrepreneurship: Entrepreneurial management. *Strategic Management Journal*, 11(S): 17–28.

Storti, C. 1989. *The Art of Crossing Cultures*. Yarmouth, Maine: Intercultural Press.

Weick, K. E. 1979. *The Social Psychology Organizing*. Reading, Mass.: Addison-Wesley.

Winogard, T. and Flores, F. 1986. *Understanding Computers and Cognition*. Reading, Mass.: Addison-Wesley.

III

THE SOCIAL STRUCTURE OF BOUNDARYLESS CAREERS

This part highlights the role of the social structure of careers in organizing work. It emphasizes the idiosyncratic characteristics of interpersonal relations that can yield benefits for innovation, flexibility, and opportunities for new alliances. At the heart of the effects of social structure on careers is their role in providing a platform for discovery by combining pieces of knowledge formerly disconnected but now recombined into novel forms with newly realized advantages. Social capital has several dimensions, including networks to access resources, and opportunities for interaction that provide for discovery. Boundaryless careers can capitalize on both.

Jerry Ellig and Tojo Joseph Thatchenkery offer a distinctive view of economics and value creation in their "Subjectivism, Discovery, and Boundaryless Careers: An Austrian Perspective." Based on the Austrian school of economics, their approach emphasizes the primacy of subjective perception and the key role of discovery in shaping career decisions. This perspective highlights five shifts in career dynamics: from objectively to subjectively validated career paths, from task emphasis to outcome orientation, from universal competencies to more heterogeneous and contextual competencies, from vertical advancement to multidirectional growth, from separation to integration of individual and company missions. The essential point they suggest is that a career always had subjective meaning to the person experiencing it, but the opportunities for discovery were often quite limited. Less-bounded careers mean that flexible, market-based forms of organization reward, and are rewarded by, people discovering their own career paths.

Holly Raider and Ronald Burt portray how social capital, the extent to which people know other people, affects their access to knowledge and other resources. Their "Boundaryless Careers and Social Capital" uses "structural hole theory" to describe how networks create value by connecting otherwise disconnected or isolated people. Entrepreneurs, broadly defined, benefit particularly by connections that enhance their social capital. The interfirm movement characteristic of boundaryless careers facilitates formation of valuable social capital by enabling construction of structural hole networks and interfirm brokerage. Firms not only gain advantages by acquiring knowledgeable employees, but also gain access to further information and influence. Thus, Raider and Burt propose that firms can be appreciated as social structures, with social capital that can be developed and maintained.

In "Global Boundaryless Careers: Lessons from Chinese Family Business," Cherlyn Granrose and B. Leng Chua continue the discussion of social networks by comparing Euro-American boundaryless careers to the interdependent, entrepreneurial networks that comprise careers in Chinese family businesses. These two models differ in that the career unit is the extended Chinese family, rather than the autonomous individual. In the extended family, reputations are defined, and networks built, not only by the exchange of favors, but also by living up to obligations. Despite the hierarchical and centralized nature of Chinese family relationships, the extended family sponsors entrepreneurial careers and widespread international business success through a focus on collective, rather than individual, gains. Granrose and Chua highlight the role of network obligations, a neglected feature in social-network theory, but a factor that can create the predictability and trust that make network organizing beneficial.

Paul Hirsch and Mark Shanley also focus on social structure. But their concern is costs to victims of transitions from bounded to boundaryless careers, as reflected in their title, "The Rhetoric of "Boundaryless": Or How the Newly Empowered Managerial Class Bought Into Its Own Marginalization." They see shifts in the structure of industry and the changing competitive environment that undermine the "sunk costs" of older workers. They see network arrangements as calling for new boundaries in order to be effective. And they see freedom to develop one's career potential as limiting, rather than expanding, career opportunities. Moreover, they suggest the boundaryless career concept may be more applicable to the United States than to other cultures. In sum, they urge better calculation of boundaryless career costs and benefits for all members of the workforce.

The shifting social structure frees resources for new uses, but can restrict access for others. Our authors remind us that social structure is a moving target, changing locally and globally. All four chapters in part III invite broad revision of our normative assumptions about the effects of social structure. And all four suggest that to appreciate this dynamic structure requires an ongoing revision of our theorizing and assessments.

10

Subjectivism, Discovery, and Boundaryless Careers: An Austrian Perspective

JERRY ELLIG AND TOJO JOSEPH THATCHENKERY

A recent *Fortune* cover story featured the new antiorganization person: a young, intelligent, hotshot MBA from a top-rated school, who doesn't want to work for a company. Instead, at age 31, he runs his own interactive-software company. "Kissing Off Corporate America," the title of the cover story, is a trend sweeping elite American business schools:

- An Opinion Research Corp. survey recently found that just 1% of the 1,000 adult respondents would freely choose to be corporate managers.
- In 1989, nearly 70% of Stanford's MBAs joined big companies. In 1994, only about half did so.
- At the University of Chicago, placement officials couldn't find enough candidates to fill up a day's worth of interviews when the cream of corporate America showed up. (Labich 1995)

All in all, it looks like William H. Whyte's (1956) "organization man" is in a midlife crisis.

Journalists' accounts link the organization man's midlife crisis to economic change. Yet perhaps paradoxically, economics has had little influence on scholars' understanding of career dynamics. Traditionally, psychology and sociology dominated the field of career studies (Van Maanen, 1977: 6–9). The relative silence of economists may have occurred because mainstream economics, under the influence of behaviorism and positivism, largely ceded the study of human perceptions and creativity to the other social sciences (McCloskey, 1983). One notable exception is the "Austrian school" of economics. Austrian economics views marketplace activity as an evolutionary process of adaptation and learning. To explain human behavior, scholars in this tradition seek to understand the intentions and purposes of the actors who are the subject of study. This focus on evolution and perception sets Austrians apart from mainstream economists, and it also offers new insights into the meaning and causes of boundaryless careers.

An Austrian approach to career theory can be summarized in the following propositions:

· A boundaryless career is subjectively defined by the career actor, who continually discovers new opportunities to develop and apply his or her abilities.
· Careers are less bounded now, because individuals have greater opportunities and rewards for discovering new career paths.
· These opportunities are the inevitable results of the market-based organizational changes that are required to accommodate knowledge-intensive work.

Two Austrian Concepts of Career Behavior

Austrian economists trace their roots to Carl Menger, a mid-nineteenth century theorist. The label *Austrian* was originally a pejorative term applied to Menger and his followers by economists of the German Historical School. The Austrians, like earlier classical and contemporary neoclassical economists, argued that deductive theorizing is an indispensable tool of economic analysis. The Historical School, in contrast, rejected deduction (and the idea of universal theories), in favor of ad hoc induction from historical and statistical studies.

Austrians accept many of the basic tenets of contemporary economic theory, such as the idea that people respond to incentives and try to do the best they can for themselves. However, Austrian economists also embrace some insights that differentiate them from mainstream economics. The two Austrian concepts most relevant to career studies are radical subjectivism, and discovery in a world of uncertainty.

Radical Subjectivism

The term *boundaryless career* describes careers that cross organizational boundaries, cross traditional boundaries within the organization, involve allegiance to a profession outside the organization, utilize networks of relationships that cross organizations, or involve extraoccupational considerations, such as the family. "Perhaps a sixth meaning," Arthur (1994: 296) suggests, "depends on the interpretation of the career actor, who may perceive a boundaryless future regardless of structural constraints." (See also Barley 1989: 49; Van Maanen, 1977.) Austrian economics takes this sixth meaning as the starting point in understanding career behavior. To understand the career choices that people make, we must understand how people perceive the various opportunities and courses of action. This method of inquiry is known as "subjectivism."

Virtually all economists say they are subjectivists. What most mean is that they assume individuals have subjective preferences and desires. People want different things with different intensities, and it is not possible to quantitatively compare the intensity of the same desire among different people. Goods and services, meanwhile, have value only to the extent that they fulfill some human need. The value that people attach to various things depends on the importance of the needs that the different things fulfill (Menger, 1981: 114–174). Economists call this insight the "subjective theory of value," and it is generally recognized as a major advance over the theories of classical economics, which sought measures of objective value for all goods.

Austrian subjectivism is much more extensive. Scholars in this tradition agree that individuals' preferences are subjective, but they don't stop there. In their view, the fundamental economic problem is not merely one of harmonizing subjective desires with an objective external world. The external world itself must be interpreted through the veil of each individual's own background, experiences, and preconceptions (Lavoie, 1990: 172). This thoroughgoing subjectivism can be traced to Menger. He emphasized that for something to be considered an economic good, people must have knowledge of its ability to satisfy their needs. He cites charms, love potions, divining rods, medicines for nonexistent diseases, and pagan idols as examples of things that can become economic goods because people perceive that they can satisfy needs (Menger, 1981: 52–53). These perceptions may be mistaken, but to understand human action, we must understand the perceptions.

This theme persists in Austrian writings throughout the twentieth century. Ludwig von Mises argued that nothing becomes a means to an end until some human being attributes meaning to it and uses it to achieve an end. For example, farmers who seek richer crops through diverse means—magic, pilgrimages, prayer, or fertilizer—are all engaged in purposeful activity, and what matters in explaining their action is that they believe the means employed will bring about the desired ends. Even profit, which people frequently speak of as an objective, monetary magnitude, is actually a subjective concept. Profit is the difference between subjectively perceived benefits and subjectively perceived costs. For many individuals, this concept of profit may well differ from the monetary profits that an external observer can calculate (Mises 1966: 37, 92–94, 97).

Nobel laureate Friedrich Hayek echoed both Menger and Mises when he wrote:

> If we wish, we could say that all . . . objects are defined not in terms of their "real" properties but in terms of opinions people hold about them. In short, in the social sciences the things are what people think they are. Money is money, a word is a word, a cosmetic is a cosmetic, if and because somebody thinks they are. (1980: 60)

A few decades later, Kirzner argued that "the subjectivist approach to social phenomena in general emphasizes that what is important about the objects that surround us is not the objects themselves, but only the knowledge and beliefs about them that inform and shape human actions" (1979: 151). More recently, O'Driscoll and Rizzo offer a succinct subjectivist statement: "The objects of economic activity are thus not even definable except in terms of what actors perceive them to be" (1985: 18). For these and similar scholars, subjective perception is a key to understanding action. (See also Machlup, 1946.)

Austrian subjectivism extends to the interpretation of others' actions and intentions, as well as impersonal objects and events (Hayek, 1980: 61). Walker and Warner offer a simple but powerful illustration:

> Take, for example, the action of one person holding out an object toward another. How are we to understand this action? Is the individual engaging in a religious ritual, is he presenting a gift, or is he simply showing the object to another? Clearly, given the individual's overt behavior, it is possible for the individual to be engaged in any one of these actions and innumerable others. The action is understood as *exchange* only after that *meaning* is attributed to that action by the individuals involved. (1992: 347)

Thus, people act and make decisions on the basis of the ways that they interpret what other people are doing. A person may ascribe a different meaning to an action, or a statement, than was intended. But it is the perception that matters for understanding people's actions. People avoid the "infinite regress" of continually interpreting others' interpretations by arriving at commonly understood, or "intersubjective," meanings (Hayek, 1980: 64; Addleson, 1994: 79; Lavoie, 1990: 177).

This subjectivist focus offers a somewhat different perspective on career studies. In the more traditional concept of careers, firms gave careers to people; the available careers were defined by slots on the firm's career ladder. In the Austrian view, each person defines his or her own career. The career is one of the mental tools the person uses to organize and make sense out of a sequence of experiences.

A striking example of the way that subjective perceptions define careers is the emergence of *virtual career communities*. Individuals dislodge their identity and often their commitment from an organization and relocate them to a career community, which may exist only in an imagined reality. An example of a virtual career community is the network often sarcastically referred to as the "Beltway bandits," in the Washington, D.C. area. The national capitol area is saturated with hundreds of small companies that have the federal government as their major client. Most of these companies employ 20 to 100 people and are highly knowledge intensive. They have flat structures with very little hierarchy. Almost all work is project oriented and has a definite time limit. The environment is highly competitive; success often depends on past performance and on the ability to carve out new ways of accomplishing tasks. People who work for such contract-oriented companies engage in a wide variety of tasks in each project. An engineer must know not only the technical aspects, but also a lot about budgeting, customer/public relations, and new business development. In highly ambiguous environments such as these, career is a very porous construct. There are very few traditional boundaries—such as job descriptions or career paths within a company—that lend tight structure to a career.

Yet career identities still exist. Individual Beltway bandits identify with a virtual community consisting of professionals engaged in similar work. It is a virtual community in the sense that no real community of like-minded people physically exists. Nevertheless, individuals possess a subjective understanding of what it means to be a Beltway bandit. Moreover, this understanding is intersubjective; two Beltway bandits meeting at a cocktail party, or at a dentist's office, share an understanding about what "the business" is, who is inside and outside the business, and what constitutes advancement in the business. Subjective meanings have thus taken the place of formal structures in defining careers.

Discovery

The Austrian contribution is distinctive not only because of radical subjectivism, but also because of its emphasis on uncertainty, creativity, and discovery.

The traditional economic approach focuses on optimization within known constraints. Economic models usually postulate that individuals maximize their utility or satisfaction, while being subject to limited resources, a given state of technology, and a given state of general knowledge. Indeed, the most common definition of economics is: the study of how individuals satisfy unlimited wants with limited resources (Kirzner, 1960). More sophisticated approaches attempt to incorporate the acquisition of new information, but in assessing whether or not to gather more information, the agent "knows precisely what it is that he does not know" (Kirzner, 1985: 17). In this way, many economists force even information into the paradigm of optimization within known constraints.

Austrians take a different view, emphasizing that the generation and use of knowledge (as opposed to information) involves breaking constraints and inventing new wants. Such changes occur not as the result of optimizing activity, but because of genuinely novel discoveries that people were previously ignorant about. The agents involved in discovery are not rational optimizers acting on given knowledge. Rather, they act on the basis of their perceptions of current conditions and their projections of the future. Discovery requires an ability to imagine the world as being somehow different than it is today, to ascertain whether it is possible to get from here to there, and to implement a plan for making the change (Woodward, Ellig, and Burns, 1994: 6).

Different Austrian authors offer different variations on this theme. At one extreme is Kirzner (1979, 1985, 1992), who emphasizes the entrepreneurial discovery of opportunities that were already inherent in the situation. A ticket scalper at a football game, for example, buys tickets from people at one entrance to a stadium, and resells them to people who value them more highly at another entrance. By buying low and selling high, the scalper captures entrepreneurial profits. The possibility of profit was inherent in the situation. The only thing preventing some people from selling their tickets to others was the fact that these groups of people did not know about the opportunity because they were on different sides of the stadium. The scalper was the person with enough insight to walk around the stadium; the possibility of profit was the incentive that encouraged him to be alert to the opportunity. For Kirzner, this discovery of existing, but hitherto unnoticed, opportunities is the essence of entrepreneurship.

Other authors place less emphasis on whether the opportunity was really already inherent in the situation, thus underscoring the entrepreneur's creative role. Schumpeter (1942) provides the best example of this view of discovery. The Schumpeterian entrepreneur is the one who develops and introduces the new product, the new source of supply, the new technology, or the new method of business organization. This type of entrepreneur does not just discover something that was "out there" but unnoticed; it would be more accurate to say that this entrepreneur introduces a novelty that no one had previously imagined.

Despite these differences between the Kirznerian and Schumpeterian entrepreneurs, they share some similarities as well. Both are engaged either in prompting new human wants or relaxing constraints on resources and knowledge. They do so by means of creative discovery, not purely by rational calculation.

Perhaps most relevant for career studies, the primacy of discovery applies not just in product markets, but to all human action. It is the ability to create and discover—not the ability to optimize within constraints—that makes human beings different from animals and plants. Experiments have amply demonstrated that even rats behave like the optimizing "economic man" of textbook fame. When faced with changes in constraints—such as an increased number of presses on a lever that are required to get a food pellet—rats respond rationally; they eat less food, because the "price" has increased. Humans, however, possess additional attributes; they can imagine alternatives that do not currently exist (Buchanan, 1982: 17). A quintessentially human characteristic is the ability to imagine oneself as a different person, and to take steps that move toward that vision:

> Once all of the possible constraints are accounted for (historical, geographic, cultural, physical, genetic, sexual), there still remains a large set of possible persons that one might imagine himself to be, or might imagine himself capable of becoming. There is room for "improvement," for the construction of what might be . . . .We move through time, constructing ourselves as artifactual persons. (Buchanan, 1979)

People "create themselves" as they seek out new ways of using their existing abilities and developing new ones. For this reason, the Austrian perspective on discovery completely undermines the notion of stable careers or career paths outlined well in advance of actual career experiences. As time passes, individuals discover new opportunities that they could not possibly have previously anticipated. These opportunities prompt each individual to reassess the type of person he or she wants to become, and thus they alter career decisions. Viewed in this way, the boundaryless career is not just a result of external influences, such as information technology or corporate downsizing. Rather, the concept of the boundaryless career is inherent in the notion of what it means to be a choosing, acting human being.

Virtual career communities provide illustrations of discovery as well as subjectivism. Due to the high degree of ambiguity, actors must try new things, which results in various discoveries: new services, new processes, and new outcomes. The high degree of experimentation and entrepreneurial activity among the Beltway bandits has thus generated numerous new career patterns—even for people who are not in the consulting business. An example is the rise of personal services. The Washington, D.C., area has the highest concentration of dual-income families in the nation, and time is a scarce commodity. It is in this context that Mr. X started doing errands for a couple who both worked. He renewed their pet owner's license, took the pet to the vet, stood in line to buy football tickets, and followed up on a real estate assessment dispute. Soon the couple referred his name to some others who needed similar services, and they, in turn offered referrals. Very soon, Mr. X had the newest career inside the Beltway: personal services! He did not know beforehand that he would find a thriving demand for personal services. In the act of performing services for others, he discovered that there was a significant marketplace demand for what he was sporadically doing.

The idea of a well-defined career path presupposes knowledge that no one has. People can look back and make sense of their actions; they can also imagine the future. But the future rarely unfolds precisely as people imagine it, because they can only learn about their abilities and opportunities by trying different things and noting the results. In other words, a career is a lifelong discovery process that cannot be planned in advance.

Boundaryless Careers: An Austrian Interpretation

For Austrian theorists, then, a boundaryless career has two essential attributes: The career is defined by the subjective perceptions of the career actor, and it continually changes as the actor discovers new opportunities and develops new abilities. The actor's career is his interpretation of past life experiences, plus his current vision of where he would like to proceed in the future.

Many changes in contemporary career dynamics involve elements of both subjectivism and discovery. Table 10.1 illustrates some of the most significant changes in the way people view their careers. In each case, careful analysis reveals the influence of the twin Austrian insights.

From Normative to Subjective Validation

When recently asked, "What is your professional identify?," a successful CPA turned doctoral candidate in a well-known research university replied: "I want to be a good husband and father." When asked to clarify, he confirmed that that indeed was his professional identity. Traditional boundaries of hierarchy, function, and geography are eroding, and in their place has emerged a new set of boundaries that is more subjectively and psychologically defined (Hirschhorn and Gilmore, 1992). The traditional model of a career is based on a consensual validation of what a "good career" is. In this model, society develops norms about the functions, responsibilities, and tasks of each career, and most people accept these social norms (Bird, 1994). In the boundaryless career, each individual finds or creates his or her own meaning.

The new types of tasks performed by both secretaries and CEOs illustrate this change. Thanks to computers, word processors, and faxes, many support functions are performed by all types of employees. If corporate executives now

Table 10.1   Traditional versus Boundaryless Career Paradigm

Traditional Career Paradigm	Boundaryless Career Paradigm
Normative: A single, externally determined view defined what a good career is.	Subjective: Actors derive the worth and significance of a career by interpreting and attaching subjective value to it.
Task orientation: Larger jobs separated into discreet units, which resulted in the proliferation of highly specialized careers.	Outcome orientation: People use whatever competencies are needed to achieve the right outcome, often blending generalist and specialist roles.
Universal career competencies: Career requires competencies in a narrowly defined field of expertise.	Contextual career competencies: Career requires diverse competencies that vary from situation to situation.
Vertical advancement: Progress is measured in terms of how quick one climbs the hierarchical ladder of position, power, and responsibility.	Multidirectional growth: Actors seek careers that are intrinsically rewarding, regardless of hierarchical movements.
Separation of organizational and personal mission: Professional or work life separate from personal or family life, except for small entrepreneurs, who tend to merge the two missions.	Integration of organizational and personal mission: Proliferation of autonomous entities within the large firm allow employees to act like business owners, facilitating integration of personal and organizational missions.

perform some secretarial functions, then what makes a secretary a secretary? Austrian subjectivism suggests that the individual makes meaning out of his or her career, instead of accepting a normative prescription generated by external agents. The secretary, like the other career actors, derives the worth and significance of a career by interpreting and attaching subjective value to it. A secretary watching the CEO type her own e-mail correspondence may feel his job is threatened if he defines his career as handling the CEO's correspondence. On the other hand, the secretary may not feel threatened—or may even feel relieved—if he defines his career as finding ways to enhance the CEO's performance. Her use of e-mail frees him to focus on other, more valuable things he can do to help her.

The shift from old paradigm to the new results from discovery processes that are fundamental to the Austrian analysis. Consider the CEO of a small company who has become a prolific user of her computer notebook. By constantly using its word-processing, e-mail, fax, and mutimedia functions to stay in touch with others and prepare presentations, she has replaced many tasks that her secretary would normally have done. However, this expansion of the range of the CEO's tasks did not result from deliberate planning and prediction. Like many users, she probably originally obtained the computer because it allowed her to carry and work on documents more conveniently than with paper files. After enjoying its word processing convenience, she may have noticed that letters took a frustratingly long time to print, mail, and receive responses on, so she investigated e-mail. Variable font sizes may also have led to the insight that the word processor could be used for preparing presentation slides, and her dissatisfaction with the resulting quality would have led to a search for more sophisticated presentation software. The CEO gradually took on more "secretarial" functions, not because she planned to take her secretary's job, but as a result of experimentation that revealed she could do much more with the computer than she initially expected. Despite this change, it is doubtful that she now thinks of herself as a secretary.

From Task Orientation to Outcome Orientation

The traditional career model categorized employees into "heads" and "hands." The heads were supposed to do the thinking, planning, and strategizing, while the hands would do the simpler, repetitive tasks. For both groups of employees, superior productivity was supposed to arise from a division of labor into ever-narrower tasks, and performance of these tasks came to define careers. In contrast, the new career environment places paramount importance on accomplishing results. Sometimes this may involve the development of highly specialized knowledge. Other times, it may require someone to be both a generalist and a specialist. The older career categories receive less emphasis as people begin to understand their careers in terms of the results they produce, rather than the tasks they perform.

The new emphasis on outcomes encourages individuals to define their careers subjectively, in ways that make sense to them, instead of their relying for their identify on external categories. In an outcome-oriented company, people move from project to project, redefining their bundles of tasks and responsibilities as they change projects (Arthur, Claman, and DeFillippi, 1995: 15–17). As a result, individuals now bear responsibility for constructing the narratives that integrate a sequence of project experiences. In addition, individuals opt to be involved in different projects, based on their own ideas of the types of skills they want to develop and, more generally, on the type of person they want to become. The company's outcome orientation creates an environment in which individuals define their own career paths.

Even on automobile assembly lines—the traditional bastion of narrow job classifications—task-oriented career definitions are gradually disappearing. This change resulted largely from automakers' desire to stimulate discovery of improved manufacturing methods, through better use of shop-floor knowledge (Womack, Jones, and Roos, 1990) In so doing, automakers hope to capitalize on the workers' "knowledge of particular circumstances of time and place," which Austrian scholars have emphasized as critical for economic progress (see Hayek, 1980; Ellig and Lavoie forthcoming.) In turn, new ways of producing cars have created new careers. For example, at a Ford plant in Michigan, many assembly line workers operate robots that manage the assembly line, drastically altering the stereotypical image of the auto worker. The new auto worker is indeed a well-trained problem solver who typically works in cross-functional teams that are focused on results rather than tasks. Thus, a set of changes that, the company hoped, would promote the discovery of new manufacturing knowledge has also facilitated the discovery of new career identities.

From Universal to Contextual Career Competencies

As firms focus on outcomes, we also see a change in focus—from universal career competencies to contextual career competencies. The traditional model often involved a narrow set of career-related competencies. Each profession had a set of core competencies, and possession of these competencies almost automatically defined one as a holder of a particular career. In contrast, the new world of boundaryless careers requires people continually to develop additional competencies useful in particular situations. A person cannot effectively employ her universal competencies unless she also masters some contextual competencies.

The changing role of physicians in different contexts illustrates the differences between subjectivist and nonsubjectivist approaches to career competencies. In the past, physicians typically needed some specific, closely related competencies: the abilities to diagnose accurately, treat promptly, and prognosticate realistically. In contemporary medicine, however, additional competencies are required that vary with each context. For example, a physician in private practice in the United States is likely to know much more about liability, insurance regulations, and billing practices than a doctor in a Veterans Affairs hospital or a doctor in Asia. The private-practice physician is now concerned not just with giving the best care, but also with a whole range of other issues. Furthermore, ignoring issues like malpractice liability or Medicare billing regulations could quickly end her medical career. Being a good physician requires not just a set of universal competencies, but other specific competencies that vary with the physician's perception of the situation. In short, the career of a physician means different things to different physicians, depending on the context.

As with other changes in career dynamics, the move from homogeneous to heterogeneous competencies is rarely planned ahead of time; people develop new competencies as they discover the need for them. A physician who became a hospital administrator provides a good example. The physician was asked to officiate in place of one who had gone on leave. When the original administrator did not return, the physician was offered the position he was temporarily filling. While serving as administrator, he discovered that he enjoyed management. At that point in his life, he liked the change and felt the new position fit well with his new, developing interests. This was an insight he did not have before taking the position. If he were asked, at the beginning, whether he would be a permanent candidate for the position, in all likelihood he would have said no.

From Vertical Advancement to Multidirectional Growth

When the meaning of a career is subjectively defined, so, too, is the meaning of career advancement. In the old model, career life was conceived in terms of "vertical growth" (Arthur, 1994; DeFillippi and Arthur, 1994; Mirvis and Hall, 1994). Many employees typically started at the lowest level, such as an assembly line or the mail room, and worked up to senior management. In the new model, one doesn't have to go *up* in order to advance; advancement has become polydirectional. As Peter Drucker recently remarked, "The stepladder is gone, and there's not even the implied structure of an industry's rope ladder. It's more like vines, and you bring your own machete" (Harriss, 1994: 117).

Career growth without climbing a ladder is a straightforward application of subjectivism. What constitutes a "better" career opportunity is subjective, so we should not be surprised that people willingly move in various directions. An engineer for an auto company provides an especially striking example. He started out as a design engineer in an auto plant; earned an MBA in finance; moved to the accounting department; and shifted again, after a few years, to marketing and then to product development. He ended up in Washington, D.C. as a lobbyist for the company. This individual was not moving up in a hierarchy. In the automobile industry, that would have meant moving up within engineering design. Ending up on Capitol Hill only removes a player from the key site of power, the firm's Detroit headquarters.

This person's range of career moves also suggests that discovery plays a significant role in career growth. It is difficult to imagine that one individual would join a company with a conscious plan to progress through design, finance, marketing, and product development, and then get to government relations. (Indeed, articulating such a plan at the outset could well keep one from getting hired in the first place!) Rather, it is much more likely that this person saw each career move as a logical outgrowth of something he had discovered in some combination of previous positions. He could not have planned this career path in advance, though, because he could not know in advance what he would learn in each job along the way.

From Separation to Integration of Organizational and Personal Mission

More than 30 years ago, Chris Argyris (1964) argued that it is inherently difficult to achieve congruence between the individual's needs and the organization's needs. This has been true in most of corporate America for years, especially in regard to integration of family and career goals. Individuals were told to adjust their career expectations to fit into preconceived slots, and "Heaven help" the rebel who insisted on dragging family or other irrelevancies into the workplace. But a new generation of business leaders has decided that if existing corporate structures keep them from following subjectively defined careers, they will bypass the bureaucracy in search of personal fulfillment. "Kissing off corporate America," the trend documented in the *Fortune* cover story cited previously, reveals a move toward congruence between individual and organizational missions.

Hotshot MBAs move toward subjective definition of their careers because they want to be excited about their work, and would like to see their careers create a positive impact on society. Their solution?: Bypass the large companies, with their bureaucracies and career ladders, and join smaller firms that give them more freedom to mix their "public" and "private" lives. Cramton (1993) illustrates that small-business owners tend to integrate their personal and business missions, at least during the firm's founding and early growth stages. Transitions in family life tend to influence business strategy, and business strategy likewise shapes family life. A colleague of ours whose family used to own two grocery stores perhaps best summarized this insight: "My dad always said, 'This family is the business, and the business is the family.' " In such an environment, the management of a small business becomes just one part of a larger, subjectively fined concept of a career.

This blending of private and public life that is found in small businesses may also offer new opportunities for entrepreneurial discovery. Some research suggests that integration of private and public lives—particularly, of work and family—promotes corporate productivity, because people traditionally made use of different capabilities in these two spheres. Integration of work and family can spark new forms of creativity as people bring the different capabilities used in their private lives to bear on business problems (see chapter 15 in this volume). Thus, the newly minted MBA who opts for a position in a small company may end up both happier and wealthier.

An Austrian Perspective on Career Evolution

Austrian theory emphasizes that for a career to be truly boundaryless, it must involve both subjective interpretation and the discovery of new opportunities. Given this definition, it is worth asking whether careers have always been boundaryless, or whether the boundaryless career is a new phenomenon.

In some sense, the first condition has always been met for all human workers. The meanings of careers have always been subjectively determined (cf. Van Maanen, 1977: 15). The big change has occurred in regard to the second element of a boundaryless career: discovery. While people were always free to interpret their careers in whatever way they wished, they frequently chose to accept the roles and responsibilities offered to them by their firms. Careers became boundaryless when individuals started discovering new roles and developing novel interpretations that gave personal meaning to these roles.

Austrian-style analysis also suggests why opportunities for discovery have expanded. The more traditional notions of career fitted in well with the ways that organizations assigned roles and responsibilities in the industrial era. During the past several decades, however, new organizational forms began to emerge as organizations struggled to harness the knowledge of all of their employees. Using hierarchy, giving orders, planning, and controlling are not especially effective means of managing workers who are expected to think.[1] The reason stems from the nature of knowledge itself: Much of the knowledge that is relevant to any production process is tacit, subjective, and subject to change. As a result, command-and-control management methods fail to use all of the knowledge that the people in the organization possess.

Knowledge work thus poses new management challenges in an organization of any appreciable size. To fully use knowledge that is tacit, subjective, and subject to change, organizations move decision-making authority to where the knowledge is, instead of carrying leaking buckets of knowledge to the top of the managerial hill. But independent spheres of authority are not enough to mobilize everyone's knowledge. In addition to autonomy, individuals need means of understanding how their decisions and actions affect the decisions and actions of others in the organization.

Austrian economists argued that free markets would inevitably replace centrally planned economies, precisely because markets prove far superior at combining autonomous decisions with communication of information about the rest of the system (see Mises, 1966; Hayek, 1980; Lavoie, 1985; Kirzner, 1985). In similar fashion, to promote the effective generation and use of knowledge, more and more firms are adopting structures that look less like authoritarian hierarchies, and more like free markets (Ellig and Lavoie, forthcoming; Gable and Ellig, 1994).

A growing literature, with few direct links to Austrian theory, documents this evolution. Some authors explicitly discuss examples of corporate "internal markets" (Halal et al., 1993). Other authors use a variety of words to characterize ongoing organizational changes. Starbuck (1992) discusses the emergence of "knowledge-intensive firms" that give employees a great deal of authority and autonomy. Additional common buzzwords include "multidimensional organizations," "virtual corporations," "intrapreneurship," "liberation management," and "market networks" (see Ackoff, 1994; Davidow and Malone, 1992; Halal, 1986, Pinchot and Pinchot, 1993; Peters, 1992).

These new types of organizations emphasize autonomy, creativity, and accountability for results, rather than following procedures or bureaucratic chains of command. The transition from a hierarchy to "internal free enterprise" holds two implications for the development of careers.

First, adoption of internal markets requires a drastic change in roles for people in the firm. Top executives will leave many more decisions to entrepreneurs in the internal market. The executive's new role will be to do only those things that lower-level units are incapable of doing for themselves.[2] For both managers and employees, the career paths available in these organizations are much less settled. The idea of advancement depends much more on the individual's own aspirations and ability to find ways to create value, and much less on externally defined concepts of what constitutes a promotion. In such an environment, each individual obviously has much greater latitude (and greater responsibility) for defining his or her own career, to give meaning to a progression of projects (Mirvis and Hall, 1994). The nature of knowledge work is driving organizational change, which, in turn, prompts people to discover new career paths.

The second implication for careers stems from the indirect effect of internal markets on the firm's external relations. In many cases, internal markets blur the distinction between "insiders" and "outsiders." Companies adopting internal markets frequently end up spinning some functions off into independent entities, owned either by their employees or by a completely different group of shareholders. Others have opted to throw internal functions open to external competition, so that outside suppliers are now privy to formerly captive internal markets. Still others keep many functions in-house, but also permit them to pursue external business (see Halal, Geranmayeh, and Pourdehnad, 1993; Ellig, 1992). Such firms do not just make use of price information internally; they also function as more-open systems, with more-permeable boundaries and greater movement of people across boundaries. In such an environment, employees make their own careers, not just by discovering opportunities inside the firm, but by coming into contact with new, external networks as well—building their "know-who" competencies (Arthur, Claman, and DeFillippi, 1995).

In short, the greater the internal-market orientation of a company, the greater is the probability of careers being boundaryless. As each business unit becomes a self-managing entity, people encounter more opportunities to develop their abilities and find new uses for them. Because internal markets give individuals greater latitude to act on and profit from the opportunities they perceive, they also give individuals greater incentives to notice new career opportunities in the first place. Thus, boundaryless careers are one unintended consequence of internal markets and other changes promoting greater autonomy for business units.

Conclusion

An Austrian approach to career theory emphasizes the primacy of subjective perception and the key role of discovery in shaping career decisions. These insights help us understand five shifts in career dynamics:

- · From normative to subjective validation;
- · From a task to an outcome orientation;
- · From homogeneous and universal competencies to heterogeneous and contextual competencies;
- · From vertical advancement to multidirectional growth; and
- · From separation to integration of personal and organizational missions.

In some sense, careers have always been subjectively interpreted, but opportunities for discovery were often limited. Careers are less bounded now because flexible, market-based organizations reward people for discovering their own career paths. Organizational change, in turn, results from the evolution toward knowledge-intensive work, and Austrian economics explains why the nature of knowledge encourages the development of flexible, market-based organizations.

Some of the insights and ideas that we have called Austrian can also be found in other approaches to career theory. The Chicago school of sociology pioneered the idea of the career as a subjective construct (Barley, 1989). Hall (1976) characterized careers as "Protean": individuals create their own careers, as the Greek god Proteus could change shape at will. Changes in organizational structure and knowledge work are often seen as key developments that make careers less bounded (Arthur 1994). The Austrian approach adds value to career studies by emphasizing the importance of the generation and use of knowledge in a dynamic world. In so doing, it provides a unifying theoretical framework that helps connect a variety of concepts and phenomena.

Notes

1. Note that our definition of *knowledge work* is not just limited to the professions, management, or high technology, but also includes any work that involves thinking. Thus, an assembly-line worker who is expected to chart the performance of machinery, and analyze reasons for malfunctions, is a knowledge worker.

2. Of course, this begs the question of how corporate executives can have the relevant knowledge to decide what the lower-level units are incapable of doing. Some authors propose using the Western-style "mixed economy" as a metaphor; the corporate central office would thus serve as an "internal government" (see Halal et al., 1993). Many Austrian economists would disagree with this approach, arguing that Western

governments already undertake many activities that can be better accomplished by other institutions in society (see, e.g., Kirzner, 1985).

References

Ackoff, Russell L. (1994). *The Democratic Corporation*. New York: Oxford University Press.

Addleson, Mark (1994). "Equilibrium versus Understanding: The Methodological Dilemma of Economists." Unpublished manuscript, George Mason University.

Argyris, Chris ([1964] 1990). *Integrating the Individual and the Organization*. Boston: Transaction Publishers.

Arthur, Michael B. (1994). "The Boundaryless Career: A New Perspective for Organizational Inquiry." *Journal of Organizational Behavior* 15, 295–306.

Arthur, Michael B.; Priscilla H. Claman; and Robert J. DeFillippi (1995). "Intelligent Enterprise, Intelligent Careers: Applying the 'New Paradigm' to Employment Practice." *Academy of Management Executive* 9, 4.

Barley, Steven R. (1989). "Careers, Identities, and Institutions: The Legacy of the Chicago School of Sociology." In M. B. Arthur; D. T. Hall; and B. S. Lawrence (eds.), *Handbook of Career Theory*. New York: Cambridge University Press.

Bird, Allan (1994). "Careers as Repositories of Knowledge: A New Perspective on Boundaryless Careers," *Journal of Organizational Behavior* 15, 325–344.

Buchanan, James M. (1982). "The Domain of Subjective Economics." In I. M. Kirzner (ed.), *Method, Process, and Austrian Economics*. Lexington, Mass.: D. C. Heath.

——— (1979). "Natural and Artifactual Man." In *What Should Economists Do?* Indianapolis: Liberty Press.

Cramton, Catherine Durnell (1993). "Is Rugged Individualism the Whole Story? Public and Private Accounts of a Firm's Founding." *Family Business Review* 6(3), 233–261.

Davidow, William H., and Michael S. Malone (1992). *The Virtual Corporation*. New York: HarperCollins.

DeFillippi, Robert J., and Michael B. Arthur (1994). "The Boundaryless Career: A Competency-Based Perspective." *Journal of Organizational Behavior* 15, 307–324.

Ellig, Jerry (1993). "Internal Pricing for Corporate Services." Fairfax, Va.: Center for Market Processes Working Paper.

Ellig, Jerry, and Don Lavoie (forthcoming). "Governments, Firms, and the Impossibility of Central Planning." In Paul Foss (ed.), *Economic Approaches to Organizations*. Aldershot, Eng.: Dartmouth Publishing.

Gable, Wayne, and Jerry Ellig (1994). *Introduction to Market-Based Management*. Fairfax, Va.: Center for Market Processes.

Halal, William E. (1986). *The New Capitalism*. New York: John Wiley.

Halal, William E., Ali Geranmayeh, and John Pourdehnad (1993). *Internal Markets*. New York: John Wiley.

Hall, D. T. (1976). *Careers in Organizations*. Glenview, Ill.: Scott, Foresman.

Harriss, T. George (1993). "The Post-Capitalist Executive: An Interview with Peter F. Drucker." *Harvard Business Review* (May-June), 115–122.

Hayek, Friedrich ([1948] 1980). *Individualism and Economic Order*. Chicago: University of Chicago Press.

Hirschhorn, Larry, and Thomas Gilmore (1992). "The New Boundaries of the 'Boundaryless' Company." *Harvard Business Review* 70(3), 104–115.

Jensen, Michael C., and William H. Meckling (1992). "Specific and General Knowledge and Organizational Structure." In Lars Wein and Hans Wijkander (eds.), *Contract Economics*. London: Basil Blackwell.

Kanter, R. M. (1989). *When Giants Learn to Dance: Mastering the Challenge of Strategy, Management, and Careers in the 1990s*. New York: Basic Books.

Kirzner, Israel (1960). *The Economic Point of View*. Princeton: Van Nostrand.

——— (1979). *Perception, Opportunity, and Profit*. Chicago: University of Chicago Press.

——— (1985). *Discovery and the Capitalist Process*. Chicago: University of Chicago Press.

Labich, Kenneth (1995). "Kissing Off Corporate America," *Fortune* (February 20), 44–52.

Lavoie, Don (1990). "Hermeneutics, Subjectivity, and the Lester/Machlup Debate: Toward a More Anthropological Approach to Economics." In W.M. Samuels (ed.), *Economics as Discourse*. Boston: Kluwer Academic Publishers, 167–184.

Machlup, Fritz (1946). "Marginal Analysis and Empirical Research." *American Economic Review* (September), 519–554.

McCloskey, Donald (1983). "The Rhetoric of Economics." *Journal of Economic Literature* 21 (June), 481–517.

Menger, Carl (1981). *Principles of Economics*. New York: New York University Press.

Mirvis, Philip H., and Douglas T. Hall (1994). "Psychological Success and the Boundaryless Career," *Journal of Organizational Behavior* 15, 365–380.

Mises, Ludwig von (1966). *Human Action*, 3d rev. ed. Chicago: Contemporary Books.

O'Driscoll, Gerald P., and Rizzo, Mario (1985). *The Economics of Time and Ignorance*. London: Basil Blackwell.

Peters, Tom (1992). *Liberation Management*. New York: Fawcett-Columbine.

Pinchot, Gifford, and Elizabeth Pinchot (1993). *The End of Bureaucracy and the Rise of the Intelligent Organization*. San Francisco: Berrett-Koehler.

Schumpeter, Joseph (1942). *Capitalism, Socialism, and Democracy*. New York: Harper.

Starbuck, W. H. (1992). "Learning by Knowledge Intensive Firms." *Journal of Management Studies* 29(6), 713–740.

Van Maanen, John (1977). *Organizational Careers*. New York: John Wiley.

Walker, Deborah, and Stuart D. Warner (1992). "The Nature of Social Reality." *Cultural Dynamics* 5, 341–355.

Whyte, William H. (1956). *The Organization Man*. New York: Simon and Schuster.

Womack, James P., Daniel T. Jones, and Daniel Roos (1990). *The Machine that Changed the World*. New York: Rawson Associates.

Woodward, Alison; Jerry Ellig; and Tom R. Burns (1994). *Municipal Entrepreneurship and Energy Policy*. London: Gordon and Breach.

11

Boundaryless Careers and Social Capital

HOLLY J. RAIDER AND RONALD S. BURT

Social capital refers to the structure of individuals' contact networks—the pattern of interconnection among the various people with whom each person is tied. The central idea behind social capital arguments is that differences in social contexts produce inequality. In fact, with regard to career attainment, social capital arguments reason that differences in social networks account for performance differences among similarly educated, able, and experienced individuals—that individuals with better social capital earn higher rates of return on their human capital.

Certain network structures are more advantageous than others. Network structures in which one is connected to diverse and disconnected individuals and social groups are a competitive advantage. Survey research documents the effects of such network structures on job seeking and on career attainment. Most familiar is Granovetter's (1974) research on white collar job seeking, which evidenced that people with weak ties to socially distant others were more successful in finding jobs than were people with only strong ties to an immediate social group. Other researchers provide corroborating evidence of the value of network ties for obtaining jobs (Boxman, De Graaf, and Flap, 1991; Lin and Dumin, 1986; Lin et al., 1981) and for creating intrafirm mobility (Burt, 1992; Flap and De Graaf, 1989; Marsden and Hurlbert, 1988; Podolny and Baron, 1994).

The concept of social capital is formalized by using structural hole theory, which describes how certain network structures offer a competitive advantage by providing access to more opportunities, and the ability to act on those opportunities (Burt, 1992). Network structures that offer a competitive advantage are large networks comprised of disconnected contacts. Disconnections among contacts are the structural holes, the presence of which enable access to diverse sets of information, control of the flow of information between disjoined parties, and determination of the form of projects that bring together disconnected others. The reasoning is that individuals who connect otherwise disconnected others are more autonomous, and have more opportunities, than individuals with smaller networks comprised of interconnected others. Details, as well as measurement and related theoretical issues, are discussed by Burt (1992).

Information and control benefits underlie the competitive advantage of having large networks with many structural holes. The information benefits of these networks include access to dissimilar information; propitious timing in receiving information; and referrals, on one's behalf, by direct contacts to distant third parties. The control benefits of having a network rich in structural holes derive from the entrepreneurial opportunities of brokering the relations between disconnected others. Like Burt (1992: 30–49, 274, note 10), we use *entrepreneur* as meaning "one who takes from between," from the French root verb *entreprendre*. In this sense, the entrepreneur is akin to *tertius gaudens* (Simmel, 1922)—the third party, who benefits from being positioned between two others with conflicting interests. There are several ways control can play out. First, disconnected parties may compete for the same relationship with a third—such as two bidders for the same contract. By informing the parties in the competition, the third party is able to negotiate more favorable terms for the contract. Second, disconnected parties can be leveraged against one another—such as leverage gained by a manager playing off the conflicting interests of marketing and finance. Third, two disconnected parties who can add value to one another are introduced by the entrepreneur, who benefits from crafting valuable projects.

Two network structures with different information and control potential are illustrated in Figure 11.1. Both Liz and Ann have five primary network ties that consume the same network time and energy. Liz's network is entrepreneurial; there are many structural holes among her primary contacts; and through her five primary contacts, she reaches 24 additional people. Ann is in a clique network; her five direct contacts are themselves interconnected. Her five ties give Liz access to five clusters of information, and position her as the broker across ten structural holes.

Ann, in contrast, reaches two clusters and only 10 people beyond her immediate five contacts. Given these network structures, Ann will enjoy fewer information and control benefits than will Liz. Ann's access to information is effectively limited to two sources, as information from 1, 2, and 3 will be redundant. Not only does Liz access five nonredundant sources of information, but the disconnections across the clusters in her network make more likely valuable referrals. Liz is also the one person in her network who receives information from all five clusters, and will be the person who first sees the value that one cluster could add to another. Ann's comments and actions will quickly be known by all 15 people in her network; while Liz is able to move more autonomously, her behavior in one cluster will probably not be known in the other clusters. Liz's network is more likely to extend to various parts of the firm and beyond, while Ann is more likely to be socially cloistered in her immediate work group.

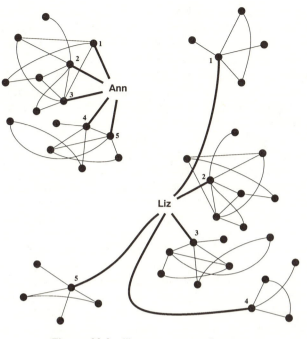

Figure 11.1   Illustrative network structures.

The Role of Social Capital

For the reasons that social capital is generally important for job seeking and career attainment, it is particularly important in boundaryless careers. With respect to getting a job, individuals in boundaryless careers are more frequently involved in job searches than are individuals in organizational careers, and so they will more frequently have occasion to call upon their contacts for information regarding opportunities. The recurrent nature of job seeking and information gathering in boundaryless careers is richly illustrated in this volume by Jones (in chapter 4), and by Baker and Aldrich (in chapter 8). The importance of contacts in the job-search process is accentuated in the context of interfirm work sequences by the absence of internal labor markets in guiding career moves (see Arthur and Rousseau, chapter 1). Given their frequent use of social networks for information about job opportunities in other firms, people in boundaryless careers will depend on their contacts for accurate information regarding potential positions and employers.

The contention that social capital is especially important for attainment within boundaryless careers is supported by arguments and evidence on the contingent value of social capital. Social capital is generally important, but is more important for people at the social frontier—people at the interface of different social worlds. For contexts in which there are no clear-cut procedures, or in which job success depends on coordinating others, or where there is recurrent negotiation with people outside the firm, social capital is more important for getting things done, getting proposals accepted, and getting buy-in. Positions at the top of the firm; positions spanning firm boundaries; and positions with few functionally equivalent peers are positions where individuals must legitimize their actions, due to the lack of acknowledged procedures or of a frame of reference provided by others doing the same kind of work (Burt, 1995). Entrepreneurial networks are especially useful in these jobs because they position the entrepreneur to be informed of the interests of others in the firm, to identify opportunities, and then develop them in ways that are likely to be valuable to the firm.

A study using a probability sample of managers in a high-technology firm provides empirical evidence of the contingent value of social capital (Burt, 1992; 1995). The significant positive association of early promotion with entrepreneurial networks, observed for managers across the firm, is even more strongly associated for managers higher up in the firm and at the boundary of the firm— such as managers in sales and service; field managers and managers in remote plant locations; and managers recently hired. These conditions are commonplace for people in boundaryless careers. People in boundaryless careers are often "recent hires" and often occupy boundary-spanning, liaison, and peripheral job positions. There is also a tendency for firms to place individuals with peripatetic work sequences in positions outside the firm's core (Wiesenfeld and Brockner, 1996). The stronger association between social capital and success that is observed in these contexts (Burt, 1995) should also be evident in boundaryless careers—within a firm and over the course of multiple-firm work sequences.

Distinguishing between voluntary and involuntary boundarylessness is helpful in understanding the role of social capital in interfirm work sequences. Aldrich and Baker (in chapter 8) report that involuntary boundaryless workers experience stigmatization in the job-search process, and suggest that they have difficulty securing subsequent jobs—illustrating kinds of outcome differences between voluntary and involuntary boundarylessness. Among both groups, those with entrepreneurial networks are likely to find better jobs, faster than those with clique networks. Still, a disparity between voluntary and involuntary boundarylessness can be accounted for by social capital influences on interfirm movement.

Voluntary boundarylessness occurs when people elect to move to a new firm, in contrast to people who find themselves boundaryless as a result of such processes as downsizing, phasing out, restructuring, or firing. The many rationales for voluntarily moving are often some variant of having advanced as far as possible at a current firm. For the voluntarily boundaryless, the fact of interfirm movement implies hearing about and landing a potentially more rewarding opportunity in another firm. Information and referral benefits of structural hole networks enable entrepreneurs to be informed of, and recommended for, opportunities in other firms, and so to become voluntarily boundaryless. Social capital effects on performance and on intrafirm mobility reinforce this association, because those with entrepreneurial networks make for more attractive candidates than their peers. Accordingly, seemingly serendipitous interfirm work sequences of the voluntarily boundaryless should be accounted for by entrepreneurial network structures.

Involuntary boundarylessness occurs when people are compelled to find a new job. Likely, these are people who expected an organizational career, but who find themselves looking for a job as a result of such events as downsizing or being fired. Ceteris paribus, they will have clique networks and, as a result, are unlikely to hear about interesting career opportunities, because information in these networks is limited and quickly redundant. The expectation of an organizational career may also have led to building contact networks consisting of people from within their current firm or workgroup. Contacts in these networks may be peers who are in similar straits and so are competitors in the job market. Contacts who themselves built networks around people in the current firm will be acquainted with information about opportunities within the firm, and relatively uninformed about opportunities outside the firm.

Formal versus Informal Relations

We have discussed how the structure of contact networks affects careers. Although the focus of this chapter is on the relationships between network structure and boundaryless careers, it is worth noting how the value of entrepreneurial network structures is dependent upon kinds of relations. Available research on career outcomes points to different network benefits of formal and informal relations (Ibarra 1992a,b; Podolny and Baron 1994). Formal relations involve those prescribed by the formal organization of a firm—such as those with a boss, subordinate, or a coworker. Informal relations, involving contacts to whom people go to for advice and discussion about important matters, obtain greater social capital value (Burt, 1995). Control benefits of entrepreneurial networks are more likely realized through informal relations because the structural hole characteristics of entrepreneurial networks are at odds with bureaucratic relations structured to maximize corporate authority and to minimize employee authority.

Information benefits of entrepreneurial networks are also better achieved through informal relations. Informal ties are conduits of unique information, information that might not be acquired through authority relations. Even for information that would transfer via formal channels, informal relations offer a timing advantage by communicating information earlier than it would officially be accessed. Referrals from informal relations can be more compelling than those from formal relations. Bosses have an interest in the performance of their subordinates, and so are expected to sponsor them, while referrals from authorities elsewhere in the firm can be more credible. Lastly, having contacts outside formal-authority relations means that one's interests are more widely represented in the firm.

The ability to mobilize social capital for constructing boundaryless careers is also affected by having social networks that enable one to circumvent formal employment-search and interview processes. As discussed earlier, clique networks and networks built exclusively around contacts in one firm are not very helpful in finding positions outside that firm. As a consequence, people with these networks tend to depend on formal channels for job-search information, such as company advertisements and placement services. Information about the best opportunities may never become widely disseminated, as firms initially post openings in-house, filling them internally, or with an external candidate who hears about the opening from a contact in the hiring firm. Prospective employers' use of in-house referrals to screen applicants adds to the competitive disadvantages of external candidates with weak social capital (Powell and Smith-Doerr, 1994). The disadvantages of using formal job-search channels offer further insight into the previous discussion of voluntary and involuntary boundarylessness. As suggested earlier, individuals who are involuntarily boundaryless are likely to have the kinds of social networks that provide few information and referral benefits, and therefore are likely to resort to formal channels for job seeking.

Interfirm Mobility and the Formation of Social Capital

The occurrence of interfirm mobility creates a contextual change that can facilitate entrepreneurial behavior. Boundaryless careers open up opportunities for interfirm coordination by positioning individuals as potential brokers between current and former employers. Interfirm movement also assists individuals in building entrepreneurial networks, by making it possible to maintain contacts across different firms and to disengage from unproductive or constraining relations.

One of the benefits of entrepreneurial networks is controlling the forms of projects that bring together disconnected parties. The interfirm movement characteristic of boundaryless careers positions people to act as brokers between current and former employers. Although many firms traditionally include boundary-spanning jobs, the rise of network forms of organizing creates an additional need for persons capable of coordinating across firm boundaries. Entrepreneurs with boundaryless careers have an edge on interfirm coordination. They may have contact networks across firms; they may have knowledge about the interests and agendas within these firms; and they may have tacit knowledge about the firms' operations. These benefits facilitate the formation of several types of brokered relations.

Familiarity with many firms enables movers to recognize where a joint venture or strategic alliance might be of mutual interest to the firms. Familiarity with these firms also enables the entrepreneur to help negotiating parties reach mutually acceptable agreements. Movers are positioned to identify how the product or services of one firm could be valuable to another, creating buyer-supplier relations. Beyond recognizing opportunities across firm boundaries, entrepreneurs can better craft and pitch a proposal because they are informed of the agenda and interests of people in the firms concerned. For example, suppose an entrepreneur's present firm, an investment bank, is competing with other banks to sell a financial service to a former firm of the entrepreneur. The entrepreneur knows that the manager with the most influence on the decision is leery of certain investment strategies and favors certain others. This information allows the entrepreneur's current firm to tailor its proposal to these preferences.

The entrepreneur enjoys referral benefits as well. Through her contacts in this former firm, the entrepreneur also has a good word put in for her with the decision-making manager. Such comments can be invaluable: "I hear you are going to be talking with Liz next week. She did a smashing job when she was with us on the Firmco account; she really knows her stuff." Knowing the personalities and interests involved, as well as the organization of the firm, the entrepreneur's company is at an advantage in the bidding to sell a product or service. A competitor in the bidding, another investment bank, has a person with a firm- centered, or clique, network in charge of a team crafting a proposal. An excellent analysis and a respected portfolio may be inadequate if the proposal happens to include investments deemed suspect by the key manager in the client firm. The clique manager's firm is also at a competitive disadvantage because she does not have contacts in the client firm to circulate positive referrals about her ability.

In addition to brokerage opportunities, people with boundaryless careers have more opportunities to construct entrepreneurial networks than do people with organization careers. Interfirm movement is an occasion to build relations with people who are unconnected to others already in a contact network, as contacts across firms are less likely to be connected than are contacts within a single firm. Each move to a new firm is an opportunity to add another, disconnected cluster, to a network. Not only does interfirm movement facilitate the building of networks for structural holes; it also makes former corporate-authority relations more valuable. When people leave a firm, they become removed from the formal authority structure and are no longer assured of receiving information that was once communicated as a matter of formal position. By maintaining contact to formal-authority relations at a past employer, one perpetuates access to some information once received as a matter of corporate authority. In this way, corporate-authority relations are recast as informal relations. In addition to these information benefits, previously formal relations can be essential contacts for referrals and for interfirm coordination. Thus, once-formal relations take on the social capital benefits of informal relations discussed earlier in this paper.

Interfirm movement is also an occasion to disengage from unproductive network relations. Unproductive or constraining ties can come in many forms. For some, it could be an uncooperative member of a production team. For others, it could be the marketing manager who does not back the R&D manager's initiatives. Whatever the reason for the difficulty, these people are unavoidable. There are three strategies for tempering awkward or troublesome relations (Burt, 1992: 230–236). One is to expand the network; the addition of new people (supporters) to the network creates alternatives to, and counterpressure on, difficult contacts. A second strategy is to embed the relationship—establish a second dimension to the relationship, so that there is more autonomy with regard to this contact in the primary domain. One example of this strategy is adding informal, socializing behavior to the relationship with a difficult formal tie. The third, and perhaps most obvious, strategy is to withdraw from the relationship—exit the relationship and focus on other contacts. Withdrawal, however, is not often a viable alternative, especially when the tie to the difficult person is imposed by the formal structure.

Interfirm movement enables practical use of a withdrawal strategy. When withdrawal is coincident with shifting employers, disengagement is a matter of letting unproductive relationships atrophy. This is more palatable than active rejection, where there is a risk of hostility or of being seen as unscrupulous, and where the clarity of dissolution precludes reactivating a tie. It is a far simpler matter to let relationships wane as one exits a firm and is no longer physically proximate to undesired contacts. Getting away from difficult people may not be sufficient justification for leaving a firm, but it is one network benefit of boundaryless careers. Coupled with an ability to maintain worthwhile contacts, people in boundaryless careers can build up entrepreneurial networks, while trimming some of the excess.

Firm-Level Effects of Social Capital

We have focused on the relationship between social capital and boundaryless careers from the perspective of the individual. Earlier, in discussing how entrepreneurs add value by coordinating disconnected others, we intimated that firms benefit from the entrepreneurial behavior of their employees. In this section, we emphasize firm-level effects of social capital and suggest a conceptualization of organization as the interface of social networks.

Both within and across firms, entrepreneurs add value by bringing together disconnected others, thereby supplanting the market as a coordination mechanism (Burt, 1995). Firms traditionally have boundary-spanning jobs—such as sales, marketing, or field managers—but the rise of network and virtual-community forms of organizing creates additional demand for individuals capable of interfirm coordination as more business takes place at the social frontier of firms (Baker, 1992; Kanter, 1989; Miles and Snow, 1986; Piore and Sabel, 1984; Powell, 1990). Strategic alliances and joint ventures are increasingly frequent forms of organization. Firms such as Benetton and Corning use these arrangements as an integral part of business strategy. Still other network forms of organizing are grounded in flexible specialization (Piore and Sabel, 1984), and in Best and Forrant's community-based specialization (see chapter 19 in this volume). A somewhat parallel development to the recognition and appreciation of relational forms of organizing is the understanding that individuals play a key role in the formation and governance of economic relations. This is diversely explicated by Eccles and Nohria (1992), Granovetter (1985), Sabel (1993), and White (1992), and it is illustrated in several case studies (Garguilo and Benassi, 1993; Larson, 1992; Uzzi, 1995).

As Arthur and Rousseau note in chapter 1 of this volume, social networks can have aggregate effects on firms as mechanisms for learning (Powell and Brantly, 1992), and as social capital (Burt, 1992; Granovetter, 1985). As mechanisms for learning, social networks are a means to accessing knowledge—improving "know-how" through "know-whom." This is a variant of our claim that there are information benefits of certain network structures that are maximized in large networks of disconnected others. Because structural hole theory provides a theoretical argument for how network benefits are dependent on network structure, we will continue our discussion in terms of general-information benefits of entrepreneurial networks. But the idea that individuals learn through social networks may make more obvious our contention that social capital can be a competitive advantage for firms in the same way it offers a competitive advantage to individuals.

Again, see Figure 11.1, but now assume Ann and Liz are interested in knowledge about production processes. As a result of the dense interconnection within the clusters to which Ann is connected, there is a good chance that know-how has already been exchanged, and that there is relative homogeneity in practice. Whereas novel-knowledge inputs from Ann's contacts are unlikely, Liz is positioned to access more alternatives, and so to be a locus of cross-fertilization that facilitates innovation. By virtue of their position in the social structure, individuals with entrepreneurial networks are better able to improve know-how through know-whom. Studies on interfirm communication illustrate the value of contacts for know-how (e.g., Hipple, 1987; and Saxenian, 1994). Moreover, Saxenian (in chapter 2 in this volume) emphasizes the link between interfirm learning processes and the emergent relative success of communicative firms in Silicon Valley over the isolationist firms along Route 128.

Direct firm-level effects of employee social capital are not limited to know-how contributions. This is evident in the investment-bank illustration we used earlier, in which the entrepreneur's information and referral placed her firm at a competitive advantage. Firms can be beneficiaries of entrepreneurial behavior on several counts. First, in term of added value: Projects coordinated by an entrepreneur are unlikely to be executed unless they serve the interests of the firm and its constituents. Although the entrepreneur may act in her own interest, her behavior is unlikely to be tolerated if it is purely selfish. Parties coordinated by an entrepreneur must also profit from the venture; projects satisfying only the avaricious intentions of a broker offer little incentive for other parties to cooperate. Second, regarding flexibility and efficiency: As Burt enumerates elsewhere (1992: 116), entrepreneurs are more effective than bureaucratic mechanisms at monitoring information, shifting from one solution to another, and in tailoring solutions to particular parties involved in a given transaction. Third, regarding performance: Information, control, and referral benefits enable entrepreneurs to better fulfill job functions (Burt, 1992). Because entrepreneurs are positioned to recognize opportunities and read agendas, they are particularly more adept in boundary-spanning positions—positions at the social frontier of a firm, and where there is need for individual coordination.

Just as interfirm movement enables individuals in boundaryless careers to build and expand entrepreneurial networks, network access of firms is extended through the networks of former employees. Granrose and Chua (in chapter 12 of this book) illustrate such strategic-network building as part of expatriate-Chinese family practice. A family business is based on primogeniture; other siblings and nonfamily employees serve limited tenures at the family firm and are expected to disperse to other enterprises, while maintaining relations with the origin family. In this way, families construct entrepreneurial networks through the social capital of family members and former employees. Past employers are beneficiaries of departures through both interfirm coordination and the extension of employers' networks into new firms. Employee departure, however, can also have undesired consequences. Firms can experience a loss when employees take with them social capital that is in some way exclusionary, such as the kind of client relations often observed in law, advertising, and medicine. Firms can also experience a loss when employees set up their own firms in competition with their former employers, or take proprietary information to an established competitor.

While structural hole theory describes how certain network structures can be a competitive advantage for firms, boundaryless careers are a mechanism for strategic construction of firm networks. Like human capital, social capital is an asset of employees. And like human capital, social capital considerations can be incorporated into human-resource management and business strategy. There may be buyers or suppliers with whom a firm would like to have better terms of trade; firms with which it would like to enter into a strategic alliance; or constraining business relations that it would like to coopt. Business and human-resource interests can be furthered by hiring from buyers, suppliers, or competitors people whose social capital makes more likely the coordination of desired strategic alliances or the negotiation of favorable terms of trade (Rousseau and Wade-Benzoni, 1994).

The Firm as Social Residue

In this section, we take firm-level effects of employee social networks a step further by introducing a conceptualization of the firm as a constellation of networks—networks that consist of both constituent actors and formal relations with other firms. The firm as a constellation of its constituent actors is apparent in the case of an individual, independent contractor—where the form of organization is coextensive with the "employee" and her network structure. It is also easily appreciated at the boundary of the firm, where coordination is dependent on individuals. Thinking of the firm as an aggregation of constituent networks is not limited to the periphery of the firm; it is also fitting where internal routine is not determined by bureaucratic procedure—such as for high-autonomy positions or for jobs with few peers. Research on internal organization of the firm suggests, in contrast to classic images of bureaucracy and vertical coordination, that many areas of internal coordination are not scripted, but, rather, are negotiated and emergent (Eccles and White, 1988). In the case of multinational firms, geographical dispersion and cultural differences result in their subsidiaries' independence from the formal organization imposed by corporate parents (Ghoshal and Bartlett, 1990). As a result, connections between units effectively function as network relations, the point being that more and more of what was once conceptualized as bureaucratically determined is now understood to evolve through kinds of network relations.

Through interaction and negotiated control, individuals, especially entrepreneurs, come to shape the form and boundaries of the organization. When the content and procedure of work is not scripted, as is increasingly the case, the shape a firm takes at any moment in time depends, in large part, on the action of its employees. Individual coordination complements and even supplants market and bureaucratic forms of coordination. A general blueprint for the structure of the firm may persist, despite changes in personnel, but extant organization is emergent from the behavior of actors in the firm, actors who are constrained or enabled by their position in the social structure. Included in this chapter are examples of how the effective form of organizing is contingent on network behavior: Entrepreneurial network behavior makes the investment-bank deal happen; know-how gleaned through know-whom leads to a new process or product; employees connected across firm boundaries, through social networks, forge a strategic alliance.

Entrepreneurial coordination of interfirm relations also affects the aggregate position of the firm. The firm is influenced by its position in interfirm networks—among buyers and suppliers as well as among competitor firms—much as industries are affected by market position among upstream and downstream industries (Burt, 1992; Raider, 1995; Talmud, 1994; Yasuda, 1993). Industries with greater interfirm coordination that trade with disorganized buyer and supplier industries have higher profit margins than industries in inferior market positions. Shifting positions among firms can affect the nature of a firm and the constraints on a firm in ways analogous to personnel flows. We propose a general notion of the firm as a social structure is needed to relate theory about the firm to sociological theory of markets as social structure (Burt, 1983; Baker, 1981; White, 1981; see also Swedberg, 1994).

Boundaryless careers reinforce a conception of the firm as social residue. The movement away from organizational careers means more ebb and flow of personnel, more-fluid firm boundaries, and more-extensive interfirm networks. Likely, this leads both to calcification of clerical duties to provide a skeleton for the firm; and to growth of social-network forms of coordination, through which entrepreneurs have the opportunity to flesh out the organization of the firm. As we have conveyed here, and as elaborated elsewhere (Burt, 1982, 1992), individual action is constrained and enabled by location in social networks. This holds true at different levels of analysis, for corporate and individual actors alike. Using structural hole theory, in combination with a boundaryless-career perspective, is a way to link these two levels of analysis for study of the firm.

Conclusions

We summarize with three broad conclusions. First, there are complementarities between boundaryless careers and social capital. Strong social capital—contact networks rich in structural holes—is particularly valuable in boundaryless careers, both for job seeking and for career attainment. For job seeking, people in boundaryless careers will frequently use their social-capital resources for job leads and employer information. People with boundaryless careers are often newcomers, and hold positions at the social frontier of firms; these are contexts in which social capital is most strongly associated with performance. We also described how structural hole theory can explain outcome differences between the involuntary and voluntary boundaryless. The association between boundaryless careers and social capital is reinforced by opportunities, presented through interfirm mobility, to construct networks rich in structural holes and to engage in entrepreneurial behavior.

Second, there are firm-level effects of employees' social capital. Firms expand their social network through new as well as departed employees, as illustrated by Chinese family practice. Firms benefit from the social capital of employees through superior performance and enhanced internal coordination. Additionally, individuals with entrepreneurial networks, and in particular those with boundaryless careers, can add value to a firm through the information benefits of these network structures. Extensive relations to people in other firms enables individuals with boundaryless careers to promote interfirm learning, to identify and develop buyer and supplier relations, and to forge strategic alliances, joint ventures, and other such network forms of organization.

Third, we suggest a conceptualization of the firm as social structure. This is motivated by three points: firm-level aggregate effects of employee social networks; sociological research on the role of individuals as mechanisms for economic coordination; and evidence that more and more of what was once thought of as determined by bureaucratic rule is emergent from network relations. As firm boundaries become even more fluid through boundaryless-career behavior, structurally driven theories of action will be powerful alternatives to traditional firm-centered theories of organizational behavior, strategy, and human resource management.

ACKNOWLEDGMENTS: We are grateful to Michael Arthur and Denise Rousseau for valuable assistance; we also thank Robert DeFillippi and Bhaven Sampat for comments and discussion.

References

Arthur, M. B. 1994. "The boundaryless career: A new perspective for organizational inquiry." *Journal of Organizational Behavior*, 15: 295–306.

Baker, W. E. 1990. "Market networks and corporate behavior." *American Journal of Sociology*, 96: 589–625.

Baker, W. E. 1981. "The social structure of a national securities market." *American Journal of Sociology*, 89: 775–811.

Baker, W. E. 1992. "The network organization in theory and practice." in R. G. Eccles and N. Nohria (eds.), *Networks and Organizations*, pp. 397–429. Boston: Harvard Business School Press.

Best, M. H. 1990. *The New Competition: Institutions of Industrial Restructuring*. Cambridge, Mass.: Harvard University Press.

Boxman, E. A. W.; P. M. De Graaf; and H. D. Flap. 1991. "The impact of social and human capital on the income attainment of Dutch managers." *Social Networks*, 13: 51–73.

Burt, R. S. 1995. "The contingent value of social capital." Manuscript, University of Chicago.

Burt, R. S. 1992. *Structural Holes*. Cambridge: Harvard University Press.

Burt, R. S. 1983. *Corporate Profits and Cooptation*. New York: Academic Press.

Burt, R. S. 1982. *Towards a Structural Theory of Action*. New York: Free Press.

DeFillippi, R. J., and M. B. Arthur. 1994. "The boundaryless career: A competency-based perspective." *Journal of Organizational Behavior,* 15: 307–324.

Eccles, R. G., and N. Nohria. 1992. "Face-to-face: Making network organizations work." In R. G. Eccles and N. Nohria (eds.), *Networks and Organizations,* pp. 288–308. Boston: Harvard Business School Press.

Eccles, R. G., and White, H. C. 1988. "Price and authority in inter-profit-center transactions." *American Journal of Sociology,* 94: S17–S51.

Flap, H. D., and N. D. De Graaf. 1989. "Social capital and attained occupational status." *Netherlands Journal of Sociology,* 22: 145–161.

Garguilo, M., and M. Benassi. 1993. "Informal control and managerial flexibility in network organizations." Working paper. Fontainebleau, France: INSEAD.

Ghoshal, S., and Bartlett, C. B. 1990. "The multinational corporation as an interorganizational network." *Academy of Management Review,* 15: 603–625.

Granovetter, M. 1985. "Economic action, social structure, and the problem of embeddedness." *American Journal of Sociology,* 78: 1360–1380.

Granovetter, M. 1995. *Getting a Job: A Study of Contacts and Careers,* 2d ed. Cambridge, Mass.: Harvard University Press.

Hipple, E. von. 1987. "Cooperaton between rivals: Informal know-how trading." *Research Policy,* 16 (6): 201-302.

Ibarra, H. 1992a. "Homophily and differential returns: Sex differences in network structure and access in an advertising firm." *Administrative Science Quarterly,* 37: 422–447.

Ibarra, H. 1992b. "Structural alignments, individual strategies, and managerial action: Elements toward a network theory of getting things done." In R. G. Eccles and E. Nohria (eds.), *Networks and Organizations,* pp. 165–188. Boston: Harvard Business School Press.

Kanter, R. M. 1989. *When Giants Learn to Dance.* New York: Simon and Schuster.

Larson, A. 1992. "Network dyads in entrepreneurial settings: A study of the governance of exchange relationships." *Administrative Science Quarterly,* 37: 76–104.

Lin, N., and M. Dumin. 1986. "Access to occupations through social ties." *Social Networks,* 8: 365–385.

Lin, N.; W. Ensel; and J. Vaughn. 1981. "Social resources and strength of ties: Structural factors in occupational status attainment." *American Sociological Review,* 46: 393–405.

Marsden, P. V., and J. Hurlbert. 1988. "Social resources and mobility outcomes: A replication and extension." *Social Forces,* 66: 1038–1059.

Miles, R. E., and C. C. Snow. 1986. "Network organizations." *California Management Review,* 28 62–73.

Nohria, N. 1992. "Information and search in the creation of new business ventures: The case of the 128 venture group." In R. G. Eccles and N. Nohria (eds.), *Networks and Organizations,* pp. 240–262. Boston: Harvard Business School Press.

Perrow, Charles. 1992. "Small Firm Networks." In R. G. Eccles and N. Nohria (eds.), *Networks and Organizations,* pp. 445–470. Boston: Harvard University Press.

Piore, M. J., and C. F. Sabel. 1984. *The Second Industrial Divide: Possibilities and Prosperity.* New York: Basic Books.

Podolny, Joel M., and James N. Baron. 1994. "Make new friends and keep the old?: Social networks, mobility and satisfaction in the workplace." Manuscript, Stanford University Graduate School of Business.

Powell, W. W. 1990. "Neither market nor hierarchy: Network forms of organization." *Research in Organizational Behavior,* 12: 295–336.

Powell, W. W., and P. Brantly. 1992. "Competitive cooperation in biotechnology: Learning through networks." In R. G. Eccles and N. Nohria (eds.), *Networks and Organizations,* pp. 366–394. Boston: Harvard Business School Press.

Powell, W. W. and L. Smith-Doerr. 1994. "Networks and Economic Life." In Neil J. Smelser and Richard Swedberg (eds.), *Handbook of Economic Sociology,* pp. 368–402. Princeton, N.J.: Princeton University Press.

Raider, H. J. 1995. "Market structure effects on R&D and innovation: Differences across industries." Paper presented at the annual meeting of the American Sociological Association, Washington, D.C.

Rousseau, D. M., and K. A. Wade-Benzoni. 1994. "Linking strategy and human resource practices: How employee and customer contracts are created." *Human Resource Management,* 33: 463–489.

Sabel, C. F. 1993. "Studied trust: Building new forms of cooperation in a volatile society." In Richard Swedberg (ed.), *Explorations in Economic Sociology,* pp. 104–144. New York: Russell Sage.

Saxenian, A. 1994. *Regional Advantage: Culture and Competition in Silicon Valley and Route 128.* Cambridge, Mass.: Harvard University Press.

Simmel, G. 1922. *Conflict and the Web of Group Affiliations.* Trans. K. H. Wolff and R. Bendix. New York: Free Press.

Swedberg, R. 1994. "Markets as social structures." In N. J. Smelser and R. Swedberg (eds.), *The Handbook of Economic Sociology,* pp. 255– 282. Princeton, N. J.: Princeton University Press.

Talmud, I. 1994. "Relations and profits: The social organization of Israeli industry." *Social Science Research,* 23: 109–135.

Uzzi, B. 1995. "The Nature of embeddedness, economic action, and organizational survival." Paper presented at the Social Organization Workshop, Graduate School of Business University of Chicago.

White, H. C. 1992. "Agency as control in formal networks." In R. G. Eccles and N. Nohria (eds.), *Networks and Organizations,* pp. 91–117. Boston: Harvard Business School Press.

White, H. C. 1981. "Where do markets come from?" *American Journal of Sociology,* 87: 517–547.

Wiesenfeld, B. M, and J. Brockner. 1996. "Toward a psychology of contingent work." In J. J. Halpern and R. S. Stern (eds.), *Debating Rationality: Nonrational Aspects of Organizational Decision Making.* Ithaca, N.Y.: ILR Press.

Yasuda, Y. 1993. "A Comparative Structural Analysis of American and Japanese Markets." Ph.D. diss., Department of Sociology, Columbia University.

12

Global Boundaryless Careers: Lessons from Chinese Family Businesses

CHERLYN SKROMME GRANROSE AND
BEE LENG CHUA

The dramatic growth of East Asian economies marks the emergent centrality of "Confucian capitalism" in the new world order (Berger, 1991; Redding, 1990; Hofestede and Bond, 1988). In particular, the growth of the "four dragons"—Singapore, Hong Kong, Taiwan, and South Korea—offers clear evidence of new global players (Woronoff, 1986). The more recent explosion of capitalism, in the People's Republic of China (PRC), Malaysia, Indonesia, Thailand, and Vietnam, echoing the economic transformation of Japan, confirms the magnitude of Asian economic development (Lord, 1995; Berger, 1991; Berger and Hsiao, 1988; Friedman, 1988; Gerlach, in press).

While the story of each of these Asian economies is unique, they share the substantial influence of emigrant Chinese family businesses expanding into international corporate networks. These firms combine the entrepreneurial spirit of Western strategy with the conservative traditions of ancient China, to create uniquely successful entities.

Academic authors have analyzed Japanese business practices regularly since World War II (Lockwood, 1954; Roberts, 1973; Ouchi, 1981; Johnson, 1982), but reports of Chinese management practices have surfaced relatively recently (Landa, 1983; Schermerhorn, 1987; Ralston et al., 1992; Lee and Chen, 1995; Naisbitt, 1996). *Megatrends Asia* claims a major shift away from Japanese economic dominance and toward Chinese and overseas Chinese influence in the Pacific region (Naisbitt, 1996). This shift signals an urgent need to understand the nature of Chinese family businesses and careers.

Careful analyses of economies with a Chinese heritage, such as Redding's

The Spirit of Chinese Capitalism (1990), describe a Confucian and a Buddhist tradition similar to some aspects of Japanese culture. However, these analyses also reveal significant differences that are based on different degrees of firm versus family loyalty; different relationships between government and private enterprise; and different levels of popular democracy (Hofstede and Bond, 1988; Redding, 1990; Berger, 1991). The comparisons indicate that it would be inaccurate to generalize from Japanese to Chinese business experience. They also suggest that analyses of Chinese business practices might yield lessons useful for developing a global perspective of careers.

This chapter examines aspects of Chinese management that may offer new insights into non-Chinese firms. It explores the internal structure and belief systems common in Chinese family firms, and compares their career patterns with new career ideas emanating from the notion of boundaryless careers. Placing boundaryless careers in a new cultural context can stimulate critical thinking that may benefit American, European, and Asian ways of looking at career phenomena. In particular, this analysis emphasizes similarities and differences in obligation, hierarchy, and identity in network-based career behavior. It also explores differences in learning, centralization, and transactional-relational ties.

Since biological membership in a Chinese family is involuntary, those family characteristics dependent on blood ties are of limited interest to others. However, Chinese businesses also foster a broader familism based on family principles, but extending beyond genetic kinship. Strong ties based on a common geography, occupation, and language, and on longstanding business activities, bind people together in many relationships similar to those of families. In addition, both Chinese firms and Western firms are increasing their workforce diversity to include members of other cultures. As a result, analysis of Chinese family businesses offers lessons for those seeking to explore boundaryless careers in non-Chinese contexts, and for those seeking to apply the construct of boundaryless careers to East-West joint-venture and employment relationships.

The Economic Importance of Chinese Family Businesses

Evidence of the importance of Chinese family businesses to East Asian economies is widespread. The importance stems jointly from these businesses' growth within single national economies and from their expansion into transnational activities (Tan, 1986).

Internal Economic Growth

The Chinese family business is the predominant form of business throughout much of East Asia. In Taiwan, the majority of the population trace their ancestry to Fukien province, in the PRC. During two decades of rapid economic growth, Taiwan has risen to the top-20 list of countries in average per capita gross national product (GNP) (Nixon, 1994). Five large family-run firms account for about 10% of Taiwan's GNP, but 901,000 small and medium-sized family firms constitute the largest economic sector (*Excellence Monthly*, 1993; *Central Daily*, 1994).

Hong Kong and Singapore also host many small, and a few very large, family firms founded by immigrants from southern China. In Hong Kong, 99% of companies employ less than 200 people, but a few large, family firms contribute a substantially larger proportion to the GNP (*Hong Kong Annual Report*, 1990). Likewise, in Singapore, the GNP has doubled from the mid-1920s to the mid-1990s and Chinese family firms have played major roles in this expansion (Singapore, 1995; Chan and Chiang, 1994; Hsieh, 1978).

In the Southeast Asian countries of Malaysia, Indonesia, the Philippines, and Thailand, the Chinese, although a minority, are a powerful economic force. In Indonesia, the Chinese comprise only 4% of the population but control 17 of the 25 largest business groups (*South China Morning Post*, 1992). In Thailand, during the 1970s, ethnic Chinese, comprising about 10% of the population, owned 90% of commercial and manufacturing assets and half of the banks' capital. In spite of the Malaysian government's efforts to redistribute the economic wealth to the indigenous majority through its five-year economic plans, that country's Chinese continue to hold on to their wealth by investing it overseas and by installing Malays on boards of directors. Likewise, less than 1% of the people in the Philippines are of pure Chinese descent, but they came to own almost 70% of the commercial entities (Omohundro, 1983).

Going Transnational

Government support, economic prosperity, and the relaxation of restrictions on capital outflow now encourage Asian companies to invest abroad. The opening up of the PRC has stimulated large investments from Hong Kong and Taiwan. Chinese family conglomerates from Indonesia, Malaysia, and Singapore are not far behind in seeking a foothold in PRC markets. Other frontiers for offshore ventures in Asia include Indonesia, Thailand, Burma, the Philippines, Malaysia, and India (Lord, 1995). These transnational activities, and popular and government support behind them, represent an evolution of extended family networks used when ancestors first ventured out of China to seek their fortunes.

Chinese families often use marriage alliances and nonpatrilineal inheritance systems to establish their external business dynasties (Wang, 1993: 193). For hundreds of years, successful merchants in Thailand and the Philippines have had their children marry members of local aristocratic or patrician families in order to ease the way for doing business smoothly. Other ties are cultivated through family members' participation in foreign higher education systems (described later in this chapter).

Strategic family alliances in the 1990s are a prominent vehicle for expansion abroad. Powerful Chinese family businesses have joined forces not only with each other, but also with indigenous family groups from the countries in which they seek to establish businesses, or with Western firms offering capital or specific know-how. One well-known joint venture includes Ong Beng Seng of Singapore, and Khin Sunda Win, who built an office complex in the capital of Burma; Khin Sunda is the daughter of Burma's prime minister. Another well-known alliance involves Li Ka-shing and Deng Zhifang, son of Deng Xiaoping, who formed the New China Hong Kong Group. Li has helped Wu Jianchang, Deng Xiaoping's eldest son-in-law, and has close links with Deng Nan, the patriarch's second daughter.

The Emergence of Chinese Family Business Activities

Both national and transnational Chinese family business activities draw on a rich history of shared social and cultural experiences. They also draw on strong traditions of management practices, family loyalty, and social networking. All of these factors underlie current business practices and career behavior.

Social Origins

The early overseas Chinese came from peasant and laboring classes. On arriving in Southeast Asia, they had few skills, few blood relatives, and limited financial resources (Limlingan, 1986). Many early immigrants could not obtain land for farming, so they became self-employed in commodity trading. The immigrants established social networks that provided food and housing, and that gave them information about business opportunities. These social networks also provided capital loans and labor for new business activities (Lim and Gosling, 1983; Landa, 1983).

An intricate system of unrenounceable work and social relationships, among close and distant family members, lends mutual support to Chinese family businesses (Wong, 1988). Chinese values and practices, including maintaining loyal, hierarchical family relationships, and preserving the family name and honor, facilitate this system. Norms of creating wealth and security for future generations, through pragmatism, hard work, and continuous learning, perpetuate the family.

In an environment of high-risk price fluctuation and minority status, trust was important to Chinese businessmen entering a new community. Trusting relationships played a particular role in supporting pre-1949 Chinese merchants, who were developing freedom from Mandarin or official control, and were entering into risky ventures (Wang, 1993). The trustworthy included kinsmen, people from their old villages in China, clansmen, friends, guild members, and those in the same dialect group—that is, "extended family" (Landa, 1983). The emphasis on trust lives on today as Chinese family businesses expand and diversify, and seek to recruit new family and nonfamily expertise into their ranks.

Social Organization and Expanded Definitions of Family

The Chinese perceive *family* differently from Western and other Asian cultures. The Chinese family includes a network of close and distant relatives, or kinsmen and clan members, as well as those not related by blood, such as people originating from the same Chinese village. Clans are defined on the basis of a shared last name, and assume some blood ties. Although a shared name may not indicate common ancestry, it is enough to claim kinship ties with strangers in a new land, and is sufficient to shape careers in directions based on trusting relationships.

Familylike forms of voluntary social organization also play an important role in identifying who can be trusted in Chinese communities (Hsieh, 1978; Mak, 1988). The voluntary associations include *hui-kuans,* dialect associations, and guilds (Tan, 1986). The *hui-kuans* are associations of members from the same village or province, embracing a larger geographic unit than members of a single blood line. Dialect associations represent larger groupings, organized according to distinctive languages, such as Hokkien, Cantonese, Hakka, Hainanese, Shanghainese, and Teochew. Guilds originated in China to represent a trade, business, or craft. Unlike modern trade unions and professional associations, the function of guilds extends beyond occupational interests to the providing of assistance, such as educational and burial aid, to members and their families. Guild members also worship patron gods of their trade or craft.

In her study of Chinese middlemen in Southeast Asia, Landa (1983) observes that social relations are placed in rank categories. Of highest status and significance are close kinsmen from the family, followed by distant kinsmen from the extended family. The third category includes the clansmen; and the fourth, the fellow villagers from China who may also use the same dialect. The fifth-ranking category is comprised of people who are not from the same village, but who share the same dialect. Those who do not use the same dialect, but are Chinese, belong to the sixth category, while the non-Chinese comprise the last category.

While the precise order of ranking may not be universal, some ranking determines the degree of relatedness or kinship, and thus the degree of trustworthiness. Kinsmen are bound by the Confucian code of ethics to conduct themselves properly in terms of their ranking in the network of relationships; so the closer the relationship, the greater the degree of obligation and trust. If trust cannot not be established on kinship bases, it has to be developed as a personal relationship of one individual to another. This is a more time-consuming, but still important, aspect of running a business, and forms a large part of the network of relationships that is the key to successful Chinese family businesses.

Cultural Roots of Chinese Firms

Chinese values, like the values of other cultures in Asia, are anchored in the Confucian philosophy. Three key values include obligation-based relationships, continuous learning, and a focus on the practical worldly existence, rather than on the spiritual realm.

An important Confucian principle linking heaven, earth, emperor, parents, and teacher (*tiān dì, jūn, fù mǔ, shī*) dictates a code of proper behavior for establishing and maintaining relationships with members of a group, initially a family, but also extending to larger units of the community and society. This principle prescribes a pattern of relationships based on fulfilling social obligations with sensitivity and reciprocity, to ensure harmony and continuity. Behavior, according to Confucian principles, enhances the reputation of one who is sensitive to obligations; and it destroys the face, reputation, and honor of one who is not fulfilling obligations (Carmody and Carmody, 1983; Chong, 1987).

There are five types of relationships—between ruler and subject, father and son, brother and brother, husband and wife, and friend and friend. Four of these reflect superior-subordinate statuses, and guide the nature of the relationship between boss and employee. The subordinate is obligated to treat the superior with deference, obey instructions, take advice, and not challenge authority. In return, the superior should show concern for the subordinate and ensure that the subordinate's needs are met, as a parent would do for a child.

The inclusion of friend-friend relationships provides rules for harmonious interactions with peers, and also provides the model for how relationships based on family are extended beyond blood kin. This is particularly important as a guideline for establishing a non-kin personal network of those who can be considered trustworthy. In these peer relationships, the key ingredients are mutual loyalty and beneficence like between father and son.

A second characteristic of Confucianism is the emphasis on education and learning (*jiào yǔ wué*) as an important mechanism for achieving a virtuous life. A network of schools and a system of promotions to government positions—based on meritorious performance in examinations—were instituted during the primary era of Confucian influence in China. A balance—between favor based on familial relationships, and favor based on education and performance—persists in political and economic systems among ethnic Chinese.

The strong emphasis given to overseas college education for children of powerful and wealthy Chinese entrepreneurs is a contemporary expression of the traditional value of education. Several examples from Hong Kong illustrate the point. The two sons of entrepreneur Li Ka-Shing are both graduates of Stanford University; although still in their 20s, both are already well immersed as executive directors in various arms of the family business. The three Kwok brothers of the Sun Hung Kai group were educated at the Imperial College, London University, as well as at Cambridge and Harvard universities. At the Wing On Group, the director is Philip Kwok, a physicist trained at MIT and Harvard University. Victor Fung and his brother, of the Li and Fung Company, hold postgraduate U.S. degrees in business administration and physics.

Returning with business degrees from Western universities, the children of Chinese family conglomerates bring with them Western management concepts and practices. This group of second-generation overseas Chinese not only gains support from the network of kinsfolk, but also brings a different set of modern management tools.

The training gained in obligation networks is frequently more important than formal education. The socialization, coaching, and mentoring aspects of paternalistic relationships (*jiā zhǎng shì*) support continuous, informal education. In particular, socialization in regard to the family business occurs during many familial interactions (Redding, 1990).

A third characteristic of Confucianism is the concentration of attention on the worldly here and now (*tiān guó*), rather than on the mystical, imagined world of deities. Reportedly, Confucius vehemently denied that his principles were religious in an otherworldly sense. He affirmed the necessity of being grounded in a practical daily reality. His practical rules for daily living include hard work (*qín*), perseverance (*yì*), frugality (*jiǎn*), and patience (*rěn*).

While honoring experience and age brings a conservative bias in traditional Chinese thinking, this focus on the practical here and now provides a counter-force grounded in contemporary daily reality. Because the rules of daily living are applied to maintain a natural order and harmony (*tiā dào yǔ zhōng hé*), they contribute both to maintenance of tradition and to adaptive responses to changing economic and cultural environments. The essence of this pragmatism is to focus on applying tradition to the current setting.

Chinese Management Practices

Chinese management principles emanating from cultural and social values include autocratic control, nepotism, and networking. Paternalism within networks of carefully prescribed relationships is a primary characteristic of the management style in Chinese companies.

The style of the patriarchal leader of the family business is generally both autocratic and decisive: The family head implements centralized decision making. Thus, decisions about careers for organizational members usually reflect the judgment of the company's owner about what will be best for the overall business and family welfare (Redding and Wong, 1986; Silin, 1976).

Children usually follow the career paths that their fathers decide for them, often taking a particular role and position in the family business. Alternatively, children are told to pursue a position in another firm; or, they are told to start a branch of the family business in another location, in order to learn a specific skill, learn about a particular business, or cement a particular relationship assumed to have a long-term benefit to the family. The education and placement of children of Hong Kong families mentioned earlier provide examples of this principle.

Control in Chinese family businesses stresses financial security, whereby access to information is restricted to trustworthy individuals, usually close family members. The need for control extends to longer-term interests in wealth accumulation and advancement opportunities. Access to financial resources, information, and career mobility is given to people whose frugality and trustworthiness are assured by "kinship, prior personal bonds, recommendation, personal dependency, or prior demonstrated loyalty, that is, seniority" (Deyo, 1983).

The Impact of Nepotism

The Confucian principle of according respect and priority to older family members (*zhūn lǎo jìn lǎo*) has traditionally meant that the eldest son succeeded the father as head of the firm. However, this tradition is balanced by a pragmatic evaluation of skill, education, and competence. The older sibling who works for the company may get a greater share because he has been involved in the company longer; however, all older sons do not take over family businesses. Younger sons, sons-in-law, or even daughters, who demonstrate superior business ability may be chosen as heirs if such choices are in the family's best interest.

In some cases, family relationships and nepotism may not be openly acknowledged. The media have noted a reluctance to disclose succession plans, and often speculate about who will take over a family business. During one interview, a son of a Hong Kong business tycoon responded to a question on succession, "I don't even know whether it's been worked out yet; . . . we never talk about it" (Johnstone and Chalkley, 1992).

The disadvantages of nepotism appear compelling. Conflict may arise when employees resent relatives or kinsmen who have an attitude that they deserve special privileges (Redding, 1990). Nepotism used to fulfill family obligations can result in employing people who are not needed, or do not have appropriate qualifications or experience. It is difficult to terminate relatives for poor performance, as this can invoke criticism from the rest of the family. A recent example of this problem involved one of Indonesia's conglomerate family businesses, which failed, in part, due to management limitations of the patriarch's son.

However, Redding (1990) argues that nepotism does not necessarily promote weakness or inefficiency. Rather, it is a way of dealing with the problem of trust in a minimally integrated society, particularly in the early years of migration. Labor costs can be lower, since relatives are more willing to work for low wages if their basic needs are taken care of in the family. Both job hunting and employee selection are made easier because of the obligation to help relatives by giving them jobs. Decisions tend to be made faster when relatives committed to obedience and loyalty are partners or employees. Placing kinsmen in responsible positions prevents dissipation of family property and profits to outsiders, and perpetuates the family name (Wong, 1988).

Initiating Networks

In the event of Chinese family migration, tradition dictates that the eldest son will remain behind to take care of the family assets, and to fulfill his filial duties of caring for the elderly parents. The younger siblings may set up new businesses elsewhere, but maintain ties with their parental origins. Thus, over time, domestic family-business networks can expand into international business networks.

Nonfamily employees and younger siblings see their days as "numbered" in a Chinese company. Positions provide exposure to needed skills and serve as stepping stones for becoming owners of new businesses. Chinese family businesses support this practice even though they lose well-trained employees. They do this because cultural beliefs affirm the importance of learning in all situations; and because family businesses cannot provide top-management positions for every family member. In addition, every spin-off yields a potential business relationship, a fact often acknowledged by a financial contribution to the departing employee's venture.

Ironically, the lack of career opportunities for younger siblings and nonfamily members in Chinese organizations has been an impetus for economic growth in indigenous Chinese communities. Redding and Tam (n.d.) note the role of this phenomenon in the growth of the Hong Kong economy during the past 30 years. The situation in Taiwan is similar: The current ratio of CEOs in the Taiwanese labor force is 2.5 CEOs for every 100 people. This high ratio arises from the large number of self-employed entrepreneurs (Peng, 1995). As the popular Chinese proverb indicates, "It is better to be the head of a chicken than the tail of an ox." Likewise, a small textile-factory owner in the PRC has been quoted: "A Shanghainese at 40 who has not yet made himself owner of a firm is a failure, a good-for-nothing" (Wong, 1988: 98).

The three top reasons that Chinese give for wanting to become entrepreneurs are: to more fully use their expertise and abilities (35.2% say this), to escape control by others (32.2%); and to have a greater chance to make money (21.3%) (Jan, 1992). The popularity of entrepreneurship and the motivation for monetary success create a strong economic impact. Also, the common career practice of new-firm formation creates a wide array of new career options.

Consolidating Network Effects

A further consequence of the exiting of younger siblings and nonfamily members is that individuals have a network of relationships, composed of both kinship ties and obligation friendships, and built during previous employment relationships. If, in a previous firm, someone trained, promoted, and helped an individual, this obligation persists and is reciprocated in the new setting. In addition, a personal network of relationships built by business transactions may be shared by old and new firms to their mutual advantage.

Chinese family businesses are now seeking to add non-Chinese business relationships to their networks, and frequently tout the mutual benefits (Brauchli and Biers, in the *Wall Street Journal,* April 19, 1995). The Chinese businesses gain sophistication and know-how, and their partners gain access to Chinese family networks. A typical example is the alliance between Malaysia's family-controlled YTL Corporation and Siemens AG, to develop electric-power plants in Malaysia. The German firm contributed technological skills, while the Malaysian firm contributed the government license and connections needed to implement the project (Brauchli and Biers, in the *Wall Street Journal,* April 19, 1995).

The result of these organizational practices is an interlinked network. The network includes firms tied by family links of siblings who founded their own businesses; offspring migrating to new locations to learn, and then returning to enrich the family business repertoire; and offspring sent to start another firm in a new location. The network also includes nonfamilial links bound by school ties, business relationships, common Chinese language, Chinese ethnicity, and occupational guilds. Nodes in the network are tied by mutual bonds of trust, loyalty, and obligation. These ties are reinforced by exchanges of goods, services, capital, information, and personnel. Hierarchy and degrees of closeness and trust define the extent of the exchanges along the network lines.

Useful Lessons from Chinese Family-Business Success

The construct of the boundaryless career seems particularly useful, because it describes facets of work lives (network links tied to reputation, learning, and the exchange of basic necessities for career opportunities) that are important in cultures as diverse as the United States, Japan, Europe, and Chinese communities in Southeast Asia (Koike, 1990; Arthur, 1994; Nohria and Eccles, 1992).

However, this chapter suggests both similarities and differences between Chinese family-business activities and Western thinking on boundaryless careers. Our principal purpose here is to draw useful lessons from Chinese family-business success so as to inform the fledgling boundaryless-careers agenda. A secondary purpose is to promote better understanding between East Asian and Western firms who exchange commerce and employees, and collaborate in the expanding arena of joint-venture opportunities.

Networks

Networks, from a boundaryless-careers perspective, not only provide gates of inclusion and exclusion; they also provide access to others' resources and information, both at the individual and firm levels of analysis. Being embedded in a professional network provides opportunities for business transactions, opportunities for interfirm mobility, and opportunities for learning and teaching as information flows among network members (Nohria, 1992).

Networks, as used in Chinese family businesses, have all of these characteristics. Like boundaryless careers, Chinese family businesses thrive on extended networks of trust arising from degrees of social linkage, and from reputations. They embody values of learning, pragmatism, and reciprocal exchange. Both family members and nonfamily peers use networks to exchange information, goods, and business services; and as vehicles through which personal industry can be rewarded through wages, training, and entrepreneurship opportunities.

However, beyond surface similarities, other characteristics of Chinese family businesses suggest new implications for the further study of boundaryless careers. Three particular characteristics—*obligation, rank ordering,* and *self-definition*—are discussed below.

Obligation (yì wú)

The reciprocal-obligation component of Chinese networks is one of their great strengths. Obligation is *assumed* between family members on the basis of the shared benefits to family welfare, and the honor brought to the family name. But among nonkinsfolk, the obligation of participating in a network is *created* as a friendship is built. Indeed, layers of obligation are carefully and slowly built through initial small favors, then intermediate moderate requests, and, later, an exchange of larger debts. For example, it is not uncommon for a person to be given, initially, a small part-time job, then a full position, and, later, funds to purchase a car and a home, or even a child's college education (Wong, 1988). Requests for favors are not made lightly, because the recipient of the request is bound, by honor, not to refuse if the request comes from a family-network member, and the act of asking incurs a future obligation. This sense of obligation, as a characteristic of network relationships, exists also in Japanese, Korean, and other Asian cultures; and in each of these cultures, careful attention to these obligations defines one's reputation (Axelrod, 1984; Ota, 1989; De Vos, 1973).

Paying more attention to the obligatory costs of networks, in addition to their opportunities, may clarify a further aspect of the role networks play in boundaryless careers. When an entire career is shaped by lifelong networks, rather than by the more-transitory networks used to obtain a single position or a few pieces of information, the accumulation of debts and obligations may become a substantial influence on the choices made by both individuals and firms.

Likewise, ignoring one's debts may be a more influential source of conflict, career stagnation, and loss of reputation than has been anticipated in writings about boundaryless careers. Current discussions of reputation in boundaryless careers focus on the reputation gained by demonstrated expertise. This is also an important source of reputation and rewards among Chinese. But examination of careers in Chinese family businesses reminds us that trustworthiness in meeting obligations is another important dimension of one's reputation. A stronger theme of trustworthiness could be a useful addition to Western ideas about boundaryless-career behavior.

Rank Ordering (wŭ lún)

A second characteristic of Chinese family-business networks is the way in which networks are ranked. As previously described, family and blood relations command the highest ranks, but are followed by six or seven decreasing degrees of closeness, from commonality of village through shared language. The ranking of the network determines the amount of shared trust, shared knowledge, and shared physical resources.

This ranked (or nested) aspect of networks raises at least two questions for boundaryless careers. First, if we apply the concept of boundaryless careers in hierarchical or high power distance cultures, do careers become boundaryless when they move beyond a single firm, such as the family business, or are the firm boundaries simply replaced by hierarchically ranked boundaries of other networks? Stated differently, what difference does it make to change the unit of analysis from the boundaries of a (familial or nonfamilial) intrafirm network to the boundaries of an extended conglomerate, an intraregional network, or an intraindustry network?

The reverse question also proves thought provoking: What happens when the notion that all networks are not equal is applied to boundaryless careers? In cultures that value equality more and value hierarchical loyalty less, what are the other dimensions along which networks might be ranked in their relevance to boundaryless careers? What kinds of differences do the dimensions selected for ranking make?

Self-definition (rén)

A third important characteristic of networks in Chinese family businesses is their function in determining a person's identity, or self-concept. Networks do this by defining a specified position, and its relationship to all other positions, for each network member.

One aspect of collectivism in cultures such as the Chinese is self-definition through "being in relationship" to others, rather than self-definition through "doing something" as autonomous behavior. For example, Ho (1993) states that in a collectivist culture, "self" means the place of the individual in a web of interpersonal relationships. Placement in the social web influences both the "social self" and the "inner self." If the inner self is defined by doing (and the "social self" is neglected) in an individualistic culture, the network may not play the same role in self-affirmation.

The group, or unit of collectivism, and the precise nature of the relationship of an individual to the group, differ in each culture, but the importance of the relationship in defining the self remains constant in collectivist cultures (Ho, 1993; Kim et al., 1994). Applying the construct of boundaryless careers to firms in cultures high in various dimensions of collectivism may prove inappropriate when the key defining process in a boundaryless career remains an individualistic, action-oriented, and self-directed one.

On the other hand, seeking to expand the definition of boundaryless careers to include collective, "being-in-relationship" perspectives raises other interesting possibilities. Is defining a career as one's position in a web of interrelated networks (such as occupational, industrial, regional, ethnic, gender, and school-cohort networks) one way of positively valuing many different career patterns, rather than valuing only vertical career progress in a large corporation? Does position in multiple networks provide a useful way of understanding entrepreneurship, product teams, and other new forms of intrafirm as well as interfirm careers? Can a collectivist view of boundaryless careers, defined by position in a network of relationships, rather than by individual career orientation, provide mechanisms to counteract the isolation and egocentrism implied in limited views of self-directed boundaryless careers?

Learning Orientation

Emphasis on learning and knowledge is another dimension that both boundaryless and Chinese family business careers have in common (Hall and Mirvis, 1994). Discussion of company and career knowledge, from a U.S. perspective, has focused on "knowing why," "knowing how," and "knowing whom" (De-Fillippi and Arthur, in chapter 7 of this volume), questions which would be familiar in a Chinese setting, also. But the answers sought to these questions, and the ways of learning, might differ.

In U.S. explanations of "knowing why" people make particular career choices include defining the self in autonomous or entrepreneurial ways (Weick and Berlinger, 1989) and balancing work and home lives through unique personal choices (Bailyn, 1993). Chinese firms offer an alternative not often considered in an era when work in the United States is so sharply separated from family life. While entrepreneurship is considered important, the Chinese define the self in terms of their collective membership in a family, and make choices in terms of what is good for the family as a whole, not what is good for any one member.

It may seem unlikely that a collectivist view of the self will become important in cultures steeped in individualism. However, in an era when many families are composed of multiple wage earners, and when entrepreneurial or corporate demands may require geographical movement, the family-welfare perspective may be helpful. It offers a way of establishing criteria for making difficult choices—criteria that may have been underutilized by Western families, and largely ignored by many non-Asian scholars.

Regarding "knowing how," the U.S. perspective emphasizes the continuous learning of job-relevant knowledge and firm-relevant knowledge from multiple sources, especially occupational and industrial communities (DeFillippi and Arthur, in chapter 7 of this volume). The Chinese perspective reinforces the emphasis on continuous learning. However, it also highlights the roles of more-experienced paternalistic mentors, and members of a common cultural group, as specific sources of knowledge. Learning from elders who are not immediate job supervisors might be easy to ignore in the struggle to stay abreast of a rapidly changing technical environment. But elders who are experienced in many domains (not just the familial) might suggest how not to repeat past mistakes when trying something new.

For example, among the Philippine Chinese, the formation of social networks incorporates features of Filipino and Chinese social relationships. These include "agnatic" or blood kin and "affinal" Filipino relatives through marriage, who may serve as trusted employees, managers, mentors, and links with the local population. The Philippine Chinese also follow the local practice of appointing godparents, or *compadres*. The godparent system allows a younger person to become attached to an older person who may not be a relative. The godparent takes the responsibility of guiding the youth and providing many kinds of assistance, including giving the younger person a job in the godparent's family business. Thus, the Philippine Chinese have a wide range of people who could best teach them and serve their business interests (Omohundro, 1983: 79).

Learning from members of a cultural-identity group is not exclusive to the expatriate Chinese. But the importance of this source of learning, when old learning networks are no longer available, is typical of Chinese expatriate experiences. Incorporating both sources of learning—from nonorganizational elders outside the firm and from other members of a cultural-identity group—into discussions of boundaryless careers may highlight new learning opportunities.

"Knowing whom" in boundaryless career behavior emphasizes developing peer contacts from interfirm and nonhierarchical networks (Nohria and Eccles, 1992). Boundaryless career perspectives assume a decline in the importance of learning from, and networking with, hierarchical superiors, such as supervisors, inside a firm. But in Chinese society, familism presumes hierarchial relationships, which exist in both intrafirm and interfirm networks. Someone who is of one's father's generation, even if not a blood relative, and even if in a different firm, still commands respect and obligation.

The presence of a clear hierarchy is one of the largest differences between the current trends to flatten Euro-American-based firms and the present realities of Chinese-based firms. In Chinese firms, the hierarchy is seen as contributing to efficiency, not detracting from it, because there are clear role relationships for everyone involved. When we apply boundaryless-career principles outside the United States, we must pay careful attention to honor the hierarchical dimensions of work life important in other cultures, such as the Chinese, the Japanese, and the Korean, even if these dimensions have been reduced in domestic U.S. settings (Hofstede and Bond, 1988).

Centralization

The assumption that new visions of careers will occur primarily in flat, participatory forms of organization based on individual autonomy does not fit the traditional Chinese organizational structure. Chinese family businesses thrive on centralized, autocratic decision making within and across multiple networks. Centralized decision making usually goes unchanged even when Chinese family members trained abroad in management techniques seek to modernize family businesses. For example, we cited the Western-educated Chinese son who did not know if his father had chosen an heir, but who soon became the head of the large family conglomerate.

In Euro-American settings, we assume that shared decision making brings added motivation to enact a decision, because one has helped make the decision, and because one has increased information through participation. In contrast, centralized decisions are enacted in Chinese organizations through motivation created by obligation, not motivation created by participation. While both ways may get the job done, boundaryless career processes may not describe Chinese experiences accurately. This difference in centralization raises a question of whether the autonomy aspect of boundaryless careers prevents applying it to Chinese family businesses or to other centralized forms of organization. If boundaryless careers are applicable, how must the concept be modified to enable application in settings where centralized decision making is the norm? Answering this question may prove crucial to successfully adapting boundaryless career principles to these types of firms.

Transactional-Relational Ties

The final characteristic shared by boundaryless careers and careers in Chinese family organizations is the belief that hard, industrious work is exchanged for the means to obtain basic necessities. However, the basis of exchange in Chinese familial firms is exactly the one being renounced by today's downsizing Western firms—namely, the relational exchange of loyalty in return for promises of shared security, a reputation, and future well-being. In the Chinese way of thinking, *relational* and *transactional* are not dichotomous terms, but, rather, are parts of the same whole. One is in a relationship that is defined by a certain form of transaction. Even if the relationship is between nonfamily members and a family firm, or between nonfamilial, occupational guild members, an expectation of a Confucian exchange of protection and well-being for loyalty and industry defines the relationship and the exchanges between those in the relationship. This raises a most challenging question for the boundaryless-careers perspective. To what extent should career scholars be developing a new definition of careers in response to Western firms' unwillingness to participate in relationships based on the loyalty and welfare of employees? Or, to what extent should we be differentiating the career characteristics of this aspect of employment life from other contemporaneous changes that influence boundaryless careers, such as network structures, computerized technologies, flexible job definitions, and continuous learning?

One lesson that Chinese family businesses may have to teach is that entrepreneurial-network structures, continuous learning, accommodation to environmental and technological change, and economic success can occur in firms whose very foundations are the long-term loyalty obligations that some contemporary U.S. firms are abandoning. Does the careers discipline want to define the new vision of careers as one which accepts, without questioning or empirically examining, the prevailing assumption that such loyalty is no longer economically feasible or culturally desirable? Or given the discipline's long history of concern with human welfare, do we wish to suggest alternatives inspired by the example of Chinese family businesses?

Conclusion

Our purpose in this chapter has been to describe the principal facets of Chinese family businesses and to relate them to the new concept of boundaryless careers. We have suggested multiple lessons drawn from our observations of expatriate-Chinese career behavior, each of which broadens the boundaryless careers agenda. The *lessons*—we use the term guardedly since there is still much to learn—may apply to Western-Chinese firm interactions, firm alliances, and cross-cultural employment of Chinese individuals.

Our closing thought for the boundaryless careers agenda is a central challenge: Is it possible to create patterns of lifelong work in network-oriented, entrepreneurial, technologically sophisticated, learning firms that have the positive characteristics of shared trust, a good reputation, employment security, rapid decision making, and easy recruitment, without the downside cost of unneeded, unqualified, or unmotivated employees? If we can explore boundaryless careers in a way that responds to this challenge, we may have learned from cross-cultural comparisons, and also built a basis for greater East-West understanding in an increasingly interdependent world.

References

Arthur, M. B. 1994. "The boundaryless career: A new perspective for organizational inquiry." *Journal of Organizational Behavior,* 15: 295–306.

Axelrod, R. 1984. *The Evolution of Cooperation.* New York: Basic Books.

Bailyn, L. 1993. *Breaking the Mold.* New York: Free Press.

Berger, P. L. 1991. *The Capitalist Revolution.* New York: Basic Books.

Berger, P. L., and M. Hsiao. 1988. *In Search of an East Asian Development Model.* New Brunswick, N.J.: Transaction Publishers.

Brauchli, M. W., and D. Biers. 1995. "Overseas Chinese reach outside the clan." *Asian Wall Street Journal,* April, 20: 1–5.

Carmody, D. L., and J. T. Carmody. 1983. *Eastern Ways to the Center: An Introduction to Asian Religions.* Belmont, Calif.: Wadsworth.

Central Daily. 1994. "A thirty thousand increase in medium and small enterprises than last year." September 14, International Edition.

Chan, K. B., and C. Chiang. 1994. *Stepping Out: The Making of Chinese Entrepreneurs.* Singapore: Prentice Hall.

Chong, L. C. 1987. "History and managerial culture in Singapore: 'Pragmatism,' 'openness' and 'paternalism.' " *Asia Pacific Journal of Management,* 4: 133–143.

DeFillippi, R. J., and M. B. Arthur. 1994. "The boundaryless career: A competency-based perspective." *Journal of Organizational Behavior,* 15: 307–324.

DeVos, G. 1973. *Socialization for Achievement.* Berkeley: University of California Press.

Deyo, F. C. 1983. "Chinese management practices and work commitment in comparative perspective." In P. Gosling and L. Lim (eds.), *The Chinese in Southeast Asia.* Singapore: Maruzen Asia.

Excellence Monthly. 1993. "Five big families taking over Taiwan." September, 109: 28–33.

Friedman, D. 1988. *The Misunderstood Miracle of Industrial Development and Political Change in Japan.* Ithaca, NY: Cornell University Press.

Gerlach, M. L. In press. "Economic organization and innovation in Japan." *Journal of Economic Behavior and Organization.*

Hall, D. T., and P. P. H. Mirvis. 1994. "Careers as lifelong learning." In A. Howard (ed.), *The Changing Nature of Work.* San Francisco: Jossey-Bass.

Ho, D. Y. F. 1993. "Relational orientation in Asian social psychology." In Y. Kim and J. W. Berry (eds.), *Indigenous Psychologies: Research and Experience in Cultural Context.* Newbury Park, Calif.: Sage, pp. 240–259.

Hofstede, G., and M. H. Bond. 1988. "The Confucius connection: From cultural roots to economic growth." *The Journal of Organizational Dynamics,* 16: 4–21.

Hong Kong Annual Report. 1990. Hong Kong Government Information Services, p. 99.

Hsieh, J. 1978. "The Chinese community in Singapore: The internal structure and its basic constituents." In P. J. S. Chen and H. D. Evers (eds.), *Studies in ASEAN Sociology.* Singapore: Chopmen Enterprises.

Jan, T. S. 1992. "Survey on the work preference of entry-level college graduates." *Management Monthly,* 215: 112–118.

Johnson, C. 1982. *MITI And The Japanese Miracle.* Stanford, Calif.: Stanford University Press.

Johnstone, R., and A. Chalkley. 1992. "Empire of the son." *Hong Kong Tatler.* January: 74–79.

Kim, U.; H. C. Triandis; C. Kagitcibasi; J. S. Choi; and G. Yoon. 1994. *Collectivism and Individualism.* Thousand Oaks, Calif.: Sage.

Koike, K. 1990. "Intellectual skill and the role of employees as constituent members of large firms in contemporary Japan." In M. Aoki; M. Gustavsson; and O. E. Williamson (eds.), *The Firm as a Nexus of Treaties.* Newbury Park, Calif.: Sage.

Landa, J. T. 1983. "The political economy of the ethnically homogeneous Chinese middle group in Southeast Asia: Ethnicity and entrepreneurship in a plural society." In *The Chinese in Southeast Asia.* Singapore: Maruzen Asia, with Economic Research Centre, and Centre for South and Southeast Asia.

Lee, Y. T., and C. C. Chen. 1995. "The effect of modernization on Chinese values and attitudes." Paper presented to the American Psychological Society, Washington, D.C.

Lim, L. Y. C., and P. L. A. Gosling (eds.). 1983. *The Chinese in Southeast Asia,* vol. 1: *Ethnicity and Economic Activity.* Singapore: Maruzen, Asia, with Economic Research Centre, and Centre for South and Southeast Asia.

Limlingan, V. S. 1986. *The Overseas Chinese in ASEAN: Business Strategies and Management Practices.* Ann Arbor, Mich.: University Microfilms International.

Lockwood, W. W. 1954. *The Economic Development of Japan, Growth and Structural Change 1868–1938.* Princeton, N.J.: Princeton University Press.

Lord, W. 1995. "Building a Pacific community." *Word Affairs Journal,* 8: 1–2.

Mak, L. F. 1988. "Chinese secret societies in the nineteenth century Straits Settlements." In Lee Lai To (ed.), *Early Chinese Immigrant Societies.* Singapore: Heinemann Asia.

Naisbitt, J. 1996. *Megatrends Asia.* New York: Simon and Schuster.

Nohria, N. 1992. "Is a network perspective a useful way of studying organizations?" In N. Nohria and R. G. Eccles (eds.), *Networks and Organizations.* Boston: Harvard Business School Press.

Nohria, N., and R. G Eccles. 1992. *Networks and Organizations.* Boston: Harvard Business School Press.

Omohundro, J. T. 1983. "Social networks and business success for the Philippine Chinese." In *The Chinese in Southeast Asia,* vol. 1: *Ethnicity and Economic Activity.* Singapore: Maruzen, Asia, with Economic Research Centre, and Centre for South and Southeast Asia.

Ota, M. 1989. "Effects of global communication networks on Japanese human resource management strategies." Paper presented at the Annual Conference of the Association for International Business. Singapore.

Ouchi, W. G. 1981. *Theory Z.* Reading, Mass.: Addison-Wesley.

Peng, T. K. 1995. "Career planning and development of managers in Taiwan." Unpublished manuscript.

Ralston, D. A.; P. M. Elsass; D. J. Gustafson; F. Cheung; and R. H. Terpstra. 1982. "Eastern values: A comparison of managers in the United States, Hong Kong, and the People's Republic of China." *Journal of Applied Psychology,* 77: 664–671.

Redding, S. G. 1990. *The Spirit of Chinese Capitalism.* Berlin, New York: Walter de Gruter.

Redding, S. G., and S. Tam. N.d. "Networks and molecular organizations: An exploratory view of Chinese firms in Hong Kong." Unpublished paper, University of Hong Kong.

Redding, S. G., and G. Y. Y. Wong. 1986. "The psychology of Chinese organizational behavior." In Michael H. Bond (ed.), *The Psychology of the Chinese People.* Hong Kong: Oxford University Press.

Roberts, J. G. 1973. *Three Centuries of Japanese Business.* Tokyo: Weatherhill.

Schermerhorn, Jr., J. R. 1987. "Organizational features of Chinese industrial enterprise: Paradoxes of stability in times of change." *The Academy of Management Executive,* 1: 343–347.

Silin, R. H. "Leadership and Values." 1976. In *The Organization of Large-Scale Taiwanese Enterprises.* Cambridge, Mass.: East Asian Research Center, Harvard University.

Singapore Facts and Pictures 1995. Singapore: Ministry of Information and the Arts.

South China Morning Post. 1992. "Adding up strength of overseas Chinese." July 25.

Tan, T. W. 1986. "Your Chinese roots." In *The Overseas Chinese Story.* Singapore: Times Books International.

Wang, G. 1993. *China and the Chinese Overseas.* Singapore: Times Academic Press.

Weick, K. E., and L. R. Berlinger. 1989. "Career improvisation in self-designing organizations." In M. B. Arthur; D. T. Hall; and B. S. Lawrence (eds.), *Handbook of Career Theory.* New York: Cambridge University Press.

Wong, S. 1988. "Emigrant Entrepreneurs." In *Shanghai Industrialists in Hong Kong.* Hong Kong: Oxford University Press.

Woronoff, J. 1986. *Japan's Commercial Empire.* Tokyo: Lotus Press.

13

The Rhetoric of
Boundaryless—Or, How the
Newly Empowered Managerial
Class Bought into Its
Own Marginalization

PAUL M. HIRSCH AND MARK SHANLEY

> "*Boundarylessness* is just another word for nothing left to lose."
> Adapted from "Me and Bobby McGee"
> © Kris Kristofferson (BMI)

Let us imagine we are looking back from the year 2000. As the 1990s drew to a close, three of the most noteworthy trends of the decade were:

1. The resurgence of such corporate "dinosaurs" as IBM, GM, and Sears, which rejoined GE, AT&T, PepsiCo, Microsoft, and Hewlett-Packard among the giants of American industry (as prophesied by Kanter, 1989);
2. The continued decline in the number of full-time employees, at all levels, employed by the increasingly profitable *Fortune* 500; and
3. The surprising decline of mid-sized corporations (between $50 and $500 million in revenue).

By the decade's end, the number of small, specialized, niche-filling businesses had mushroomed. Their customers were largely the restructured "lean and mean" giant companies that had outsourced all but their "core competencies," and had become more "virtual" corporations. As the networks of relationships between firms were extended to the global marketplace, via the proliferation of strategic alliances and, to a lesser extent, mergers and acquisitions, they also succeeded in reducing their expenses for employee benefits to their lowest levels in 30 years.

The essays in this book focus on the implications, for employment and careers, of the organizational reshaping of large firms—from a world of static and formal hierarchies to one of flat, flexible, and dynamic networks. This world is generally depicted as being filled with opportunities for personal development and fulfillment—indeed, empowerment—as well as for enhanced value creation and productivity. These opportunities are available to those who learn to manage boundaryless careers and to network effectively (Baker 1994). But even as we look forward to a boundaryless world that has not yet unfolded, its report card seems to have already arrived, with an impressive chorus of almost uniformly high evaluations. Indeed, when chapter 1 of this volume characterizes the boundaryless world as a welcome opportunity to supplant the evils of bureaucracy and the "Orwellian Legacy" they leave behind, the normative overtones seem clear.

Before joining the celebration, we believe some cautions are warranted concerning such a rapid and unchallenged entry into this brave new world. Still unclear are the sources, contours, and implications of boundaryless careers for society and social structure. Particularly neglected have been the costs of transition for major segments of the workforce—older employees who lose out in the stepped-up tournaments of the new organizational era, and their younger peripheralized counterparts. Until now, the main focus has been on the beneficiaries of the concept of a boundaryless career. To this, we will add a more balanced consideration of those who lose out, sampling less on the dependent variable of winners only.

Balanced against the increased opportunities for a minority of professionals, American society in the 1990s also witnessed the following: an upsurge in white-collar crime; an increase in bank robberies by unemployed professionals; continued dramatic downsizings of both large corporations and government agencies; the rise of alienated militias, bombings, and greater violence; and greater overall inequality. These are correlates of reduced, rather than enhanced, opportunities. Therefore, before we can all sing the unqualified praises of this new utopian *eschaton*, it is important to begin sorting out who will bear the costs of reaching it.

It is toward a better understanding of both the broader ramifications of the boundaryless revolution and its career implications that we now turn. Specifically, we address

- The connection between boundaryless careers and the decline of vertical integration;
- Winners and losers in the new "freelance economy" (Kiechel, 1994);
- The dubious contribution of network theory to the unqualifiedly positive view of the boundaryless concept;
- The continued importance of boundaries for both stability and predictable relationships;
- Social problems on the road to implementing a boundaryless society;
- Why the boundaryless concept may be peculiarly American and more difficult to adopt outside the United States.

Looking Backward: Rattles on the Vertical Chain

To understand boundaryless careers, it is important to examine the growth of the boundaryless-employer organization that makes the new career patterns so important. Continuing our look back from the year 2000, two additional noteworthy trends we experienced were a proliferation of strategic alliances and joint ventures as alternatives to either internal development or mergers and acquisitions; and the continued reorientation of up to 80% of the workforce to professional and quasi-professional service activities, and away from manufacturing. These developments extended insights and observations made during the 1990s by, among others, Quinn (1992); Harrison (1994); Bleeke and Ernst (1993); and Rousseau (1995)—all of these portended the shift from bounded to boundaryless careers.

Within firms, the contest for legitimacy pitted building a firm's managerial labor force from within, on the basis of long-term, firm-specific experience, against relying on ad hoc project-management teams, with needed skills purchased on a spot basis from external labor markets. It was resolved in favor of more ad hoc project teams, whose members were paid a premium for market-recognized value (Burton and Moran, 1995; Davidow and Malone, 1991). As Bridges (1994) observed, employees, increasingly, no longer had jobs in the conventional sense of the term. Rather, they performed tasks for firms, but the length of these associations, and the linkage of jobs and one's package of skills with careers, had become disconnected.

As the job was now conceived, the new norm became the boundaryless career. In this context, the term *boundaryless* is largely a shorthand descriptive term summarizing the large-scale macro-adaptation of society to its turn-of-the-new-century's economic and technological environment. Considering the strong redefinition of work this entailed, what else might account for its near-overnight adoption?

Large firms have responded to these new environmental opportunities and demands by changing how they manage themselves and define their employees. Rather than big corporations becoming dinosaurs, these companies have shed the earlier era's employment arrangements, substituting the newer, more-ad hoc, and boundaryless definition. Borrowing a famous phrase from a different time, "The firm is dead, long live the firm!"

Following the merger waves around the turn of the century, market imperfections, government regulations, and technological limitations allowed large firms to gain and hold dominant positions in critical industries, for reasons of both market power and efficiency. Large firms grew larger, to escape the rigors of competition and take advantage of new opportunities for economies of scope and scale. They also grew through the absorption of critical buyers and suppliers along their vertical chain, when the benefits of vertical integration exceeded its costs of inflexibility and slower response (Williamson, 1985). As Chandler (1977) and others have shown, firms thereby internalized transactions that had previously been made in the marketplace.

In the 1980s and 1990s, all three of these conditions changed in directions that made it difficult for large, vertically integrated firms to respond to market demands with the same flexibility of smaller, market-specialist firms. Developments in information and communications technology made it possible for individuals and small firms to be much more efficient in their information processing and coordinative activities, relative to larger firms (Quinn, 1992). The development of global markets increased competition and promoted small-firm entry into heretofore stable oligopolistic markets, and forced large firms to become more efficient. Finally, government deregulation in such critical sectors as air travel, health care, trucking, and financial services forced firms to face competition that they had not faced before.

These changes not only affected Western (and especially American) firms. The late 1980s saw the almost-simultaneous demise of centralized Communist economic regimes in Eastern Europe and the former Soviet Union. Command economies also fell into disfavor in Latin America and Asia. In all of these areas, there has been an increasing emphasis on market, rather than bureaucratic, models; privatization; entrepreneurship; deregulation; and a more competitive firm response to market conditions. Observers of these changes have attributed them to the same factors that are producing "postindustrial" economies in the West, including increased information-processing needs and the demands for technological innovation (Fukuyama, 1992; Buckley and Ghauri, 1994).

The innovative organizational changes that gave rise to the boundaryless firm were thus predictable responses to these new environmental conditions. In economic terms, whereas before, the market was imperfect and hierarchy relatively more desirable, the market is now less imperfect and, consequently, hierarchy no longer seems so equal to the task. Under such conditions, it is reasonable to expect that firms would try to pare themselves down to those activities at which they were most adept; to cut costs where possible; and to leave less critical or noncore tasks to market specialists (Bettis et al., 1993).

Organizationally, what makes the problem of strategic adaptation to major environmental changes so interesting, however, is that prior strategic success may delay or prevent firms' adapting to changed conditions. It is very difficult to turn large firms around and undo a history of once-upon-a-time strategic choices so as to strike a new balance with changed conditions (Pettigrew, 1985).

Large firms face enormous problems in adapting to major environmental changes. First, it is hard to know when strategic changes are needed. A history of success may blind managers to changes in basic conditions. Knowing that change is needed is also not the same as knowing which changes to make. It is seldom clear which activities are core and critical ones, and which activities can be spun off or closed down. In addition, current accounting and control systems can seldom identify the economic value added by particular activities and programs. (This is one reason why activity-based systems are growing in popularity—e.g., see Datar et al., 1991.) Finally, knowing which changes are needed does not mean that they can be implemented successfully. Strategic assets are difficult to redeploy, and their value is often contingent on a given state of the environment (Ghemawat, 1991). In addition, resistance to change, on the part of employees and managers, can blunt the implementation of those changes that can be accomplished (Pettigrew, 1985).

Sunk Investments and Boundaryless Careers

If large firms have problems adapting, consider the even-greater problems faced by their employees. Any employee brings to the job a set of resources that varies in the degree to which it is valued on external, versus internal, labor markets (Becker, 1993). At one extreme, an employee may possess only generic knowledge and skills that can be employed equally well in any of several firms—specialized knowledge of the regulations governing all the firms in an industry would be an example. At the other extreme, the employee may possess skills that improve the productivity of a current employer, but are of little or no value to other firms—expertise in a firm's idiosyncratic production practices, or its personnel and administrative procedures, would constitute this type of resource.

The concept of a career within a single firm (a bounded career) means that the employee bets on the use of his or her human capital, emphasizing investments in firm-specific knowledge and skills, relative to knowledge and skills that are more easily tradable in labor markets. The boundaryless career is most important for individuals who have made, or are contemplating, bets against investing in firm-specific knowledge. Entrepreneurs, for example, usually choose a career without boundaries, while professionals still retain numerous boundaries in their careers, albeit not necessarily organizational ones (see chapter 20).

Career investments can be irreversible. While it may not be hard to change employers early on—during the first or second job—it can be difficult to go back and restart a career after ten or twenty years. Even when midcareer changes occur, they frequently do not put an individual in a superior rank or position against employees beginning their first career with comparable credentials (Rosenbaum, 1984). The choice of the employee to pursue an organizational career will thus be a profitable one as long as the firm in which an individual works continues to be organized in such a way that careers are possible and valued by top management.

When large firms restructure and downsize, however, these career possibilities change drastically. It is important to note, however, that major changes will have different implications for different types of employees. Whether employees find the world of the boundaryless career to be beneficial or hostile depends on their particular resources, the extent of personal investments in those resources, and the degree to which their capabilities are valued by the firm in its new strategic situation. The variations in incentives provided, and in what firm-specific investments we may expect from employees with boundaryless careers, are summarized in Table 13.1.

Core Employees: A Temporary Elite

There may still be significant intraorganizational career potential following restructuring, but only in areas identified as core (Bettis et al., 1993)—in those areas, the level of competition for career positions will be high. While individuals in core areas may continue their careers within a single firm, external labor markets may still be important for these individuals to ensure that their employer pays them premium wages for their contributions. Core employees may need to certify their value to employers through their ability to generate compet-

Table 13.1 Differential Rewards for Types of Boundaryless Employees

Type of Employee	Investments, Firm Specific	Rewards for Firm-Specific Investments	Rewards for Being Boundaryless
Core	Yes	Yes, until no longer in the core	No, but must remain valuable to employer
Newer-employee peripherals	No	No, but investments are avoided	Yes, will keep skills portable
Older-employee peripherals	Yes	No, so these employees lose out	Late-entrant chances poor; will keep trying

ing offers from other firms. Overall, the advent of the boundaryless career bodes well for core employees (Davis-Blake and Uzzi, 1993). In areas outside the core, however, there will remain far fewer organizational jobs, in the traditional sense, for those seeking to build careers (Bridges, 1994).

Even core status, however, may be highly contingent in a boundaryless world. It is not clear that top managers will know which of their functions are core ones, and which are not. Mistakes are likely. Even without mistakes, the new orientation of the firm to market and stakeholder demands means that *which* employees are designated as core employees will depend on the particular strategy the firm is following at a given time. As strategies shift, due to new-market entry, innovation, and regulatory change, whole groups of core employees may suddenly become dispensable. Over time, given the potential for strategic shifts and mistakes, firms can come to have no core functions left intact, in which case no group of employees will be secure.

New Employees: Avoiding Firm-Specific Investments
Located at the other extreme from core employees with long tenure are new employees at the start of their careers. The advent of a boundaryless world may force these employees to reevaluate their career prospects within a given firm, and, quite likely, could lead them to change jobs and employers if they do not see sufficient prospects in their current situation. These new employees are at times referred to by the dismissive sobriquet "slackers" (as in the *Wall Street Journal* column Hal Lancaster authored—"You May Call Them Slackers: They Say They're Just Realistic")—and frequent reevaluations of their career prospects ensue. While this process may be stressful, it is not much different from the process that these individuals already face, in a boundary-filled world, at the start of their careers. When entering a firm initially, employees have few firm-specific resources and are thus well suited to enter external labor markets, if that is needed. This means that the advent of the boundaryless career will not have much of an impact on those who are just beginning their careers. The advent of boundarylessness could even make younger employees without significant career investments more attractive to employers, since these employees are unburdened by firm-specific knowledge and skills from previous jobs.

The boundaryless career will be most relevant for longer-term employees, whose sunk career investments are suddenly called into question by the threat of restructuring. Their knowledge and skills are no longer valued by their "home" firm and were never strongly valued by other firms. For these employees, the principal issues involved in boundaryless careers concern making the best of a bad situation. These people must reorient themselves to the marketplace and make sure that their career development builds general, rather than specific, assets. At the same time, they face the additional problem of finding an alternative use of their firm-specific knowledge and skills, without sacrificing their marketability.

For whom, then, is the boundaryless career idea important? It is not important for individuals at the start of their careers, since it requires little change in the types of choices that these individuals already must make. It is more important for core employees who happen to be valued by their firms, but only because the bets placed by these employees have turned out favorably, at least for the present. For these individuals, however, careers are not boundaryless. Rather, these are the exceptions to the trend toward boundaryless careers, and it is as exceptions that core workers will find the boundaryless world to be one of opportunity.

When all is said and done, the boundaryless career is most important for those individuals with the most to lose from its arrival—employees with significant sunk career investments that are rendered obsolete by changes in business conditions and practices. For these individuals, the advent of the boundaryless career is not an opportunity, but is the occasion for scrambling to keep a bad situation from getting worse, and to salvage something from prior career investments. Focusing on boundaryless careers in terms of opportunity, empowerment, freedom, and the dynamism of entrepreneurs glosses over the serious and difficult career problems the new organizational era poses for long-term career employees.

The Dubious Contribution of Network Theory: Rainmaker Nodes, Asymmetric Power Relations, and Controlled Chaos Below

The concept of networking gained currency among managers during the late 1980s, and skyrocketed as it became readily apparent that successful managers were those who could make the best use of social networks both within their own firm and between their firm and other firms. When it became clearer that downsizings would replace internal labor markets, and that long-term employment relationships with a single firm were less and less likely for most individuals, networking ideas became more popular as necessary adjustments to the onset of boundarylessness.

In *Pack Your Own Parachute*, an early recognition of this trend, Hirsch (1987) defined the networking "free-agent manager" as embodying the following maxims:

1. Cultivate networks; maintain visibility.
2. Return recruiters' calls; maintain marketability.
3. Avoid overspecialization; maintain generality.

4. Avoid long-term and group assignments: maintain credibility.
5. Keep your bags packed; maintain mobility.

Hirsch continued: "These guidelines maximize the psychological and occupation freedom managers need to do best in a world of increasingly unreliable corporate employers. 'Get ready to leave' was the main message of the last chapter. 'Be streetsmart and realistic' are the bywords to master in this one."

As internal mobility tournaments gave way to crossing organizational boundaries to succeed in a profession, network theory, with its clear implications for managing a boundaryless career, became increasingly important. The recommendations of network analysts—such as: "build relationships"; control information; develop contacts (*network* is now a verb); and exploit the strength of weak ties—certainly appear in tune with a management environment in which individuals will need to rely on their personal resources, without the aid of in-house organizational sponsors and job ladders on which to build their careers.

In retrospect, however, as the implications of boundaryless firms became clearer, we can see that while the recommendations of network analysts were methodologically on target—indeed, a key task of managing careers is managing networks of relationships —they failed to address several fundamental downside problems raised by the boundaryless concept. Indeed, as careers became increasingly stochastic, we see that the more the idea of networks was discussed without reference to social context, the closer it approached the view of a firm as the "nexus of contracts" seen by agency theorists (Alchian and Demsetz, 1972; Jensen and Meckling, 1976). The individual in these networks soon joined other (self-employed) actors in a more perfectly competitive market, in which most were powerless to influence the price offered for their services. We conclude that boundaryless careers reduced the power of individual employees and professionals in the face of market forces.

Let's take a closer look at why network theory needs boundaries. Nearly every social situation can indeed be characterized in terms of a network, whether one is discussing formal organizations or commodity exchanges. If that is true, however, then network ideas apply as much to bounded as to boundaryless environments. What is lacking in popularizations extolling the virtues of network ideas, especially as they apply to careers, is a realistic discussion of the social structures that networks require, and of the advantages that networking derives from bounded and structured environments.

Individuals lose out when the structure of networks does not support successful networking. The importance of such network ideas as structural equivalence (Burt, 1992) and embeddedness (Granovetter, 1985) depends on the structured nature of the social fields within which networks form. Burt (1992) makes this clear with his idea of structural holes—that is, gaps in relationships that can be effectively managed by skillful individuals. For networks to offer opportunities to individuals, such as through the spanning of structural holes, they must be sparse and structured. Liaison or gatekeeper roles in a population are examples of network positions that offer possibilities for personal power through the spanning of structural holes. If a network were too dense—if nearly everyone in it had relationships with everyone else—then occupying a particular position in the network would be of no consequence, since others would not need to go through a particular party to reach one another.

Looking at networking and boundaryless careers, without recognizing the importance of structure for network opportunities, has fed right into the redefinition of the firm as a nexus of contracts that, in turn, released and encouraged managers and professionals to network and contract more freely—(like the "free agents" described by Hirsch 1987). The powerful, but much less clearly recognized, correlate was that the same redefinition also enabled the more sophisticated large firms to contract much more selectively and provide jobs, subcontracts, and strategic alliances, through a small pool of highly networked brokers ("rainmakers") for professional jobs and services. While the resultant form of migrant labor for some classes of professional workers was packaged with more dignified adjectives ("empowered independent contractors," for example), the downward shift in power and benefits for the more isolated and dependent-on-contracts professional labor force meant, in network-theory terms, that access to knowledge about job opportunities was increasingly centered on a smaller number of nodes within firms. To have access to the best network positions required being employed in the firm.

The popularizations of best-sellers and business-press articles on how to reposition one's skills and learn to network (e.g., Bridges, 1994a, and "Rethinking Work," in *Business Week,* Oct. 17, 1994), reflected more the increasing powerlessness and insecurities of a horde of newly detached and isolated professionals, who were seeking scarce opportunities, than a growing sophistication of management techniques or a stronger power base for these professionals.

Professional skills and postgraduate training became more of a growth industry during the 1980s and 1990s, as these newly isolated skilled workers sought new credentials. An increasingly heard ironic joke during this time was that the main beneficiary of the boundaryless career would be the trainers and therapists, who gained mobility and income from the resultant insecurities of others. Needless to say, this fostered a lonely life of reading self-help books, in which only a lucky few can drive to work listening to their audio versions.

Why Boundaries Are Needed: The Connection between Organizational Parameters and Occupational Freedom

A serious problem with ideas such as the boundaryless firm and the boundaryless career is not just that much of the vision of the world that they presume remains to be clearly spelled out. These ideas also carry with them the clear implication that formal boundaries, per se, are bad and restraining. This orientation to boundaries is misguided, both in general and in the case of careers. We suspect—much like the old proverb that argues against throwing out the baby with the bathwater—that the rhetoric here is overstated and confuses the general category of all formal boundaries with a particular application, such as the large corporation.

A critical point missed by the overgeneralized negative attribution to boundaries is that formal boundaries provide limits within which individuals exercise discretion. Eliminating boundaries will not render individuals free, but, instead may increase the external constraints on individual actions and their unpredictability. This intuition of freedom through restraint is critical in theories of constitutionalism and constraints on democratic decision making (Elster and Slagstad, 1988). Given that large firms often are intermediary governance structures between individuals and the state (Lindblom, 1977), the importance of boundaries for both firms and societies remains a critical idea for discussion.

As discussed above, the normative orientation of the boundaryless career rhetoric is generally positive and oriented to freedom and empowerment. Employees will now be able to develop their potential to the fullest—indeed, they will need to do so to survive in the boundaryless world. They will not be hemmed in by restraining career choices and organizational inertia. Instead, they will be free to take advantage of new and better opportunities as they develop. The net positive effects of boundaryless careers for individuals will come about through the enhancement of their personal autonomy and capabilities.

It is quite possible that these claims for the boundaryless career are inaccurate and misleading on several points. A plausible case can be made for the boundaryless organization and career as threats to freedom, rather than opportunities for its expansion. Freedom to develop one's career potential may come from, rather than in spite of, boundaries. Taking away career and organizational boundaries can thus have the effect of limiting, rather than expanding, freedom.

What benefits for an individual come from the pursuit of a traditional (bounded) career? A traditional career offers the individual an opportunity to link jobs together, to learn from prior jobs and greatly enhance value to the firm by way of coordinated investments in human resources. In addition, the likelihood that a traditional career can be pursued within a firm is beneficial to an individual because it reduces the uncertainty about career investments and the distraction of having to continually maintain one's personal resources for possible reentry into external labor markets. This is one advantage of opportunities afforded by a career within a firm, although it does not come with guarantees, and neither party is locked into maintaining the relationship indefinitely—for example, managers have always heard from headhunters.

As firms come to rely more on external, rather than internal, labor markets to meet their needs, it is likely that individual freedom is diminished, rather than being increased. In responding to external labor-market demands, individuals gain the nominal choice of a wider range of employment. If labor markets are competitive, however, this wider choice is deceptive since employment will depend more on what the market will pay for a given set of credentials and experience at a given time.

As conditions associated with boundaryless firms continue, it is also likely that the internal labor markets will be perceived as being too slow to match employee capabilities with employer needs within a firm. Labor economists have long noted the transaction-cost issues associated with internal labor markets and firm-specific human resources, both for firms and employees (Rosen, 1993). Because of these issues, a well-functioning internal labor market needs to be supported by a comprehensive personnel system that combines incentive and reward structures with training, testing, assignment, and turnover-management functions.

As restructuring becomes commonplace in large firms, it is possible that these personnel matching and support functions will be victims of cost-cutting pressures, since they are not clearly profit centers, and their link to firm performance is hard to document clearly. As that occurs, the personnel function of a firm may be increasingly reduced, so that eventually the personnel office will be little more than a focal point for the processing of new hires, layoffs, and retirements, as well as a broker for matching buy-and-sell requests for intrafirm transfers. In an era where educational systems have failed to prepare people adequately for occupational demands (see chapters 18 and 21), the weakening personnel function increases the personal costs of organizational restructurings.

Even in subunits and for particular jobs and tasks, the arrival of the boundaryless firm will place new constraints on individual career development. As more recourse is made to the market, both for outsourcing activities and securing new project teams, the status of subunits and their employees will become less clear. Each new round of activity will potentially subject subunits to a zero-based decision regarding whether or not it should continue to exist.

Employees can, therefore, become distracted and unfocused in two ways: They can be distracted by the tendency for subunits to perform a broader scope of activities, in an effort to justify their existence to top management; they can also be distracted and constrained by interruptions in their activities by top managers or other unit managers. Distractions give rise to a new nexus of contracts, but one comprising increasingly weak or ambiguous contracts filled with transitions and instability that employees read as "no guarantees" (Rousseau, 1995). Boundaryless firms exacerbate these distractions because their subunits lack standards (e.g., clear cultural norms or specified contractual performance terms) to use in defending their discretionary actions.

Consider the case of an electrical engineer with 20 years' experience as an employee at AT&T's Bell Labs. As noted in "The New Deal: What Companies and Employees Owe One Another" (O'Reilly, 1994: 46):

> He can be notified at any time that his job is "at risk." That means that Bell Labs is cutting back people in his area of discipline, that his skills are obsolete, and that he had one of the poorer job evaluations in recent years.
>
> Even if there are no layoffs and his evaluations are good, he cannot relax. His engineering projects typically last a year or two, and when they end he must find another project to work on. If he can't find another job at the company within a few months, he must leave. . . . "They expect me to recognize that the box I'm working on now will be a microchip in a year, with ten times as much software, and to be ready." His concerns, in order of urgency: "What project will I be on in six months, what will my role in the project be, and will I have a job?"

Looking back from the vantage point of the year 2000, we now see that the boundaryless career led to less, rather than more, freedom for individual-career development. Individuals had fewer jobs available to them within firms, and fewer opportunities to link jobs together into a manageable career. As they entered external labor markets, individuals were increasingly subject to the ebbs and flows of the market, against which they had little influence. Within firms, internal labor markets became less of an integrated system for matching a firm's needs and its human resources, and more of a simple brokering function for job hunters within the firm, a function fraught with transaction costs for individuals and managers. Within jobs, there were also new constraints on the ability of individuals to see beyond individual projects and to rely on a definition of their tasks and their unit's mission as bases for guiding action.

Rose-Colored Glasses and the Strong Likelihood That America's Boundaryless Concept Is Not Exportable

So why is it that the early reports on the boundaryless career have been so positive? This question is answerable once two factors are recognized. First, Americans are already more mobile and less tied to any forms of tradition than participants in virtually any other national culture. Second, across all populations of innovators, the first movers are often the most talented and visibly successful; and when those behind them seek to follow, they may be less gifted, and/or there may be fewer opportunities remaining.

Before we can generalize from the successes of this likely atypical and unusually successful sample of first movers, a more comprehensive analysis must also at least take into account that new careers are also inherently difficult to manage, represent losses for many other employees, present limited growth opportunities for those outside the core functions, and can actually restrict an individual's freedom to engage in career development.

The nonrepresentative experiences of the American professionals who first moved into boundaryless careers, and the inherent difficulties of these new careers, help explain why the "transition period" has proven rougher and more awkward than what the positive early projections of many had anticipated. To better understand the difficulties of this transition, one needs to further distinguish among at least three broad occupational groups in American society, cite their relative numbers, and note the prospects for upward mobility among them. We have already focused (as do most of the chapters in this book) on the winners' circle—the subgroup of (largely) professionals who will either gain, or stand to lose the least, in the move to a boundaryless career. Below this elite group of highly skilled and well-networked professionals, we have the harsher realities of employed, but less highly skilled and easily replaced, workers, for whom *boundaryless* initially translates to job insecurity; and a growing population of those who are unemployed, undereducated, and/or between jobs, many of whom possess skills for which there is a declining market (auto repairing, or assembly-line production, for example) and only positions at lower wages.

For those who aspire to join the boundaryless elite, American society provides a strong cultural tradition (dating back to voyaging to America and, later, reading career guidebooks like Dale Carnegie's) of individualism and do-it-yourself self-reliance. This tradition continues in the proliferation of best-selling books on repositioning oneself in today's changing job markets. In emphasizing the payoffs for self-reliance and hard work in a new world of opportunities (a rhetoric Eccles and Nohria [1992], document), the discontent is minimized for those who would otherwise feel disenfranchised. For many, there is a long-run lower probability of dramatic success. Americans' tradition of optimism, however, still strains to highlight the opportunities, rather than the threats, and the upside, rather than the downside.

The generally positive emphasis on the boundaryless firm and its consequences may also stem from an emphasis on the end point to which workforce trends are leading, with less emphasis on the costs of the transition and the difficulties in reaching this end state. While such an emphasis is understandable, it is also simplistic. Most interesting organizational problems are transitional ones. In addition, the social costs incurred by these transitions, when they significantly affect large numbers of individuals, are not just "noise" that needs to be endured so that the benefits of a more stabilized equilibrium state can be realized. On the contrary, if transitional costs are sufficiently high, they can generate a political/governmental response that can call the entire direction of change into question.

An international example of this, in a world of cultural traditions far less optimistic and less open to radical changes than the United States, is the experience of nations in the former Soviet empire. Without these supporting traditions, and without an infrastructure and markets that can provide resources to back the new boundaryless employers and boundaryless careers, political and social stability come under far more severe challenges. By transferring the assumptions of a stable supporting external environment, within which big organizations could downshift (privatize) and persuade former employees of the good life ahead, Sachs (1993) and other American economists have severely underestimated the social and political costs of transitions to more competitive market economies in national settings where they have no cultural or historical grounding.

The political repercussions of imposing such "shock therapy" on most nations in Eastern Europe have been both underestimated and severe. In other parts of the world, the disestablishment of large organizations, and the substitution of the more boundaryless social structure and ideology, have also had to proceed more slowly. To explain why these have taken root as quickly and effectively as they have in the United States requires a greater appreciation of this nation's more unique historical path and cultural traditions than is usually noted, when discussions advocating more boundarylessness neglect to specify in which social contexts it is most likely (and, we would add, least likely) to thrive.

A related point, regarding the United States, concerns the growing population of workers who are unemployed, undereducated, and/or between jobs. These people are more likely to reject the rhetoric of opportunity in the more boundaryless world. It is here that we will find the most anger, social disorganization, crime, and violence, with the least buy-in to the idea that in the new boundaryless society, opportunity is available, much less unlimited. As the gap between those possessing skills marketable in the future and those lacking them increases, it is widely anticipated that the growing economy for the first group of skilled technicians, possessing the right jobs, will not trickle down to the second group, consisting of permanently low-income and/or unemployed—that, in short, economic inequality in the United States will become more pronounced. A major, developing political problem will be the need to address issues such as how to find work for the less skilled, when many of the jobs they formerly could take are no longer available in this country. In fact, while some of the boundaryless professionals in the most desirable jobs are being paid well to eliminate those very jobs for the less skilled, through better technology, the wider social costs of these changes will continue to increase. The externalities for the world of increasingly outsourced and virtually boundaryless corporations will still need to be addressed by the society.

Conclusion

In this chapter, we looked back from the year 2000 and noted that not all workers benefited from the shift of employment arrangements from relatively stable relationships to the more temporary world of boundaryless organizations and careers. We are concerned about what lies beyond 2000 as well. There are clearly some skill sets and occupations that will do better in the future. While there are also strong macroeconomic forces that will continue to push for fewer commitments to labor in a more global economy, there also remain many uncertainties about how these changes will be, and should be, accomplished. At this point, neither the end point of the social-change process we are going through, nor its costs and/or optimal arrangements, have been carefully thought through; nor can they be easily anticipated. And, while we have stressed that much of this change may be inevitable, we also note that the rhetoric about the boundaryless career has almost euphorically predicted a better world for all. We argue that celebrating the good fortunes of those who come out ahead from these large-scale changes may exclude the self-marginalizing managers enshrined in our title. It is far more responsible and appropriate to better calculate the costs and benefits of these changes, across larger groups of people affected, and then to begin policy discussions about establishing more safety nets for those adversely impacted. Other writers have proposed infrastructure changes that this new era may require (e.g., Bridges, 1994b; Heckscher, 1995). Both the toll of transition and the costs entailed in the new organizational era itself warrant continuing attention.

ACKNOWLEDGMENTS: We wish to thank Robert DeFillippi for his helpful comments.

References

Alchian, A. A. and Demsetz, H. (1972). Production, information costs, and economic organization. *American Economic Review, 62:* 777–795.

Baker, W. E. (1994). *Networking Smart: How to Build Relationships for Personal and Organizational Success.* New York: McGraw-Hill.

Becker, G. S. (1993). *Human Capital,* 3d ed. Chicago: University of Chicago Press.

Bettis, R. A.; Bradley, S. P.; and Hamel, G. (1992). Outsourcing and industrial decline. *Academy of Management Executive, 6:* 7–22.

Bleeke, J., and Ernst, D. (1993). *Collaborating to Compete*. New York: Wiley.

Bridges, W. (1994a). "The end of the job." *Fortune*, Sept. 19, 1994, pp. 42–47.

Bridges, W. (1994b). *JobShift: How to Prosper in a Workplace without Jobs*. Reading, Mass.: Addison-Wesley.

Buckley, P. J., and Ghauri, P. N. (eds.). (1994). *The Economics of Change in East and Central Europe*. London: Academic Press.

Burt, R. S. (1992). *Structural Holes*. Cambridge, Mass.: Harvard University Press.

Burton, T. T., and Moran, J. W. (1995). *The Future-Focused Organization*. Englewood Cliffs, N.J.: Prentice Hall.

Business Week (1994). "Rethinking work: The new world of work." Oct. 17, 1994, pp. 74–96.

Chandler, A. D. (1977). *The Visible Hand: The Managerial Revolution in American Business*. Cambridge, MA: Belknap.

Datar, S.; Kekrem, S.; Mukhopadyay, T.; and Svaan, E. (1991). Overloaded overheads: Activity-based cost accounting of materials handling for cell manufacturing. *Journal of Operations Management, 10:* 119–137.

Davidow, W. H., and Malone, M. (1992). *The Virtual Corporation*. New York: HarperCollins.

Davis-Blake, A., and Uzzi, B. (1993). Determinants of employment externalization: The case of temporary workers and independent contractors. *Administrative Science Quarterly, 29:* 195–223.

Eccles, R. G., and Nohria, N. (1992). *Beyond the Hype: Rediscovering the Essence of Management*. Boston: Harvard Business School Press.

Elster, J. and Slagstad, R. (eds.). (1988). *Constitutionalism and Democracy*. Cambridge, Eng.: Cambridge University Press.

Fukuyama, F. (1992). *The End of History and the Last Man*. New York: Free Press.

Ghemawat, P. (1991). *Commitment: The Dynamic of Strategy*. New York: Free Press.

Granovetter, M. S. (1985). Economic action and Social structure: The problem of embeddedness. *American Journal of Sociology, 91:* 481–510.

Harrison, B. (1994). *Lean and Mean: The Changing Landscape of Corporate Power in the Age of Flexibility*. New York: Basic Books.

Heckscher, C. (1995). *White Collar Blues: Management Loyalties in an Age of Corporate Restructuring*. New York: Basic Books.

Hirsch, P. M. (1993). Undoing the managerial revolution? Needed research on the decline of middle management and internal labor markets. In *Explorations in Economic Sociology*, edited by Richard Swedberg. New York: Russell Sage Foundation: 145–157.

Hirsch, M. (1987). *Pack Your Own Parachute: How to Survive Mergers, Takeovers, and Other Corporate Disasters*. Reading, Mass.: Addison-Wesley.

Jensen, M. C., and Meckling, W. H. (1976). Theory of the firm: Management behavior, agency costs, and ownership structure." *Journal of Financial Economics, 3:* 305–360.

Kanter, R. M. (1989). *When Giants Learn to Dance*. New York: Simon and Schuster.

Kiechel, W. (1993). How we will work in the year 2000. *Fortune* (May 17): 38–52.

Lancaster, H. (1995) You may call them slackers: They say they're just realistic. *Wall Street Journal,* (August 1): B1.

Lindblom, C.E. (1977). *Politics and Markets*. New York: Basic Books.

O'Reilly, B. (1994). The new deal: What companies and employees owe one another." Fortune (June 13): 44–48.

Peters, T. J. (1994). *The Tom Peters Seminar*. New York: Vintage Books.

Pettigrew, A. (1985). *The Awakening Giant: Continuity and Change at ICI.* Oxford, Eng.: Blackwell.

Quinn, J. B. (1992). *Intelligent Enterprise.* New York: Free Press.

Rosen, S. (1993). Transaction costs and internal labor markets." In Williamson, O. E., and Winter, S. G. (eds.), *The Nature of the Firm: Origins, Evolution, and Development.* New York: Oxford University Press.

Rosenbaum, J. E. (1984). *Career Mobility in a Corporate Hierarchy.* New York: Academic Press.

Rousseau, D. M. (1995). *Psychological Contracts in Organizations.* Newbury Park, Calif.: Sage.

Sachs, J. (1993). *Poland's Jump to the Market Economy.* Boston: MIT Press.

Williamson, O. E. (1985). *The Economic Institutions of Capitalism.* New York: Free Press.

IV

PERSONAL DEVELOPMENT AND GROWTH ALONG THE BOUNDARYLESS CAREER PATH

The revolution in careers and work challenges conventional views of personal development, self-expression, and success. The challenge suggests new metrics for both gauging personal accomplishment and making life choices. This part of the book addresses how an individual's development throughout the life span is affected by boundaryless careers. Particular attention is given to the effects of job changes, family circumstances, gender, and minority-group membership.

In "Psychological Success and the Boundaryless Career," Philip Mirvis and Douglas (Tim) Hall argue that the boundaryless career could be a bane or a boon to people's experience with psychological success. They describe how workers will have to deal with aging over several career cycles, integrate diverse experiences into their identities, and come to terms with new employer-employee relationships. They introduce the idea of finding psychological success in one's life work, encompassing not only a job and a firm, but also work as a spouse, parent, community member, and self-developer. They anticipate that a future "path with a heart" will mean, for many, using social networks, rather than company networks, as principal sources of identification.

Joyce Fletcher and Lotte Bailyn's "Challenging the Last Boundary: Reconnecting Work and Family" continues the call for reducing boundaries in life sectors outside work. However, Fletcher and Bailyn argue that the separation of work and family continues to be maintained by a rigid and intractable boundary. They emphasize that firms—not just workers and their families—pay a high price for this intractability, and that competitiveness suffers. Perversely, firms' resistance to family variables is based on an expressed desire to remain competitive. Fletcher and Bailyn propose ways of rethinking the meaning of work and nonwork so that each can make a positive contribution to the other.

David Thomas and Monica Higgins, in "Mentoring and the Boundaryless Career:

Lessons from the Minority Experience," suggest that extrafirm networks are particularly important for career development. They also suggest that these extrafirm networks are traditionally emphasized in the minority community and among minority members of predominately white firms. Traditional assumptions about developmental relationships, particularly intrafirm mentoring, are biased toward the majority experience. However, minorities are more likely to consciously develop extrafirm networks, relationships which are particularly important for both personal and community development. The result of changing employment patterns will be that networks of mentors, sponsors, and special peers will increasingly become similar for majority and minority workers.

Continuing the theme that changing career structures will reveal the advantageous experiences of women and minorities, Nanette Fondas addresses "Feminization at Work: Career Implications." Going beyond a demographically driven view of feminization by the numbers, she explores the increasing employment of women in all classes of work, to describe a broad assimilation of feminine values and skills into modern organizational arrangements. Newly valued capacities include the ability to manage multiple roles and diverse interdependencies; maintenance of both an other-orientation and broader social identity; and emphasis on flexibility. The difference between disconnected work experiences and a boundaryless career may lie in a met-askill—the capacity for the adjustment of both men and women as they move in and out of different work settings.

Personal and career development are inherently intertwined. Each of our authors makes a case for the revolution in the personal development, self-expression, and accomplishment that people seek in the new organizational era.

14

Psychological Success and the Boundaryless Career

PHILIP H. MIRVIS AND DOUGLAS T. HALL

Definitions of work, nonwork activities, and careers are changing in America, Japan, and parts of Europe. A decade-and-a-half of corporate downsizing and broad-based deindustrialization has seen employers reduce staffs, shut down facilities, and make more use of consultants and the contingent workforce. As a result, notions of cradle-to-grave job security have been shattered, along with the psychological contract binding people to companies (DeMeuse and Tornow, 1990; Rousseau and Wade-Benzoni, 1995). Leisure time is decreasing in the United States (Schor, 1991), and recent surveys find over half of the nation's workers pining for more time with family and friends (Galinsky and Friedman, 1993). It seems working people are struggling to manage the boundaries between work and other parts of their lives, while trying to preserve some semblance of a career in the face of an uncertain future.

The New World of Work

Restructuring in the United States and elsewhere stems from the globalization of the economy and the movement to information-driven, increasingly service-based lines of business. The future projection is that large firms, through multiple divisions as well as joint ventures, regional alliances, and private-public partnerships, will dominate major markets, while entrepreneurs, franchisers, and small businesses will provide raw materials and technologies; handle support services; distribute goods; and, at the same time, reach niches with their own products and services. This will see companies routinely reshaping and resizing themselves, regularly buying and selling off businesses, and periodically partnering with other institutions. These flexible firms, whether flying the flag of federalism or operating as virtual corporations, are coming to be called boundaryless organizations.

Under the most optimistic scenarios, people working in these organizations are expected to move seamlessly across levels and functions, through different kinds of jobs, and even from company to company through a boundaryless career. All of this will presumably be aided by new types of university, technical, and corporation-based education; increased flextime, sabbaticals, and work-at-home options; so-called mommy and daddy career tracks; and all sorts of other support services, programs, and groups (cf. Parker and Hall, 1993). Scholars and practitioners are currently developing a picture of the boundaryless organization (cf. Davis, 1995; Howard, 1995). But, up to this point, we have only the barest outline of tomorrow's boundaryless career.

Indeed, it still looks ragged: people working long and hard and, in many cases, scared. Transitions from work to the home to work, from assignment to assignment, and from company to company—voluntary and otherwise—seem abrupt, frenzied, and fractious. Levels of unemployment and underemployment are high, and advanced technology is eliminating clerical and semiskilled blue-collar jobs at a worrisome pace (Rifkin, 1994). Meanwhile, older workers, in particular, are being cut adrift from corporate moorings (cf. Hall and Mirvis, 1993). Much has to do with the fact that needed transitional structures and mechanisms—flexible work options; retraining and redeployment programs; family support services; and career planning and placement assistance—are not yet in place to sustain the boundaryless career (c.f. Mirvis, 1993). Meanwhile, people bemoan casualties of mergers and acquisitions; sympathize with victims of layoffs and downsizing; and shake their heads at the shrinking few who remain loyal to their employers, typecasting them as modern-day Willie Lomans.

Our aim here is to look at the pluses and minuses of the boundaryless career in regard to what Hall (1976) terms "psychological success." This refers to the experience of achieving goals that are personally meaningful to the individual, rather than those set by parents, peers, an organization, or society. Most studies of this concept have focused on how people set expectations of task accomplishment or goals of career advancement. Looking ahead, the boundaryless career will offer a broad and diverse array of task stimuli. Thus the keys to experiencing psychological success will be people's abilities to make sense of their constantly changing work agenda and to integrate their work experiences into a coherent self-picture. It also seems likely that many of the factors that support and reinforce psychological success in a career—such as job security, ever-increasing levels of income, and the status that derives from one's position and employer—will be less available and more chancy in the workplace of the future. This means that many more working people may have to reexamine their career aspirations and look to other sources of psychological success, or else risk disappointment and a sense of failure.

As straightforward as this sounds, setting new standards of success promises to be complicated for working people, who will be asked to do more at work and in the way of personal development while, at the same time being pressed by the demands of change and pulled by family, home, and civic obligations. How will people find the time to figure out what is personally meaningful for them? They will also have fewer stable attachments—in the workplace and in mobile communities—through which to gauge who they are and what they might become. How can people form a new work identity without trustworthy role models, close peers, and a supportive reference group?

These are but a few of the challenges to redefining psychological success that people will encounter as they embark on a boundaryless career. At the same time, since this career will provide so few external guideposts and guarantees of success, there will be little choice but to look inside oneself and probe personal values to fashion some kind of career-development plan and identity in this new working world. This sort of introspective life-planning can be a lonely pursuit, undertaken in off-hours, and steered by self-assessment tests, self-help books, and job-placement agencies. However, there is also reason to believe that the boundaryless career could itself offer new opportunities, stimuli, relationships, and networks that people can use to remake themselves and redefine their standards of psychological success. To develop this point, we will begin with a closer look at these new kinds of organizations and careers.

The Boundaryless Organization and Career

Models of the boundaryless organization date from the 1960s, when, for example, Bennis and Slater (1968) argued that "democracy is inevitable," and advised organizations to devise "temporary" structures to respond to rapid changes in their environments. The next decade witnessed "collateral" forms of organization, in which temporariness would be built into project groups; "parallel" structures in which semipermanent committees of workers and managers would oversee change efforts; and the "matrix" organization, which institutionalized cross-functional linkages and boundary-spanning work roles (Zand, 1974; Galbraith, 1977; Davis and Lawrence, 1977). By the 1980s, change had sped up to such a point that organizations began an era of ongoing restructuring exemplified by new work designs; total quality management (TQM) programs; and mergers, acquisitions, divestitures, and cross-company ventures, in the service of reinventing the corporation (for reviews, see Lawler et al., 1992, and Mirvis and Marks, 1992).

Today, this tumult is encapsulated in models of the boundaryless organization. Handy (1989) describes one such configuration in the form of a shamrock with three leafs. The first leaf—and the most important for continuity and organizational survival—contains a core staff of managers, technicians, and professionals. These are highly skilled individuals who are expected to make a major commitment to the organization, and who derive a lot of their sense of identity from it. The second leaf contains contractors, and specialized people and firms, often outside the organization, who serve a variety of needs, including supply, distribution, and routine control functions. Their work is not part of the essential core technology and competence of the firm, and can usually be done better, faster, and cheaper by someone else in a smaller, more specialized, and autonomous position. The third leaf includes the contingent labor force—part-timers and temporary workers who provide a "buffer" for the core workforce of a firm.

The logic behind the three leaves is that they enable an organization to get a richer picture of its environment and to flexibly respond to opportunities and threats—without a lot of overhead and bureaucracy. Specialists in organization design (cf. Emery and Trist, 1973; Weick, 1977; Cohen and March, 1986; Wheatley, 1993) contend these advantages come from having sufficient variety in structure and skill, such that a firm can better sense and interpret the complexity of its environment. In turn, a minimum of critical specification of job duties, coupled with the creation of more or less self-contained work units, allow companies to respond flexibly and fully to new circumstances. Finally, and the key to the success of the boundaryless organization, is its capacity for self-design in these circumstances. This means moving people quickly into new assignments, forming them into new structures, and having them hit the ground running.

Extrapolating from these principles, Hall and Mirvis (1994) argue that people will need more varied work experience to cope with complexity and change in their task environments. They will also need to be flexible and to have the competencies required to self-design much of their personal and career development (DeFillippi and Arthur, 1994). In turn, the ability to learn-how-to-learn will be crucial to their success in cobbling together an enriching career path (cf. Weick and Berlinger, 1989; Hall, 1991). Likely as not, working people tomorrow will have the opportunity to acquire and apply these skills as they move around the boundaries of organizations, retrain themselves or return to school, and otherwise adjust to changes in the employment market. This makes people's know-how, self-direction, and learning-ability the core competencies for navigating the boundaryless career. The question of interest here, however, is: Where are the psychological shoals?

What Is Different about the Boundaryless Career?

Much of the theory and research on careers over the last 40 years has focused on the ways people work their way up in an organization, emphasizing career stages, life cycles, and ladders (cf. Hall et al., 1986). This notion of a career was forged in the post-World War II era and appealed to people who grew up during, or heard firsthand stories of, the Great Depression and the war. Many entered the workforce in the 1950s with the idea of a lifetime career with one employer. Those who began their careers in the next 30 years recognized, to some extent, the necessity of frequent job changes; but most were still imbued with expectations of upward mobility, and looked forward to mastering a job and then savoring the intrinsic and material satisfactions of seniority.

In the case of the boundaryless organization, however, career development may be more cyclical—involving periodic cycles of reskilling. In addition, it will be marked by more lateral, rather than upward, movement and will culminate in a phased retirement. The problem is that this model of career progress is new and not yet accepted as the norm: It seems the antithesis of the onward-and-upward ideal that fires the success ethic. What is more, it does not fit the more conservative, but realistic, notion that, through hard work and diligence, one can make it in a chosen field of endeavor. Accordingly, one major psychic challenge for working people will be the need to adjust their expectations about continuous upward mobility and career progress.

It seems inescapable, too, that in the decades ahead, workers will have to change jobs, companies, and even occupations over their life course. Even work for a single employer will feature frequent job rotation, developmental assignments, and transitions from the first to the second and third leaves of a company. Movement across these work boundaries promises to tax even the most adaptable worker. To complicate matters, there will continue to be work and home boundaries to manage: The number of dual-career couples will continue to increase, and, whether coupled or not, many who will have to cope with complex working conditions will also have to concern themselves with childcare and elderly care. The resulting sense of role overload and conflict will pose countless practical problems, and could even further fragment people's work identities and family systems (cf. Hage, 1995).

Finally, it seems likely that the locus of career-development responsibility will shift even more so to the individual, in part because boundaryless organizations will not be able to meaningfully plan an employee's career—there will be simply too much uncertainty about future organizational needs to chart out prospective career paths and steer people through prescribed developmental sequences. This means that the individual will truly be on his or her own in developing a career. As appealing as this may sound to self-starters and self-developers, the sense of being part of something larger than oneself, of having elders to guide a career, and of having the opportunity to mentor young people, serves an important psychic function for all who are members of a firm. Finding a substitute for organizational identification is yet another psychic challenge that will face those charting a boundaryless career.

A Protean View of Careers

To better conceptualize these psychological challenges, and identify ways that people might address them, it is necessary to decouple the concept of a career from its mooring in any one organization and, indeed, from its exclusive association with paid employment. One recommendation is to see careers as being "protean" (Hall, 1976). The term is taken from the name of the Greek god Proteus, who could change shape at will, from fire to a wild boar to a tree, and so forth. This career concept can be defined as follows:

> The protean career is a process which the person, not the organization, is managing. It consists of all the person's varied experiences in education, training, work in several organizations, changes in occupational field, etc. The protean career is not what happens to the person in any one organization . . . (Hall, 1976: 201)

There are several advantages that accrue from this career concept. First, it opens up new ways to think about work over time. Most employers tend to think about career development in terms of individuals who are developing from the early-to-middle stages of their employment, and then either "plateauing" or "dropping off," in terms of what they have to offer the organization (Barth et al., 1993). The protean concept, however, also encompasses careers marked by peaks and valleys, by early or late blooming, and by movement from one line of work to another (Hall, 1993).

Second, it enlarges what we might call the career space. There is a tendency to associate a career with paid work and to draw sharp distinctions between people's work and nonwork lives. A more elastic concept, however, acknowledges that work and nonwork roles overlap and shape jointly a person's identity and sense of self. In practical terms, an enlarged definition of career space enables people to seriously consider taking time off to spend with their growing children, or to care for aging parents, under the rubric of attaining psychological success. Already there are examples of people "downshifting" in their careers to pursue hobbies or regain peace of mind; doing volunteer work to give back to the community; and, of course, pursuing the option of working at home where housework can spill over into paid work and visa versa (cf. Hyatt, 1990).

Finally, this career concept opens up new ways to think about the relationship between employers and employees. There is evidence that at least some of the most able and ambitious working people are taking charge of their work careers by choosing to "pack their own parachute," rather than following any corporation's definition of career development (Hirsch, 1987). These free-agent managers and professionals, (like their counterparts in sports) are constantly on the lookout for better situations, more money, or extra leverage. Yet even these stars have to contend with the problems of self-definition and normlessness that come from having to assume new roles in new situations, and from lacking long-term identification with a "home" team. Making sense of, and coming to terms with, the boundaryless career may be even more of a challenge to those who have neither the talent nor means to live like stars.

In sum, the protean-career concept gives us a more flexible way to see careers unfolding over time and in space. While it shifts responsibility for career development even more clearly to the individual, it also opens up new possibilities on how to think about and plan a career.

Aging over Career Cycles

As people work their way through the boundaryless organization, we expect them to periodically plateau, or to pass their prime, during their career years. Research on plateauing indicates that a worker has become "mature" when she or he has become established in a line of work, and when chances of upward mobility slow down or stop. In fields with drastically shorter product- and technology-cycle times, becoming established occurs in the 20s or the 30s (Hall, 1985). Looking ahead, it could be that just as the product life cycle is shortening in many industries, so, too, will the career cycle of many employees.

One way to help people develop over the course of a boundaryless career is to keep them moving through a number of career cycles of exploration-establishment and maintenance-disengagement, rather than trying to prolong the maintenance stage of their career (see Figure 14.1). In a career path in the

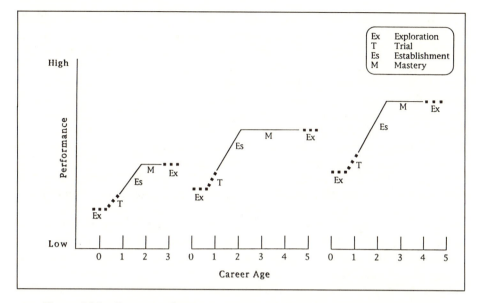

Figure 14.1 Career stages (learning versus age). The new model: Learning stages.

shamrock type of organization, for instance, people might work in core areas for a time; take a job at a supplier company or consulting firm; work as an individual contractor on selected projects; and then return to the fold as a senior core contributor and mentor.

The practical and psychological benefits of seeing careers in terms of re-peated developmental cycles could be substantial. For instance, a second cycle of career exploration might encourage a young person—after working for a time to pay off school debts—to go overseas (as retirees often do) to rethink earlier career decisions. In the same way, it might invite an older person—after experi-encing several cycles of disengagement—to become engaged again by working part-time in a service outlet (as young people often do), rather than retiring to the Sunbelt. The notion of going back to school to earn a degree, or gain new skills, or simply for self-improvement, also fits comfortably into a career concept of several cycles. So, too, does the decision of a sociologist to start over, in computer programming, or that of a programmer to move into social service. At this point, these kinds of career moves do not fit mainstream models of career development, but they are examples of boundaryless careers.

There will, of course, be material and psychological costs to this sort of career development pattern. For example, people who, more or less, start over in a new occupation will have less overall lifetime earnings than would accrue in the traditional single career path. Changing companies can also be costly: Early-retiring executives earn, on average, less than 85% of their former salary when they move to another company, and skilled manufacturing workers earn an even lesser percentage when they move to the service sector (Willis, 1987; Fisher, 1988). Furthermore, taking into account the costs of retraining and rede-ployment, plus the value of lost earnings, the boundaryless career may well prove less remunerative than the stable career paths of the past.

As to the psychological fallout, researchers have amply documented the emotional toll of an unexpected job loss (Brockner et al., 1985), and of the tensions associated with "hanging on" versus "letting go," even in the case of a planned change in jobs or employers (Bridges, 1980). Sarason (1977) notes, as well, that many working people are imbued with the "one life/one career" perspective, which makes the idea of a career change especially threatening. If we add to this the problems of unlearning familiar work routines and skills and learning new ones, the boundaryless career could be fraught with trauma.

This suggests that one important way to experience psychological success during the ups and downs of career cycles is to cultivate adaptability. Hall (1986) refers to this as a "metaskill" as it enables people to accommodate to new tasks and relationships, and to incorporate new roles and responsibilities into their personal identities. What is important to recognize, moreover, is that personal adaptability is much sought after by boundaryless organizations: It is what they look for when they hire from the outside, and what they try to develop in their high-potential employees. One survey of U.S. firms with 100 or more employees found that 56% offered personal-growth training to their employees (Gordon, 1988). It is not hard to imagine leading firms offering seminars on boundaryless career management as part of their training portfolio in the future. Indeed, companies may pay a "learning bonus" to employees that begin a new and organizationally valued career cycle, and a premium for the new skills that are mastered. The main point is that people who can adapt to the challenges of aging over several career cycles will have increased security within their organizations, and a better chance of finding a rewarding job if they choose to leave their company or be laid off.

Clearly, it will be important to study how and when people learn to adapt to change in a career marked by several cycles. To what extent is career adaptability a function of one's personality or age and stage, rather than a function of a skill and an outlook that can be developed? This is a practical question because the shamrock-type organization may offer career paths akin to the "farm system" in professional baseball—drawing young people from supplier plants and consulting firms after they have gained some seasoning; trading players and acquiring free agents during their mid-careers; and then farming out older workers to serve as mentors and coaches. This career path fits with developmental models of the seasons of life. Yet former stars often turn out to be the worst coaches, in part because they cannot adapt to the idea of aging in a short-time-span career. Are the tensions between hanging on and letting go different for people at different points in their lives? Could the demands of aging cyclically in a career speed up, in any way, the psychological changes associated with chronological aging?

It will also be important to study what organizations can do to help people adapt: What personal-growth training and developmental assignments best prepare people to become engaged in new career cycles and disengage from old ones? Should the boundaryless organization provide a safety net, incentives, and coaching to promote exploration and career learning, or put more emphasis on opportunities, competition, and self-help? Finally, we need to know the kinds of firms and industries for which it makes strategic sense to invest in employee adaptability versus hiring talented outside contractors and free agents (cf. Marks, 1993; Useem, 1993).

An Integrated Identity

A recent survey finds that three out of five American workers rate the effect of a job on their personal and family life as "very important" in making employment decisions—far more so than wages, benefits, and even job security (Galinsky and Friedman, 1993). With 87% of the American workforce living with at least one family member, finding time for spouses, children, parents, or partners is a major priority for more and more people. The survey reports that nearly half of the workforce rates the family-support policies of employers as a key consideration in their job choice.

Demographic shifts in the workforce, coupled with the increased priority many people place on their family and personal life, make it imperative that companies respond to work/family issues. Hall and Parker (1993) argue that just as companies are becoming more flexible in structure, staffing, and work systems, so, too, they need to be more flexible in the way they view work roles. Indications are that more and more firms are offering, say, flextime, work-at-home options, part-time employment, and even job sharing and career breaks, under the rubric of work/family programming (Parker and Hall, 1993). Furthermore, the temporariness of work assignments in the future (cf. Bridges, 1994), coupled with advances in telecommunications technology, will afford many more people the opportunity to work part-time, or from their home, or on a seasonal basis.

In so doing, however, the boundaryless career may well complicate and change people's work identity. To this point, many people have encapsulated their work, job, and employer in their work identity. As all three will change more often in a boundaryless career, the question of "What do I do?" may be raised more frequently and insistently. Moreover, people who are part of a dual-career couple, or who have children, or who care for their elders, have to contend not only with changing expectations of their roles, but also with more options about how they might fill them. The key point here is that as new career options open up boundaries around work, so, too, will they open up boundaries of identity.

Of course, people's work identity is but one aspect of their larger sense of self; or, expressed another way, identity is made up of a collection of subidentities (Hall and Schneider, 1973). The syndrome of "career success/personal failure," identified by Korman and Korman (1980), illustrates how some organization men compartmentalize their lives and fulfill their work goals at the expense of other subidentities. The ranks of women caught up in this syndrome also seem to be growing. In some respects, the boundaryless career could heighten this self-fragmentation: The combination of the psychic challenge and financial insecurity, for instance, could prove to be a narcotic for workaholics (cf. Machlowitz, 1978). On the other hand, the boundaryless career could afford people the flexible time and space to explore other life roles more fully and even expand their sense of self.

More-flexible career options, in turn, give people the freedom to change their career orientations over their lifetime. To illustrate: If we take seriously the notion that people will age over a period of several career cycles, then an early-career male, needing more education to move up the career ladder, may choose instead to emphasize his parental role—take more time off to be with his young children—and switch gears to a balanced identity, thereby putting off an MBA until his mid-30s or later, or not do it at all. In the same way, a midcareer women, who has peaked early in a small-employer or functional-career track, may rev up by moving to a nonprofit service organization or simply by increasing her volunteer work.

Naturally, there are financial and psychological costs in changing one's identity. However much a job or career change might enhance one's self-picture, moving into a job in the nonprofit sector, or working part-time, or in other ways limiting one's earning potential, may put an added burden on spouses or children to make up the difference—or else the change necessitates a lowering of one's lifestyle. Attempts to find balance in an organization may also prove costly: Even seemingly family-friendly firms give the most kudos to those who sacrifice their personal and family time to make heroic contributions. Indeed, a common complaint of the many women and the fewer men who have tried to adopt a balanced orientation in their work and family responsibilities is that their reputations, advancement potential, and, ultimately, their incomes have all suffered (Googins, 1990).

As to the psyche, it is hard to imagine dedicated careerists, whether in Japan or the United States or Europe, letting go of their emphasis on corporate advancement and achievement in order to, say, take extensive time off to care for an aging parent and develop a more expansive view of their purpose in life. Indeed, studies of high-achieving career women find that many attempt to be a supermom—combining work success with model child rearing—and then experience commensurate levels of fatigue and burnout. It doesn't help, of course, that their spouses eschew doing a larger share of household chores.

Hall (1986) calls the development of personal identity another "metaskill" needed to experience psychological success over the course of a career. The boundaryless career challenges people to make sense of and integrate many more stimuli and experiences into their sense of self. A once-favored notion is that people compensate for a lack of psychological success in one life sphere by putting more of their time and energy and identity into another. One limitation of this concept is that it treats identity as a fixed asset. Another is that it neglects the ways that experiences in many spheres have crossover effects and shape people's myriad subidentities—what has been called the "spillover" theory (cf. Staines, 1980; Voydanoff, 1989; Howard, 1992).

It will indeed be important for researchers to assess how people's experiences in their multiple and fast-changing roles spill over and shape their identities as they move through a boundaryless career. There has already been a major study of the ways that work affects family life (Evans and Bartolome, 1980).

More studies show how family experiences shape the way that people go about their work (cf. Barnett, 1993). Questions: Do managers who become active and loving parents learn to handle people more effectively? Do people who have complex and demanding home and personal responsibilities feel more pressured by their workloads? Or, can they handle them better? What is of interest here is how people transfer learning from setting to setting and how they integrate their experiences in different settings into their larger self-picture.

It will also be worthwhile to study what kinds of employers and employment conditions facilitate identity development. Obviously, companies that offer flexible employment options give people the chance to take on a balanced career orientation and adjust their work commitments over time, in line with their family and nonwork needs. But when is flexibility countermanded by the message that the most successful people "eat, sleep, and breathe" their jobs? What is of interest here is how people sort through mixed messages about paths to success, and come to terms with the trade-offs and compromises they must make—and what happens when they are not able to integrate experiences into a coherent identity.

Employer-Employee Relations

Rousseau (1990), drawing from legal scholars, has identified two types of employment contracts: transactional and relational. A transactional contract is defined in terms of a monetary exchange over a specified period of time, with the employer contracting for specific skills used for specific tasks, and then compensating the skill holder for a satisfactory performance. A relational contract, by comparison, is not time bound; rather, it establishes an ongoing relationship between the person and the organization, and involves the exchange of both monetary and nonmonetary benefits, including mutual loyalty, support, and career rewards. From this vantage point, one way to view the contemporary psychological contract between employers and employees is to say that it is shifting from a relational contract to a transactional one.

Who is likely to offer, and get, each type of contract in the years ahead? Setting this in a framework of strategic human-resource management, Rousseau argues that "make"-oriented firms, in Miles and Snow's (1984) terms, are more likely to establish relational contracts with people, while "buy"-oriented organizations are more likely to offer them transactional contracts. Using Handy's (1989) framework, we can also hypothesize that those employees in the core of a business are more apt to have a relational contract, while those on the second and third leaves will have a transactional employment arrangement.

It is also possible that transactional contracts will become the norm in industry, particularly in the United States. For instance, many of the traditional, career-oriented employers—IBM, Hewlett-Packard, and AT&T, among others—are increasingly hiring managerial and professional talent from outside and making continued employment explicitly contingent on the fit between people's competencies and business needs. This ethic reaches its logical conclusion in Jack Welch, CEO of General Electric, who contends that GE offers its people a "one-day contract."

Our own view is that boundaryless organizations will use both relational and transactional contracts—and in potentially very innovative ways. For instance, some employees might be treated like "partners," with a share in ownership, participation in profit sharing, and even emeritus status after eventual retirement. Now these terms generally apply to top-level managers and high-level individual contributors. In the future, they may also extend to customer-service representatives, lathe operators, or programmers who are on a career learning path and acquiring the varied skills and experience needed for flexible assignments throughout an organization. By contrast, some otherwise highly paid professionals and managers, deemed specialists, might work on a fee-for-services basis and be treated more or less as "hired hands." It is also possible that firms will have long-term contracts with, say, a consultant or a key service provider, and will offer employment on a project-by-project basis to an early retiree—a former executive or technician.

This shift in employment boundaries is bound to have an impact on people's psychological boundaries. For some people, periodic and unpredictable changes in their employment status and degree of membership in a company are certain to create confusion and upset. Add to this the stress of changing assignments, work groups, work location, plus the possibility of unemployment, and the likely result is a fragmentation and, ultimately, a loss of identity. In a very real sense, a firm's boundaries will not hold people as firmly as in the past. Others, however, will experience more degrees of freedom than ever before. Not only will it be easier for people to change jobs and employers; there will be less stigma attached to it—whether the action is voluntary or forced. In addition, it may also be easier for people to return to a previous employer. Companies such as GE, which used to frown on people's departures from the firm, have begun to rehire former employees as a way of obtaining skilled talent and capitalizing on their shorter start-up time and learning curve. In this sense, the permeability of employment boundaries gives people more psychological freedom to explore new identities and even return to old ones with a richer sense of themselves.

It is also possible that transactional employment will give a boost to people's self-esteem. Under the relational contract, the locus of responsibility is on the employer: Job security is a company policy. Hence employees can attribute steady pay increases and employment to standard practice, rather than to their own unique effort and performance. As a result, to take an example, people who have plateaued in job-secure organizations are never sure of their status: Are they really seen as contributing, or are they being kept on and humored because of their firm's loyalty to longtime employees? This uncertainty can involve a vicious cycle affecting job performance and development. After all, why should plateaued employees upgrade their skills or take on developmental assignments when, in any case, they will be valued and kept on?

By comparison, under the transactional contract, the locus of responsibility is squarely on the individual: He or she is employed based on current value to the organization. The resulting sense of self-responsibility means that people can attribute continued employment to their own efforts and achievements. This also puts added responsibility on them to continue to learn new skills, take on developmental projects, and further develop their core identities. This scenario becomes a virtuous cycle wherein people continue to add value to themselves and are seen as adding value to their employer.

What about organizational identification? Under the relational contract, through promotion from within, mentoring and socialization, and various rites of acculturation, many employees come to identify with an organization. In some cases, they fully internalize company values and link their identities to their organization. Although this varies by national and corporate culture (cf. Etzioni, 1961; Ouchi, 1981), one's level of identification is often expressed in response to the question: "What do you do?" People who have a sense of togetherness at their firm typically respond: "I work for company X."

Under the transactional contact, by contrast, identity develops more around a person's skills and competencies, since these comprise the currency he or she has to exchange. Today, this marks the identity of many skilled professionals, whose response to the standard query is, usually: "I do Y." It may come to define many more who pursue a boundaryless career in the future. In principle, this self-description is not associated with any particular organization—the organization is simply the place where professionals do their work. On the other hand, firms will likely find that their primary competitive advantage lies in people who have the skills, know-how, and discretion to manage the demands of fast-changing work situations. Hence it is expected that many employers will try to capitalize on people's commitments to their work, by making sure that they provide them with challenging and stimulating opportunities to do their own thing.

All of this raises some important questions for further research. For example, are people more apt to feel a sense of psychological failure under conditions of a relational contract or a transactional contract? In the former case, one may see oneself as having let down peers and the organization, incurring a shameful feeling and a loss of self-worth. At the same time, companies that offer relational contracts to employees often have support systems to help people cope with failures and to provide coaching and training to ensure that they can learn from their mistakes. By contrast, to the extent that people hired for assignments receive more cues that success is attributable to their distinct effort and skill, so, too, will they get more signals that failure is due to their deficiencies. Furthermore, transactional workers may not have access to an organization's support system or be given a second chance to redeem themselves. On the contrary, when their transactional contract is not renewed, the explicit and public message will be that they no longer add value to the company.

Other questions concern the roles people will play based on their employment contract. For instance, even when people are achieving success in transactional employment, they may feel that they are only partially included in the core work and culture of a company. While this can free them, it can also limit people's influence in an organization and leave them feeling left out of things. At the same time, movement across boundaries in a company may give people more contacts and networks and a fuller and deeper picture of what is going on in the firm. Whether or not this gives them more influence and a sense of belonging depends, in part, on how employees play their multiple roles and how they are seen in a company: Are they repositories and disseminators of knowledge (cf. Nonoka, 1988), or just transitory figures who come and go?

It is also valuable to study further the impact of choice in these different employment contracts. To the extent that employers chose to offer employees relational contracts in past decades, they are seen today as unilaterally changing the terms to a transactional basis. This has heightened fears of job insecurity (Mirvis, 1992) and bred employee mistrust of companies (Mirvis and Kanter, 1992). It is also seen as a factor in the crimes of revenge committed against management by displaced employees, and in the turnabout-is-fair-play job hopping among those with the wherewithal to move nimbly from company to company.

At the same time, those who pursue a boundaryless career, by choice and without the baggage of evening the score, may experience a greater sense of control over their relationship with an employer. Leinberger and Tucker's (1991) study of the sons and daughters of the "organization men" profiled by Whyte (1956) is instructive in this regard. They find these offspring make work and job choices contingent on the fit to their lifestyles, family situations, and personal values. In so doing, they seem to be fashioning a protean-career identity and applying new standards of psychological success in their employment decisions.

Psychological Success and a Life's Work

At this point, however, the movement toward the boundaryless organization is well ahead of acceptance of the boundaryless career. Many people have resisted letting go of the apparent ideal of a lifetime of work in one firm, as well as the stability offered by predictable career paths. As a consequence, when moved laterally, laid off, or forced to retire early, they experience their loss of status or employment in relational terms: They were "seduced" by their companies and then "betrayed," "jilted," and "abandoned" (cf. Lewicki, 1981; Mirvis and Marks, 1992).

One prominent way in which working people have coped with their disillusionment is by sliding into cynicism (Kanter and Mirvis, 1989). In so doing, they lower their expectations of, and commitments to, an employer, keeping their emotions in check and lowering their temperatures to a bearable degree. To this extent, cynicism is a functional reaction as it shields people from disappointment. At the same time, it plays havoc with the heart and hampers relationships with a spouse, family, and friends (Williams, 1989).

As more and more people embark on boundaryless careers, however, new and better coping strategies will recommend themselves. One possibility is that people will identify themselves more with their work than with any particular organization. Many self-employed consultants already pursue these kinds of careers, and their attachments to organizations may be a harbinger of things to come: As some describe it, rather indelicately, it's just "sex," not "marriage." Carried to the extreme, of course, this equates with fee-for-service prostitution and threatens to fully depersonalize the employer-employee relationship.

As cold and calculating as this sounds, two factors will likely work against a purely transactional relationship between corporations and their workers. First, firms are constantly being judged on how they manage people. On this count, it is worth noting that companies who downsized in the late 1980s, but did not retrain and redeploy their people, are having a hard time recruiting new people; they have acquired a bad reputation (Marks, 1993). Second, companies who have taken a lead in responding to new conditions facing their business typically invest more in employee development and do more to retain their people (cf. Mirvis, 1993; Denison, 1990).

Carrying this point forward, we believe that leading companies will make every effort to attract and retain people under guidelines: that they change jobs frequently, willingly move laterally, and take increased responsibility for developing themselves and their careers. This warms up transactional employment and has a company offering people stimulation, opportunities, and developmental experience in exchange for professional work. Life in the boundaryless organization could also prove nourishing and enhance prospects of psychological success. No doubt, task challenges and new relationships, when successfully managed and formed, will add significantly to people's sense of achievement and enrich their social networks. It is also likely that these organizations will provide chances for people to, say, teach in public schools; work on community projects; participate in foreign joint ventures; and get involved in environmental projects—all of these might expand their self-images and introduce them to new aspects of who they might become. The irony is that boundaryless organizations could offer, to those employees able to negotiate its waterways, the opportunity to have a one-company career, gain a position of prominence and influence, and serve socializing and mentoring roles.

It will be useful to study the conditions under which people grow from this kind of diverse, potentially identity-stretching experience, and to determine when it overwhelms them and causes a psychic shutdown. Possibly, there will be points of optimal stretch where people can assimilate the rich variety of stimuli into their self-picture, but beyond which they become saturated and lose their self-identity (cf. Gergen, 1991). In addition, it is worth examining the conditions under which people respond to this stretching by showing loyalty to their companies, versus maintaining the emotional distance that keeps them free to attend to the other demands and interests in their lives.

Our own hunch is that more of tomorrow's boundaryless workers will set their own career course. Surveys and studies over the past three decades have amply documented American workers' desires for interesting work, personal growth, and self-fulfillment on the job (cf. Yankelovich, 1981; Pascarella, 1984). It may be, however, that some have "maxed out" in their quest for stimulation at work and, instead, seek other sources of satisfaction. Maccoby (1988) finds, as an example, finds a new character type emerging in the workforce—the self-developer, who wants to master a skill but also explore and play; who seeks knowledge but also balance between work and other life pursuits. It could be that the interesting, fast-changing, and emotionally demanding work offered by tomorrow's organizations will not prove to be the be-all and end-all for the self-developer. Aspirations of getting more time with family and pursuing personal goals hint at other dimensions to their identities. To the extent we can set aside simplistic notions that self-actualization is the pinnacle of human motivation, this makes room to consider how family feeling, community membership, and spirituality are transcendent aims of human development.

In this light, Hall and Mirvis (1994) hypothesize that people's core identities may be enlarged by incorporating what we call a commitment to their life's work. In this framework, a person's identity deepens not only through cumulative work experiences and career achievements but also through work as a spouse, parent, and community member, and especially through work on one's identity. In many respects, the boundaryless career will give people the freedom and flexibility to more fully engage in their life's work and to find, where desired, greater balance in their lives. It will, however, be incumbent on individuals to integrate these diverse work and life experiences into their larger sense of self. They will also have to accept the financial and psychological trade-offs that follow from the choice of a balanced career. Such choices can, of course, deepen the self: The process is referred to as finding one's "calling" (Peck, 1993). Shepherd (1984) calls it simply "the path with a heart."

Where will people find role models and the social support needed to follow a self-styled path with a heart? For a period of time, anyway, this career orientation may be suspect in organizations and, alternatively, bring envy and disparagement from coworkers and superiors. As the boundaryless career becomes more commonplace, however, one will find many more fellow travelers to provide guidance and some companionship. In this case, it will be important to study what tomorrow's freelancers call their kingdom. Kahn (1992), for example, finds that people's social connection to coworkers enhances their "psychological presence" at work. Does this mean, as Bennis and Slater (1968) hypothesized, that the capacity to quickly form close, personal, authentic relationships with new people in new settings will be required for people to work effectively and derive social satisfaction in temporary work situations? How about people who are shy, or introverted, or have a prickly disposition, or who choose to work at home—how will they get the social support needed to sustain a boundaryless career?

We expect that many more working people in the future will use their social networks, rather than their organizations, as focal sources of identification. These networks, incorporating not only colleagues from past and present work assignments, but also fellow members of the PTA, maybe some neighbors, as well as spouses and children, could well provide a needed emotional anchor for those who opt for a boundaryless career. Furthermore, we expect to see more people joining any of a myriad of voluntary associations, ranging from social support groups and service clubs to religious and cultural groups, to regain a sense of connection heretofore provided primarily by their companies. It is not hard to imagine people in boundaryless careers responding to the standard query with the reply "I do lots of different things," and then elaborating on work projects; their roles as coparents or as single ones; their pursuit of personal goals; and their membership in one social group or another. To this extent, they will have found a home in a complex social network and, possibly, it will be just as flexible, flawed, and enriching as the network of the person who asked them the question.

ACKNOWLEDGMENTS: Modified from an article originally published in *Journal of Organizational Behavior, 15,* 1994, 365–380.

References

Barnett, R. (1993). "Work/family experiences and distress: Exploring gender effects." Wellesley, Mass.: Wellesley College, Center for Research on Women.

Barth, M. C.; McNaught, W.; and Rizzi, P. (1993). "Corporations and the aging workforce." In P. Mirvis (ed.), *Building the Competitive Work Force.* New York: Wiley.

Bennis, W. G., and Slater, P. (1968). *The Temporary Society.* New York: Harper and Row.

Bridges, W. (1980). *Transitions.* Reading, Mass.: Addison-Wesley.

Bridges, W. (1994). *JobShift.* Reading, Mass.: Addison-Wesley.

Brockner, J.; Davy, J.; and Carter, C. (1985). "Layoffs, self-esteem, and survivor guilt: Motivational, affective, and attitudinal consequences." *Organizational Behavior and Human Decision Processes, 36:* 229–244.

Cohen, M. D., and March, J. G. (1986). *Leadership and Ambiguity.* 2d ed. Boston: Harvard Business School Press.

Davis, D. D. (1995). "Form, function, and strategy in boundaryless organizations." In A. Howard (ed.), *The Changing Nature of Work.* San Francisco: Jossey-Bass.

Davis, S. M., and Lawrence, P. R. (1977). *Matrix,* Reading, Mass.: Addison-Wesley.

DeMeuse, K. P., and Tornow, W. W. (1990). "The tie that binds—has become very, very frayed!" *Human Resource Planning, 13:* 203–213.

DeFillippi, R. J., and Arthur, M. B. (1994). "The boundaryless career: A competency-based Perspective." *Journal of Organizational Behavior, 15,* 4: 307–324.

Emery, F. E., and Trist, E. L. (1973). *Toward a Social Ecology.* London: Tavistock.

Etzioni, A. (1961). *A Comparative Analysis of Complex Organizations.* New York: Free Press.

Evans, P., and Bartolome, F. (1980). *Must Success Cost So Much?* New York: Basic Books.

Fisher, A. B. (1988). "The downside of downsizing." *Fortune,* May 23: 42.

Galbraith, J. R. (1977). *Organizational Design.* Reading, Mass.: Addison-Wesley.

Galinsky, E., and Friedman, D. (1993). *National Study of the Changing Workforce.* New York: Families and Work Institute.

Gergen, K. (1991). *The Saturated Self: Dilemmas of Identity in Contemporary Life.* New York: Basic Books.

Googins, B. (1991). *Work/Family Conflicts: Private Lives—Public Responses.* New York: Auburn House.

Gordon, J. (1988). "Who's being trained to do what?" *Training,* October: 51–60.

Hage, J. (1995). "Postindustrial lives: New demands, new prescriptions." In A. Howard (ed.), *The Changing Nature of Work.* San Francisco: Jossey-Bass.

Hall, D. T. (1976). *Careers in Organizations.* Glenview, Ill.: Scott, Foresman.

Hall, D. T. (1985). "Project work as an antidote to career plateauing in a declining engineering organization." *Human Resource Management, 24:* 271–292.

Hall, D. T. (1991). "Business restructuring and strategic human resource development." In P. B. Doeringer et al. (eds.), *Turbulence in the American Workplace.* New York: Oxford University Press.

Hall, D. T. (1993). "The 'new career contract': Alternative career paths. Paper presented at Fourth German Business Congress on Human Resources, Cologne.

Hall, D.T., and Mirvis, P. H. (1993). "The new workplace: A place for older workers?" *Perspective on Aging,* October-December: 15–17.

Hall, D.T., and Mirvis, P. H. (1995). "Careers as lifelong learning." In A. Howard (ed.), *The Changing Nature of Work*. San Francisco: Jossey-Bass.

Hall, D. T., and Parker, V. A. (1993). "The role of workplace flexibility in managing diversity." *Organizational Dynamics,* Summer: 4–18.

Hall, D. T., and Schneider, B. (1973). *Organizational Climates and Careers: The Work Lives of Priests*. New York: Academic Press.

Hall, D. T., and Associates. (1986). *Career Development in Organizations*. San Francisco: Jossey-Bass.

Handy, C. (1989). *The Age of Unreason*. Boston: Harvard Business School Press.

Hirsch, P. (1987). *Pack Your own Parachute*. Reading, Mass.: Addison-Wesley.

Howard, A. (1992). "Work and family crossroads spanning the career." In S. Zedeck (ed.), *Work, Families, and Organizations*. San Francisco: Jossey-Bass.

Howard, A. (1995). "A framework for work change." In A. Howard (ed.), *The Changing Nature of Work*. San Francisco: Jossey-Bass.

Hyatt, C. (1990). *Shifting Gears*. New York: Fireside.

Kahn, W. A. (1992). "To be fully there: Psychological presence at work." *Human Relations, 45,* 4: 321–349.

Kanter, D. L., and Mirvis, P. H. (1989). *The Cynical Americans*. San Francisco: Jossey-Bass.

Korman, A. K., and Korman, R. (1980). *Career Success/Personal Failure*. Englewood Cliffs, N.J.: Prentice-Hall.

Lawler, E. E.; Mohrman, S. A.; and Ledford, G. E. (1992). *Employee Involvement and Total Quality Management: Practices and Results in Fortune 1000 Companies*. San Francisco: Jossey-Bass.

Leinberger, P., and Tucker, B. (1991). *The New Individualists*. New York: HarperCollins.

Lewicki, R. J. (1981). Organizational seduction: Building commitment to organizations. *Organizational Dynamics,* Autumn: 5–21.

Maccoby, M. (1988). *Why work?* New York: Simon and Schuster.

Machlowitz, M. (1978). *Workaholics*. Reading, Mass.: Addison-Wesley.

Marks, M. L. (1993). "Restructuring and Downsizing." In P. Mirvis (ed.), *Building the Competitive Work Force*. New York: Wiley.

Miles, R. E., and Snow, C. C. (1984). Designing strategic human resources systems. *Organizational Dynamics,* Summer: 36–52.

Mirvis, P. H. (1992). Job security: Current trends. In L. K. Jones (ed.), *The Encyclopedia of Career Change and Work Issues*. Phoenix: Oryx Press.

Mirvis, P. H. (ed.). (1993). *Building a Competitive Workforce: Investing in Human Capital for Corporate Success*. New York: Wiley.

Mirvis, P. H., and Kanter, D. L. (1992). Beyond demographics: A psychographic profile of the workforce." *Human Resource Management, 30,* 1: 45–68.

Mirvis, P. H., and Marks, M. L. (1992). *Managing the Merger*. Englewood Cliffs, N.J.: Prentice-Hall.

Nonaka, I. (1988). Toward middle-up-down management: Accelerating information creation. *Sloan Management Review,* Spring: 9–18.

Ouchi, W. A. (1981). *Theory Z: How American Business Can Meet the Japanese Challenge*. Reading, Mass.: Addison-Wesley.

Parker, V., and Hall, D. T. (1993). Workplace flexibility: Faddish or fundamental? In P. Mirvis (ed.), *Building the Competitive Work Force*. New York: Wiley.

Pascarella, P. (1984). *The New Achievers*. New York: Free Press.

Peck, M. S. (1993). *A World Waiting to Be Born*. New York: Bantam.

Rifkin, J. (1994). *The End of Work*. New York: Putnam.

Rousseau, D. M. (1990). New-hire perceptions of their own and their employer's obligations: A study of psychological contracts. *Journal of Organizational Behavior, 11:* 389–400.

Rousseau, D. M., and Wade-Benzoni, K. A. (1995). Changing individual-organizational attachments: A two-way street. In A. Howard (ed.), *The Changing Nature of Work*. San Francisco: Jossey-Bass.

Sarason, S. (1977). *Work, Aging, and Social Change*. New York: Free Press.

Schor, J. B. (1991). *The Overworked American*. New York: Basic Books.

Shepherd, H. A. (1984). On the realization of human potential: A path with a heart. In M. B. Arthur; L. Bailyn; D. J. Levinson; and H. A. Shepherd (eds.), *Working with Careers*. New York: Graduate School of Business, Columbia University.

Staines, G. (1980). Spillover versus compensation: A review of the literature on the relationship between work and nonwork. *Human Relations, 33:* 111–129.

Tichy, N., and Sherman, S. 1993. *Control your Destiny or Someone Else Will: How Jack Welch is Making General Electric the World's Most Competitive Company*. New York: Doubleday/Currency.

Voydanoff, P. (1989). Work and family: A review and expanded conceptualization. *Journal of Social Behavior and Personality, 3,* 4: 1–22.

Useem, M. (1993). Company policies on education and training. In P. Mirvis (ed.), *Building the Competitive Work Force,* New York: Wiley.

Weick, K. E., and Berlinger, L. R. (1989). Career improvisation in self-designing organizations. In M. B. Arthur; D. T. Hall; and B. S. Lawrence (eds.), *Handbook of Career Theory*. New York: Cambridge University Press.

Weick, K. E. (1977). Organization design: Organizations as self-designing systems." *Organizational Dynamics,* Autumn: 38–49.

Wheatley, M. J. (1993). *Leadership and the New Science: Learning about Organization from an Orderly Universe*. San Francisco: Berrett-Koehler.

Whyte, W. (1956). *The Organization Man*. New York: Simon and Schuster.

Williams, R. C. (1989). *The Trusting Heart*. New York: Times Books.

Willis, R. (1987). What's happening to America's middle managers? *Management Review,* January: 24–33.

Yankelovich, D. (1981). *The New Rules*. New York: Random House.

Zand, D. (1974). Collateral organization: A New Change Strategy." *The Journal of Applied Behavioral Science, 10:* 63–89.

15

Challenging the Last Boundary: Reconnecting Work and Family

JOYCE K. FLETCHER AND LOTTE BAILYN

The needs of today's business enterprises—responsiveness, adaptability, flexibility, and creativity in responding to global markets and to customers—are increasingly identified with their ability to cross internal and external boundaries, boundaries that for years have been considered inviolate. Indeed, boundary crossing is quickly becoming the hallmark of a new approach to business, one that has been called "co-opetition" (Lipnack and Stamps, 1993). The centerpiece of this approach is a recognition of the added value that comes from bridging barriers that traditionally have fostered competition, rather than cooperation, such as barriers between marketing, engineering, and research and development; barriers with external suppliers; and even competitive barriers between companies within the same industry (Handy, 1989; Ring and Van de Ven, 1994; Wheatley, 1993). In the words of Jack Welch, CEO of General Electric (quoted in Slater, 1994: 110):

> Boundarylessness means engaging every mind on every problem, leaving no one out, weighing no one's ideas heavier because of the color of their collar or their skin, their gender, their nationality, or whatever. We find again and again that every barrier that divides us, between engineering and manufacturing, between us and suppliers or us and customers, between the preconceived view we have of Jakarta or Shanghai and the view we know of Boston or Des Moines, between genders, between races, every barrier—serious or silly—is a speed bump that slows us down and deprives us of the quickness we must have to capture the opportunity that is out there in abundance.

From the individual employee's point of view, this new form of organization implies the necessity, or perhaps the opportunity, to forge one's own career, over time, to meet one's personal needs. Such a career —in which workers move with ease across organizational and functional boundaries—is likely to be entre-

preneurial or professional, rather than bureaucratic (Kanter 1989), and it therefore changes the social contract between employees and employers. The employment contract is no longer based on job security in exchange for loyalty and
commitment. Instead, workers are assumed to be responsible for their own employability, and, in return, companies are challenged to offer interesting, important work; increased freedom and control; and the experience and training
needed to enhance individuals' marketable skills (Hakim, 1994).

The successful worker in this new world is a systems thinker, one who can
think holistically and is comfortable operating in this more complex environment of more permeable boundaries. It is a worker who, for example, can integrate and capture the synergy between marketing and engineering goals; or who
can anticipate the skills that will be needed in the next generation of products,
and can step across the boundaries of occupational specialization to acquire
them (Hammer and Champy, 1993; Nonaka, 1994; Senge, 1990). But despite
this new respect for boundary crossing, one boundary remains "off limits" in
this discussion—the boundary between work and family (Bailyn, 1993). Indeed,
the worker implicit in the boundaryless form of organization continues to be
one whose ability, willingness, and energy to focus on work, and to develop
new marketable skills, are unconstrained. Family and community involvement
are considered irrelevant to the development of the new entrepreneurial, self-
employed worker, except as a possible alternative for those who choose balance
over other career orientations, such as "getting high on work" or "getting
ahead" (Derr, 1986). This view of family as adversarial to the needs of work
leads to a rather paradoxical vision of boundaryless organizations filled with
workers who have the skills to capture the synergy in crossing functional and
occupational boundaries, but who nonetheless feel the need to maintain the
strict separation of work and family.

The irony is that by shifting the responsibility of career development from
the employer to the employee, the careers enabled by the this new organizational
form *should* be able to help individuals integrate work and family more easily.
The problem, however, is that nothing in the new employment relationship challenges the underlying sense that work and family spheres are adversarial—that
they represent an either-or situation for both the employee and employer. In
fact, this sense of competing, adversarial spheres runs so deep that even when
bridging this boundary is listed as one of the meanings of a boundaryless career
(Arthur, 1994; Mirvis and Hall, 1994), the two sides are often cast unwittingly
as oppositional; and the goal of balance is seen as an individual choice achieved
through rejecting—either permanently or for a short time during child-rearing
years—career opportunities in order to put personal or family needs first.

It is our contention that such an adversarial, zero-sum view is not necessary. The goal of this chapter is to explore this hypothesis by challenging the
separation of work from family in order to identify the potential for synergy in
the reconnection of these two spheres, which might benefit both individuals and
the companies in which they work. It draws on the findings of a major research
study that challenged this boundary and highlighted the potential for synergy.[1]

Work and Family as Separate Spheres

The boundary between work and family is rooted in societal beliefs about the necessity of keeping the public and private spheres of life separate. These two spheres are generally conceptualized as competitive, adversarial arenas, where the goal is balance between the two, rather than systemic boundarylessness or integration. Traditional approaches to work and family are rooted in this assumption of separation, and in an image of an ideal worker who not only has a firm boundary between the two, but is able and willing to put the work sphere ahead of the family sphere. This is most easily demonstrated through a close examination of the assumptions underlying typical company responses to work-family concerns. The traditional response to issues of work and family has focused on designing policies and practices to help "special-needs" employees (employees with visible outside responsibilities) more closely resemble "ideal" workers (employees with no visible outside responsibilities). The assistance typically offered has taken the form of work-family benefits, such as on-site day care, elder-care referral services, and flextime. These forms of assistance are intended to help employees with family responsibilities meet the existing demands of the workplace. The business argument for providing such assistance has to do with changing demographics and a projected increase in the number of these special-needs employees. The underlying assumption is that helping these employees makes good business sense, since family demands are assumed to create stress and tension that could affect productivity (cf. Rodgers and Rodgers, 1989). Opportunities for leaves from work, which would permit workers to manage this boundary more easily by themselves, have generally not been part of the American response to these issues.

What is problematic about this traditional approach is that it casts those who have outside interests and responsibilities as an aberrant subset for whom special accommodations must be made in order to free them to be productive organizational citizens (Fletcher, 1995). We know, however, that this aberrant subset actually represents the norm, and that the notion of separate spheres is more a cultural myth than a reality for most workers. For example, studies that explore the effects of work on family suggest that there are a number of work factors—such as degree of control, peer relationships, and job demands—that have a significant effect on family functioning (Barling, 1994, Barnett, 1994; Galinsky and Friedman, 1993; Hunt, 1994). Likewise, there are many studies that demonstrate the positive and negative effects of family circumstances on workers' well-being and effectiveness (e.g., Barnett, 1994, Kriegsman and Hardin, 1974, cited in Barling, 1994).

Despite this personal experience of interdependence, the workplace rewards those individuals who are able to keep these responsibilities and interests hidden, and who can maintain the myth that the two spheres are separate and discrete (Fletcher, 1994a; Johnson, 1994). Because of the cultural emphasis on the separation of spheres, the image of an ideal worker remains that of one who can maintain a strict boundary between work and personal life. In a study of employees in the publishing industry in the United Kingdom, for example, it was found that keeping one's private life entirely separate from one's work was reported by both men and women to be one of the main criteria of occupational success (Walsch and Cassell, 1995). Another study found that even when organizations have progressive work-family policies, employees experience severe informal pressure not to take even the minimum work-family benefits guaranteed by law. Not only were high-level female managers who had taken only a few weeks' maternity leave held up as role models for junior managers; but one of the highest compliments paid to these women was to have it said that "you'd never even know she has a family" (Collinson and Collinson, 1995). Thus, although all workers live in an interdependent world of paid employment and outside interests and responsibilities, those (often women) who are unable or unwilling to hide these outside activities suffer career repercussions.

Another problem with this traditional framing of work and family issues is that it casts the two spheres not only as separate, but as having competing interests. Thus, it not only frames organizational success as dependent on workers who demonstrate their commitment through a willingness to sacrifice family for work; but it frames family success as dependent on individual members who demonstrate their commitment through a willingness to sacrifice career success for family. Findings from the work-family research study (Bailyn et al., 1995) in which we were involved indicate that this pitting of family versus work leads to mistrust and suspicion on both sides. For example, the assumption that committed workers will put work first leads to a situation in which a worker who asks for changes in work processes or practices in order to meet family needs is seen as a less-than-committed worker. The underlying assumption is that these requests are in the individual's best interest, but will have a negative impact on company goals. They therefore must be tightly controlled. When granted, these accommodations are often treated as "rewards" for past performance or as an expression of a manager's sensitivity to extreme employee need (Johnson, 1994). The motivation for management in considering these requests is quite limited and stems from a belief that companies must be sensitive to the needs of this ever-increasing pool of special-needs workers, or that they will suffer the consequences in problems with employee recruitment and retention.

Likewise, management requests for work-process improvements to enhance productivity or cost effectiveness are often met with worker mistrust and suspicion. Such changes are assumed to benefit the firm at the expense of the individual. Because the "time saved" is assumed to go to the company, many workers fear—especially in these times of downsizing—that increases in productivity will lead to either further reductions in staff or increases in workload. Thus, workers have a limited motivation to be fully engaged in the process of work innovation because they assume they will not share the benefits of these efforts. As a result, the internal desire to strive for excellence is often undermined, rather than being tapped, and the company's need to change is thwarted.

This adversarial framing of individual and organizational interests stands in sharp contrast to the "boundaryless-organization" goal of capturing the synergy between previously separate entities. Despite a recognition that a synergy between competing elements is useful in the boundaryless form of organization, the possible synergy that could be captured by moving from the current framing of work and family as competing spheres has been ignored. We argue that not only does a synergistic approach to work and family have the potential to align individual and business concerns in a way that releases new energy and yields mutual benefits; but that when this boundary between work and family is *not* connected, key business goals are likely to be invisibly, but surely, undermined.

The Organizational Costs of Separation

When marketing and engineering take a zero-sum approach to resource alloca-tion, or assume a zero-sum allotment of organizational rewards, their competi-tive interactions are likely to create the "speed bumps" that Jack Welch speaks of eliminating. So, too, in the work-family arena, the zero-sum assumption of separate spheres and adversarial interests creates a similar, but largely unrecog-nized, set of speed bumps that constrains the ability to innovate work practices and structures. Recent research suggests that the assumed separation of the pub-lic and private domains of life operates to dissociate the skills and values associ-ated with the public sphere from those associated with the private sphere (Fletcher, 1994a; Gordon, 1991; Jacques, 1992). The result is that skills associ-ated with the public sphere, such as rationality, linear thinking, autonomy, and independence, are more easily recognized as the core competencies that individu-als and companies need. As a result, these skills tend to be used as "ability signals" (Rosenbaum, 1989) denoting career potential, while skills commonly associated with the private sphere of life—such as empathy, nurturing, collabo-ration, and attending to the emotional context of situations—are less valued in organizational settings and, indeed, are often considered inappropriate in the workplace.

There is a growing body of work, however, that suggests that business has much to gain by encouraging the blending of these two sets of skills and values in their workers. For example, an in-depth study of decision making among 24 major American executives (Everett et al., n.d.) identified a small group of "principled risk takers," whose business decisions included at least one that reflected social or environmental values. One of the key findings about this group was their sense of wholeness: They were "concerned not only with mate-rial and short-term well-being but with subjective experience and long-term con-tinuity as well" (Everett et al., p. 26). In contrast, the more conventional deci-sion makers completely separated their business decisions from the values of their personal lives. The point is not that environmental decisions are necessarily an end in themselves, but that strict compartmentalization of decisions denies to the business world the approaches that have been successfully applied in pri-vate life. What, for example, is one to make of the successful manager of a bank who was very nervous because his sister was applying for a job at the same bank. When asked to explain, he replied: "She might not like the person I am at the bank."

What we are suggesting is that the expertise that people acquire in caring for their families and participating in community affairs, although different from the skills usually used at work, is directly in line with the needs of modern firms. If, as Bird (1994) suggests, a career is the accumulation of knowledge that is based on work experiences, we add the notion that careers can also benefit from the accumulation of knowledge from the personal or private sphere of life.

In our study, we found employees who tried to bring private-sphere skills to their work. Although these efforts had demonstrable benefits for the business, they were often undermined by the traditional assumption of public/private-life separation. For example, Fletcher's (1994a) research study of female engineers found a way of working—relational practice—that was rooted in a model of effectiveness and achievement that relied on private-sphere skills. These engineers went out of their way to enable the achievement, of coworkers; to treat them with respect; and to take their preferences, feelings, and likely emotional responses into account when making decisions. Although these activities enhanced organizational learning and the effectiveness of decision making, Fletcher found that these behaviors were not noted as evidence of competence but, instead, were viewed as manifestations of personal attributes or inadequacies. Thus, although the workers were intending to innovate work practices by crossing the boundaries between the public and private spheres of life at the individual, internal level, this boundary-crossing behavior was rejected as inappropriate. Importantly, the motivation for engaging in this kind of behavior was suspect, and people who did it were assumed to be incompetent, or operating from a belief system that was inconsistent with business goals. This misinterpretation of the motivation underlying the behavior constrains the ability to innovate work practices by crossing the public/private boundary, and limits innovations to work practices that rely on standard skills, traditional measures of effectiveness, and narrow definitions of business needs.

In another case, we found that the assumption that work innovations—motivated by a desire to integrate the work and personal aspects of one's life—are not in the company's best interest can actually work *against* the realization of business goals. Two workers—one in sales and one in management—requested a job-sharing arrangement that would allow them to spend more time with their respective families. As our research associate Maureen Harvey notes, the extensive proposal they devised, outlining the specific ways in which business needs would be met under the new arrangement, had the added benefit of suggesting a way to revamp the sales-management training program. The proposal (as outlined) included an apprenticeship training model, whereby the sales representative took on limited management responsibilities under the tutelage of a sales manager. Such an apprenticeship could have improved the current organizational practice of "throwing" sales people into management with little training, which was generally accepted as detrimental to organizational goals. Despite this potential advantage, the proposal was rejected. Because the motivation for the proposal was viewed as stemming from a private-sphere concern (wanting to have more personal time), rather than a public-sphere concern (wanting to increase company effectiveness), it was narrowly interpreted as an employee-benefits request. The innovative apprenticeship approach to training and developing sales managers got lost in this narrow interpretation, and an opportunity for rethinking standard operating procedures, and capturing the synergy in crossing the work and family boundary, was missed.

The recent decision, by some large corporations, to set up virtual offices is yet another good illustration of how a firm boundary between work and family undermines the goal of mutuality and misses an opportunity for synergy. For many years, advocates of work-family integration have proposed work-at-home options as a solution to some of the dilemmas of integration. Despite evidence that those who work at home match or exceed on-site workers in productivity, these proposals are typically rejected by managers, who fear that this arrangement will undermine their accepted procedures of supervision and control (Bailyn, 1989; Perin, 1991). Even though the technology is available to make this a potential win-win situation, management has generally not seen this workplace change as an opportunity to reconsider accepted work practices, and therefore has failed to capture potential employee energy to rethink existing job arrangements. We suggest that underlying this reluctance is the belief that individual and organizational interests are irrevocably at odds on this issue, and that rearranging work to suit work-family integration would inevitably incur a cost in company effectiveness that must be tightly controlled. Ironically, the decision to introduce the virtual office now—as real estate prices and cost-cutting pressures give management energy to reconsider the issue of working from home—is unlikely to generate the kind of synergy we believe is possible. Front-line employees, operating under the same set of assumptions about the strict separation and assumed adversarial nature of public- and private- sphere interests, are unlikely to engage fully and wholeheartedly in restructuring the work and ironing out the kinks in innovations that are now perceived as springing solely from organizational constraints on resources.

The Organizational Benefits of Connection

To reap the benefits of connection requires a shift from a context of competing interests to one of mutuality. As Ring and Van de Ven (1994) note, bridging will work only when both sides have a high commitment to the relationship and an expectation of mutual benefit and reciprocity. In contrast to competitive interactions, mutuality implies a belief in the possibility of mutual benefits, an openness to change, and a level of trust and goodwill that is often absent from organizational efforts. Mutuality in the work-family arena can lead to two important characteristics absent from the examples above: truly innovative thinking, and heightened energy and motivation to make the changes work.

Opportunities for innovation are enhanced because a key element of mutuality is an openness to being influenced by the other side's perspective and needs (Jordan et al., 1992). In an organizational context, this translates into a willingness, on both sides, to push the boundary of standard operating procedures in order to enable each side to achieve its goals. Thus, mutuality goes beyond identifying shared goals or joint projects. Rather, it implies a partnership that is characterized by an openness and a willingness to expand standard solutions and traditional beliefs about the way to achieve one's own goals (Fletcher, 1994b). In contrast to the virtual-office scenario described above, it implies a recognition that this expansion is not a "giving up" in a zero-sum game, but an opportunity for creativity and innovation, where something that is beneficial in new ways, to both parties, might emerge. It is a way of dealing with the different needs and circumstances of an increasingly heterogeneous workforce that depends on learning from diversity, rather than merely managing or valuing it (Bailyn, 1993).

Again, data from our action research project illustrate one way in which connecting work and family needs can lead to revolutionary thinking about work-practice innovations. At one of the sites we studied, work-family negotiations had always centered on individual negotiations with managers to have them grant flextime arrangements. The precondition for these arrangements was that an employee had to show how business needs would be met by the options. The catch-22 was that business needs not only were nonnegotiable, but were so narrowly defined that the options for meeting them were severely constrained. With systems, structures, and general practices off the table, the only innovations open to individuals were those within the scope of their own jobs. Even more problematic, the system could only accommodate just so much individual "jiggling" before it would break down, so the number of flexible arrangements was strictly controlled, often dispensed on the basis of a very narrow definition of personal need. As a result, both sides of the work-family boundary suffered: Few individuals were granted the flexibility they needed to integrate their work and personal lives, and those whose requests were granted often experienced backlash from other team members; at the same time, the company's standard operating procedures and narrow definition of business needs remained unchallenged and rigidly in place.

On the basis of work with our research team, designed to reconnect work and family, the manager of the unit, on a trial basis, opened up the use of work-family policies and flexible options to all employees, regardless of family situation or intensity of need. This made wants equivalent to needs and avoided the backlash from selective flexibility. As a result of this initiative, nearly everyone worked out a different schedule, and the site experienced a reported 30% decrease in absenteeism as employees could plan for doctors' appointments and other scheduled absences. The workers reported greater customer satisfaction since the hours of customer-service coverage actually increased; and greater team morale since perceived managerial favoritism was reduced, and employees now had more control over both their work and their personal lives. And, because of this more inclusive environment, it was no longer possible to deal with employees' work-family issues on an individual basis, the work groups began to decide collectively how to structure and schedule work. This allowed these groups to move to self-managed teams; who not only managed their schedules but also began to have a say about work assignments and team-member selection and evaluation.

It is worth noting that the mutuality in this approach is qualitatively different from the atmosphere of entitlement that often characterizes employee/company interactions in the work-family arena. Human-resource representatives often note that no matter how many benefits exist, employees continually are pushing for more. By the same token, employees, particularly in this era of downsizing, often feel that no matter how much they give or how many sacrifices they make, companies want more. Thus, the individual/organizational boundary is one that is perceived as being crossed only through careful negotiation, where one side's own interest is carefully guarded against the insatiable appetite of the other side.

In contrast, when mutuality, rather than entitlement, is the context, not only are energy and enthusiasm for joint solutions generated, but determination and persistence in making those solutions work are unleashed. A good example of the difference was found at one of our study sites, where the researchers recommended establishing a cross-functional team comprised of sales, service, and business operations, to create more opportunities for work-family flexibility through coverage and collaboration. While, in a previous effort to enhance company effectiveness, such a cross-functional team had been tried but soon abandoned, in this case the team effort was a success. As one participant noted, "There is tremendous energy now to make this thing work. I mean, I really care about this because if it succeeds, then maybe I'll be able to live a normal life and see my kids once in a while. We are going to *make* this work!" And work it did. Members of the team have been meeting for many months, sharing information, making joint sales calls, covering for each other, and working collaboratively to service some key accounts. Sales are up; the service department has been better able to plan installations and coordinate preventive maintenance, which has reduced emergency calls; and the business-operations people have made better connections across functions—all of these are benefits of mutuality.

A final site from our study again shows the synergy possible by connecting employees' personal concerns to business needs. At this site—housing a product-development team—we found that the pressure to shorten time in getting products to markets created such a perpetual sense of crisis that not only the engineers' lives, but their ability to produce the product in good time, were undermined. Hours were long and unpredictable, creating personal issues for the engineers. And even though management was aware that this crisis was detrimental to their business goals, they were unable to change this mode of working. Our analysis of this situation led to a collective decision to restructure the use of time in such a way as to lessen the sense of crisis. Through detailed tracking of how engineers spend time at work, Perlow (1995) ascertained that in order to solve the crisis of the moment, engineers interrupt others on an as-needed basis. These constant interruptions make it difficult for them to get their own work done, and thus perpetuate the crisis mode of working. Further, she found that in such an environment, all interactions are perceived as interruptions, so the contribution to the work process that is made by certain critical interactions is not appropriately valued. Jointly with the members of the software team, she designed a way of separating the day into "quiet time" and "interactive time." This restructuring of daily activities gave the engineers time to work on their individual deliverables without interruptions, while, at the same time, helping them to appreciate the importance of interactions that coordinate and further the overall goals of the project. The results were positive for all: The product was launched in record time; managers changed in the direction of less surveillance; the engineers gained by having more control of their lives; and everyone became more aware of the role of constructive interactions in preventing a perpetual state of crisis. As one engineer reported: "It's not that I spend less time at work—but I can finish what I need to and don't have to take the worries home."

Conclusion

It seems clear that there are many benefits to be gained, both for companies and for individuals, when the last boundary—the one between work and family—is challenged. What perhaps is not as apparent, but may be more dangerous to ignore, is that *not* challenging this boundary has the potential to undermine the very efforts firms are undertaking to compete in the global economy. Indeed, the reason many companies give for maintaining the strict separation of work and family—by, for example, cutting back on traditional work/family benefits, demanding longer and longer hours, and downsizing—is that these changes are required in order to maintain a competitive edge. What is missing in this argument is the recognition of the costs of ignoring this last boundary.

To create the synergy that our study has shown to be possible, we believe boundaryless, reengineered forms of organization must incorporate a new vision of an ideal employee. This employee's value lies not in her or his ability and willingness to put work first, but in the ability to operate as an individual who reconnects work and family in ways that benefit both. Only by valuing equally the skills, values, and needs of the private sphere, and incorporating these as legitimate input into all efforts at reengineering and work-process redesign, can the synergy we have found be generally available. Because of the deep cultural divide between public and private life, such a transformation will not be easy. Indeed, the very notion of career is an *individual* concept, rooted in ideas of individual choice, fit, and trade-offs. The kind of approach we are advocating, however, is *systemic,* rooted in an appreciation of the interdependent nature of organizational and individual concerns, as well as of the interdependent nature of work and family. It is important, therefore, that discussions of the boundaryless career do not inadvertently reinforce the status quo by ignoring these critical boundaries. Just as the boundaryless form of organization challenges the tight link between an employee and the employer, so should the boundaryless career challenge the belief that work must come first, and that there is a clear separation between the person as worker and that person in the private domain.

There is also a societal reason for bridging the public/private boundary. The exclusive emphasis on the public realm of paid employment exacerbates the growing "crisis of care"—care of children, elders, communities—which has potentially grave social consequences. As Friedlander (1994) notes, the irony is that although there is a growing awareness that companies must be viewed as entities operating in larger societal and global systems, when it comes to work and family, the view of individuals remains narrowly focused and tightly bounded within the public sphere, with little recognition of the family, community, and societal systems within which all individuals operate. Further, as Rhona Rapoport (1995) has said, the segregation of personal and family life from work life, with work taking priority, is not the only way to organize the relationship between work and personal life. We need to be aware of its consequences and to consider alternatives to our multinational corporations' exporting of this pattern to other parts of the world.

For all these reasons it is imperative to challenge this last boundary and to reconnect work and family—for the sake of individual well-being, of families and communities, and of productive and effective workplaces.

Note

1. This four-year study, "Work-Family Partnership: A Catalyst for Change," was funded by the Ford Foundation through research grant 910–1036. The research team included Lotte Bailyn, Deborah Kolb, Susan Eaton, Joyce Fletcher, Maureen Harvey, Robin Johnson, and Leslie Perlow, with Rhona Rapoport as the consultant. See Bailyn et al. (1995) for a summary report of this project.

References

Arthur, M. B. 1994. The boundaryless career: A new perspective for organizational inquiry. *Journal of Organizational Behavior,* 15: 295–306.

Bailyn, L. 1993. *Breaking the Mold: Women, Men, and Time in the New Corporate World.* New York: Free Press.

Bailyn, L. 1989. Toward the perfect workplace? [A study of home-based systems developers in the United Kingdom] *Communications of the ACM,* 32: 460–471.

Bailyn, L.; D. Kolb; S. Eaton; J. Fletcher; M. Harvey; R. Johnson; and L. Perlow. 1995. *Summary report: Work-family partnership: A catalyst for change.* Ford Foundation Action Research Project. Cambridge, Mass.: MIT.

Barling, J. 1994. Work and family: In search of more effective workplace interventions. In C. L. Cooper and D. M. Rousseau (eds.), *Trends in Organizational Behavior.* Chichester, Eng.: Wiley.

Barnett, R. 1994. The good news is the bad news was wrong: Reexamining gender-bending roles in the 1990s. Paper presented at the Radcliffe College Alumnae Association and Harvard/Radcliffe Club of Philadelphia, October.

Bird, A. 1994. Careers as repositories of knowledge: A new perspective on boundaryless careers. *Journal of Organizational Behavior,* 15: 325–344.

Collinson, M., and D. Collinson. 1995. "Corporate liposuction" in the UK financial services. Paper presented at the Labor Process Conference, Blackpool, Eng., April.

Derr, C. B. 1986. *Managing the New Careerists.* San Francisco: Jossey-Bass.

Everett, M.; J. E. Mack; and R. Oresick. N. d. "Reinventing the corporate self: The inner agenda for business transformation." Unpublished manuscript. Cambridge, Mass. Center for Psychology and Social Change.

Fletcher, J. K. 1995. The work-family business imperative: Where's the beef? Symposium talk presented at Academy of Management Annual Meeting, Vancouver, B.C., August.

Fletcher, J. K. 1994a. *Toward a theory of relational practice in organizations: A feminist reconstruction of "real" work.* Ph.D. diss. Boston University.

Fletcher, J. K. 1994b. Castrating the female advantage: Feminist standpoint research and management science. *Journal of Management Inquiry* 3 (1): 74–82.

Friedlander, F. 1994. Toward whole systems and whole people. *Organization,* 1: 59–64.

Galinsky, E., and D. Friedman. 1993. *National Study of the Changing Workforce.* New York: Families and Work Institute.

Gordon, S. 1991. *Prisoners of Men's Dreams*. Boston: Little, Brown.

Hakim, C. 1994. *We Are All Self-Employed*. San Francisco: Berrett-Koehler.

Hammer, M., and J. Champy. 1993. *Reengineering the Corporation: A Manifesto for Business Revolution*. New York: Harper Business.

Handy, C. 1989. *The Age of Unreason*. Boston: Harvard Business School Press.

Harvey, M. 1994. Personal communication.

Hunt, J. 1994. The effects of work group culture on work/family stress. Ph.D. diss. Boston University.

Jacques, R. 1992. Re-presenting the knowledge worker: A poststructuralist analysis of the new employed professional. Ph.D, diss., University of Massachusetts.

Johnson, R. 1994. Where's the power in empowerment? Definition, difference and dilemmas of empowerment in the context of work-family management. Ph.D. diss., Harvard University.

Jordan, J.; A. Kaplan; J. B. Miller; I. Stiver; and J. Surrey. 1991. *Women's Growth in Connection*. New York: Guilford Press.

Kanter, R. M. 1989. Careers and the wealth of nations: A macro-perspective on the structure and implications of career forms. In M. B. Arthur; D. T. Hall; and B. S. Lawrence (eds.), *Handbook of Career Theory*. New York: Cambridge University Press.

Kriegsman, J. K., and Hardin, D. R. Does divorce hamper job performance? *The Personnel Administrator*, 19: 26–29.

Lipnack, J., and J. Stamps. 1993. *The TeamNet Factor: Bringing the Power of Boundary Crossing into the Heart of Your Business*. Essex Junction, Vt.: Oliver Wright Publications.

Mirvis, P., and D. T. Hall. 1994. Psychological success and the boundaryless career. *Journal of Organizational Behavior*, 15: 365–380.

Nonaka, I. 1994. A dynamic theory of organizational knowledge creation. *Organization Science*, 5: 14–37.

Perin, C. 1991. The moral fabric of the office: Panopticon discourse and schedule flexibilities. In P. S. Tolbert and S. R. Barley (eds.), *Organizations: Organizations and Professions*. Greenwich, Conn.: JAI Press.

Perlow, L. 1995. The time famine: An unintended consequence of the way time is used at work. Ph.D. diss., MIT.

Rapoport, R. 1995. Global forces and corporate responses. Symposium paper presented at the Work/Life Issues Conference, Northeastern University, Boston.

Ring, P. S., and A. Van de Ven. 1994. Developmental processes of cooperative interorganizational relationships. *Academy of Management Review*, 19: 90–118.

Rodgers, F. S., and C. Rodgers. 1989. Business and the facts of family life. *Harvard Business Review*. November/December: 121–129.

Rosenbaum, J. E. 1989. Organization career systems and employee misperceptions. In M. B. Arthur; D. T. Hall; and B. S. Lawrence (eds.), *Handbook of Career Theory*. New York: Cambridge University Press.

Senge, P. 1990. *The Fifth Discipline: The Art and Practice of the Learning Organization*. New York: Doubleday/Currency.

Slater, R. 1994. *Get Better or Get Beaten!* Burr Ridge, Ill.: Richard D. Irwin.

Walsch, S., and C. Cassell. 1995. *A Case of Covert Discrimination: Report of the Women in Management Study*. London: Book House Training Centre.

Wheatley, M. 1993. *Leadership and the New Science*. San Francisco: Berrett-Koehler.

16

Mentoring and the Boundaryless Career: Lessons from the Minority Experience

DAVID THOMAS AND MONICA HIGGINS

> The fundamental premise of the new model executive . . . is, simply, that the goals of the individual and the goals of the organization will work out to be one and the same. The young men have no cynicism about the "system," and very little skepticism . . . . They have an implicit faith that The Organization will be as interested in making use of their best qualities as they are themselves, and thus equanimity they can entrust the resolution of their destiny to the Organization . . . The average young man cherishes the idea that his relationship with The Organization is for keeps.
>
> William H. Whyte Jr.
> *The Organization Man* (1956)

> The social contract between employees and employers, in which companies promise to ensure employment and guide the career of loyal troops, is dead, dead, dead.
>
> Hall Lancaster (columnist), "Managing Your Career"
> *Wall Street Journal* (November 29, 1994)

Just as there was little debate in the late 1950s about Whyte's pronouncement, today there is widespread agreement with Lancaster's. A radical change has occurred: Employers no longer act out of a parental-like obligation to ensure the security of their employees. Just doing your job and being loyal no longer guarantees your career. Today, the new employment contract is more "adultlike" (Kissler, 1994). The focus is on finding a decent match between what the firm needs and what the individual needs, and this fit is sought by the individual, who is now in charge of his or her own career. Perhaps the most significant implication is that the firm can no longer be the anchor for one's professional sense of self and definition of psychological success. The individual now has the responsibility to develop what Hall (1986) calls a "metaskill"—cultivating adaptability by adopting new work roles and experiences and assimilating them into an integrated sense of identity.

But where are the "psychological shoals" for us (Mirvis and Hall, 1994) as we go through this dramatic transformation of work and identity? To whom will we turn for help in developing a strong internal anchor in our professional lives? Important insights and answers to this question lie in examining the career experiences of those whose perspectives were not represented in Whyte's study, and who, perhaps, have never been able to rely solely on predominantly mainstream corporations and institutions in the way he describes.

Minorities, especially those in management and the professions,[1] have seldom enjoyed the privilege of having "implicit faith" in the corporation's promises to recognize their abilities or to provide them with an affirming sense of professional identity (Dickens and Dickens, 1982; Davis and Watson, 1982; Ely, 1995). In addition to limitations and barriers posed by overt discrimination, they often are made to feel an acute tension, and an incongruence between their identities as racial minorities and women and their occupational roles. Some respond by trying desperately to rid themselves of patterns of dress, speech, behavior, or attitudes that bespeak an affinity for these group identities. The more isolated the individual, the more extreme and maladaptive the response is likely to be. (Bell, 1990; Ely, 1995). A more frequent and adaptive response has been to build social networks that extended beyond the boundaries of the workplace to form relations with others, in support of their personal and professional development (Thomas, 1990; Ibarra, 1995).

In this chapter, we propose that, like racial minorities and women, all other individuals working in the new boundaryless-career environment will need to look beyond the confines of their firms to those who can help them integrate an internal, or subjective, sense of themselves and their profession with an ever-changing external career reality. Multiple developmental relationships, including extrafirm relations, will be necessary to provide the kinds of psychosocial and instrumental career support that will enable individuals in today's environment to develop a strong professional identity and, hence, navigate their own careers. As a result, the balance of internal and external developmental relationships of majority workers will resemble that of minority workers in years gone by.

Drawing from a network of developmental relationships to advance one's career is not a new concept. Kram, in her seminal work on mentoring at work wrote that "relationship constellations . . . enable individuals to maintain high performance levels as well as a continued sense of well-being" (1985: 158). What is new is the notion that a primary focus of career development will be on help providers who reside outside one's place of work. Indeed, only one of Kram's eight tentacles of her "relationship constellation" is labeled as being "outside work," and this she defines narrowly as "outside work friends." Rather, we suggest that social networks that extend beyond firm boundaries, into multiple arenas such as professional associations, community groups, and one's former educational institutions, will all constitute critical sources of help in this new work environment. Hence, we adopt an even broader view of developmental relationships, by extending the definition to incorporate those ties that reside outside the boundaries of the organization and include, but are not limited to, friendship circles.

What we are suggesting, then, is that individuals in today's boundaryless-career environment need to adopt a *cosmopolitan* orientation toward work, where cosmopolitan is defined as a more outward, or externally oriented, perspective (Gouldner, 1957). This should help them to relinquish the old employment contract—in which working hard in one firm was rewarded financially and with job security—in favor of a new contract, which is marked by increased risk and interfirm mobility, but also by increased flexibility in the creation of one's career.

The Minority Experience

Minorities have not opted for boundaryless careers, and yet the portfolio of developmental relationships they have tended to develop mirrors what we predict will be true for all individuals pursuing boundaryless careers in the future. In 1990, Thomas's research demonstrated that African-Americans tend to have broader support networks than whites. He found that African-Americans had more extradepartmental and extrafirm relationships, and more relationships with other blacks and with white females. Minorities—in this case blacks—formed mentoring relationships with other blacks that went beyond the boundaries of the primary work unit, while also maintaining developmental relationships with whites inside their departments. Ibarra (1995) also found that high-potential racial minorities were more likely than their white high-potential counterparts, and non-high-potential minorities, to have relationships outside their primary work units.[2] Her work suggests a positive relationship between the development of external ties and enhanced opportunity structures for minorities. Using both internal and external ties to enhance one's career is an important lesson that can be learned from the minority experience, and one which we will explore in depth in this chapter.

Denton (1990), looking specifically at African-American women's networks, found that many of the contacts they relied on for emotional support were with black women outside their companies. They valued this external support for its contributions to both their work and nonwork lives. Bell (1990), looking at the same group of women, noted the bifurcation of many of their lives into two distinct nonoverlapping worlds, one black and the other white; the stress associated with this bore an inverse relationship to the degree of nonoverlapping social networks in these two worlds. Thomas (1989) detailed the difficulties experienced by African American women, which inhibit their ability to form close and supportive work relationships with white male superiors. Relationships between these women and white men were socially distant because of their lack of identification with one another, and because of the issues of public scrutiny and peer resentment encountered when the relationships did form.

Recent work by Ibarra (1992, 1993a) suggests that white women may also adopt more functionally differentiated networks of relationships than their white male counterparts. Women face the problem of a lack of same-gender identity-group ties in the upper echelons of companies. Their token status (Kanter, 1977) in many corporations leads female managers to develop cross-gender developmental relationships with senior-level white males, so that they may gain the career support and the legitimacy they need to advance professionally (Ibarra, 1993a; Burt, 1992). Like racial minorities, women also tend to seek help elsewhere; they develop broad social networks comprised of multiple developmental relationships.

Identity-Group Relations and Network Composition

To understand what drives this pattern of findings, we need an interpretative focus that helps us to understand the relationship between social identity, including one's race and gender, and the professional role one assumes in the firm. Intergroup theory posits that individuals working in firms belong to two types of groups: identity groups, which share characteristics such as race, ethnicity, age, and gender; and firm-defined work-groups, which share participation in some function, hierarchy, or task in the firm (Alderfer, 1987). Identity-group members adopt similar worldviews, while work-group members adopt similar organization views. According to this theory, both individuals and firms are constantly managing the tensions and potential conflicts between these two types of group membership (Thomas and Alderfer, 1989).

How identity and work groups are embedded in the firm is a major determinant of how individuals experience and respond to these tensions (Alderfer and Smith, 1982). When there is a high degree of correlation between identity- and work-group memberships, and when this mirrors power relations and social stratification at more macro levels, such as society or the community, a state of congruent embeddedness exists. Such is the case when, for example, racial minorities predominate in low-status, low-skilled positions, with only token representation in managerial or executive jobs. In these instances, corporate norms, values, and practices are likely to affirm the cultural tastes of whites and to treat whiteness as normative and being a nonwhite as a deficit. Under these conditions, racist stereotypes and assumptions are also more likely to go unexamined and to influence careers. (Thomas and Alderfer, 1989).

It is under these conditions of embeddedness that women and racial minorities have sought to obtain the career and psychosocial support necessary for their career development. Career support refers to the coaching, feedback, exposure, and challenging assignments that help to advance one's career (Kram, 1985). Psychosocial support refers to those things which facilitate the development of professional identity; promote a sense of self-efficacy; and engender positive attachments to one's work group, profession, and/or firm (Kram, 1985). These include role modeling, counseling, and affirmation. An important and documented source of developmental support lies in relationships with mentors and sponsors inside the organization (Thomas and Kram, 1988). Mentors typically provide both types of support, while sponsors provide only career support.

Also, Kram and Isabella (1985) illustrate the critical and often overlooked developmental roles that peers play as sources of information, career advice, and emotional support.

In a survey of over 300 developmental relationships in one congruently embedded firm context, Thomas (1990) found that cross-race and cross-gender developmental relationships provide less psychosocial support than do same-race and same-gender relationships. Thomas (1986) also found that minorities receive less psychosocial support from their work-group peers than do whites in the same company. A lack of psychosocial support from within the firm is posited to be what leads blacks to look outside traditional organizational boundaries for same-identity-group mentors (Thomas and Alderfer, 1989). And, since fewer blacks tend to be in upper-level positions of power and control in corporations, blacks may find it necessary to adopt a portfolio of developmental relationships that consists of intrafirm ties that provide career support, and extrafirm ties that provide psychosocial support. This broad constellation of developmental relationships enables blacks to gain the benefits of both types of support and, hence, cope with the bicultural stress (Bell, 1990) that results from the clash between the views of their identity and work groups.

Having networks of developmental relationships that provide both psychosocial and career support enables individuals to handle the tensions they may feel from a lack of overlap or congruence between the dominant sociocultural views and values of their identity groups and their firms. These relationships thus enable individuals to gain a positive sense of their professional identity—an integrated sense of themselves and their professional role at work. Over time, these developmental relationships can help individuals develop "career anchors," or a sense of what they value, believe, and are good at (Schein, 1993). And, in arriving at this total career self-concept, individuals will find ways to reconcile their subjective views of work, and the role work plays in their lives (the internal career aspects), with the actual job sequences, institutional constraints, and other realities they face (the external career aspects) (Derr and Laurent, 1989).

Minorities look beyond firm boundaries for help in developing their professional identities, because the people inside their workplace often cannot provide the internal sense of a career that is so crucial to building a total career self-concept. At the most elemental levels, and early in their careers, incentives to do this relate to a lack of role models. More fundamentally, however, they are driven by the lack of a supportive relationship between their identity-group membership and the cultural assumptions that often undergird their work roles, and by the constraining nature of the context in which minorities work.

Specifically, a study by Ibarra (1993a) suggests that the structural nature of the employment context in which people work can have direct and different effects on the network composition of minorities (both women and racial minorities), compared to that of their white male counterparts. Indeed, minorities tend to have a very different "opportunity context" for the development of professional relationships, due to the differences minority and majority individuals experience in the availability of same identity group contacts in their firms. The higher proportion of women and recial minorities located in lower-power and lower-status positions tends to render minorities' same-group ties less instrumental. Further, the cross-sex, cross-race nature of minorities' contacts with members of the firm's dominant coalitions renders minorities' instrumental resources less strong.

As a result, if minorities were to restrict themselves to intrafirm developmental relationships, then their personal networks would be composed of fewer strong instrumental ties, and fewer dual-purpose ties that could provide both the career and psychosocial support needed to develop a strong professional identity. In response to this constraining opportunity context, minorities have sought relationships outside the traditional boundaries of work and, as a result, have developed broader constellations of developmental relationships than their majority counterparts. Therefore, while there may indeed be no gender and race differences found in the frequency of mentoring (Dreher and Ash, 1990; Ragins & McFarlin, 1990), the composition of networks of developmental relationships of minorities has looked different from that of majority workers.

Similar Melody, Different Keys

We predict that the developmental networks of all workers will increasingly reflect the tendencies we have observed in the social networks of racial minorities and women. This trend results from the fact that minority and majority workers are playing a similar melody but in different keys. What exactly is this similar melody? It is the psychological instability that emanates from a work context that does not affirm salient and important aspects of one's personal identity, or provide sufficient information and guidance to sustain one's career growth and development.

In a boundaryless career environment, majorities will also experience a more acute tension between their personal identities, work roles, and firms, but for different reasons than minorities have experienced this tension in the past. Specifically, majorities will find that the flux in firm membership in this new boundaryless career environment will drive them to look outside their immediate workplace for the assistance necessary to advance in their careers and to create a stable and integrated sense of professional identity. As we noted, minorities have sought assistance from those outside their work environments due to a clash between minority identity and firm and work-group cultural assumptions. These differences reflect the different keys to the similar melody minorities and majorities will play while advancing their individual careers in the new work environment.

In the past, majority individuals have generally enjoyed a fine match between their identity and firm-based work groups. Today, however, majority employees must "say good-bye to the world that [gave] them their identity and their feelings of competence" (Bridges, 1994: 196). Why?—because work roles and firm membership are constantly changing, and, as a result, the groups' views are in constant flux. Furthermore, the workplace is becoming increasingly diverse, and with greater interfirm career mobility, majority individuals will be less open to compromising important parts of their personal identities for the organization. Consequently, a nice, neat match between the worldviews of the majority's identity group and the firm views of the majority's work role is virtually impossible.

The result? It is no longer clear how one's internal sense of a career will match up with aspects of one's external career, since the latter will always be on the move. As Mirvis and Hall explain, in order "to find meaning in this mix, people will have to 'make sense' of their constantly changing work agenda and integrate varied experiences into a coherent self-picture" (1994: 366–367). Without strong internal career anchors, individuals will not be able to integrate their sense of self with their professional experiences, leading to an underdeveloped professional identity.

The Lessons: Changes in Sociological and Psychological Realities

What does this changing nature of career development and the new look for constellations of developmental relationships imply for individuals and how they think about their careers? We believe that four important lessons can be drawn from the examination of minority career experiences, and of the similar strain that majority workers will experience as they try to develop a strong professional identity in the new boundaryless career environment.

First, individuals will need to spend more time and energy anchoring themselves internally in both their work and nonwork lives. This involves integrating one's diverse set of experiences into a more expanded and grounded sense of one's self. As Mirvis and Hall (1994) note, individuals' core identities will be enlarged by their commitment to their "life's work," to a "place with a heart."

Second, individuals will need to keep a constant eye on the external progress of their careers. "Security" in the boundaryless work environment resides in the person, rather than in the position (Bridges, 1994) or institution. This external, market-oriented approach may seem a bit unnerving at first, but as many have pointed out, it also opens up new options for work and identity (Mirvis and Hall, 1994). Moving beyond the firm where one works and thinking more broadly, to recognize the boundarylessness of careers and the many relationships that will come from outside the organization, will enable individuals to attain "psychological success."

Third, the structure of relationship networks and, in particular, of developmental relationships, will change in this new boundaryless career environment. We may refer to an individual's network, or constellation, of developmental relationships as a portfolio of relationships that individuals "carry" around with them and draw on for advice and support as they make choices in their careers. In the past, the portfolio of developmental relationships for majorities was characterized by strong intrafirm ties, from which individuals derived both career and psychosocial support. In the boundaryless-career environment, the portfolio will shift such that it is comprised of both intrafirm and extrafirm ties, with extrafirm ties providing both career and psychosocial support. In short, individuals will have broader, although not necessarily less strong, portfolios of developmental relationships.

Fourth, this new portfolio balance for majority employees will resemble that for minority employees. However, this is not to say that the various factors precipitating the change for majority individuals will not affect minority individuals as well. On the contrary, since minorities still will not find their identity group's views properly represented in the organization, and since they, too, will face the problem of changing organization-group membership, minorities will have an even greater need for extraorganizational ties to help them develop strong career anchors. As a result, matching one's internal career ties with one's external career ties will be even more difficult for minorities in the future, making it all the more important for minority individuals to find strong developmental relationships.

The Relational Context of the Boundaryless Career

We have argued that minorities have tended to develop broad constellations of developmental relationships, and that majority employees will follow this same pattern in the future.

But why are the above mentioned changes occurring? Is it simply that individuals and their mentors are shifting in and out of firms, and that this is driving people to develop broader and more differentiated support networks? We think not. The external realities of work and life have shifted dramatically, such that multiple factors are driving the changes in how individuals view their own career development and developmental relationships and also, in the types of assistance they seek (Kotter, 1995). These changes may be identified at the individual, interpersonal, organizational, and societal levels.

At the individual level, people will no longer aim to get ahead or move up in only one organization. Rather, careers will develop cyclically and involve lateral and interfirm career moves. Individuals will spend less time trying to maintain their positions, and will spend more time cycling repeatedly through the career stages of exploration, establishment-maintenance, and disengagement (Mirvis and Hall, 1994). Career cycling offers individuals more opportunities to develop a variety of supportive relationships. For this reason alone, we may expect to find more differentiated support networks for employees in the future.

On the other hand, such constant shifting can be quite draining for majority and minority workers alike. The increase in responsibility for one's own career, coupled with the need for two incomes to support a family nowadays, can lead to stress and role overload. With increased entrepreneurial activity occuring as individuals manage their own careers, the line between work and family life will become increasingly blurred. And, unfortunately, recent research suggests that there is much that still needs to be accomplished in restructuring and rethinking the way work gets done, so that we will be able to close the gap between the needs of organizations and the personal and family needs of employees (Bailyn, 1993).

To sort through the demands and joys of work and family life, psychosocial support such as encouragement, caring, and friendship from multiple mentoring relationships may be helpful. Moreover, given this new and more elastic view of careers, in which work and nonwork roles overlap, individuals may find that this type of support is most useful when it comes from people who understand their multiple roles and, hence, don't necessarily work in the same company. At the individual level, then, workers in the new boundaryless work environment will strive to find people who can help them integrate the many facets of their varied work and nonwork lives into a coherent and whole self. Bridges (1994) termed this sense of wholeness "integrity," which, together with identity, can create a solid sense of self.

At the interpersonal level, we have already mentioned the fact that mentors and sponsors will be experiencing cyclicality in their own careers as well as increased interorganizational mobility. This movement will lead, in a very direct fashion, to broader constellations of relationships, including extrafirm relationships, for protégés. We may also expect this increase in mobility to drive individuals to create and maintain, in an indirect fashion, broader support networks. One way to understand this is to begin by considering one's career as the information and knowledge that is created as a result of a person's work experiences (Bird, 1994). As Bird explains, knowledge may be passed from person to person within or outside a workplace, either tacitly or explicitly. In the boundaryless career environment in which people are constantly joining and leaving firms, tacit knowledge that exists within the firm must be made explicit on an ongoing basis. Therefore, articulation (moving from tacit to explicit knowledge creation) will be critical in a boundaryless work environment.

Articulation hinges on interaction at the interpersonal level. Bird (1994: 338). predicts that this emphasis on articulation or making tacit information explicit, will mean that "interaction will be more loosely structured and less likely to be situated within the organization. Instead, it may occur within a person's own network of acquaintances, or it may occur through professional gatherings and conferences." Therefore, we may expect that individuals will seek out and maintain extrafirm developmental relationships in order to acquire information and knowledge that will help them develop their own careers. Indeed, professional associations, such as the Boston Women in Communications Association and the National Association of Black Engineers, have recently begun mentoring programs within their groups to make explicit the tacit knowledge their members have gained through their many work experiences. As such, these mentoring relationships are extra-firm and yet they provide a rich source of career support for individuals managing their own careers.

At the organizational level, dramatic change in the structure of firms in recent years continues to impact individuals' career development. Downsizing or resizing has become epidemic, with large corporations cutting positions at all different levels. In the first half of 1994 alone, over 300,000 workers were laid off. As one commentator put it, "Welcome to the company that isn't there" (*Business Week,* October 14, 1994: 86–87). By taking on temporary or part-time workers, firms are making their boundaries more permeable. According to a recent business report, over a quarter of those employed today work on some sort of contract basis (*Business Week,* October 14, 1994: 85). All of these changes have had a dramatic impact on how people think about their careers and their career development.

This part-time status, the changing job responsibilities and tasks, and the uncertainty associated with ongoing restructuring, all lead to a very fuzzy definition of one's external career. How can an individual match a sequence of job experiences with any traditional kind of job profile or any coherent professional identity? Extrafirm mentors who see their protégés in a variety of work and nonwork settings can help individuals stay grounded in their core values and their beliefs about who they are and how their identity fits into their many roles as professionals. Such mentors can provide psychosocial support in times of transition (and there will be many of those), and they can provide career advice so that the transitions employees do make are aligned with their sense of professional identity.

At the societal level, we are witnessing a shift to a much more cosmopolitan orientation toward both work and life. Entire communities are relinquishing their local views of enterprise in favor of a more global, or market-oriented, perspective. This is reflected in the way communities of individuals develop resources, form alliances, and draw on institutions that extend beyond geographical and industry boundaries (Kanter, 1994).

This shift at the societal level has implications for the structuring of careers. Using her macroperspective on careers, Kanter (1989) defined three primary career forms: (1) bureaucratic, defined by the logic of advancement, and for which the key resource is one's hierarchical position; (2) professional, defined by one's craft or skill, and for which the key resources are knowledge and reputation; and (3) entrepreneurial, defined by its key resource—the capacity to create valued outputs. Kanter argues that the recent proliferation of downsizing and flattening of corporations has led to a decline in the bureaucratic career form and to an increase in professional and entrepreneurial career forms.

Individuals with professional careers tend to have weak loyalty to any one employer. Their motto could be, "Have reputation, will travel" (Kanter 1989). Entrepreneurial career actors don't aim to move up in one firm but, rather, to expand the territory below them and, in some shape or form, to create their own ventures. For either of these two types of career forms, work identities will not be defined by an attachment to any one employer. Rather, they may be defined by the professional associations or entrepreneurial groups that people belong to. Consequently, in this new world of work, we may expect individuals to have networks of relationships that are not moored in any one organization. Such relationship constellations will enable individuals to develop professional identities apart from that of their place of work, and to develop a cosmopolitan orientation toward their work and career development.

For minorities, the breadth of their developmental networks has stemmed from efforts to cope with the realities and limitations imposed by their relationships to the groups and organizations in which they work. For majorities, a similar clash will exist, but it will be due to a constant change in organization membership, not to a change in identity-group views, or to the way these ideas are reinforced by society.

Conclusion

Everyone managing a career in a boundaryless career environment will need to seek extrafirm ties. For majorities and minorities alike, looking outside for help will become a necessary and important part of developing a solid professional identity. Extraorganizational ties constitute only one aspect, then, of the cosmopolitan orientation that we will all need to adopt in this new work environment.

It is important to state, however, that by pointing to similarities in the patterns of developmental experiences for minority and majority groups, we in no way mean that there has been any substantial leveling of the playing field for minority and majority employees. Indeed, ample evidence suggests that there are still very real barriers to minority mobility, marked by limited access to resources and professional opportunities in companies; whites still maintain the dominant positions of decision-making authority and power in most corporations. Moreover, the stereotypes and cognitive mind-sets established in years gone by continue to be reinforced in today's work settings and society, making race and gender very important, even unique, contributors to the career-development experiences of minorities. Therefore, we may expect to witness similar patterns in developmental experiences for minorities and majorities, but these similar patterns will be driven by combinations of different factors.

Of course, there are costs associated with managing one's career and a broader network of developmental relationships. Creating and maintaining such a network takes time and energy—which may take away from one's work and/or nonwork life. Indeed, Ibarra's (1993b) research found that women who developed more functionally differentiated networks had weaker links to those people who had access to centralized and important resources. It could be, then, that maintaining a broader network may necessitate giving up some benefits that come with strong ties, such as trust. Still, research has not substantiated whether network breadth and intimacy are negatively correlated (Ibarra, 1993b).

In order to sidestep these pitfalls, individuals will need a supportive organizational context in which to forge extrafirm relationships. Employers will need to encourage the development of human and social capital in their employees. Understandably, some firms as well as individuals will find this new employee-employer relationship uncomfortable. Employees may suspect that certain corporate initiatives, such as training programs or conferences, are being used as weeding-out vehicles. Moreover, employers may feel that by providing such opportunities, they run the risk of eventually losing some of their best workers.

While these concerns may be very real, they fail to consider the alternative: Not encouraging a cosmopolitan outlook for employees who are bound to cross firm boundaries, sooner rather than later, can backfire. The risk is that these folks may get "crushed," or feel isolated, in their work; they may never develop commitments; they may constantly underachieve on the job; and they may fail to develop a professional identity.

On the positive side, expecting and encouraging employees to have multiple and extrafirm relationships can benefit the company. By getting employees connected externally to professional associations, for example, the knowledge they pick up, as well as the valuable ties they develop, can help the firm gain the information and the access to resources that will help it stay competitive in the marketplace. In short, by developing a cosmopolitan orientation in one's employees and their relationships, firms can themselves develop a more cosmopolitan, and less myopic, outlook.

Notes

1. In this chapter, we use the term *minority* to refer to both racial minorities and women. While we recognize that there are some unique and different challenges facing these two groups, there are also important similarities. One such similarity is the tendency to develop extrafirm developmental relationships—the focus of this chapter.

2. The term *high-potential* refers to individuals who are viewed, by their firm's top management, as candidates for high-level executive positions.

References

Alderfer, C. P. 1987. An intergroup perspective on group dynamics. In J. Lorsch (ed.), *Handbook of Organizational Behavior:* 190–222. Englewood Cliffs, N.J.: Prentice Hall.

Alderfer, C. P., and K. K. Smith. 1982. Studying intergroup relations embedded in organizations. *Administrative Science Quarterly,* 27: 35–65.

Bailyn, L. 1989. Understanding individual experience at work: Comments on the theory and practice of careers. In M. B. Arthur; D. T. Hall; and B. S. Lawrence (eds.), *Handbook of Career Theory:* 477–489. New York: Cambridge University Press.

Bailyn, L. 1993. *Breaking the Mold: Women, Men, and Time in the New Corporate World.* New York: Free Press.

Bell, E. L. 1986. *The Power Within: Bicultural Life Structures and Stress among Black Women.* Ph.D. diss., Case Western Reserve University.

Bell, E. L. 1990. *The bicultural life experience of career-oriented black women. Journal of Organizational Behavior,* 11: 6.

Bird, A. 1994. Careers as repositories of knowledge: A new perspective on boundaryless careers. *Journal of Organizational Behavior,* 15: 325–344.

Bridges, W. 1994. *JobShift: How to Prosper in a Workplace without Jobs.* Reading, Mass.: Addison-Wesley.

Burt, R. 1992. *Structural Holes.* Cambridge: Harvard University Press.

Business Week. 1994. The new world of work: Beyond the buzzwords is a radical redefinition of labor. October 14: 76–87.

Davis, G., and Watson, G. 1982. *Black Life in Corporate America.* New York: Doubleday.

Denton, T. C. 1990. Bounding supporting relationships among black professional women. *Journal of Organizational Behavior,* 11: 6.

Derr, C. B., and Laurent, A. 1989. The internal and external career: A theoretical and cross-cultural perspective. In M. B. Arthur; D. T. Hall; and B. S. Lawrence (eds.), *Handbook of Career Theory:* 454–471. New York: Cambridge University Press.

DeFillippi, R. J., and Arthur, M. B. 1994. The boundaryless career: A competency-based perspective. *Journal of Organizational Behavior,* 15: 307–324.

Dickens, F., and Dickens, J. B. 1992. *The Black Manager.* New York: AMACOM.

Dumaine, B. 1996. Why do we work? *Fortune,* December 26: 196–204.

Dreher, G. F., and Ash, R. A. 1990. A comparative study of mentoring among men and women in managerial, professional, and technical positions. *Journal of Applied Psychology,* 75: 539–546.

Eden, D., and Aviram, A. 1993. Self-efficacy training to speed reemployment: Helping people to help themselves. *Journal of Applied Psychology,* 78 (3): 352–360.

Ely, R. 1995. Organizational demographics and the dynamics of relationships among professional women. *Administrative Science Quarterly,* 39: 203–238.

Ely, R. 1995. The power in demography: Women's social construction of gender identity at work. *Academy of Management Journal,* 38 (3): 589–634.

Gouldmer, A. W. 1957. Cosmopolitans and locals: Toward an analysis of latent social roles. *Administrative Science Quarterly,* (December) 281–306 and 440–480 (March).

Hall, D. T. 1986. Breaking career routines: Midcareer and identity development. In D. T. Hall et al. (eds.), *Career Development in Organizations:* 120–159. San Francisco: Jossey-Bass.

Hill, L., and Kamprath, N. 1991. Beyond the myth of the perfect mentor: Building a network of developmental relationships. Boston: HBS Publishing, Teaching Note, 9–491–096.

Ibarra, H. 1992. Homophily and differential returns: Sex differences in network structure and access in an advertising firm. *Administrative Science Quarterly,* 37: 422–447.

Ibarra, H. 1993a. Personal networks of women and minorities in management: A conceptual framework. *Academy of Management Review,* 18 (1): 56–87.

Ibarra, H. 1993b. Untangling the web of interconnections: Pragmatics of gender differences in managerial networks. Working paper, Division of Research, Harvard Business School.

Ibarra, H. 1995. Race, opportunity, and diversity of social circles in managerial networks. *Academy of Management Journal,* 38 (3): 673–703.

Kanter, R. M. 1977. *Men and Women of the Corporation.* New York: Basic Books.

Kanter, R. M. 1989. Careers and the wealth of nations: A macro-perspective on the structure and implications of career forms. In M. B. Arthur; D. T. Hall; and B. S. Lawrence (eds.), *Handbook of Career Theory:* 506–521. New York: Cambridge University Press.

Kanter, R. M. 1994. What thinking globally really means: Organizational change and the rise of "collaborative advantage." Speech delivered to Academy of Management, August 16, Dallas.

Kissler, G. D. 1994. The new employment contract. *Human Resource Management,* 33 (Fall) 335–352.

Kotter, J. P. 1995. *The New Rules: How to Succeed in Today's Postcorporate World.* New York: Free Press.

Kram, K. E. 1985. *Mentoring at Work: Developmental Relationships in Organizational Life.* Glenview, Ill.: Scott, Foresman.

Kram, K. E., and M. Isabella. 1985. Mentoring alternatives: The role of peer relationships in career development. *Academy of Management Journal,* 28: 110–132.

Labich, K. 1993. The new unemployed. *Fortune,* March 8: 40–57.

Lancaster, H. 1994. Managing your career: A new social contract to benefit employer and employee. *Wall Street Journal,* November 29: B1.

McCauley, C. D., and Young, D. P. 1993. Creating developmental relationships: Roles and strategies. *Human Resource Management Review,* 3 (3): 219–230.

Mirvis, P. H., and Hall, D. T. 1994. Psychological success and the boundaryless career. *Journal of Organizational Behavior,* 15: 365–380.

Ragins, B. R., and McFarlin, D. B. 1990. Perceptions of mentor roles in cross-gender mentoring relationships. *Journal of Vocational Behavior,* 37: 321–339.

Schein, E. H. 1993. *Career Anchors: Rediscovering Your Real Values.* Amsterdam: Pfeiffer.

Senge, P. M. 1990. *The Fifth Discipline: The Art and Practice of the Learning Organization.* New York: Doubleday.

Thomas, D. A. 1986. *An intraorganizational analysis of black and white patterns of sponsorship and the dynamics of cross-racial mentoring.* Ph.D. diss., Yale University.

Thomas, D. A. 1990. The impact of race on managers' experiences of developmental relationships. *Journal of Organizational Behavior,* 11: 479–492.

Thomas, D. A. 1993. Racial dynamics in cross-race developmental relationships. *Administrative Science Quarterly,* 38: 169–194.

Thomas, D., and Alderfer, C. 1989. The influence of race on career dynamics theory and research on minority career experiences. In M. B. Arthur; D. T. Hall; and B. S. Lawrence (eds.), *Handbook of Career Theory:* 133–158. New York: Cambridge University Press.

Thomas, D. A., and Kram, K. 1988. Promoting career enhancing relationships: The role of the human resource professional. In M. London and E. More (eds.), *Employee Career Development and the Human Resource Professional:* 49–66. Westport, Conn.: Greenwood.

Zellner, W. 1995. The rules of the game in the new world of work. *Business Week,* October 17: 98–100.

17

Feminization at Work: Career Implications

NANETTE FONDAS

Recently arguments have appeared in both business publications and academic journals that suggest a "feminization" is occurring in the workplace (Fondas, 1993; Jenson, Hagen, and Reddy, 1988; Lee, 1994; Lenz and Myerhoff, 1985; Lunneborg, 1990; Reskin and Roos, 1990; Smith and Smits, 1994). *Feminization* is used generally to refer to the rising rate of female participation in the paid labor force and its effect on occupational sex composition (Jensen, Hagen, and Reddy, 1988; Johnston and Packer, 1987) and to women's entry into customarily male fields, such as law, business, and medicine (Cohn, 1985; Reskin and Roos, 1990). "Feminization" is also used to refer the spread of characteristics culturally ascribed to females and thus held to be feminine in society. Ann Douglas (1977) introduced this usage in *The Feminization of American Culture*, when she documented the spread of domesticity throughout the mass culture of Victorian America. Drawing on Douglas's definition, in *The Feminist Case against Bureaucracy*, Ferguson (1984) used feminization to refer to the spread of traditionally feminine traits—such as supportiveness and attention to others—to bureaucratically defined subordinates. Similarly, Calas and Smircich (1993) adopted this definition in their description of the continued subordination of women in global workforce. Fondas (1993) followed in this tradition by describing "feminized" managers whose careers are now characterized by temporary, subcontracted, part-time, ad hoc, and insecure employment arrangements. These concepts are used in this chapter to describe feminization and its implications for organizing and managing within the context of boundaryless careers.

Women Cross the Boundary from Unpaid to Paid Work

Women have always "worked" (Kessler-Harris, 1981); but their entry into the paid labor force, outside the home, occurred later than it did for men, and it is continuing today. Indeed, women are the only demographic group whose paid labor outside the home increased continually during this century. At some time, older men, teenagers, and even middle-aged men decreased their employment rates (Goldin, 1990: 10). In 1900, only 19% of women were in the labor force, but by 1950, 34% were working. Since then, women's participation in the labor force has risen steadily, hitting 58% in 1990, and it is expected to rise to 61% by 2000 (Shribman, 1992). Labor statistics show that 73% of women between the ages of 25 and 54 were working in 1988, and that by 2000, 81% of that group will work (Marsh, 1991). As females continue entering the labor market, both their labor-force participation rate and their percentage of the workforce are rising. In 1970, women workers numbered 32 million, constituting 38% of the workforce; by 1990, they numbered 57 million, constituting 45% of the workforce (U.S. Department of Labor, 1995). By 2005, women workers are projected to number 72 million, or 47% of the work force (U.S. Department of Labor, 1995).

Not only have women entered the labor force in large numbers, but also they have made inroads into what traditionally were male-dominated occupations and professions, particularly those requiring advanced education. For example, while women constituted only 3% of the lawyers in 1960, they constituted 7% by 1975 and more than 20% by 1988. Women architects represented 4% of the profession in 1975, but by 1988 they represented 15%. Similarly, women were 10% of the physicians in 1975, but by 1988 they constituted 20% (AFL-CIO, 1992). These percentages are likely to increase further, as the number of women graduating from professional schools rises (Johnston and Packer, 1987).

Management is one occupation where women have made substantial inroads. Their 43% share of all managerial jobs (U.S. Department of Labor, 1995) is approaching their 46% share of the workforce. This represents a gain of 147% over their 17% share of managerial jobs in 1970. Although women hold only 25% of the managerial jobs in the 200 largest companies (Sharpe, 1994), their control of smaller companies has escalated: 30% of all sole proprietorships are owned by women (Marsh, 1991). Jacobs (1992: 282) called this entry by women into management "the most dramatic shift in the sex composition of an occupation since clerical work became a female-dominated field in the late 19th century."[1]

Statistical analyses of women's entry into previously male-dominated fields present a picture of occupations that are moving toward parity with females' representation in the labor force as a whole. An unresolved question, however, is whether an occupation becomes feminized when its status and wages have begun to decline—prompting male flight and further female entry, and, consequently, resegregation of the occupation, which further erodes its status and pay (Reskin and Roos, 1990). Occupational groups in which this has occurred include teachers, typesetters, bank tellers, book editors, pharmacists, bartenders, telephone operators, insurance adjusters, and real estate agents (Cohn, 1985; Davies, 1982; Reskin and Roos, 1990; Strober, 1984). By contrast, a study of computer programmers by Wright and Jacobs (1995) found that men did not leave computer work as women entered this field, and earnings were not in decline prior to, or subsequent to, women's entry. Nor did occupational segregation follow women's entry into medicine, law, or management (Jacobs, 1989, 1992).

These findings highlight the characteristics of the fields in which feminization apparently produces no adverse effects. Computer programming, in particular, is characterized by circumstances that, Reskin and Roos (1990) argue, are important to fostering occupational integration: It is a job that is growing in an entrepreneurial field; it has not been historically sex-typed; and it demands specialized skills requiring education and training. This confluence of job and labor market features may currently be relatively uncommon (Stone, 1995: 422), but such features become increasingly prevalent as the boundaries in and around organizations and jobs are removed. So, for example, as the hierarchically bounded middle-management job is replaced by the boundaryless project-management job, parity between females and males should be achievable. Similarly, differences between male and female pay and participation rates should diminish as the traditional first-line supervisor's job is supplanted by the boundary-spanning team-leader role.

Career and Cultural Implications of Workforce Feminization

Females' rising participation in the workforce has allowed them to enhance their own careers and those of other women—in part, because of the effect of their increasing size as a minority group relative to that of the male-majority group. As Rosabeth Moss Kanter (1977) argued in *Men and Women of the Corporation,* when only a small proportion of a group possesses a particular characteristic, such as being female, this characteristic becomes the basis on which members are distinguished. Those in the majority exaggerate what they have in common with one another and how they differ from those in the minority. Kanter concluded that as the numbers of minority- and majority-group members became more balanced, the salience of the distinguishing characteristic—in this case, gender—would diminish. This suggests that females' rising participation in various fields should lead to better working conditions for women, such as less discrimination and more opportunities for career advancement.

Kanter's perspective is sometimes countered by Blalock's (1967) argument that a minority group's increasing size poses a threat to the majority group's share of resources. As a result, the majority will resist the minority group's progress, becoming more antagonistic toward the minority. Until recently, there was little evidence to support or refute either argument. Today, anecdotal evidence of a backlash against affirmative action suggests Blalock's thesis is correct (cf. *Newsweek,* 1995a, 1995b). But a study by Jacobs (1992) supports Kanter's view that women gain strength in numbers—that increasing their representation in a field or a company improves their position. Jacobs found that the substantial growth of women in management has coincided with a narrowing of the difference between male and female managers' wages and authority, not a widening of the difference, as the backlash argument suggests. An implication of this is that as women increase their numbers within organizations and fields, they gain political strength. This translates into more allies, mentors, role models, and networks, which are all essential to women trying to advance their own careers and help other women do so.

Indeed, strength in numbers will prevent women's demands from falling on deaf ears, and their influence on the culture at large will be profound. Females' rising labor-force participation has enabled them to become a powerful demographic group, to which the market must increasingly respond. Already, the presence of large numbers of females in the workforce is causing demands for equal pay, child-care programs, flexible hours, portable benefits, telecommuting, job sharing, tax breaks, household help, and other services designed to accommodate their needs and desires. For women (and, increasingly, men), the career concept is inextricably linked to these needs. That is, for most women to build careers over time, they must find sustainable ways to cope with unpaid work responsibilities, such as care of children and other dependents (e.g., parents); household chores and home administration; and all else comprising the "second shift" (Hochschild, 1989) that women work at home. Carrying the burden of this unpaid work is one reason most women's careers have not fit the so-called traditional model (Marshall, 1989) of upward advancement, with its assumption of a support system in the form of a stay-at-home spouse. Even women who have successfully advanced report that they intend to truncate their careers. In a study of women executives in the *Fortune* 1000 industrials and the *Fortune* 500 service companies, 77% said they would retire early, due to burnout created by an absence of better support systems for coping with so many demands on their time (Perry, 1993).

Companies can ill-afford to lose valuable employees who experience burnout from shouldering many unpaid work responsibilities. As women continue entering occupational groups and professions, companies will need to accommodate their needs. As they do so, they will further actuate feminization. Two case studies illustrate how this happens. In one of these, *Re-making Love: The Feminization of Sex*, Ehrenreich, Hess, and Jacobs (1986) explain how, during the sexual revolution of the 1960s, women's changing sexual attitudes created a great capitalist opportunity. Market forces responded to women's new demands—for clothes, books, and so forth—and then, in turn, institutionalized these tastes in the wider culture. A similar process is described by Douglas (1977) in *The Feminization of American Culture:* Between 1820 and 1875, Victorian ladies comprised the bulk of the dependable reading public; they were the prime consumers of American culture. Authors catered to their desire for sentimental novels. The ladies' taste exerted an enormous influence on the culture, feminizing it, while Melville, Thoreau, and other purveyors of the masculine culture were ignored (Douglas, 1977).

Soon after the year 2000, women again are likely to exert a great influence on the wider American culture. By then, they are projected to comprise approximately half of the workforce (U.S. Department of Labor, 1995). If current trends continue, well over half of the mothers with children under age 3 will work outside the home, and over two-thirds of women with children under age 18 will do so (Shellenbarger, 1992). The salient needs and demands of females in the workforce will exert great pressure on existing employers and social institutions. These will include the demand for making high-quality child care universally available and affordable, so that women can maintain their careers, and not be forced to suboptimize on what has been called the "mommy track" (Schwartz, 1989). Another demand will be for more flexible work hours and work arrangements, such as job sharing. Since most families will include two careers, companies will be pressured to provide more and better relocation and career-change assistance for the spouses of people they try to recruit. Companies will have to heed calls to create a truly "woman-friendly" work situation. Today, the efforts at this are criticized as being, at best, slow efforts, and at worst, superficial, public relations stunts. But, as the case studies suggest, the marketplace will in time respond to women's demands, and employers and society will make substantive changes, institutionalizing women's preferences, in order to enhance productivity and profitability.

Men at Work: Being "Feminized" by New Career Realities

As mentioned at the beginning of this chapter, *feminization* refers not only to women's increasing participation in the workforce, but also to the spreading of career or other characteristics traditionally associated with females to males. It is in this sense that I describe men in the workforce as being "feminized" by the new career realities they face. The restructuring of American industry in the past two decades has caused even previously successful men to experience such things as the devaluation of their work, the loss of secure employment arrangements, more part-time and temporary positions, more-frequent career shifts in lateral or downward directions, and increasing ambivalence about the role of work in their lives. For men, these career realities differ enormously from those of men of the post–World War II generation. They resemble instead the themes that historically dominated females' careers.

To understand the effect of these new career realities, we must remember that for American men, masculinity means primarily being a good provider (Bergmann, 1986; Showalter, 1991). Yet the workforce has undergone so much merging, consolidating, downsizing, and delayering that it has become difficult for them to fulfill their breadwinner role as easily as in the past. For the first time, millions of white-collar jobs have been eliminated, along with manufacturing and other blue-collar jobs. Like the steel and auto workers of the early 1980s, most of the white-collar people will never get back the jobs, earnings position, security, or special status that large companies offer (*Business Week*, 1992).

This economic restructuring has actually been occurring far longer than the recent wave of mergers and downsizing indicates. Economists explain that the average American's wages rose continuously for 26 years after the end of World War II. But since 1973, average family income has managed to increase only at a rate of 0.04% a year, compared with 2.72% over the 15 years prior to 1973. This near-invisible gain was achieved only because more mothers and wives entered the labor force (Harrison and Bluestone, 1988; Heilbroner, 1991; Levy and Michel, 1991).

The restructuring has meant that, for the first time, white males have had to accept substandard wages, substandard pensions, and substandard fringe benefits—an experience previously endured only by women and blacks (Barlett and Steele, 1992). One reason is that more than 75% of new jobs are in services, which do not pay as well as manufacturing jobs. Faced with less opportunity in factories, some men have moved into services and, also, retail sales—industries that traditionally hired women. These jobs pay 15–33% less than what men under age 30 make in factories; and they pay even less than they did formerly (*Business Week*, 1991).

Managers, too, who lost their jobs when investment bankers and corporate raiders wrested control of corporations from them, have found their breadwinner role curtailed. Many of them have found work on a temporary basis as consultants, but their wages do not approach their former executive salaries (Bennett, 1990; *Business Week*, 1992). As the concepts of subcontracting and "just-in-time hiring" take hold, many managers are finding themselves part of the peripheral workforce, where they are needed only on a part-time basis. One needs only to recall the words *Kelly Girl* to realize that the occupational status of part-time, marginal employees has traditionally been reserved for females.

This underscores the fact that the reality of diminished economic and career prospects is not just about money, but also about loss of status and identity. Many men derive their sense of identity and self-worth from a prospering career and find it difficult to take what might be considered a step backward (Rotundo, 1993; Seidler, 1994). As Amanda Bennett concluded in *The Death of the Organization Man,* when companies eliminated hierarchies, and thousands of "organization men" were terminated in the 1980s, it "wasn't just a matter of salary, and not just a matter of prestige. It was a real social system within which a person's professional status was defined. . . . It gave them a clear-cut way of measuring their progress and of being content with it. It gave them an identity" (1990: 40). Many men—who face permanent loss of the income, possessions, and status long considered the defining accoutrements of their breadwinner role in middle-class society—now find themselves adrift without a sense of personal identity for the present, or of economic security for the future. This is a painful reversal of the male, white-collar expectation that the next job will always be better. Further, the declining fortunes of the middle class are expected to continue through the 1990s and beyond, as the economic restructuring continues (Barlett and Steele, 1992: 27).

This situation has led some experts to conclude that coping with downward mobility will be the most important economic and social issue of the next decade (*Business Week*, 1992). According to Katherine Newman, who conducted a study of downward mobility in the American middle class:

> Downward mobility strikes at the heart of the "masculine ideal" for the American
> middle class. When the man of the house has failed at the task that most clearly

defines his role, he suffers a loss of identity as a man. When this is coupled with the admirable efforts of a wife to salvage the situation by going out to work, the man's response may be intensified feelings of impotence and rage. (1988: 139)

To make matters worse, children's reactions to role shifts between mothers and fathers are "filled with contradictions. . . . When fathers would try to help out with housework, to ease the burdens on now-working wives, they would sometimes run afoul of their children. Kids found it confusing and shameful when their fathers took on what they perceived as 'feminine' tasks, particularly if this behavior was in full view of the local community" (Newman, 1988: 118).

In an era of diminished expectations and new career realities, with upward advancement through single organizational hierarchies no longer being assured, men's "career themes" (as noted by Van Maanen, 1977) are beginning to resemble those of females: Their career paths are not "straight-forward and predictable but idiosyncratic and confusing" (Kanter, 1989: 85; see also, Kotter, 1995). They may need to be mobile in order to sustain employment and career development, but they are tied to a geographical area by the income needed from a spouse's job. Their hopes and expectations may be dashed when they face "glass ceilings" due to corporate restructuring, and other barriers to the traditional notion of advancement in a single company or career. Some may have to hold more than one job, experiencing overload, exhaustion, and the stress of balancing multiple commitments. Such career themes were once almost exclusively the province of females. Today, they have come to characterize men's careers as well.

Feminization in a Boundaryless Context

Women have penetrated previously male-dominated occupational groups and professions, and they have climbed to ever-higher rungs on the corporate ladder, only to find that ladders are being removed as part of the restructuring and "reengineering" of corporate America. Men, too, have been struck by the dismantling of hierarchies and the walls of separation between departments, divisions, and corporate fiefdoms. Further, both women and men now confront the challenge of a career that is not bounded by full-time, secure jobs and single-firm employment arrangements. What implications, then, do diminished boundaries have for feminization, and vice versa?

The coincidence of females' inroads into paid occupations and the diminution of boundaries around companies, jobs, and careers may be a setback for women. But it is one that may be more than offset by the fact that managing and organizing in a boundaryless context favors female sensibilities. Traits that are needed in this more fluid context are not those culturally ascribed to men—rationality, self-interest, toughness, domination—but, rather, are traits traditionally held to be feminine ones. The classical, masculine notion of managerial work as consisting of planning, ordering, directing, and controlling emphasizes rational, hierarchical, heroic management properties. These are seen as a major cause of U.S. firms' diminishing competitiveness in the 1970s and 1980s. In their place, a less bounded job has emerged—one that requires a person to do things via cooperation and a shared influence; to build relationships and connections with others, both inside and outside the boundaries created by job descriptions, departmental lines, and chains of command. Hierarchical relationships are supplanted by egalitarian partnerships to enhance personal and organizational effectiveness.

In a boundaryless context, the individual is not at center stage, making decisions, but shares responsibility and the limelight; individuals are not the sole source of expertise and solutions—they alone do not drive and steer the operation, but share that authority with others. This requires they be open, egalitarian, and focused on others, not on themselves. It requires them to reduce uncertainty through unity and cooperation, not separation and control. It requires an agility at nurturing relationships.

In a boundaryless context, managing and organizing require people to focus on helping and developing others. Managers no longer command, direct, and regulate workers, but, instead, support them and empower them to exercise their skills and capabilities to the fullest extent. This requires that they teach and influence others without dominating them, and that they facilitate the process of solving problems, without supplying all the answers. It requires responsiveness to others, interpersonal sensitivity, a comfort with interdependence, and a focus on the needs of others.

All of these are traditionally identified in our culture as feminine traits (Bakan, 1966; Eisler, 1987). Females are credited with greater sensitivity and responsiveness to other people's needs and motivations, which enable them to forge social alliances by managing interpersonal relationships (Janeway, 1971; Ferguson, 1984). The traditional feminine role emphasizes a focus more on process than on outcomes such as winning and losing (Gilligan, 1979, 1982). Its orientation is toward the collective interest and typically includes showing a wide interest in, and solidarity with, others (Ferguson, 1984; Glennon, 1979). It is a way of being involved in the world that Bernard (1981) concludes is characterized by mutuality, cooperation, and affiliation, and that therefore facilitates the maintenance of social structures.

While feminine traits promise to fit the demands of managing and organizing in a boundaryless context, the female experience may offer both women and men an example of the boundaryless career. Having historically had so few opportunities to advance in hierarchical settings, women may feel a sense of familiarity with the demands and constraints of ladderless, boundaryless careers. Traditional female experiences may, therefore, help us understand the nature of a boundaryless career.

One such experience is that of entrepreneurship. Historically, women have faced impediments to career advancement in large corporations—for example, discrimination and sexual harassment. One response has been for them to flee corporations in favor of starting their own businesses: Entrepreneurship has been a more hospitable outlet for their business savvy. Today, approximately 6.5 million businesses are owned by women. One out of ten workers is employed by women-owned companies, more than the number employed by the *Fortune* 500 worldwide (Lee, 1994). This move away from corporate careers, and toward entrepreneurial careers, has allowed women to avoid the glass ceiling and to build personal wealth and economic power. It has provided them with employment, often more flexible than that available from traditional employers, and with skill-building opportunities. But entrepreneurship is highly risky and has the downsides of insecurity and marginality. Nevertheless, the female experience is proving prophetic for contemporary men. In a recent study of 115 members of the Harvard Business School class of 1974, Kotter (1995) found that many have decided to forgo a traditional career of striving to move slowly up a company's hierarchy. Instead, they have decided to jump off the ladder to smaller companies, despite higher levels of risk. Why? They wanted to increase their compensation, but also their level of impact on a company and their speed in career development.

Another way the female experience may reveal the nature of the boundaryless career is in the manner in which an identity is built around both work and nonwork activities. Historically, a woman measured her success by personal achievements, such as the success of her family and social relations. More recently, women have added their own career achievements to their measure of success; but as Ferguson (1984: 98) argues, women located at the lower rungs in company hierarchies continue to value personal relations over career goals. Even higher-placed women today are often ambivalent about labeling themselves "successful," unless they are satisfied with their personal lives and personal accomplishments (Lenz and Myerhoff, 1985: 94). Mary Catherine Bateson (1989) captured the essence of this traditional female career experience in her observation that men build careers while women "compose" lives.

The era of boundaryless careers calls for men, especially, to reassess the value of personal, nonwork activities to their lives and goals. According to Mirvis and Hall (1994), boundaryless careers call for people to follow a path of building an identity through career achievement as well as through their "life's work"—work as a spouse, parent, volunteer, caretaker, mentor, and neighbor. Much as women have always done, men will need to balance their personal and work commitments, if they hope to avoid a crisis when their outmoded assumptions collide with reality. They will have to define success not only as a job well done, but as a life well lived.

Note

1. Across specific industries, women's participation in management varies. Women constitute 41% of the managerial personnel in the finance, insurance, and real estate industry; 39% in services; 39% in retail trades; 26% in transportation, communications, and public utilities; 21% in wholesale trades; 16% in manufacturing; 15% in agriculture; 10% in construction; and 10% in mining (U.S. Department of Labor, 1995). There is also a wide variation within these industries in women's share of management jobs. For example, in public utilities, 52% of the managers at US West are women, but at Ohio Edison only 3% are women. In financial services, 66% of the managers at Wells Fargo are women, while at Loews, only 17% are women. In the consumer noncyclical industry, 45% of the managers at U.S. Healthcare are women, but at Archer-Daniels-Midland, only 6% are women (Sharpe, 1994).

There is also a wide variation across industries in the level of managerial jobs held by women and men: Women are still clustered primarily in lower-level jobs, and second-arily in middle-management jobs. The 1995 Federal Glass Ceiling Commission reports that women still hold only 5% of the top management jobs, but that is a threefold increase from the mid-1980s, when they held only 1.5% (U.S. Department of Labor, 1995). Senior women have made other inroads: A study of women executives in the Fortune 1000 industrials and *Fortune* 500 service companies reported that the percentage with the title "executive vice president" more than doubled in ten years, from 4% to 9%. Those holding "senior vice president" jobs also rose, from 13% to 23%, over the same period (Perry, 1993).

References

AFL-CIO. 1992. *Breaking the Barriers: White-Collar Women on the Move.* Publication no. 92–1. Washington, D.C.: Department for Professional Employees, AFL-CIO.

Bakan, D. 1966. *The Duality of Human Existence.* Boston: Beacon.

Barlett, D. L., and J. B. Steele. 1992. *America: What Went Wrong?* Kansas City: Andrews and McMeel.

Bateson, M. C. 1989. *Composing a Life.* New York: Atlantic Monthly Press.

Bennett, A. 1990. *The Death of the Organization Man.* New York: William Morrow.

Bergmann, B. R. 1986. *The Economic Emergence of Women.* New York: Basic Books.

Bernard, J. 1981. *The Female World.* New York: Free Press.

Blalock, H. M., Jr. 1967. *Toward a Theory of Minority-Group Relations.* New York: Wiley.

Business Week. 1992. Downward mobility. March 23: 56–63.

Business Week. 1991. What happened to the American dream? August 19: 80–85.

Calas, M. B., and L. Smircich. 1993. Dangerous liaisons: The "feminine-in-management" meets "globalization." *Business Horizons,* March-April: 71–81.

Cohn, S. 1985. *The Process of Occupational Sex-Typing: The Feminization of Clerical Labor in Great Britain.* Philadelphia: Temple University Press. 1985.

Davies, M. 1982. *Woman's Place is at the Typewriter: Office Work and Office Workers, 1870–1930.* Philadelphia: Temple University Press.

Douglas, A. 1977. *The Feminization of American Culture.* New York: Avon Books.

Ehrenreich, B.; E. Hess; and G. Jacobs. 1986. *Re-making Love: The Feminization of Sex.* New York: Anchor.

Eisler, R. 1987. *The Chalice and the Blade.* San Francisco: Harper.

Ferguson, K. E. 1984. *The Feminist Case Against Bureaucracy.* Philadelphia: Temple University Press.

Fondas, N. 1993. The feminization of American management. In D. Moore (ed.), *Academy of Management Best Paper Proceedings.* Atlanta: Academy of Management, 358–362.

Gilligan, C. 1982. *In a Different Voice: Psychological Theory and Women's Development.* Cambridge, Mass.: Harvard University Press.

Gilligan, C. 1979. Woman's place in man's life cycle. *Harvard Educational Review,* 49, November: 431–446.

Glennon, L. M. 1979. *Women and Dualism.* New York: Longman.

Goldin, C. 1990. *Understanding the Gender Gap: An Economic History of American Women.* New York: Oxford University Press.

Harrison, B., and B. Bluestone. 1988. *The Great U-turn.* New York: Basic Books.

Heilbroner, R. 1991. Lifting the silent depression. *New York Review of Books,* XXXIII (17): 6–8.

Hochschild, A. 1989. *The Second Shift*. New York: Viking Penguin.

Jacobs, J. A. 1989. *Revolving Doors: Sex Segregation and Women's Careers*. Stanford, Calif.: Stanford University Press.

Jacobs, J. A. 1992. Women's entry into management: Trends in earnings, authority, and values among salaried managers. *Administrative Science Quarterly*, 27: 282–301.

Janeway, E. 1971. *Man's World, Woman's Place*. New York: Delta Books.

Jenson, J.; E. Hagen; and C. Reddy (eds.). 1988. *Feminization of the Labor Force: Paradoxes and Promises*. New York: Oxford University Press.

Johnston, W. B., and A. E. Packer. 1987. *Workforce 2000: Workers and Work for the Twenty-First Century*. Indianapolis: Hudson Institute.

Kanter, R. M. 1977. *Men and Women of the Corporation*. New York: Basic Books.

Kanter, R. M. 1989. The new managerial work. *Harvard Business Review*, 67 (6): 85–92.

Kessler-Harris, A. 1981. *Women Have Always Worked*. New York: Feminist Press.

Kotter, J. P. 1995. *The New Rules: How to Succeed in Today's Postcorporate World*. New York: Free Press.

Lee, C. 1994. The feminization of management. *Training*, November 25–31.

Lenz, E., and B. Myerhoff, 1985. *The Feminization of America*. Los Angeles: Jeremy P. Tarcher.

Levy, F., and R. C. Michel. 1991. *The Economic Future of American Families*. Washington, D.C.: Urban Institute Press.

Lunneborg, P. 1990. *Women Changing Work*. New York: Bergin and Garvey.

Marsh, B. 1991. Women in the work force. *Wall Street Journal*, October 12: B3.

Marshall, J. 1989. Re-visioning career concepts: A feminist invitation. In M. B. Arthur; D. T. Hall; and B. S. Lawrence, (eds.), *Handbook of Career Theory*. New York: Cambridge University Press.

Mirvis, P. H., and D T. Hall. 1994. Psychological success and the boundaryless career. *Journal of Organizational Behavior*, 15: 365–380.

Newman, K. S. 1988. *Falling from Grace: The Experience of Downward Mobility in the American Middle Class*. New York: Vintage Books.

Newsweek. 1995a. Affirmative action: Race and rage. April 3: 22–33.

Newsweek. 1995b. What about women? March 27: 22–26.

Perry, N. 1993. More women are executive VPs. *Fortune*, July 12: 16.

Reskin, B. F., and P. A. Roos. 1990. *Job Queues, Gender Queues: Explaining Women's Inroads into Male Occupations*. Philadelphia: Temple University Press.

Rotundo, E. A. 1993. *American Manhood: Transformations in Masculinity from the Revolution to the Modern Era*. New York: Basic Books.

Schwartz, F. 1989. Management women and the new facts of life. *Harvard Business Review*, 67 (1), January-February: 65–76.

Seidler, V. J. 1994. *Unreasonable Men: Masculinity and Social Theory*. London: Routledge.

Sharpe, R. 1994. Women make strides but men stay firmly in top company jobs. *Wall Street Journal*, March 29: A1.

Shellenbarger, S. 1992. Women with children increase in work force. *Wall Street Journal*, February 12: B1.

Showalter, E. 1991. Selling sugar and spice. *Los Angeles Times Book Review*, October 20: 1.

Shribman, D. 1992. Working women tend to be alienated, vocal and inclined to Clinton. *Wall Street Journal*, October 15: A1.

Smith, P. L., and S. J. Smits. 1994. The feminization of leadership? *Training and Development*, February: 43–46.

Stone, P. 1995. Assessing gender at work: Evidence and issues. In J. A. Jacobs (ed.), *Gender Inequality at Work:* 408–423. Thousand Oaks, Calif.: Sage.

Strober, M. H. 1984. Toward a general theory of occupational sex segregation: The case of public school teaching. In B. Reskin (ed.), *Sex Segregation in the Workplace: Trends, Explanations, Remedies:* 144–156. Washington, D.C.: National Academy Press.

U.S. Department of Labor, Glass Ceiling Commission. 1995. *Good for Business: Making Full Use of the Nation's Human Capital.* Washington, DC: Government Printing Office.

Van Maanen, J. 1977. Experiencing organization: Notes on the meaning of careers and socialization. In J. Van Maanen, (ed.), *Organizational Careers: Some New Perspectives:* 39–41. London: Wiley.

Wright, R., and J. A. Jacobs. 1995. Male flight from computer work: A new look at occupational resegregation and ghettoization. In J. A. Jacobs (ed.), *Gender Inequality at Work:* 344–378. Thousand Oaks, Calif.: Sage.

V

SOCIAL INSTITUTIONS IN THE NEW ORGANIZATIONAL ERA

In this part of the book, broad societal changes, brought on by organizational transformation, are seen to place new pressures on social institutions. The authors highlight effects on the civil society, regional development, the structure of occupations, and educational institutions. Boundaryless careers thus become societal concerns that public policy must address and that social institutions must accommodate.

Charles Perrow's "The Bounded Career and the Demise of the Civil Society" is a bold critique of the legacy of the modern corporation. Perrow attributes the weakening of the educational system, conflicts between work and family, and the losses in pensions and health care that displaced workers experience to the absorption of these functions by the modern firm. Now that firms are shedding responsibility for employee education, family support, and benefits, a void is created since the broader society had already ceded these functions to the firm. The demise of civil society means that people can no longer obtain basic benefits of citizenship in the broader community. Dependence on the firm, which now divests itself of such commitments, creates broad public-policy concerns that must be addressed before boundaryless careers can be enjoyed without undue vulnerability and strain.

Michael Best and Robert Forrant's "Community-Based Careers and Economic Virtue: Arming, Disarming, and Rearming the Springfield Metalworking Region" introduces the role of the region as a resource for boundaryless careers. They argue that community-based careers are an alternative to lifelong careers in big companies. Community-based careers exist, they note, where members of an industrial community (e.g., metalworkers in a region), "over a lifetime, may work for or manage a series of loosely coupled or networked small and medium-sized enterprises" within a specific geographic area. To do so, however, requires us to guard against large-firm intrusion and emergent dependency. It also requires clear education-to-work channels and supportive governmental policies. One response to this need for improved education-to-work channels is the reemergence of occupational community learning, affirmed also by Pamela Tolbert.

Tolbert's "Occupations, Organizations, and Boundaryless Careers" suggests an increasing centrality of occupations in new career arrangements. People's occupationally based careers provide a means for signaling their competence in an era when ability to deliver outcomes is critical but not easily assessed or tested directly. Tolbert suggests ways for individuals to manage their careers through occupational structures; marketable competencies developed over time; and a social network which recognizes their value. She proposes multiple changes that regulatory bodies—including educational and credentialing institutions—must address in realizing the benefits of occupations in the new era.

James Rosenbaum and Shazia Rafiullah Miller's "Moving In, Up, or Out: Tournaments and other Institutional Signals of Career Attainments" highlights a key issue in boundaryless careers: Employee mobility requires effective signals—dependable information about individuals' past achievements. Mobile individuals can succeed, and firms benefit, from their experience only if individuals can get credit for past achievements and firms can recognize these achievements. Rosenbaum and Rafiullah Miller review how signals often get lost in hiring, promotions, and exiting, and note the harmful consequences for individuals' careers, employer selections, employee motivation, and societal efficiency. They discuss practices that can improve the creation and transmission of appropriate signals; some institutions which are experimenting with such practices; and directions for further institutional reforms.

In sum, this part's authors point the way toward innovations in public policy that would enhance social prosperity and ease individual transitions into the new organization era. In addition to supportive governmental policies (local, state, and federal), other institutions, particularly those which can offer credible signals of an individual's skills and knowledge, have a role to play, too. Occupational accrediting bodies and schools emerge as key contributors to a boundaryless careers future. Firms and their workers would face severe handicaps in trying to face that future alone.

18

The Bounded Career and the Demise of the Civil Society

CHARLES PERROW

From the late nineteenth century to about 1973, U.S. organizations—public and private—steadily increased in size. Since 1973, selected evidence has shown that for-profit organizations have been decreasing in size; for example, the size of the top *Fortune* 500 has declined by about 8%. (I do not know of similar data on nonprofit and government organizations.) This decrease is small and predictions of the demise of the giant corporation are premature; indeed, the merger rate increased in the first half of the 1990s. Nevertheless, the downsizing of for-profit organizations has prompted attention to boundaryless careers, as evidenced in this book. I welcome anything that increases one's independence from large organizations (Perrow, 1992). I am also sure that for a small minority of the workforce, new technologies and structures make it possible for more people than ever before (in this century) to have a career that takes more of its gratification from exercising one's skills and enjoying satisfaction from one's output, rather than from wages and benefits.

But I suspect that for every satisfying boundaryless career that opens up, there are five to ten dead-end and degrading ones created, and one or two people left unemployed for a long stretch. The following figures from various government and other sources are from 1985 to 1989, and things can't have changed too much since then. It was predicted that the five fastest-growing occupations for the late 1980s would be low-technology janitorial, custodial, medical, sales, and restaurant jobs, and they were growing six times as fast as the five fastest-growing high-technology occupations. The occupation of building custodian accounted for more jobs than the five fastest-growing high-technology occupations combined. It was predicted that by 1995, only 6% of jobs would be sufficiently technologically oriented to require two or more years of college.

However, even aside from the crucial issue of the number and distribution of boundaryless careers, the focus on careers—on work life—has largely ne-glected the implications for nonwork life of those negatively affected by brief organizational tenures—the vast majority of those who bear the brunt of our failure to compete.

In this chapter, I will argue that over the last 100 years, organizations that employ large numbers of people have wittingly and unwittingly "absorbed" many segments of society that were organized around small groups and small, independent organizations—what I will call "civil society." (The term is differ-ent from that which means the private, as distinguished from the state, aspects of social life; as will be explained, in my usage, civil society is organized on the basis of citizenship; and the organizational society, on the basis of the employ-ment contract.) My observations are relevant to U.S. organizations, although related trends have been experienced in other industrial societies.

Due to the failure of many large economic organizations to compete inter-nationally, and due to the continued substitution of capital for labor, large eco-nomic organizations are now disgorging parts of the society they had absorbed. That is, with regard to one aspect of the absorption thesis—benefits—they are (1) cutting benefits for their remaining workers; (2) placing some in part-time and contingent positions without benefits; (3) sending others to small subcon-tractors who cannot afford benefits; and (4) simply laying still others off, forcing them to find low-wage, no-benefits positions wherever they might, or to become marginal entrepreneurs, or unemployed. However, civil society—that which lies outside the employment contract—has been weakened, and the benefits that have increasingly become a condition of work are less and less available as a condition of citizenship. I do not have any evidence on the number of people in each category that once enjoyed an organizationally sponsored substitute for civil society but no longer do, but it is presumably large enough to warrant the concern of this chapter.

Civil society, in this view, consists of networks of ties and obligations that depend on status (citizenship, and such things as parentage, ethnic and religious identification, and locality), and not on the contract (e.g., jobholding, credentials such as education, and private property). Civil society provides access to *collec-tive goods* needed for a civilized existence, such as socialization mechanisms; medical and nursing care; sustenance, if one is unemployed or incapacitated; religious and secular counseling; recreation; education; friendships; mate selec-tion; child care; and old-age care. A strong civil society may not be egalitarian. While those with more property, education, or more valued religious and ethnic/racial characteristics will be favored in getting the benefits of civil society, an effective civil society keeps such inequalities within bounds and assures an ade-quate minimum for all who have citizenship status. Having a strong society independent of the employment relationship means a sufficiently high benefits level that precludes extensive dependency upon employers.

Employee benefits such as health care, pensions, and parking lots are the most readily acknowledged society benefits being delivered as a condition of employment. But there are also more subtle sociopolitical processes that the large organization shapes or controls, such as the determination of residence patterns; friendship opportunities; mate selection; political socialization; and most broadly, the ways in which social reality is constructed—for example, the reinforcement of what Polanyi (1957) has called a "market mentality." At the turn of the century, organizations employing about 50 to 100 would be considered as having a large enough workforce to absorb some of civil society; at present, it would be those employing 500 or more. Employee benefits were few before World War II, and it was after the war that we saw the great expansion of sociopolitical aspects of organizational absorption. But I hope to show that this process began in the late nineteenth century. It was both an unwitting and a witting absorption on the part of employers.

Regarding unwitting absorption, as organizations grew large, they became the locus of social interactions that occurred because of the employment contract, rather than civic status. For example, I suspect that one's friends and one's marriage partner were less likely to come from one's neighborhood, church, or lodge connections (status groups) than from one's place of employment, and less likely to be dependent on one's rank or level within the place of employment. The organization's employment practices thus shaped social interactions, largely, though not entirely, unwittingly. The viability of these social opportunities outside the employment contract—those shaped by one's civil status—was reduced. Indeed, as a colleague, Sue Hudd (in a personal communication), points out, federally mandated practices, such as parental leave, may, in part, arise to fill the civil society void.

On the other hand, I would argue (but am unlikely to empirically prove) that the interest in having employees who were dependable and politically reliable encouraged the provision of social service benefits, with employers hiring psychologists, sociologists, and religious and medical personnel. The witting part of this was that the type of services provided and the conditions of their availability had to match the interests of management. But unwittingly, the availability of these services in the civil community, where they were not conditions of the employment contract, was relatively diminished, even if the services grew absolutely as civil society came to need or value more of them.

Perhaps unwittingly also, large organizations generated externalities that small organizations were not likely to generate. Large organizations begot other organizations to clean up after them—and the techniques were celebrated as innovations, and the outputs were included in the index of the gross national product. The remedial organizations, in turn, created their own externalities, because of their size and activities, further drawing in people and services from civil society.[1] One obvious example is the way that urban crowding gave rise to the development of low-cost public transportation, which, in turn, prompted demands for private automobiles and publicly financed highways.

Whether they wished to or not, large places of employment, to offset these externalities, came to provide ameliorative services to their employees: locked facilities and surveillance personnel, parking lots, medical facilities, safety inspectors, citizenship programs, space for political activities, United Fund drives, information on political candidates, and time off for voting, for example. These now essential civic functions were no longer provided by small, responsive, and independent groups and organizations of the polity. Some of these ameliorative services became defined as benefits, and were even subject to collective bargaining. Wage controls during World War II spurred the growth of benefits immensely, and bargaining over benefits became a standard union practice, furthering the absorption of civil society. Management has always sought to reduce benefits, and fought the demand for new ones. But I suspect that giving some benefits was more attractive to management than giving pay raises, because their value was dependent on long periods of service—an organizational dependency—and the cost of the benefits was reduced with high volume. The benefits were certainly valuable to labor as untaxed income. The taxing powers of the state have been slow to acknowledge this.

It is important to distinguish my account of the absorption of civil society by large organizations from the account, popular through the 1970s and early 1980s, of the shift from community to society, or from *gemeinschaft* to *gesellschaft*—the terms made popular by the German social theorist Ferdinand Tonnies (1887).[2] The image I wish to present of U.S. civil society in the late eighteenth and early nineteenth century requires neither a loving family and friends nor geographical stability, though these may have been more in evidence than today. Instead, my account emphasizes small units of production; broad, if shallow, skills; multiple sources of sustenance; long-term employment arrangements; and relatively open community decision making.[3] Also, in contrast to other accounts, my own emphasizes the distinctive characteristics of dependency on a wage, on working for someone else; and on unobtrusive controls in bureaucracies.

I should also note that this discussion omits the piece of the argument concerned with organizations' accumulation of wealth and power. Let me say simply that I assume that wealth and power are always favored over their absence, when that choice is available. But I argue that some systems structure choices such that they can generate much more inequality than others. In contrast to other nonsocialist industrialized nations, the U.S. system has generated a high degree of wealth and power concentration, with large organizations as a primary device behind that concentration. The society of organizations provides the context in which careers need to be understood.[4]

The Circumstances of Employment and Absorption

My argument rests on the claim that most people work for wages or a salary, either in large organizations or in small organizations that are dependent on large ones for their business or their existence. While we are accustomed to thinking of big government, big business, and, until recently, big labor, and seeing the very large organizations as the most significant actors in society, the demographics of workplaces are actually complex and somewhat obscure. Some large assumptions I make are unsupported by reliable or convincing data, some of which may be impossible to gather. At present, I can offer only some suggestive data.

In 1780, it is estimated that 80% of the working population was self-employed; by 1880, this figure had dropped to 37%; by 1974, it was only 8%. This is a dramatic increase in the proportion of people working for someone else's power, wealth, or privilege. And the size of organizations has grown over the century. By 1986, in the private sector, 65% of all employees were in firms with 100 or more employees; 50% in firms of over 500 (Small Business Administration, 1988). And I suspect it is much the same in government organizations. You might have heard differently, heard that about 95% of the employed work in *establishments* with under 50 people. But these include all the franchises, where there may be only 10 people. Citibank or Burger King are two of the giant firms that tell people what to do and, increasingly, how to live.

What kind of a society is being created within the large employing organizations, or through the dense clusters of smaller organizations that attach themselves to the big ones and are dependent upon big ones for their existence? It is a rationalized, controlled, surrogate society. For employees of the large organizations, the bureaucracy has increasingly become more than a source of wages and salaries, which can then be freely spent on the products that other bureaucracies choose to produce. The big bureaucracy is increasingly a source of benefits that can be obtained only by being an employee.

Employee benefits went from a trivial 3% of wages and salaries back in 1929 to 35.5% by 1986 (Enslow 1991).[5] Many of the benefits are not freely chosen by employees; nor is their vendor; and if not used—if one does not need counseling or want to use a gym—they are lost by the employee. Think of the variety that might be produced, the wide range of goods and services that small firms and local governments might have to provide, if paychecks of all employees increased by one half. To use the title of one of Milton and Rose Friedman's books (1980), they would be "free to choose" between this or that doctor or health plan; free to go to a gym or a psychotherapist of their choice, or to neither; to demand a bus route from the city, rather than a company parking space; and to picnic with a religious or ethnic group, rather than the company.

I think it makes a difference in the relative strength of society (as opposed to organizations) if the organization is the source of the services discussed below, or the arbiter of their availability—my list here is gleaned from personnel journals and business reports.

Of course, health care leads the list: Without a job at a decent-sized company, health care for most is unaffordable; and comprehensive medical care has become a necessity, largely because of the pollution, addictions, diets, and accidents that our organizations generate. Think only of the advertisements for dangerous lifestyles. One's ability to change employers is drastically limited by health-care provisions; people stay in low-level jobs because of vested health coverage. But some also provide, with the complicity of the IRS, pretaxable accounts for hearing aids, glasses, health-related travel, and 15-minute on-site massages (to offset company stress).

But the company goes deeper, with nutritional counseling, and back-care, substance-abuse, and stress-control programs (could they be company related?). The company goes still deeper with financial incentives for fulfilling its definition of wellness, rewarding the lifestyles that other companies draw one away from; and taxing smokers that the tobacco industry, with government subsidies, tries to create; criticizing overweight—which is in part due to our junk-food industry—and those with the high blood pressure that the competitive company creates. Companies fire or do not hire those suspected of genetic traits the company's own processes might fatally stimulate.

Recreation is an essential service, and the firms shape it with vacation-planning services, company vacation resorts, travel services, and sports facilities and sports programs. Resort hotels flourish in hosting the company's annual convention, where no civil society dare intrude; other employees in the firm or travel bureau provide one with the cues as to the appropriate kind of vacation and even its location, where company bonding can take place.

Financial services are shaped with financial planning; investment and tax advice; house and auto insurance at reduced rates; and special rewards for voluntary savings plans, to instill the rationality our economy counts on. Employees retire or are laid off, of course, so there is retirement counseling; outplacement services; incentives to save for (possibly sudden) retirement; and, since employees are often required to move, relocation services, including finding a house in the right suburb. (William H. Whyte, Jr., was memorable on this in his prescient *The Organization Man,* way back in 1956.)

Education is a big service, with tuition, time off, and loan assistance provided; and grants to schools where employees do volunteer work. This is not the community-embedded education of civil society; the employer is the purchasing agent and educational services are his customers. Extending the organization into the community is furthered by providing time off for parent-teacher conferences or for the first day of school for kids; information on summer-camp options; programs for presumably independent public schools to develop company-related curriculums and discuss aspects of corporate life with students (kind of like getting a Mobil ad on the editorial page of the *New York Times*); and on-site, before-school and after-school programs, to, as one company says, "show kids they are going to work just as their parents do." Showing kids this reality is a key socialization task in an organizational society. There is even a program (started in 1993) to bring one's kid to work for a day, to legitimate one's absorption in the company.

Many of the abovementioned company services touch the family, but there is more: There are elder-care referral services; employee benefits for what are now called "domestic partners"; adoption assistance; high-school graduation gifts; not just day-care centers, but summer camps for employees' children, with bus transport; child-development seminars at lunchtime; special phones to call home to latchkey kids, if one does not rank high enough to have a phone on one's desk; programs for kids to fill those organizational gaps on holidays and the first week of school vacation; Saturday child care during the tax-season rush at an accounting firm; maternal and also paternal medical leave; parenting courses; courses on "balancing" the family and one's organizational career—a significant "tilt," I would think, to turn a status privilege into a contract one; and even programs on the development of family goals—presumably by hiring group leaders who understand the employer's interest in family goals. Then there is the provision of religious facilities on the premises and, to round out the full life in a society of organizations, grieving provisions and funeral services.

Finally, the area of personal services is not neglected, with firms providing on-site beauty parlors, on-site department-store branches, sensitivity training for managers, sensitivity training and conflict resolution for gays and lesbians, sex therapy, and, of course, all forms of psychological counseling.[6] Where you live, who you socialize with, and make friends with and even mate with are all influenced by organizations—and not so indirectly.

We applaud these; we count as progressive the employer, the firm, or the university that supplies our needs through these services, some of them tax-avoiding devices that, we should note, are thus financed by the less fortunate employees in the marginal organizations that don't provide them. But they are *not* gifts; they are payments in lieu of wages or a salary, and, as such, will be devised to shape our behavior and our consciousness in unobtrusive ways, thereby taking a bit of choice that once was outside the employment contract—and was embedded in local and personal relations—and giving it to the bosses.

It may even be a compassionate organizational gesture, to be welcomed in a society where compassion, like child care, seems harder and harder to find. But that is just the point. What happened to the source of that compassion? The groups that had provided it in the past are now too weak to carry the burden, are on contract to the organization, or have disappeared entirely.[7]

All these societal services could come from small, local, and more or less autonomous groups and organizations, what we once thought of as those making up the community—but not in the face of large organizations, including government organizations, that have competing vested interests. It's true that we have a lot of small organizations and especially small voluntary organizations (there has been an explosion of NPOs—non profit organizations), but they are either weak and vulnerable, or, if successful, often quietly sponsored by big organizations. Mothers against Drunk Driving could be described as a profitable scam financed by the auto and liquor industries to blame drivers, rather than the organizational products—beer ads to encourage drinking, and dangerous cars to get to the party.

If the services I have enumerated are a condition of employment, rather than citizenship, then the logic of profit maximization in the private sector, and of power and job security in the public sector, will distort the choices available to employees. If, in contrast, the services are a condition of citizenship, then citizens can shape the choices, independent of who they work for, and can have a say even if they are not part of the labor force.

How We Got There

What has brought about the absorption of civil society by U.S. organizations? I do not think it is the inevitable logic of history, the implacable rationalization of the world that Max Weber saw, for there were choice points in U.S. history. Other nations tried and retained alternative arrangements less dependent on organizational largesse. Nor is it wholly the distinctive U.S. culture, which somehow sprang from the enterprise of its citizens and its new political institutions, although that is a part of it. It is, rather, a confluence of unique and exceptional conditions that made possible a new social form—modern bureaucracy—that was once unleashed by the leading economic power on the planet, and is still spreading throughout it.

In the nineteenth century, the United States went from dependency upon mother England to being the world's greatest economic power; from an economy where an organization with over 10 employees was rare to one where an organization with thousands was commonplace; from substantial economic equality to a plateau of inequality higher than that of almost all other industrialized nations—a plateau that would persist through the present time, despite unions and progressive reforms (Williamson and Lindert, 1989). To achieve this growth, organizations needed resources; and the natural resources were abundant and easily claimed, from nature and the Native Americans. The human resources flowed out of crowded Europe, and a population explosion occurred that so frightened Malthus and brought attendant social dislocations. America's greatest product in the nineteenth century, one historian remarked, was people. Most of that product was imported, although often in an unfinished state.

There are three components that make our society of organizations possible: wage dependency, which made citizens available for organizations; the externalization of the social costs of extensive organized activity, which hid the costs from citizens; and the development and spread of a novel form of bureaucracy—"factory bureaucracy"—which made controls unobtrusive.

Wage Dependency

With the first textile-mill towns, we had our first large organizations of hundreds of employees. Three distinct models developed: the boarding-house model, associated with the Lowell mills in Massachusetts; the family-employment model, centered around New Bedford; and the artisan model of Philadelphia. The boarding-house mills were the largest. It took new towns with five-story buildings in order to concentrate and service 500 or 1,000 employees in an area within walking distance of work. The employees were women recruited initially from the surrounding farms. These were the first instances of a society of organizations. The owners built dormitories, stores, schools, and churches because there was no infrastructure present, and without some minimal civil society, they could not attract workers.

Those mills that were built in decaying coastal towns did not need to provide either infrastructure or supervised living; the employees were unemployed families and immigrants, already there and dependent, rather than farmers' daughters. Working conditions appear to have been worse in these mills, and children were a majority of the workforce. Both the boarding-house and the family-labor types were mass-production operations—cheap goods were produced in large quantities, with little change in the production technology. Both models, spurred on by the availability of immigrant labor, grew towns that featured nonpaternalistic employment practices. The towns came to resemble the lack of social concern that marked the big firms of the end of the century, which gave rise to de-skilling and indifferent exploitation (Scranton, 1983).

The third form—the artisanal mills of Philadelphia—emphasized quality goods, rapid changes in styles and technologies, and a more skilled workforce that moved rather freely among the mills. The artisanal mills were locally owned, changed ownership frequently, did not amass fortunes and widespread investments, and were small and innovative parts of a variegated and adaptive economy. The artisanal form characterized most of industry until late in the century, when mergers and market control were possible because of centralized capital.[8] It was the railroads that were the change agent for the massive transformation that would occur.

Three perspectives are important for understanding the railroads. One is that the emphasis on bureaucratic rationalization and control in this new industry laid the groundwork for large organizations with rationalized structures in other industries (Chandler, 1977). Another perspective contrasts the "institutional logic" of three countries in order to explain why the new industry was state controlled from the start in a strong state, France; experienced mixed control in Britain; and was privatized in a weak state, the United States (Dobbin, 1994). A third perspective argues that the railroads concentrated capital in the investment houses of New York, which took capital out of private, family, and dynasty hands and "socialized" it through stock offerings. Then, when railroad securities failed massively in 1893, capital moved suddenly to industrial firms, prompting the incorporation and mergers of large firms (Roy, 1996).

The availability of capital coincided with the emergence of cheap, electric trolley lines in the 1880s. Until then, the growth of most organizations was capped at a couple of hundred employees. Cities other than the few mill towns had to be clusters of small enterprises, and each ward had its own bakeries, breweries, cobblers, and stables (Warner, 1968). Wage work, people felt, should supplement farming or other trades during slack seasons; and even those largely dependent on wages should be able to hunt, fish, gather fuel, and garden to maintain some independence (Keyssar, 1986).[9] Fortunes were made from trades, where organizational size was very low—five or ten people; but few fortunes could be made from the new industrial revolution until mass transport of workers and goods allowed for mass organizations.

Steadily, however, a fully wage-dependent population was created from the waves of immigrants and the offspring of farmers. The new large organizations drove the small ones out with their market power and scale economies, or swallowed them up under one gigantic roof, gradually substituting machines and unskilled tasks for the craft skills the workers had entered with (Hershberg, 1981). In turn, a large service industry grew out of the need to feed, clothe, and house the dependent workers, who could no longer do these things for themselves. We take it for granted today that 90% of us will work for someone else, and be fully dependent upon wages and salaries for our living. But this idea was so foreign to the nineteenth century that slavery was the only precedent, other than the military, for such an unwholesome state of dependency—hence, the terms *wage slavery* and *the industrial army*.

Externalities

The new organizations were immensely productive and the society benefited from industrialization; from the discipline created by having a wage-dependent population; and from the mass-production economies of large organizations.

But there were also substantial costs that need not have been born. Most were obvious and noted at the time, but they were, as we say, "externalized." That is, the costs were not included in the price of the goods or services—which would make rational choice among alternatives possible—but were passed on, in a hidden form, to the society, and generally to the weaker parts of it. For example, the cost of producing goods or services in ever larger organizations meant more money had to be spent on transportation, and more time on the journey to work, than if organizations had remained small; urban crowding increased and living spaces grew smaller; sewage and pollution problems multiplied; and freedom to change employers—seeking the best or the fairest—had to decline as a smaller number of organizations employed a larger percentage of the nonagricultural labor force.

The scale of production probably contributed to the fearful rise in accidents, to the point where, as late as 1910, nearly one-quarter of the full-time workers in the iron and steel industries suffered some type of injury each year. In one Carnegie mill alone, one quarter of the recent immigrants there were injured or killed each year between 1907 and 1910—3,723 in all, in these three years (Guttman, 1977: 30). Indeed, externalities such as pollution and crowding became, perversely, business opportunities and spawned ever-larger organizations, such that a good part of what we declare as progress today is only a case of cleaning up the externalities that our large organizations create as they make progress. The externalities included pollution, crowded cities, transportation costs, industrial accidents, the dislocation of business cycles, and the exhaustion of natural resources. Big organizations grew out of the need to handle them.

A significant consequence of passing off on the rest of society—and generally its weaker parts—the social costs, resource costs, and environmental costs of organized activity, on a large scale, was a transfer of wealth from the weaker parts to the elites that ran the big organizations. Profits rose in the private sector and new fortunes were made. In the government sector, needed services became numerous and more costly, requiring more taxes and more employees, and thus raising managers' salaries and increasing their power.

Gradually, some of the costs were internalized, through workmen's compensation and unemployment insurance and some government-mandated fringe benefits. But it is only in the last 10 years, after nearly two centuries of industrialization, that we are seriously beginning to measure these costs and require that the price of goods and services reflect them, as in effluent charges, environmental-impact assessments, and restrictions on auto travel to work. By and large, the nineteenth century and a good part of the twentieth have been a free ride for organizations that has contributed to our growth in income inequality, and then to its persistence. Most other industrialized countries have long internalized many more of the social, environmental, and resource costs of industrialization. With all the advantages we had in resources and a nearly empty continent, the United States could have done much better than it did. With a weak central government during the first 120 years or so of industrialization, it is not surprising that business and industry could so easily remain untaxed in these areas.

Bureaucracy

Large organizations raised a problem of control, especially with an untrained workforce, and one that began realizing that its dependency on wages was lasting. The direct method of control—direct supervision—was costly except for the most visible, routine, and noninterdependent tasks. Another method—decentralization with skilled workers that could coordinate themselves—meant expensive workers with a high level of bargaining power. A third form of control, neither direct nor delegated to professionals, proved to be as important as any new technology the nineteenth century produced—bureaucracy. It was an unobtrusive form of control, rather than reactive, as direct order giving was. It was vested in rules and regulations, and in surveillance of the product, rather than the process. It was also more exquisite and detailed than delegation of control to professionals, and offered minimum bases for employee bargaining.

Large-scale organizations have been around for centuries, building the pyramids or Venetian ships, establishing religions, fighting wars, administering kingdoms. But only with industrialization—and initially with the factory, then the railroads—did the elements of factory bureaucracy come together in a large number of organizations, enough of them for the organizational pattern to be readily and easily adopted by all new organizations, public and private, in the growing economy.

Briefly, bureaucracy meant centralized control in one office manned by full-time professionals; a hierarchy that subdivided the increasingly complex work processes and established clear lines of authority and accountability; formalization of the hierarchy through job titles, and formalization of all processes through rules and regulations, which can control without direct observation; formal training standards for all but the lowest positions; and, finally, specialization of tasks and standardization of inputs, outputs, and processes. It was a magnificent social invention because formal rules and regulations generated less reaction than barking orders did, and required less supervision.

In the world's history, no elites have had such a productive, economical, and safe means of domination. As Weber put it at the time, all else is dilettantism, and he cited speed, precision, calculation, predictability, impersonality, and accountability as bureaucracy's virtues (Weber, 1968; Collins, 1986). Guaranteed a labor force through wage dependency, and able to ignore the externalities because of weak government, the economic elites found the use of bureaucratic controls smoothed the radical cutting edges of democracy. Naturally, bureaucracy quickly spread from factories to schools, hospitals, prisons, government bureaus, churches, and voluntary organizations. Indeed, all organizations realized its virtues, and all could grow to substantial sizes without losing their all-important control.

Absorption over the Past 100 Years

Without large organizations, there could be no absorption of civil society by organizations, of course, and wage dependency, externalization, and bureaucracy made the large organizations possible. But what was the absorption that,

I claim, took place? Such things as organizationally approved sex therapy and a department-store branch at work were to come much later. In the nineteenth century, the organization had fewer and far cruder concerns about the lives of its employees. Some worked hard to control drinking and used the religious revivals to advocate good Protestant lifestyles. Foremen were advised to go to church or lose their positions. But the new organizations were less notable for their concern with the employee's soul than for their lack of concern with the civil society around them. Indeed, it was their largely unwitting weakening of civil society in the nineteenth century that required organizations to do more absorbing in the twentieth.

Wage dependency destroyed varied work activity; broad, if shallow, skills; independent and multiple sources of sustenance; and the fusing of work and the community, or economics and society, and their mutual enrichment. In the early nineteenth century, work and social life were not very distinguishable. One lived where one worked, or nearby, with children under one's feet and helping; there was less segregation of tasks by gender, and one had greater social ties with one's employees. (In the late twentieth century, the line between work and society once again became blurred, as noted at the beginning of this chapter, but this time, social life was trimmed and packaged to fit the needs of the big organization, rather than the small employer adjusting to the social demands of workmates, customers, and family.)

With full employee dependency on year-round wages from a large employer, the economy developed specialized, standardized, and largely repetitive jobs that were as socially *dis*embedded as possible. It also required enormous geographical mobility as areas prospered and declined, disrupting neighborhoods and dictating new residence patterns. Always a restless people, by necessity, the immigrants and the subsequent generations, as the bountiful lands opened up, speeded up their circulation with the advance of industrialization and its large organizations. The victim was decentralized, localized, civil society, with a stable membership.

The externalities gave birth to huge (for the time) government public-works programs, pollution abatement, crowding, crime, and disease. The externalities overwhelmed local government, and the traditional sources of recourse, such as local churches, neighborhood associations, charities, and even the orphanages and workhouses. Village resources gave way to city and state organizations, with standardization, specialization, and cultural explanations given—for the social problems they dealt with—that blamed the victims of layoffs and accidents (Lubove, 1965).

Bureaucracy extracted its toll on the civil society and on the local, familial forms of socialization and community bonding. New "habits of the heart" had to be instilled in the immigrants and the huge population of child laborers. As Herbert Guttman notes, "In the 1880 manuscript census 49.3 percent of all Paterson boys and 52.1 percent of all girls aged *11–14* had occupations listed by their names" (1977: 47). Child labor rose as the prosperity of industry rose, until the technology made children inefficient. Twice as many children under 12 were working in Rhode Island in 1875 than there had been in 1851 (Ware, 1931: 76). Punctuality, obedience, deference, impersonality, and narrow specialization was the lot of the workforce, eroding or rendering useless the traditional socialization patterns of the small-firm, farm, village, kinship, ethnic, and religious ties. Identity was transferred to the organization, away from one's home, neighborhood, skill, and generation. One was someone who worked at the mill or the factory.

These were mainly destructions of the civil society; as yet, the organizations provided little in return. Yes, the standard of living rose, but equality, resources, and civil society declined, unnecessarily so. The decline of civil society was, of course, resisted, and there is good evidence of family ties persisting in the work setting (Harevan, 1991). There is also evidence of the work crews being ethnically and religiously homogeneous, and of settlement patterns being homogeneous under the right conditions. And there are the redoubtable achievements of the progressive era in the 1920s. Of course, new skills appeared and waves of immigrants at the bottom pushed the older settlers up into the middle class. Cultural activities increased, as did educational levels. But in every case—where one lived; the skills one owned; the value system one continually reconstructed; and the educational choices one had—in every case, the employing organization extracted its loyalties and exerted its subtle or quite overt control.

By the time World War II was over, three large changes had modified the control of the organization over its employees. First, starting feebly in the progressive era in the 1920s, government began to force organizations to internalize some social costs, especially in the accident, the unemployment, and, then, the health area. Second, technological change required more skills and less brute strength, increasing the investment in employees and improving their treatment. Third, labor organized the large mass-production factories and extracted the first of the fringe benefits, using, ironically, the employing organization as the basis for meeting the needs that the civil society it had weakened could no longer provide. But this gave the organizations control over the benefits, and a strong say in what benefits there would be. The professions, interested in their own growth and dominance, cooperated with big business and big government, and became big enough to do their own absorbing of what remained of independent society.

By 1950, there seemed to be no countertrend; little resistance; and even little sense that what was happening was novel, and far from past ideals. We identified our welfare with big organizations, and the wages and salaries and benefits and services they increasingly provided. Since then, the process has speeded up, being falsely analyzed as the workings of a free market in social goods, when the market has all but disappeared into the employment contract. We now have the list of services and fringes I cited previously, and a society with few spaces for small, independent groups and organizations of any consequence. We also have the unmanageable scale of complex interactions in a tightly coupled, high-powered system.[10] We keep trying, with self-help groups, entrepreneurship, and small service firms, to provide some alternative. But these are either the trivial flotsam and jetsam of a declining economy, satellites of the big organizations, or desperate and doomed attempts to "organize," often bureaucratically, an independent society.

Finally, a brief word about other industrialized societies: We did not take the route of the Soviet Union and other command economies where the distinction between organizations and society was almost nonexistent—where it was one big, impossibly inefficient organization controlling most of social life, a kind of nationwide Lowell textile mill/town. But we also did not take the route of Europe, where the state gave people access to decisions about social services, and broke the close connection between a firm and a living. Education, retraining, relocation, and social services provided by elected governments have restrained the absorption there, although it is still marked. The most fascinating cases are those areas of Europe where networks of small firms outcompete the big firms, as in northern Italy; there, local civil society is reemerging and is vibrant, with local-government autonomy and a high degree of citizen participation (Perrow, 1992; Putnam, 1994). But how much of our economic machine can be decentralized in this fashion is unclear, and it may be only a small faction. We find almost no small-firm networks revitalizing local government and communities in the United States, which clings to the ideal of huge organizations and a market economy in all things economic and social. We are a population whose egalitarian and democratic culture is endangered. It was not inevitable, but the branches of a path-dependent history are so thoroughly embedded in everything, down to our self-conceptions and our cognitive processes, that reconnecting to past branches, to explore the alternatives not taken, is quite unlikely.

Conclusion

To return to the themes of this book, then, I welcome the emphasis upon careers; it is an important topic. But I fear that it signals an emphasis only on the few who "don't have to work for any particular company," rather than on the great majority of the employed population. Small firms abound, but as Harrison (1994) argues, they may be less responsible for new-job generation than recent conventional wisdom would have us believe. Harrison also alerts us that the "collapse of large firms" that Arthur and Rousseau refer to in chapter 1 of this book may be misperceived. Some are downsizing; others are merging. The downsizing is producing erratic and downwardly mobile careers for the perhaps 10% of the employees of big firms that are being let go, leaving slightly smaller big firms still in command of the field. Indeed, large U.S. firms have recently gotten leaner, challenged by large foreign firms with more sensible and flexible structures; but this does not signify boutique careers, except for people with scarce skills.

I have argued elsewhere, perhaps too passionately, for the social value of small-firm networks, as opposed to large firms, since the networks distribute wealth and power and avoid some externalities that choke communities (Perrow, 1992). In several industrialized countries, they have indicated a possibility that theorists of capitalism, on the Left or Right, never envisioned; and for this reason, they are very interesting and present a powerful critique of managerial capitalism. But I think the future of these small-firm networks is precarious, and their growth to greater significance unlikely.

Two additional things worry me about the new concern with careers. First, I hope it does not distract us from the continued study of organizations, since this is the independent variable still shaping the dependent variable—careers. Second, I hope it does not signify a further diminishment in the study of jobs, especially the kind of low-level, contingent, and part-time jobs—even if they require computer work-station literacy—that our economy is overwhelmingly creating.

Finally, I have argued that big organizations—firms, nonprofits, and government—have absorbed much of what was small, local, and independent in civil society. There is less of society for the unemployed, the part-timer, and the benefitless employee to draw on when they leave the big organization or get their benefits cut. Rebuilding that local society, in a passionately market-oriented, self-interest-maximizing nation, will be very difficult. Along with the other tenured authors of chapters in this book, I am among the precious few who have careers independent of particular organizations, and the social resources to ignore the passing of a civil society that is not dependent on an employment contract.

The challenge, then, is not to pick and study elite careers from the comfort of privileged vantage points. It is to find ways to reverse the absorption of civil society by employing organizations, and, simultaneously, to rebuild that society. If—and only if—the study of boundaryless careers can help respond to that challenge, it is to be welcomed.

Notes

1. A large proportion of the remedial organizations are government ones, although this is changing. Government, or the state, is insufficiently theorized in my argument, I am often told. Yes, the state is pallid in the present account, and its distinctive nature is not theorized, and rightly so, because in one sense it is *organizations* that count, whether state or private. Just by being big, organizations of any pedigree have an impact, and distinguishing public and private ones is not as crucial as my critics believe. Indeed, it is insufficiently theorized, and unfortunately so. Independent of their organizational properties, large government organizations do manage power and tilt playing fields and privilege particular groups and classes. Tentatively, I view the United States as a nation with a very weak state until after World War II, and I find the large organizations in the private sector to be dominant in shaping society. After World War II, the prosperity gave the government some room to have an independent agenda; its own organizational needs grew more important; and a wider variety of citizens began to call on or use the state than ever before—in some cases, because of the disappearance of civil society. The state has been filling in. I need to theorize it more than I have here.

2. As Bender (1984) notes, it is not a case of either/or—the modern city is full of the community as well as the impersonal society. But the image of the community, in the decline of community literature, emphasizes personal, affective relations and long traditions born of settled living arrangements going back generations. And Bender might have stressed, more than he does, that the rural town or the village of the past had its share of *gesellschaft* characteristics, such as impersonality (to strangers), contracts (including marriage ones, ones with servants, or with slaves), and self-interested behavior (on the part of community elites, landowners, clergy).

3. Nor does my "society of organizations" necessarily include all the sins of *gesell-*

schaft—in particular, universalism and impersonality. Particularism and personal relations can thrive in large organizations. We find in large organizations a *gemeinschaft* of a sort, but one that is on organizational terms, even though it is readily embraced by employees as more or less genuine. Far more important for me than impersonality and universalism (the blight of the *gesellschaft* critique), are wage dependency and bureaucratic characteristics that find no mention in Bender's (1984) exhaustive account.

4. The missing argument is part of a broader study of the society of organizations, in which I am presently engaged (see Perrow, 1991).

5. The ratios of direct pay to benefits are more extreme for executives. Their direct pay was, by 1985, just 44% and by 1990, 34% of the total remuneration. By 1990, 66% of the total remuneration of executives came as organizationally determined and controlled perks, long-term incentives, and benefits (Enslow, 1991).

6. Most of these benefits are described in *Employee Benefit Plan Review* for the years 1990—1992; for the others, see the journals *Across the Board, Personnel Journal,* and *Training and Development* for these years.

7. I know my long list of services that the enlightened employer now provides was poorly provided in 1820, if at all. But most of these services now exist, to redress the social costs of large-scale organizations that hardly existed before organizations appeared and generated such social costs. And with the wealth of the United States, we might expect these and more services to be available now as a right of citizenship in a civil society, and thus be provided collectively, by government, if they cannot be generated by small voluntary or familial units. (This is the European model.) Instead, they are a condition of employment at a progressive organization.

8. For the classic works on the textile mill towns, see Dublin (1979), Josephson (1949), and Ware (1931). On the Philadelphia model, see Scranton (1983). On company towns, see Brandes (1970), although Brandes does not emphasize that company towns grew in times of labor shortages, and were abandoned, except in the most remote locations, in times of labor excess.

9. The first factories, all small, in England, and some of those in the United States, had to draw on paupers and prisoners (Clawson, 1980; Pollard, 1965). The United States recruited abroad, and a significant proportion of early factory labor was indentured.

10. In brief, the argument is that "degrees of freedom" were wrung out of the system as units became larger and relied more and more on interactions with other large units; unexpected interactions, following even small failures, increased, and the tight coupling of large units prevented the quick recovery from failure and led to a cascade of increasingly disastrous failures. This argument is developed, for high-technology systems with catastrophic potential (such as nuclear power plants), in Perrow (1984, 1994).

References

Bender, T. (1978). "Introduction: The Meanings of Community" and "Social Theory and the Problem of Community." In *Community and Social Change in America.* New Brunswick, N.J.: Rutgers University Press.

Bender, T. (1984). "The Erosion of Public Culture: Cities, Discourses, and Professional Disciplines." In *The Authority of Experts,* edited by Thomas L. Haskell, pp. 84–106. Bloomington: Indiana University Press.

Brandes, S. D. (1970). *American Welfare Capitalism, 1880—1940.* Chicago: University of Chicago Press.

Chandler, A. D., Jr. (1977). *The Visible Hand.* Cambridge: Harvard University Press.

Clawson, D. 1980. *Bureaucracy and the Labor Process.* pp. 41 -70. New York: Monthly Review Press.

Collins, R. (1986). *Weberian Sociological Theory*. Cambridge, Eng.: Cambridge University Press, chap. 2.

Coolidge, J. (1942). *Mill and Mansion: A Study of Architecture and Society in Lowell, Massachusetts, 1820– 1865*, p. 106. New York: Columbia University Press.

Dobbin, F. (1994). *Forging Industrial Policy: The United States, Britain, and France in the Railway Age*. New York: Cambridge University Press.

Dublin, T. (1978). *Women at Work*. New York: Columbia University Press.

Enslow, B. (1991). "Up, Up and Away." *Across the Board,* July/August, pp. 18–25.

Friedman, M., and R. Friedman (1980). *Free to Choose,* San Diego: Harcourt Brace Jovanovich.

Guttman, H. G. (1977). *Work, Culture and Society*. New York: Vintage Books.

Hareven, T. K. (1991). "The History of the Family and the Complexity of Social Change." *American Historical Review,* vol. 96, no. 1 (February), p. 95.

Harrison, B. (1994). *Lean and Mean: The Changing Landscape of Corporate Power in the Age of Flexibility*. New York: Basic Books.

Hershberg, T., ed. (1981). *Work, Space, Family, and Group Experience in the Nineteenth Century, Essays Toward an Interdisciplinary History of the City*. New York: Oxford University Press.

Josephson H. (1949). *The Golden Threads*. New York: Duell, Sloan, and Pearce.

Keyssar, A. (1986). *Out of Work: The First Century of Unemployment in Massachusetts*. New York: Cambridge University Press.

Lubove, R. (1965). *The Professional Altruist: The Emergence of Social Work as a Career, 1980–1930*. Cambridge, Mass.: Harvard University Press.

Perrow, C. (1984). *Normal Accidents: Living with High-Risk Technologies*. New York: Basic Books.

Perrow, C. (1991). "A Society of Organizations." *Theory and Society,* vol. 20, pp. 725–762.

Perrow, C. (1992). "Small-Firm Networks." In N. Nohria and R. G. Eccles (eds.), *Networks and Organizations*, pp. 445–470. Boston: Harvard Business School Press.

Perrow, C. (1994). "Accidents in HighRisk Systems," *Technology Studies,* vol. 1, no. 1, pp. 1–20.

Polanyi, K. (1957). *The Great Transformation*. Boston: Beacon Press.

Pollard, S. (1965). *The Genesis of Modern Management*. London: Edward Arnold.

Putnam, R. (1984). *Making Democracy Work*. Cambridge, Mass.: Harvard University Press.

Roy, W. G. (1996). *Socializing Capital: The Rise of the Large Industrial Corporation in America*. Princeton, N.J.: Princeton University Press.

Scranton, P. (1983). *Proprietary Capitalism: The Textile Manufacture at Philadephia, 1800–1885*. New York: Cambridge University Press.

Small Business Administration (1988). *Handbook of Small Business Data*, p. 203. Washington, D.C.: Small Business Administration, Office of Advocacy.

Tonnies, F. ([ca. 1887], 1940). *Fundamental Concepts of Sociology,* translated by Charles Loomis. New York: American Book Co.

Ware, C. F. (1931). *Early New England Cotton Manufacturers*. Boston: Houghton Mifflin.

Warner, S. B., Jr. (1968). *The Private City: Philadelphia in Three Periods of Growth*. Philadelphia: University of Pennsylvania Press.

Weber, M. (1968). *Economy and Society,* edited by Guenther Roth and Claus Wittich, vol. 1, pp. 212–225. New York: Irvington Publications.

Williamson, J. G., and P. H. Lindert (1980). *American Inequality: A Macro-Economic History*. New York: Academic Press.

19

Community-Based Careers and Economic Virtue: Arming, Disarming, and Rearming the Springfield, Western Massachusetts, Metalworking Region

MICHAEL H. BEST AND ROBERT FORRANT

With the occurrence of a dramatic downsizing of big corporations, the opportunity for a life-long career within one company is increasingly unrealistic. What are the alternatives? In this chapter, we explore the idea of a community-based career, in which members of an industrial community, over a lifetime, may work for or manage a series of loosely coupled or networked small and medium-sized enterprises within a geographical region.

Industrial districts in other regions have demonstrated that networked groups of small firms can be internationally competitive. These districts involve considerable mobility across firms, of both people and knowledge. They also involve interfirm institutions of cooperation that facilitate the entry of new firms and the provision of collective services. In describing common features of industrial districts in northern Italy, the Italian economist Sebastiano Brusco (1992) stresses that within such communities, the shared range of values and body of knowledge are "so important that they define a cultural environment." He adds that constituent firms are "also linked to one another by very specific relations in a complex mix of competition and co-operation."

A class of successful industrial districts seems to have self-organizing capabilities that do not require the leadership of a single dominant company that acts as a system integrator. Numerous examples of such self-organizing capabilities within groups can be found in the natural world, such as a migrating flock of geese that fly in a V-shaped formation with continually revolving positions; or a school of minnows that reshape its collective shape as it swims through shallow areas. However, the understanding of such collective behavior lags behind the observation of its existence.

How self-organizing capabilities function in social organizations, in generating group identities, is not clear, either, but again, examples exist. In fact, the very existence of a language community suggests that a self-organizing ability is an important aspect of human life. At a different level, organizations such as Alcoholics Anonymous seem to function without a hierarchy or central direction. But all such human communities and organizations do have rules, formal and informal, that shape the actions of participants. Consequently, it would be hard to imagine that an industrial district that is comprised only of atomistic enterprises could exist; interactions across firms, intermediary organizations, and other means of connecting must be established and nourished.

These issues are of concern for many reasons, but, particularly, to provide insights into how to cope with the rapid and widespread downsizing of many big corporations, and the resulting erosion of skills and corporate careers. Cases of regions that combine competition and cooperation, both in other countries and in America's own history, may provide insights into how to cope with this emerging challenge. We explore such issues through a comparison of three periods in the history of the Springfield, Massachusetts, metalworking region along the Connecticut River valley: before, during, and after the organization of the region's metalworking activities by vertically integrated, bureaucratic enterprises.

Central to our analysis of the events at Springfield is "economic virtue"—a theme concerned with interdependent themes of personal integrity, skill development, and industry awareness. Our analysis offers economic virtue as an alternative to the simplistic notion of "economic man," which we portray as underlying Springfield's demise.

Unfortunately, there was a lack of a conceptual analysis of the role that community institutions of cooperation played in the success of the Springfield metalworking region, before the emergence of big firms. This lack of analysis contributed to subsequent behavior that undermined the economic virtue required to make the region work. Today, the region must rebuild economic virtue without the technical advantage that Springfield enjoyed in the early decades of the nineteenth century. It remains an open question whether the community's memory is strong enough to overcome the handicap of being left behind in a number of areas crucial to sustaining industrial success.

Arming the Region: The Origins of Community-Based Careers

In the early 1800s, the Springfield Armory was the hub of an industrial district, along the Connecticut River valley, populated by networked groups of small metalworking and machine-making firms.[1] By the turn of the century, Springfield was a diversified manufacturing center with over 300 firms and thousands of skilled workers producing a variety of products. Springfield had indeed earned the nickname "Industrial Beehive."

The origin of the Industrial Beehive was the concept of interchangeability—an idea that drove the U.S. Army's sponsorship of contracts for the purchase of muskets. The Springfield Armory converted the concept into a working principle for the production of muskets, under which individual parts were no longer hand-fitted, or filed to fit, into individualized guns but, instead, could be "promiscuously" inserted into standardized guns. The advantages for the army were enormous—it no longer needed skilled craftsmen behind the battle lines to repair weapons; a broken part could simply be replaced by a new, interchangeable one.

The new "American system" of production redefined the requisite skills of the craftsman and opened up the age of the specialist machine. The growth of the emerging metalworking industrial district was based on three interrelated factors: technological innovation and diffusion, generated initially by the Springfield Armory; a diverse nucleus of locally owned machine-tool builders who, in turn, became refiners and transmission agents of technical innovations across a broad range of industries; and a base of skilled workers capable of handling the precision machinery required to turn out world-class products.

Bruce Tull's archival research at the armory reveals that the Civil War witnessed the "zenith" of the armory's role as a technology diffusion and training center.[2] To quote Tull:

> If there was still any question on how to produce precision componentry in the North, the Civil War was a period of massive diffusion of "armory practice." Hundreds of firms subcontracted to produce either complete arms or components, and the Armory continued its practice of openly sharing its machinery patterns with virtually every contractor, subcontractor or machine builder in the northern states. Noted machinery builders such as Providence Tool Company's Frederick Howe, and William Sellers & Co., borrowed Armory designs, and spent time in the Armory viewing operations. Use of Armory patterns was so widespread that the Armory began assessing standardized charges of 1/2 cent per pound for castings made from Armory patterns to compensate for wear and tear. (1995)

Springfield became a diversified manufacturing region dotted with small and medium-sized metalworking companies that, collectively, employed thousands of engineers and skilled and semiskilled machinists, who produced machine tools, assemblies, and components for the nation's machine-tool, automobile, steel, and electrical-equipment industries. These firms were supported by small, highly specialized tool-and-die shops and foundries engaged in the production of fixtures, tooling, gauges, and made-to-order components.[3] The machine-making industry was a "transmission agency" that spread an innovation (developed in a particular application) to users in entirely different industries (Rosenberg, 1963).

The development and diffusion of skills, through movements of skilled workers within and across industries, represent an example of how networks, even in the early nineteenth century, served as learning systems that linked skill development, innovation, and careers. Historian Patrick Malone refers to a 1917 article in the *American Machinist,* in which author George Sawitzke, himself a superintendent at the Osborn Manufacturing Company, notes that "many good ideas are gathered from the rank and file and it is to the foreman's best interests to bring out the best that is in his men"; foremen were indeed admonished to "accept the best and use it to the shop's betterment" (Malone, 1988: 64).

Malone summarizes how the transmission of skills, both vertical and horizontal, took place in the armory: "Surely the successful foremen at Springfield had always followed this practice; most of them had risen from the rank and file in the production shop or had served an apprenticeship under a skilled machinist." This "shop culture" placed a high value on practical experience; promoted participation in machine design and incremental innovation; and, as Malone indicates, "encouraged respect for the ideas of 'practical men' (1988: 64). Such an approach to careers and learning was fundamental to the success of the metalworking industry in Springfield, Massachusetts, throughout the nineteenth century and the first half of the twentieth century.

The Springfield metalworking district in this period illustrates the three themes of economic virtue: Personal integrity is indicated in the district's reliance on skilled workers to both submit and exchange their ideas; skill development is reflected in the system's reliance on the recruitment and persistent cultivation of precision machining skills; and industry awareness is suggested in the broad reliance on workers as the transmission agents for further innovation. None of these observations is consistent with the narrow self-interested assumptions of "economic man." Instead, they reflect alternative assumptions of economic virtue, embedded in the ongoing career behavior of district participants.

However, the metalworking district along the Connecticut River valley was not a case of a pure industrial district without a single central hub similar to those described by Brusco and others. It had a single enterprise—the government-owned Springfield Armory—that acted as a system organizer. The armory was crucial to rapid growth and technology diffusion, and fostered the specialization and differentiation common to industrial districts. In fact, it had much in common with the Japanese production system that was to emerge later: It combined a hub factory with interfirm networking.[4]

The Springfield Armory, like the Japanese hub firm, did not generate a managerial hierarchy to coordinate, plan, and allocate resources, as did the later American corporate bureaucracy, as described by Alfred Chandler. The functions of the armory—namely, training, technology diffusion, and collective services—cannot be ignored. But the district generated rapid advances in productivity, as demonstrated by its success in the marketplace, without a hierarchy and the associated corporate career patterns. The managerial focus was on the shop floor in hundreds of small shops.[5]

As giant, vertically integrated corporations began to emerge elsewhere in America, it was assumed the Springfield enterprise system was obsolete. The economies of scale of big business would transcend the "mature" Springfield system, just as the American system would replace the British craft-based system early in the twentieth century. No other model was considered. Assumed obsolete, the Springfield model was pushed aside.

Disarming the Region: The Erosion of Economic Virtue

Well into the twentieth century, Springfield firms continued to be noted internationally for their machine-tool innovations.[6] At the same time, firms began to grow in size. The Stacy Machine Works invented the first upright drill. The Bauch Machine Tool Company specialized in threading machines and worm gears, universal joints, and cutting tools. The Hampden Grinding Wheel Company developed and produced its own brand of precision grinding wheels. In 1930 the Moore Drop Forging Company was one of the largest firms in the city, with 1,400 workers producing bases and beds for machine tools for export worldwide. Storm Drop Forge's 1,000 employees manufactured custom-ordered forging out of steel, brass, and bronze, for export worldwide. In 1910, Van Norman engineers and machinists designed and built the first milling machines with adjustable cutter heads, and the first cutter grinders. The Westinghouse Electric and Manufacturing Company, the city's largest manufacturing firm in the early 1930s, with 4,500 employees, was purchasing annually close to one million dollars' worth of tooling and fixtures from local machine shops.

The industrial success of the area was dependent on a base of skilled machinists. William Cooper, director of the U.S. Bureau of Foreign and Domestic Commerce, noted, in 1930, that in Springfield "the large number of successful firms, including Van Norman, Chapman Valve, Westinghouse, and Bosch relied on worker skills to design and build new equipment and products" (Artman, 1930: xi).[7]

Springfield's employment growth was twice the state's average growth between 1937 and 1947. Metalworking firms reported shortages of skilled machinists and started up training programs. The armory had 500 employees enrolled in vocational-school night courses in 1940, and 1,000 in 1941. Westinghouse, Van Norman, and American Bosch established a collaborative training program of their own, using another local vocational high school. The program consisted of classroom instruction in shop mathematics and blueprint reading, and hands-on training in the setup and operation of a variety of machine tools.

But even with these efforts, in the words of a plant manager of one program-sponsoring firm: "Skilled mechanics who understand their machines have this year been at a premium. Specialization over a period of many years has led to a large group of just machine operators. They could pull a lever, but that was about it" (*Springfield Republican,* October 25, 1936). Somewhere along the line, the industrial district was losing its innovativeness and its skill base. Big firms appeared to be consuming without replenishing the skill base of the region, which had been built up over many generations.[8]

Declining performance became a public issue with the announcement of a study of the New England economy—it was initiated by President Truman's Council of Economic Advisers, and the findings were published in 1951. The council expressed its concern that present-day owners had become more conservative and had "turned their attention away from industrial progress" in order to preserve the status quo. In the study report's introduction, they argued that:

> To some extent manufacturing success in the 19th century and the early part of the 20th century seems to have bred lethargy and complacency among New England industrialists, which handicapped the region in its competition with newer regions. The gap between ownership policies motivated by short-run financial considerations and the need for long-run modernization, research and product development has also intensified manufacturing problems in New England. (Council of Economic Advisers, 1951: xxii)

The impact of this changed behavior was felt in Springfield. By the early 1950s, skill development, technological innovation, and the diffusion of new production methods lessened. There is little evidence of the types of collaboration found earlier, either between firms, or between managers and workers. In fact, management determined that there was little to gain from pressing for relationships with shop-floor workers that included their participation in such things as shop-floor layout, new-product design, new-machinery purchases, and quality-improvement strategies. Respect for the ideas of "practical" men was replaced with a management paradigm: that dedicated production machinery, college-educated engineers, and a top-down approach to work were the elements of modern organization of production.

According to the president's council, regional solutions for the slowing New England economy depended on a recapturing of earlier production advantages derived from technological innovation and the skills of employees. But instead of this, Springfield firms disbanded apprenticeship programs and cut back on worker training. They concentrated instead on training foremen to get the work out, and eliminated longstanding union-management production committees.

For a short time, the Korean War rearmament boom acted like a pressure-release valve and made it possible for firms to ignore their internal and external problems. But it was not enough to stimulate sustainable growth and fend off plant closings, as shown in Table 19.1. The assumption that highly skilled metalworking plants were somehow insulated from the more familiar textile- and shoe-mill closings proved painfully incorrect. The Indian Motorcycle Company failed in the late 1950s. Package Machinery moved its production facilities out of the city; and the East Springfield Westinghouse plant, which employed 4,600 people in 1950—one out of every seven workers in the city—began a slow, painful 12-year phase out; its gates were locked in 1970. Even the armory, the city's third largest employer, and a symbol of manufacturing innovation, finally closed down in 1968. By the 1960s, the Industrial Beehive had been renamed the "City of Homes." The production workforce was slashed at nearly every large plant in the city. Closings, not innovative breakthroughs in machine-tool technology, captured the headlines (D'Amato, 1985).

In a closing that symbolized everything that was wrong with the city's manufacturing base, the former American Bosch plant shut its doors in 1986: On February 4, 1986, United Technologies Corporation (UTC), now the owner of

Table 19.1 Permanent Layoffs and Closings of Springfield-Area Metalworking Companies in the Mid-1980s

Company	Status	No. of Jobs Eliminated	Closure Date	Years in City	Peak Employment since 1960
American Bosch	Closed	1,000	2/86	80	1,800
Chapman Valve	Closed	250	6/86	100+	2,700
Springfield Foundry	Closed	75	4/86	100+	—
Portage Casting	Closed	60	8/86	36	100
Van Valkenberg	Closed	40	7/86	100+	135
Wico Prestolite	Closed	250	3/82	80	675
Rafferty Brown Steel	Closed	50	11/85	40	—
Van Norman	Closed	275	10/83	90	1,200
Plainville Casting	Closed	65	4/87	65	75
Oxford Precision	Closed	60	9/86	40	120
Easco Hand Tool	Downsized	2,000	1980s	75	2,200
Columbia Bicycle	Closed	250	6/88	80+	800
Package Machinery	Closed	400	9/88	100+	950
Atlas Copco	Downsized	565	1980s	70+	800
Kidder Stacy	Closed	90	9/89	100+	250
Rexnrod C'belt	Closed	200	6/89	100+	575
Northeast Wire	Closed	35	1990	22	110
Storm Drop Forge	Layoffs	125	1980s	60+	250

NOTE: With the exception of Plainville Casting, Rafferty Brown Steel, and Oxford Precision, all plants were unionized. All but two of the closed companies, representing all but 475 of the lost jobs, were not locally owned; 15 of 18 firms had been bought out since 1959, and 13 of them since 1979.

SOURCE: R. Forrant. 1988. "Plant closings and major layoffs in Springfield, MA." Springfield: Machine Action Project.

the 76–year-old plant, announced it would have to close the factory. The announcement was the culmination of a series of permanent layoffs made by UTC after it acquired the facility in 1978.

From World War II until its closure, wild swings in employment at the Bosch plant made training difficult and expensive. There was little continuity in the workforce to help plant managers introduce new manufacturing and quality-control procedures. Moreover, the prevailing management paradigm treated workers as a homogeneous "factor of production" that could be bought and sold in the marketplace, and worker skills as replaceable by high-tech machines. "Economic man" was not only a concept in economic theory; it became a product of management practices. Meanwhile, workers and union leaders realized that job security was tenuous. Bosch management and the union fought over job classifications, rates of piecework pay, and such things as whether rates included sufficient time to do quality checks on parts being produced.

These were the wrong arguments to be having. While many Bosch workers were highly skilled, they were not allowed to apply their skills toward in-plant decisions. As a result, negative dynamics were set in motion: Any management attempts to cut piece rates, change the incentive system, alter inspection techniques, or change job descriptions were met by the various means at the workers' disposal, including the grievance-and-arbitration procedure; articles in their union newspaper; strikes; and individual and organized shop-floor resistance to technical change. In addition, both the organization of production and the sustained confrontations with management signaled a loss of connection that workers had had with the circumstances of their industry—a connection which had been a strength in the old armory days.

The negative dynamics of management presuppositions and the matching economistic (wage) union response eroded the surviving tenets of economic virtue. Lack of inclusion of workers in management, particularly after the active role they had played during the war years, signaled distrust, rather than personal integrity; short-term employment (cycles of layoffs and movement from firm to firm) undermined skill development; and workers were trapped in an adversarial dialogue that presumed, rather than questioned, the health of the employing industry and its member companies. Not surprisingly, the large firms were ill-prepared to meet the emerging new and more comprehensive performance standards of cost management, quality control, flexibility, production time, and innovativeness.

Rearming the Region: Restoring Economic Virtue

The closing of American Bosch, the last of the large employers, signals the transition to a third period in the history of the Springfield metalworking region—a period of restoring economic virtue. The handmaiden of the new period was the Machine Action Project (MAP), established, in the aftermath of the Bosch closing, by the Commonwealth of Massachusetts's Executive Office of Economic Affairs, to determine, and then respond to, the needs of the small, precision metalworking firms that remained in the region. The first task of the two-person MAP staff was to conduct an audit of the region's metalworking shops.[9]

Close to 100 firms were visited to determine the strengths and weaknesses of the entire group of companies, so that regional needs could be assessed and services devised to offer assistance. MAP's initial mission was to assist the transition away from metalworking. But with 350 firms and 15,000 jobs remaining, a different focus emerged. The small firms that remained provided a link to the original strength of the city: its skill base. Could a regional strategy be developed that utilized this strength? Before this question could be answered, a paradox had to be addressed. The numerous plant closings suggested an overabundance of machinists in the region. But help-wanted ads in the newspapers suggested otherwise: The frequency of ads for machinists did not seem to change even as the Bosch plant shut its doors. Both demand for, and supply of, machinists were present but the market for them did not seem to close. What was going on?

The paradox was explained by a comparative survey of the skills of several hundred laid-off workers and those individuals employed in Springfield-area small shops (Forrant and Roditi 1987). The results are shown in Table 19.2.

Workers losing their jobs at the region's large companies were machine operators—they lacked the set up, blueprint-reading, and math skills required by the small precision shops. The small firms produced in small-lot sizes, which meant frequent setups, and small size meant training workers to set up and

Table 19.2   Likelihood of Having Certain Machinists' Skills (by percent of workers surveyed)

Skill	Small Firms	Large Firms
Operating at least three different machine tools	66%	20%
Setting up at least three different machine tools	47	14
Tool sharpening	47	20
Assembling parts from blueprints	35	16
Inspecting machine parts	60	28

SOURCE: R. Forrant and H. Roditi. 1987. "Disjuncture in the Hampden County metalworking labor market and what to do about it." Springfield, Mass.: Machine Actioon Project.

operate several machines. Flexibility was not an objective of the large firms, which specialized tasks and workers and minimized setups with long runs of the same product. The relative lack of investment by large firms in the skills of workers was further demonstrated by a MAP survey that compared employee-training rates for computer-numerical-controlled (CNC) machine tools: 21% of workers in small firms, as opposed to 3% of workers in large firms. The multiple skills demanded for flexible production by the small shops did not match the specialized skills of workers displaced by the large firms.

Training and Technical-Assistance Programs

On the basis of these findings, programs were put in place to prepare dislocated workers to assume positions in the smaller firms. At the same time, technical high schools altered their curricula to emphasize the teaching of setup skills.[10] The firm visits also revealed that while firms had purchased state-of-the-art, computer-controlled machine tools, most lacked the personnel to repair the equipment. This meant that when the machines failed, shops lost valuable production time waiting for the machine-tool firm to send out repair personnel. A training consortium was established by a dozen firms, the local technical college, and MAP, to design a curriculum for the repairing and installation of computer-controlled machinery. The course was made available in the evening to currently employed workers, and during the day to dislocated workers with either a machining or electronics background. The program trained over 100 workers in its first year.

However, MAP was not set up to become a permanent agency. Thus, during the Spring of 1993, MAP sought ways to merge its activities into a revitalized and upgraded local chapter of the National Tooling and Machining Association (NTMA). Together, MAP and the NTMA developed a proposal whereby they would join with the five largest state economic-development and training organizations, to put together a training and technical-assistance program for the region. From joint discussions, the Tooling and Machining Education, Training, and Technology Network was born.

While the NTMA is the financial entity responsible for the network, it is collaboratively administered and jointly funded by industry and several public sector partners, the most important being the Bay State Skills Corporation. Its stated mission is to improve the manufacturing capability of the hundreds of small and medium-sized metalworking firms dotting the Connecticut River Valley.[11] Day-to-day operations, hiring, and fiscal matters are handled by the executive committee of the 50-firm local chapter of the NTMA.

The network is an integral part of the local NTMA chapter's attempt to implement its mission statement: "to become an exclusive resource center for Western Massachusetts precision custom manufacturers by providing training, continual education, shared technology, marketing and networking, government activities and association services."

NTMA-sponsored programs include, first, an array of education opportunities for advancing metalworking skills of individuals and groups—including a 23–week, hands-on training program that prepares graduates for jobs in precision machine shops; evening skills-upgrading courses for managers and workers; and group workshops and seminars on topics such as International Standard 9001/2 on manufacturing-supplier classifications, how to survive defense downsizing, and how to identify new market opportunities. The courses are announced in a monthly newsletter mailed to over 400 machine shops.

A second service involves skill upgrading offered at the firm level. In 1994, 50 firms took advantage of a broad range of NTMA-sponsored workshops, seminars, and hands-on courses. The list of offerings included: CNC Milling; CNC Turning; Interpreting Engineering Drawings; Computer-Aided Design; Computer Machine Tool Programming; Technical Math; In-Process Work Flow Management; and ISO 9000.

Third, with state and federal financial assistance, the program offers in-plant technology assistance and modernization projects. Individual projects include the reorganization of the work flow on a plant's existing assembly line; the development of software to automate job orders; assistance in preparing a marketing strategy; and the reorganization of a product line into a manufacturing cell. Group projects include *kaizen* (continuous improvement) training; International Standard 9001; rapid prototyping; and a joint marketing program for the entire chapter. Each of these projects is approved by a five-person review team. To facilitate interfirm learning, companies have to agree to share the general results of their project. Firms are also required to underwrite half the total cost of these projects.

Six NTMA firms joined together in 1991 to establish MechTech, an innovative four-year apprenticeship program. MechTech is a nonprofit corporation that hires workers and assists them in achieving both an associate's degree in manufacturing technology and a toolmaker's apprenticeship. MechTech's students rotate through several shops over a four-year period, learning all aspects of the tooling and machining industry. In addition, they attend classes two evenings a week at Springfield Technical Community College.

MechTech pays participants' wages, benefits, and tuition and charts their progress in the shops. Participating firms envision program graduates as becoming the next generation of industry managers and owners. Member firms signed a contract whereby they agreed to rotate the students among the firms. This was a major hurdle to overcome since it raised shop owners' fears that someone would "steal" their manufacturing secrets or customers and give them to a competitor. However, for the apprenticeship to work, rotation was essential for providing students with hands-on exposure to the various aspects of the industry—no single small firm could do this. The shops have also agreed not to hire students until they have completed the program, no matter how badly they may need help. This bears out the participating firms' high level of commitment to training, since there is no guarantee that students will want to go to work at one of the MechTech firms.[12]

Sixteen firms have participated in drafting a strategic plan for the NTMA chapter. The plan is going to further raise the stakes, by determining how the chapter can provide technical services to members and become both a center for the promotion of advanced manufacturing technologies and a marketing arm for firms. This ambitious scope of work is a far cry from what had been the chapter's central function—namely, to run an entry-level training school. Bringing a strategic orientation to considerations of training and service programs also serves to link skill and industry awareness. Instead of the air of distrust that had divided worker from manager, and firm from firm, the various networking activities allow breathing space for personal integrity and concentrate the energies of industry leaders on developing services that advance industry capabilities.

The chapter is, in part, a social organization. But it has become much more. It is a vehicle for pursuing a skill-based strategy in a region that cannot compete on the basis of low cost. As illustrated in Figure 19.1, the chapter has assumed the lead role in rebuilding the skill and technical infrastructure of the region. The chapter is quite fortunate in having an active core of members interested in education and training; many of them completed an apprenticeship program themselves when they were younger. Their own career paths—from apprentice to skilled machinist, to firm owner—provide ample testimony as to the importance of education and training in sustaining an industry that depends on skill for its survival.[13]

More than an appreciation of education is involved in explaining the active participation of community elders in the development of industrywide education and skill-upgrading programs. These programs themselves provide structures so that people who, in their youth, benefited from the opportunity to plug into an industry can give something back to the industry in their older years. They do not want the industry to die—it is an issue of personal integrity for the older generation. With the establishment of networking agencies, industry-community members have the opportunity to be active participants in the shaping of their industry, an opportunity that was never made available in the large-firm era.

Both business organization and management roles are being redefined as firms move to skill-based and networking strategies. As we noted previously, the old management paradigm treated workers as a homogeneous factor of production that could be bought and sold in the marketplace, and worker skills as replaceable by high-tech machines. The elements of economic virtue—namely, personal integrity, skill development, and industry awareness—were ignored; consequently, economic performance, good and bad, was explained in terms that obscured the real forces driving production and competitiveness.

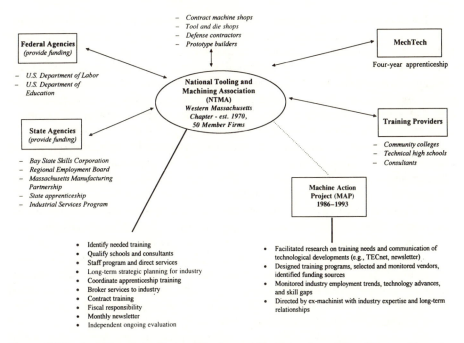

Figure 19.1 Activities of the National Tooling and Machining Association, Western Massachusetts chapter (350 firms).

Once more in the Springfield area, economic virtue is being fostered by an interfirm agency committed to shared skill development and technology diffusion. A constructive dynamic between economic virtue and business organization is emerging to replace the negative dynamic that led to the closing of all of the area's larger firms. The new dynamic taps the stock of stewardship of those in their late-career years (Arthur and Kram, 1989), but it is a stewardship directed toward regional, rather than corporate, welfare. The process is reinforced by the community's investment in transferable, rather than firm-specific, skills.

Dynamic Industrial Districts and Economic Virtue

The question is: Can the region be rearmed? We argue that rearming the region will depend, in part, on the refinement of an economic-development vision that accounts for cooperative activities of the type that restores economic virtue.

The new competitive dynamics create both challenges and opportunities for learning districts to develop as models of industrial organization. Success depends on being both innovative and productive. Product-led competition has increasingly pressed firms to reduce cycle times for existing products and new designs and to meet cost and quality standards. Meeting these more demanding performance standards requires that business enterprises organize according to the new principles of multiproduct flow (replacing a task-oriented layout with a process-oriented layout); project-driven, team-centered work organization; and process integration over local optimization. The new principles can be established within networked groups of firms or within a large, project-driven company. Examples of the former include the fashion-industry districts of northern Italy; and of the latter, 3M, Motorola, and Hewlett-Packard.

In the transition to the new competitive dynamics, small firms have an advantage: Many have not been organized into fragmented fiefdoms in which power and status are tied to control over occupational and departmental specialties. Cellular manufacturing and self-directed work teams can often be developed without the social inertia that is built into most big enterprises.

The challenge for the smaller enterprises is twofold: first, to convert the challenges of globalization and technical change into opportunities for establishing competitive advantage based on combining established skills with technical advances and world-class manufacturing practices; and second, to network with other specialist producers that are proactively addressing the challenge of the new competition. From this perspective, successful industrial development is about, in part, developing cooperative capabilities in a variety of forms, including teamwork within enterprises and networking across enterprises.

Firms, big and small, do not compete alone in the global economy, but as members of networked groups of firms. The networks are formal and informal vehicles for converting individual firms into interdependent groups or business systems capable of acting on shared interests.

Networks connect both firms specializing in complementary activities and firms cooperating to support common services offered by intermediary agencies. But networks are more than agents of coordination—they become part of a dynamic between interfirm and intrafirm organizations. The third dimension of economic virtue—industry awareness—is, in part, the link between networks and individuals. Networks assist the formation of industry awareness, and a group awareness that allows for a strategic assessment of a region's competitiveness against other regions. The strengths and weaknesses, and the obstacles and opportunities, of a regional group of enterprises can then become subjects of debate and, potentially, effective public policy to promote regional competitiveness.

Inadvertently, the armory, in the formative years of the Springfield metalworking district, played such a role, as an investor in skills, a coordinator of activities, and supplier of common services. In the big-firm era, firms became autarchic and, equally inadvertently, eroded economic virtue by eroding the infrastructural support of a common skill base and the goodwill between management and labor that had contributed to the diffusion of technical and organizational innovations in the earlier period. By failing to invest in worker skills or promote industry awareness, they further undermined community resources. The lack of industry awareness shown by both management and labor left the region without a vehicle for acting on shared concerns, such as requisites for sustaining a competitive metalworking region in a rapidly changing environment.

Developing the capabilities to network, manage joint projects, and articulate common needs is about establishing the common good in a world of interdependencies. A vibrant industrial community, like a healthy polity, is capable of defining and pursuing actions that advance the common good. To take the analogy a step further, a healthy polity depends on, draws from, and replenishes civic virtue; a healthy industrial district depends on, draws from, and replenishes economic virtue.

The argument is not that networking depends on trust or even personal integrity. Trust is not enough. In fact, the large corporation relied on trust—a trust that said "trust the corporation." In too many cases, this was not a trust based on mutual respect and shared understanding. While this may have worked in the past, it left many firms ill-equipped to compete against the new product-led competition that has emerged in recent decades.

The idea of economic virtue is one that locates trust within an interactive dynamic involving personal integrity, skill, and industry awareness. Industry awareness, as community consciousness, is distinct from loyalty to a single firm—as such, it reins in free-riding employees that receive the benefits of a company's investment in education but then move on to another firm, leaving the investing firm with the costs. There is indeed little free-riding limiting investment in worker skills in an industrial district. People want to be able to change jobs by moving across companies, but less so across communities.

The task of nurturing civic virtue is not a problem for networked groups of small firms alone. The failure of economic theory to account for economic virtue sustains a free-market ideology which ignores organizational capabilities both within and across enterprises. Such policies risk undermining the supply of economic virtue that is required to make not only industrial districts, but markets and bureaucracies, function. This risk is particularly acute in the case of skill generation and technology diffusion.

Conclusion

In this chapter, we have described a historically successful case of regional industrial development driven by a networked group of firms, which occurred before the time of organizationally based careers anchored in the corporate revolution. When Springfield earned the nickname "Industrial Beehive," it was a diversified manufacturing center with over 300 firms and thousands of skilled workers producing a variety of products.

While the Springfield metalworking region was never dominated by *Fortune* 500 enterprises, it did come to be dominated by firms with 1,000–2,000 employees for nearly a 50-year period. From the end of World War II through the late 1980s, the region lacked the technological-diffusion capacity of an earlier period, and its skill base dissipated. The decline of the larger enterprises has been followed by a new period in which business-and-government partnerships have sponsored industrial-community-building institutions in forms reminiscent of the earlier period. The boost in intrafirm and interfirm learning in Springfield in recent years has better prepared participating firms to take advantage of the opportunities afforded by the new competition and to, potentially, set in motion a new dynamic, between specialist firms and innovation networks, based on skill development and rapid technology diffusion.

Both in the past and the present, within the same locality, the idea of community-based careers has come alive. Hopefully, this time around, the concept of community-based careers, like that of industrial districts, can itself become a term that shapes both public discourse and institution building. Hopefully, too, the neglected elements of economic virtue concerned with personal integrity, skill development, and industry awareness can be restored. Springfield may well be privileged in having the resource of an industrial heritage that can be reclaimed.

ACKNOWLEDGMENTS: The authors would like to thank Michael Arthur, who, besides encouragement, left a major imprint on the organization and content of this chapter; and Roopa Majithia, for research and graphics assistance.

Notes

1. References to the Springfield armory are found in Best (1990); Deyrup (1948); Forrant (1994); Frisch (1972); Hounshell (1984); and Tull (1995).

2. Tull also explores a series of links in an emerging national system of innovation involving the U.S. Army's Ordnance and Engineering departments, national and armory testing labs, and experiments conducted at the armory. Teams of officers were sent to Europe as part of efforts by Presidents Adams and Jefferson to establish America's first engineering program at West Point, and, in Tull's words, "to visit cannon foundries, small arms manufactories, fortifications, etc., and purchase books, sample arms, maps and scientific instruments" (1995).

3. Hounshell points out that two keys to armory success were an early reliance on private arms contractors as a source of innovation, and for improvement in inspection methods; the region's reputation for quality work was enhanced as innovations in inspection methods spread to other shops (1984: 33–34, 44). Hounshell cites Deyrup (1948) for documentation of instances when the armory's patternmakers and skilled foundrymen made "castings of valuable machines developed by outside contractors."

4. The task of the Japanese hub, or "focal," factory has been to integrate design, engineering, and production in order to do product development (Fruin, 1992). Unlike the American model of big business, the Japanese model does not involve extensive vertical integration and internalization of parts, components, and subassemblies within a single firm or lead manufacturer.

5. The armory was not the only hub. By the 1870s, an industrial concentration had grown up around the Wason Car Manufacturing Company. Founded in 1846, Wason produced railroad cars for virtually every major rail line in the United States and exported to China, Brazil, Venezuela, and Canada. At its height in the 1870s, Wason employed close to 700 people. The Smith Carriage Company built carriages and wagons sold across the country and in Europe. In 1892 it built the body for the first gasoline-powered automobile built in the United States. In 1895 the first major U.S. automobile corporation, the Duryea Motor Wagon Company, turned out its first cars. The Knox Automobile Company and the Indian Motorcycle Company were also incorporated. Both firms were owned, in part, by the J. Stevens Arms and Tool Company, which built several of the production machines and tools for both companies. Other firms engaged in the development of many new processes and products. A cylindrical paper-making machine, built and operated by Ames and Company in 1822, revolutionized the industry. Also, envelopes, dictionaries, lawn mowers, elevators, and motorcycles were made in Springfield factories.

6. This section draws heavily from Forrant (1994), in which a full set of citations can be found.

7. Artman's report was based on information, gathered from close to 5,000 manufacturers, regarding methods of manufacturing, plant organization, and marketing strategies, and supplemented by federal manufacturing census data. It contains richly detailed analyses of the metalworking, machine-tool building, textile, leather, paper, printing and publishing, and wood and furniture industries.

8. While the emerging firms were not large by standards of big business, they were large by standards of metalworking and machine-making sectors, and many of the larger enterprises were bought and sold by *Fortune 500* companies. (For example, United Technologies purchased and eventually closed down American Bosch.)

9. Springfield, the largest city in the region, has a population of approximately 150,000. Together, the surrounding communities in the Connecticut River valley account for an additional 450,000. In that region, MAP determined there were close to 350 metalworking firms with a workforce of 15,000. For how firms interacted, see Forrant, Cann, McGraw (1991); and Forrant and Cann (1993). The 1993 study noted that the region's dependence on a few dominant companies in the slow-growth defense and minicomputer industries meant that "the links in the chain that supplied high skill/high wage work to small manufacturing firms have been weakened and in some cases broken" (p. 3).

10. MAP received a grant from the Massachusetts Department of Education, and used the funds to purchase a curriculum—developed by an industry trade group, the National Tooling and Machining Association—for five schools. Training was also provided to 20 instructors, to help them utilize both the new curriculum and to update them on the latest manufacturing technologies.

11. The network never came up with a formal name. It is currently directed by the western Massachusetts chapter of the National Tooling and Machining Association. The NTMA is a national organization of contract machine shops and has a membership of approximately 2,700 firms in 55 chapters.

12. MechTech's brochure describes the program this way: "MechTech's comprehensive training program equips apprentices/employees with skills necessary for challenging, rewarding, and limitless career opportunities. The unique industry rotation system provides greater exposure to equipment, techniques, and applications than any single training site could afford. It also develops human relations skills and an adaptability to varying working conditions."

13. The total budget for these ten projects is $128,000; the total cost to firms is $64,000.

References

Arthur, M. B., and K. E. Kram. 1989. "Reciprocity at work: The separate, yet inseparable possibilities for individual and organizational development." In M. B. Arthur; D.T. Hall; and B. S. Lawrence (eds.), *Handbook of Career Theory*, pp. 292–312. New York: Cambridge University Press.

Artman, C. 1930. *Industrial Structures of New England: Part I of the Commercial Survey of New England*. Washington, D.C.: Department of Commerce.

Best, M. H., and R. Forrant. In press. "Creating industrial capacity: Pentagon-led versus production-led industry strategies." In J. Michie and J. G. Smith (eds.), *Restoring Full Employment*. Cambridge, Eng.: University Press.

Best, M. H. 1990. *The New Competition*. Cambridge, Mass.: Harvard University Press.

Brusco, S. 1992. "Small firms and the provision of real services." In F. Pyke and W. Sengenberger (eds.), *Industrial Districts and Local Economic Regeneration*, pp. 177–197. Geneva: International Institute for Labour Studies.

Council of Economic Advisers. 1951. *The New England Economy: A Report to the President*. Washington, D.C.: Government Printing Office.

D'Amato, C. 1985. *Springfield—350 Years: A Pictorial History*. Charlottesville: University of Virginia Press.

Deyrup, F. J. 1948. "Arms makers of the Connecticut River valley: A regional study of the economic development of the small arms industry, 1798–1870." *Smith College Studies in History*, 33.

Forrant, R. 1994. "Skill was never enough: American Bosch, Local 206, and the decline of metalworking in Springfield, Massachusetts, 1900–1970." Ph.D. diss., University of Massachusetts.

Forrant, R., and E. Cann. 1993. "The demise of the Massachusetts defense connection." Springfield: Machine Action Project.

Forrant, R.; E. Cann; and K. McGraw. 1991. "Phoenix or dinosaur: A survey of western Massachusetts metalworking." Springfield: Machine Action Project.

Forrant, R., and H. Roditi. 1987. "Disjuncture in the Hampden County metalworking labor market and what to do about it." Springfield: Machine Action Project.

Frisch, M. 1972. *Town into City: Springfield, Massachusetts, and the Meaning of Community, 1840–1880*. Cambridge, Mass.: Harvard University Press.

Fruin, W. M. 1992. *The Japanese Enterprise System*. Oxford, Eng.: Oxford University Press.

Hounshell, D. 1984. *From the American System to Mass Production, 1800–1932*. Baltimore: Johns Hopkins University Press.

Malone, P. M. 1988. "Little kinks and devices at the Springfield Armory, 1892–1918." *Journal of the Society for Industrial Archeology*, 14 (1): 59–76.

Rosenberg, N. 1963. "Technological change in the machine tool industry, 1840–1910." *Journal of Economic History*, pp. 414–446.

Springfield Republican. 1936. October 25, p. 2c.

Tull, B. 1995. "The Springfield Armory as early industrial policy." Ph.D. diss., University of Massachusetts.

20

Occupations, Organizations, and Boundaryless Careers

PAMELA S. TOLBERT

It does not take a particularly perspicacious observer to note that industrial societies are characterized by a wide variety of work careers—careers that are linked to very different types of labor markets and employment relationships. These differences are denoted in contemporary research by an array of terms and associated acronyms—*firm internal labor markets* (FILMs), *occupational labor markets* (OLMs), *secondary labor markets* (SLMS), and so forth (see Althauser and Kalleberg 1981). Although such conceptual distinctions clearly imply variations in career patterns, the notion of *career,* nonetheless, has come to be strongly associated with a particular employment relationship—a relationship characterized by long-term employment with a single employer, and involving movement through a series of interconnected, and increasingly prestigious and powerful jobs arranged within a hierarchy.

The predisposition to identify careers, at least implicitly, with this type of employment may be partly a reflection of underlying cultural assumptions about effective forms of organizing work and, in particular, the acceptance of the ideal type of bureaucracy as an implicitly prescribed model for organization. So, for example, in his original articulation of this model, Weber (1947) attributed the success of bureaucracy as a contemporary form of organization, in part, to this employment structure. By offering individuals opportunities for upward mobility, contingent on demonstrated merit and performance, Weber argued, bureaucracies link individual success to the enterprise's success and are thereby able to effectively secure employees' commitment to the achievement of the enterprise's objectives (see also Barnard 1938; Simon 1945).[1]

Whatever the source, contemporary preoccupation with careers formed within the boundaries of a single firm or agency is reflected both in the psychologically oriented literature on careers and in the extensive literature in economics and sociology on internal labor markets. It's not clear, however, that lifetime, or even relatively long-term, employment with a single employer has ever been the dominant career pattern in the United States. Moreover, as this book has underscored, this type of career pattern appears to be in decline in this country, as firms increasingly seek to adapt to turbulent economic conditions through "externalization" (Pfeffer and Baron, 1988) and "flexible staffing" (Milkovich and Boudreau, 1994; Noe, Hollenbeck, Gerhart, and Wright, 1994).[2]

Thus, researchers recently have begun to give greater attention to the implications of boundaryless careers for individuals, organizations, and the larger society (Arthur, 1994). As others in this book and elsewhere have noted (e.g., Spilerman, 1977; Rosenfeld, 1992), the notion of a career, in its most fundamental form, denotes a sequence of jobs—a sequence that is patterned by what Braude (1975: 112) obliquely refers to as "some containing social structure." It is this patterning that distinguishes careers from simple job histories (Van Maanen and Barley, 1984). The modifier, *boundaryless,* as Arthur and Rousseau indicate in chapter 1, is intended to underscore the declining significance of organizations as a "containing social structure" that produces the patterning in job sequences.

But boundarylessness should not necessarily be interpreted to mean patternlessness. The central premise of this chapter is that, as organizations become less important in defining career pathways and boundaries, occupations will become increasingly *more* important. While occupational demarcations have always had a significant, albeit often unacknowledged, impact on individual career patterns, the significance of such demarcations for careers is likely to be heightened by current trends in employment relationships.

In this chapter, then, I review the sociological literature on occupational labor markets and on the structure of professional occupations, in an effort to shed light on a number of issues associated with occupationally based careers. Of specific concern are three questions: What kinds of job and occupational characteristics foster such careers? When occupations become the major locus of careers, what are the consequences for organizations? And finally, what are some of the key career-management issues for individuals pursuing occupationally based careers?

Historical Backdrop: Research on Occupations and Careers

Sociological research on occupations and careers was originally motivated by an interest in the way in which industrial systems of production shaped and reshaped social institutions and patterns of social relationships. Reflecting this concern, much of the early research on occupations consisted of rich ethnographic case studies of workers in a given occupation, as suggested by the titles of such books as *Saleslady* (Donovan, 1929); *Man on the Assembly Line* (Walker and Guest, 1952); *Men Who Manage* (Dalton, 1959); *Professional Soldier* (Janowitz, 1960); and *Wall Street Lawyer* (Smigel, 1964). Career processes—gaining entrance into an occupation, changing jobs and getting promoted, retiring from work—were examined in such studies as only one part of the larger research enterprise of understanding work and social relationships.

An alternative approach to the analysis of careers, although one that still reflected recognition of critical occupational influences, developed in the years following World War II, and focused on the probabilities and determinants of shifts between jobs and between occupations. Based on work histories of a sample of respondents surveyed in Ohio and in Oakland, California (Form and Miller, 1949; Lipset and Bendix, 1952a, 1952b; Lipset and Malm, 1955), early research in this vein explored differences among occupational groups in terms of patterns of occupational persistence, job tenure, and shifts among occupational categories.[3] General findings from the different studies were largely corroborative: They indicated that white-collar and skilled workers had much more stable careers (defined by continuous employment in a single occupation and with a single employer) than semiskilled and unskilled workers; that career shifts within manual, and within nonmanual, occupations were much more common than career shifts across the manual/nonmanual boundary (bridging occurred most often among respondents who were self-employed at some point in their careers); and that chances of upward mobility were affected both by respondents' own educational achievements and by the occupational status of their fathers.[4]

The latter finding served as an initial point of departure for a substantial body of research on the determinants of social mobility (e.g., Blau and Duncan, 1967) generated by sociologists throughout the 1960s and 1970s. Partially driven by the popularity of regression analysis, which was designed for use with continuous (not categorical) dependent variables, research on social mobility during this period focused primarily on quantitative measures of career attainments, such as earnings and occupational prestige; the central debates in the area centered on the relative importance of individuals' ascribed characteristics (for example, social class background) compared to achieved characteristics (such as level of education completed) as determinants of such career outcomes. The implication of earlier studies—that occupational categories were likely to be associated with qualitative boundaries to mobility (presumably due to occupationally specific knowledge of work content and particular skills)—was largely ignored.

However, studies by economists and sociologists in the 1970s (e.g., Doeringer and Piore, 1971; O'Connor, 1973; Edwards, Reich, and Gordon, 1975; Bibb and Form, 1977), predicated on the notion of separate and distinctively different labor markets in the United States, led to a renewed interest in structural economic divisions as determinants of individual career outcomes. In its most basic form, this research posits two different systems of employment relationships, each associated with correspondingly different labor markets and individual career patterns. In one system, jobs are arranged in ladders involving progressive skills, with well-defined ports of entry and, to varying degrees, points of intersection with other, higher-reaching ladders in an organization (Rosenbaum, 1984; Osterman, 1984; DiPrete and Soule, 1988). The career patterns, or movements of individuals between jobs, in such systems are comparatively orderly and predictable. In the other system, jobs are characterized as being largely unconnected, neither requiring nor providing specialized skills; and incumbents are typified by a relatively short organizational tenure and, presumably, disorderly, unpredictable job sequences. Although occupational differences are implicitly embedded in this sort of conceptualization of employment patterns, the specific independent effects of firm-based job definitions, occupational categories, and industrial boundaries on career processes and outcomes were often blurred and largely unexplored in analyses done in this tradition (Baron and Bielby, 1980).

Other problems and limitations of particular models of economic segmentation have been highlighted (Kalleberg and Sorensen, 1979; Zucker and Rosenstein, 1981), but the focus of this general line of work—on the effects of economic structures on career patterns—provided an important corrective to the severe neglect of such structures in much of the preceding work on social mobility. For our purposes, the notion of different types of labor markets provides a particularly useful point of departure for thinking about the nature of boundaryless careers.

Variations in Labor Markets and Career Patterns

The trend toward limited-term employment relationships and the changes in career patterns that accompany this trend reflect the response of many contemporary businesses to increasingly turbulent economic conditions. Greater levels of uncertainty in organizational operations, created by increased competition in product markets and rapid rates of change in core technologies, have led many firms to seek flexibility through the reduction of permanent employees and the increasing use of subcontractors or temporary employees (Carey and Hazelbaker, 1986; Swinnerton and Wial, 1995). Short-term, project-based employment has long been characteristic of some types of jobs and some occupational groups (e.g., construction workers, film crews and studio musicians, agricultural workers), but it appears that such employment arrangements are now being extended to a wider proportion of the workforce.

Some jobs and occupations appear to be more vulnerable to the transformation to contingent status than do others (Baron, Davis-Blake, and Bielby, 1986; Davis-Blake and Uzzi, 1992), but few appear to be completely immune (see Nelson, 1988; Belous, 1989; Feinstein, 1989; Williams, 1989; Magner, 1995). College faculty provide a good example of an occupational group in which the norm of long-term employment, made unusually explicit in the form of tenure contracts, is being eroded. In 1984, approximately 12% of all full-time faculty held "temporary" (nontenure-track) positions (American Association of University Professors 1986); by 1992, that figure had risen to nearly 20% (*1994 Almanac of Higher Education:* 65). In addition, over a third of 510 higher education institutions surveyed in 1992 indicated that the number of positions held by temporary faculty had increased since the previous year; less than 15% reported a drop. Similarly, a recent survey of the earnings of temporary workers included an array of occupational groups rarely thought of as being "temps," such as managers, computer systems analysts and scientists, engineers, and registered nurses (Williams, 1989).

Thus, the evidence suggests that a growing number of jobs and occupations are joining the ranks of those traditionally associated with boundaryless careers. However, relatively little attention has been given to the analysis of the conditions that affect the occurrence of such career patterns. Here, two conditions are considered: the level of human asset specificity associated with particular jobs; and the degree of codification of occupations.

Human Asset Specificity: Internal versus External Labor Markets

It may be useful to begin this section by considering the relationship between jobs and occupations. While specific positions (jobs) within firms are usually associated with particular occupations, the required skills and responsibilities assigned by different employers to a job can vary considerably within occupations. Thus, the duties and knowledge required of a waiter in a small pizza restaurant are only loosely related to those of a waiter in a large, four-star restaurant with a sophisticated and demanding clientele. Similarly, the job of an accountant in a small, local practice, that of a lower-level, junior member of an accounting department in an international business corporation, and that of a senior partner in an elite accounting firm differ markedly in the kinds of skills and knowledge required. A critical dimension along which jobs vary, in this respect, is the degree to which they involve human asset specificity—skills and knowledge that are unique to a firm, and/or that are required by a firm and are not readily available in the labor force (Williamson, 1981). As the foregoing examples are intended to illustrate, jobs may vary on this dimension independent of the status of the larger occupation with which they are identified.

The degree of human asset specificity usually serves as a critical determinant of whether or not a job is part of an internal labor market. The relatively high search and replacement costs for employees with a high level of human asset specificity make it rational for firms to create internal labor markets—a series of interlinked, progressively higher-status and higher-paying positions—to retain such individuals (Becker, 1957; Doeringer and Piore, 1971; Williamson, 1981). The way particular jobs are defined by employers, then, determines whether they are likely to be part of an internal or an external labor market.

Jobs that are part of internal labor markets are not, by definition, normally associated with boundaryless careers. But there are also distinctive differences among the career patterns associated with jobs in external labor markets. The existing literature on segmented labor markets suggests two distinctive career forms that could be described as boundaryless, in the sense of being characterized by relatively high rates of interfirm mobility. In one form, high rates of interfirm mobility are accompanied by low levels of interoccupational mobility; Althauser and Kalleberg (1981) identify this with occupational labor markets. The other form is characterized by high rates of both interfirm and interoccupational mobility; this form is most likely to be found in what have been labeled secondary labor markets. Thus, a key source of the differences between labor markets associated with boundaryless careers lies in the structure of occupations.[5]

Codification: Occupational versus Secondary Labor Markets

Occupations represent a particular type of social group, one whose major bonds are specifically economic (Weber, 1968: 342–345).[6] Pursuit of collective economic interests normally leads occupational groups to seek both broad and exclusive jurisdictions—that is, to claim, as the exclusive domain of group members, as wide an array of work activities as possible (Berlant, 1975). Exclusivity and breadth are, oftentimes, competing objectives: The broader the array of work activities an occupational group lays claim to, the more likely it is to become embroiled in jurisdictional disputes with other occupational groups that also seek to define the activities as part of *their* domain.

Abbott (1988), in an insightful analysis of relations among occupational groups, identifies three main loci of jurisdictional conflicts: the legal arena, public opinion, and the workplace. Successful assertion of jurisdictional claims in all three arenas entails what Bridges and Villemez (1991) refer to as *codification*. Drawing on Boisot and Child's (1988) usage, this term denotes the degree to which occupations are commonly identified with a clearly defined set of skills and knowledge, and with a distinctive set of tasks or problems to which these skills and knowledge are applied. It thus implies the existence of social understandings about the "bundles" of work activities for which an occupational-group member can and should be responsible. Bridges and Villemez argue that such understandings provide the crucial foundation of occupational labor markets, allowing "*both* prospective employers and prospective employees [to] know what they are getting into when hiring workers or accepting jobs" (Bridges and Villemez, 1991).[7]

What are the conditions that are associated with higher levels of codification? The literature on the development of professions provides some useful insights on this point (e.g., Caplow 1954; Goode 1957; Wilensky 1964; Cullen 1978). Key characteristics that have been identified with professional occupations include highly standardized education/training requirements; the existence of strong occupational associations; and strong member identification with the occupation. Whether these characteristics define critical differences between professional and nonprofessional occupations per se is moot (as is the general utility of this distinction; see Tolbert 1990), but quantitative evidence does suggest that these attributes distinguish importantly among occupations. An analysis of characteristics of over 250 occupations by Cullen (1978: 208–209) shows that the broad occupational categories of professional and technical workers, and of crafts and kindred workers, have consistently higher mean scores on these dimensions, as compared to other occupational groups. These two broad categories encompass a wide range of occupations—accountants, architects, dental hygienists, carpenters, brick and stone masons, shoe repairmen, tool and die operators, among others—but they are linked by virtue of having relatively well-defined work tasks and responsibilities, and requisite skill and knowledge bases (that is, by being highly codified).

The degree of occupational codification, in turn, is predicated on the ability of group members to develop a dominant paradigm (Kuhn, 1962)—that is, the ability to reach an internal consensus on a definition of relevant work activities and the application of appropriate work techniques and procedures for the occupational group. A second factor is the level of resources that can be mobilized from among group members and from other groups in society, resources that can be applied in influencing both public opinion, in general, and legislative bodies, in particular (Larson, 1977). Occupational groups are more likely to become highly codified, then, as the degree of self-conscious collective organization increases among the members, and as the level of resources that can be accessed by and from individual members increases. An extreme form of codification of occupations is represented by a legal monopoly, based on the provision of strong state sanctions that protect the occupational group's claims to work domains and practitioner requirements. When occupational groups are able to use such sanctions effectively to limit entry into the group, members' economic interests are likely to be advanced (Holen, 1965). But even in the absence of such sanctions, codification facilitates the employment of individuals with the appropriate occupational credentials, since those lacking such credentials are less likely to be seen as eligible candidates for particular work activities.

Occupational labor markets, then, rest on codification; secondary labor markets are most likely to contain jobs associated with occupations that are not highly codified. This is not intended, however, to imply that all jobs in less-codified occupations are in secondary labor markets. As suggested previously, the level of codification of the occupation and the degree of human asset specificity of particular jobs may vary independently. "Idiosyncratic jobs" (Miner, 1987, 1991), for example, are probably more likely to be found in less-codified occupations (such as sales or management), but may, nonetheless, be part of an internal labor market because they entail a high degree of human asset specificity.

In sum, jobs in secondary labor markets are likely to be characterized by general skills that are widely distributed in the population and to be in occupations that are less codified. Jobs in internal labor markets, on the other hand, may be drawn from highly codified or not very highly codified occupations, but are more likely to involve firm-specific and less widely distributed skills. As Bridges and Villemez's (1991) analysis indicates, it is quite possible that jobs associated with occupational labor markets will be found in internal labor markets (for example, professors, graphic designers, engineers); these markets are not necessarily mutually exclusive. Table 20.1 shows the implications of my argument concerning the effects of the codification of occupations and the level of asset specificity of jobs on forms of labor markets and associated career patterns.

Current trends in organization, and particularly the reduction of internal labor markets by many contemporary organizations that seek to increase flexibility through subcontracting and contingent employment, can be predicted to

Table 20.1 Types of Labor Markets, by Job and Occupational
Characteristics

Codification of Occupations	Human Asset Specificity Required by Jobs	
	High Degree	Low Degree
Highly codified	ILM/OLM[a]	OLM
Not highly codified	ILM	SLM[b]

[a] ILM: internal labor markets; OLM: occupational labor markets
[b] SLM: secondary labor markets

lead to the increasing codification of occupations, and to the increasing dominance of boundaryless careers via an expansion of occupational labor markets.

Expansion of Occupational Labor Markets and Boundaryless Careers

Greater use of contingent employees makes increasing codification of occupations advantageous from both employers' and employees' points of view (Bridges and Villemez, 1991). For employers, codification helps to define relevant skill packages for particular types of work, and provides preexisting standards (as defined by the occupational group) for evaluating the suitability of candidates for jobs. Possession of group-approved credentials provides some assurance that candidates do in fact have the requisite training and skills to carry out the jobs. Thus, codification contributes to the reduction of costs of recruitment for organizations—an important consideration when repeated rounds of hiring are at stake, as they are with the employment of contingent workers.

The use of existing occupational standards in the construction of jobs within organizations is one facet of what Barley and Tolbert (1991) have referred to as the "occupationalization" of organizations. Zucker (1991) also discusses some of the advantages that occupationalization provides for organizations in terms of internal performance evaluation. She argues that when judgments of work quality are an important component of performance evaluation, occupational members outside the firm generally provide information that is more thorough and more valuable than that obtained internally. Codification also provides advantage from an employee's standpoint. By ensuring that they have credentials and training that are deemed to be relevant for particular types of jobs, individuals can enhance their marketablity. Moreover, to the degree that occupational groups succeed in gaining control of entry requirements and standards of practice, both through influencing social definitions of appropriate credentials and training, and through shaping formal legislation on licensing and peer-review requirements, members of those occupational groups are likely to benefit from the existence of favorable supply/demand conditions.

Thus, there are a number of reasons to expect that the increased reliance on contingent employment arrangements, by both private firms and public agencies, will lead to the expansion of occupational labor markets. Such expansion rests, in large part, on the rate at which "communities of practice" develop and become institutionalized within occupations; this, in turn, will have implications for employers' management practices, as well as for employees' career-management strategies.

Implications for Occupational Communities

"Communities of practice"—individuals who actively share a core body of tacit knowledge that is necessary for the execution of concrete, everyday work tasks (Latour, 1986; Lave and Wenger, 1990; MacKenzie and Spinardi, 1995)—provide the foundation for occupations. Occupations become increasingly codified as a consequence of associational processes within communities of practice, as described by Van Maanen and Barley (1984), and of progressive recognition of common material interests among members (Larson, 1977; Berlant, 1975). It is such recognition that typically leads to the creation of some sort of organizational mechanism for pursuing collective interests—that is, a national association, or a set of cooperatively related associations. As I argued earlier, the existence of a strong association can be taken as an important indicator of codification.

Formal associations usually play a critical role in diffusing tacit knowledge among occupational-group members, both through providing opportunities for social contact among individuals, and through the creation of standardized education and training requirements. The latter task is often a highly contentious (albeit crucial) element of codification: It is bound up with adjudication of internal disputes among members over definition of task boundaries and appropriate techniques for conducting the tasks (Abbott 1988). Thus, for example, the American Medical Association succeeded in making allopathy (as opposed to the rival approach of homeopathy) the basis of medical treatment procedures through the standardization of medical education (Starr, 1982). (The AMA's drive for educational standardization was greatly aided by the widespread distribution of the "Flexner Report," a scathing review, based on a study funded by the Carnegie Foundation, of the state of medical education at the turn of the century.) More recently, association-led struggles to standardize occupational-training requirements similarly have been evinced in such emergent occupations as employee-assistance counseling (Osagie, 1995) and human-resource management (Ritzer and Trice, 1969).

Thus, contemporary changes in employment and career patterns set the stage for increasing codification of occupations; in response, many occupations are likely to witness increasing associational growth and activity, especially activity involving educational credentialing. Closer personal ties to other occupational-group members—created through participation in associations—in conjunction with more standardized training and educational backgrounds, can lay the foundation for the formation of stronger occupational identities for individuals. This, in turn, may have implications for effective work-design and reward systems.

Implications for Work-Design and Reward Systems

The literature on professionals in organizations offers a number of relevant and potentially important insights concerning the impact of occupationally based careers on employment relationships. A central debate in this literature revolves around the issue of whether there is an inherent conflict involving what Freidson (1971) terms "occupational versus administrative principles of control." This debate can be traced to a now-famous footnote by Talcott Parsons (1947), who, in translating Weber, pointed out that Weber's discussion of the bureaucratic organization appeared to conflate two very different sources of authority—one of which is based on the possession of expert knowledge in a particular substantive area; and the other, based on an individual's position in an organizational hierarchy. As Parsons points out, these are very different, and not necessarily compatible, bases on which assertions of authoritative control may rest.[8]

Thus, Freidson identified the occupational principle of control with general social deference to the judgments of members of particular occupational groups, based on the groups' successful claims to an exclusive body of knowledge and area of practice. In contrast, according to the administrative principle of control, responsibility for direction of work and coordination among interdependent workers is determined by individuals' positions in an organizational hierarchy; such authority, presumably, is based on beliefs about the superior knowledge of organizational operations and functioning that is possessed by individuals at given hierarchical levels.

Based on this distinction, early research often assumed that the employment of professionals in organizations inevitably resulted in high levels of conflict for organizations, and in work alienation for individual professionals. Kornhauser (1962), for example, in a study of scientists employed in industry identified four key issues on which professional/organizational conflicts frequently occurred: recruitment (professionals value technical competence, while managers value administrative potential); organization of work (professionals prefer same-discipline groups, while managers favor mixed task forces); assignment of group leadership (professionals choose individuals with high professional status as leaders, while managers choose individuals with a strong administrative orientation as leaders); and outcome of scientific research (professionals follow norms of research dissemination to colleagues, while managers tend to view findings as proprietary). Similar points of conflict have been documented in other research (e.g., Daniels 1969; Zahn 1969; Perrucci 1980).

However, research by Gouldner (1957) showed that significant variations in professionals' orientations toward their work could affect such conflict. His study of university faculty suggested that individuals he classified as cosmopolitans, those whose identification with their occupational group was much stronger than that with their university, were relatively more likely to experience conflict with the administration than were locals—individuals with a stronger loyalty to the local institution than to their occupation. Other studies, covering a range of occupations, have provided additional documentation of the variability in relative levels of occupational and organizational commitment among professional employees (Reissman, 1949; Friedlander, 1971; Aranya and Ferris, 1984; Gunz and Gunz,

1994). More recent studies, however, have called into question the assumed polarity of the cosmopolitans/locals distinction, suggesting that high levels of occupational commitment are, not incompatible with high levels of organizational commitment, and that these two forms of commitment are, in fact, positively correlated (Aranya and Ferris, 1984; Gunz and Gunz, 1994).

From a managerial perspective, these recent findings are promising, suggesting that contingent employment arrangements will not necessarily limit organizations' ability to attract employees who are both technically proficient and attentive to organizational rules and requirements. However, since mobility prospects for individuals in occupationally based careers are likely to be affected more by their standing and reputation in their occupational group than in a given organization, effective work design for people pursuing such careers will almost certainly have to take this into consideration. Organizational time horizons associated with boundaryless careers will affect the perceived value of acquiring skills and knowledge unique to the organization (Mannix and Loewenstein, 1993); employees are likely to be motivated most by work that permits the enhancement of occupationally valued skills. Thus, if tasks require the development of skills and knowledge that are unique to the organization, extra rewards or other forms of motivation may need to be associated with them if contingent employees are to be used effectively.

Similarly, potential conflict between professional and organizational bases of authority may be realized more frequently when employees have shorter-term employment horizons. The greater an individual's long-term career independence from a particular organization, the more likely he or she may be to resist control of work by those lacking specific occupational expertise, since their evaluations of performance are apt to be given less weight within the occupational community. This implies that effective management of such employees will require organizations to emphasize technical expertise and reputation in making hiring decisions about permanent employees, who will be responsible for supervising contingent employees.

This, in turn, may accelerate an existing trend toward the occupational segmentation already noted in some professions. Arguing against analysts who forecast widespread deprofessionalization as a consequence of the increasing employment of members of traditional professions (such as doctors and lawyers) by bureaucratic organizations (Haug, 1975; Toren, 1975; Rothman, 1984), Freidson (1984) points out that organizational employment in itself is not sufficient evidence of declining professional control of work, and that members of occupational groups considered to be professions are almost always under the direct supervision of members of the same group. He argues, instead, that bureaucratic employment is leading to changes in the internal organization of many professions, and, specifically, to the emergence of a more formalized stratum of administrative elite who serve as managers and supervisors of rank-and-file practitioners (see also Finlay 1983; Abbott 1988; Tolbert and Stern 1991). If Freidson's arguments are correct, selected members of occupational groups are likely to serve as increasingly important gatekeepers for long-term career success. This, in turn, has implications for strategies used by individuals in managing occupationally based careers.

Implications for Individual Career Strategies

Other chapters in this book detail the role of individual's characteristics in determining boundaryless careers (see the chapters in part IV, especially); thus, I will just touch on a few issues briefly. One implication of the preceding argument is that individuals' connections to occupational networks, and, particularly, to occupational members who serve as organizational gatekeepers, are likely to become increasingly important determinants of career outcomes. While the effect of social networks on job-search outcomes has long been recognized (Granovetter, 1974), extraorganizational networks, particularly occupational networks, are likely to be especially important to the development of boundaryless careers. Existing evidence that the educational institution from which an individual graduates has strong effects on career outcomes is consistent with this idea (Caplow and McGee, 1958; Crane, 1970; Judge, Cable, Boudreau, and Bretz, 1994). From the individual's standpoint, then, graduating from the "right" institution, and participating in occupational associations and other occupationally based social groups, may become increasingly important components of effective career-management strategies.

There is some evidence, however, suggesting that women and minorities have less access to network connections and are often less able to utilize the connections they have (Brass, 1985; Thomas, 1990; Burt, 1992). Ibarra (1992), for example, in a study of advertising managers and professionals found that men are most likely to have both affective and instrumental network ties to other men. Women exhibited a more differentiated pattern of network ties: They were more likely to have affective ties to other women, but to have instrumental ties to men. These findings are consistent with explanations emphasizing preferences for similar others, and with those emphasizing strategic status-seeking efforts in networks (since men are more likely to be in resource-controlling positions). Ibarra suggested that the differentiated patterns of ties among women resulted in weaker network connections, which in turn contributed to gender-based inequality in organizational power.

Relatedly, Burt (1992) found that weak ties were less advantageous for women than for men; women's mobility hinged on the existence of strong ties to strategic partners. The degree to which such findings support the blunt conclusion drawn by Brass (1985: 340)—that "encouraging women to form networks with other women . . . may be unnecessary or, at worst, nonproductive"—can be debated. However, they do suggest that women—and, by extension, members of other groups that are not socially dominant—need to give particularly careful thought to network relations and strategies in managing their careers.

One potentially positive effect of boundarylessness on individuals' careers may be the lessening of the frequently observed relationship between age and unfavorable mobility outcomes. The tendency for interfirm mobility to slow markedly as individuals age has been well documented (see Baker and Aldrich's discussion in chapter 8), and research examining the effects of such mobility on career outcomes (Spilerman, 1977; Kalleberg and Hudis, 1979; DiPrete and

Krecker, 1991) indicates a reason for this pattern: Changes in employers at later stages of an individual's life are often associated with income loss. However, while the evidence on late-career, interfirm, within-occupation job changes is limited, it suggests that such changes are less likely to have negative consequences when careers are occupationally based (Kalleberg and Hudis, 1979). Thus, age considerations per se (that is, as distinguished from other age-related factors, such as technical obsolescence) may be less of a career-management issue for those in boundaryless careers.

Conclusion

The central premise of this chapter is that a likely but unintentional consequence of employers' efforts to gain greater operational flexibility through the use of contingent employees will be the increased centrality of occupations as the primary loci of individual careers. Using this premise, I have considered how the changes in employment patterns, and a shift toward occupationally based careers, may produce changes in occupations, firms, and individual career strategies.

Occupations, in this scenario, assume an increasingly important role in defining work processes and arrangements within firms, as well as in allocating individuals to statuses within the system of societal stratification. For the use of contingent employees to be efficient, organizations must define work tasks in packages that can be readily parceled out to employees who have preexisting knowledge and skills relevant for such tasks. As occupations become more codified, they are likely to exert considerable influence on organizations' definitions of such packages, and on the definition of skills needed for particular types of work activities. In this context, members of a given occupational group are in the best position to assess the level of occupational qualifications possessed by individuals and, thus, are likely to serve as key agents in determining the suitability of candidates for contingent work.

These arguments point to the need for increased attention to research on processes through which occupations develop and change, and on the effects of occupational influences on both organizational and individual outcomes. Abbott's (1988) work offers important, trail-breaking insights on the first issue, but much empirical and theoretical work remains to be done in following up on these insights. Similarly, early work by Form and Miller (1949), and by Spilerman (1977), on the effects of occupations on individual career patterns offers promising leads for further research, but, to date, relatively little has been done to follow these leads. And as yet, very few studies have explicitly addressed the problem of how occupational developments influence organizational structures, and vice versa. (Studies by Jacoby [1985], and by Baron, Dobbin, and Jennings [1986], of the development of the field of human resource management represent two notable exceptions, and perhaps models for future work.) The most general implication of the occupational analysis presented here is that a full understanding of the rise and nature of boundaryless careers necessarily must rest on the concatenation of such lines of research.

ACKNOWLEDGMENTS: The helpful comments and suggestions that Michael Arthur, Peter Sherer, and John Van Maanen gave me on an initial draft of this chapter are very gratefully acknowledged.

Notes

1. While Weber was clearly aware of both organizational and social problems associated with bureaucracy, he nevertheless argued (1947: 337) that the bureaucratic form of organization was, "from a purely technical point of view, capable of attaining the highest degree of efficiency and is in this sense formally the most rational known means of carrying out imperative control over human beings. It is superior to any other form in precision, in stability, in the stringency of its discipline, and in its reliability."

2. There is a question about whether average employment tenure is, in fact, declining. For example, based on a comparison of the average length of tenure of workers in 1979 and 1988, Osterman (1992) concluded that tenure rates were basically stable over the 10-year period. Swinnerton and Wial (1995), on the other hand, using similar data for the period 1979 to 1991, but a different analytic approach, argued that a general decline in job stability had occurred during this period. This conclusion is consistent with evidence of a substantial increase in temporary employment during the 1980s (Feinstein, 1989; Williams, 1989). It's possible that increases in the average tenure of full-time employed workers may have occurred simultaneously with increases in layoffs and temporary employment, if employees with shorter tenures (regardless of age) were most likely to be laid off, and if firms tended to rehire laid-off employees as temporary workers. In the latter case, both firms' reports and employees' own reports of employment tenure could be problematic.

3. This work—and most work on occupations today—is based on some variant of the occupational schema first developed by Alba M. Edwards for the U.S. Census Bureau in the 1940s, which was aimed at grouping together occupations that "connoted a common life style and social characteristics" (Reissman, 1959: 145). His original set of categories included, in order of social ranking: professionals, proprietors/managers/officials, clerks/kindred workers, skilled workers/foremen, semiskilled workers, unskilled workers.

4. Unfortunately, these studies fail to provide information on the distribution of men and women among the respondents, consequently precluding inferences about possible gender effects on the findings. Later work that followed from these studies also often ignored sex differences, frequently relying only on samples of male employees.

5. Although most work on internal labor markets does not differentiate between forms of careers within organizations, a logical distinction could also be drawn among those involving movement across occupational boundaries and those that did not involve occupational shifts.

6. Van Maanen and Barley (1984) make a persuasive case for viewing occupations as communities—social groups bound together by a shared normative order and affective ties. However, while occupational groups often acquire communal qualities, members are connected, fundamentally, by a common market-exchange relationship, rather than by blood ties, geographic closeness, or other social factors.

7. It should be recognized that the concept of codification has a close connection to two other commonly used concepts in the sociological literature on organizations and occupations: institutionalization and professionalization. *Institutionalization* has been used to refer to the processes through which commonly held expectations of behavior and form are generated and take on a "rulelike status in social thought and action" (Meyer and Rowan, 1977: 341). The emphasis on social understandings as a crucial determinant of social action and outcomes is thus common to the concepts of institution-

alization and codification. The latter concept, as used here, at least, is a narrower one, referring specifically to processes involving creation and change in occupations. *Professionalization* is another term often used to describe evolutionary processes of occupations (Abbott, 1988), but carries with it the connotation of increasing occupational prestige and autonomy. The concept of codification lacks this latter connotation. Therefore, even at the risk of contributing to the unfortunate spread of multisyllabic turns in academia, I follow Bridges and Villemez's use of the term *codification* here.

8. Weber's neglect of this distinction may well stem from his reliance on the Prussian army as a prototypical bureaucratic organization. In the military, the overlap between individuals' expertise, in terms of knowledge of military strategy and tactics, and their hierarchical position is likely to be considerable.

References

Abbott, Andrew. 1988. *The System of Professions*. Chicago: University of Chicago Press.

Althauser, Robert, and Arne Kalleberg. 1981. "Firms, occupations and the structure of labor markets: A conceptual analysis." Pp. 119–152 in I. Berg (ed.), *Sociological Perspectives on Labor Markets*. New York: Academic Press.

American Association of University Professors. 1986. "Report on full-time non-tenure-track appointments." *Academe* 72 (July–August): 14a–19a.

Aranya, N., and K. R. Ferris. 1984. "A reexamination of accountants' organizational-professional conflict." *Accounting Review* 69: 1–15.

Arthur, Michael. 1994. "The boundaryless career: A new perspective for organizational inquiry." *Journal of Organizational Behavior* 15: 295–306.

Averitt, Robert. 1968. *Dual Economy: The Dynamics of American Industry Structure*. New York: Norton.

Barley, Stephen, and Pamela Tolbert. 1991. "Introduction: At the intersection of organizations and occupations." *Research in the Sociology of Organizations* 8: 1–13.

Barnard, Chester. 1938. *Functions of the Executive*. Cambridge, Mass.: Harvard University Press.

Baron, James, and William Bielby. 1980. "Bringing the firm back in: Stratification, segmentation and the organization of work." *American Sociological Review* 45: 737–765.

Baron, James; Alison Davis-Blake; and William Bielby. 1986. "The structure of opportunity: How promotion ladders vary within and among organizations." *Administrative Science Quarterly* 31: 248–273.

Baron, James; Frank Dobbin; and P. Devereaux Jennings. 1986. "War and peace: The evolution of modern personnel administration in U.S. industry." *American Journal of Sociology* 92: 250–283.

Becker, Gary. 1957. *Economics of Discrimination*. Chicago: University of Chicago Press.

Belous, Richard. "How human resource systems adjust to the shift toward contingent workers." *Monthly Labor Review* : 7–12.

Berlant, Jeffrey. 1975. *Profession and Monopoly*. Berkeley: University of California Press.

Bibb, Robert and William Form. 1977. "The effects of industrial, occupational and sex-stratification on wages in blue-collar markets." *Social Forces* 55: 974–996.

Blau, Peter, and Otis D. Duncan. 1967. *American Occupational Structure*. New York: Wiley.

Boisot, Max, and John Child. 1988. "The Iron Law of Fiefs: Bureaucratic failure and the problem of governance in the Chinese economic reforms." *Administrative Science Quarterly* 33: 507–527.

Brass, Daniel. 1985. "Men's and women's networks: A study of interaction patterns and influence in an organization." *Academy of Management Journal* 28: 327–343.

Braude, Louis. 1975. *Work and Workers: A Sociological Analysis.* New York: Praeger.

Bridges, William, and Wayne Villemez. 1991. "Employment relations and the labor market: Integrating institutional and market perspectives." *American Sociological Review* 56: 748–764.

Burt, Ronald. 1992. *Structural Holes: The Social Structure of Competition.* Cambridge Mass.: Harvard University Press.

Caplow, Theodore. 1954. *Sociology of Work.* New York: McGraw-Hill.

Caplow, Theodore, and Reece McGee. 1958. *The Academic Marketplace.* New York: Basic Books.

Carey, Max, and Kim Hazelbaker. 1986. "Employment growth in the temporary help industry." *Monthly Labor Review* (April): 37–44.

Chronicle of Higher Education. 1994. *1994 Almanac of Higher Education.* Chicago: University of Chicago Press.

Crane, Diana. 1970. "The academic marketplace revisited." *American Journal of Sociology* 70: 953–964.

Cullen, John. 1978. *The Structure of Professionalism.* New York: Petrocelli.

Dalton, Melville. 1959. *Men Who Manage.* New York: Wiley.

Daniels, Arlene. 1969. "The captive professional: bureaucratic limitations in the practice of military psychiatry." *Journal of Health and Social Behavior* 10: 255–265.

Davis-Blake, Alison, and Brian Uzzi. 1993. "Determinants of employment externalization: A study of temporary workers and independent contractors." *Administrative Science Quarterly* 38: 195–223.

DiPrete, Thomas, and Margaret Krecker. 1991. "Occupational linkages and job mobility within and across organizations." *Research in Social Stratification and Mobility* 10: 91–131.

DiPrete, Thomas, and William Soule. 1988. "Gender and promotion in segmented job-ladder systems." *American Sociological Review* 55: 757–773.

Doeringer, Peter, and Michael Piore. 1971. *Internal Labor Markets and Manpower Analysis.* Lexington, Mass.: Heath.

Donovan, Frances. 1929. *Saleslady.* Chicago: University of Chicago Press.

Edwards, Richard; Michael Reich; and David Gordon. 1975. *Labor Market Segmentation.* Lexington, Mass.; Heath.

Feinstein, Selwyn. 1989. "More small firms get help from rent-a-boss services." *Wall Street Journal* (January 25): B1.

Finlay, William. 1983. "One occupation, two labor markets: The case of longshore crane operators." *American Sociological Review* 48: 306–315.

Form, William, and Delbert Miller. 1949. "Occupational career pattern as a sociological instrument." *American Journal of Sociology* 54: 317–329.

Friedlander, Fred. 1971. "Performance and orientation structure of research scientists." *Organizational Behavior and Human Performance* 14: 169–183.

Freidson, Eliot. 1971. "Professions and the occupational principle." Pp. 199–238 in E. Freidson (ed.), *Professions and their Prospects.* Beverly Hills, Calif.: Sage.

———. 1984. "The changing nature of professional control." *Annual Review of Sociology* 10: 1–20.

Goode, William. 1957. "Community within a community." *American Sociological Review* 22: 194–200.

Gouldner, Alvin. 1957. "Cosmopolitans and locals: Toward an analysis of latent social roles, Part I." *Administrative Science Quarterly* 2: 281–305.

Granovetter, Mark. 1974. *Getting a Job: A Study of Contacts and Careers*. Cambridge Mass.: Harvard University Press.

Gunz, Hugh and Sarah Gunz. 1994. "Professional/organizational commitment and job satisfaction for employed lawyers." *Human Relations* 41: 801–827.

Haug, Marie. 1975. "The deprofessionalization of everyone?" *Sociological Focus* 3: 197–213.

Holen, Andrew. 1965. "Effects of professional licensing arrangements on interstate labor mobility and resource allocation." *Journal of Political Economy* 73: 492–498.

Ibarra, Herminia. 1992. "Homophily and differential returns: Sex differences in network structure and access in an advertising firm." *Administrative Science Quarterly* 37: 422–447.

Jacoby, Sanford. 1985. *Employing Bureaucracy*. New York: Columbia University Press.

Janowitz, Morris. 1960. *Professional Soldier: A Social and Political Portrait*. New York: Free Press.

Judge, Timothy; Daniel Cable; John Boudreau; and Robert Bretz. 1994. "An empirical investigation of determinants of executive career success." Working paper 94-08, Center for Advanced Human Resource Studies, School of Industrial Relations, Cornell University.

Kalleberg, Arne, and Paula Hudis. 1979. "Wage change in the late career: A model for the outcomes of job sequences." *Social Science Research* 8: 16–40.

Kalleberg, Arne, and Aage Sorensen. 1979. "The sociology of labor markets." *Annual Review of Sociology* 5: 351–379. Palo Alto, Calif.: Annual Reviews.

Kornhauser, William. 1962. *Scientists in Industry: Conflict and Accommodation*. Berkeley: University of California Press.

Kuhn, Thomas. 1962. *The Structure of Scientific Revolutions*. Chicago: University of Chicago Press.

Larson, Megali. 1977. *The Rise of Professionalism*. Berkeley: University of California Press.

Latour, Bruno. 1986. "Visualization and cognition: Thinking with eyes and hands." *Knowledge and Society* 6: 1–40.

Lave, J., and E. Wenger. 1990. *Situated Learnings: Legitimate Peripheral Participation*. New York: Cambridge University Press.

Lipset, Seymour, and Reinhard Bendix. 1952a. "Social mobility and occupational career patterns: Stability of jobholding." *American Journal of Sociology* 57: 366–374.

———. 1952b. "Social mobility and occupational career patterns: Social mobility." *American Journal of Sociology* 57: 494–504.

Lipset, Seymour, and F. Theodore Malm. 1955. "First jobs and career patterns." *American Journal of Economics and Sociology* 14: 247–261.

MacKenzie, Donald, and Graham Spinardi. 1995. "Tacit knowledge, weapons design and the uninvention of nuclear weapons." *American Journal of Sociology* 101: 44–99.

Magner, Denise. 1995. "Tenure re-examined." *Chronicle of Higher Education* (March 31): A17.

Mannix, Elizabeth, and George Loewenstein. 1993. "Managerial time horizons and interfirm mobility: An experimental investigation." *Organizational Behavior and Human Decision Processes* 56: 266–284.

Meyer, John, and Brian Rowan. 1977. "Institutionalized organizations: Formal structure as myth and ceremony." *American Journal of Sociology* 83: 340–363.

Milkovich, George, and John Boudreau. 1994. *Human Resource Management*. Burr Ridge, Ill.: Irwin.

Miner, Anne. 1987. "Idiosyncratic jobs in formalized organizations." *Administrative Science Quarterly* 32: 327–351.

———. 1991. "Organizational evolution and the social ecology of jobs." *American Sociological Review* 56: 772–785.

Nelson, Robert. 1988. *Partners with Power*. Berkeley: University of California Press.

Noe, R. A.; J. R. Hollenbeck; B. Gerhart; and P. M. Wright. 1994. *Human Resource Management: Gaining a Competitive Advantage*. Burr Ridge, Ill.: Irwin.

O'Connor, James. 1973. *Fiscal Crisis of the State*. New York: St. Martin's.

Osagie, Sylvester. 1995. "Processes of occupational emergence: A study of employee assistance." Unpublished manuscript, School of Industrial and Labor Relations, Cornell University.

Osterman, Paul. 1984. "White-collar internal labor markets." Pp. 163–189 in P. Osterman (ed.), *Internal Labor Markets*. Cambridge: MIT Press.

———. 1992. "Internal labor markets in a changing environment: Models as evidence." Pp. 273–208 in D. Lewin; O. Mitchell; and P. Sherer (eds.), *Research Frontiers in Industrial Relations and Human Resources*. Madison, Wis.: Industrial Relations Research Association.

Parsons, Talcott. 1947. "Introduction." In M. Weber, *Theory of Social and Economic Organization*. New York: Oxford University Press.

Perrucci, Robert. 1980. "Whistle-blowing: Professionals' resistance to organizational authority." *Social Problems* 28: 149–164.

Pfeffer, Jeffrey, and James Baron. 1988. "Taking the workers back out: Recent trends in the structuring of employment." *Research in Organizational Behavior* 10: 257–303. Greenwich, Conn.: JAI Press.

Reissman, Leonard. 1949. "A study of role conception in bureaucracy." *Social Forces* 27: 305–310.

———. 1959. *Class in American Society*. New York: Free Press.

Ritzer, George, and Harrison Trice. 1969. *An Occupation in Conflict: A Study of the Personnel Manager*. Ithaca, N.Y.: ILR Press.

Rosenbaum, James. 1984. *Career Mobility in a Corporate Hierarchy*. New York: Academic Press.

Rosenfeld, Rachel. 1992. "Job mobility and career processes." *Annual Review of Sociology* 18: 39–61.

Rothman, Robert. 1984. "Deprofessionalization: The case of law in America." *Work and Occupations* 11: 183–206.

Simon, Herbert. 1945. *Administrative Behavior*. New York: Free Press.

Smigel, Ernest. 1964. *Wall Street Lawyer: Professional Organizational Man?* New York: Free Press.

Spilerman, Seymour. 1977. "Careers, labor market structure and socioeconomic achievement." *American Journal of Sociology* 83: 551–593.

Starr, Paul. 1982. *Social Transformation of American Medicine*. New York: Basic Books.

Swinnerton, Kenneth, and Howard Wial. 1995. "Is job stability declining in the U.S. economy?" *Industrial and Labor Relations Review* 48: 293–304.

Thomas, David. 1990. "The impact of race on managers' experiences of developmental relationships." *Journal of Organizational Behavior* 11: 479–492.

Tolbert, Pamela. 1990. Review of Andrew Abbott's *The System of Professions*. *Administrative Science Quarterly* 35: 217–218.

Tolbert, Pamela, and Robert Stern. 1991. "Organizations and professions: Governance structures in large law firms." *Research in the Sociology of Organizations* 8: 97–118.

Toren, Nina. 1975. "Deprofessionalization and its sources." *Sociology of Work and Occupations* 2: 323–337.

Van Maanen, John, and Stephen Barley. 1984. "Occupational communities: Culture and control in organizations." *Research in Organizational Behavior* 6: 287–365.

Walker, Charles, and Avery Guest. 1952. *Man on the Assembly Line.* Cambridge, Mass.: Harvard University Press.

Weber, Max. 1947. *Theory of Social and Economic Organization.* New York: Oxford University Press.

———. 1968. *Economy and Society: An Outline of Interpretive Sociology.* New York: Bedminister Press.

Wilensky, Harold. 1964. "The professionalization of everyone?" *American Journal of Sociology* 70: 137–158.

Williams, Harry. 1989. "What temporary workers earn: Findings from new BLS survey." *Monthly Labor Review* (March): 3–6.

Williamson, Oliver. 1981. "The economics of organizations: The transaction-cost approach." *American Journal of Sociology* 83: 548–577.

Zahn, Gordon. 1969. *The Military Chaplaincy: A Study of Role Tension in the Royal Air Force.* Toronto: University of Toronto Press.

Zucker, Lynne. 1991. "Markets for bureaucratic authority and control: Information quality in professions and services." *Research in the Sociology of Organizations* 8: 157–190.

Zucker, Lynne, and Carolyn Rosenstein. 1981. "Taxonomies of institutional structure: Dual economy reconsidered." *American Sociological Review* 46: 860–884.

21

Moving In, Up, or Out: Tournaments and Other Institutional Signals of Career Attainments

JAMES E. ROSENBAUM AND
SHAZIA RAFIULLAH MILLER

The End of the Company Man

The company man, if not entirely extinct, is a rapidly dying species. As with many endangered species, his environment has changed and become inhospitable, and a new species, more adaptive to the changed environment, is taking his place. This person is known as the mobile worker, and the environment is the boundaryless career. Mobile workers identify themselves by the skills and positions they have achieved, not by their affiliation with a particular institution. Their careers are delineated not by the traditional constraints of an institution, but only by their ability to navigate the new boundaryless terrain. While the old company man moved up the company ladder, mobile workers move up any ladders onto which they can get a foot. They rise in their careers by hopping from firm to firm, with an eye toward ever-better positions, and the firms which employ them often benefit by gaining ambitious employees who bring new ideas, creativity, and the enthusiasm of new blood.

Yet for mobile workers to succeed, and for firms to take full advantage of this type of employee, workers must get credit for their past achievements, and firms must be able to recognize applicants' achievements. The boundaryless career depends on effective signals—dependable information about the type and quality of work individuals have done in the past

Unfortunately, individuals are turning into mobile workers faster than employers are developing ways to create and manage the signals required. In spite of the great need involved when bringing in (hiring), moving up (promoting), and moving out (terminating) employees, institutions do not provide easily readable signals about how individuals are doing. Firms expect to hire qualified employees, but they often do not get good information to use in making hiring decisions. While firms expect to base promotions on dependable information, promotion committees often use distorted information. Firms expect terminated employees to sell themselves on the labor market, but these employees often have difficulty informing potential employers about their past achievements.

Overall, firms do not give or receive good information about individuals' capabilities, and, as a result, firms' decisions are flawed and their employees fail to get recognition for their past achievements. Because firms lack the capability of conveying good signals about employees' value, both firms and individuals fail to realize the full benefits of the new mobility. When the mobile worker is unable to get credit for past accomplishments, this failure casts a pall over the morale of other workers, which reduces commitment. Hiring firms, in turn, suffer as they are unable to assess job applicants on their merits or deficiencies. Society also suffers an efficiency loss when individuals and institutions are unable to coordinate the best fit between employee and job (Spence, 1974; Wanous, 1980; Stumpf, 1981).

Our chapter arises from a recent study of employer hiring practices. First, we found that employers have many complaints about the capabilities of their job applicants and of those they hired. Second, many employers fail to give clear signals to candidates about how to prepare and whether to apply, because they are reluctant to state formal selection criteria. Third, many applicants have difficulty demonstrating their value to potential employers, because their previous institutions failed to give them relevant signals about their value. Fourth, institutions which do not provide relevant signals find a decline in the motivation and commitment of their members. While these observations come from a study of hiring, this chapter will show their relevance to promotions and outplacement. We will also describe some new efforts that have been used to improve the signaling process, thereby enabling firms and society to benefit more fully from the potential of the mobile worker.

Why Individuals, Firms, and Society Need Strong Signals

Americans strongly believe individuals are responsible for their own destiny. This belief formerly applied to finding a job and succeeding in it; it now also applies to keeping one's resume current, knowing when to leave, and knowing how to find the next job. It is evident in the oceans of self-help books on how to succeed. Even more penetrating analyses, such as Paul Hirsch's *Pack Your Own Parachute* (1987), resort to individualistic approaches when it comes to recommending practical actions and describing how individuals can package themselves to be desirable to future employers. While this advice is certainly valuable, it does not address the larger contextual difficulties that make it difficult for individuals to present prospective employers with trustworthy information on their own merits.

Job seekers' primary obstacle is a lack of credible information about their achievements. Most rely on resumes, but as comedian Dave Barry (1986) observes, "Your resume is more than just a piece of paper: it is a piece of paper with lies written all over it." Resumes are job seekers' main method for describing their performance and abilities, yet as Barry points out, they are not particularly trustworthy and, thus, not always effective.

Thus, while individuals are responsible for making their own careers, their ability to do so depends on whether the infrastructure enables them to convey their experience and accomplishments in a trustworthy manner. Moreover, as labor-market theory suggests, their ability to do so has important implications for individuals, firms, and society as a whole.

Obviously, individuals must convey trustworthy information about their accomplishments in order to get jobs that build on their previous experience. Past employers can present this information more convincingly than individuals, but they do not usually do so. Firms rarely provide other employers with any information on past employees that goes beyond neutral statements indicating starting and ending dates, salary, and title. Moreover, the information firms do provide is hard to interpret. While companies mark employees with a wide range of signals of their value, the diversity across different firms results in a mixture of titles and levels that means very little outside the company. At one institution, becoming vice president is a major achievement, the result of hard and innovative work, while at others, it comes from longevity and is a position held by many. An operations engineer can be responsible for directing multimillion-dollar operations or for lubricating a few machines. Individuals who have held demanding positions need to be able to convey the value of their achievements if they are to be appropriately placed in the next job; they need their prospective firm to understand the language of value used by their old firm, in order to retain their earned status.

Firms also need strong signals to recognize individuals' value. As this chapter will show, firms need signals in order to hire the most capable applicants, to decide on promotions, and to preserve morale during downsizing.

In an increasingly competitive world economy, society as a whole also needs strong signals to make maximum use of its human capital and not waste it through mismatched jobs and employees. Yet while the supply of human skills is increasingly provided by one set of institutions and used by another, there remains little incentive for a provider to give trustworthy signals to a potential user. This has long been true of the training provided in schools, and it is increasingly true of workers' employment experiences as job mobility increases. Schools rarely focus on how to provide good signals to employers, and firms do so even less. When employers fail to detect and make use of workers' previously acquired skills, employers and society lose the benefits of previous investments.

While economic theory recognizes the crucial need for information, in practice it is often ignored. For example, an economics research firm recently bragged about the efficiency of its travel budget procedure: It gave invited visitors a fixed amount for travel expenses and let them make their own decisions about how to spend it. Unfortunately, this group of economists did not tell recipients the rules until the end of the visit; consequently, the system did not affect anyone's decisions. Similarly, as we note below, employers rarely communicate their hiring and promotion criteria, so individuals often fail to prepare for the specific demands of desirable jobs. Society and firms lose by facing ill-prepared candidates and having insufficient information for identifying the most appropriate candidates. The lack of good information is clearly a serious barrier to making the best use of the mobile worker's boundaryless career.

Human Capital Theory and the Tournament: Traditional Signals

The need for signals within the occupational structure first developed from a critique of human capital theory. Human capital theory suggests that individuals are hired and promoted on their skills and experience (Becker, 1962). However, the theory assumes that employers get perfectly credible information about an individual's human capital. While the expected output of a piece of machinery is easily measured, people's capabilities are not. Signaling theory recognizes that "information is a valuable resource" (Stigler, 1961: 213); and, as with other resources, economic decisions must be made about the cost-effectiveness of alternatives. Since obtaining information about applicants' true human capital is costly, employers resort to "signals"—indicators of individuals' value that are easily obtained (Arrow, 1973; Spence, 1974).

The resume is one such inexpensive source of information; however, as comedian Barry warned, resumes give hard-to-interpret information that cannot always be trusted. It is not surprising, then, that employers have often wanted other signals of a person's value when making hiring and promotion decisions. In the era of the company man, companies made their judgments about individuals' value by gauging their past success in their career history (Kanter, 1977; Lawrence, 1987). One model of this process—the tournament model—suggests that individuals are assessed according to the speed by which they advance in a promotion-based hierarchy, with "fast risers" being seen as having more ability than those who advance more slowly (Rosenbaum, 1979, 1984). Thus, managers essentially use an age of employees-by-position matrix to assess whether one has moved up faster or slower than average, which, in turn, is used to signal one's ability to progress further.

Inferring ability from one's previous mobility is not an entirely arbitrary one. A selection early in a career is a sign of one's ability. In addition, early selection also allows individuals to receive new training and experiences that increase their capabilities. Thus, even if tournaments sometimes overlook some good people, reaching down to someone who was overlooked earlier would ignore the experience accumulated by early winners. The "rich get richer" because their early wins give them increased experience and training. As a result, the tournament essentially creates a shorthand for managers to identify their rising stars.

The tournament model continues to have relevance even in the era of the mobile worker. Employers can still partially rely on promotion histories to assess the worth of potential employees. However, the vast differences in the meanings of various titles across companies and the unreliability of the sources make this method much more difficult to use across institutions than within them.

Moreover, in spite of a roughly meritocratic logic, the tournament is highly troubling in that opportunities are limited on the basis of crude indicators of merit that have serious defects. In particular, if an individual fails to rise for any reason, the failure is attributed to a low level of ability. The most obvious victims of such faulty inferences are the large numbers of employed women. While the speed of a career trajectory might be informative for a man with few responsibilities at home, it is far less informative for a woman (or man) who have taken time off to care for children or elderly parents. Arriving at a midmanagement post by age 35 might be considered slow for a person working consistently since age 22, but be considered rapid for a person who had taken five years off for child rearing. Indeed, the current concern about locating social practices that create the "glass ceiling" in the country-club locker room ignores the ways that tournament inferences devalue women's careers by evaluating them on the basis of artificial timetables. In addition, the tournament system penalizes late entrants to the competition—an increasing problem as a growing number of people change jobs and careers. The remedy for these defects is to create better signals of ability to replace the crude ones currently being used.

How Employers Currently Use Signals

In this section, we will describe three domains in which signals can be institutionalized. First, hiring—can firms devise hiring procedures so that they receive better signals of applicants' human capital? Second, promotions—can firms institutionalize signals that can be better used inside the firm? Third, terminations and voluntary exits—can firms devise procedures that give employees better signals of their human capital and accomplishments? We will note how these challenges have been handled in the past and show that the old functions of human-resource departments (training and counseling) are not enough and suggest some appropriate reforms.

Hiring

As we noted, firms need to receive strong signals about candidates in order to make good hiring decisions, and it is hard to get good information from resumes or from previous employers. Firms also need to send good signals about their hiring needs and requirements in order to encourage people to become appropriately prepared, and to allow applicants to determine for themselves whether they qualify for jobs, thereby saving both individuals and firms from wasting time on unpromising interviews in cases where basic qualifications are not met.

A good way to understand how employers actually use signals is to study their hiring of recent high-school graduates. The skills demanded by nonexempt jobs (open to outsiders) are relatively easy to assess, and by focusing on the pool of new high school graduates, we can examine the influence of schools' formal evaluations (transcripts) in the hiring process.

Human capital theory assumes that employers have no difficulty in identifying applicants' human capital and in getting adequate workers. However, employers' needs are not being met, and many employers lament the poor academic skills of high school graduates (National Academy of Sciences, 1984). In interviews with a sample of 51 employers, in Chicago and its western suburbs about their hiring practices, many employers report that they waste a lot of time in interviewing people who are not even close to meeting their needs.[1] Others note that they make many mistakes when hiring employees without the skills or traits required. They report having new hires with serious reading, writing, and math deficiencies, including a stockroom worker who did not understand decimals, secretaries who could not spell simple words, and production workers who could not use a ruler. They note that employees often fail to come to work, come late, show poor cooperation with supervisors and coworkers, and fail to complete assigned tasks. Their complaints imply that they could improve their selections and better meet the needs of their workplaces, if they could get signals of applicants' academic skills and work habits, and if they could transmit signals to potential applicants about how to prepare for their jobs.

However, despite these complaints, employers rarely use the grades of new high school graduates in making hiring or pay decisions (Crain, 1984; Bills, 1988; Bishop, 1989; Rosenbaum and Kariya, 1991). Our study found that employers hiring for jobs in manufacturing, transportation, and business/office occupations are reluctant to use formal selection criteria. They do not like being bound by formal systems or requirements, and they are more comfortable trusting their "gut feelings" in brief interviews (Rosenbaum and Binder, 1994). They are particularly skeptical about information from schools, including transcripts which are readily available and used by colleges. Employers say that school transcripts and other information are not relevant to work, and many believe teachers evaluate students on irrelevant criteria. Similarly, a 1994 survey of all of the public high schools in Delaware found that, although Delaware employers hire thousands of recent high-school graduates, "few bother to look at records of attendance and punctuality or find out how well applicants have done academically" (Hill, 1995).

Thus, while employers suffer when applicants have poor academic skills, they fail to acquire information that would improve their selections, and they fail to inform students that they want applicants with better academic skills. Because of their reluctance to state formal procedures, employers are forced to interview large numbers of applicants who do not meet minimum requirements, and who did not realize how they could have prepared for employment. Lacking good signals from schools, employers must rely on less-reliable information from resumes and short interviews. However, while those who conduct employment interviews often have great confidence in their powers of insight, it has long been known that such interviews are notoriously bad predictors of subsequent performance (Campbell et al., 1970). Indeed, some employers are aware that they waste a lot of time in interviewing unqualified applicants, and that they still make many mistakes.

At the same time that employers complain that high school graduates often cannot write, spell, do basic math and that they are often absent, late, lazy, and uncooperative, few employers hire based on school information such as attendance, tardiness, grades, or teachers' recommendations. While school information has limitations, it is likely that math grades convey information about math skills, and that school attendance records and deportment ratings might help employers predict which individuals will have good attendance records and cooperative attitudes at work. As some employers admit that 15-minute interviews do not enable them to predict applicants' levels of effort or cooperation, they might get more reliable information from teachers' impressions from one or more school years. This same set of information is used to convey information to colleges about students' skills and efforts; yet employers fail to utilize such potentially pertinent information. The breakdown in the transfer of information prevents the labor market from functioning efficiently.

Moreover, these employer actions undermine the effectiveness of schools in preparing future workers and in providing employers with useful information. Because employers rarely use information from schools, school staff do not believe they can help students get jobs. In interviews with school counselors, we found that while they spend considerable time in providing information to colleges, they view employers as not interested in school information (Rosenbaum, Miller, and Krei, 1995). Even some vocational teachers believe this and do not try to provide signals about their students to employers (Rosenbaum and Jones, 1995).

A high school's failure to serve employers may affect the operation of the high school itself. The poor motivation of work-bound students is a major problem in schools. Staff often blame students' poor motivation on a deficiency in their personalities; yet this may not be the whole explanation. If schools do not provide relevant signals to employers, then work-bound students will see little reason to work hard in school (Stinchcombe, 1965). Students who feel the school is not helping their future opportunities exert less effort (Rosenbaum and Nelson, 1994) and have lower levels of achievement (Mickelson, 1990). When asked what incentives a school offers for work-bound students to get good grades, teachers and counselors could not identify any reason for students to get grades above the minimum needed to pass. One teacher noted that when a student was offered a chance to improve from a just-passing grade to a better grade, the student replied, "Why would I want to do that?" The teacher had no answer. While it is possible that some youths have motivational deficiencies, it is hard to identify motivational deficiencies if schools offer no incentives.

In contrast, in Japan and Germany, students have clear incentives for school efforts (Hamilton, 1990; Rosenbaum and Kariya, 1991). These countries have strong and trusted relationships between schools and employers, and students' grades affect the jobs they get after graduation. As a result, students in Japan and Germany work hard in school, and the level of academic achievement of work-bound youths in these countries is much higher than that of their counterparts in the United States (Rosenbaum, 1992).

However, we discovered that some American employers have long-term relationships with one vocational teacher or a few (Rosenbaum and Jones, 1995). In these relationships, employers trust teachers to recommend qualified students, and they are rarely disappointed with the results. Because these teachers value their relationships with employers, employers can be confident that teachers will not jeopardize their long-term relationships by recommending a poorly qualified student. Therefore, employers usually hired students strongly recommended by these teachers. About one-quarter of the vocational teachers we interviewed reported having such relationships, and, like employers, they report that these relationships offer them a chance to help a promising student find a job. The teachers confirmed that they would never jeopardize their relationship with an employer by recommending a poorly qualified student, because they would lose the opportunity to help future students.

These findings suggest several conclusions. First, despite their strong complaints about applicants' academic skills, many employers avoid using selection criteria relevant to their complaints. Second, school staff, by failing to offer useful signals about their work-bound students, also failed to motivate these students. Third, the fact that a few employers had found informal ways to get useful information suggests that useful information does exist in schools; that this information comes from trusted relationships with teachers, rather than from schools, suggests that in the more individualistic United States, it is easier to construct interpersonal, rather than institutionalized, transfers of trusted information. Fourth, the lack of a trusted method of transferring information on human capital from one institution to another can result in unmotivated, uninvolved individuals, a threat for both schools and companies.

The information on how employers hire experienced employees is more limited, but it also suggests a failure in the flow of information between institutions. High schools are rarely used as sources of experienced employees; employers prefer to recruit from other employers (Bureau of National Affairs, 1979). However, the information that they get from other companies, and from applicants themselves, is inadequate, and many firms feel the need to use company-administered tests in the hiring process (Arvey, 1979; Cascio and Silbey, 1978). The research has not, however, focused on how many employers have strong conviction about these tests. Research has also not addressed the question of how many employers tell applicants what skills are required to pass their tests and get jobs in their firms. The literature notes clearly that the imperfect flow of information has made good person-and-job matching difficult to achieve (Dyer, 1973; Lippman and McCall, 1976). Companies, individuals, and society are losing from the failure to match employees' skills to appropriate jobs.

Promotions

Since signals are needed when information is imperfect, one might expect the signaling model not to apply to promotions where formal policies can define promotion criteria explicitly, and where information about criteria can easily be communicated within the firm. However, firms do not always clearly specify their promotion criteria. Managers in the same firm differ on what is important, and their descriptions even change during different interviews (London and Stumpf, 1982: 225–227); these changes are not the result of mental confusion—procedures have been found to vary over time and in different circumstances (p. 214–216). London and Stumpf found that "many of the managers interviewed either had no clear decision-making strategy [about promotions] or evolved a strategy while making the decision." (p. 214). Thus, it appears that employees do not receive clear signals about what is necessary for them to be promoted, because the criteria are actually unclear.

Managers find the fuzziness to be useful—it allows them to figure out what is needed and how to proceed, and even how to redefine criteria to fit available information on candidates and attributes of the candidate pool. "Selection standards may be set after discovering what types of information are available. The number of candidates may determine how carefully the decision maker can review each one" (London and Stumpf, 1982: 215).

Yet, in spite of the value of flexibility for decision makers, the failure to provide clear criteria can create problems for candidates and for the company. "Not formulating a strategy may lead to disappointment in finding qualified candidates, having the recommended candidate rejected, or not being able to obtain the release of the most qualified person" (London and Stumpf, 1982: 215). Moreover, this flexibility fails to provide signals about what the system wants. Individuals do not know what they are supposed to do to get promoted; so some highly capable people devote efforts to irrelevant activities, or to activities that actually hurt their careers. The firm suffers because individuals are not maximally preparing themselves for the firm's needs, and the firm consequently loses some capable people due to random mistakes. The trade-off, then, is between managers' desire to keep their options open, and individuals' and firms' needs for clear goals and criteria. While it would be imprudent to curtail managers' freedom entirely, providing some clear guidelines and criteria would serve as a compromise that need not unduly fetter managers and would significantly improve the information provided to candidates.

The second problem with promotions is that the signals provided about potential candidates are not reliable. It is generally assumed that the information passed along within a firm is undistorted, so signaling theory does not apply. However, "supervisors are sometimes reluctant to provide names of qualified subordinates for fear of losing good people who could develop in their own departments. [In addition], some supervisors may give positive recommendations to subordinates they would rather lose" (London and Stumpf, 1982: 214). Even internal systems are flooded with false positives and false negatives, arising more from vested interests than from candidates' attributes. When valid information competes with vested interests, the former is sometimes sacrificed. The victims in this sacrifice are both the firm, which does not get the best people for its openings, and the individual, who is prevented from rising because supervisors do not want to lose their good workers.

Third, while it is certainly easier for promotion committees to get information about internal candidates than to get it about external ones, the former is still imperfect, because committee members rarely know all candidates well. To make up for this, promotion committees typically resort to inferring ability from an employee's promotion history, using the already mentioned flawed tournament outcomes as signals of ability, and excluding many excellent candidates from consideration (Rosenbaum, 1984).

Thus, as in the example of hiring practices, promotions exhibit some of the same elements noted earlier: Promotion committees do not identify their selection criteria, and they do not obtain relevant signals about applicants. In this case, we see indications that managers intentionally avoid stating their criteria, and the same potential consequences still arise: Managers get inappropriate candidates, inappropriately prepared candidates, inappropriate information, and demoralized employees who did not anticipate their failures. Meanwhile, individuals being considered for promotions tend to assume that promotion committees are well informed about their performance; so these individuals are slow to realize that information about their performance is not always reliably transmitted. As a result, their performance does not decline until after they have been passed over for promotions several times—after their career is seriously sidetracked (Rosenbaum, 1989).

Terminations and Voluntary Exits

Institutions' weak signals about employees' worth also magnify the damage from terminations. Terminations are always hard on company morale, but the way former employees rebound, after being fired, has a significant effect on how the remaining employees respond at-their-jobs. The traditional intrafirm career system tried to create orderly careers and prevent demotions and terminations in order to protect morale; encourage long-term decisions, rather than short-term opportunism; help create a workforce that knew the firm well; and eliminate a possible reluctance to train subordinates by assuring that underlings would not be used as replacements (Doeringer and Piore, 1971; Goode, 1967). While many of the reasons for such a system remain important, the old system of handling them is disappearing. Employees no longer have any assurance that if they do good work, they will not be terminated, and that the cumulative advantage of their hard work and experience will not be lost. Such a situation limits employee loyalty and investments in long-term company success. To alleviate this problem, employers need to offer some assurance that good work will be rewarded by career progression or by desirable positions and projects, even if they are at another firm.

Employers also face severe workplace demoralization when people are actually terminated. Hughes Consultants found that survivors of downsizing go through very predictable, negative stages of emotion, including lower morale and productivity, increased absenteeism, and more unplanned resignations of key employees (Sherer, 1993). With the wave of downsizing continuing, as shown by an American Management Association (AMA) (1994) survey—which found that 25% of human-resource managers plan to make further workforce reductions—the issue of demoralization remains a pressing one.

Many employers have turned to outplacement services to reduce the damage done during workforce reductions. In 1994, the same AMA survey found 58% of downsizing firms offered outplacement assistance to all displaced employees and 84%, to at least some; in total, 1.4 million people received outplacement services that year (Mergenhagen, 1994). The first goal of outplacement services is to reduce the laid-off employee's psychic stress by providing one-on-one counseling. This type of assistance is used primarily to prevent the employee from taking detrimental action against the institution, through lawsuits or even violence. It is also designed to help the individual prepare mentally for a job search and new employment. These services also aim to help individuals get new jobs through various procedures, ranging from helping to prepare new cover letters and resumes to actually finding new jobs.

While outplacement can be helpful, it does little to help employees mitigate the stigma of being jobless. Moreover, job-placement results from outplacement services are highly variable; so surviving employees have difficulty assessing their own chances. Thus, while outplacement sometimes helps individuals, it does not necessarily reduce either the damage from employees' general uncertainty about long-term rewards or the deleterious effects of terminations on morale.

While the need for good signals of an employee's worth are of great importance for an exiting employee, standard signaling problems are exacerbated during downsizing. Former employees can request reference letters, although this is often not possible if whole divisions have been restructured and the supervisors are laid off along with their subordinates. Reference letters are an even less plausible option if individuals choose to leave. Yet signaling reforms could help employees get proper credit for their work. In turn, this would improve the morale of surviving employees, who can assess their own value and the ways it translates into subsequent employment. Employees and employers could benefit from signaling reforms, which could greatly improve the benefits of outplacement.

Prospective Reforms

While individuals and companies need clear signals about job requirements and performance, the current system rarely provides them. Companies have relied on shortcuts that, while reasonably reliable in the past, are becoming less effective due to the changing workforce. Reforms could help create good systems and good signals could reduce the damage caused by information distortions.

The barriers which hinder the creation of clearly defined selection criteria are somewhat arbitrary and not very deeply held. While Americans do not like being pinned down to clear criteria and rigid systems, they use them often enough. Colleges have entrance criteria, firms often have selection tests, and unions have seniority requirements. Some law schools even provide potential applicants with a grid which charts the percentage of acceptances from combinations of test scores and grades. In many venues, the benefits gained by well-defined criteria are considered well worth the costs of limiting flexibility. To take advantage of the increased mobility in the workplace, institutions must define clear guidelines for advancement, regardless of company of origin, and encourage greater use of interpersonal and institutional connections in conveying that information.

Reforming Hiring

While flexible hiring criteria may serve managers' immediate needs, they have serious failings for firms. To get appropriate candidates to apply and to encourage potential applicants to appropriately prepare themselves, firms must send clear signals of their hiring needs and their selection criteria. Employers who state that they expect strong academic skills will encourage potential applicants to prescreen themselves, so that they do not waste their time with jobs they cannot get. If firms notified students that they use grades or academic tests in hiring, then students would prepare themselves accordingly.

For example, a two-year business college in Chicago specializing in preparing people for secretarial and clerical fields, tells its students that it will place them according to the grades they get in their studies. This system gives students clear incentives to do well in their classes and to learn the information presented. Businesses readily hire this college's graduates, because they know that they can rely on the graduates to be well prepared and able to respond to task demands. Similarly, an unidentified technical college makes the same promise, and analyses show that the correlation between grades and starting salaries of this school's graduates is over .90, with virtually no differences by race or gender (Roze and Curtis, 1990). Some graduate schools of management recommend students for the best jobs on the basis of grades and area of training (Burke, 1984). While explicit criteria reduce firms' flexibility in these cases, they increase firms' ability to get the kind of people they need, and firms benefit from students' improved motivation and preparation, and from getting useful information on their applicants. Explicit criteria also provide potential employees with a clear message of firms' needs, which encourages appropriate preparation and prescreening, and therefore better-quality applicants.

Reforming Promotions

Current employees can also benefit from explicit criteria. Employees who know how they will be judged for the next promotion can focus on those activities which are valued by the firm, and will not waste their time following unappreciated lines of work. Of course, creating and using prestated criteria limits managers' flexibility, but managers gain by getting better-prepared candidates, and less disgruntlement from the many who can plainly see that they do not meet the criteria.

While business likes to disparage the federal bureaucracy, business could benefit by considering the benefits of its evaluation system, which conveys valued information inside and between agencies. This system relies heavily on regular written evaluations based on a formal criteria. Although these criteria are designed for internal use, the evaluations are understood across agencies. Managers use these criteria to make their annual assessment of each individual's skill development and accomplishments. The assessment takes the form of a rating system followed by individualized comments that support the rating in each category. At assessment time, employees receive explicit feedback about their level of performance—about areas where they need to work to be promoted, and about areas where they need more experience. Similarly, those who receive consistently poor ratings come to realize that they are not doing well and might be better off elsewhere. Moreover, federal employees know these ratings are valuable even if they leave their agency, because their achievements in one federal position will be recognized by any other federal agency. Clear criteria allow managers to make better decisions and allow employees to be better prepared.

While businesses are skeptical about such formal procedures, it is important to recall the disadvantages of the informal procedures in many firms. Despite official policies for periodic performance evaluations in some firms, many managers avoid this unpleasant task—in what Hall (1976) has called "the vanishing performance evaluation." In one firm, employees who had been rated unpromotable only learned of these ratings many years after the decision had been made (Rosenbaum, 1989). This evasiveness might succeed in keeping employees striving for promotions for a few extra years, but their subsequent anger at the evasiveness might last for several decades. Of course, managers resent any limitations on their discretion in making informal decisions about their subordinates, but subordinates tend to view such flexible, informal decisions as arbitrary, and they can lead to resentment and even litigation (Rousseau, 1995: 75).

Explicit evaluations also help reduce the loss of talent that arises from poor employee-manager matches. Talented employees who do not work well with their supervisors tend to get poor training and preparation (Berlew and Hall, 1966). While the worst mismatches are obvious, explicit evaluations help subordinates quickly realize when their talents are not being recognized, and they can request a shift to another supervisor. Besides providing the possibility for a second opinion, this procedure can reduce the chances that managers will underrate valued subordinates to avoid losing them to another department. Formal evaluations help employees see which managers help their subordinates' careers, and talented employees will seek positions with them. Indeed, increased information is likely to benefit talented employees, good managers, and the entire firm.

Reforming Outplacement

Explicit evaluations are particularly beneficial when firms are downsizing. When departing employees can get good jobs elsewhere, surviving employees suffer less anxiety about their former colleagues' prospects, and will be heartened about their own job prospects, if they have to find new employment. Better signals thus offer a supplement to outplacement.

Firms need to provide the kind of signals of employees' worth that are understood and trusted outside the firm. Many firms provide recommendations when they terminate employees, but these recommendations often are mistrusted. Evaluations would have far greater credibility if they were part of a formal evaluation system that could be used both internally and externally and included a history of evaluations written long before termination; an outside employer is likely to give more credibility to an evaluation which was written for internal use than to one written solely at the time of termination. For skilled workers, a system of skills certification is most appropriate, whereas managers need clear-cut records of responsibilities, tasks, and accomplishments.

If employees could have records of their past performance sent to potential employers, they would have reason to keep up their performance level, even in times of job uncertainty, and good employees would have an easier time finding a new job, because they would have reliable documentation of their accomplishments. This would also help downsizing firms by softening the blow termina-tions have on morale, and would help hiring firms choose a better workforce.

Besides rationalizing performance appraisals, firms could also go one step further and establish job-placement linkages. The organizational-behavior litera-ture has long argued that supervisors have an obligation to help their subordi-nates' careers, within the company (Hall, 1976). In the era of the mobile worker, the appropriate extension of this idea is that supervisors have an obliga-tion to help individuals with the next step in their careers, whether inside or outside the company. The linkage model offers one method of doing so.

The linkage model is an extension of networking. Rather than employees relying on personal connections, the linkage model offers employees the benefit of the connections of the supervisor and the firm, in finding appropriate employ-ment, with supervisors helping place their former employees in appropriate jobs. Firms can develop and cultivate such connections through suppliers and custom-ers, and these connections can be used to further strengthen these relationships through an interlinked workforce. Individuals could be placed with connected firms, who would trust the other firm to send only appropriate candidates in order to preserve their long-term connections.

While such linkages are currently rare, there are several reasons to believe they could become more common. First, in an era when there is an increasing emphasis on good fit over a simple case of high quality, one employer's medio-cre data-entry clerk is another's outstanding telemarketer. This notion of a good fit focuses on placing employees in situations where they can make the best use of their talents and skills, and it deemphasizes areas where individuals are defi-cient. With a focus on fit, supervisors are more aware of their employees' need to make the best use of their skills, and they are more willing to help them.

Second, firms are not islands—nearly all firms are connected to other firms which perform interrelated functions. These connected firms are the ideal links through which to send (and receive) employees, because the trust is already there, and the employee is already familiar with the basic workings of the indus-try. Moreover, as we shall note, firms which have tried these methods have found that they benefit not only from improved morale and lower unemployment-compensation costs but also from stronger relationships with suppliers and customers.

This method has been tried in several different arenas. Japanese firms use this method widely, transferring surplus workers to suppliers or subsidiaries during periods of contraction (Plath, 1983). Similarly, some American school-teachers have created links with employers in order to get their students jobs after high school (Rosenbaum and Jones, 1995), and some American employers have begun experimenting with such a model (Rosenbaum and Binder, 1994).

Some recent actions by American firms deserve special attention, for they illustrate the fact that some employers are aware of the potential benefits from such connections and have concluded that it is worthwhile to help their dis-placed workers find appropriate new employment. The armed forces, where over 200,000 jobs are being eliminated, are the biggest example of this. The military has taken responsibility for helping its former personnel find civilian jobs (Caudron, 1992; Overman, 1993). Fifty-five job-assistance centers worldwide, staffed with 286 counselors, have two types of referral systems: The Defense Outplacement Referral System (DORS), a data base of miniresumes, allows service personnel and their spouses to list their names, qualifications, and the type of job sought on a system—which employers access using a touch-tone telephone. An employer can receive as many as 25 resumes per day by fax, and up to 100 resumes by mail the next day. The second system is the electronic Transition Bulletin Board, which employers use for posting job descriptions which personnel can look at on their own, or with the help of job counselors. The Defense Department will soon offer one further piece of assistance: certificates which translate military skills into their civilian equivalent, so that employers can more easily recognize which personnel have the skills they seek.

The military is not the only place where we see such assistance. Rhino Foods, a specialty dessert maker faced with layoffs, asked its workers for alternative suggestions (Cronin, 1993). One came up with the idea of contracting people out to other employers. Management agreed, and the human resources director set out to screen potential placements. Employees who volunteered to be sent elsewhere were assured of the same pay, but warned that if they were fired at their new job, they would also lose their positions at Rhino. Employees were sent to various other firms, including two of Rhino's biggest customers, and reinstated at Rhino when its business picked up. At the end of the experience, Rhino management people felt that this arrangement had been less expensive than layoffs would have been and that they had gained a more loyal workforce. In addition, some employees returned to Rhino with ideas for how to improve the business.

When Home Life Insurance merged with Phoenix Mutual Life of Hartford, nearly 500 jobs were eliminated. Home Life, however, decided to take responsibility for finding its employees new positions, either with the now-merged companies, or at another company (Daniele, 1992). Along with more traditional outplacement services, Home Life went so far as to run newspaper ads for its employees.

Metropolitan-Mount Sinai Medical Center was faced with a similar situation when it closed its doors in the summer of 1991 (Eubanks, 1992; Matthes, 1992). Rather than terminate its workforce, its parent company, Health One, tried to place Mount Sinai's staff in new positions. Approximately one-third of its former workforce accepted early retirement, one-third went to affiliated or competing hospitals, and one-third got help in finding jobs through Health One's efforts. In terms of the latter, the company provided career-transition assistance, job fairs, and retraining. Overall, almost 90% of the 1,200 employees were placed in new positions, and only eight employees applied for unemployment. The results had bottom-line benefits—Health One saved $18 million in unemployment payments.

Some downsizing agencies have implemented "job bridging"—a combination of career counseling and outplacement support (Liebman and McCarthy, 1993). In particular, the placement offices try to match employees with appropriate jobs. Directly addressing the potential for demoralization, counselors try to ensure that only qualified applicants apply for the open positions, to protect employees from another rejection and to maintain credibility among potential employers. While many of the employers who help place their workers do so through a sense of responsibility, they also do so because it is good business; it improves employee morale and the public's image of the firm.

Disincentives to Sending Good Signals

Rationalizing employer/employee relations is not a new idea; it harks back to two of the fundamental goals of good management: disseminating information and motivating employees. The most closely related widespread movement for such changes is known as management by objectives (MBO). Under this management technique, a manager and a subordinate decide the goals on which the subordinate will be judged (Drucker, 1954; Ivancevich and Matteson, 1987). Although this method took a step toward more objective measures of employee performance, it was sometimes an empty exercise. While the idea of involving employees in setting the criteria on which they will be judged is appealing, managers need to get certain goals met, and employees have little alternative but to agree to them. Pretending employees had some say in the matter was sometimes a frustrating charade.

A related effort—performance-appraisal systems—is a step in the right direction. While these take many forms, they are all used for evaluating employees' performance. In our view, these systems could be more effective motivators if appraisals were codified into signals readily understood outside the firm. Indeed, most firms do not clearly define their appraisals in a form that could be used outside the firm, and internal appraisals are rarely available for external purposes. These appraisals have a great deal of credibility within firms, and if they were made more readily available and understandable to other firms, then employees' value would be more easily recognized by other firms. Admittedly, such codification would sometimes be difficult, but there are many times when it would be simple. What is most clear is that we do not know how difficult it would be, because few firms have made the effort.

Conclusion

While it is widely recognized that businesses and individuals need good information to make good decisions, the exchange of information within and between firms remains haphazard and unreliable. Because of unreliable information on individuals' value, labor markets are unable to function smoothly. More standardized procedures for the creation and transmission of information would allow individuals, firms, and society to take full advantage of people's skills and capabilities.

While some dismiss these problems as inevitable and as solvable only by cumbersome bureaucracies, we have proposed that personal and institutional linkages can address these problems. Both kinds of linkages have their advantages. Personal linkages, relying on relationships built between people, offer the advantages of interpersonal trust. Individuals who work with one another are more likely to know and trust the evaluations of the other. Personal linkages are also easier to implement, for they do not require the cooperation of others in the industry, or the company, to make them useful. Any set of personal linkages that is used will help improve the flow of information and the job fit for the hiring employer and the employee. However, personal linkages mean that the employee and hiring employer can only get reliable information from a specific, limited set of sources.

Formal institutional linkages, on the other hand, provide readily available credentials for any employee and employer to use. They create institutional standards and criteria which can be universally understood and easily transferred, even by those who do not know the potential employee. If such signals are widely used, they will open up a whole range of opportunities for firms and mobile workers. They also offer an ease of transmission. Such information can be transferred from one human-relations department to another, freeing supervisors from this task.

While there are trade-offs involving the two linkage models, perhaps the ideal system would offer a combination of the two. If these formal assessments were on file, for employees to use when necessary, and supervisors also took an active responsibility in helping displaced employees, the value of both personal and impersonal signals would create the most complete assessment of an employee's strengths and weaknesses and allow for the most appropriate job fit. Such changes will not come easily, but they will be necessary if individuals, firms, and society are to gain the benefits of boundaryless careers.

ACKNOWLEDGMENTS: We thank Amy Binder, Molly Burke, Mark Granovetter, Stephanie Jones, Virgina Mills, Karen Nelson, Kevin Roy, and Melinda Scott Krei for their assistance in various phases of this chapter, as well as Michael B. Arthur, Denise M. Rousseau, and Bob DeFillippi for their helpful suggestions on an earlier draft. Support for this work was provided by the Spencer Foundation, the W. T. Grant Foundation, the Pew Charitable Trusts, and the Center for Urban Affairs and Policy Research at Northwestern University.

Note

1. We excluded industries which we thought likely to offer only "youth jobs," such as restaurants, grocery stores, and other service industries that offer little room for advancement. We included both large and small companies, with a range of less than 10 employees to over 80,000, and emphasized medium-sized firms.

References

American Association of Management. 1994. *1994 AMA Survey of Downsizing and Assistance to Displaced Workers.* New York: American Management Association.

Arrow, Kenneth J. 1973. "Information and Economic Behavior." In *Collected Papers of Kenneth J. Arrow,* vol. 4, chap. 11. Cambridge, Mass.: Belknap.

Arvey, R. D. 1979. *Fairness in Selecting Employees.* Reading, Mass.: Addison-Wesley.

Anonymous. 1993. "More Cuts . . . Deeper Cuts . . . and More Help for Employees." *HR Focus,* 70(11): 24.

Axmith, M. 1981. "The Act of Firing: A Constructive Approach." *Business Quarterly*, 46(1): 36–45.

Barry, Dave. 1986. *Claw Your Way to the Top: How to Become the Head of a Major Corporation in Roughly a Week.* Emmaeus, Penna: Rodale Press.

Becker, G. 1962. "Investment in Human Capital: a Theoretical Analysis." *Journal of Political Economy*, 70: 9–44.

Berlew, D. E., and Hall, D. T. 1966. "The Socialization of Managers." *Administrative Science Quarterly*, 11: 207–223.

Bills, D. 1988. "Educational Credentials and Hiring Decisions: What Employers Look for in Entry-Level Employees." *Research in Social Stratification and Mobility* 7: 71–97.

Bishop, J. 1989. "Why the Apathy in American High Schools?" *Educational Researcher*. 4(1): 17–28.

Bureau of National Affairs. 1979. *Recruiting Policies and Practices*. (Personnel Policies Forum Survey no. 120). Washington, D.C.: Bureau of National Affairs.

Burke, M. A. 1984. "Becoming an MBA." Ph.D. diss., School of Education, Northwestern University.

Cascio, W. F., and Silbey, V. 1978. "Utility of the Assessment Center as a Selection Device." *Journal of Applied Psychology*, 64: 107–118.

Campbell, J. P; M. D. Dunnette; E. E. Lawler III; and K. E. Weick, Jr. 1970. "Managerial Behavior, Performance, and Effectiveness." New York: McGraw-Hill.

Caudron, Shari. 1992. "Recruit Qualified Employees from the Military." *Personnel Journal*. 71(5): 117–119.

Crain, R. 1984. *The Quality of American High School Graduates: What Personnel Officers Say and Do*. Center for the Study of Schools, Johns Hopkins University.

Cronin, Michael P. 1993. "Employee Swapping." *Inc.*, 15(13): 165.

Daniele, Elizabeth. 1992. "Our Loss Is Your Gain." *Insurance and Technology*, 17(8): 52.

Doeringer P., and Piore, M. 1971. *Internal Labor Markets and Manpower Analysis*. Lexington, Mass.: Lexington Books.

Drucker, P. 1954. *The Practice of Management*. New York: Harper and Row.

Dyer, L. D. 1973. Job-Search Success of Middle-Aged Managers and Engineers. *Industrial and Labor Relations Review*, 26: 969–979.

Eubanks, Paula. 1992. "Finding Jobs for 1,200 Laid-Off Employees: Health One's Goal." *Hospitals*, 66(1): 43–44.

Gibson, Virginia M. 1994. "Organizations Must Adapt to Employees' Changing Needs." *HR Focus*, 71(3).

Goode, William J. 1967. "The Protection of the Inept." *American Sociological Review*, 32(1).

Hall, D. T. 1976. *Careers in Organizations*. Pacific Palasades, Calif.: Goodyear.

Hamilton, Stephen F. 1990. *Apprenticeship for Adulthood*. New York: Free Press.

Hill, Douglas M. 1995. "Hire Education." *Education Week*, 33: (May).

Hirsch, Paul. 1987. *Pack Your Own Parachute*. Reading, Mass.: Addison-Wesley.

Ivancevich, J. M., and Matteson, M. T. 1987. *Organizational Behavior and Management*. Plano, Tex.: Business Publications.

Kanter, Rosabeth Moss. 1977. *Men and Women of the Corporation*. New York: Basic Books.

Kariya, Takehiko, and Rosenbaum, James E. 1995. "Institutional Linkages Between Education and Work as Quasi-Internal Labor Markets." *Research in Social Stratification and Mobility*, 14: 99–134.

Lawrence, B. S. "An Organizational Theory of Age Effects." *Research in the Sociology of Organizations,* edited by S. Bacharach and N. DiTomaso. Greenwich, Conn.: JAI.

Liebman, Helene G., and McCarthy, Steve. 1993. "Job Bridging: Downsizing without RIFs." *Public Manager,* 22(2): 25–27.

Lippman, S. A., and McCall, J. J. 1976. "The Economics of Job Search: A Survey, Part I: Optimal Job Search Policies." *Economics Inquiry,* 14: 155–189.

London, Manuel, and Stumpf, Stephen A. 1982. *Managing Careers.* Reading, Mass.: Addison-Wesley.

Matthes, Karen. 1992. "The Pink Slip Turns into Something Rosier." *Management Review,* 81(4): 5.

Mergenhagen, Paula. 1994. "Job Benefits Get Personal." *American Demographics,* 16(9): 30–36.

Mickelson, Roslyn A. 1990. "The Attitude-Achievement Paradox Among Black Adolescents." *Sociology of Education,* 63: 44–61.

Miller, Michael V., and Robinson, Cherylon. 1994. "Managing the Disappointment of Job Termination: Outplacement as a Cooling-Out Device." *Journal of Applied Behavioral Science,* 30(1).

Myers, Jeffrey, E. 1993. "Downsizing Blues: How to Keep Up Morale." *Management Review,* 82(4): 28–31.

National Academy of Sciences. 1984. *High Schools and the Changing Workplace: The Employers' View.* Washington, D.C.: National Academy Press.

Overman, Stephanie. 1993. Heroes for Hire. *H R Magazine,* 38(12): 61–62.

Plath, D. W. 1983. *Work and Lifecourse in Japan.* Albany, N.Y.: SUNY Press.

Rosenbaum, James E. 1979. "Tournament Mobility: Career Patterns in a Corporation." *Administrative Science Quarterly,* 24: 220–241.

Rosenbaum, James E. 1984. *Career Mobility in a Corporate Hierarchy.* New York: Academic Press.

Rosenbaum James E. 1989. Organizational Career Systems and Employee Misperceptions. Pp. 329–353 in M. Arthur; D. Hall; and B. Lawrence, eds., *Handbook of Career Theory.* New York: Cambridge University Press.

Rosenbaum, James E. 1992. *Youth Apprenticeship in America.* New York: W. T. Grant Commission on Youth and America's Future.

Rosenbaum, James E., and Binder, Amy. 1994. "Do Employers Really Believe They Need More Educated Youth?" Paper presented at the meeting of the American Sociological Association.

Rosenbaum, James E., and Jones, Stephanie A. 1995. "Creating Linkages in the High School-to-Work Transition: Vocational Teachers' Networks." In M. Hallinan, ed., *Making Schools Work.* New York: Plenum Press.

Rosenbaum, James E., and Kariya, Takehiko. 1989. "From High School to Work: Market and Institutional Mechanisms in Japan." *American Journal of Sociology.* 94: 1334–1365.

Rosenbaum, James E., and Kariya, Takehiko. 1991. "Do School Achievements Affect the Early Jobs of High School Graduates in the U.S. and Japan?" *Sociology of Education,* 64: 78–95.

Rosenbaum, James E.; Kariya, Takehiko; Settersten, Rick; and Maier, Tony. 1990. "Market and Network Theories of the Transition from High School to Work." *Annual Review of Sociology,* 16: 263–199.

Rosenbaum, James E.; Miller, Shazia Rafiullah; and Krei, Melinda Scott. 1995. "Gatekeeping in an Era of More Open Gates: High School Counselors' Views of Their Influence on Students' College Plans." Working paper (WP-95–11). Chicago: Center for Urban Affairs and Policy Research.

Rosenbaum, James E.; and Nelson, Karen A. 1994. "The Influence of Perceived Articulation on Adolescents' School Effort." Paper presented at the American Educational Research Association.

Rousseau, Denise M. 1995. *Psychological Contracts in Organizations*. Thousand Oaks, Calif.: Sage.

Roze, M., and Curtis, M. 1990. "Alumni Survey." Unpublished report from an unidentified technical college.

Sherer, Jill. 1993. "Corporate Culture: Lessening the Impact of Layoffs on Survivors." *Hospitals and Health Networks,* 67(11): 64.

Smith, Bob. 1994. "Cease Fire! Preventing Workplace Violence." *HR Focus,* 71(2): 116–117.

Spence, A. M. 1974. Market Signaling: *Information Transfer in Hiring and Related Processes*. Cambridge, Mass.: Harvard University Press.

Stigler, G. J. 1961. "The Economics of Information." *Journal of Political Economy,* 69: 213–225.

Stinchcombe, Arthur. 1965. *Rebellion in a High School*. New York: Quadrangle Books.

Stumpf, Stephen E. 1981. "The Effects of Career Exploration on Organizational Entry and Career Related Outcomes." Working paper, New York University.

Wanous, J. P. 1980. *Organizational Entry: Recruitment, Selection, and Socialization of Newcomers*. Reading, Mass.: Addison-Wesley.

22

Conclusion: A Lexicon for the New Organizational Era

MICHAEL B. ARTHUR AND DENISE M. ROUSSEAU

Chaos is not bad,
it is what is.
Bercquist, 1993

This book has dealt with change—in "the new organizational era." Change has been examined through a new conceptualization of careers—boundaryless careers—which replaces more circumscribed conceptualizations that have come before. The chapters in this book have extended our exploration of change along the new pathways that boundaryless careers suggest. These pathways have led to new perspectives on the world of work, and new viewpoints on what we once took to be familiar. In response, this chapter offers a brief guide to the new pathways: We offer a lexicon, of meanings old and new, delineating the phenomena brought into view. Our lexicon is directed at both those who study and those directly engaged in boundaryless career activity.[1]

What we saw in the 1980s as short-run cost cutting—shaving off excesses in the internal labor market to pay off corporate debt services from mergers and acquisitions—has become a prolonged groping for more efficient, adaptive, and imaginative ways to organize work. The transition from circumscribed careers to boundarylessness confronts researchers and workers with a problem outside their experience. No norms and few models exist to tell us how to evaluate, plan, analyze, review, promote, or enact a boundaryless career. Of all changes, the most fundamental are changes in assumptions—about the way the world works, what concepts mean, and what is real. The emergence of a more fluid reality for careers should create some empathy for the ancient Celts (Cahill, 1995) who believed in shape-shifting—people taking new forms at will (from rocks to wolves, and so on). In the same sense that Weick characterizes his chapter on enactment and the boundaryless career as a "story of shifting identities," shape-shifting is a process not readily amenable to those whose preferred reality is continuous and constant. The shape of work—how people organize themselves and each other—is obviously shifting, and shifting is becoming the shape of work.

This book's contributors offer a lexicon: new meanings for old concepts, and new concepts that encompass novel meanings. Appropriating old terms for new meanings surfaces old assumptions and replaces them with new premises. Assumptions—powerful beliefs normally invisible to the holder—function like the lens of the eye. Everything we know about the world we know through the lens of our assumptions, a lens we cannot usually see.[2] We see careers and organization through our concepts of what organization or careers should be. Our lexicon bears examination.

> BOUNDARY Old meaning: a limit; the division between familiar and hostile territory. New meaning: something to be crossed in a career behavior, or in managing complexity.

Old boundaries involved time, territory, and technology (Miller, 1969). The differences they created between people who worked the day or graveyard shift, in Arkansas or Ontario, or on a production line or with a telephone were palpable sources not only of distinct rewards and values but also of fundamental conflicts that made interdependence something to avoid. Technology now means that time can be bridged, and distance affords less distinction. Ijiri (1993) maintains that "technology has made complexity friendly" and taken the adversarial sting out of differences. Fletcher and Bailyn (chapter 15 in this volume) suggest a new concept, that of "co-opetition"—of managing relations between interdependent groups, such that the old meaning of *boundary* disappears. The old boundaries confined people to linear career paths, a functional focus, and narrow specialization. As people encounter nonlinear, cumulative, multifunctional experiences, they cannot know today how their skills will be deployed tomorrow. As people break more and more boundaries, they become unable even to see them. Boundarylessness is the inevitable result.

Boundarylessness means that we will all have a tougher time studying organizational parts in isolation. Over two decades ago, Simon (1973) argued that organizations were nearly decomposable, that a part had dynamics separate from other parts and from the larger whole, and could be studied in isolation. We now understand better the danger of fragmentation. This decomposability is certainly less true today. When Peters (1991) argued that what the United States needed was a "declaration of interdependence," he challenged the notion of decomposable work and workers. Practically speaking, this means, for instance, that job analysis can no longer be done on individual jobs, but must be work-flow analysis, which captures the essence of constituents, collaborations, multiple work flows, and partnerships. As dynamic organizing supersedes formal organization, network analysis will likely capture more accurately the structure of work than any formal chart can. We are going to be much more aware of the limitations of assessments made of any particular work unit, and much more curious about interunit connections.[3]

CAREER Old meaning: a course of professional advancement; usage is restricted to occupational groups with formal hierarchical progression, such as managers and professionals. New meaning: the unfolding sequence of any person's work experiences over time.

Career was once a concept commonly restricted to selected kinds of workers. As popularly conceived, work experiences labeled careers affected only people whose work changed over time, whose skills were progressively built on those previously acquired, and who enjoyed institutional rewards for advancing in sequence. Left out were blue-collar workers, who had jobs, rather than careers (Thomas, 1989); housewives and homeworkers; and any others not directly participating in the traditional labor force. The new organizational era introduces change into virtually all work, and alters the skill base as well as the incentives for skill development. All work involves a sequencing of experiences that must be understood. What has changed is the set of standards for gauging the meaning and utility of these experiences.

The concept of a career always did provide for a broad interpretation of the effects of work and time (Arthur, Hall, and Lawrence, 1989). What was lacking was a willingness to apply the concept without preconceived status rigidities. Management researchers, in particular, have compounded the myth that managers and professionals had careers but that others did not. The emerging new meaning of *career* emphasizes that people create meanings out of life experiences to build a sense of psychological success (see Mirvis and Hall, chapter 14 in this volume). People may also format their same life events differently in constructing their resumes (see Weick, chapter 3 in this volume). Disconnecting a career from status and hierarchy dislodges the assumptions behind career success. Careers are now improvised along with the work flows in which people participate, and success has its own meaning for each improviser.

ORGANIZATION Old meaning: a legal entity defining authority relations and property rights. New meaning: organizing through networks, value chains, and so on—a more dynamic, process-centered usage.

Organization has meant the formal structuring of work performed within a legal entity, which held intellectual-property rights to work done within it in exchange for pay and, under certain conditions, job-property rights. Hierarchical control permitted the organization of work to stay the same even when the people changed. The new interdependence among work and workers means that organization has given way to organizing, in which cooperative teams act as building blocks for work. These teams span traditional organizational boundaries, bringing the environment *inside,* so to speak. Organizing not only reflects the entire value chain that produces goods and services but also and builds teams across functions and across suppliers, producers, distributors, and customers. Organizing is evident in discovery and learning (see Ellig and Joseph, chapter 10 in this volume), which accrue to people and leave firms vulnerable when people move. Knowledge that was once seen as a property of the employing organization is now seen to reside in the careers of its frequently temporary employees (see Bird, chapter 9 in this volume).

Historically, organizations were a lot like board games, in that they had their own rules, which could not be questioned. Now, legitimacy is becoming a constant question, since rules are localized and temporary. Reduced emphasis on a hierarchy in modern work settings implies that people need to voluntarily accept the terms of agreements before they will provide input (Rousseau, 1995). The social elements of employment (cooperation, mentoring, collective learning) cannot be developed unless members agree to fulfill complementary roles, in contrast to the technical requirements that mechanistic organizations used to dictate. The more that social elements of work dominate preset technical demands, the more incomplete will be the a priori information on how to work together, and the greater the number of issues requiring agreement (Ellig and Joseph, chapter 10 in this volume). But what a significant array of issues to agree on: intellectual-property rights; information flows and communication, including sharing of data through enterprise integration; deliverables and accountabilities that change, project by project. The disappearance of external guides to work organization may well reverse the predominance of routine- over nonroutine-information processing, changing profoundly the way future workers think about their work.

> EMPLOYMENT Old meaning: the action of employing a person; alternatively, a state of being employed, or a person's regular occupation or business. New meaning: a temporary state, or the current manifestation of long-term employability.

Our authors have implied that employment is a dependent state (Perrow, chapter 18) or a system in need of reform (Rosenbaum and Miller, chapter 21). Nonetheless, the essential meaning of *employment* remains much the same, although the vehicle providing employment may differ. Early usage of *employment* as a state referred to having people in one's service, and personal service is surely the earliest concept of employment. The large body of employment law, however, is rooted not in master-servant relations but in agency, where rights of firms and of members address the fact that firms risk their owners' money (Stinchcombe, 1986). The old model of employment envisioned that firms and the jobs within them were permanent. Internal labor markets consisted of sturdy, inflexible ladders. Since the Industrial Revolution had consolidated work so that it was done at one time and place under managerial control, people were largely dependent on firms for work. Perrow would suggest that this dependency has been exacerbated—despite the weakening of managerial control—by the erosion of the civil society, which does not provide the "life supports" (health-care, retirement, or child-care benefits) that firms came to absorb.

Many contributors to this volume recast employment along the lines of Kanter's (1989) notion of employability. The concern is less with the availability of standard jobs than it is with the marketability of cumulative personal skills. Employment increasingly focuses less on filling predetermined work roles, and more on cultivating and using skills and capabilities. In the process, employment is coming to mean something at once more exciting and more temporary, driven by shifting personal competencies (DeFillippi and Arthur, chapter 7); by project activities (Jones, chapter 4; Weick, chapter 3); and by discovery (Ellig and Joseph, chapter 10; Miner and Robinson, chapter 5).

OCCUPATION Old meaning: a habitual course of action, a set of tasks associated with requisite skills and codified knowledge; a basis for credentials. New meaning: an anchor for lifelong learning; a basis for network participation.

Occupation has its roots in the holding of land, evolving into the possession of an office or title. To occupy means to take possession of something. Property rights are at the heart of the concept of an occupation, although it increasingly became a sort of intellectul-property right, a claim to the possession of knowledge and, importantly, to the use of that knowledge. Occupations stake a claim. Critical dimensions that distinguish occupations identify them with a set of clearly defined skills, and a defined set of tasks to which these are applied (Bridges and Villemez, 1991). Tolbert adds that *occupation* implies social understandings about the "bundles" of work activities for which an occupational group's members are responsible. An occupation is an ability signal conveying to prospective employers what they are getting when hiring workers. Historically, occupational-group entry was often controlled by regulations of external bodies (e.g., state bar exams for lawyers, licensing for psychologists, time served for bricklayers). An occupation was a claim to ability. But since some jobs lack clearly defined tasks and prespecified requisite skills, they may or may not comprise an occupation. Idiosyncratic jobs, enacted by workers based on unique understandings, look less like the possession of an office and more like the creation of one (see Miner and Robinson, chapter 5 of this volume).

It appears that the time-honored meaning of an occupation is strengthened in the new organizational era. Reliance on contingent employees increases the value of occupational-group memberships as ability signals because demonstrated ability to produce results is prized. Marketability of workers is also enhanced in occupations that convey the relevant credentials and training. Tolbert (chapter 20) forecasts that reliance on contingent employment should strengthen and expand occupational labor markets. Miles and Snow (chapter 6) argue that fourth-wave organizations will function like umbrellas, bringing together component firms and networks on the basis of their own distinctive competencies—a network of occupations. Occupations are a socially acceptable way for one group of people to persuade others that they are capable of doing work that is otherwise difficult to monitor or control.[4] But this raises a question about whether there is sufficient structure and flexibility in the education and credentialing systems to make occupations efficient signaling devices. Continuous vocational education, according to Baker and Aldrich, is needed to accelerate the pace at which new skills are learned, to avoid having 1 year of experience repeated 20 times, as opposed to 20 years of experience. Despite the in-service training of teachers and nurses, occupations traditionally have struggled to balance the valuing of work experience with the obsolescing of established skills. As a result, the new meaning of occupations as creators of knowledge has yet to be fully realized.[5]

ENVIRONMENT Old meaning: external conditions outside the boundaries of the organization. New meaning: interdependent constituents in a network or value chain.

When we saw organizations as entities, we saw their environments as being comprised of external markets and social forces outside the firm. We also saw environments as being mandated to be beyond the firm's direct control, due to antitrust and other institutional constraints. In this view, the environment was the residual, everything the organization was not. This environment-as-the-residual was always a less-than-true situation, particularly in certain societies. In Japan, interfirm alliances, coupled with governmental relations, created a higher level of managed competition and interdependence, making the concept of organizational environment a rather redundant one.

Although laws in the United States and other Western countries have not necessarily caught up with the escalating interdependence among firms, our concept of the environment surely has shifted from "whatever the organization is not" to interdependencies that must be managed. Environment in the new era means a complex value chain of customers, suppliers, original equipment manufacturers, and end users, some of whom play multiple roles in the same network. The environment now comprises both internalized relationships and externalized work flows. Careers paths follow the course that the environment lays. Just as the environment-as-the-residual kept work and workers within the organization, the interdependent chain of constituents that the environment has become provides greater flexibility of experience and movement.

NONWORK   Old meaning: the worker's life outside work. New meaning: Is there one?

One seemingly durable boundary remains between work and family. Despite the fact that more people than ever are finding mates at work, combining business trips with sightseeing, and working at home, family life is still largely outside the boundary of work. It used to be that "real men didn't type," but the task was relabeled keyboarding and word processing and it became acceptable. Paternal leave, however, although ostensibly available, is often not culturally acceptable. Becoming part of the set of "pseudo-benefits" that workers have but cannot take (as is also the case when they try to use all of their allotted vacation time), paternal leave and other family-related arrangements affirm the durability of the separateness of work and family in modern society. Fletcher and Bailyn (chapter 15) join with Mirvis and Hall (chapter 14) in strenuously voicing the societal failure this represents, along with its wearying ramifications for family members who work. A ray of hope may be found in some of the more technologically sophisticated firms, such as Hewlett-Packard, which use technology that bridges time and space to reduce travel times for workers and to increase time spent with family (e.g., video and CD-ROM demonstrations of products, or redrawing sales territories based on operations-research analyses of single-day-travel and return schedules).

However, while technological solutions may make family life more convenient for workers, they do not change the institutional assumptions regarding work and family. Fletcher and Bailyn emphasize that nonwork aspirations, competencies, and experiences can bring innovations to the workplace. Also, while Fletcher and Bailyn's emphasis is on family, nonwork can also mean leisure. The need for leisure to provide both relaxation and growth is poorly understood, but we anticipate that it may have a more important place in the new boundaryless career arena.

> GROUP Old meaning: interdependent individuals within a social unit, such as a firm or a voluntary association. New meaning: interdependent individuals who identify psychologically with one another.

Historically, groups were building blocks for the formal organization, in which work flows created the intermediate units between the individual and firm levels of analysis. Groups were seen to have common member interests, and group theory taught us how cohesion could be leveraged, and intergroup conflict contained, to the greater benefit of the firm. Such theory saw group identity as subordinate to the firm, and responsive to motivation on the firm's behalf.

The new groups are, more commonly, interfirm phenomena (see Bird, chapter 9 in this volume), consisting of networks of contractors, independents, and entrepreneurs (see Jones, chapter 4), and of work- and nonwork-based relationships (Thomas and Higgins, chapter 16). Interdependent interests replace common interests, and groups integrate the interests of multiple firms, rather than subordinating their interests to those of a single firm. (An example is a product-design team consisting of suppliers, customers, engineers, and marketing experts.) In Miles and Snow's "fourth-wave" form of organization (chapter 6), such groups will provide the glue to bind multifirm agendas together and to hold individual firms to communal agendas. Such new theory sees group identity as external to any one firm, yet essential in making multiple firms cohere.

> LEARNING Old meaning: acquisition of knowledge committed to memory, typically by individuals. New meaning: a multilevel phenomenon, which includes creation and acquisition of knowledge, collective processes for shared interpretation, and patterns of adaptation and transformation.

Historically, learning was individually centered, focused on the acquisition and retention of information (Berryman and Bailey, 1992). At its most extreme, the old view held that individuals were passive vessels into which knowledge was poured. In the traditional model, skills and knowledge transfer worked best when acquired in an environment dedicated to learning (e.g., a training program or school). In firms, the focus has been on defining required skills by analyzing jobs into component tasks, specifying work methods in detail and finding the best way to do each task—which is then reinforced by drills and practice. More recent excursions into "organizational learning" (Senge, 1990; Nonaka and Takeuchi, 1995) have suggested how firms learn as collectives. Consistent with Weick (see chapter 3 in this volume), these contemporary theories see learning as social construction and emphasize the advantages of "learning by doing."

Extending the social construction perspective, our authors here highlight multiple levels of learning. Even individual classroom learning can have regional, transferable qualities (Rosenbaum and Miller, chapter 21). Collective learning is treated as an interfirm social interaction (Bird, chapter 9; Miner and Robinson, chapter 5), as a property of occupational groups (Tolbert, chapter 20), or of industry communities (Best and Forrant, chapter 19). Firm-centered approaches to learning seem, increasingly, too narrow to reflect the organizing revolution of knowledge-based work and workers. The watering holes frequented by Silicon Valley engineers—which Saxenian describes in chapter 2—offer ample evidence of unbounded knowledge transfer, of new processes and problem solving, that occurs over beers. Career-enhancing experiences will, of necessity, build personal and collective learning.

>REGION Old meaning: an area with a definite extent and character; an administrative division. New meaning: an interactive array of geographical, societal, and company resources.

The importance of a region for social interaction was presumed to have been eroded by the "company man's" presumed dependence on the employer firm (see Rosenbaum and Miller, chapter 21 in this volume). The rise of the multinationals, and the emergence of the "global village," could be taken to suggest regions as being even less significant than before. Porter's (1990) surprising emphasis on regions in *The Competitive Advantage of Nations* was seen by some to be out of character.

Yet, region is a factor that is everywhere in our discussion of boundaryless careers. Regions bind complex technologies and human capabilities across small firms to provide a competitive edge (see DeFillippi and Arthur, chapter 7). A regional skill base provides resources for renewed and sustainable development, and capitalizes on proximity as a necessary condition of knowledge transfer (see Best and Forrant, chapter 19). Regions afford an opportunity for both information exchange among producers and shared identities among boundaryless workers (see Saxenian, chapter 2). Regionally-based information channels share information with competitors as well as compatriots, as manifested in the "business-affairs underground" that Jones describes in chapter 4. Boundaryless-career workers are well advised to build ties to regional networks, and even to choose the region in which they will work, with future learning opportunities in mind. Meanwhile, the region emerges as an increasingly important subject for social science research. New models of career development, technological change, and learning will surely fail us unless they incorporate regions, and regional factors such as industry concentration and social networks, into their analyses.

>CIVILITY Old meaning: the status of citizenship; the state of being civilized, freedom from barbarity. New meaning: community membership where entitlements are coupled with responsibilities, an infrastructure sustaining and enhancing social and personal relations.

Civility implies both allegiance to a social order and obligations derived from it. The original term, with its Roman roots, implied a freedom from barbarity, both in terms of deportment and manners and through benefits derived from the infrastructure citizens could access. The root concept of *civicus* refers to private rights, those held by citizens, the body of which form Perrow's (chapter 18) notion of a civil society. The term *civility* can be applied to persons, to the milieu in which they live and work, or to the larger society. But the growth of large organizations, enhancing their control over work behaviors, has unwittingly absorbed many segments of society, at least in the United States, and made movement outside organization walls truly dangerous for people (see Perrow, chapter 18). Health-care and pension benefits, once markers of an employer of choice, are now markers of intransigence (Lucero and Allen, 1994). For the new, and, in effect, self-employed boundaryless worker, an entirely new infrastructure, a new civility, as it were, is needed to provide medical and dental coverage, security during old age, and mobility.[6] As employers now divest themselves of broad social functions, a multilevel infrastructure outside firms is pressed to respond. Best and Forrant (chapter 19) suggest that an appropriate governmental response is possible if agencies are able to test and revise their assumptions.

A new civility is needed. Its desiderata include portable health and retirement benefits, easy access to quality training and lifelong education, refreshers and updates, and access to labor markets where one's reputation is known. People starting boundaryless careers now or in the future should fare better than those who began in an earlier era (see Baker and Aldrich, chapter 8 in this volume), because some of the institutional barriers to boundaryless careers (e.g., lack of benefit portability) have been reduced over time. In times of change, the challenge is not only to spot and understand the slippage, disharmony, and conflict that mark transition, but also to separate the products of transition from long-present institutional failures that transition makes salient. Large organizations have altered our social ecology: The atmosphere, resources, and population patterns have adapted to their presence. A new ecology of civility is needed to sustain boundaryless careers, and boundaryless careers will contribute to this new ecology.

> TRANSITION Old meaning: the movement between states. New meaning: prevailing cycles of change and adaptation, including stages of preparation, encounter, adjustment, stabilization, and renewed preparation.

Anomalies abound in the new organizational era, signs of pervasive transitions. Anachronistic secondary schools can yield a high dropout rate and few job opportunities after high school graduation, and yet the system drones on (see Rosenbaum and Miller, chapter 21 in this volume). A labor glut in one industry sector can coexist beside shortfalls in neighboring sectors (see Best and Forrant, chapter 19). Obsolete models of career success make failures out of competent people who are held accountable to outmoded yardsticks (see Mirvis and Hall, chapter 14). Yet for each of these anomalies, the instincts of social science are the same: to repair the wrong by installing a new stasis to replace the old. As the world has changed, both organizational and career research have hardly begun to adjust their methods to the new phenomena under study (Miles and Creed, 1995).

However, transitions can be seen as involving an ongoing process that may continue indefinitely, a new societal pattern consistent with the continuous enactment cycle Weick (chapter 3) has articulated. Weick notes that there are transition cycles with stages of preparation, encounter, adjustment, stabilization, and renewed preparation. Entrepreneurs move from opportunity to opportunity, refugees move from country to country and through shifting occupations and social status, and displaced housewives move through successive transitions from school to work and new personal relationships. To the person making multiple fresh starts, life is full of what Weick (and Mischel, 1977) refer to as weak situations. Information is incomplete and people fill in the blanks along the way. In doing this, people in weak situations become strong forces shaping the situations in which they find themselves. Weick pursues the argument to offer the idea that such weak situations enhance long-run adaptability, as opposed to short-run efficiency. People carve out careers of their choice by moving through successive weak situations.

> FEMINIZATION Old meaning: the growth in female members in a workforce, or occupational or social group. New meaning: the induction of female values.

Multiple statistics about the emergent numbers of working women, notably in management, and parallel debates about persistent "glass-ceiling" effects that still restrict women's advancement, reflect a view of feminization-by-numbers. Many firms—prominently, for example, the Big Six accounting firms—would have struggled to stay in business into the 1990s if they had not shifted dramatically toward recruitment of women. Yet, the statistics and debates ignore fundamental differences in the psychological makeup of Western men and women (see Fondas, chapter 17 in this volume).

The real issue in terms of changing concepts and organizations is not the presence of women per se but the feminization of work and workers. *Feminization* refers to the spread to the workforce and, indeed, more broadly, to society, of characteristics previously attributed to women. It means that skills typically associated with women become characteristic of both men and women (see Fondas, chapter 7; Weick, chapter 3). Successful men need the skills women typically have (and, of course, successful women need the skills men typically have). Boundaryless careers in organizing networks necessitate multitasking, accelerated skills in relationship management, blurred boundaries between roles, and the need to change one's style of behavior, depending on whom one is dealing with.[7] The shift toward the new organizational era suggests more interdependent people, informed by, but liberated from, traditional sex-role characteristics.

> SELF Old meaning: individual psychological identity defined by the boundaries of a physical body; alternatively, an independent being. New meaning: individual psychological identity defined by interdependence with others; alternatively, an interdependent being.

The issue of feminization is linked to a broader issue about society's most fundamental assumption—a sort of "mother of all assumptions"—the conception of self. From the Western concept of the independent self flow many other assumptions and their manifest values: behavioral consistency, self-expression (e.g. speaking one's mind), personal achievement as psychological success (Markus and Kitayama, 1991). In contrast, collectivist, non-Western, societies assume an interdependent self, in which psychological identity flows from one's relations to others. Manifest values of an interdependent self include behavioral flexibility, other-orientation, and group accomplishments as features of psychological success. Yet, the sheer growth of interdependence—and of the number of ties integral to doing work organized into networks and value chains—necessitates a more complex view of self, which, in turn, involves responsibilities and skills in dealing technically, socially, and personally with network partners. Changes in skills are insufficient to accommodate the new demands of interdependence. Working closely with lots of different people necessitates changes in one's comfort levels for ambiguity and connection. It requires adjustments in communication style, even changes in language, accommodations to distinct work styles, and arrangements that mandate flexibility. If the self is being drawn to interdependence, might it become a more interdependent self?

Currently, a battle is being waged around the independent and interdependent self. Throughout this book, some authors have lauded aspects of the newly hyphenated self: self-employment, self-empowerment, self-support or self-insurance, self-designed careers. These have much in common with the old concept of one's own efficacy, in which an individual's sense of personal capabilities promoted an internal locus of control and reified the boundaries between the person and the larger environment. Thomas and Higgins (chapter 16 in this volume) suggest that strong internal career anchors help to integrate minority members' sense of self with their professional experiences. They argue that one needs a sense of wholeness to have a solid sense of self. This Western point of view seems at odds with the view that a sense of self comes from harmonious interpersonal relations. Could these prescriptions for minorities reflect paths to success in a majority world, where the independent self is affirmed in myths of success and hard work? Granrose and Chua (chapter 12 in this volume) illustrate how far removed from a view of self as interdependent the traditional West and its organizations have been. Ellig and Joseph (chapter 10 in this volume) suggest a shift from separation to integration of personal and company missions, with considerable opportunity, in any and all missions, for creation and discovery. Personal identity can be created, reified, or challenged by the successive changes in work experiences (see Baker and Aldrich, chapter 8 in this volume).

OUR LEXICON REMAINS incomplete. But we hope our readers can now pick up the task themselves. As you encounter the new organizational era, ask yourself what changes accrue by thinking about a boundaryless, rather than a bounded, career world. Ask also what changes accrue in life outside work, to which work inevitably connects. We are confident you will pick up and amplify the story in your own work and research experiences.

One term excluded from our lexicon is the one from our opening quotation—CHAOS. For years, chaos was something we sought to avoid, as advice about "getting a qualification," "dressing for success," or becoming a "one-minute manager" filled the personal-help bookshelves. When that advice began to fail, another suggestion, "Pack your own parachute," emerged, a hint of the new era to come, an invitation to float above the chaos, in the air of free agency. Hirsch and Shanley now decry the costs of free agency, leaving the impression that you may pack your own parachute, but perhaps it would be better to simply deplane.

Yet chaos has itself become respectable. It has shifted from meaning everything undesirable to being the principal factor behind what we now see as an orderly universe (Wheatley, 1994). And chaos is, in many ways, the handmaiden of boundaryless careers—a source of vitality and movement, that which makes the unusual usual. We may wish that both chaos and boundaryless careers would go away, but, in our better judgment, we know they will not. Moreover, if we embrace them, we may surprise ourselves at the pace at which our new appreciation grows.

ACKNOWLEDGMENTS: We thank Kerr Inkson for cogent comments on an earlier draft of this chapter.

Notes

1. Rousseau and Wade-Benzoni (1995) offer a lexicon for the changing employment relationship, in which the terms have acquired very different meanings. In the present context, we observe that there are numerous newly created terms as well as shifting meanings.

2. Myopia or far-sightedness become apparent only when one has been shown what 20–20 vision "looks like."

3. Where boundaries remain part of a group's identity (e.g., a nation, or a profession), despite interdependence, a challenging question needs some answers: How do we overcome the endemic in-group/out-group conflict prevalent in social psychological research? Particularly, we refer to the work of Insko et al. (1990), who observe that whenever there is a marker of group differences, negative attributions and resulting dysfunctional behaviors work against integration and collaboration.

4. Note here that we are using the term *occupation* broadly, going beyond restrictive trades that jealously guard the control their members possess. Rather, consistent with Tolbert, we are focusing on membership in a community identifiable by its knowledge base and its commitment to lifelong development of expertise.

5. With a new-hire rate that is 60% female, and losses of upward of 50% over five years, Deloitte and Touche is always training. Today, its audit partners can also spend time training the suppliers of training (e.g., university instructors who, in turn, will teach junior auditors). Occupational knowledge is being recodified by practitioners.

6. Surprisingly, academia offers a model of mobility with security, in the form of the longstanding reliance on TIAA-CREF as a pension fund for teachers; offering vesting after a few years with an employer, TIAA-CREF is portable and supplementable. The infrastructure which will support boundarylessness, from a benefits perspective, does not readily exist in other industries.

7. According to a recent article in the *New York Times* (May 31, 1995), she already contributes more to the total household (through activities both at home and work) than he does, suggesting the economic value associated with feminine skills.

References

Arthur, M. B.; Hall, D. T.; and Lawrence, B. S. (1989). *Handbook of Career Theory.* New York: Cambridge University Press.

Bercquist, W. (1993). *The Postmodern Organization.* San Francisco: Jossey-Bass.

Berryman, S. and Bailey, T. (1992). *The Double Helix of Education and the Economy.* New York: Columbia Teachers College, Institute on Education and the Economy.

Bridges, W., and Villemez, W. (1991). Employment relations and the labor market: Integrating institutional and market perspectives. *American Sociological Review, 56,* 748–764.

Cahill, T. (1995). *How the Irish Saved Civilization.* New York: Doubleday.

Hirsch, P. M. (1987). *Pack Your Own Parachute.* Reading, Mass.: Addison-Wesley.

Ijiri, Y. (1993). Complexity and technology. Paper presented at Graduate School of Industrial Administration, Deans's Conference, Carnegie Mellon University, Pittsburgh, Pa.

Inkso, C. A.; Schloper, J.; Hoyle, R. H.; Dardis, G. J.; and Graetz, K. A. (1990). Individual-group discontinuity as a function of fear and greed. *Journal of Personality and Social Psychology, 58,* 68–79.

Kanter, R. M. (1989). *When Giants Learn to Dance: Mastering the Challenge of Strategy, Management and Careers in the 1990s.* New York: Basic Books.

Lucero, M. A., and Allen. R. E. (1994). Employee benefits: A growing source of psychological contract violations. *Human Resource Management, 33,* 425–446.

Markus, H. R., and Kitayama, S. (1991). Culture and self: Implications for cognition, emotion, and motivation. *Psychological Review, 98,* 224–253.

Miles, R. E., and Creed, W. E. D. (1995). Organizational forms and managerial philosophies. In L. L. Cummings and B. Staw (eds.), *Research in Organizational Behavior,* vol. 17. Greenwich, Conn.: JAI Press.

Miller, E. (1969). Technology, territory, and time: The internal differentiation of complex production systems. *Human Relations, 12,* 243–272.

Mischel, W. (1977). The interaction of person and situation. In D. Magnuson and N. S. Endler (eds.), *Personality at the Crossroads.* Hillsdale, N.J.: Erlbaum.

Nonaka, I., and Takeuchi, H. (1995). *The Knowledge-Creating Company.* New York: Oxford University Press.

Peters, T. (1991). A declaration of interdependence. *San Jose Mercury,* July 4.

Porter, M. E. (1990). *The Competitive Advantage of Nations.* New York: Free Press.

Rousseau, D. M. (1995). *Psychological Contracts in Organizations: Written and Unwritten Agreements.* Newbury Park, Calif.: Sage.

Rousseau, D. M., and Wade-Benzoni, K. A. (1995). Changing individual-organization attachments: A two-way street. In A. Howard (ed.), *The Changing Nature of Work.* San Francisco: Jossey-Bass.

Senge, P. M. (1990). *The Fifth Discipline: The Art and Practice of the Learning Organization.* New York: Doubleday.

Simon, H. A. (1973). The organization of complex systems. In H. H. Patee (ed.), *Hierarchy Theory: The Challenge of Complex Systems.* New York: Braziller.

Stinchcombe, A. (1986). Contracts as hierarchical documents. In A. Stinchcombe and C. Heimer (eds.), *Organizational Theory and Project Management* (pp. 121–171). Oslo: Norwegian University Press.

Thomas, R. J. (1989). Blue-collar careers: meaning and choice in a world of constraints. In M. B. Arthur; D. T. Hall; and B. S. Lawrence (eds.) *Handbook of Career Theory.* New York: Cambridge University Press.

Wheatley, M. J. (1994). *Leadership and the New Science: Learning about Organizations from an Orderly Universe.* San Francisco: Bennett-Koehler.

Index